THE ROUGH GUIDE TO
POLAND
WITHDRAWN

This eighth edition written and researched by
Jonathan Bousfield

with additional contributions by
Mark Salter, Hilary Heuler and Stuart Wadsworth

**ROUGH
GUIDES**

Contents

Introduction to
Poland

Of all Europe's countries, Poland is the one that has changed the most in recent decades. All of its major cities have been through a process of major reinvention, opening flashy new museums, laying out new parks and brushing up their heritage with a spate of renovation. Gleaming corporate skyscrapers have taken root in Warsaw, the one East European capital that looks like a city of the future as well as a monument to the past. And yet, at the same time, the country remains deeply traditional: folk culture is still an integral part of the contemporary scene, religious festivals are enthusiastically observed and vast tracts of rural Poland retain an unhurried, un-modernized feel. There's an awful lot of wild nature, too, from the drifting dunes of the Baltic coast to the dense forests of the east, and the magnificent mountain chains that mark the country's southern borders.

Poland's transformation is all the more remarkable when one considers that it was a **communist**-ruled one-party state from the late 1940s until 1989. In many ways it was Poland's resistance to communism that kicked off the whole system's collapse, with the birth of the **Solidarity** trade union in 1980 – and the imposition of martial law in 1981 – demonstrating that communism throughout Eastern Europe had gone into irreversible decline. Two decades of non-communist governments have wrought profound changes on the country, unleashing entrepreneurial energies and widening cultural horizons in a way that pre-1989 generations would have scarcely thought possible. Most importantly, the country has a radically different look about it, having exchanged the greyish tinge of a state-regulated society for the anything-goes attitude of private enterprise – and all the billboards and window displays that go with it.

Much of Poland's recent transformation is a direct consequence of joining the **European Union** in 2004. Almost all of the things built in Poland in the ensuing years were paid for, either wholly or in part, by EU funds. EU membership has also seen the exodus of Poles seeking work in other member states (a number that peaked at over 2 million in 2007), reducing unemployment at home and bringing money into the local economy through remittances sent back to the mother country. More Europeans (usually tourists) are visiting Poland, too, thanks in part to budget airlines – there's hardly a single Polish city that doesn't have some kind of connection with the UK, Ireland or Europe at large. However, attitudes to the EU remain ambiguous in Poland itself. EU membership has allowed foreign investors to buy up large chunks of the Polish economy, and also encouraged (either consciously or not) the growth of a cosmopolitan, liberal culture of which many conservative Poles disapprove.

Indeed, Polish society outside the big cities remains fundamentally traditional, maintaining beliefs and a sense of nationhood in which the **Catholic Church** occupies a central position. During periods of foreign oppression – oppression so severe that Poland as a political entity has sometimes vanished altogether from the maps of Europe – the Church was always the principal defender of the nation's identity, so that the Catholic faith and national independence have become fused in the Polish consciousness. The physical presence of the Church is inescapable wherever you travel, whether in Baroque buildings, roadside shrines or images of the national icon, the Black Madonna of Częstochowa.

Poland is also a remarkably ethnically homogenous place. The country's significant **Jewish** community, numbering some 3.2 million in 1939, was almost entirely wiped out during the Holocaust. Before World War II Poland included eastern territories that harboured significant Belarusian and Ukrainian minorities, but in 1945 the **Soviet**-dominated nation was given new borders, losing its eastern lands to the USSR and gaining tracts of formerly German territory in the west. Germans were expelled, to be replaced by Polish migrants from the east, with the result that the population of Poland today is far more uniformly "Polish" than in any previous century.

Unsurprisingly, symbols of Polish **national heritage** are everywhere, from

---

FACT FILE

• **Poland** occupies a vast swathe of territory in north-central Europe, bordered by Germany to the west, the Czech Republic and Slovakia to the south, and Ukraine, Belarus, Lithuania and Russia to the east.

• Much of northern and central Poland is made up of **agricultural plainland** and gently rolling countryside, although the Tatra and Carpathian **mountains** in the south provide a dramatic contrast.

• Its **population** of 38.5 million is predominantly both Polish and devoutly **Catholic**, although, unsurprisingly for a country which has changed its borders many times in the past, significant pockets of Ukrainians, Belarusians, Bojks and Łemks exist in the east of the country.

• Traditionally, Poland is known for its ship-building, coal and steel **industries**, although these days cosmetics, medicines and textile products – often made under licence for Western conglomerates – are increasingly important sources of foreign income.

• Poland's national tipple, **wódka**, dates back to the early Middle Ages, when the first Polish vodkas appeared. Called *gorzałkas*, they were primarily used as medicines.

• About thirty percent of the country is covered by **forest**. This includes Białowieża Forest, one of last surviving stretches of primeval forest in Europe.

the beautifully restored Old Towns of the main cities to the former aristocratic palaces of the east. One of the hallmarks of the new Poland is its ability to give this heritage contemporary shape, evidence of which is provided by the plethora of outstanding, media-savvy **new museums** that have sprung up all over Poland, from the POLIN Museum of the History of Polish Jews in Warsaw, to the European Solidarity Centre in Gdańsk, the Emigration Museum in Gdynia, the Brama Poznania in Poznań, the Stara Kopalnia in Wałbrzych, the Silesia Museum in Katowice, the Home Army Museum in Kraków… the list goes on. There's arguably no other country in Europe that has laid its history and culture out for the visitor in such an accessible, well-designed way.

Where to go

Poles delineate their country's attractions as "the mountains, the sea and the lakes", their emphasis firmly slanted to the traditional **rural heartlands**. However, the last two decades have seen the inexorable rise of Poland's **cities** as the main motors of cultural change, and it's these that have sprung into the international consciousness as

JEWISH HERITAGE

The history of Poland is inexorably linked to that of its **Jewish** population which, before World War II, comprised roughly ten percent (three million) of the country's total – Europe's largest Jewish community and the world's second largest after the USA. Of the current world Jewish population of fifteen million, over half are thought to be related to Polish Jewry.

Poland's Jewish communities were largely wiped out during the **Holocaust**, and many of the neighbourhoods where they lived were destroyed – either during the war or as a consequence of post-war urban development plans. However, there is much in the way of **Jewish heritage** still to see, from the beautifully restored synagogues of Tykocin (see page 184), Włodawa (see page 205), Zamość (see page 216) and elsewhere, to the evocative streets and squares of Kazimierz, the animated former Jewish quarter of Kraków (see page 319). The POLIN Museum of the History of Polish Jews in Warsaw (see page 71) makes for essential viewing, pulling all the strands of Jewish heritage together in spectacular, inspirational fashion. Many will feel the need to visit the former camps at Auschwitz-Birkenau (see page 309), a place that – due to the sheer weight of physical evidence and survivor testimony – has come to symbolize the Holocaust as a whole.

THE HISTORIC PORT OF GDAŃSK

hot-tip destinations for those who want to soak up central European history, immerse themselves in the arts, or stay up all night sampling hipster pubs, vodka bars and DJ-powered dancefloors. Poland can boast seven urban agglomerations of half a million people or over, each of which has its own personality, gastro-scene and distinctive nightlife, not to mention a wealth of (frequently very new) museums. Most regional cities have airports served by international budget carriers, ensuring that you're spoiled for choice when it comes to deciding where to start and finish your trip.

Kraków, the ancient royal capital, is the real crowd-puller for Poles and foreign visitors alike, rivalling the central European elegance of Prague and Vienna. This is the city where history hits you most powerfully, in the royal Wawel complex, in the fabulous open space of the Rynek, in the one-time Jewish quarter of Kazimierz, and in the chilling necropolis of nearby Auschwitz-Birkenau, the bloodiest killing field of the Third Reich. Kraków is also the gateway to the **Tatras**, a rugged mountain range of truly alpine grandeur that offers any number of epic walks.

No longer the grey city of Eastern European stereotype, the capital **Warsaw** is ebullient, forward-looking and multi-layered, a mosaic of fast-changing neighbourhoods that provides an endless source of fascination. West of Warsaw, surprise package **Łódź** would never have featured on any tourist map a decade ago; the red-brick factories of the erstwhile mill-town now house art galleries, nightlife quarters and a state-of-the-art planetarium.

To the north, the historic port of **Gdańsk** – which together with neighbouring Sopot and Gdynia forms the coastal sprawl known as the **Tri-City** – presents a dynamic brew

BEETROOT

Anyone spending time in Poland should be sure to drop any preconceptions they might have about **beetroot**. The vitamin B-rich super-vegetable is ubiquitous in Polish cuisine, regardless of whether you're eating in the fancy restaurants or the street-corner canteens. A side-salad of grated beetroot is the traditional accompaniment to almost every main course, and beetroot is also the staple ingredient in **barszcz** (borsch), the sweet-and-sour soup that features on almost every menu. Polish borsch usually comes in the form of a clear soup, although plenty of chunkier versions are also available. The bright-pink *Chłodnik Litewski* (Lithuanian cold borsch), a chilled beetroot soup mixed with sour cream, is the perfect summertime refresher.

of culture, commerce and seaside hedonism set against a townscape reminiscent of the mercantile towns of the Netherlands. Gdańsk is also a useful jumping-off point for the extraordinary desert-like dunes of the **Słowiński National Park** and the formidable castles constructed by the Teutonic Knights at **Malbork**, **Kwidzyn** and other strategic points along the **River Vistula**. Nearby **Toruń** is one of the most atmospheric and beautiful of the old Hanseatic towns in the area.

The best entry point for Poland's **lake district** is the relaxed small city of **Olsztyn**, which lies a brief hop away from the wood-shrouded waterways of Mazuria and northern Podlasie. Podlasie's capital is **Białystok**, a springboard for the eastern borderlands, where restored synagogues and onion-domed Orthodox churches vie for attention with Tatar mosques. Straddling the Belarusian frontier is the **Białowieża National Park**, site of one of Europe's last surviving primeval forests and home to a herd of European bison.

The main urban centre of eastern Poland is **Lublin**, which boasts a famously beautiful, Baroque-flavoured Old Town, and provides access to two of the best-preserved small towns in Poland: riverside **Kazimierz Dolny** and magnificent, Renaissance **Zamość**. The southeastern corner of Poland is one of the most rewarding areas of the country for slow unhurried touring; both the **Beskid Niski** and the mysterious, bare-topped **Bieszczady** are a hill-walker's delight, while local villages are famous for their immaculate wooden churches.

The western corner of Poland also has its fair share of captivating highland landscapes, with the stark green-brown **Karkonosze** attracting hordes of summer hikers and winter skiers. Silesian coal-belt capital **Katowice**, once the epitome of urban boredom, has successfully reinvented itself as a post-industrial metropolis of cultural attractions and music festivals.

Main centre of the southwest, **Wrocław**, is a complex synthesis of German and Polish cultures that offers grand architecture from all epochs, leafy riverside walks and a famously unrestrained nightlife. The other great historic city of western Poland is **Poznań**, a bustling business-oriented place with an arty, alternative edge, and a dizzying number of characterful bars and bistros. Marking the country's northeastern corner, the port city of **Szczecin** is an alluring tangle of nineteenth-century boulevards and shipyard cranes, and is a useful stepping stone en route to the pristine white-sand beaches of the **Baltic Coast**.

AVERAGE TEMPERATURES AND RAINFALL

	Jan	March	May	July	Sept	Dec
KRAKÓW						
max (°F)	32	45	67	76	67	38
max (°C)	0	7.2	19.4	24.4	19.4	3.3
Rainfall (mm)	28	35	46	111	62	36
GDAŃSK						
max (°F)	35	40	59	70	64	38
max (°C)	1.7	4.4	15	21.1	17.8	3.3
Rainfall (mm)	33	27	42	84	59	46
WARSAW						
max (°F)	32	41	67	76	67	36
max (°C)	0	5	19.4	24.4	19.4	2.2
Rainfall (mm)	27	27	46	96	43	44

When to go

Spring and **summer** are arguably the ideal seasons for travel: outdoor café life is taking over the cities, the countryside is vividly colourful and Poland's unspoilt lake and mountain areas are perfect for exploration. If you're heading for the Baltic Coast or the lake district then it might be worth delaying your trip until July or August, when the water is warm enough for bathing and there are enough visitors around to generate an invigorating holiday vibe.

Autumn can be a spectacular time to tour the countryside, with the rich colours of the fall heightened by brilliantly crisp sunshine. In **winter** the temperature drops rapidly, icy Siberian winds blanketing many parts of the country with snow for anything from one to three months. It can be a magical time to visit cities, with Christmas markets and a seasonal party atmosphere enlivening Kraków and other urban centres. In the mountains, skiers and other winter sports enthusiasts will find themselves in their element.

PIESKOWA SKAŁA CASTLE

Author picks

Our indefatigable author, Jonathan Bousfield, has travelled the length and breadth of Poland to bring you some unique travel experiences. Here are some of his personal favourites.

Baltic beaches Poland's Baltic shores are characterized by miles and miles of white sand. Join the crowds in chic Sopot (see page 129), or stroll the endless strands of Łeba (see page 449) or Hel (see page 136).

Folk art Whether in Warsaw's ethnographic museum (see page 64), the "painted" village of Zalipie (see page 320) or the wooden churches of the southeast (see page 248), you're sure to find a feast of visual inspiration in Poland's traditional arts.

Cities that never sleep Cafés, bistros, bars and craft beers have changed the face of Polish socializing, especially in Kraków (see page 304) and Wrocław (see page 381), where there always seems to be one more bar round one more corner.

Castles As one might expect from a country with such a dramatic history, castles come in all shapes and from all epochs in Poland. Malbork (see page 143) is perhaps the best known, although the hillside-hugging Pieskowa Skała (see page 316), the abandoned Krzyżtopór (see page 215) and the refined aristocratic seat of Książ (see page 388) all possess an undeniable aura of their own.

Industrial heritage The red-brick architecture of Poland's former industrial heartlands is at its best in Łódź (see page 94), whose factories (many now repurposed) provide the city with its defining architectural stamp. In Katowice (see page 344) and Wałbrzych (see page 386), coal-mining heritage has been spectacularly transformed into modern museum attractions.

Summer in Warsaw The Polish capital moves outdoors as soon as the weather warms up, with hordes of locals flocking to the weekend Breakfast Market (see page 84) or descending on the Vistula riverfront (see page 64) to stroll, cycle or linger in alfresco bars.

> Our author recommendations don't end here. We've flagged up our favourite places – a perfectly sited hotel, an atmospheric café, a special restaurant – throughout the Guide, highlighted with the ★ symbol.

LUBIATOWO BEACH, BALTIC COAST
TRADITIONAL PAINTED HOUSE, ZALIPIE, MAŁOPOLSKA

20

things not to miss

It's not possible to see everything that Poland has to offer in one trip – and we don't suggest you try. What follows, in no particular order, is a selective taste of the country's highlights: outstanding buildings, historic sites and natural wonders. All entries have a page reference to take you straight into the guide, where you can find out more.

1

1 RYNEK GŁÓWNY, KRAKÓW
See page 261
A spectacular medieval market square, packed with fine architecture, in a country that's famous for them.

2 WOODEN CHURCHES
See page 249
An age-old form of folk architecture still preserved in rural corners of the country. One of the most spectacular examples is at Kwiatoń in the Beskid Niski.

3 ZAMOŚĆ
See page 216
A model Renaissance town, stuffed with the palaces and churches built by the Zamoyskis, one of the country's leading aristocratic families.

4 EUROPEAN SOLIDARITY CENTRE, GDAŃSK
See page 122
Commemorating the Solidarity protest movement of the 1980s, this museum is an absorbing and inspiring tribute to non-violent revolutions everywhere.

5 THE TATRAS
See page 324
Poland's prime highland playground is a paradise for hikers, with everything from relaxing rambles in sub-alpine meadows to hair-raising mountain ridge walks.

6 WAWEL, KRAKÓW
See page 276

One of the most striking royal residences in Europe and a potent source of national and spiritual pride.

7 LUBLIN
See page 194

A jewel of an Old Town and a large student population make Lublin the liveliest and most rewarding of Poland's eastern cities – and one that's relatively undiscovered.

8 THE BIESZCZADY
See page 239

The grassy summits and bald ridges of the Bieszczady mountains provide Poland with some of its most alluring and accessible walking terrain.

9 POLIN MUSEUM OF THE HISTORY OF POLISH JEWS, WARSAW
See page 71

When it comes to fabulous new museums, this is the most fabulous of all: a virtuoso exercise in history-telling, housed in a stunning contemporary building.

10 KAZIMIERZ DOLNY
See page 208

Beautifully preserved small town and age-old centre of Jewish culture, now popular with Warsaw's media set, who descend en masse on summer weekends.

11 ULICA DŁUGA, GDAŃSK
See page 117

A stroll down one of Poland's most beautiful set-piece streets will take you past a string of opulent town houses, recalling the mercantile dynasties that once made Gdańsk great.

12 SŁOWIŃSKI NATIONAL PARK
See page 450

Trek across Sahara-like dunes just outside the seaside town of Łeba, pausing to sunbathe, birdwatch or explore World War II rocket installations along the way.

13 RAFTING ON THE DUNAJEC
See page 337

Drift down the River Dunajec as it winds its way between the craggy peaks of the Pieniny mountains.

14 VISTULA RIVERBANK, WARSAW
See page 64

Centre of the capital's social life come summer, when city folk descend to stroll, sunbathe or sup the evening away in the waterside bars and clubs.

15 KATOWICE
See page 344

The ugly duckling of Polish tourism is suddenly its brightest up-and-coming star, thanks to a post-industrial cocktail of repurposed coal mines, new museums, lively nightlife and big-hitting festivals.

11

12

16 WROCŁAW
See page 364
Wrocław's historic core is an exhilarating mixture of architectural influences, from Flemish-style Renaissance mansions to the glorious Gothic monstrosity of its town hall.

17 KSIĄŻ
See page 386
Of all Poland's palaces, it's Książ that most looks the part – a turreted hilltop hulk with jaw-droppingly lavish interiors.

18 BIAŁOWIEŻA NATIONAL PARK
See page 187
One of the most extensive areas of primeval forest in Europe is also famous for being home to a beast indigenous to Poland: the European bison.

19 MALBORK CASTLE
See page 143
The Teutonic Knights lorded it over northern Poland for more than 200 years, and this rambling complex of fortifications is their most imposing monument.

20 AUSCHWITZ-BIRKENAU
See page 309
The notorious concentration and extermination camp offers profound insights into the nature of human evil.

17

18

19

20

Itineraries

Most visitors to Poland head straight to Kraków, but there's much more to the country than its crowd-pulling ancient capital. These itineraries will give you a taste of Poland's variety and diversity, from industrial-heritage cities to historic towns and beautiful highland landscapes.

GRAND TOUR

Our Grand Tour concentrates on the most rewarding of the country's great towns and cities. It will easily fill two weeks.

❶ Warsaw The most changed capital city in Europe and an endless source of fascination, Warsaw is the obvious place to begin or end your travels. See page 50

❷ Łódź Don't be tempted to miss out Łódź, a short train ride west of Warsaw. This former industrial grime-bucket has reinvented itself as a red-brick heritage city packed full of diversions. See page 94

❸ Gdańsk Next, head north to this multi-layered, energetic port city, a seductive mixture of waterside warehouses, Gothic churches, canal-spanning bridges and shipyard cranes. See page 112

❹ Toruń A university town rich in fine monuments, the former fortress of Toruń offers a crash-course in Polish history and culture. See page 148

❺ Poznań A couple of hours' train ride from Toruń, Poznań is a microcosm of contemporary Poland, with a beautifully preserved historic centre bordered by go-ahead business districts, nightlife areas and the quiet cathedral quarter of Ostrow Tumski. See page 404

❻ Wrocław The capital of Lower Silesia is the site of a famously charming main square, and a lovely riverside characterized by small islands and bridges. See page 364

❼ Kraków The cavalcade of churches, palaces and civic buildings that make up Poland's most popular city is truly stunning. See page 258

❽ Auschwitz-Birkenau This enduring symbol of the Nazi epoch is a necessary day-trip from Kraków. See page 309

❾ Lublin Finish your journey in Lublin, the most welcoming place in Poland's east, with a compact, magical Old Town and a clutch of summer festivals. See page 194

THE HIGHLANDS

This two-week tour focuses on the stark beauty of Poland's highland areas.

❶ Jelenia Góra With its charming market square, this is a fitting introduction to southern Poland; the dark, bare-topped Karkonosze mountains lie half-an-hour to the south. See page 389

❷ Wałbrzych This former coal-mining town is one of the fascinating spots in the south, with industrial heritage, Nazi-era underground bases and the splendid Książ castle all on its doorstep. See page 386

❸ Kudowa-Zdrój It's a short hop by train from Wałbrzych to this quaint spa resort, with walking trails stretching up into the Table Mountains. See page 398

❹ Cieszyn Head east to Cieszyn, one of Poland's most attractive market towns, with a knot of quaint streets descending towards the River Olza and the Czech border. See page 356

❺ **Zakopane** Always crowded but never less than charming, Zakopane offers immediate access to some stunning alpine walking in the Tatra Mountains. See page 327

❻ **Szczawnica** A short hop east of Zakopane, the enchanting village of Szczawnica is a great base from which to embark on the Czarny Dunajec raft trip. See page 339

❼ **Gorlice** This peaceful town is the ideal base from which to visit historic Biecz and the beautiful churches of Kwiatoń and Sękowa. See page 248

❽ **The Bieszczady** From Gorlice, head southeast to the grassy-ridged Bieszczady – Poland's most alluring mountain range. See page 239

THE EASTERN BORDERLANDS

Explore the historic small towns and multicultural resonances of the country's eastern borderlands on this ten-day tour.

❶ **Białystok** The biggest city of Poland's northeast, underrated Białystok offers an easy-going blend of Neoclassical architecture and restful parks; quaint little towns like Tykocin and Supraśl are only a short hop away. See page 178

❷ **Białowieża** A short bus ride takes you to one of the last stretches of primeval forest in Europe, home to a flourishing population of hairy bison. See page 189

❸ **Lublin** Next, head south to Lublin; the nooks and crannies of its Old Town are among the most evocative in Poland. See page 194

❹ **Kazimierz Dolny** If there was a competition for loveliest small town in Poland then Kazimierz – a short hop from Lublin – would be the major contender, with its well-preserved centre and charming riverside setting. See page 208

❺ **Zamość** Laid out by sixteenth-century town planners, Zamość is a beautifully preserved monument to the Polish Renaissance. See page 216

❻ **Rzeszów** From Zamość, head south to Rzeszów, the capital of the southeast. It has one of the most animated main squares in the country, and makes an excellent base from which to visit the fabulous palace at Łańcut. See page 224

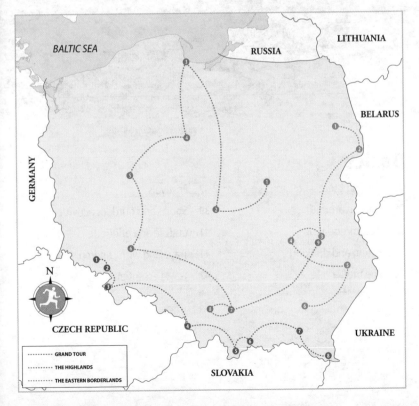

BIESZCZADY MOUNTAINS

Basics

Getting there

The easiest way to reach Poland is by air, with direct flights from the UK, Ireland and North America, and indirect flights from Australasia. Travelling overland from Britain is a relatively long haul, and you'll save little, if anything, going by train, although with an InterRail pass you can take in Poland as part of a wider European trip. Approaching Poland by car or bus from the UK involves a journey of at least 1,000km and takes the best part of two days.

Airfares always depend on the season. Peak times for flights to Poland are May to September, and around the Easter and Christmas holidays; at these times be prepared to book well in advance. Fares drop during the "shoulder" seasons (April and Oct); and you'll usually get the best prices during the low season (Nov–March, excluding Easter and Christmas). The skiing season in southern Poland (Dec–March) ensures that in some regional airports (notably Kraków) there never really is a low season.

The best deals are usually to be found by booking through discount travel websites or the websites of the airlines themselves.

Flights from the UK and Ireland

With a flying time of 2 hours 30 minutes and plenty of airlines to choose from, getting to Poland **from the UK** by air is relatively problem-free. The sheer number of routes on offer ensures that there are plenty of potential entry points to Poland.

Cheapest are the budget airlines. **EasyJet**, (Ⓦeasyjet. com) offers flights from Belfast, Bristol, Edinburgh, Manchester and London Gatwick to Kraków. **Ryanair** (Ⓦryanair.com) flies from Birmingham, Bournemouth, Bristol, Dublin, East Midlands, Edinburgh, Glasgow, Liverpool, London Luton, London Stansted and Shannon to Gdańsk, Katowice, Olsztyn, Poznań, Rzeszów, Szczecin, Warsaw Modlin, Warsaw Chopin and Wrocław. Finally, **Wizzair** (Ⓦwizzair.com) has flights from Aberdeen, Belfast, Birmingham, Bristol, Doncaster, Glasgow, Liverpool and London Luton to Gdańsk, Olsztyn, Poznań, Katowice, Lublin, Warsaw and Wrocław. Bear in mind the cheap-flight market is in a state of constant fluidity and there may be changes in operators and routes in the future.

Most useful of the mainstream airlines is **British Airways** (Ⓦba.com), who fly from London Heathrow to Warsaw and Kraków; and Poland's national carrier **LOT** (Ⓦlot.com), who fly from London Heathrow to Warsaw, with connecting flights to Polish regional cities.

From Ireland, Aer Lingus (Ⓦaerlingus.com) fly direct from Dublin to Warsaw, while Ryanair serve almost every major Polish city. From Northern Ireland easyJet offer flights from Belfast to Kraków.

Flights from the US and Canada

From the USA, LOT (Polish Airlines; Ⓦlot.com) offers flights to Warsaw from New York, Chicago and Los Angeles, and to Kraków from Chicago. Approximate fares in high season are: New York–Warsaw US$1800; Los Angeles–Warsaw US$2800; Chicago–Warsaw/Kraków US$1900. If you're coming from another part of the USA, LOT will connect you with a domestic carrier, United Airlines (Ⓦunited.com) being their favoured partner. Several other carriers, including British Airways (Ⓦba.com), Austrian Airlines (Ⓦaustrian.com), Swiss Airlines (Ⓦswissair.com) and Lufthansa (Ⓦlufthansa.com) have flights from the USA to Warsaw via their European hub cities. Delta (Ⓦdelta.com) has flights connecting via Paris.

From Canada, LOT operates a direct service to Warsaw from Toronto. Fares cost at around CAN$2600. Starting from another Canadian airport, Air Canada (Ⓦaircanada.com) will connect you with LOT's Toronto flight for a reasonable add-on fare. Discount agents sometimes come up with cheaper deals involving other major airlines which fly daily to Warsaw, but require a change of plane in Western Europe – British Airways flies to Warsaw via London, CSA (Czech Airlines; Ⓦczechairlines. co.uk) via Prague, Lufthansa via Frankfurt, and Swiss via Zürich. The cost of these occasionally turns out slightly cheaper than LOT, depending on the route.

A cheaper option is to book a flight **to London** on a major airline and then connect to Warsaw or Kraków using Ryanair, easyJet or one of the other budget

---

A BETTER KIND OF TRAVEL

At Rough Guides we are passionately committed to travel. We believe it helps us understand the world we live in and the people we share it with – and of course tourism is vital to many developing economies. But the scale of modern tourism has also damaged some places irreparably, and climate change is accelerated by most forms of transport, especially flying. All Rough Guides' flights are carbon-offset, and every year we donate money to a variety of environmental charities.

carriers (see page 25). Return flights with Virgin Atlantic (ⓦ virginatlantic.com) cost US$1700 from New York to London Heathrow. This will give you the option of a stop in London, but as the budget flights leave from smaller airports, you'll need to cross the city to catch your second flight: plan carefully.

Flights from Australia, New Zealand and South Africa

Although there are no direct flights to Poland from Australia or New Zealand, there are plenty of one- or two-stop alternatives. **From Australia**, typical one-stop routings with Qantas Airways (ⓦ qantas.com) involving European hubs such as London, Frankfurt or Vienna tend to be expensive, with the average return fare from Sydney, Melbourne or Perth to Warsaw or Kraków hovering around the AUS$2700 mark. Cheaper deals involve a combination of airlines and two stops en route: Sydney–Kuala Lumpur–Vienna–Warsaw or Sydney–Bangkok–Frankfurt–Warsaw are typical examples. Fares on these routes are around AUS$1800.

From New Zealand, Air New Zealand (ⓦ airnz.co.nz) flies from Auckland to London and Frankfurt (with a stop in Los Angeles, Vancouver or elsewhere), where you can pick up connecting flights to Warsaw and other Polish cities. All other flights from New Zealand involve at least two stops. Return fares start at around NZ$3000 in high season.

There are no direct flights to Poland **from South Africa**, but plenty of airlines offer one-stop flights via European hubs such as London or Frankfurt. Flying from Johannesburg to Warsaw with British Airways or Lufthansa costs around ZAR 8700, and takes 18–24 hours.

Trains

Travelling by train to Poland, though relaxing and leisurely, can't compare price-wise with taking the plane. The fastest option **from London** involves taking the Eurostar from St Pancras to Brussels, and then continuing across Belgium and Germany to Berlin, where you can pick up expresses to Warsaw, Poznań, Wrocław or Kraków. None of these options take longer than 24 hours – although the possibility of overnight stopovers in Brussels and/or Berlin may well persuade you to take your time. It is difficult to book the whole journey in one go however; using the German railway website ⓦ bahn.com enables you to book a trip in two separate legs (London–Berlin and Berlin–Warsaw). A return ticket for the whole journey will set you back around £180, more if you book a couchette or sleeper for the overnight part of the journey.

Rail passes

If you're planning to visit Poland as part of a more extensive trip around Europe, it may be worth buying a **rail pass**. Poland is covered in the InterRail pass scheme, which is available to European residents. Non-European residents can make use of the Eurail pass. Further details of these passes can be found on ⓦ eurail.com and ⓦ raileurope.com.

InterRail

InterRail passes can be bought at Voyages SNCF in the UK and come in over-26 and (cheaper) under-26 versions. They cover most European countries, including Poland and all the countries you need to travel through in order to get there. A pass for five days' travel in a fifteen-day period (£233 for adults, £180 for those under 26) will just about suffice for a trip to Poland and back; although a more leisurely approach would require a pass for seven days' travel within one month (£277 and £221 respectively), or ten days within one month (£323 and £262). You can also get passes for continuous travel for periods of fifteen days (£364 and £303), 22 days (£426 and £335) or one month (£550 and £429). InterRail passes do not include travel between Britain and the continent, although pass-holders are eligible for discounts on rail travel in the UK and on cross-Channel ferries.

Eurail

Non-European residents qualify for the **Eurail Global pass**, which must be purchased before arrival in Europe from selected agents in North America, Australia and New Zealand or from Voyages SNCF in London. The pass allows unlimited free first-class train travel in over twenty European countries, including Poland and most of its immediate neighbours. The pass is available in increments of fifteen days (US$685), 22 days (US$881), one month (US$1081) and two months (US$1524). A Eurail Global Flexi pass will give you ten days' first-class travel in a two-month period for US$804.

If you're under 28, you can save money with a **Eurail Global Youthpass**. Options include US$705 for one month's continuous travel, US$448 for fifteen days' continuous travel or US$526 for ten days' travel in a two-month period (all second-class fares).

Buses

Bus travel is an attractively cheap way of getting to Poland although the journey itself is relatively dull unless you have a penchant for northern European motorway landscapes. Virtually all Polish towns of any size are covered from a wide range of UK departure points, with the most reliable services being operated by **Eurolines**. They run regular services from London to Warsaw and Kraków (usually with a change in Berlin) and a whole host of other Polish cities. Return tickets for Warsaw start at around £130 (with minimal reductions for under 26s, senior citizens and children). Tickets can be bought at any National Express office in the UK, and will include connecting fares from anywhere outside London.

Better deals might be available from **Polish-run companies**, especially if you're travelling from outside London. The ⓦvoyager.pl website deals with online reservations for a variety of companies and routes. Prices hover around the £120 mark for a northern England–Poland return.

Driving

Driving to Poland **from the UK** means a long haul of 1000km from Calais or Ostend to the Polish border – and another 450–500km from there to Warsaw or Kraków. Flat out, and using the **Channel Tunnel**, you could do the journey to the border in eighteen hours, but it makes more sense to allow longer, breaking the journey in central Germany.

The most convenient **Channel crossings** are P&O Ferries' and DFDS Seaways' services from Dover to Calais, the DFDS Seaways service from Dover to Dunkirk, or the Eurotunnel from Folkestone to Calais. From any of these ports, the most popular and direct route is on toll-free motorways all the way, bypassing Brussels, Düsseldorf, Hannover and Berlin. The most convenient ferry routes from the north of England are the P&O North Sea Ferries services from Hull to Rotterdam and Zeebrugge, and DFDS's Newcastle–Amsterdam service.

AGENTS

North South Travel UK ☎ 01245 608 291, ⓦ northsouthtravel. co.uk. Friendly, competitive travel agency, offering discounted fares worldwide. Profits are used to support projects in the developing world, especially the promotion of sustainable tourism.

STA Travel UK ☎ 0333 321 0099; US T 1 800 781 4040; Australia ☎ 134 782; New Zealand ☎ 0800 474 400; South Africa ☎ 0861 781 781; ⓦ statravel.com. Worldwide specialists in independent travel; also student IDs, travel insurance, car rental, rail passes, and more. Good discounts for students and under-26s.

Trailfinders UK ☎ 020 7368 1200; Ireland ☎ 01 677 7888, ⓦ trailfinders.com. One of the best-informed and most efficient agents for independent travellers.

RAIL CONTACTS

CIT Holidays Australia ☎ 1300 380 992, cit.com.au
Deutsche Bahn UK ☎ 0871 880 8066, ⓦ bahn.com. Timetable

information and through ticketing on European routes.
Eurostar UK ☎ 03432 186 186, ⓦ eurostar.com.
Rail Plus Australia ☎ 1300 555 003, ⓦ railplus.com.au. Sells Eurail and Eurostar passes.

The Man in Seat 61 ⓦ seat61.com. Enthusiast-run site packed with information on all aspects of international rail travel, including tips on the best way to reach Poland by train, and how to book. Far more reliable than any of the official sites.

Trainseurope UK ☎ 0871 700 7722, ⓦ trainseurope.co.uk. Tickets from the UK to European destinations, InterRail and other individual country passes.

Voyages SNCF UK ☎ 0844 848 5848, ⓦ uk.voyages-sncf.com. Agents for Eurail, InterRail and Eurostar.

BUS CONTACTS

Eurolines UK ☎ 0871 781 8181, ⓦ eurolines.com.
Voyager ⓦ voyager.pl.

FERRY CONTACTS

DFDS Seaways UK ☎ 0871 574 7235 & 0871 522 9955, International ☎ +44 330 333 0245, ⓦ dfdsseaways.co.uk. Dover to Dunkirk; Dover to Calais; Newcastle to Amsterdam.

P&O Ferries UK ☎ 08716 642 121, International ☎ 01304 863 000 ⓦ poferries.com. Dover to Calais; Hull to Rotterdam; Hull to Zeebrugge.

CHANNEL TUNNEL

Eurotunnel UK ☎ 0844 335 3535, International ☎ +33 810 630 304, ⓦ eurotunnel.com.

TOUR OPERATORS

Adventures Abroad UK ☎ 00 800 665 03998, USA and Canada ☎ 1 800 665 3998, ⓦ adventures-abroad.com. Exclusive Poland tours plus Poland/Baltics/Central Europe combinations.

American Travel Abroad US ☎ 1 800 228 0877, ⓦ amta.com. Poland specialists offering flights, hotels, car rental and escorted tours.

Chopin Express Tours Canada ☎ 1 800 533 0369, ⓦ chopintours. com. City breaks and a big choice of escorted tours covering folklore, history and culture.

Cresta UK ☎ 0844 800 7020, ⓦ crestaholidays.co.uk. City breaks in Kraków and Warsaw.

Eastern Eurotours Australia ☎ 1800 242 353, ⓦ easterneuro tours.com.au. Flights, accommodation, city breaks and guided tours.

Exodus UK ☎ 0203 811 4374, ⓦ exodus.co.uk. Nine-day treks in the Tatras, snowshoeing trips, and two-week tours mixing Central European destinations.

Explore UK ☎ 01252 883 505, USA ☎ 1 800 715 1746, Canada ☎ 1 888 216 3401, Australia ☎ 1300 439 756, ⓦ exploreworldwide.com. Hiking tours in the Tatra mountains, cycling tours, and multi-country tours taking in Polish and East European cities.

Kirker Holidays UK ☎ 020 7593 1899, ⓦ kirkerholidays.com. City breaks and tailor-made holidays in Kraków, Gdańsk and Warsaw.

Naturetrek UK ☎ 01962 733 051, ⓦ naturetrek.co.uk. Expertly led wildlife treks concentrating on seasonal fauna (there's one tour each in winter, spring and autumn).

PAT (Polish American Tours) US ☎ 413 747 7702 or 1 800 388 0988, ⓦ pattours.com. Hotel bookings, car rental, and a range of escorted tours with historical or folklore themes.

Polorbis UK ☎ 020 7624 1123, ⓦ polorbis.co.uk. Weekend breaks in Warsaw, Kraków and Gdańsk, and 7- and 14-day tours of the country's top sights.

Regent Holidays UK ☎ 02035 532 735, ⓦ regent-holidays. co.uk. City breaks and tailor-made itineraries in Poland and neighbouring countries from a long-standing specialist.

Roadscholar US ☎ 1 800 454 5768, ⓦ roadscholar.org. Specialists in educational and activity programmes for senior travellers, offering general Central European art-and-culture tours and Polish heritage tours.

Visas and red tape

Citizens of EU countries (including the UK, for as long as it remains part of the EU), the USA, Canada, Australia and New Zealand can stay in Poland for up to ninety days without a **visa**. Once the ninety days are up, you have to leave the country or apply for a residence permit. Nationals of other countries should check current visa regulations with the nearest Polish consulate before setting out. Visa requirements do sometimes change and it is always advisable to check the current situation.

POLISH EMBASSIES ABROAD

Australia 7 Turrana St, Yarralumla, Canberra, ACT 2600 ☎ 02 6272 1000, ⓦ canberra.msz.gov.pl.

Canada 443 Daly Ave, Ottawa, Ontario K1N 6H3 ☎ 613 789-0468, ⓦ ottawa.msz.gov.pl.

Ireland 5 Ailesbury Rd, Ballsbridge, Dublin D04 W221 ☎ 01 283 0855, ⓦ dublin.msz.gov.pl.

New Zealand Level 4, Solnet House, 70 The Terrace, Wellington ☎ 04 499 7844, ⓦ wellington.msz.gov.pl.

South Africa 14 Amos Street, Colbyn 0083, Pretoria ☎ 12 430 2631, ⓦ pretoria.msz.gov.pl.

UK 47 Portland Place, London W1B 1JH ☎ 0207 2913 520, ⓦ london.mfa.gov.pl.

US 2640 16th Street NW, Washington, DC 20009 ☎ 202 499-1700, ⓦ waszyngton.msz.gov.pl.

Getting around

Poland's transport infrastructure has undergone considerable improvement in the last decade. Faster intercity rail services, new highways and an improved choice of long-distance buses have all made travel easier, ensuring that you can fit a lot more of the country into your trip. Be aware, however, that away from the main intercity routes, bus and train services are still slow, and poor or busy roads mean that you won't get around much quicker by car. Although transport costs are rising, the price of public transport tickets and car hire remains lower than in Western Europe.

By train

The Polish **railway companies** operate a multiplicity of trains, and tickets valid for one type of service are rarely valid for another. Thanks to recent track improvements, intercity services are on the whole much quicker than they used to be (Warsaw–Kraków takes 2hr 25min; Warsaw–Gdańsk 2hr 50min; Warsaw–Poznań 3hr 40min). Away from these prime routes, however, journey times are much slower, and a leisurely approach to rail travel is advised. Some big-city train stations have been completely modernized, are easy to navigate, and have a range of shopping and eating facilities; others feature inadequate information displays and long queues for tickets.

Train companies

The biggest of the rail companies is **PKP InterCity** (ⓦ intercity.pl), which runs Express InterCity Premium (EIP), Express InterCity (EIC), InterCity (IC), EuroCity (EC) and TLK trains. EIP use modern Pendolino trains and run on premium routes (such as Gdańsk–Warsaw–Kraków or Warsaw–Gdańsk); while EIC and IC trains are almost as fast and comfortable as EIP but use slightly older locomotives and carriages. EC trains are intercity services that run between Polish cities and destinations in neighbouring countries. TLK (which stands for Twoje Linie Kolejowe or "Your Own Railway") are cheaper intercity services that use older carriages (usually compartment trains with limited legroom), but are only slightly slower than their EIP, EIC and IC equivalents.

The **PolRegio** company (ⓦ polregio.pl) is responsible for running local or cross-country trains that travel at slower speeds than their PKP equivalents and stop at a lot more stations en route. There is also a large number of **local train companies** operating services in specific regions. For example, Koleje Mazowieckie (ⓦ mazowieckie.com.pl) operate local trains in Warsaw and central Poland; Koleje Dolnośląskie (ⓦ kolejedolnoslaskie.eu) operate trains in Wrocław and Lower Silesia; and Koleje Śląskie (ⓦ kolejeslaskie. com) provide services in Katowice and Upper Silesia. To complicate matters further, the **Warsaw Municipal Transport** company (ZTM; ⓦ ztm.waw.pl) operate commuter trains in and around the capital.

Ticket prices for PolRegio and the regional train companies are significantly lower than those charged by PKP InterCity, but train quality can be unpredictable – many services use modern comfortable rolling stock, others still use rattly old carriages with uncomfortable seats.

Tickets

Tickets for one type of train are not valid for another, so always be precise about which train you wish to travel on when buying your ticket. At many stations (especially the bigger ones), tickets for **PKP InterCity** services are sold from one counter (displaying the PKP InterCity logo), while tickets for PolRegio and local trains are sold from another – so check that you are in the right place before you start queueing. In big-city stations like Warsaw Centralna and Kraków Główny, international tickets are sold at a separate counter.

Reservations (miejscówka; 5zł) are obligatory on EIP, EIC, IC, EC and TLK services. **Ticket prices** are highest on the premium, EIP, EIC or EC services – a TLK service is often an affordable alternative. For example, a second-class single ticket from Warsaw to Kraków costs around 150zł on the EIP Pendolino service (2hr 25min); 60zł on a TLK train (2hr 50min). Tickets for all PKP InterCity services can be purchased online on the PKP website; buying tickets online over a week before the date of travel can be significantly cheaper than buying them on the day. First class (pierwsza klasa) coaches are usually 25–50 percent more expensive than second-class (druga klasa) – worth considering if you are travelling on TLK trains, where second-class accommodation is prone to sardine-like conditions, especially at weekends or during holidays.

Discounted tickets (ulgowy) are available for senior citizens and for children aged between 4 and 10 years; those under 4 travel free, though they're not supposed to occupy a seat. For students, ISIC cards no longer entitle you to discounted travel within Poland. InterRail and Eurail passes are valid in Poland (see page 26).

If you've boarded a train without the proper ticket (or if you are starting your journey from an unstaffed station with no ticket-buying facilities), seek out the **conductor**, who will sell you the right ticket.

Overnight trains

Some long intercity journeys (for example from Kraków to Szczecin or from Zakopane to Gdańsk) can be made **overnight**, with trains conveniently timed to leave around 10 or 11pm and arrive between 6 and 9am. For these, it's advisable to book either a **sleeper** (sypialne) or **couchette** (kuszetka) in advance; the total cost will probably be less than a room in a cheap hotel. Sleepers cost about 150zł per head in a three-bunk compartment (though it's rare that all three beds are used), complete with washbasin, towels, sheets, blankets and a snack. At about 120zł, couchettes have six bunks and also come with sheets, a blanket and a pillow.

Booking a sleeper or couchette is often done at a separate counter (look for the bed logo). Since many officials in smaller stations don't speak English, a good way to get the precise ticket you want is to write all the details down and show them at the counter.

Station practicalities

In train stations, the departures are normally listed on **yellow posters** marked odjazdy, with arrivals on **white posters** headed przyjazdy. Fast trains are marked in red and slower local services in black. An "R" in a square means that seat reservations are obligatory. Additionally, there may be figures at the bottom indicating the dates between which a particular train does (kursuje) or doesn't (nie kursuje) run – the latter usually underlined by a warning wiggly line. The platform (peron) is also indicated.

Information counters, if they exist, are usually heralded by long queues and often manned by non-English-speaking staff. Train times can be looked up on the internet on ⓦrozklad-pkp.pl or on the ever-reliable ⓦbahn.com.

Polish stations have a rather confusing **platform numbering** system, in which one set of numbers refers to the platforms themselves and another set of numbers refers to the tracks on either side – so take care that you board the right train. Electronic departure boards are yet to be installed in many smaller Polish stations, and trains don't always display boards stating their route, so it pays to ask before boarding.

The main station in a city is identified by the name Główny or Centralny. These are open round the clock and usually have such **facilities** as waiting rooms, toilets, kiosks, restaurants, snack bars, cafés, and luggage lockers. Facilities on the trains are much poorer, though EIP and EIC trains have a buffet car.

By bus

Poland's **bus network** (often referred to as "PKS" after the state-run company that used to operate it) consists of a multitude of regional and national companies, and is extraordinarily comprehensive. It's in rural districts not touched by the railway network that buses come into their own, although a growing number of bus companies are offering intercity routes that provide a viable alternative to rail travel. One of these is **Polski Bus** (ⓦpolskibus. com), who run fast, comfortable services between Warsaw and major cities – although they only sell tickets online or by phone, and frequently stop at locations different from the main bus stations.

Elsewhere, popular routes linking major towns and cities (such as Kraków–Zakopane or Warsaw–Białystok) are usually operated by comfortable modern vehicles with onboard wi-fi. Some popular routes are handled by fast minibuses – be aware that they have a small number of seats and tickets sell out quickly. Out in the provinces, vehicles are more likely to be old, smelly and uncomfortable. Rural journeys can be time-consuming because of poor road quality – in some areas buses rarely exceed an average of 30km per hour.

Noticeboards show departures (*odjazdy*) and arrivals (*przyjazdy*) not only in the bus stations, but on all official stopping places along the route. "Fast" (*pospieszny*) buses (which carry a small supplement) are marked in red; slow in black. As at the train stations, departures and arrivals are marked on different boards, so make sure you're looking at the right one. It's very rare to find an English speaker in the average Polish bus station, so it's best to write your destination down to avoid any confusion.

Tickets

In towns and cities, the main bus station (*dworzec autobusowy* or *dworzec PKS*) is usually alongside the train station. Tickets can be bought in the terminal building. **Booking** in the terminal ensures a seat, as a number will be allocated to you on your ticket. However, the lack of computerized systems means that many stations cannot allocate seats for services starting out from another town. In such cases, you have to wait until the bus arrives and buy a ticket – which may be for standing room only – from the driver. The same procedure can also be followed (provided the bus isn't already full to overflowing) if you arrive too late to buy a ticket at the counter. Some of the bigger bus companies offer student discounts, so it always pays to ask.

By car

Poland's recently-expanded **motorway** network ensures fast links between some of the main cities: the main routes are Warsaw–Łódź, Łódź–Gdańsk, Łódź–Wrocław, Łódź–Poznań and Wrocław–Katowice–Kraków. However, there's a dearth of multi-lane highways away from these routes, ensuring that you'll spend much of your time trailing behind a stream of slow-moving cars and lorries. Poland's rural backroads are quiet and hassle-free by comparison, and – providing you have a decent map – present the perfect terrain for unhurried touring.

If you're **bringing your own car**, you'll need to carry your vehicle's registration document. If the car is not in your name, you must have a letter of permission signed by the owner and authorized by your national motoring organization. You'll also need your **driving licence** (international driving licences aren't officially required, though they can be a help in tricky situations), and you may need an international insurance green card to extend your insurance cover – check with your insurers to see whether you're covered or not.

Car rental

Car rental in Poland works out at about 120–180zł a day and 700–800zł a week for a Nissan Micra or equivalent with unlimited mileage. A Volkswagen Passat or equivalent will cost fifty percent more. Cars can be booked through the usual agents or in Poland itself: all the four major operators have their own agents in most of the big Polish cities. Cars will only be rented to people over 21 (or for some types of vehicle, over 25) who have held a full licence for more than a year.

CAR-RENTAL AGENCIES

Avis Ⓦ avis.com
Budget Ⓦ budget.com
Europcar Ⓦ europcar.com.pl
Hertz Ⓦ hertz.com.pl
Joka Ⓦ joka.com.pl
SIXT Ⓦ sixt.pl

Rules of the road

The main rules of the road are pretty clear, though there are some particularly Polish twists liable to catch out the unwary. The basic rules are: traffic drives **on the right**; it is compulsory to wear **seat belts** outside built-up areas; children under 12 years of age must sit in the back; seat belts must be worn in the back if fitted; headlights must be switched on at all times; and right of way must be given to public transport vehicles (including trams). Driving with more than 0.2 promile (parts per thousand) of alcohol in the bloodstream (about equivalent to one glass of beer or wine) is strictly prohibited, as is talking on hand-held **mobile phones** while driving.

You're also required to carry a red warning triangle, a first-aid kit and a set of replacement bulbs, and display a national identification sticker. **Speed limits** are 50kph in built-up areas (60kph from 11pm to 5am), 90kph on country roads, 100kph on main highways, 120kph on dual carriageways, 140kph on motorways, and 80kph if you're pulling a caravan or trailer. Speed traps are common, particularly on major trunk roads such as the Gdańsk–Warsaw route, so caution is strongly advised, especially on the approach to, and when travelling through, small towns and villages. Fines for transgressors are administered on the spot.

Fuel

Poland's roads are pretty well served with **filling stations**. Many stations in cities and along the main routes are open 24 hours a day, others from around 6am to 10pm; almost all out-of-town stations close on Sundays. Unleaded fuel (*benzyna bezołowiowa*) and diesel are available at most stations. Carrying at least one fuel can permanently topped up will help to offset worries in rural areas.

Car crime

Car-related crime – both simple break-ins and outright theft – can be a problem in Poland, with foreign-registered vehicles one of the major targets. In big towns especially, always park your vehicle in a **guarded parking lot** (*parking strzeżony*), never in an open street – even daylight break-ins occur with depressing frequency. Never leave anything of importance, including vehicle documents, in the car. Guarded lots are not too expensive (about 30zł a day, more in major city centres) and in most towns and cities you can usually find one located centrally – the major hotels almost always have their own nearby. If you have a break-in, report it to the police immediately. You're unlikely to get anything back, but you'll need their signed report for insurance claim purposes back home.

Breakdowns and spares

The national **breakdown emergency number** is ☎9637. If you have insurance against breakdowns, the tow will be free.

The wide range of cars now available in Poland means that you will not have problems finding **spares** for major Western makes. If it's simply a case of a flat tyre, head for the nearest sizeable garage.

By plane

The domestic network of **LOT** (Ⓦlot.com), the Polish national airline, operates daily flights from Kraków to Gdańsk, and from Warsaw to Gdańsk, Katowice, Kraków, Poznań, Rzeszów, Szczecin and Wrocław – each of which take about an hour. Bookings are best done online, although tickets can also be bought from high-street travel agents in Polish cities. Prices vary according to how far in advance you book and which day you choose to travel – expect anything between 200zł and 650zł each way.

By bike

Cycling is an ideal way to see a predominantly rural country like Poland. Particularly on the backroads, surfaces are generally in good shape, and there isn't much **traffic** around – anyone used to cycling in Western European traffic is in for a treat. An additional plus is the mercifully flat nature of much of the terrain, which allows you to cycle quite long distances without great effort. You'll need to bring your own bike and a supply of basic spares like inner tubes and a puncture repair kit: except in a few major cities like Warsaw and Kraków and a number of southern mountain areas like the Bieszczady, **bike rental** and spare part facilities are still a comparative rarity.

Taking your bike on **trains** isn't a problem as long as there's a luggage van on board: if there isn't you usually have to sit with it in the last carriage of the train where, if you're lucky, there'll be fewer passengers; either way there's a nominal fee. **Hotels** will usually put your bike either in a locked luggage room or a guarded parking lot. You need to exercise at least as much caution concerning security as you would in any city at home: strong locks and chaining your bike to immobile objects are the order of the day, and you should always try to take your bike indoors at night.

City transport

Trams are the basis of the public transport system in nearly all Polish cities. They usually run from about 5am to 11pm, and departure times are clearly posted at the stops. **Tickets** can be bought from newspaper kiosks and can only be used in the city where they were bought. On boarding, you should immediately validate your ticket in one of the machines; checks by inspectors are rare, but they do happen from time to time. Note that some tickets have to be validated at both ends (arrows will indicate if this is so); this is for the benefit of children and senior citizens, who travel half-price and thus have to cancel only one end per journey. Tickets are frequently valid for a particular time-span – so if you have a 30-minute ticket you won't need a new ticket each time you change from one tram to another providing the 30 minutes aren't up.

Tram tickets are valid on **municipal buses**, and the same system for validating them applies. Note

ADDRESSES

In Poland the street name is always written before the number. The word for street (**ulica**, abbreviated to ul.) or avenue (**aleja**, abbreviated al.) is often missed out – for example ulica Senatorska is simply known as Senatorska. The other frequent abbreviation is pl., short for **plac** (square). See page 482 for details on the most common street names.

that on both buses and trams, **night services** are often priced differently to daytime services and require different tickets.

Taxis

The price of **taxis** is cheap enough to make them a viable proposition for regular use during your visit. **Taxi ranks** are usually easy to find outside stations and in town centres. Make sure you choose a taxi with an illuminated sign on its roof bearing the company name and phone number. If you pick up a taxi in the street, you're more likely to pay above-average prices; the safest and cheapest option is to ring a quoted taxi number and order one. Generally speaking, you should expect to **pay** 15–25zł for a cross-city journey, depending on your time of travel (prices are fifty percent higher after 11pm). Prices are also raised by fifty percent for journeys outside the city limits. However, costs are always negotiable for longer journeys – between towns, for example – and can work out very reasonable if split among a group.

The app-based taxi service **Uber** is available in several major cities across Poland and may expand further in future. For a full list consult ⓦ uber.com/cities.

Accommodation

Accommodation will probably account for most of your essential expenditure in Poland. Prices have risen in recent years, although bargains are still easy to come by – especially in the rural resort areas favoured by the Poles themselves. Most hostels, hotels and campsites offer free wi-fi.

Hotels

There's a growing range and diversity of **hotel accommodation** in Poland, although standards of service and value for money vary widely from place to place. The international five-star grading system is in use and is a reasonably accurate guide to quality. As a general rule, one-star hotels provide rooms with a bed and not much else; two-star hotels offer rooms with at least an en-suite shower; and three-star hotels are likely to provide you with a telephone and a TV. Anything four-star or five-star is in the international business or luxury league. **Breakfast** is usually included in the room price; we have noted exceptions in the reviews.

There are very few one-star hotels in Poland (and those that exist are probably not worth recom-

mending). There is however a huge choice of **two- and three-star hotels**, and these come in all shapes in sizes – from concrete blocks built in the 1960s and 1970s to suburban villas converted into hotels by enterprising owners. Many fine nineteenth-century hotels have ended also up as two- and three-star hotels, especially near main railway stations in Kraków, Poznań and Wrocław. Prices and quality vary considerably in this category, but for a standard medium-range double room expect to pay anything from 160zł to 220zł a night – significantly more in Warsaw and Kraków. The oldest of these two- and three-star hotels often have a few cheap rooms with shared facilities as well as the standard en suites which are invariably offered to new arrivals – there will be a substantial difference in price, so always ask.

Five-star hotels are still something of a rarity outside Warsaw and Kraków, but **four-star** establishments are mushrooming all over the place, largely thanks to the booming numbers of business travellers. Many major **international hotel chains** have built brand-new hotels in Poland's major cities, some of which (such as the new *Hiltons* in Warsaw, Wrocław and Gdańsk) have made a major contribution to the urban scene. There is also a growing number of new-build **boutique hotels** and design hotels offering a dose of urban style to art-conscious travellers, especially in popular city-break destinations such as Kraków, Gdańsk, Poznań and Wrocław. Double-room prices at this level start at about 360zł, although you may well find significant reductions at weekends.

Hostels

Poland's cities are increasingly well-served by backpacker-oriented hostels providing neat and tidy **dormitory accommodation** and a friendly atmosphere. They're invariably equipped with kitchens,

---

ACCOMMODATION PRICES

Unless specified otherwise, prices given in this book are quoted per night for the **cheapest double room** in high season, including breakfast. For **hostels,** we quote the per-person rate for a dorm bed, as well as the price of private rooms where available. For **campsites**, we give the price for a tent pitch for two people plus a car. All necessary taxes and service charges are included in the quoted rates.

The majority of places will expect you to pay in złoty, though prices are often quoted in euros.

washing machines and common rooms, and aren't subject to curfews. Most backpacker hostels also offer a handful of **self-contained doubles** – they're not always cheap, but are perfect if you want to enjoy the hostel atmosphere but require privacy at the same time. Prices for dorm beds are around the 60–80zł mark; while doubles start at around 150zł. We have noted in the reviews where there is an extra charge for **breakfast**.

If you are in a town which doesn't have any backpacker hostels, bear in mind that many of Poland's two- and three-star hotels (see page 32) have rooms sleeping three or four people – ideal for groups travelling together.

Apartments

An increasing number of establishments in Warsaw, Kraków and other cities are offering **serviced apartments** in modern blocks. These usually offer the same comforts as a three-star hotel or above, but come with the added advantage of a small kitchenette (breakfast won't be provided) and – depending on what size of apartment is available – the chance to spread yourself out a bit more than you would do in a hotel room.

Prices depend on how many of you are sharing, but are usually slightly cheaper than the equivalent level of accommodation in a hotel. Always enquire about the dimensions of an apartment before committing yourself: some are generously proportioned, others are little more than glorified cupboards.

B&Bs, pensions and rural homestays

There's a growing number of urban **B&Bs** in Poland, though so far this phenomenon is limited to Warsaw, Kraków and a few other cities. Ranging in style from cute converted attics, flats and houses to purpose-built blocks that resemble hotels in all but name, many of these places ooze with character due to the individual tastes of the owners.

Outside the main cities, some of Poland's best accommodation deals can be found in the growing stock of **pensions** (*pensjonaty*) situated in major holiday areas – especially in the mountains, the Mazurian lake district, and along the coast. There's no hard and fast rule governing what constitutes a pension in Poland: some are actually full-size hotels that use the **pensjonat** title to convey a sense of cosiness and informality; others are private houses transformed into family-run B&Bs.

In addition, an increasing number of Polish farmers are offering B&B-style accommodation (known as **agroturystyka**) in order to augment their income. As well as being ideal for those seeking rural tranquillity, they also offer the chance to observe a working farm and sample locally produced food and drink.

All of the above tend to offer simple en-suite rooms, often equipped with the additional comforts of a fridge and an electric kettle. Rates are usually between 120zł and 300zł per double, depending on style, and include breakfast.

The local tourist information office (if there is one) will have lists of local pensions and rural homestays.

Private rooms

You can get a **room in a private house** (*kwatera prywatna*) in many parts of the country. In urban areas these tend to be located in shabby flats, which may be situated some way from the centre of town. You will be sharing your hosts' bathroom, and breakfast will not be included. In lake, mountain and seaside resorts, however, hosts are often more attuned to the needs of tourists and may provide rooms with an en-suite bathroom, electric kettle, and even TV. Staying in private rooms doesn't necessarily constitute a great way of meeting the locals: some hosts will brew you a welcome glass of tea and show a willingness to talk; most will simply give you a set of house keys and leave you to get on with it.

Local travel agencies undertake the job of allocating rooms – otherwise the local tourist information centre will hand out a list of addresses. Expect to pay around 40zł per person per night.

At the unofficial level, many houses in the main holiday areas hang out signs saying *Noclegi* (lodging) or *Pokoje* (rooms). It's up to you to bargain over the price.

Mountain huts

In mountain areas, a reasonably generous number of **mountain huts** (*schroniska*), many of them PTTK-run (see page 46), enable you to make long-distance treks without having to make detours down into the villages for the night; they are clearly marked on hiking maps. Accommodation is in very basic dormitories but costs are nominal and you can often get cheap and filling hot meals; in summer, the huts can be very crowded indeed, as they are obliged to accept all comers. As a rule, the refuges are open all year round but it's always worth checking for closures or renovations in progress before setting out.

Campsites

There are some five hundred **campsites** throughout the country, classified in three categories: category 1 sites usually have amenities such as a restaurant and showers, while category 3 sites amount to little more than poorly lit, run-down expanses of grass; category 2 sites could be anywhere in between.

Apart from a predictably dense concentration in the main holiday areas, sites can also be found in most cities: the ones on the outskirts are almost invariably linked by bus to the centre and often have the benefits of a peaceful location and a swimming pool. The major drawback is that most are open between May and September only, though a few do operate all year round. Prices usually work out at a little under 20zł per tent or caravan space plus 20zł per person, and 15zł per vehicle.

One specifically Polish feature is that you don't necessarily have to bring a tent to stay at many campsites, as there are often **bungalows** or **chalets** for rent, generally complete with toilet and shower. Though decidedly spartan in appearance, these are good value at around 50zł per head. In summer, however, they are usually booked long in advance.

Eating and drinking

Poland has a distinctive national cuisine, with trademark dishes like *pierogi*, potato pancakes, pork chops and roast joints of poultry ensuring that there's plenty to work your way through while you're here. As in much of northern Europe, traditional Polish cooking is strong on calories, although fresh vegetables and salads are an ever-present part of the culinary scene.

Poland's cities are increasingly cosmopolitan places, and – whether you're aiming for fast food or fine dining – international food is never hard to find.

Restaurants, caféterias and cafés

There's a high concentration of **restaurants** (*restau-racja*) in tourist-trodden areas of Warsaw, Kraków and other major cities, ranging in style from upmarket

establishments with French-flavoured menus to unpretentious, informal places serving Polish staples at moderate prices. Out in the provinces, the choice is more limited, with most restaurant menus sticking to the simpler Polish dishes.

One type of eating place you'll find throughout Poland is the **cafeteria** (usually called *bar mleczny* or **"milk bar"**, although in Kraków and the south they're more commonly labelled *jadłodajnia*), where customers order their food at the counter and then await a shout from the kitchen indicating that their chosen dish is ready. These cafeterias are often the best places to find the full repertoire of traditional Polish food, and prices are reassuringly cheap.

Cafés (*kawiarnia*) usually concentrate on food of the ice cream and cakes variety, although several also offer salads, sandwiches and other light meals.

An increasing number of cafés and restaurants now offer a **breakfast** menu – particularly useful if you are staying in a hostel or private apartment where breakfast is not served.

Costs

The **cost** of main courses in Polish restaurants hover between 20zł and 60zł, depending on the estab-lishment, although there are plenty of filling soups and simple dishes (such as the popular Polish staple *pierogi*) that cost considerably less than this. **Tips** aren't usually given in a cafeteria, but in restaurants and cafés with table service it's polite to leave ten percent or round up the bill to the nearest convenient figure.

Local dishes

Most restaurants and caféterias will offer a broadly similar menu of Polish standards, kicking off with a solid repertoire of **soups**. Most famous of these is **borsht** (*barszcz*), a reddish beetroot-flavoured broth with a mildly sweet-and-sour taste. Three more soup staples are the tangy rye-based *żurek*, the barley-and-potato soup *krupnik* and the thick beany *fasolka*.

One undoubted Polish culinary classic is the **pierog** (plural *pierogi*), a small parcel of dough stuffed with a variety of savoury or sweet fillings. *Pierogi ruskie* come with potato and soft white cheese; *pierogi z kapustą I grzybami* are filled with cabbage and mushrooms; *pierogi z mięsem* with minced meat. *Pierogi* are usually boiled; many places also offer baked *pierogi* (*pierogi z pieca*) which have crunchy crusts and are usually bigger than the boiled version – be careful how many you order.

Other ubiquitous national specialities include **bigos** (a filling stew comprising a mixture of meats, cabbage, mushrooms and spices), **gołąbki** (cabbage leaves stuffed with rice and meat) and **placki** (potato pancakes), either served on their own with sour cream or covered in **goulash** (**gulasz**).

Otherwise, the basis of most main courses is a fried or grilled cut of **meat** in a thick sauce, most common of which is the **kotlet schabowy**, a pork cutlet which is often fried in batter. Other favourites include **flaczki** (tripe cooked in a spiced bouillon stock with vegetables – usually very spicy), and **golonka** (pig's leg with horseradish). Roast duck with apples is the standout poultry dish.

Fish and chips is very much a Polish staple in sea, lake and mountain areas: halibut (*halibut*) and cod (*dorsz*) are popular along the Baltic coast; zander (*sandacz*) and perch (*okoń*) rule the roost in the lakes, while mountain trout (*pstrąg*) is most common in the south.

Main meals usually come with a side order of **salad** (*surówka*), which in Poland usually means grated carrot, beetroot and cabbage. As far as **desserts** are concerned, cheesecake (*sernik*) and apple pie (*szarlotka*) both have the status of national culinary institutions, while pancakes (*naleśniki*) filled with a variety of sweet fillings also crop up on pretty much every menu.

Vegetarians

A meal without meat is a contradiction in terms for most Poles, and vegetarians will often be forced to find solace in customary standbys like omelettes, cheese-based dishes and salads. Thankfully, Kraków and a handful of other cities now boast a sprinkling of dedicated vegetarian cafeterias, and most mainstream restaurants have a (albeit limited) vegetarian section in the menu. Crucially, Poland's main centres have a growing number of good-quality **Italian restaurants**, where Mediterranean salads and meat-free pastas are the order of the day.

Vegetarian dishes are listed on menus as **potrawy jarskie**; other useful phrases are *bez mięsa* ("without meat") and *bez ryby* ("without fish").

Drinking

Most **daytime** drinking takes place in a **kawiarnia**, or café, which range in style from functional places with plastic furniture to grand nineteenth-century establishments with apron-wearing staff and a full menu of patisserie-style goodies. From here onwards however distinctions become rather blurred, with places that call themselves **pubs** or **bars** catering for coffee-drinkers during the daytime and serious beer- and spirit-guzzlers come the

evening. There's certainly no shortage of characterful night-time drinking holes in the major cities, with candlelit bohemian haunts, flashy disco-pubs and swanky cocktail bars all vying for custom.

Tea and coffee

Tea (*herbata*), is usually served black, so you will need to specify if you want it with milk (*z mlekiem*). The quality of **coffee** (*kawa*) varies considerably from place to place, with international-style coffee bars in city centres serving up espresso, cappuccino and other Italian-inspired brews; while provincial cafés and train station snack bars offer a dispiriting brown liquid made by dumping grounds (or instant powder) in a cup and pouring water over them. If you're anything of a coffee connoisseur it's best to stick to the classier-looking places. In the cheaper cafés, coffee is served black unless you ask otherwise, in which case specify with milk (*z mlekiem*) or with cream (*ze śmietanką*).

Soft drinks

A full range of international soft drinks is available in Poland. Look out also for the Polish-made range of **John Lemon 'lemonades'** (they actually come in all kinds of fruit flavours including pear, plum, rhubarb and quince), which are only lightly fizzy and are free of artificial preservatives.

Alcoholic drinks

Night-time drinking venues all offer a broad range of international drinks, although traditional Polish spirits – especially **vodka** – frequently occupy pride of place. There has been a revolution in Polish **beer**-drinking over the last few years, with the unexciting lagers produced by mass-market breweries (such as Żywiec, Tyskie and Lech) increasingly challenged by characterful **ales and craft brews** churned out by small, local producers. An increasing number of

---

STREET FOOD AND SNACKS

Despite the onward march of the **kebab stall** (there's hardly a single high street in Poland without one), indigenous snack food has proved surprisingly resilient to globalization. The **fried fish stall** (*smażalnia ryb*) is a ubiquitous sight in seaside, lake and mountain resorts. In towns and cities, the best bet for a substantial post-pub bite is the **zapiekanka**, a baguette-like piece of toasted bread topped with cheese, mushrooms and a choice of other toppings.

city-centre bars will have a selection of small-brewery beers in the fridge, and there's a growing number of multi-tap pubs with a seasonally-changing choice of brews chalked up on a board beside the bar. The town brewery in Miłosław near Poznań (see page 413) is one example of a small facility reactivated in the 1990s and now producing a wide range of highly original ales. Craft breweries are all over the place; Trzech Kumpli and Pinta are leading examples of Poland's growing number of "**flying breweries**" – beer makers that don't have their own base but use small breweries throughout the country to turn out excellent limited-edition beers.

The media

As you would expect from a country of nearly 40 million people, Poland boasts newspapers, magazines and websites devoted to just about everything. The problem is finding quality sources of information in the English language. If you just want to read international news and lifestyle magazines, there's a wide range available in big-city multimedia stores.

Newspapers and magazines

One Polish daily **newspaper** that has become a major European media institution is *Gazeta Wyborcza* (ⓦ wyborcza.pl), founded in 1989 as the main organ of the anti-communist opposition. *Gazeta* is strong on investigative journalism and intellectual comment, and fiercely retains its liberal political stance. Its main competitor is *Rzeczpospolita*, originally the official voice of the communist government, and now an influential right-wing broadsheet.

Glossy monthly **magazines** are devoured as eagerly in Poland as anywhere else. Home-grown women's magazines like *Ewa* and *Twój Styl* have been joined by Polish-language versions of *Cosmopolitan*, *Marie Claire* and others; the worldwide explosion in men's lifestyle magazines has been mirrored here too.

English-language publications

As far as English-language media are concerned, the *Warsaw Voice* (a web-zine which is also published on paper four times a year; ⓦ warsawvoice.pl), is slanted towards political and business news. The *Warsaw Insider* (produced monthly on paper and distributed free in hotels and restaurants; ⓦ warsawinsider.pl) is far superior when it comes to lifestyle, culture, local knowledge and good writing. The web-based *Kraków Post* (ⓦ krakowpost.com) offers a mixture of local news and lifestyle features.

Western newspapers and magazines are widely available in the big cities. The biggest selection is offered by the Empik chain of multi-media stores.

TV and radio

Poland's state broadcaster **TVP** has a reputation for slavishly following the dictates of whichever party happens to be in power, although a scattering of privately-owned TV channels ensures a degree of political pluralism. The regular diet of game shows, soap operas and American films doesn't differ that much from anywhere else in Europe, although Polish TV has managed to preserve a few quirks of its own – notably the tendency for foreign imports to be dubbed by a single **lektor**, who reads all the parts in the same voice. Most hotel TVs offer a selection of cable or satellite channels, although Polish-language stations predominate – only higher-end hotels offer a genuine choice of English-language programmes.

The state radio broadcaster **Polskie Radio** (ⓦ the news.pl) broadcasts in English via the internet and also has English-language feature content on its website.

VODKA

Vodka (*wódka*) is very much the national drink, and most self-respecting bars will have a broad selection in stock. Vodka is usually served on its own, without ice (vodka bottles are usually kept ready-chilled in the bar's fridge), in a shot glass measuring anything from 30 to 50ml, and is usually downed in one – although Poles may forgive foreigners who prefer to sip their spirits. Most Polish vodka is made from grain and has a subtle grainy taste. Speciality vodkas include **Żubrówka**, made in Eastern Poland and flavoured with the local bison grass, and **Żołądkowa Gorzka**, an amber-coloured herbal vodka that is relatively sweet in taste and works excellently as a digestif. **Wiśniówka** (cherry vodka) is another popular shot.

The most sought after Polish vodka is **Starka**, a bronze-coloured grain spirit that is only bottled after being aged for several years in barrels. Starka tastes as exquisite as an aged malt whisky, and costs just about as much too.

EASTER WEEK

The highlight of the Catholic year is Easter (*Wielkanoc*), which is heralded by a glut of spring fairs, offering the best of the early livestock and agricultural produce.

Easter Week kicks off with **Palm Sunday** (*Niedziela Palmowa*), when palms are brought to church and paraded in processions. Often the painted and decorated "palms" are handmade, sometimes with competitions for the largest or most beautiful. The most famous procession takes place at Kalwaria Zebrzydowska near Kraków (see page 313), inaugurating a spectacular week-long series of mystery plays, re-enacting Christ's Passion.

Good Friday (*Wielki Piątek*) sees visits to mock-ups of the Holy Sepulchre – whether permanent structures such as at Kalwaria Zebrzydowska (see page 313) and Wambierzyce in Silesia (see page 397), or ad hoc creations, as is traditional in Warsaw. **Easter Saturday** (*Wielka Sobota*) is when baskets of painted eggs are taken along to church to be blessed and sprinkled with holy water. The consecrated food is eaten at breakfast on **Easter Day** (*Niedziela Wielkanocna*), when the most solemn Masses of the year are celebrated. On **Easter Monday** (*Lany Poniedziałek*) girls are doused with water by boys to "make them fertile" (a marginally better procedure than in the neighbouring Czech Republic where they're beaten with sticks). Even in the cosmopolitan cities you'll see gangs of boys waiting in the streets or leaning out of first-floor windows waiting to throw water bombs at passing girls.

Festivals

One manifestation of Poland's intense commitment to Roman Catholicism is that all the great feast days of the Church calendar are celebrated with whole-hearted devotion, many of the participants donning the colourful traditional costumes for which the country is known.

As a supplement to these, Poland has a calendar bursting with **cultural festivals**, particularly in the fields of film, music and drama. As well as a strong ethnic/folk music scene, there are an increasing number of open-air **pop/rock festivals** in summer.

Events calendar

Precise dates of cultural festivals can change from one year to the next, so check websites or local tourist information offices before travelling.

JANUARY/FEBRUARY

Epiphany (Dzień Trzech Króli) Everywhere. January 6. Groups of carol singers move from house to house, chalking the letters K, M and B (symbolizing the three Kings: Kaspar, Melchior and Balthazar) on each doorway as a record of their visit. The chalk marks are usually left untouched throughout the coming year, thereby ensuring good fortune for the household.

MARCH/APRIL

Review of Stage Songs (Przegląd Piosenki Aktorskiej) Wrocław Ⓦ ppa.wroclaw.pl. Mid-March. Singer-songwriters, experimental musical theatre and intellectual cabaret, with a fair smattering of international guests.

Katowice Street Art Festival Katowice Ⓦ katowicestreet artfestival.pl Late March to early April. Mural painting, plein-air installations and arty street performance characterize this innovative event.

Misteria Paschalia Kraków Ⓦ misteriapaschalia.com. Easter week. Festival of religious music through the ages.

Easter Beethoven Festival Warsaw Ⓦ beethoven.org.pl. Easter week. Works by Beethoven and other classical composers, frequently with a sacral theme.

Warsaw Theatre Meetings (Warszawskie Spotkania Teatralne) Warsaw Ⓦ warszawskie.org. April. Arguably the top domestic drama event of the year, with innovate productions from leading theatres all over Poland.

Jazz on the Oder (Jazz nad Odrą) Wrocław Ⓦ jnofestival.pl. Mid-April. Five days of top-quality international jazz ranging from big bands to freeform improvisation.

MAY

Probaltica Toruń Ⓦ probaltica.art.pl. Early May. Orchestral and chamber music featuring musicians from the Baltic and Scandinavian regions.

Night of the Museums (Noc muzeów) Venues all over Poland. Mid- to late May. Museums and galleries open up in the evening for free, generating an atmosphere of cultural carnival.

Kraków Film Music Festival (Festiwal muzyki filmowej) Kraków Ⓦ fmf.fm Mid- to late May. A celebration of soundtracks and film scores featuring orchestral concerts in various venues and an accompanying programme of lectures.

International Festival of Orthodox Church Music (Miedzynarodowy festiwal muzyki cerkiewnej) Hajnówka Ⓦ festiwal-hajnowka.pl. Late May. Haunting choral music from Orthodox choirs, with guest ensembles from all over Eastern Europe.

Contact Theatre Festival (Kontakt) Toruń Ⓦ teatr.torun.pl. Late May. One of Europe's foremost theatrical events, featuring outstanding drama from all over the continent. Even-numbered years only.

Łańcut Music Festival (Muzyczny festiwal w Łańcucie) Łańcut Ⓦ filharmonia.rzeszow.pl. Late May. Chamber music from some top international performers, with concerts taking place in southeast Poland's most sumptuous palace.

Kraków Film Festival (Krakowski festiwal filmowy) Kraków Ⓦ krakowfilmfestival.pl. Late May to early June. International festival of documentaries, animated films and shorts.

Corpus Christi (Boże Ciało) Everywhere. Late May or early June. Colourful processions take place everywhere where there is a church dedicated to Corpus Christi. The most famous takes place in Łowicz, where celebrations take the shape of a colourful folkloric pageant.

JUNE

Orange Warsaw Warsaw Ⓦ orangewarsawfestival.pl. Early June. Two- or three-day rock festival held at an out-of-town racecourse. There's a good mix of Polish and international acts – previous headliners include Beyoncé, Kings of Leon and Muse.

Dragon Parade (Parada smoków) Kraków Ⓦ paradasmokow.pl. First or second Sat in June. A fantastic parade of dragons on Kraków's main square followed by a *son et lumière* show by the river.

Hetman's Fair (Jarmark Hetmański) Zamość Ⓦ zdk.zamosc. pl. First or second weekend in June. Folk and crafts fair with market stalls and live music.

Midsummer's Eve (Wianki) Venues across Poland. June 23 or nearest weekend. Traditionally celebrated by virgins throwing wreaths into rivers while bonfires are lit on the water's edge, Wianki is nowadays celebrated with outdoor pop concerts and fireworks.

Malta Theatre Festival Poznań Ⓦ malta-festival.pl. Late June to early July. Outstanding modern drama, visual arts and music, with performances making full use of the city's outdoor spaces. A big feature of the festival is the series of lakeside gigs by international names (Manu Chao and Portishead have appeared in recent years).

Festival of Folk Bands and Singers (Festiwal kapel i śpiewaków ludowych) Kazimierz Dolny Ⓦ kazimierzdolny.pl. Late June. Traditional musicians from all over Poland ripping it up on an outdoor stage.

Festival of Jewish Culture (Festiwal kultury żydowskiej) Kraków Ⓦ jewishfestival.pl. Late June to early July. Ten days of theatre, film, workshops, discussions, and stomping klezmer music on an outdoor stage.

Open'er Gdynia Ⓦ opener.pl. Late June to early July. Poland's biggest commercial pop rock festival, with international acts entertaining a 100,000-strong crowd on an airfield outside Gdynia. Radiohead, Florence + the Machine and Red Hot Chili Peppers are among recent headliners.

Warsaw Summer Jazz Days Warsaw Ⓦ warsawsummerjazzdays. pl. Late June to early July. Jazz, jazz-rock and fusion from around the world in venues across town.

JULY

Different Sounds (Inne Brzmienia) Lublin Ⓦ innebrzmienia.eu. Early July. Free music festival on a city-centre meadow, featuring world music, alt rock and folk with a strong East European flavour.

Tauron New Music Festival (Tauron Nowa Muzyka) Katowice Ⓦ festiwalnowamuzyka.pl. Early July. Electronic music from dance-oriented beats to the avant-garde, performed in a range of post-industrial spaces.

Jazz in the Old Town (Jazz na Starówce) Warsaw Ⓦ jazznastarowce.pl. July & Aug. Summer-long season of Saturday-evening concerts on the Old Town Square.

Jarocin Jarocin (east of Poznań) Ⓦ jarocinfestiwal.pl. Early to mid-July. Poland's longest-standing alternative rock gathering, with (mostly Polish) punk music ancient and modern figuring heavily. Open-air, with tent site provided.

Przystanek Woodstock Kostrzyn (south of Szczecin) Ⓦ woodstock festival.pl. Mid-July. Open-air free festival of alt-rock, reggae and world music with anti-globalization, peace-and-solidarity theme.

Lemko Vatra (Łemkowska Watra) Zdynia (south of Gorlice) Ⓦ watrazdynia.pl. Second-to-last weekend of July. Open-air folklore festival celebrating the culture of the Lemkos, pastoral inhabitants of the Polish Carpathians.

Crossroads (Rozstaje) Kraków Ⓦ etnokrakow.pl. Late July. A week of world music from Poland and abroad, with some concerts on the main square, others in indoor concert venues.

Globaltica Gdynia Ⓦ globaltica.pl. Late July. Impressive world music weekender in a seaside park.

Magicians' Festival (Carnaval sztukmistrzów) Lublin Ⓦ sztukmistrze.eu. Late July. Inspired by Isaac Bashevis Singer's novel *The Magician of Lublin*, this street festival packs magicians, acrobats, musicians and all manner of entertainers into Lublin's Old Town.

St Dominic's Fair (Jarmark św. Dominika) Gdańsk Ⓦ jarmardominika.pl. Late July to mid-Aug. Three weeks of markets, craft stalls and outdoor concerts.

Audio River Płock Ⓦ audioriver.pl. Late July to early Aug. Long weekend of cutting-edge dance music and underground electronica beside the River Vistula, attracting the big names of the genre.

Shakespeare Festival (Festiwal Szekspirowski) Gdańsk Ⓦ teatrszekspirowski.pl. Late July to early Aug. Highly regarded drama festival featuring groundbreaking interpretations of the bard from around the world.

Two Riversides (Dwa Brzegi) Kazimierz Dolny and Janowiec nad Wisłą Ⓦ dwabrzegi.pl, Ⓦ kazimierzdolny.pl. Late July to early Aug. Independent film, world music and art exhibitions take over towns on opposite banks of the River Vistula.

Beskidy Culture Week (Tydzień Kultury Beskidzkiej) Żywiec Ⓦ rok.bielsko.pl. Late July to early Aug. Two festivals in one, with a three-day meeting of Polish highland folk groups (*Festiwal Górali Polskich*) swiftly followed by an international folklore festival (*Międzynarodowe Spotkania Folklorystyczne*).

AUGUST

New Horizons (Nowe Horyzonty) Wrocław Ⓦ nowehoryzonty. pl. Early Aug. Big international film festival featuring many of the best new movies from around Europe. Accompanying concerts and clubbing events round out the programme.

Chopin Festival (Festiwal Chopinowski) Duszniki-Zdrój Ⓦ festival.pl. Early Aug. Top international piano-playing talents pay tribute to Chopin in a charmingly old-fashioned spa resort once patronized by the maestro himself.

Off Festival Katowice Ⓦ off-festival.pl. Early to mid-Aug. Top-notch alternative rock with an international line-up, in a lakeside park just outside Katowice.

Jagiellonian Fair (Jarmark Jagiellonski) Lublin Ⓦ jarmark jagiellonski.pl. Mid-Aug. One of the biggest folk, craft and historical-reenactment fairs in the country, with stalls filling the city's Old Town.

Feast of the Assumption (Święto Wniebowzięcia NMP). Everywhere. Aug 15. The most important of the many holidays honouring the Virgin Mary, Assumption is marked all over Poland with Masses, processions, and pilgrimages to Marian shrines.

Kraków Live Kraków Ⓦ livefestival.pl. Mid-Aug. Two-day rock-pop festival featuring major international headliners, held in a field east of the centre.

International Festival of Highland Folklore (Międzynarodowy festiwal folkloru ziem górskich) Zakopane Ⓦ festivale.zakopane.pl. Mid- to late Aug. Folk groups from the mountain regions of the world, with a strong Polish presence.

Singer Festival Warsaw Ⓦ festiwalsingera.pl. Late Aug to early Sept. A week of concerts, film screenings and markets in celebration of Warsaw's Jewish heritage.

SEPTEMBER

Wratislavia Cantans Wrocław Ⓦ nfm.wroclaw.pl. Early to mid-Sept. Choral music over the centuries, performed by outstanding choirs and soloists from around the globe.

Dialogue of Four Cultures (Festiwal dialogu 4 kultur) Łódź Ⓦ 4kultury.pl. Early to mid-Sept. Art, theatre and music representing Polish, Jewish, German and Russian cultural traditions.

March of the Dachshunds (Marsz Jamników) Kraków. First or second Sun in Sept. Sausage dogs wearing fancy dress are paraded through town from the Barbakan to the main square.

Sacrum Profanum Kraków Ⓦ sacrumprofanum.com. Mid- to late Sept. Modern music from contemporary classical to the avant garde, featuring anything from Steve Reich to Aphex Twin, with concerts in atmospheric (frequently post-industrial) venues.

Warsaw Spring (Warszawska Jesień) Warsaw Ⓦ warszawska-jesien.art.pl. Mid- to late Sept. One of Europe's most formidable festivals of contemporary music, inaugurated in the early 1960s and still going strong.

Festival of Polish Feature Films (Festiwal polskich filmów fabularnych) Gdynia Ⓦ festiwalgdynia.pl. Mid- to late Sept. Poland's answer to the Oscars, with the year's best domestic features competing for top prizes.

OCTOBER

Łódź Design Festival Łódź Ⓦ lodzdesign.com. Early Oct. Week-long celebration of Polish and international design with exhibitions, talks and workshops throughout the city.

Opowiadania Short Story Festival Wrocław Ⓦ opowiadanie. org. Early Oct. Literary readings featuring Polish and international authors (so there will be some events in English).

Warsaw Film Festival (Warszawski festiwal filmowy) Warsaw Ⓦ wff.pl. Early to mid-Oct. Ten-day celebration of independent filmmaking with a sizeable international contingent.

Unsound Kraków Ⓦ unsound.pl. Early to mid-Oct. Mind-bending selection of experimental music, electronic music and DJ music

performed in a variety of venues.

Conrad Festival Kraków Ⓦ conradfestival.pl. Late Oct. International literary festival attracting a slew of big-name guests, with (frequently English-language) readings and panel discussions.

NOVEMBER

All Saints' Day (Dzień Wszystkich Świętych). Everywhere. Nov 1. The most important Catholic feast of the autumn, with families visiting cemeteries to pay their respects to the departed. Flowers, wreaths and candles are laid on tombstones.

Camerimage Bydgoszcz Ⓦ camerimage.pl. Late Nov to early Dec. Film festival with the accent on cinematography, featuring screenings and lectures by the world's great camera operators.

DECEMBER

Advent market (Targi Bożonarodzeniowe) Kraków. Throughout Dec. Craft stalls selling jewellery, accessories, woodcarving, speciality foodstuffs and mulled wine fill the main square.

St Barbara's Day (Barbórka) Mining towns throughout Poland. Dec 4. This is the traditional holiday of all miners, with special Masses held for their safety as a counterweight to the jollity of their galas.

St Nicholas Folk Festival (Mikołajki Folkowe) Lublin Ⓦ mikolajki. folk.pl. Early to mid-Dec. Traditional music from Poland and beyond.

Christmas Eve (Wigilia). Everywhere. Dec 24. Families gather for an evening banquet (traditionally of twelve courses to symbolize the number of the Apostles) before attending midnight Mass.

Sports and outdoor activities

For a growing number of visitors, it's the wide range of outdoor pursuits Poland has to offer that constitute the country's chief lure. Most obvious of these are the hiking opportunities provided by the extensive national (and regional) parks, several of which incorporate authentic wilderness areas of great beauty.

Hiking

Poland has some of the best **hiking** country in Europe, especially in the mountainous regions on the country's southern and western borders. There's a full network of marked trails, the best of which are detailed in the Guide. Many of these take several days, passing through remote areas served by mountain huts (*schroniska*; see page 33). However, much of the best scenery can be seen by covering sections of these routes on one-day walks.

Unless you're in the High Tatras (see page 334), few of the one-day trails are especially strenuous, and although specialist footwear is recommended, well-worn-in sturdy shoes are usually enough.

Skiing

Poland's mountainous southern rim provides some good **skiing** opportunities, seized on, in season, by what can often seem like the country's entire population. The best and most popular ski slopes are in the **Tatras**, the highest section of the Polish Carpathians, where the skiing season runs from December through to March. Although still in the shadow of the Alps and other well-known European resorts, **Zakopane** (see page 327), the resort centre of the Tatras, has acquired a strong and growing international following, not least in the UK, where a variety of travel operators specialize in cheap, popular skiing packages.

Less dramatic alternatives to the Tatras include the **Karkonosze** resorts of Karpacz (see page 392) and **Szklarska Poręba** (see page 392); the **Beskid Śląski** resort of Szczyrk (see page 355); and the **Bieszczady** (see page 239), a favourite with cross-country skiers.

One great advantage with all these is that they are relatively unknown outside Poland, although, consequently, facilities are fairly undeveloped – usually involving a single ski lift and a limited range of descents. These smaller resorts are perhaps better suited to individual tourists than Zakopane, which can be jam-packed with groups throughout the ski season.

Kayaking and sailing

Large stretches of lowland Poland are dotted with lakes, especially Mazuria (see page 156) in the northeast of the country, and it is relatively easy for travellers to rent a variety of watercraft – from simple kayaks to luxury yachts – once they arrive. Most people content themselves with a day or two on the water, although the number of navigable waterways in Mazuria ensures there's a host of lengthy **canoeing and kayaking** itineraries to choose from, often involving overnight stops at campsites or hostels en route. The most popular of these are the **Krutynia River Trail** in Mazuria (see page 163), which takes a week to complete or can be handled in sections; and the three-day journey down the **Czarna Hańcza** river (see page 173).

Well-equipped marinas at Mikołajki (see page 169), Giżycko (see page 164) and Ruciane-Nida (see page 171) are packed in the summer months. Simple sailing boats are easy enough to rent at these places; although at least one member of your party will need sailing experience if you want to hire a bigger craft.

Fishing

Especially in the outlying regions of the country – where the rivers are generally less polluted – **fishing** is a popular pastime. The season effectively runs all year in one form or another, with winter fishing through holes in the ice and on the major Mazurian lakes, and fishing for lavaret with artificial spinners in summer. The best fishing areas include the Mazurian lakes (pike and perch), the Bieszczady, notably the River San and

---

TOP TEN NATIONAL PARKS

The sheer diversity of landscapes in Poland is revealed by its **national parks**, which cover a range of natural wildernesses, from high alpine mountains to blustery Baltic shores.
Białowieża National Park Dense primeval forest, containing some of the last European bison. See page 189
Biebrza National Park An area of squelchy wetlands popular with migrating birds. See page 186
Bieszczady National Park Eerily beautiful grassy ridges, set in the sparely populated southeast. See page 239
Karkonosze National Park Stark, bare mountains rising towards the Czech frontier. See page 392
Ojców National Park Picturesque limestone gorge just north of Kraków. See page 315
Pieniny National Park Compact but spectacular group of rocky peaks, right next to the Tatras. See page 338
Roztocze National Park Gently rolling, forested hills, and unspoilt rivers perfect for kayaking. See page 220
Słowiński National Park Otherworldly landscape of shifting sand dunes and tranquil pines. See page 450
Tatra National Park Awesome cluster of grey peaks hovering above high-altitude lakes. See page 334
Wielkopolska National Park A patchwork of lakes and forests that makes for perfect walking terrain, just south of Poznań. See page 421

its tributaries (trout), and the southeast in general. For details on how to buy compulsory fishing **licences**, contact the National Tourist Office (see page 46).

Spectator sports

The Polish media devote a vast amount of coverage to team games as diverse as **basketball** (*koszykówka*), **handball** (*piłka ręczna*) and **volleyball** (*siatkówka*). One sport that enjoys enormous popularity in Poland is **speedway** (*żużel*). Most enormous cities boast a team and a stadium, although it's in the industrial conurbations of the southwest that the sport arouses the greatest passions. Events usually take place on Saturdays; street posters advertise times and venues.

Football

Football (*piłka nożna*) remains the only sport that commands a genuine mass following nationwide. Franz Beckenbauer described the Polish national side as "the best team in the world" in 1974's World Cup, when they were unlucky to finish only in third place. The Poles remained a significant force in the world game for the next decade, with players such as Grzegorz Lato, Kazimierz Deyna and Zbigniew Boniek becoming household names. The Polish teams from the 1990s to the 2010s have been comparatively anonymous, frequently qualifying for major competitions only to perform disappointingly once they get there.

Despite receiving blanket coverage from the country's private TV stations, Polish **league football** is currently in the doldrums: few clubs are rich enough to pay the wages of top players, and the country's best talents ply their trade in Germany, Italy or elsewhere. Wisła Kraków and Legia Warsaw enjoy the biggest countrywide following, although it's Cracovia Kraków (formed in 1906) that claims to be the oldest in the country. Other teams with proud historical pedigrees are the Silesian trio of GKS Katowice, Ruch Chorzów and Górnik Zabrze; and the two Łódź sides, LKS and Widzew.

The football **season** lasts from August to November, then resumes in March until June. You shouldn't have trouble buying tickets (40–50zł) on the gate for most games, although you may be asked to show ID before being subjected to a spot of vigorous security frisking. For details of results and **fixtures**, check out the Polish Football Federation's website Ⓦpzpn.pl.

Culture and etiquette

As a nation in which roughly 85 percent of the population declare themselves to be Catholic, Poland is a comparatively conservative country, especially in the countryside. Poland's young tend to be more relaxed than their parents, displaying a fully globalized fashion sense and a hedonistic approach to weekend socializing. Poles of all ages tend to be warm, hospitable, and helpful towards strangers when approached.

Tipping in Poland is not expected if you are buying a drink in a bar or ordering a meal in a café. If you are ordering a round of drinks in an establishment where there is table service, or eating in a restaurant, then you should leave 10 percent or round up the bill to a convenient figure.

Smoking is not permitted in restaurants, cafés or bars unless an isolated room is set aside for this purpose (and in practice only a small number of bars and very few restaurants have this facility). Smoking is usually permitted on the outdoor terraces of eating and drinking establishments, although some restaurants enforce no smoking zones here too.

Traditionally, visitors to Polish churches are expected to **dress modestly** – no shorts for men, no bare arms for women. Although a younger generation of Poles is increasingly stretching these dress-code boundaries, visitors should opt for a conservative approach. It is considered rude for visitors to look around churches during Mass.

Travelling with children

Poles are in general family-oriented and child-friendly, and children are generally welcome in cafés and restaurants.

International brands of **formula milk**, **nappies** and other essentials are available in supermarkets and

TOP FIVE THINGS TO DO WITH KIDS

Copernicus Centre, Warsaw See page 64

Boat trips on the Mazurian Lakes See page 165

The Stanisław Lem Garden of Experiences, Kraków See page 294

Dragon Parade, Kraków See page 308

Kolejkowo Model Railway, Wrocław See page 372

convenience stores throughout Poland. If you are travelling with children who require regular **medication** then bring enough to cover your trip, as you may find it difficult to replenish your stocks in Polish pharmacies without a prescription from a local doctor.

Breast-feeding in public is frequently unavoidable if you are on the road (Polish mothers have to do it too) but should be done discreetly in order to avoid upsetting conservative sensibilities – keep a shawl handy for draping over the shoulder. If you need a public toilet with **nappy-changing facilities**, then shopping malls and big-city railway stations are the best places to look.

Local **transport** is free for the under-7s, while children aged 18 or under are entitled to a reduced ticket (*bilet ulgowy*), usually half price. On trains, children under 4 travel free while older kids get a 37 percent discount.

Museums and attractions often offer free entry for the under-7s and reduced ticket prices for under-18s. Buying a **family ticket** (*bilet rodzinny*; usually covering 4–5 family members) is frequently the cheapest option.

Looking for **hotel rooms** can be a complicated business. Some establishments will provide cots at no extra cost, or child beds at fifty percent of full cost. Many hotels have three- or four-bed rooms which suit families travelling with children. However not all hotels have rooms big enough to accommodate extra beds and might offer families two separate double rooms instead.

Travel essentials

Costs

Although **costs** are on the rise in Poland, it's still a reasonably inexpensive destination compared to Western Europe. Hotel and restaurant prices are at their highest in Warsaw, Kraków and other major cities, although outside these areas a little money can go a long way.

Accommodation is likely to prove your biggest expense. Hostel beds in the main cities cost around 60–80zł; while simple double rooms in pensions and rural B&Bs start at around 120zł. Good three-star hotels cost around 180zł for a double room in the provinces, double that in Warsaw, Kraków and Gdańsk.

Prices for **public transport** are relatively low – tickets for the new breed of InterCity trains are pricier than in the past, but still cheaper than in Western Europe. Travelling across half the length of the country by TLK trains or by bus can still cost under 100zł. Similarly, you are unlikely to fork out much more than 20zł to visit the more popular **tourist sights**, with half that the normal asking price.

If you are shopping in markets for picnic ingredients during the daytime and sticking to the cheaper cafés and bars in the evening, then 50zł per person per day will suffice for **food and drink**. In order to cover a sit-down lunch and a decent dinner followed by a couple of night-time drinks, then a daily outlay of 100zł per person seems more realistic. Pushing the boat out in fine restaurants and fancy cocktail bars will set you back even further.

Crime and personal safety

The biggest potential hassle for visitors to Poland comes from **petty crime** – notably hotel-room thefts and pickpocketing in crowded places such as train stations (especially in Warsaw) and markets. A few common-sense precautions should help you avoid trouble: display cameras, fancy mobile phones and other signs of affluence as little as possible;

DISCOUNTS

ISIC cardholders can pick up all kinds of discounts, with some hostels offering ten percent reductions, and most museums offering significant savings on entrance charges. A handful of bus companies, several theatres, and even some high-street pizzerias are among the other organizations offering a small discount.

Over-65s are usually entitled to discounts of up to fifty percent in museums, attractions and on public transport – although in most cases you have to be from an EU country or an EU-associate country to qualify for this. **Children** receive discounted travel and are often offered free or reduced admission at museums and other attractions.

never leave valuables in your room; and keep large sums of cash in a (well-hidden) money-belt. Theft of Western **cars** and/or their contents is something of a national sport in Poland.

Your best protection against crime is to take out **travel insurance** before you go. If you do have anything stolen, report the loss to the police as soon as possible, and be patient – filling in a report can take ages. The chances of getting your gear back are virtually zero. You should always keep your **passport** or European ID card with you, even though you're unlikely to get stopped unless you're in a car; Western number plates provide the excuse for occasional unprovoked spot checks. It's also a good idea to make a photocopy of the information-bearing page of your passport. This will help your consulate to issue a replacement document if you're unlucky enough to have it stolen.

It's a good idea to write your name and mobile phone number on important documents or inside bags. If you do accidently leave your belongings somewhere, it's highly likely that a good citizen or conscientious police officer will get in touch.

Cultural organizations abroad

All the major English-speaking countries have **Polish cultural organizations** that are worth contacting if you want to learn more about the country or if you have Polish heritage yourself. Some of the more active groups around the globe include the Polish Cultural Institute in London (Ⓦpolishculture.org.uk), and the Polish Cultural Institute in New York (Ⓦpolishculture-nyc.org).

Electricity

Poland uses the standard Continental 220 volts. Round two-pin **plugs** are used.

Health

Citizens of EU countries are entitled to free emergency health care in Poland providing they are in possession of an EHIC (**European Health Insurance Card**). At the time of writing, British citizens were still covered by the EHIC scheme, but given the 2016 Brexit vote, checking the situation via Ⓦehic.org.uk is advisable before you travel. Lengthy courses of treatment (as well as any prescribed drugs) must be paid for, however, so it's sensible to take out adequate **health insurance**. North Americans, Canadians, Australians and New Zealanders ought to arrange full insurance before leaving home.

Inoculations are not required for a trip to Poland. Drinking **tap water** is perfectly safe.

TIPPING
In restaurants and cafés that have table service it's usual to leave a ten percent **tip** or round up the bill.

Pharmacies

Simple complaints can normally be dealt with at a regular **pharmacy** (*apteka*), where medicines are dispensed by knowledgeable staff. In every town there's always at least one *apteka* open 24 hours. In the cities, many of the staff will speak at least some English. If you are currently taking prescription medication, bring enough supplies to last your trip; pharmacies can't dispense prescription drugs without a note from a local doctor, which can be time-consuming to obtain. Generic non-prescription painkillers and flu remedies can be purchased in supermarkets.

Hospitals

For more serious problems, or anything the pharmacist can't work out, you'll be directed to a public **hospital** (*szpital*), where conditions will probably be cramped, with more patients than beds and a lack of resources. Health service staff are highly qualified but heavily overworked and scandalously underpaid. Hospital patients may be required to pay for the better-quality medicines, and will probably need friends to bring food in for them. If you are required to pay for treatments or medication, remember to keep receipts for your insurance claim.

Private clinics

In the larger cities you can opt for **private healthcare**. Kraków and Warsaw now have a considerable number of private health clinics, often staffed by good English speakers. Access to doctors may be quicker if you go private, but you will still need the funds (or the insurance) to cover the costs. See the relevant city listings for details.

Insurance

The EHIC scheme only covers the bare essentials of emergency medical care, and all visitors would do well to take out an **insurance policy** before

EMERGENCY PHONE NUMBERS
Police (*policja*), **Fire brigade** (*straż pożarna*) and **Ambulance** (*karetka*) ☎112

travelling to cover against theft, loss and illness or injury.

Internet

Most hostels, hotels, cafés and bars in Polish cities now offer **free wi-fi**. Free wi-fi is also available in the central squares of many cities (Kraków included), and in the ticket halls of large mainline railway stations. Once you get away from urban areas, wi-fi is less widespread (and even when present may not actually work). Due to the increased availability of wi-fi, **internet cafés** are now rather hard to find in Poland, but are listed in the Guide where relevant. Usage rarely costs more than 6zł/hr.

Laundry

Self-service facilities are virtually non-existent in Poland – although most towns do boast a laundry (*pralnia*), these tend to concentrate exclusively on dry-cleaning. Some of them offer service washes, too. You can get things service-washed in the more upmarket hotels, but at a cost.

Left luggage

Most train and bus stations of any size have **luggage lockers**. Big-city train stations are often open 24 hours; elsewhere, take note of the station building's opening and closing times. Lockers come in different sizes and can cost anything between 6zł and 24zł for 24 hours – be sure to have a selection of coins at the ready as they are not equipped to give change.

LGBT travellers

Although homosexuality is legal in Poland, it remains something of an underground phenomenon, and public displays of affection between members of the same sex may provoke outrage and hostility, especially outside the big cities. Warsaw has a small

gay scene, and major cities such as Kraków, Gdańsk and Wrocław do at least have a number of bohemian bars and clubs which welcome people of all persuasions. Annual '**Tolerance Marches**' organized by the LGTB community are a regular fixture in Warsaw (June) and Kraków (April/May), although both are occasionally met by counter-demonstrations mounted by radical conservatives.

Maps

The best maps of Poland are those produced by local publishers **Demart,** although there are a number of other firms producing accurate national and regional maps in a variety of scales, as well as detailed city maps (*plan miasta*) of almost every urban area in Poland.

Hiking maps (*mapa turystyczna*) of the national parks and other rural areas are produced by an array of companies. They're universally clear and simple to use, although it's wise to choose a larger-scale map – 1:25,000 or greater – if you want to walk a particular route. The best places to buy maps are the Empik multimedia stores found in big city centres – although most other bookshops and newspaper kiosks will carry a small selection.

Money

The Polish unit of currency is the **złoty** (abbreviated to zł). It comes in notes of 10zł, 20zł, 50zł, 100zł, 200zł and 500zł; and coins in 1, 2 and 5zł denominations, subdivided into **groszy** (1, 2, 5, 10, 20 and 50). Currently the **exchange rate** is around 4.70zł to the pound sterling, 4.20zł to the euro and 3.70zł to the US dollar, but future fluctuations are possible.

Prices of hotels and other tourist services are often quoted in euros, although payment is made in złoty.

Exchange

The easiest place to change money is at an **exchange bureau** (*kantor*). Very often little more than a simple booth with a cashier sitting behind a

---

ROUGH GUIDES TRAVEL INSURANCE

Rough Guides has teamed up with **WorldNomads.com** to offer great travel insurance deals. Policies are available to residents of over 150 countries, with cover for a wide range of adventure sports, 24hr emergency assistance, high levels of medical and evacuation cover and a stream of travel safety information. Roughguides.com users can take advantage of their policies online 24/7, from anywhere in the world – even if you're already travelling. And since plans often change when you're on the road, you can extend your policy and even claim online. Roughguides.com users who buy travel insurance with WorldNomads.com can also leave a positive footprint and donate to a community development project. For more information, go to ⓦ roughguides.com/travel-insurance.

thick plate of glass, these can be found on the main streets of virtually every Polish town. They tend to work longer hours than regular banks (in big cities some *kantors* are open 24 hours a day), usually offer competitive exchange rates and rarely charge any commission. Be aware, however, that it pays to shop around in well-touristed parts of Warsaw and Kraków, where a *kantor* on the main street will offer a substantially less advantageous rate than a similar establishment in a side alley nearby.

Exchange rates at Polish **banks** (usually open Mon–Fri 7.30am–5pm, Sat 7.30am–2pm) tend to be the same from one establishment to the next, although banks are much more subject to long queues and usually deduct a commission.

It's wise to avoid changing money in hotels as they tend to offer poor exchange rates or charge large commissions.

Credit cards and ATMs

ATMs are ubiquitous in urban areas: you'll find them dotted around main squares and in shopping malls. When withdrawing money, many ATMs will offer to bill you in your home currency rather than złotys, on the basis that this will allow you to see clearly the exchange rate being charged – it is best to refuse this as the rates applied are usually disadvantageous compared to the ones normally applied by your bank at home.

Major **credit and debit cards** are accepted by supermarkets, travel agents and almost all hotels, restaurants and shops – except in small towns and villages, where some establishments still refuse plastic. You can also arrange a cash advance on most of these cards in big banks.

Opening hours

Most **shops** are open on weekdays from 10am to 6pm, on Saturdays until 2 or 3pm. Big-city shopping malls have longer hours and frequently stay open all day on Saturdays and Sundays. In addition, all city centres and small towns have a number of small supermarkets and **convenience stores** (Żabka and Biedronka are two nationwide chains) which are open 6am–11pm seven days a week.

Street kiosks, where you can buy newspapers and municipal transport tickets, are generally open from about 6am to 5pm, although many remain open for several hours longer.

As a rule, **tourist information offices** are open from 9 or 10am until 5pm (later in major cities) during the week; hours are shorter on Saturdays and Sundays.

Banks are usually open weekdays 7.30am–5pm, and on Saturday from 7.30am to 2pm. **Post office**

PUBLIC HOLIDAYS

The following are national public holidays, on which you can expect some shops, restaurants and most sights to be closed. It's well worth checking if your visit is going to coincide with one of these to avoid frustrations and disappointments. It's particularly worth noting that because Labour Day and Constitution Day are so close together, most businesses (including the majority of banks and shops) give their employees a full four days of holiday.

January 1 New Year's Day
January 6 Epiphany
March/April Easter Sunday
March/April Easter Monday
May 1 Labour Day
May 3 Constitution Day
May/June Pentecost Sunday
May/June Corpus Christi
August 15 Feast of the Assumption
November 1 All Saints' Day
November 11 Independence Day
December 25 Christmas Day
December 26 St Stephen's Day

hours are usually Monday to Friday 7/8am–8pm, with some open on Saturday mornings; smaller branches usually close at 6pm or earlier.

Visiting hours for tourist sights

Visiting times for **museums** and historic monuments are listed in the text of the Guide. They are almost invariably closed one day per week (usually Mon) and many are closed two or three days per week. The rest of the week some open for only about five hours, often closing at 3pm, though 4pm or later is more normal.

Visiting **churches** seldom presents any problems: the ones you're most likely to want to see are open from early morning until mid-evening without interruption. However, a large number of less famous churches are fenced off beyond the entrance porch by a grille or glass window for much of the day; to visit them properly, you'll need to turn up just before or after Mass – first thing in the morning and between 6 and 8pm. Otherwise it's a case of seeking out the local priest (*ksiądz*) and persuading him to let you in.

Post

Big-city **post offices** (*Poczta*) are usually open Monday to Friday from 7/8am until 8pm, with some open on Saturday mornings. Smaller branches usually close at 6pm, often earlier in rural areas. A restricted range of services is available 24 hours a day, seven days a week, from post offices in or outside the main train stations of major cities.

Each post office bears a number, with the head office in each city being no. 1. Theoretically, each head office has a **poste restante** (general delivery) facility: make sure, therefore, that anyone addressing mail to you includes the no. 1 after the city's name.

Mail to the UK takes four days, a week to the US, and is a day or so quicker in the other direction. It costs 5zł to send a card or 50g letter to Europe (including the UK), the USA, Australia or New Zealand. Anything of value or importance should be sent by registered post (*polecona*; letters from 16.00zł). **Postboxes** are red.

Phones

Travellers with GSM **mobile phones** will find that almost all of Poland enjoys coverage – apart from the odd remote mountain valley. If you are a resident of an EU country or an EU associate country you can use your mobile phone in Poland without incurring punishingly-high roaming costs. However, you should check the terms of your package to find out exactly how much you will be paying for calls and internet usage outside your own network.

Local operators like T-Mobile, Orange, Play and Plus sell **pre-paid SIM cards** and top-up vouchers so you can use the local network while you're here. Some mobile phones automatically block if you insert a new SIM card into them, however, so check with your operator before trying this out.

Public payphones have almost died out in Poland due to the ubiquity of mobile phones. In theory they still exist, and telephone cards (*karta telefoniczna*) can be bought at post offices and Ruch kiosks. However, the time it takes to actually locate a still-working public telephone ensures that you are highly unlikely to rely on them as a means of communication. Far better to find the nearest wi-fi zone and use your mobile phone to make a phone call using one of the **apps** (such as Skype, WhatsApp or Viber) that enable free phone calls over the internet.

Remember that calls from hotels are far more expensive than any other option.

Time

Poland is one hour ahead of GMT and six hours ahead of EST. Polish Summer Time lasts from the beginning of April to the end of October.

Toilets

Public toilets (*toalety*, *ubikacja* or WC) can be found at most bus and train stations, and usually cost 2–3zł. The days when you had to buy toilet paper by the sheet are numbered, but there may be a rural toilet somewhere in Poland where it still happens. Gents are marked ▼, ladies ● or ▲.

Tourist information

Poland has a **National Tourist Office** with branches in a number of European countries and the US (see below). Within Poland, most towns and cities now have a tourist information centre (often known as **informator turystyczny** or "IT") run by the local municipality, offering full hotel listings, accommodation bookings and a range of brochures and maps (which are usually for sale rather than given away free). Sometimes the tourist information centre shares space with a privately run travel agency, and is rather more geared to selling tours and travel tickets than handing out unbiased information. Many provincial towns, especially those that see few tourists, have yet to establish tourist information centres of any kind.

One useful organization that has offices in many Polish towns is the **PTTK** (⑩ pttk.com.pl) – which translates literally as "The Polish Country Lovers' Association" – an organization that gives out information, sells maps and also runs many mountain huts, hostels and hotels. PTTK offices can often book basic accommodation and provide a wealth of local advice, although staff might not speak any language other than Polish.

TOURIST OFFICES ABROAD

UK Level 3, Westgate House, West Gate, London W5 1YY ☎ 0300 303 1812, ⑩ poland.travel/en-gb.
US 5 Marine View Plaza, Hoboken, NJ 07030 ☎ 201 420-9910, ⑩ poland.travel/en-us.

Travellers with disabilities

An increasing amount of attention is being paid to the needs of the disabled (*niepełnosprawni*) in Poland, with an increase in the number of buildings and public facilities that are **wheelchair accessible**. Most new buildings and tourist attractions built over the last ten years will be equipped with lifts and wheelchair ramps, although there is still a long way to go in adapting the rest of Poland's existing infrastructure.

The majority of set-piece **museums** in Warsaw, Kraków, Wrocław and other major cities are now

JEWISH TOURISM

Almost all of Poland's cities and towns had large pre-Holocaust Jewish populations, and are increasingly receptive to the needs of organized **heritage tours** and individuals seeking out family roots. Kraków – site of the thriving Jewish suburb of Kazimierz and within visiting distance of Holocaust memorials such as Auschwitz-Birkenau – is particularly well organized in this regard. If you find yourself hunting around the back streets of a town in search of Jewish buildings and monuments, the basic words and phrases to know when asking for directions are synagogue (*bóżnica* or *synagoga*) and Jewish cemetery (*cmentarz żydowski*). Many of the Polish-Jewish organizations listed below can be extremely helpful in providing further information and contacts.

POLISH-JEWISH ORGANIZATIONS

Emanuel Ringelblum Jewish Historical Institute ul. Tłomackie 3/5, Warsaw ☎ 22 827 9221, ⓦ jhi.pl. Archives, exhibitions, library and bookshop.

Foundation for the Preservation of Jewish Heritage in Poland (Fundacja Ochrony Dziedzictwa Żydowskiego) ☎ 22 436 6000, ⓦ fodz.pl. Information on Jewish monuments and synagogues throughout the country.

Jewish Community of Warsaw (Gmina Wyznaniowa Żydowska) ul. Twarda 6, Warsaw ☎ 22 620 4324, ⓦ warszawa.jewish.org.pl. Headquarters of the Jewish community in the capital.

Jewish Community Centre of Kraków ul. Miodowa 24, Kraków ☎ 12 370 5770, ⓦ jcckrakow.org. The Kraków Jewish Community's cultural centre, organizing cultural events, lectures and facilitating contacts.

Judaica Cultural Centre ul. Meiselsa 17, Kraków ☎ 12 430 6449, ⓦ judaica.pl. Cultural centre in the heart of the Kazimierz district, with a library, reading room, gallery, café and bookshop.

Virtual Shtetl ⓦ sztetl.org.pl. Jewish history site which functions as virtual museum, travel guide and cultural news magazine.

---

wheelchair accessible, although there remain plenty of prominent exceptions that remain difficult to get in and out of.

An increasing number of **hotels** in big cities, especially those of four stars and above, have access and rooms designed for the disabled. The downside is that the majority of these places are expensive, meaning that such provision is still, by and large, a luxury; and because the number of rooms with facilities for the disabled are limited, they sell out fast – advance reservations are essential.

Public transport has improved enormously in recent years. Newer buses and trams in Warsaw, Kraków and other big cities are equipped with hydraulic platforms to ease wheelchair access. The electronic arrivals boards at each bus and tram stop use wheelchair symbols to designate which of the approaching vehicles offers access. The Warsaw metro boasts lifts at each station, although they're badly signed from the surface. Most railway stations in big cities now have lifts to all the platforms – but, again, this is by no means universal.

USEFUL CONTACTS

State Fund for the Rehabilitation of the Disabled (Państwowy Fundusz Rehabilitacji Osób Niepełnosprawnych) al. Jana Pawła II 13, Warsaw ☎ 22 505 5500, ⓦ pfron.org.pl.

ⓦ **niepelnosprawni.pl** An invaluable source of news, views and links for those who can read Polish.

ⓦ **turystykadlawszystkich.pl** Allows you to search for hotels, restaurants and sights that are wheelchair accessible, but their database hasn't been updated for several years.

Working in Poland

Nationals of EU member states can work in Poland with a minimum of paperwork. Citizens of other countries will need to find an employer who is prepared to apply for a work permit on their behalf. There is a booming international business scene in cities like Warsaw, Gdańsk and Poznań, although the average monthly wage in Poland remains somewhere in the vicinity of €1000.

The popularity of learning English has mushroomed in recent years, leading to a constant demand for native-language **English teachers** both in the state education system and in the private language schools that have sprung up all over the country. However, you'll probably need a TEFL certificate or equivalent in order to secure a job at any but the most fly-by-night organizations. Some of the bigger English-teaching organizations actually organize TEFL courses in Polish cities, and may well help you get a job there once you've qualified. Vacancies are sometimes advertised in the education supplements of Western newspapers; otherwise it's a question of touting your CV around the language schools and making use of local contacts once you arrive.

Warsaw

PLAC WILSONA METRO STATION

1 Warsaw

With a history writ large with destruction and regeneration, Poland's two-million-strong capital Warsaw (Warszawa) is one of the great shape-shifters of the European continent. Razed by the Germans in 1944 and given a Stalinist architectural makeover in the 1950s, it became a byword for concrete brutalism in the decades that followed. Currently reaffirming itself as a muscular regional centre of business and finance, Warsaw is going through a metamorphosis as far reaching as those of the past. Bold contemporary buildings, state-of-the-art museums, destination restaurants and bar-filled bohemian quarters are the new landmarks of a restless metropolis. The idea of Warsaw as a grim East European city is nowadays the most dated travel cliché of them all.

Few European cities have reinvented themselves so often and at such speed, and at times it can seem as if several different Warsaws exist within the same geographical space. The reconstructed Old Town stands a stone's throw away from concrete developments of the socialist era, which in turn give way to the glittering, skyscraper-city office developments of today. Perhaps the most striking example of urban reinvention is the city's relationship with the river itself, where newly built walkways, outdoor bars and shore-to-shore ferry services have added a new layer of outdoor zest to Warsaw's ever-changing image.

Marking the northern end of the city centre, the busy **Old Town** (Stare Miasto) and the quietly atmospheric **New Town** (Nowe Miasto) provide the historic focal point. Rebuilt from scratch after World War II, the districts are home to the most striking examples of the capital's reconstruction. South from the Old Town, the grand, 2km-long **Krakowskie Przedmieście** street leads towards the city's modern commercial heart, the Śródmieście district, rebuilt in a haphazard manner following World War II and now the subject of major investments. Despite a glut of new high-rise constructions, the city skyline is still dominated by the Palace of Culture and Science (Pałac Kultury i Nauki), Stalin's enduring legacy to the citizens of Warsaw. Northwest of here, in the **Muranów** and **Mirów** districts, is the former **ghetto** area, where numerous monuments bear poignant testimony to Warsaw's lost Jewish population.

South of the city centre, a procession of open boulevards passes the delightful gardens of **Łazienki Park** before culminating at the stately king's residence at **Wilanów** on the southern outskirts of the city. Over on the eastern bank of the River Vistula, the emerging café- and bar-culture of suburbs like **Praga** and **Saska Kępa** provide an authentic flavour of contemporary Warsaw life.

Brief history

For a European capital city, Warsaw entered history late. Although there are records of a settlement here from the tenth century, the first references to anything resembling a town

Highlights

❶ Warsaw's Old Town A testament to Poland's postwar efforts to reconstruct itself after World War II, this historic town centre was re-created from almost nothing after being razed by the Nazis. See page 53

❷ West bank of the Vistula In summer the west bank of the river throngs with strollers, cyclists and patrons of the open-air waterfront bars. See page 64

❸ Copernicus Science Centre Offering a wealth of hands-on experiments, this is one of the most spectacular children's play centres ever conceived. See page 64

❹ Palace of Culture and Sciences A colossal monument to the ideological certainties of the Stalinist period, this imposing monolith is still the defining feature of downtown Warsaw's skyline. See page 67

❺ Łazienki Park The most elegant of Poland's urban parks, crisscrossed with oak-lined promenades. See page 74

❻ POLIN Museum of the History of the Polish Jews Epic in scale, and a beautiful piece of architecture to boot. See page 71

❼ Neon Museum The soft glow of neon is very much a Polish visual trademark; this unique collection of neon signs is a tribute to its enduring allure. See page 78

HIGHLIGHTS ARE MARKED ON THE MAP ON PAGE 54

1

date from the mid-fourteenth century. Warsaw served as the ducal capital of Mazovia until the death of the last duke in 1526, when its incorporation into Polish royal territory radically improved its fortunes. Following the Act of Union with Lithuania in 1569 the Polish parliament, or Sejm, decided to base itself in Warsaw due to its conveniently central geographic location. The crowning glory came in 1596, when **King Sigismund III** moved his capital from Kraków to its current location.

From the Deluge to the Partitions

Capital status inevitably brought prosperity, but along with new wealth came new perils. The city was ravaged by foreign armies three times during the "Swedish Deluge" of the 1650s, before being extensively reconstructed by Poland's **Saxon** kings. Poles tend to regard the **eighteenth century** as the golden age of Warsaw, when its concert halls, theatres and salons were prominent in European cultural life. The **Partitions** abruptly terminated this era, as Warsaw was absorbed into Prussia in 1795. Napoleon's arrival in 1806 gave Varsovians brief hopes of liberation, but after the collapse of his Moscow campaign in 1812, Warsaw was integrated into the Russian-controlled **Congress Kingdom of Poland**. The failure of the **1830 uprising** brought severe reprisals: a generation of patriots were exiled and all places of learning were closed.

World War I and World War II

Warsaw's position as the westernmost major city in the Tsar's domain brought

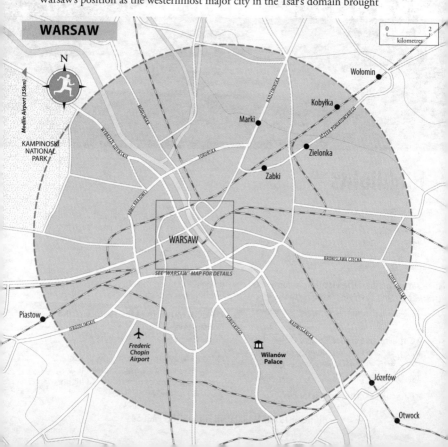

1

commercial prosperity towards the turn of the century. The Germans occupied the city early in World War I and the Tsarist Empire never returned; with the restoration of Polish independence, Warsaw reverted to its position as capital. The 1920s and 1930s were a time of economic and cultural efflorescence; the population rose to 1,300,000 in 1939, of which roughly one third were Jews.

The Nazi conquest of Poland in September 1939 was followed by the progressive annihilation of the city. Members of the Polish intelligentsia were shot out of hand in order to deprive the city of any leadership. Warsaw's Jews were crammed into a ghetto before being deported, train by train, to the extermination camps. The **Ghetto uprising** of April 1943 was a heroic but unsuccessful attempt to save what was left of the community.

In August 1944, virtually the whole of the remaining Polish civilian population participated in the **Warsaw Uprising**, an attempt both to liberate the city and to ensure the emergence of an independent Poland. It failed on both counts. Hitler, infuriated by the resistance, ordered the total elimination of Warsaw, with the SS systematically destroying what remained of its buildings. By the end of the war, 850,000 Varsovians – two-thirds of the city's 1939 population – were dead or missing. Photographs taken immediately after the **liberation** in January 1945 show a scene not unlike Hiroshima: General Eisenhower described Warsaw as the most tragic thing he'd ever seen.

Postwar Warsaw

The momentous task of **rebuilding** the city took ten years. Aesthetically the results were mixed, with acres of socialist functionalism spread between the Baroque palaces, but it was a tremendous feat of national reconstruction nonetheless. The last quarter century has seen Warsaw change yet again, with an influx of foreign capital funding the construction of a high-rise business district. Warsaw's role as co-host of the Euro 2012 football championship provided the spur to a series of **infrastructure projects** – totally rebuilt railway stations, extended metro lines and train links to the airport among them – that transformed the city into one of the most user-friendly in Europe.

The Old Town

The term **Old Town** (Stare Miasto) is in some respects a misnomer for the historic nucleus of Warsaw. Sixty years ago, this compact network of streets and alleyways lay in rubble – even the cobblestones are replacements. Yet surveying the tiered houses of the main square, for example, it's hard to believe they've been here only decades. Some claim that the restored version is an improvement on the original, perhaps because the architects worked from Baroque-era drawings by Bellotto, nephew of Canaletto, rather than prewar photographs showing nineteenth-century alterations. Today, although the streets of the Old Town are thronged with tourists, Varsovians themselves can be in short supply; with the shift of Warsaw's centre of gravity south from the Old Town the area around the main Rynek is now more historical cul-de-sac than heart of the modern city.

Castle Square

Castle Square (Plac Zamkowy), on the south side of the Old Town, is the obvious place to start a tour. Here the first thing to catch your eye is the bronze **statue of Sigismund III**, the king who made Warsaw his capital. Installed on his column in 1640, Sigismund suffered a direct hit from a tank in September 1944, but has now been replaced on his lookout; the base is a popular and convenient rendezvous point.

Royal Castle

pl. Zamkowy 4 • ⓦ zamek-krolewski.pl

Once home of the royal family and seat of the Polish parliament, Warsaw's seventeenth-

1

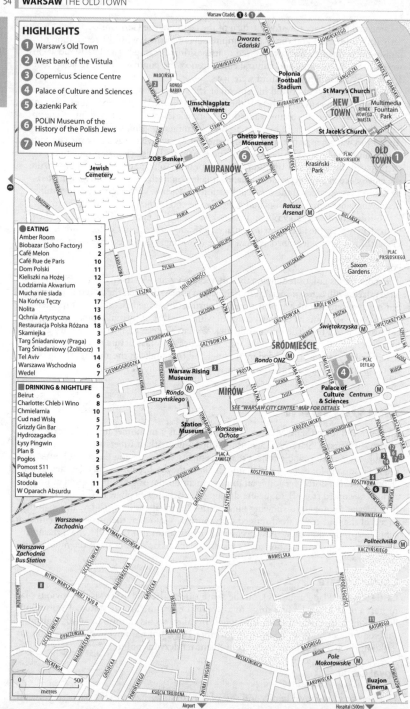

HIGHLIGHTS

1 Warsaw's Old Town

2 West bank of the Vistula

3 Copernicus Science Centre

4 Palace of Culture and Sciences

5 Łazienki Park

6 POLIN Museum of the History of the Polish Jews

7 Neon Museum

● EATING

Amber Room	15
Biobazar (Soho Factory)	5
Café Melon	2
Café Rue de Paris	10
Dom Polski	11
Kieliszki na Hożej	12
Lodziarnia Akwarium	9
Mucha nie siada	4
Na Końcu Tęczy	17
Nolita	13
Qchnia Artystyczna	16
Restauracja Polska Różana	18
Skamiejka	3
Targ Śniadaniowy (Praga)	8
Targ Śniadaniowy (Żoliborz)	1
Tel Aviv	14
Warszawa Wschodnia	6
Wedel	7

■ DRINKING & NIGHTLIFE

Beirut	6
Charlotte: Chleb i Wino	8
Chmielarnia	10
Cud nad Wisłą	5
Grizzly Gin Bar	7
Hydrozagadka	1
Łysy Pingwin	3
Plan B	9
Pogłos	2
Pomost 511	5
Skład butelek	1
Stodoła	11
W Oparach Absurdu	4

Warsaw Citadel,

Dworzec Gdański

Warsaw's Old Town

West bank of the Vistula

Copernicus Science Centre

Palace of Culture and Sciences

Łazienki Park

POLIN Museum of the History of the Polish Jews

Neon Museum

SŁOMIŃSKIEGO

MŁOCIŃSKA

RONDO BABKA

Polonia Football Stadium

St Mary's Church

NEW TOWN

Multimedia Fountain Park

Umschlagplatz Monument

MURANOWSKA

St Jacek's Church

RYNEK NOWEGO MIASTA

OLD TOWN

Ghetto Heroes Monument

ZOB BUNKER

MURANÓW

Krasiński Park

PLAC KRASIŃSKICH

Jewish Cemetery

ANIELEWICZA

DZIELNA

Ratusz Arsenal

BIELAŃSKA

PAWIA

DZIELNA

NOWOLIPIE

SOLIDARNOŚCI

PLAC PIŁSUDSKIEGO

KAROLKOWA

ŻYLNIA

SOLIDARNOŚCI

OGRODOWA

ELEKTORALNA

Saxon Gardens

LESZNO

CHŁODNA

KRÓLEWSKA

PRÓŻNA

WOLSKA

JAKTOROWSKA

GRZYBOWSKA

TWARDA

Świętokrzyska

SIEDMIOGRODZKA

KAROLKOWA

TOWAROWA

Warsaw Rising Museum

PROSTA

SIENNA

ŚRÓDMIEŚCIE

Rondo ONZ

MIRÓW

PLAC DEFILAD

Rondo Daszyńskiego

ZŁOTA

Palace of Culture & Sciences

Centrum

Station Museum

Warszawa Ochota

JEROZOLIMSKIE

NOWOGRODZKA

SEE "WARSAW CITY CENTRE" MAP FOR DETAILS

WSPÓLNA

HOŻA

WILCZA

PLAC ZAWISZY

KOSZYKOWA

KOSZYKOWA

Warszawa Zachodnia

GRÓJECKA

RASZYŃSKA

NOWOWIEJSKA

Warszawa Zachodnia Bus Station

FILTROWA

Politechnika

BITWY WARSZAWSKIEJ 1920 R.

GRZYMAŁY KOPIŃSKA

WAWELSKA

KACZYŃSKIEGO

SZCZĘŚLIWICKA

BIAŁOBRZESKA

GRÓJECKA

NIEPODLEGŁOŚCI

BOHATERÓW

OPACZEWSKA

BANACHA

BATOREGO

DICKENSA

BIAŁOBRZESKA

Pole Mokotowskie

ROSTAFIŃSKICH

BRUNA

RAKOWIECKA

Iluzjon Cinema

KSIĘCIA TROJDENA

ZWIRKI I WIGURY

0 — 500
metres

Airport

Hospital (500m)

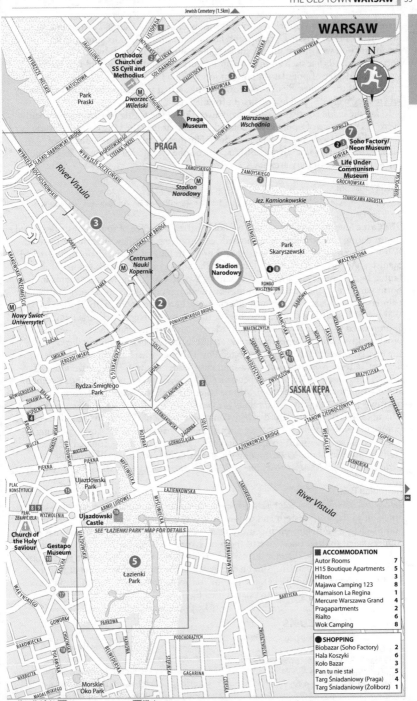

WARSAW

N

Jewish Cemetery (1.5km)

Orthodox Church of SS Cyril and Methodius

Park Praski

Dworzec Wileński

Praga Museum

Warszawa Wschodnia

PRAGA

Soho Factory/ Neon Museum

Life Under Communism Museum

Stadion Narodowy

Jez. Kamionkowskie

Park Skaryszewski

Stadion Narodowy

RONDO WASZYNGTON

River Vistula

Centrum Nauki Kopernik

Nowy Świat-Uniwersytet

SASKA KĘPA

Rydza-Śmigłego Park

River Vistula

Ujazdowski Park

Ujazdowski Castle

SEE "ŁAZIENKI PARK" MAP FOR DETAILS

Church of the Holy Saviour

Gestapo Museum

Łazienki Park

Morskie Oko Park

Warsaw Music Society

Wilanów

■ ACCOMMODATION

Autor Rooms	7
H15 Boutique Apartments	5
Hilton	3
Majawa Camping 123	8
Mamaison La Regina	1
Mercure Warszawa Grand	4
Pragapartments	2
Rialto	6
Wok Camping	8

● SHOPPING

Biobazar (Soho Factory)	2
Hala Koszyki	6
Koło Bazar	3
Pan tu nie stał	5
Targ Śniadaniowy (Praga)	4
Targ Śniadaniowy (Żoliborz)	1

1

century **Royal Castle** (Zamek Królewski) was dynamited by German troops in the aftermath of the Warsaw Uprising, and lay in ruins until 1971. Its subsequent reconstruction was one of the pet projects of communist leader Edward Gierek, who correctly judged that such an investment in patriotic symbolism would win him a significant degree of popular support. In July 1974 a huge crowd gathered to witness the clock of the domed Sigismund Tower being started up again – the hands set exactly where they were stopped by the first Luftwaffe attack.

Today the castle consists of three main attractions. The Castle Museum is the main event – a sequence of opulently-decorated rooms that take the visitor through various stages of the palace's history. The next-door Tin-roofed Palace offers a display of Caucasian kilims; while the Kubiski Arcades on the east side of the castle host some intriguing contemporary art shows.

Castle Museum

May–Sept Mon–Wed, Fri & Sat 10am–6pm, Thurs 10am–8pm, Sun 11am–6pm; Oct–April Tues–Sat 10am–4pm, Sun 11am–4pm • 30zł; free on Sun; audio guide 17zł

The **Castle Museum** kicks off with a no-holds-barred sequence of sumptuously decorated rooms dating from the time of eighteenth-century King Stanisław August Poniatowski. Polish restorers scoured the sale rooms of Europe to find tables and chairs that matched Stanisław August's tastes, although many of the artworks are originals, scooted into hiding by percipient employees at the start of World War II. The **Matejko rooms** in the north wing are crammed with paintings by the doyen of nineteenth-century Polish painters, Jan Matejko. Equally magnificent is the **Canaletto Room**, with its views of Warsaw by Bernardo Bellotto, a nephew of the famous Canaletto – whose name he appropriated to enhance his reputation. Marvellous in their detail, these cityscapes provided invaluable information for the architects involved in rebuilding the city after the war. Next door is the richly decorated **Royal Chapel**, where an urn contains the heart of Tadeusz Kościuszko, the swashbuckling leader of the 1794 insurrection, and hero of the American War of Independence. After walking through the **King's Bedroom** and the sumptuous **Marble Room**, visitors enter the **Ballroom** with its allegorical ceiling paintings symbolizing the *Apotheosis of the Genius of Poland*. It was in the Senators' Chamber that the famous **Third of May Constitution**, one of the radical highpoints of European constitutional history (see page 457), was passed in 1791. The sightseeing route continues downstairs to a collection of Old Master paintings donated by the Lanckoronski family in 1994. Among the star turns here is a compelling pair of Rembrandts: *Girl in a Picture Frame* and *Scholar at a Writing Desk*, both from 1641.

Tin-roofed Palace

May–Sept Mon–Wed, Fri & Sat 10am–6pm, Thurs 10am–8pm, Sun 11am–6pm; Oct–April Tues–Sat 10am–4pm, Sun 11am–4pm • 15zł

Stuck on to the southeastern end of the castle is the so-called **Tin-Roofed Palace** (Pałac pod Blachą), a mid-eighteenth-century residence that gets its name from the tiles of copper-plated tin that once covered the roof. Expensively restored in 2008, the palace holds one of the world's largest displays of oriental carpets, donated to the Royal Castle by collector Teresa Sahakian. Also on show are the residential apartments of Prince Józef Poniatowski (1763–1813), the patriot and soldier who took part in Napoleon's ill-fated Russian campaign of 1812, and died fighting for the French at the Battle of Leipzig a year later.

Kubicki Arcades

Access from ul. Grodzka • Daily: May–Sept 11am–10pm; Oct–April 11am–6pm • Free

The castle's east-facing terrace rests on a series of barrel-vaulted, arched spaces known as the **Kubicki Arcades** (Arkady

TOP FIVE MUSEUMS

Warsaw Museum see page 57
POLIN Museum see page 71
Warsaw Rising Museum see page 72
Katyń Museum see page 73
Neon Museum see page 78

Kubickiego). Constructed in the 1820s, these hangar-like red-brick spaces are now used as exhibition spaces for contemporary art shows. Running alongside the arcades are the palace **gardens**, a neat patch of lawns and topiary that stretches as far as the main riverbank road, the Wisłostrada.

St John's Cathedral

ul. Świętojańska 8 • Mon–Sat 10am–5pm, Sun 3–5pm • ☎ 22 831 0289

St John's Cathedral (Archikatedra św. Jana) is the Old Town's principal place of worship, an early fourteenth-century structure sporting a distinctive red-brick stepped gable. Some of the bitterest fighting of the Warsaw Uprising took place around here, with German tanks entering the church after destroying its southern side: you can see sections of caterpillar tracks built into the wall along ulica Dziekania. Down in the **crypt** lie the graves of several illustrious Poles, Nobel-prize-winning novelist Henryk Sienkiewicz and pianist-politician Ignacy Jan Paderewski among them.

Old Town Square

The compact **Old Town Square** (Rynek Starego Miasta) is one of the most remarkable examples of postwar reconstruction in Europe. Flattened during the Warsaw Uprising, the three-storey merchants' houses surrounding the square have been scrupulously rebuilt to their seventeenth- and eighteenth-century designs, multicoloured facades included. By day the buzzing Rynek teems with visitors, who are catered for by buskers, artists, cafés and *dorożki*, horse-drawn carts that clatter tourists around for a sizeable fee. Plumb in the centre is a gurgling fountain with a statue of the **Warsaw Mermaid** (Syrena), the city's symbol.

Warsaw Museum

Rynek Starego Miasta 28–42 • Tues–Sun 10am–7pm • 20zł; free on Thurs • ☎ 22 277 4402, ⓦ muzeumwarszawy.pl

Reopened in 2017 following years of renovation, the **Warsaw Museum** (Muzeum Warszawy) takes up a large part of the north side of the square; the entrance is through a house called the Pod Murzynkiem ("Under the Negro"), a reference to the inn sign that used to hang above the doorway. The core exhibition, entitled the "Things of Warsaw", pieces together the capital's history through a compelling collection of household objects, old photographs, theatre posters, fashion magazines and private mementos.

The city walls

The alleyways of Warsaw's Old Town are bordered to the west by a lengthy section of **city wall**. The rebuilt fortifications feature walkable ramparts, pointy-roofed watchtowers and a grassy former moat filled with apple trees. Most poignant of the memorials along Podwale – the open path surrounding the walls – is the **Little Insurgent** (Mały Powstaniec), a bronze figure of a small boy with an oversized helmet carrying an automatic rifle. This solitary figure commemorates the numerous children and teenagers who fought and died in the Warsaw Uprising (see page 70), many of whom were recruited from boy-scouting organizations. The most impressive part of the old fortifications is the sixteenth-century **Barbakan**, which formerly guarded the Nowomiejska Gate, the northern entrance to the city.

The New Town and around

Immediately north of Warsaw's Old Town is the **New Town** (Nowe Miasto), an artisan quarter which dates (despite its name) from the early fifteenth century. The New Town's main artery is ulica Freta, site of some fine old Baroque buildings.

1

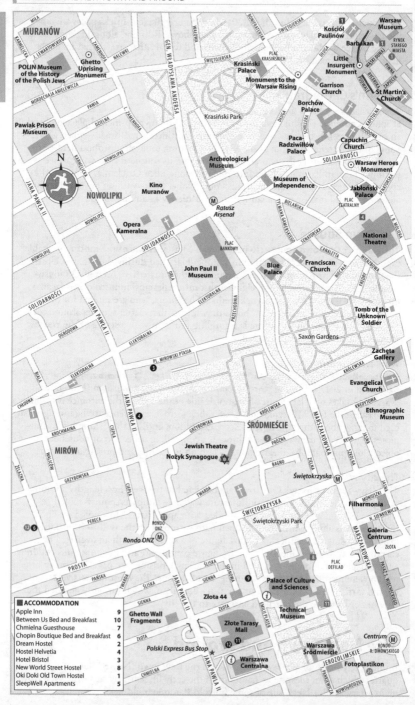

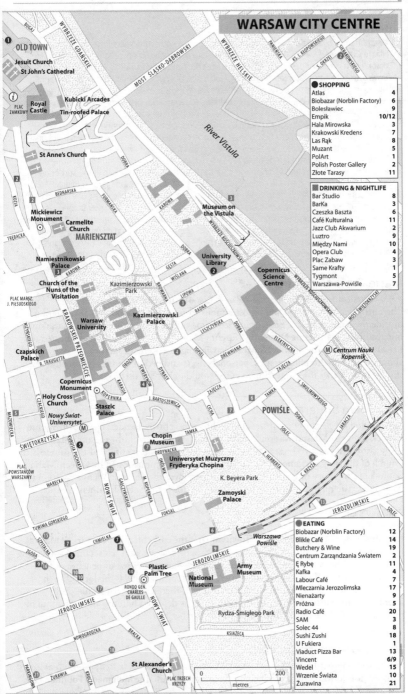

WARSAW CITY CENTRE

1

● SHOPPING

Atlas	4
Biobazar (Norblin Factory)	6
Bolesławiec	9
Empik	10/12
Hala Mirowska	3
Krakowski Kredens	7
Las Rąk	8
Muzant	5
PolArt	1
Polish Poster Gallery	2
Złote Tarasy	11

■ DRINKING & NIGHTLIFE

Bar Studio	8
BarKa	3
Czeszka Baszta	6
Café Kulturalna	11
Jazz Club Akwarium	2
Luztro	9
Między Nami	10
Opera Club	4
Plac Zabaw	3
Same Krafty	1
Tygmont	5
Warszawa-Powiśle	7

● EATING

Biobazar (Norblin Factory)	12
Blikle Café	14
Butchery & Wine	19
Centrum Zarządzania Światem	2
Ę Rybę	11
Kafka	4
Labour Café	7
Mleczarnia Jerozolimska	17
Nienażarty	9
Próżna	5
Radio Café	20
SAM	3
Solec 44	8
Sushi Zushi	18
U Fukiera	1
Viaduct Pizza Bar	13
Vincent	6/9
Wedel	15
Wrzenie Świata	10
Żurawina	21

Map labels: OLD TOWN, Jesuit Church, St John's Cathedral, Royal Castle, PLAC ZAMKOWY, Kubicki Arcades, Tin-roofed Palace, St Anne's Church, Mickiewicz Monument, Carmelite Church, MARIENSZTAT, Namiestnikowski Palace, Church of the Nuns of the Visitation, PLAC MARSZ. J. PIŁSUDSKIEGO, Kazimierzowski Park, Warsaw University, Kazimierzowski Palace, Czapskich Palace, Copernicus Monument, Holy Cross Church, Nowy Świat-Uniwersytet, Staszic Palace, Chopin Museum, Uniwersytet Muzyczny Fryderyka Chopina, K. Beyera Park, Zamoyski Palace, PLAC POWSTAŃCÓW WARSZAWY, Plastic Palm Tree, National Museum, RONDO GEN. CHARLES DE GAULLE, Army Museum, Rydza-Śmigłego Park, St Alexander's Church, PLAC TRZECH KRZYŻY, Museum on the Vistula, University Library, Copernicus Science Centre, Centrum Nauki Kopernik, POWIŚLE, Warszawa Powiśle, River Vistula

Streets: WYBRZEŻE GDAŃSKIE, MOST ŚLĄSKO-DĄBROWSKI, WYBRZEŻE HELSKIE, WYBRZEŻE KOŚCIUSZKOWSKIE, MOST ŚWIĘTOKRZYSKI, BEDNARSKA, FURMAŃSKA, DOBRA, KAROWA, GESTA, WIŚLANA, LIPOWA, BROWARNA, RADNA, LESZCZYŃSKA, DOBRA, DREWNIANA, ELEKTRYCZNA, ZAJĘCZA, J. SMULIKOWSKIEGO, TRĘBACKA, KOZIA, NIEZYMERSKIEGO, KRAKOWSKIE PRZEDMIEŚCIE, R. TRAUGUTTA, OBOZNA, SEWERYNÓW, DYNASY, TOPIEL, KARASIA, J. BARTOSZEWICZA, CICHA, TAMKA, MAZOWIECKA, T. CZACKIEGO, KOPERNIKA, ORDYNACKA, OKÓLNIK, SMOLNA, KUBUSIA PUCHATKA, ŚWIĘTOKRZYSKA, WARECKA, NOWY ŚWIAT, M. KOPERNIKA, GAŁCZYŃSKIEGO, FOKSAL, TUWIMA GÓRSKIEGO, CHMIELNA, ZGODA, SZPITALNA, ZGODA, JEROZOLIMSKIE, BRACKA, NOWOGRODZKA, KSIĄŻĘCA, ŻURAWIA, KRUCZA, PARNINGOWA, SOLEC, C. KRZYŻA, Z. HERBERTA, S. JARACZA, ZAJĘCZA, L. HERBERTA

0 — 200 metres

BUGAJ, PANIEŃSKA, KS. J. KŁOPOWSKIEGO, J. OKRZEI, J. SIERAKOWSKIEGO

1

MARIE CURIE (1867–1934)

One of many Poles to rise to fame abroad rather than at home, the Nobel Prize-winning scientist **Marie Curie** (née Maria Skłodowska) was born into a scientifically oriented Warsaw family. After completing her secondary education at the city's Russian lyceum, Curie went on to study at the **Sorbonne** in Paris, subsequently landing a job in the laboratory of the noted physicist Gabriel Lipmann. She married fellow researcher **Pierre Curie** in 1895, beginning a partnership that was to result in a number of spectacular scientific achievements. First came the discovery of polonium – so named in honour of her native country – in summer 1898, and soon afterwards, **radium**. Following her colleague Henri Becquerel's discovery of the phenomenon she eventually dubbed "radioactivity", Curie set to work on systematic research into the revolutionary new field. As a result, Marie Curie, Pierre Curie and Becquerel were jointly awarded the **Nobel Prize** in 1903. Pierre's sudden death in 1906 was a heavy emotional blow, but led to Curie's appointment to his professorship, making her the first woman ever to teach at the Sorbonne. A second Nobel Prize, this time in chemistry, came in 1911 for the isolation of pure radium.

Throughout the 1920s Curie travelled and lectured widely, founding both the Curie Foundation in Paris and the Radium Institute in her native Warsaw in 1932, to which her sister Bronia was appointed director. Constant exposure to radiation took its toll, however, Curie dying of leukaemia in 1934. The scientific community mourned the loss of one of its outstanding figures, a woman whose research into the effects of radioactivity pioneered both its medical and research-oriented applications, simultaneously paving the way for subsequent developments in nuclear physics.

Marie Curie Museum

ul. Freta 16 • Tues–Sun: June–Aug 10am–7pm; Sept–May 9am–4.30pm • 11zł • ☎ 22 831 8092, ⓦ muzeum-msc.pl

The birthplace of one of Poland's most famous women, **Maria Skłodowska** – better known outside the country by her French married name of Marie Curie – now houses the small but absorbing **Marie Curie Museum** (Muzeum Marii Skłodowskiej-Curie), dedicated to her life and work. The double Nobel Prize-winning discoverer of radium (see above) is commemorated with photographs, personal effects and period laboratory instruments similar to ones that the pioneering scientist would once have used.

New Town Square

Surrounded by elegantly reconstructed eighteenth-century facades, **New Town Square** (Rynek Nowego Miasta) was once an important commercial hub, and nowadays hosts a lively cluster of cafés and restaurants. Tucked into the eastern corner of the square is the **Church of the Holy Sacrament** (Kościół Sakramente), commissioned by Queen Maria Sobieska in memory of her husband Jan's victory over the Turks at Vienna in 1683 (see page 456). The highlight of the calm, white interior is the Sobieski funeral chapel.

St Mary's Church
ul. Przyrynek 2

Just off the northern edge of New Town Square, the early fifteenth-century **St Mary's** (Kościół Mariacki) is one of the oldest churches in Warsaw, and has retained something of its Gothic character despite later remodellings. Staggered rows of benches outside provide a wonderful viewing point across the river. St Mary's was the local church of Maria Skłodowska-Curie as a girl and, fittingly, there's a modern **statue** of the scientist on the embankment just outside. Curie is depicted holding aloft a symbol of polonium, the element she discovered in 1898.

Multimedia Fountain Park

Skwer im. I Dywizji Pancernej • Fountain May–Sept 8.30am–10.30pm; Multimedia Shows on Fri & Sat 9/9.30pm • Free • ⓦ estrada.com.pl

Situated just downhill from the New Town in a green park, the **Multimedia Fountain Park**

1

(Multimedialny Park Fontann) has become one of the most popular attractions in the city since first opening in 2011. By day, the spurting waters provide entertainment for strollers and kids. On weekend nights, the fountain becomes the scene of an ambitious multimedia spectacle powered by choreographed curtains of water, coloured lights, lasers and pounding amplified music. These shows usually have a folk-tale or children's-story narrative (in 2017 it featured a monster known as the Basilisk); crowds have been known to top 30,000.

Monument to the Warsaw Uprising

Bringing an inspirational touch of wartime drama to **plac Krasińskich,** a prominent road junction just west of Warsaw's Old and New Towns, the **Monument to the Warsaw Uprising** was commissioned by Poland's communist authorities in 1989 – a belated response to years of campaigning by veterans and their families. Somewhat dwarfed by the garishly green pillars of the National Court building behind it, the monument occupies the spot where AK (Home Army) battalions launched their assault on the Nazis on August 1, 1944.

A STROLL ALONG KRAKOWSKIE PRZEDMIEŚCIE

A popular promenading route lined with cafés, churches and former palaces, **Krakowskie Przedmieście** is the kind of place you'll find yourself strolling along more than once during your stay. The following account of the street's notable sights runs from north to south.

Standing at the northern end of Krakowskie Przedmieście, the eighteenth-century facade of **St Anne's Church** (Kościół św. Anny) is one of the outstanding examples of the boulevard's dominant Neoclassical style. A few steps further south, the **Adam Mickiewicz Monument** (Pomnik Adama Mickiewicza) was unveiled on the centenary of the national poet's birth in 1889, before a twelve-thousand-strong crowd, despite a ban on rallies and speeches. Just behind the statue stands the seventeenth-century **Carmelite Church** (Kościół Karmelitów), founded by King Władysław IV in 1637. Burned by the Swedes some eighteen years later, the church was extensively rebuilt in the eighteenth century, when it received its distinctive globe-capped facade – one of the first examples of genuine classicism in Poland.

Further south, fronted by an imposing equestrian statue of Józef Poniatowski (see page 56), the **Namiestnikowski Palace** (Pałac Namiestnikowski) is a Neoclassical pile dating from 1819, built on the site of the seventeenth-century palace where the Constitution of May 3, 1791 was passed. The present building was witness to the signing of the Warsaw Pact in 1955, at the height of the Cold War, and 34 years later, in spring 1989, it hosted the "Round Table" talks between the country's communist authorities and the Solidarity-led opposition. The palace was Poland's official presidential residence from 1994 until 2010, and still serves as the seat of the presidential secretariat and the venue for high-level receptions.

A stately ensemble of creamy-coloured Neoclassical buildings comprises the main campus of **Warsaw University** (W uw.edu.pl), entered via a grand-looking gateway bearing statuettes of Urania and Athena. Established in 1818, the university was closed by the tsar in punishment for the 1831 Insurrection, and remained closed until 1915. During the Nazi occupation, educational activity of any sort was made a capital offence, and thousands of academics and students were murdered. On the main courtyard, the old library stands in front of the seventeenth-century **Kazimierzowski Palace** (Pałac Kazimierzowski), once a royal summer residence and now home to the rector.

Towering over the southern end of Krakowskie Przedmieście is the twin-towered **Baroque Holy Cross Church** (Kościół św. Krzyża), which was ruined by a two-week battle inside the building during the Warsaw Uprising. Photographs of the distinctive stone figure of Christ left standing among the ruins became poignant emblems of Warsaw's suffering and now hang in the first chapel to the right of the altar. The church is also known for containing **Chopin's heart** – it's in an urn standing within a column on the left side of the nave.

Marking the southern end of Krakowskie Przedmieście and the beginning of Nowy Świat, the **Copernicus Monument** (Pomnik Mikołaja Kopernika) was commissioned by Polish patriots from leading Danish sculptor Bertel Thorvaldsen in 1822. It portrays the great astronomer holding his revolutionary heliocentric model in one hand, a pair of compasses in the other.

The monument comprises two sculptural groups, one depicting AK insurgents surfacing from manholes on to the street to begin their attack on the Germans, the other illustrating their forlorn retreat back into the sewers. Many drowned in the sewers, were killed by grenades thrown into the tunnels, or were shot upon emerging, although a hundred or so did make it to freedom.

TOP 5 WARSAW ICONS
The Warsaw Mermaid see page 57
Monument to Marie Curie see page 60
The Plastic Palm Tree see page 66
The Palace of Culture and Sciences see page 67
The National Stadium see page 79

1

Krakowskie Przedmieście and around

Heading south from the Old Town, the elegant boulevard known as **Krakowskie Przedmieście** – which becomes Nowy Świat (see page 65) in its southerly reaches – is one of central Warsaw's main arteries. Just west of Krakowskie Przedmieście lie several museums and galleries, many ranged around the focal point of **plac Piłsudskiego**.

John Paul II Museum

pl. Bankowy 1, enter from ul. Elektoralna • Tues–Sun: May–Sept 10am–5pm; Oct–April 9am–4pm • 15zł • ⓦ mkjp2.pl

Housed in a rotunda-shaped building that once held the Stock Exchange and National Bank, the **John Paul II Museum** (Muzeum Kolekcji im. Jana Pawła II) comprises the art collection assembled by wealthy émigré Zbigniew Carroll-Porczyński and donated to the Polish Catholic church in 1986. The hall is hung with more than eighty portraits, including some by Velázquez, Rembrandt, Titian and Tintoretto (or, more often, their workshops). Other highlights include Impressionist works such as the early and typically brooding *Farm in Hoogeveen* by Van Gogh, and *Still Life with Cauliflower* by Renoir.

Plac Piłsudskiego

An important focal point to the west of Krakowskie Przedmieście, **plac Piłsudskiego** is a broad flagstoned space occupying the former site of an eighteenth-century Royal Palace, blown up by the Germans in 1944. Placed beneath the palace's surviving arches is the **Tomb of the Unknown Soldier**, comprising eternal flame, a military guard and, chiselled into the pillars, the names of all battlegrounds that saw Poles in action.

Looming over the northern end of the square is Sir Norman Foster's love-it-or-hate-it **Metropolitan** office block, a huge glass-and-concrete doughnut (with a fountain-splashed plaza in the middle instead of the jam).

Saxon Gardens

Making up a handsome chunk of west-central Warsaw are the popular promenades of the **Saxon Gardens** (Ogród Saski), laid out for August II by Tylman van Gameren in the early 1700s and landscaped as a public garden in the following century. Some elements of the original park survived, notably the scattering of Baroque sculptures symbolizing the Virtues, Sciences and Elements, an elegant nineteenth-century fountain pool above the main pathway, the old **water tower** (Warsaw's first) built by Marconi in the 1850s, and the park's fine crop of **trees**, more than a hundred species in all.

Zachęta Gallery

pl. Małachowskiego • Tues–Sun noon–8pm • 15zł; free on Thurs • ⓦ zacheta.art.pl

Built at the turn of the twentieth century as the headquarters of the Warsaw Fine Arts

Society, the **Zachęta Gallery** (Galeria Zachęta) was one of the few large buildings in central Warsaw left standing at the end of World War II. The stucco decoration in the entrance stands in dramatic counterpoint to the changing exhibitions of modern and contemporary art, many featuring big-name international artists.

Ethnographic Museum

l. Kredytowa 1 • Tues, Thurs & Fri 10am–5pm, Wed 11am–7pm, Sat noon–6pm, Sun noon–5pm • 12zł; free on Thurs • ☏ 22 827 764 146, ⓦ ethnomuseum.pl

Folk traditions play an important role in Poland's identity, something that Warsaw's **Ethnographic Museum** (Muzeum Etnograficzne) shows off to captivating effect. The first room cheekily wrong-foots the viewer by displaying Polish folk artefacts alongside pieces of costume and sculpture from Africa, Asia and the Pacific – a tribute to the globe-trotting private collectors who brought their treasures back to Warsaw, and an introduction to the science of ethnography as a whole. Next comes a beautifully arranged collection of Polish **folk instruments**, accompanied by miniature loudspeakers that you press against your ear to get an idea of what they sound like. Pride of place goes to the two-storey gallery of **costumes**, which includes traditional garb from all over Poland alongside examples of the way in which folk motifs have been employed by the modern fashion industry. Side rooms introduce **seasonal rites**, with displays of Palm Sunday palms made from dried flowers, painted Easter eggs, and more.

The west bank of the Vistula

Nowhere in Warsaw has changed quite so completely in recent years as the **west bank of the Vistula**, an urban asset almost completely ignored until 2010, when the Copernicus Science Centre opened its doors. Since then, a riverside **foot- and cycle-path** has been built along the riverbank, and a host of summer-only **bars** have sprouted up along the route. With the National Stadium (see page 79) rearing up hypnotically on the opposite side of the river, it's a hugely popular strolling venue during the day, and a favourite location for alfresco drinking in the evening.

Copernicus Science Centre

Wybrzeże Kościuszkowskie 20 • April–June Tues–Fri 8am–6pm, Sat & Sun 10am–7pm; July & Aug Tues–Sun 9am–7pm; Sept–March Tues–Fri 9am–6pm, Sat & Sun 10am–7pm; roof garden Tues–Sun: May–Aug 10am–8pm; Sept & Oct 10am–5pm • 27zł, family of four 72zł • ☏ 22 596 4100, ⓦ kopernik.org.pl • Metro Centrum Nauki Kopernik

One of Europe's boldest hands-on family attractions, the **Copernicus Science Centre** (Centrum Nauki Kopernik) occupies a cool slab of contemporary architecture on the banks of the Vistula. Designed by Polish architects RAr-2, it's an exciting space to visit, its partly see-through ceiling supported by grey girders, with exhibits spread across two open-plan floors.

The museum is divided into several zones: nearest the entrance is **Buzz!**, a play zone for 4- to 6-year-olds full of simple but effective science games. Also on the ground floor is **Re-generation**, a series of interactive games and quizzes intended for "young adults" that deal with flirting, dating and mating. The **Thinkatorium** poses challenges to visitors

> **TOP FIVE THINGS TO DO OUTDOORS**
>
> Take in the **son-et-lumiere** at the Fountain Park, see page 60
> Admire the views from the **rooftop gardens**, University Library, see page 65
> Stroll the avenues of **Łazienki Park**, see page 74
> Walk the **riverside path** on the east bank of the Vistula, see page 77
> Pull up a deckchair at the *Cud nad Wisłą* bar, see page 89

of all ages (build a flying machine, build a bridge, and so on) and provides them with basic household items in order to undertake their task. Further sections (Roots of Civilization, Humans and the Environment, Lightzone, and On the Move) include a plethora of sound-and-light effects, physical tests and mind-bending challenges. Park strollers and serious horticulturalists alike will be wowed by the centre's **rooftop garden**, with its hardy riverside plants and cross-Vistula views.

Museum on the Vistula

Wybrzeże Kościuszkowskie 22 • Tues–Thurs noon–8pm, Fri noon–10pm, Sat 11am–8pm, Sun 11am–6pm • Free • Ⓦ artmuseum.pl • Metro Centrum Nauki Kopernik

A cube-like pavilion that popped up on the riverbank in spring 2017, the **Museum on the Vistula** (Muzeum nad Wisłą) is the temporary home of the Museum of Modern Art in Warsaw, an institution that is currently awaiting construction of a new and permanent seat on plac Defilad, right beside the Palace of Culture and Science (see page 67). The wooden pre-fab will stay in its present location for three or four years, by which time it is hoped that the new premises will be finished. It's certainly a welcome addition to the riverside scene, with changing contemporary art exhibitions, a popular café and occasional cultural happenings on the wooden decking outside.

University Library Roof Garden

ul. Dobra 55/66 • Daily: April & Oct 8am–6pm; May–Sept 8am–8pm • Free • Ⓦ buw.uw.edu.pl • Metro Centrum Nauki Kopernik

In a city well served with attractive open spaces, the **University Library Roof Garden** (Ogród na dachu Biblioteki Uniwersytetu Warszawskiej) ranks as one of the most unusual. It consists of the **lower garden**, an attractive grassy parkland complete with duck pond; and the **upper garden** on the roof itself, featuring ground-creepers, dwarf shrubs, junipers and lots of ornamental grasses. There are great views of Warsaw, and the library atrium (open to non-readers) is full of cafés and snack bars – useful if you are roaming this part of town.

Nowy Świat and around

The continuation of Krakowskie Przedmieście is **Nowy Świat** ("New World"), an area first settled in the mid-seventeenth century. The southern end of this wide boulevard, closed to traffic at weekends, has a decent concentration of restaurants, bars and cafés, and is frequently a good place to start or end an evening out.

Chopin Museum

ul. Okólnik 1 • Tues–Sun 11am–8pm • 22zł • ☎ 22 441 6251, Ⓦ chopin.museum

Arguably the jewel of Warsaw's cultural crown, the state-of-the-art **Chopin Museum** occupies the Ostrogski Palace, a late seventeenth-century structure that has been fabulously restored. With historical exhibits augmented by snatches of music, computer-screen visuals and English-language audio snippets, it's a fascinating museum that works on several levels. There's even a room reserved for 3- to 10-year-olds, complete with touch-screen Chopin jukebox and other educational aids. Musical **instruments** on display include a fine example of a so-called "giraffe" – an upright grand piano with a sensually curvy frame – and, on the first floor, an 1840 piano used by Chopin himself. The **Nohant Room** (named after George Sand's country estate) is filled with the sound of piped birdsong and contains pictures of Sand, Chopin and other houseguests, notably Romantic painter and Chopin enthusiast Eugene Delacroix. A darkly funereal final chamber displays Chopin's death mask and a lock of the composer's hair. The museum puts on summertime Sunday **concerts** in Łazienki Park (see page 74) and at Żelazowa Wola (see page 108).

1

THE PLASTIC PALM TREE

Sprouting up from the central reservation of a roundabout marking the junction of al. Jerozolimskie and Nowy Świat, the 15m-high plastic palm tree is one of Warsaw's more unusual contemporary icons. Officially entitled **Greetings from Jerusalem Avenue** (Pozdrowienia z alej Jerozolimskich; ⓦ palma.art.pl), it was erected by artist Joanna Rajkowska in 2002, with the Middle Eastern palm serving as an intentionally exotic pointer to Warsaw's historic role as a centre of Jewish settlement. Despite attracting controversy, the palm currently enjoys the blessing of the city authorities and looks set to stay in its current location – the fact that it still provokes debate only adding to its status as an artwork.

National Museum

al. Jerozolimskie 3 • Tues, Wed & Fri–Sun 10am–6pm, Thurs 10am–9pm • 15zł; permanent collection free on Tues • ☎ 22 621 1031, ⓦ mnw.art.pl

Immediately east of Nowy Świat's junction with aleja Jerozolimskie, the **National Museum** (Muzeum Narodowe) is a daunting grey-brown building that was considered a masterpiece of modern functionalism when first built in the 1930s. High-profile temporary exhibitions are held alongside the epoch-spanning permanent collection.

The ground floor

Highlight of the ground floor is the stunning collection of art from Faras, a town in **Nubia** (present-day Sudan), excavated by Polish archaeologists in the early 1960s. On show are carvings, columns and 69 murals dating from between the eighth and thirteenth centuries. The earliest paintings – notably *St Anne*, *Ammonius the Anchorite* and *SS Peter and John the Evangelist* – are powerful images comparable in quality with later European Romanesque works. The west wing of the ground floor is taken up with displays of **Egyptian mummies**, **Greek** red-figure vases and **Roman** statuary.

Also on the ground floor is a rich collection of m**edieval art**, with a kaleidoscopic array of carved and painted altarpieces. Note in particular the lovely late fourteenth-century polyptych from Grudziądz castle; a magical, dream-like fifteenth-century *Annunciation with Unicorn* from Wrocław; and a c.1500 polyptych from Pruszcz depicting the Passion, whose turbulent and dramatic crowd scenes involve over 100 wood-carved figures.

The first floor

Much of the first floor is given over to **Polish painting**. Important works include the *Battle of Orsza*, painted in the 1520s by a follower of Lucas Cranach the Elder and depicting the Polish-Lithuanian rout of the Muscovite army on the banks of the River Dnieper in 1514. Centrepiece of the eighteenth-century gallery is Jan Matejko's huge *Battle of Grunwald*, showing the defeat of the Teutonic Knights by Polish and Lithuanian forces in 1410. A dreary nineteenth-century section suddenly bursts to life with canvases by artists from the Młoda Polska movement (see page 270), with Stanisław Wyspiański's pastel portraits a particular stand-out. Roomfuls of twentieth-century art include a disturbingly mesmerising *Surrealist Execution* (1949) by Andrzej Wroblewski; and *Bus* by Bronisław Wojciech Linke (1961), a phantasmagoric vision of various Poles stuck together in the public transport conveyance of the title.

The second floor

The museum's top floor contains mixed galleries of **European old masters** and applied arts, so that canvases are frequently displayed alongside the furniture and porcelain that would have been in fashion at the same time. Painting highlights include *A Venetian Admiral* by Tintoretto, and a characteristically seductive *Virgin and Child* by Sandro Botticelli.

Army Museum

al. Jerozolimskie 3 • Wed 10am–5pm, Thurs–Sun 10am–4pm • Main exhibition 15zł; outside display 3zł; free on Sat • ⓦ muzeumwp.pl

There are grandiose plans to move the **Polish Army Museum** (Muzeum Wojska Polskiego) to a new site in the Citadel (see page 72), but for the time being it continues to occupy the east wing of the National Museum. It's certainly an inspiring collection, frequently focusing on objects and personalities that represent Polish history at its most iconic, including the famous "whistling" eagle-feather wings once worn by the fearsome Polish hussars. A section on World War I captures the pathos of Poles forced to fight and die under foreign imperial flags, while a hall of weapons and uniforms recalls the Poles who fought for the British army, navy and airforce on all fronts during World War II. Outside, there's a big collection of **heavy combat equipment**, from sixteenth-century cannons through to modern tanks, planes and missiles.

Centrum and around

The modern commercial heart of Warsaw, **Śródmieście** or "City Centre", lies some 2km southwest of the Old Town. Its main point of reference is the Centrum metro station, located at the major crossroads formed by **ulica Marszałkowska** and **aleja Jerozolimskie**. Looming above the junction is the **Palace of Culture and Sciences**, a notorious monument to Stalinist megalomania. Further west still, beyond Warszawa Centralna train station, a growing collection of **skyscrapers** epitomizes the changing face of Warsaw city life. Daniel Libeskind's sail-shaped Zlota44 apartment block, spearing up above Centralna station, is probably the most famous, although the 220m-high Warsaw Spire (designed by Jaspers Eyers Architects), 1km west, gives it a run for its money.

Palace of Culture and Sciences

Entrance on pl. Defilad • Interior lift to viewpoint daily 10am–8pm, until 11pm on Fri & Sat May–Sept • 20zł • ⓦ pkin.pl

Towering over everything in the modern centre of Warsaw is the **Palace of Culture and Sciences** (Pałac Kultury i Nauki, or PKiN for short), a gift from Stalin to the Polish people, and not one that could be refused. Officially dubbed "an unshakeable monument to Polish-Soviet friendship", the palace was completed in 1955 after three years of work by 3500 construction workers brought specially from Russia for the job. This neo-Baroque leviathan provokes intense feelings from Varsovians: some residents maintain that the best **views** of Warsaw are from the palace's top floor – the only viewpoint from which one can't see the building itself – while others are willing to grant it a sinister kind of elegance, especially when compared to the glass skyscrapers that have sprouted up nearby.

Inside, a **lift** whisks visitors 114m up to the thirtieth-floor platform from which, on a good day, you can see out into the plains of Mazovia. Parts of the marble-and-chandelier interior can be visited if you're visiting one of the palace's theatres or bars – such as *Café Kulturalna* (see page 87) – or have tickets for a concert at the famous **Congress Hall** (Sala Kongresowa). One truly epoch-defining gig to take place here was the appearance of the Rolling Stones in 1967 (a time when Western groups hardly ever made the trip to Eastern Europe), an event that exerted a profound influence on an audience that had never before seen a microphone stand wielded in such an overtly sexual way.

Technical Museum

pl. Defilad 1 • Tues–Fri 9am–5pm, Sat & Sun 10am–6pm • 25zł • ⓦ mtip.pl

Occupying the southwest wing of Warsaw's Palace of Culture and Science, the **Technical Museum** (Muzeum Techniki) offers an extensive parade of technological curiosities, ranging from the bafflingly boring to the truly revelatory; in the latter category is a German-made **Enigma code machine** of the late 1930s (see page 412). Elsewhere, models of Vostok and Gemini **spacecraft** recall the Cold War space race, while a "**Glass Maid**" (Szklana panienka) – a see-through model of a female body – lights up on the hour at weekends to show different internal organs and bodily functions (extra 2.50zł).

1

TOP 5 HISTORIC NEIGHBOURHOODS

Ulica Freta and the New Town see page 57
Krakowskie Przedmieście see page 63
MDM see page 68
Praga see page 77
Saska Kępa see page 79

The Fotoplastikon

al. Jerozolimskie 51 • Wed–Sun 10am–6pm • 6zł

For a bizarre voyage back into the world of pre-World War I popular entertainment look no further than the **Fotoplastikon**, an original 1905 contraption that stands preserved in a curtained chamber just off aleja Jerozolimskie. The barrel-shaped apparatus contains a fast-changing sequence of photographic slides that offer the illusion of being in 3D – which must have been an exciting novelty to audiences at the turn of the twentieth century. Perch on a stool and peer through goggle-shaped sights to see the parade of images, most of which shed fascinating light on the changing face of Warsaw through the ages.

The MDM area: Plac Konstytucji and Plac Zbawiciela

Few places bear more eloquent witness to Warsaw's periodical changes of image than the area around **plac Konstytucji** ("Constitution Square"), 1km south of the Centrum metro station. Site of a major Stalinist-era construction project in the early 1950s, the area is characterized by cooly imperious lines of grey-brown apartment blocks, many decorated with socialist-realist reliefs of workers, architects, scientists and other builders of socialism. The project went under the name of **MDM** (Marszałkowska Dzielnica Mieszkaniowa, or the "Marszałkowska Residential District"), an acronym by which the area is still colloquially known.

The MDM project extended south to include **plac Zbawiciela**, a pretty circular square where a sequence of imposing colonnades was constructed around the central traffic roundabout. What makes plac Zbawiciela such an extraordinarily beautiful place is the way that these Stalinist-style arcades harmonize so perfectly with the twin-towered, neo-Gothic **Church of the Holy Saviour** (Kościół Najświętszego Zbawiciela) that rises imperiously over the square's southern rim.

The MDM area now contains some of the most expensive real estate in the capital, with a growing roster of restaurants, cafés and bars giving the whole place the aura of a highly desirable neighbourhood.

Station Museum

ul. Towarowa 3 • Daily 10am–6pm • 12zł • ☎ 22 620 0480 • Metro Rondo Daszynskiego, or Warszawa Ochota train station

Located on the site of Warsaw's former main railway station (before it was moved 1km east in the 1960s), the **Station Museum** (Stacja Muzeum) brings together a fantastic collection of railway memorabilia and vintage locomotives. Models of steam engines throughout the ages fill the main halls, with particular focus on the triumphs of Polish engine construction. Star of the show is the pea-green, streamlined PM36-1, built in Chrzanów in 1937, but never put into full-scale production due to the outbreak of World War II. Outside stand long lines of locos and rolling stock, including an olive-green armoured train complete with revolving gun turret.

Mirów, Muranów and around

West of central Warsaw, the sprawling housing estates and tree-lined avenues of the **Muranów** and **Mirów** districts are home to an important clutch of museums and memorials dedicated to the horrors of World War II. Warsaw was for centuries one of the great Jewish centres of Poland, and by 1939 there were an estimated 380,000 Jews living here, one-third of the city's total population. Although Warsaw's Jewish community was spread throughout the city before World War II, it was in Mirów and Muranów that they were most concentrated, and it was here that the Nazis created a **Jewish Ghetto** in October 1940 (see page 69). Following the wholesale obliteration of the area both during and after the 1943 Ghetto uprising, the streets today bear little resemblance to their former selves: some changed their name or course, or simply disappeared altogether, making it difficult to gain an impression of what the ghetto area once looked like.

The Jewish ghetto wall

In the courtyard of the Henryk Sienkiewicz Lyceum on the corner of Sienna and Jana Pawla; courtyard open Mon–Fri during daytime

Marking the southern end of the former Jewish Ghetto is one of the few surviving fragments of the 3m-high wartime **ghetto wall**, wedged between Sienna and Złota streets. Comprising two short sections of brick, it stands as a poignant testimony to the rude separation of the ghetto – so close, and yet so far from life on the other side. The isolation was never absolute; post and phone communication with the "Aryan" sector continued long into the Nazi occupation, and food was continually smuggled into the starving ghetto, despite the threat of instant execution for anyone caught doing so. A small commemorative plaque records former Israeli president Chaim Herzog's official unveiling of the monument in 1992, along with a map showing you just how much of Warsaw the ghetto covered.

Nożyk Synagogue and around

ul. Twarda 6 • Mon–Fri 9am–7pm, Sun 11am–7pm • 10zł • ☎ 22 620 4324, ⓦ warszawa.jewish.org.pl

A stately ochre structure opened in 1902 and currently the main place of worship for Warsaw's Jewish community, the **Nożyk Synagogue** (Synagoga Nożyków) is the only one of the ghetto's three synagogues still standing; the majestic Great Synagogue on ulica Tłomackie – which held up to three thousand people – was blown up by the Nazis and is now the site of a skyscraper. The Nożyk's refined interior is full of Moorish design details that were popular with Jewish architects before World War I, with delicate arcades and balustrades, and oriental-inspired furnishings.

Before you leave the area, walk across plac Grzybowski to **ulica Próżna**. This street has somehow survived the ravages of war and reconstruction, and is the only place where you can get an idea of what the old ghetto area once actually looked like.

THE WARSAW GHETTO AND THE GHETTO UPRISING

In October 1940, 450,000 Jews from Warsaw and the surrounding area were sealed behind the walls of the Nazi-designated ghetto area, creating the largest **ghetto** in Nazi-occupied Europe. By 1941, nearly one and a half million Jews from all over Poland had been crammed into this unsanitary zone, with starvation and epidemics the intended consequence. By mid-1942, nearly a quarter of the ghetto population had died, a plight communicated to the Allies by a series of forthright reports from the Polish underground.

Deportations to the death camps from Umschlagplatz (see page 71) began in summer 1942, with 250,000 or more taken to Treblinka (see page 71) by mid-September. The Nazis moved in to "clean out" the ghetto in January 1943, by which time there were only 60,000 people left. Sporadic resistance forced them to retreat, but only until April, when a full-scale Nazi assault provoked the **Ghetto uprising** under the leadership of the **Jewish Combat Organization (ŻOB)**. For nearly a month, Jewish partisans battled against overwhelming Nazi firepower, before the ŻOB's bunker headquarters, on the corner of ulica Miła and ulica Zamenhofa, was finally surrounded and breached on May 9, following the suicide of the legendary Mordechai Anieliewicz and his entire ŻOB staff. A few combatants survived and escaped to join up with the Polish resistance in the "Aryan" sector of the city, as did the musician Władysław Szpilman, subject of Roman Polański's Oscar-winning movie The Pianist. Of those remaining in the ghetto, 7000 were shot immediately, the rest dispatched to the camps. On May 15, Jürgen Stroop, commander-in-chief of the German forces, reported to Himmler, "The Jewish quarter in Warsaw no longer exists."

1

Pawiak Prison Museum

ul. Dzielna 24/26 • Wed–Sun 10am–5pm • 10zł • ☎ 22 831 9289, ⓦ muzeum-niepodleglosci.pl/pawiak.html

Built during the Tsarist period to incarcerate Polish patriots, the notoriously grim Pawiak Prison was subsequently used by both the Polish interwar state and World War II Nazi occupiers to lock up successive generations of political undesirables. The prison was blown up by the Nazis in August 1944, and the **Pawiak Prison Museum** (Muzeum Więzienia Pawiak) now occupies a modern pavilion in a small corner of this once huge complex. It's the World War II period that figures most strongly in the museum display, with photos and mementoes commemorating the many members of the Polish intelligentsia who were

---

THE 1944 WARSAW UPRISING

Of the many acts of resistance to the savage Nazi occupation of Poland, the 1944 **Warsaw Uprising** was the biggest. After years of clandestine activity, summer 1944 seemed to offer the best opportunity for the **Polish Home Army** (Armia Krajowa or AK) to emerge from the underground and undertake offensive action. With Nazi forces reeling under the impact of the Red Army's westward advance, a German withdrawal from Warsaw began to seem a possibility. However, the AK was confronted by an agonizing dilemma: on one side, they were strongly urged by the Allies to cooperate with advancing Soviet forces in driving back the Nazis; on the other, the AK knew that Poland would fall under Soviet domination unless they opened up an autonomous front of their own.

THE ATTACK

Throughout July 1944, AK Commander **Tadeusz Bór Komorowski** hesitated over which course of action to take. With the arrival of the first Soviet tanks across the Vistula in the Praga district, the decision to launch a single-handed attack on the Germans was taken and, on August 1, the main Warsaw AK corps of around 50,000 poorly armed troops sprang an assault on the city centre. For the first few days the element of surprise enabled AK forces to capture large tracts of the city. By August 5, however, the tide was beginning to turn. Supported by dive bombers, Nazi troops began clearing out the insurgents, treating both combatants and civilians as legitimate targets for reprisals. The Nazi recapture of the Wola district on August 11 was followed by the massacre of more than 8000 civilians. Even worse followed in Ochota, where more than 40,000 were murdered. Hospitals were burned to the ground with all their staff and patients, women and children were tied to the front of German tanks to deter ambushes, and rows of civilians were marched in front of infantry units to ward off AK snipers.

With German troops driving the partisans into an ever-diminishing pocket, the AK made the decision to abandon the centre. On September 2, around 1500 surviving AK troops, along with more than 500 wounded, descended into the **city sewers** through a single manhole near plac Krasiński – an event imprinted firmly on the national consciousness in large part thanks to Wajda's legendary 1957 film *Kanał*.

SURRENDER AND THE AFTERMATH

Fighting continued for another month in isolated pockets until October 2, when General Bór and his troops finally **surrendered** to the Germans. Heavy AK casualties – around 20,000 dead – were overshadowed by huge losses (estimated at some 225,000) among the civilian population. With the AK and almost the entire population of Warsaw out of the way, Nazi demolition squads set about wiping the city off the map, dynamiting building after building until the city centre had to all intents and purposes ceased to exist.

The most controversial aspect of the Uprising remains the lack of **Soviet intervention**. The Soviet tanks that had reached Praga sat idly by throughout September 1944 as the Germans pounded the city across the river. Equally significantly, the Soviets repeatedly refused Allied access to Soviet airbases for airlifts of supplies to the beleaguered insurgents. Poles have always maintained that Stalin simply allowed the Germans a free hand in annihilating AK forces, therefore making it easier for the Soviet Union to impose its will on a leaderless Poland.

Over seventy years on, the heroic, yet ultimately tragic, events of the autumn of 1944 remain firmly lodged in the national memory, at once a piece of history whose interpretation remains controversial, and a potent source of national self-definition.

held and tortured in the cells. Outside the museum is a striking monument in the shape of an elm tree; the original tree, a much-loved Warsaw icon covered in post-war plaques honouring the Pawiak's victims, died in 2004 and had to be carted away.

POLIN Museum of the History of the Polish Jews

ul. Mordechaja Anielewicza 6 • Mon, Thurs & Fri 10am–6pm (last entry at 4pm), Wed, Sat & Sun 10am–8pm (last entry at 6pm) • 25zł; free on Thurs • ☎ 22 471 0301, ⓦ jewishmuseum.org.pl

Opened on April 20, 2013, on the seventieth anniversary of the Warsaw Ghetto uprising, the **POLIN Museum of the History of the Polish Jews** (Muzeum Historii Żydów Polskich) is the kind of museum that gets you excited as soon as you see it looming up in front of you. Designed by Finnish architect Rainer Mahlamäki, the building takes the fittingly dramatic form of a four-storey cube rent down the middle by a huge, cave-like fissure.

Inside, slogan-like captions fill entire walls, models and reproductions bring past epochs to life, and full use is made of reproduction posters, photographs and newsreel clips as the story of Poland's Jews enters the twentieth century. By focusing on the Jewish presence in Poland (a story that starts in earnest as early as the thirteenth century), the museum functions as an all-embracing panorama of Polish history in general, whether highlighting the tolerant multiculturalism of the Polish-Lithuanian Commonwealth prior to the Partitions, or the turbulent multi-ethnic urban life that characterized many a Polish city up until World War II. One outstanding exhibit is the replica of a painted wooden ceiling from the long-disappeared seventeenth-century synagogue in Gwoździec near Kraków, reconstructed from old photographs and featuring abstract patterns, fantastical beasts and zodiac signs. A café and restaurant serve up Jewish feast-day fare such as roast goose and *gefilte fisch*.

Ghetto Heroes Monument

pl. Bohaterów Getta

Unveiled in 1948 on the fifth anniversary of the Ghetto uprising, the stark **Ghetto Heroes Monument** (Pomnik Bohaterów Getta) recalls both the immense courage of the Jewish resistance, and the helplessness of the deportees, to moving effect. It was actually built from blocks ordered from Sweden by Hitler in 1942 to construct a monument to the Third Reich's anticipated victory.

The Path of Remembrance

Laid out in the 1980s, a series of memorial plaques known as the **Path of Remembrance** mark the main locations of the Warsaw ghetto, mapping out a commemorative geography of the community's suffering. Starting from plac Bohaterów Getta, then moving north along ulica Zamenhofa to the Umschlagplatz on ulica Stawki, nineteen granite blocks engraved in Polish and Hebrew honour important individuals and events of the ghetto. Along the way the route takes you past the grass-covered memorial mound covering the site of the **ŻOB Bunker** at ul. Miła 18 (see page 69) – the mound's height represents the level of rubble left after the area's destruction. In many of the surrounding streets you'll find houses built on a similar level, as the postwar communist authorities simply went ahead and constructed new housing blocks on the flattened remains of the ghetto.

Umschlagplatz

Located on the edge of a housing estate in northern Muranów, **Umschlagplatz** is where Jews were loaded onto cattle wagons bound for Treblinka and the other death camps. A simple white marble monument was raised here in the late 1980s; designed to resemble the cattle trucks used in the transportations, it is covered inside with a list of four hundred Jewish first names, symbolizing the estimated 300,000 Jews deported from here. A stone stands at

1

the exact point from which the trains departed. Across the road, one of the few surviving prewar buildings (no. 5/7) was the house of the SS commander supervising operations.

Jewish Cemetery

ul. Okopowa 49 • Mon–Thurs 10am–5pm, Fri 9am–1pm, Sun 9am–4pm; men should cover their heads – skullcaps are provided • 10zł • ☎ 22 838 2622, ⓦ warszawa.jewish.org.pl • Tram #22 west from Warszawa Centralna, or bus #180 north along Krakowskie Przedmieście

Established in 1806, the **Jewish Cemetery** (Cmentarz Żydowski) contains the graves of more than 250,000 people, and is one of the few Jewish cemeteries still in use in Poland today. This site was left almost untouched during the war, due to the fact that, unlike in smaller Polish towns, the Nazis didn't need the materials for building new roads. The tombs range from colossal Gothic follies to simple engraved stones. Scattered among the plots are the graves of eminent Polish Jews including **Ludwig Zamenhof**, the inventor of Esperanto (see page 181), early socialist activist **Stanisław Mendelson** and writer **D.H. Nomberg**. Also worth seeking out is a powerful sculpted monument to Janusz Korczak, erected in his honour in the 1980s.

Warsaw Rising Museum

ul. Grzybowska 79 • Mon, Wed & Fri–Sun 10am–6pm, Thurs 10am–8pm • 20zł; free on Sun; audio guide 10zł • ⓦ 1944.pl • Metro Rondo Daszyńskiego, or tram #12, #22 or #24 from Warszawa Centralna west to "Grzybowska"

Housed in a century-old former power station in southwestern Mirów, the **Warsaw Rising Museum** (Muzeum Powstania Warszawskiego) honours the heroism of August 1944 (see page 70) with a compelling and highly moving multimedia display. Sections detailing life within Warsaw before and during the Uprising make full use of contemporary newsreels and photographs. Crucial to the collection is a series of **photographs** by former PE teacher, Olympic javelin thrower and Polish officer **Eugeniusz Lokajski**, who after being taken prisoner in 1939 by the Soviet army escaped to Nazi-occupied Warsaw and opened a photography studio. He remained in the city throughout the occupation, commanded a platoon in the Uprising and died in a house on Marszałkowska in September 1944, leaving a legacy of more than one thousand photos. A life-size model of an American Liberator B24 bomber recalls limited Allied attempts to supply the insurgents from the air, while there's also a reconstruction of part of the sewer system through which combatants fled the destroyed city. Outside is a park with a 156m-high wall inscribed with the names of several thousand soldiers who died in the struggle.

Warsaw Citadel

Overlooking the Vistula some 2km north of Warsaw's Old Town, the crescent-shaped fortress known as the **Citadel** (Cytadela) was built by the Russians in 1832–4 in response to the uprising of November 1830, when Tsarist troops briefly lost control of the Polish capital. The site has been earmarked as the future site of the Polish Army Museum (see page 66), although it will be a few more years before this plan reaches fruition. For the time being the bulk of the citadel is out of bounds save for the two **museums** that already exist: the Museum of the Tenth Pavilion near the citadel's northern tip; and the Katyń museum at the opposite, southern end. A grassed-in former moat runs around the citadel's western rim, providing a perfect strolling ground and vantage point from which to admire the citadel's grizzled red-brick fortifications.

Museum of the Tenth Pavilion

Accessed through the Brama Bielańska gate, just off the Wybrzeże Gdańskie highway • Daily except Tues 10am–5pm • 10zł • ⓦ muzeum-niepodleglosci.pl/xpawilon • Metro pl. Wilson

The part of the citadel housing the **Museum of the Tenth Pavilion** (Muzeum X Pawilonu) was used as a prison right from the start, but put to particularly grim use following the uprising of 1863. Corridor after corridor of bleak cells recall the misery of incarceration; the memorial display devoted to leader of the uprising Romuald Traugutt records the fact that he was hanged outside the citadel in 1864. Among those incarcerated here in later years were pre-World War I nationalist leaders Roman Dmowski and Józef Piłsudski, both now honoured with photographs and mementoes. One notorious inmate of the Tenth Pavilion who is conspicuous by his absence from the display is "Iron" Feliks Dzierżyński, the goat-bearded Bolshevik and godfather of the KGB who was imprisoned here by the Tsarist authorities four times in the years before World War I.

Katyń Museum
ul. Jana Jezioranskiego 4; enter through the Nowomiejska Gate on the south side of the citadel • Wed 10am–5pm, Thurs–Sun 10am–4pm • Free • ☎ 261 878 342, ⦿ muzeumkatynskie.pl • Metro Dworzec Gdański

Commemorating the murder of over 20,000 Poles by Soviet security forces in spring 1940 (see page 73), the **Katyń Museum** (Muzeum Katyńskie) employs atmospheric lighting, sombre music and chilling sound effects (such as the screech of railway wagon wheels) to create a powerful feeling of impeding tragedy. The key narrative elements – the Nazi-Soviet pact of August 1939, the combined Nazi-Soviet invasion of September, and the incarceration of Polish officers by the Soviets – are thoughtfully presented with a mixture of photos, maps and archive film. It's with the personal belongings recovered from mass graves (water bottles, tobacco pouches, pipes, spectacles), arranged in little wooden compartments, that the display is at its most poignant.

The Royal Parks and around

The former **royal parks** south of the centre are one of Warsaw's most attractive features. Half a kilometre south of the National Museum, the park surrounding **Ujazdowski Castle** adjoins the luxuriant public gardens that make up **Łazienki Park**. A further 3km southeast is **Wilanów**, the former estate of King Jan III Sobieski and site of his sumptuous palace. The so-called **Royal Way** (Trakt Królewski) – which starts in the Old Town's Castle Square and heads south along Krakowskie Przedmieście, Nowy Świat, aleja Ujazdowska, ulica Belwederska and ulica Sobieskiego – runs past all of the parks.

THE KATYŃ MASSACRE

Following the Nazi-Soviet attack on Poland in September 1939, Poland's eastern territories were absorbed into the USSR, and thousands of Polish soldiers and civilians were imprisoned or deported to other parts of the Soviet Union – an estimated 10,000 Poles, for example, ended up in Kazakhstan. **Polish officers** were separated from other ranks and interned in special camps, where they were joined by several thousand police officers, scoutmasters, lawyers and even priests. In March 1940, Soviet security chief **Lavrentiy Beria** decided to murder them, on the basis that they may, in future, form the nucleus of an army hostile to the interests of the USSR. An estimated 22,000 Poles were shot in April and May 1940 in various locations.

The killing site at **Katyń Forest** in western Russia (where 4408 are known to have been murdered) became synonymous with the massacre as a whole, as it was the first mass grave to be excavated. The site was discovered by Nazi occupiers in 1943, and immediately exploited by the Germans in their **propaganda war** with the Soviet Union. The Soviets countered with the claim that it was the Germans who had killed the Poles with the intention of pinning it on the Soviets. Even after the war, the Polish (communist and therefore pro-Soviet) government continued to broadcast the lie that Katyń was the work of the Germans, even though the bulk of Polish society knew otherwise. Only in 1989 was the truth officially admitted.

It was during commemorations to mark the seventieth anniversary of the massacre in 2010 that a Polish aircraft carrying President Lech Kaczyński and 95 others crashed near Smolensk in western Russia, killing all on board. The power of Katyń as a symbol of Polish martyrdom has exerted a somber influence over Polish society ever since.

1

Ujazdowski Castle: the Contemporary Art Centre

ul. Jazdów 2 • Tues, Wed & Fri–Sun noon–7pm, Thurs noon–9pm • 12zł; free on Thurs • ☎ 22 628 1271, Ⓦ u-jazdowski.pl • Metro Politechnika, or bus #116, #180 or #E2 from Krakowskie Przedmieście to pl. na Rozdrożu

Squatting amidst greenery just north of Łazienki Park, some 2km south of central Warsaw, **Ujazdowski Castle** (Zamek Ujazdowski) is a rebuilt Renaissance structure once inhabited by King Sigismund August's Italian-born mother Bona Sforza. It's now home to the **Contemporary Art Centre** (Centrum Sztuki Współczesnej), one of the city's leading venues for modern art shows. As well as organizing themed exhibitions, the centre mounts innovative theatre, film and video events. The building also contains an excellent café and restaurant (see page 87), as well as a well-stocked art bookshop.

Gestapo Museum

al. Szucha 25 • Wed–Sun 10am–5pm • 10zł • ☎ 22 629 4919 • Metro Politechnika, or bus #116, #180 or #E2 from Krakowskie Przedmieście to pl. na Rozdrożu

Popularly known as the **Gestapo Museum** (its proper title is the Mausoleum of Struggle and Martyrdom, or Mauzoleum Walki i Męczeństwa), the basement space underneath the current Ministry of Education, just west of Ujazdowski Park, is where World War II German security police tortured civilians suspected of resistance activity. You can peek into the grim cells and read the stories of the inmates, the atmosphere of dread enhanced by atmospheric lighting and sound effects such as dripping water, screams and the percussive chak-chak of an interrogator's typewriter. One of the many resistance heroes who passed through here before being transferred to Pawiak (see page 70) to be further tortured and ultimately murdered was **Antoni Kocjan**, who discovered evidence of the German V2 rocket programme and fed the British with the information they needed to bomb factories and launch sites.

Łazienki Park

Entrance on al. Ujazdowskie • Daily 8am–sunset • Bus #116, #180 or #E2 from Krakowskie Przedmieście

Arguably Warsaw's most luxuriant public space, **Łazienki Park** (Park Łazienkowski) stretches for 2km alongside the southbound aleja Ujazdowskie. Once a hunting ground on the periphery of town, the area was bought by King Stanisław August in the 1760s and turned into an English-style park with formal gardens. A few years later the Neoclassical **Island Palace** was built across the park lake. Designed for the king by the Italian architect Domenico Merlini, it's a fitting memorial to the country's last and most cultured monarch. Before this summer residence was commissioned, a **bathhouse** built by Tylman van Gameren for Prince Stanisław Lubomirski stood here – hence the name, "Łazienki" meaning simply "baths".

The oak-lined promenades and pathways leading from the park entrance to the palace are a favourite with tourists and Varsovians, many of the latter coming prepared to feed the park's resident fauna, which include peacocks, squirrels and mandarin ducks. On summer Sundays, **concerts** take place under the watchful eye of the ponderous Chopin Monument, just beyond the entrance, as well as in the Cadet School by the Island Palace. On the way down to the lake you'll pass a couple of the many buildings designed for King Stanisław by Merlini; the **New Guardhouse** (Nowa Kordegarda), just before the palace, is now a pleasant terrace café.

The Island Palace

Łazienki Park • Mon 10am–2pm, Tues–Sun 10am–6pm • 25zł; free on Thurs • Ⓦ lazienki-krolewskie.pl

The **Island Palace** (Pałac na Wyspie), named after its location on a mid-lake strip of land connected by ornate bridges, is the smallest of Warsaw's royal palaces. Nazi damage to the building itself was fairly severe, but many of the lavish furnishings, paintings and sculptures survived, having been hidden during the occupation.

Cadet School

Łazienki Park • Mon 10am–2pm, Tues–Sun 10am–6pm • Free

The two-storey Neoclassical building next to the Island Palace originally housed the kitchens and administrative offices, but subsequently served as a **Cadet School** (Podchorążówka) – it was here that trainee officers hatched the anti-tsarist conspiracy that resulted in the November 1830 uprising. The building now contains a hall devoted to composer **Ignacy Jan Paderewski**, whose body was returned to Warsaw from the US in 1992. Much of what's here was bequeathed to the country by the exiled Paderewski in his will, with pride of place going to the grand piano he used at his longtime home on the shores of Lake Geneva.

Myślewicki Palace

Łazienki Park • Mon 10am–2pm, Tues–Sun 10am–6pm • 10zł; free on Thurs

The crescent-shaped **Myślewicki Palace** (Pałac Myślewicki) was a present from King Stanisław August to his nephew Prince Józef Poniatowski. Well-preserved frescoes and ceiling paintings provide an insight into the aristocratic tastes of the time, and there is an abundance of fine turn-of-the-nineteenth-century furniture. The building was used as a state residence during the communist period, when Indian premier Indira Gandhi and US President Richard Nixon figured among the guests.

White House

Łazienki Park • Mon 10am–2pm, Tues–Sun 10am–6pm • 6zł; free on Thurs

West of the Island Palace, the **White House** (Biały Domek) was built in the 1770s by Merlini for King Stanisław August's favourite mistress. It retains the majority of its original eighteenth-century interiors, including a dining room decorated with a wealth of grotesque animal frescoes, and an octagonal-shaped study which features enjoyable trompe l'oeil floral decoration.

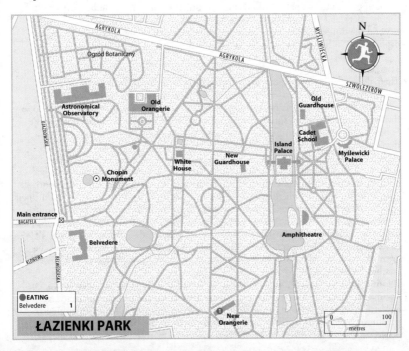

1

Old Orangerie

Łazienki Park • Mon 10am–2pm, Tues–Sun 10am–6pm • 20zł • Free on Thurs

Just northwest of the White Pavilion, the **Old Orangerie** (Stara Pomarańczarnia) contains a well-preserved wooden theatre (one of the few in Europe to retain its original eighteenth-century decor) with royal boxes and seating for more than two hundred.

Belvedere

At the southern end of the park stands the **Belvedere** (Belweder), another eighteenth-century royal residence redesigned in the 1820s for the governor of Warsaw, the tsar's brother Konstantine. It has been the official residence of Polish presidents ever since the end of World War I – save for a short period between 1994 and 2010, when heads of state resided in the Namiestnikowski Palace on Krakowskie Przedmieście (see page 62).

Wilanów

ul. Stanisława Kostka Potockiego 10/16, 9km south of the centre • **Palace** May to mid-Sept Mon, Wed, Sat & Sun 9.30am–6pm, Tues, Thurs & Fri 9.30am–4pm; mid-Sept to April Mon & Wed–Sun 9.30am–4pm; last entry 1hr before closing • 20zł; free on Thurs; audio guide 12zł • **Gardens** Daily 9am–dusk • 5zł; free on Thurs • ☎ 022 544 2700, ⓦ wilanow-palac.pl • Bus #116, #180 or #E2 from Krakowskie Przedmieście

The most beautiful of Warsaw's palaces, **Wilanów** is tucked away on the southwestern fringes of Warsaw, and makes an easy excursion from the city centre. Nicknamed the Polish Versailles, it was originally the brainchild of King Jan Sobieski, who purchased the estate in 1677 and spent nearly twenty years turning it into his ideal country residence. In 1797 the palace came under the ownership of Stanisław Kostka Potocki, who set about transforming Wilanow into both a shrine to Sobieski and a private museum based on his own art collection. Packed full of opulent furnishings and old masters, it's very much a tourist favourite.

The approach to the palace takes you past former outhouses, including the smithy, the butcher's and an inn. The **entrance gates**, where you buy your tickets, are just beyond the domed eighteenth-century **St Anne's Church** (Kościół św. Anny) and the ornate neo-Gothic Potocki mausoleum across the road.

The palace

The palace is laid out in a horseshoe plan, with a central core flanked by a pair of projecting wings. The classical grandeur of the **facade**, complete with Corinthian columns, Roman statuary and Latin inscriptions, reflects Sobieski's original conception; the centrepiece, a golden sun with rays reflecting from decorated shields bearing the Sobieski coat of arms, clarifies the fundamental idea: the glorification of Sobieski himself.

Entrance to the palace's rooms is via the basement, where seasonally-changing history exhibitions are held. A spiral staircase leads to the **picture galleries**, which hold a particularly fine collection of coffin portraits (a popular form of seventeenth-century popular art in which images of the deceased were painted onto the end of their coffins). Another undoubted highlight is Angelika Kauffman's delicate portrait of Ana Potocka, Stanisław Kostka Potocki's daughter-in-law. Downstairs from here on the palace's ground floor, the **Etruscan Study** is filled with third- and fourth-century BC vases collected in Naples by Potocki. The adjoining hall is dominated by one of the great masterpieces of Neoclassical portraiture, *Stanisław Kostka Potocki on Horseback* by Jacques-Louis David.

Some of the most lavish interiors are to be found in the **rooms of Queen Maria Kazimierza**, Jan Sobieski's French-born wife. The ceiling painting of the Marriage of Vertumnus and Pomona in the Queen's Antechamber is an allegory of Sobieski's pursuit of Maria, who initially turned him down in favour of landowning magnate Jan Sobiepan Zamoyski. After Sobieski's **library**, with its marble-tiled floor and allegorical

1

ceiling paintings, comes the small **study** (subsequently memorial chapel) where Sobieski died in 1696. Hanging in tribute is an impressive portrait of the king clad in classical-era armour, the work of Sobieski's court painter Jerzy Eleuter Siemiginowski.

The palace gardens

The gate on the left side beyond the main entrance opens onto the stately **palace gardens**. Overlooking the garden terrace, the palace's graceful rear facade is topped by statuary featuring a golden sundial, designed by Gdańsk astronomer Jan Hevelius, on the southern side. The fresco sequence punctuating the facade shows scenes from classical literature, notably the *Aeneid* and the *Odyssey*. The Baroque gardens reach down to the waterside, continuing rather less tidily along the lakeside to the north and south. Beyond the Orangery is the romantic **English Landscape Park,** modelled on eighteenth-century gardens in Britain.

Poster Museum

l. St. Kostki Potockiego 10/16 • Mon noon–4pm, Tues, Thurs & Fri 10am–4pm, Sat & Sun 10am–6pm • 11zł; free on Mon • ☎ 22 842 2606, ⓦ postermuseum.pl

Located near the main gates of the Wilanow palace gardens, the **Poster Museum** (Muzeum Plakatu) pays tribute to an art form that has long been a Polish speciality. Stylish theatre and film posters of the 1950s and '60s placed the country at the forefront of graphic design, as evidenced by the seasonally revolving display of posters taken from the museum's huge archive. The museum's modern annexe (reached via a short walk across the back garden) displays a valuable collection of international posters, including some Art Nouveau gems from *belle époque* Paris.

Praga

Metro Dworzec Wileński; tram #21 or #25 from Centrum; tram #4, #13, #23 or #26 from the Old Town

Despite being a short hop over the River Vistula from the Old Town, the gritty suburb of **Praga** looks and feels like a wholly different city: no wonder Praga residents tend to say "I'm going to Warsaw" when crossing the Śląsko-Dąbrowski bridge. Out of range of the main World War II battles, Praga retains much of its prewar architecture, and is a good place to get an idea of what central Warsaw might have looked like had the Germans not razed it in 1944. Not surprisingly, it was in Praga that Roman Polański shot the street scenes for his movie *The Pianist*. Nowadays Praga is in the throes of change; the artists and bohemians who started the transformation of the district a decade ago have been followed by the gentrifiers and loft-developers, and the extension of Warsaw's metro network to this side of the river has brought Praga much closer to the commercial energies of the city centre. Praga retains its gritty sense of otherness, however; cobbled streets and former factories contribute to a post-industrial aesthetic, and the area's cafés and pubs still seem a touch more underground than those elsewhere.

The riverside path

Unlike the western bank of the Vistula, which has been paved and adapted to leisure-time use, the river's **eastern bank** has been purposefully left to its own devices – a narrow belt of forest, wetland and sandbank that remains rich in bird- and insect-life. Several sandbanks become deckchair-covered **beaches** in summer, and the winding **foot-and cycle-path** that runs almost interrupted along the eastern bank of the river is popular year round. In many ways the path represents Warsaw's best urban hike – a semi-woodland trail that runs under dramatic bridges and offers expansive views of the city centre. The stretch from northern Praga to Saska Kępa (see page 79) makes for an easy hour-long stroll.

1

Orthodox Church of St Mary Magdalene

al. Solidarności 52 • Mon–Sat 11am–4pm, Sun 1–4pm; services daily at 9am & 5pm

Built to serve the army of Tsarist bureaucrats that inhabited Praga in the nineteenth century, the **Orthodox Church of St Mary Magdalene** (Cerkiew św. Marii Magdaleny) is one of the few remaining signs of the former Russian presence. A large neo-Byzantine structure topped by a succession of onion domes, its original mid-nineteenth-century interior decoration remains intact. If you visit during services you will probably hear the excellent **choir** in action.

Praga Museum

ul. Targowa 50/52 • Tues, Wed & Fri–Sun 10am–6pm, Thur 10am–8pm • 15zł; free on Thurs • ☎ 22 518 3430, ⑩ muzeumpragi.pl • Metro Dworzec Wileński

Housed in a three-storey townhouse on Praga's main street, the **Praga Museum** (Muzeum Warszawskiej Pragi) is an affectionate portrait of the local community, concerning itself with social and lifestyle history rather than the onward march of meaningful dates. The story of the suburb is told through an imaginative combination of photos, household objects and audio-visual recordings relating Praga inhabitants' recollections of growing up in the area. Out in the museum courtyard is a nineteenth-century Jewish prayer hall once used by merchants at the nearby Różycki market, containing painstakingly-restored murals and friezes.

Neon Museum

Soho Factory, ul. Mińska 25 • Mon, Wed–Fri noon–5pm, Sat 11am–6pm, Sun 11am–5pm • 10zł • ⑩ neonmuzeum.org • Tram #3, #6 or #22 to Gocławska

Occupying one of the handsome red-brick halls of the Soho Factory (a refurbished former munitions works now taken over by creative industries and restaurants), Warsaw's **Neon Museum** (Muzeum Neonów) is both a groundbreaking contribution to Poland's design heritage and one of the most visually ravishing things you are likely to see while you're here. Neon signs advertising shops, restaurants and public spaces were a frequent feature of Polish cities in the 1960s and '70s, when they became something of an urban visual trademark. Museum co-founder Ilona Karwińska started photographing and rescuing old neons back in 2005 – the museum (opened in 2012) was the result of several painstaking years of research and restoration. It has proved hugely influential in promoting a nationwide neon conservation boom, and has also sponsored the commissioning of new neon signs – notably the *Miło cię Widzieć* ("Nice to see you") neon that stretches along the Gdański bridge at Praga's northern end.

Life Under Communism Museum

ul. Mińska 22 (entrance from ul. Głucha) • Mon–Fri 10am–4pm, Sat & Sun 11am–5pm • 8zł • ☎ 664 828 243, ⑩ czarprl.pl • Trams #3, #6 or #22 to Gocławska

Located in an anonymous-looking block just off ulica Mińska, the **Life Under Communism Museum** (known as Czar PRL in Polish, or "Charm of the People's Republic") comprises a mock-up of a communist-era flat, complete with 1970s furniture, children's dolls, reel-to-reel tape-recorders and vinyl LPs. What it reveals is that life under communism in its middle years – despite supplies of the things you needed potentially running out at any moment – was far from grey. The children's books on the shelves include some great examples of illustration and design, while period fashion magazines demonstrate that the Western world did not always have a monopoly on glamour. It was a great time to be a Polish sports fan, too: a football report from a copy of a newspaper dated October 16, 1973, describes an epochal 1–1 draw against England at Wembley (Poland went on to play in the 1974 World Cup; England did not).

National Stadium

1

al. Poniatowskiego 1 • **Viewing Point** Daily 10am–9.30pm • 12zł • **Guided tours** Mon–Fri 2pm, Sat & Sun 2.30pm • 42zł • ☎ 22 295 9595, ⓦ en.pgenarodowy.pl • Metro Stadion Narodowy, or tram #7, #8, #9, #21, #24 or #25 to Rondo Waszyngtona

Built in preparation for the Euro 2012 football championship, co-hosted by Poland and Ukraine, the magnificent **National Stadium** (Stadion Narodowy) lords it over Warsaw's riverscape from its shoreside perch in southern Praga. It is particularly impressive at night, when lights play across its surface to mesmerising effect. On non-match days, visitors are allowed access to a **viewing point** up in the stands for views over the pitch. There's also a once-daily English-language **guided tour** of the arena, taking in much of the backstage stuff you rarely see – changing rooms, pitch-side tunnels, VIP areas and so on. As well as hosting football, the stadium is also the venue for major rock and pop concerts.

Saska Kępa

Tram #7, #8, #9, #21, #24 or #25 to Rondo Waszyngtona

Immediately south of the new National Stadium lies one of Warsaw's most characterful suburbs, one that has remained largely unchanged since its interwar heyday. It was in the 1920s and '30s that **Saska Kępa** became popular with Poland's middle classes, sprouting street after street of Bauhaus-inspired urban villas. It's this architectural heritage that makes the suburb such a fascinating place to wander, with leafy residential streets lined with the kind of perfectly-proportioned three-storey cubes that once gave modern architecture a good name. Boasting a handsome clutch of good-quality cafés and restaurants, especially on the main strip, **ulica Francuska**, the district is an increasingly fashionable destination for fans of strong caffeine and contemporary cuisine.

ARRIVAL AND DEPARTURE

WARSAW

BY PLANE

FREDERIC CHOPIN AIRPORT

Locally still known as Okęcie, Frederic Chopin airport (flight information ☎ 22 650 4220, ⓦ warsaw-airport.com), handles both international and domestic flights, and is 8km southwest of the city.

Trains Suburban SKM trains (4.40zł) serve the airport station. S3 (hourly) runs through Warszawa Centralna, Warsaw's main station (20min), before heading east across the river to Warszawa Wschodnia; S2 (every 30min) runs through Warszawa Śródmieście, right next door to Warszawa Centralna (20min), before continuing to Warszawa Wschodnia. In addition local rail operator Koleje Mazowieckie runs trains between the airport and Warszawa Centralna (hourly; 20min; 6.80zł; SKM tickets not valid).

Buses Bus #175 (every 10–15min; 4.40zł) runs to Warsaw Old Town in about half an hour, passing Warszawa Centralna and Krakowskie Przedmieście on the way. From about 11pm to 5am, night bus #N32 (2 hourly) heads from the airport to Warszawa Centralna.

Taxis Ignore all drivers waiting in the building and only go with taxis waiting outside the terminal in marked taxi ranks; the trip to the centre will cost 40–50zł, fifty percent more at night.

MODLIN AIRPORT

Primarily used by Ryanair flights, but looking to expand carriers and routes in the future, Modlin airport (flight information ☎ 22 315 1880, ⓦ modlinairport.pl) is 40km north of Warsaw near Nowy Dwor Mazowiecki.

Trains A shuttle bus runs from the airport terminal to Modlin station, from where Koleje Mazowieckie trains run to and from Warszawa Centralna (every 30min; 1hr; 17zł).

Buses Modlin Bus (ⓦ modlinbus.pl) run from outside the airport terminal to Warsaw's Palace of Culture and Sciences (every 40min; 50min; 23zł when bought online, 33zł from the driver).

Taxis A taxi from Modlin to the centre will set you back 200zł.

BY TRAIN

Warszawa Centralna The main train station, served by all the main national and international routes, is bang in the centre of Warsaw's main business and shopping district. Bus #175 will save you the 30min walk into the Old Town. Taxi ranks are outside the main door. The station's layout is confusing: the main ticket hall is at ground level, while an underground warren of corridors leads to the platforms: allow plenty of time for buying tickets and finding your train.

Other stations Most trains also stop at Warszawa Wschodnia (East) station, out in the Praga suburb, or Warszawa Zachodnia (West), in the Ochota district – the latter is also the site of the main bus station (see page 80). Both stations have regular connections to Centralna. Warszawa Śródmieście station, just east of Warszawa Centralna, handles local traffic to suburban destinations.

1

Tickets When buying tickets for domestic services remember to specify which service you want to travel on: tickets for regional trains will not be valid for PKP Intercity or the SKM (Warsaw overground) services. Tickets for international services can be bought from the international counters at Warszawa Centralna.

Information For train information visit ⓦ rozklad-pkp.pl. Destinations Białystok (8 daily; 2hr 30min); Bydgoszcz (6 daily; 3hr 35min); Częstochowa (8 daily; 2hr 30min–2hr 50min); Gdańsk/Sopot/Gdynia (12 daily; 3hr 15min–3hr 45min); Katowice (9 daily; 3hr 20min–3hr 40min); Kraków (16 daily; 3hr 25min–3hr 45min); Lublin (6 daily; 3hr); Łódź Fabryczna (Mon–Fri hourly, Sat & Sun every 2hr; 1hr 30min–2hr 30min); Łowicz (10 daily; 1hr–1hr 30min); Olsztyn (4 daily; 2hr 50min); Poznań (10 daily; 3hr 30min–4hr); Przemyśl (1 daily; 7hr 20min); Rzeszów (4 daily; 5hr 40min–6hr 20min); Sochaczew (hourly; 40min–1hr); Suwałki (2 daily; 4hr 30min); Świnoujście (2 daily of which 1 overnight; 9–10hr); Szczecin (6 daily; 5hr 30min–6hr 20min); Toruń (8 daily; 2hr 45min); Wrocław (5 daily; 4hr 45min–5hr 15min); Zakopane (1 daily; overnight; 9hr). International destinations Berlin (3 daily; 6hr 45min); Bratislava (1 daily; 7hr 50min); Budapest (2 daily of which 1 overnight; 10hr 30min–12hr); Kiev (1 daily; overnight; 16hr); Prague (2 daily of which 1 overnight; 8hr 30min–10hr); Vienna (2 daily of which 1 overnight; 8hr 30min–10hr).

BY BUS

Warszawa Zachodnia Warsaw's main bus station (Warszawa Zahodnia PKS; information ☎ 703 403 330, ⓦ dawz.pl) handles a motley collection of domestic and international services, especially to cities throughout the Ukraine. It is 3km west of the centre right next to Warszawa Zachodnia train station (see page 79). From here, a short train ride will take you in to Warszawa Centralna – virtually every eastbound municipal bus will take you there too; #127 continues on to pl. Bankowy on the fringes of the Old Town.

Polski Express A lot of domestic intercity bus routes are handled by Polski Express (ⓦ polskiexpress.com), who use departure and arrival points in the vicinity of Warszawa Centralna train station and only sell tickets online.

Lux Express Services to and from Vilnius (with onward connections to Riga and Tallinn) are handled by Lux Express (ⓦ luxexpress.eu), who use bus stands near Warszawa Centralna.

BY CAR

Car rental Avis, Frederic Chopin airport (☎ 022 650 4872, ⓦ avis.pl); Budget, Frederic Chopin airport (☎ 022 650 4062, ⓦ budget.pl); Hertz, Frederic Chopin airport (☎ 022 650 2896, ⓦ hertz.com.pl); Joka, ul. Okopowa 47 (☎ 022 609 181 020, ⓦ joka.com).

GETTING AROUND

BY PUBLIC TRANSPORT

Warsaw municipal transport authority (ZTM) operates an integrated bus, tram, metro and SKM suburban train network, with ZTM tickets valid for all four modes of transport. The major points where overground and underground public transport lines meet are Centrum, 400m east of the Warszawa Centralna train station in Śródmieście, and pl. Bankowy near the Old Town.

Metro The Warsaw metro consists of two lines running roughly north–south and east–west respectively; the lines cross over at Świętokrzyska.

Trams and buses Trams are extraordinarily useful in covering almost all areas of central Warsaw not covered by the metro; buses fill in any further gaps.

Suburban trains SKM overground trains run east–west through the city, calling at Warszawa Wschodnia, Warszawa Powiśle, Warszawa Śródmieście, Warszawa Centralna and Warszawa Zachodnia as they go. You can only use ZTM tickets (not regular train tickets) on these services, so check departure info before jumping aboard.

Ferries From May to mid-Sept there are a number of ferries crossing the River Vistula. Useful routes include Multimedia Fountain Park to Praga; Cypel Czerniakowski to Saska Kępa; and from the western end of the Poniatowski bridge to the National Stadium. The ferries (noon–7pm; every 20–30min) are free but can only take about a dozen people at a time.

Operating hours Regular municipal transport routes close down around 11–11.30pm; from 11.15pm to 4.45am a confusing array of night buses leaves from behind the Palace of Culture and Sciences on ul. Emilii Plater at 15 and 45 minutes past the hour.

Tickets Tickets (bilety) can be bought from any newspaper or tobacco kiosk sporting the "MZK" logo, from ticket machines at some central stops, and from ticket machines inside most trams, buses and overground trains. Single-fare tickets valid for any journey lasting up to 75min (with unlimited changes of modes of transport) cost 4.40zł; a 20min version costs 3.40zł. It's more economical to buy a 24-hour pass (bilet dobowy; 15zł), three-day pass (bilet trzydniowy; 36zł) or a weekend ticket (bilet weekendowy; valid from 7pm Fri to 8am Mon; 24zł). Students under 26 with a valid ISIC card can buy all tickets at half-price. Punch your ticket in the machines on board or at the metro entrance – pleas of ignorance don't cut much ice with inspectors, who'll fine you 200zł on the spot if they catch you without a validated ticket.

Information Timetable information ☎ 19115, ⓦ ztm.waw.pl.

1

BY TAXI

Warsaw taxi drivers have a better reputation than they used to but foreigners may still be overcharged, especially at the airport and train station. All reputable taxis bear a driver number and the taxi company's name, logo and telephone number: avoid any vehicles that are less clearly marked. Taxis booked by phone are often cheaper than those picked up at a rank.

Fares There's an initial charge of 6zł, followed by around 3–4zł per kilometre, 4.50zł per kilometre after 10pm and on Sun.

Firms Reputable companies include MPT (☎ 19191), Ele (☎ 22 811 1111), Sawa Taxi (☎ 22 644 4444) and Super Taxi (☎ 19622). Switchboard operators at these firms usually speak English.

BY BICYCLE

The provision of cycle lanes has improved immeasurably in Warsaw in recent years, although there are still many streets that don't have them. It is legal to cycle on pavements, but remember that pedestrians have right of way.

Bike rental Veturilo (☎ 19115, ⊕ veturilo.waw.pl) have a comprehensive network of bike pick-up and drop-off points throughout the city; register via the internet and then hire bikes using your smartphone. A good mainstream bike rental store is Wygodny Rower, ul. Smolna 10 (Mon–Fri 11am–7pm, Sat 10am–4pm; 40zł/24hr, plus 200zł deposit; ☎ 787 386 386, ⊕ wygodnyrower.pl).

INFORMATION

Tourist information centres Warsaw's municipal tourist office (☎ 22 194 31, ⊕ warsawtour.pl) operates several tourist information centres (Informacja Turystyczna, or IT) in the city, with English-speaking staff. They can provide information on accommodation throughout Warsaw, and handle hotel bookings. There are branches at the Palace of Culture and Sciences (entrance on the western side of the building; daily: May–Sept 8am–7pm; Oct–April 8am–6pm); in the Old Town at Rynek Starego Miasta 19/20/21 (daily: May–Sept 9am–8pm; Sept–April 9am–6pm); and at Frederic Chopin airport's arrival hall (daily 9am–7pm).

Maps The tourist office gives away an excellent map of the central area with sights and hotels marked; good plans of the whole city cost around 30zł and are widely available.

ACCOMMODATION

The range of accommodation options in Warsaw is comparable with those of any other European capital city, with a lot of **upmarket hotels** aimed at business and well-heeled travellers, a reasonable handful of **backpacker hostels**, and an increasing number of apartments and private flats advertised on websites like booking.com and airb&b. What makes the city slightly special is the growing number of urban **guesthouses** and **boutique B&Bs** that offer a mixture of intimacy, character and value-for-money. **Camping** in Warsaw's suburbs is a reasonable option if you don't mind being a lengthy public transport ride away from the centre.

HOTELS AND B&BS

★ **Apple Inn** ul. Chmielna 21, Lok. 22B ☎ 601 746 006, ⊕ appleinn.pl; map page 58. On the top floor of an apartment block in a perfect Śródmieście location, offering large-ish rooms with neat contemporary decor. Breakfast is in the *Vincents* café downstairs, but there's a shared kitchen (with free tea and coffee) in the B&B itself. **300zł**

★ **Autor Rooms** ul. Lwowska 17/7 ☎ 797 992 737, ⊕ autorrooms.pl; Metro Politechnika; map page 54. One of the most imaginative apartment-conversions in Warsaw (the owners work in the creative industries, hence the 'Author' tag), this place offers both class and kookiness. Rooms boast a mixture of original pre-World War I features and modern design touches (including graphic art on the walls), and there's a lovely communal breakfast table and a small kitchen. **400zł**

★ **Between Us Bed & Breakfast** ul. Bracka 20 ☎ 603 096 701, ⊕ between-us.eu; map page 58. Located in a converted apartment above the *Między Nami* café (see page 88), this bright B&B offers a combination of down-to-earth domesticity with arty touches, including works by contemporary photographers adorning the walls. There are tea- and coffee-making facilities in the communal hall; breakfast is downstairs in the café. **360zł**

Chmielna Guesthouse ul. Chmielna 13 (reception at Nowy Świat 27) ☎ 022 828 1282, ⊕ chmielnabb. pl; map page 58. Surprisingly intimate place for such a central location, with seven rooms arranged around a spacious living room and adjoining kitchen. Some rooms are quite small and share a bathroom in the hallway, but all are chicly decorated with soothing colours, hardwood floors and small TVs. Breakfast is eaten around a big communal table. **220zł**

★ **Chopin Boutique Bed and Breakfast** ul. Smolna 17, Lok. 7 ☎ 22 829 4800, ⊕ bbwarsaw.com; map page 58. Characterful rooms on two floors of an old apartment block, featuring original parquet floors and stucco – most of the furniture is verging on the antique. The B&B lives up to its name with daily piano recitals in a room next to the reception. The generous buffet breakfast (extra 40zł per person) is consumed at a long communal table. **350zł**

H15 Boutique Apartments ul. Poznańska 15 ☎ 22 553 8700, ⊕ h15boutiqueapartments.com; map page 54. This beautifully converted 1892 building, set on an increasingly popular street for drinking and dining, gives you a taste of the high life that is almost quite affordable. Most rooms have wood floors, high ceilings and a Pop Art design style that includes some attractive artwork on the walls. Huge bathrooms and walk-in cupboards are a feature of the larger doubles. There's a top-notch restaurant in the bright atrium, where breakfast (extra 65zł per person) is also served. 540zł

★ **Hilton Warsaw** al. Grzybowska 63 ☎ 22 356 5555, ⓦhiltonhotels.com; Metro Rondo Daszyńskiego; map page 54. The high-rise *Hilton* stands in the midst of the city's soaring office blocks (grab a corner room for spectacular views) and is right next door to the baton-shaped Warsaw Spire. With gym, pool, and the kind of attention-to-detail service that you would expect at this level, it's a difficult place to tear yourself away from. Breakfast extra 88zł per person. 980zł

Hotel Bristol Krakowskie Przedmieście 42/44 ☎ 22 551 1000, ⓦhotelbristolwarsaw.pl; map page 58. Opened in 1901, the legendary *Bristol* is the finest Art Nouveau building in the city, and slap bang in the centre. Though it's been completely modernized, the rooms have retained a lot of historic character and are superbly comfortable. 900zł

Mamaison Le Regina ul. Kościelna 12 ☎ 22 531 6000, ⓦmamaisonleregina.com; map page 58. Boutique hotel in a restored eighteenth-century palace in the New Town, with individually designed rooms, crisp service and a lovely courtyard. *Mamaison's* sister-hotel *Diana* on ul. Chmielna is a worthy alternative. Breakfast extra 99zł per person. 540zł

Mercure Warszawa Grand ul. Krucza 28 ☎ 22 583 2100, ⓦmercure.com; map page 54. Handily located for shopping and nightlife, this startlingly pretty concrete 1950s hotel has been completely overhauled inside and now has sparkling modern rooms. It can be a real bargain if you book over the internet and avoid busy weekends. Breakfast extra 65zł per person. 535zł

★ **Rialto** ul. Wilcza 73 ☎ 22 584 8700, ⓦrialto.pl; map page 54. A delightful boutique hotel in Art Deco style, within easy strolling distance of the Palace of Culture and Sciences and the pl. Konstytucji neighbourhood. Rooms are large and luxurious, and furnished with stylish period touches, right down to the 1920s-style light switches. With high standards of comfort and service, this is one place for which it's well worth pushing the boat out. Rates can drop dramatically if you book online and choose dates carefully. Breakfast extra 80zł per person. 800zł

HOSTELS

Dream Hostel Krakowskie Przedmieście 55 ☎ 22 419 4848, ⓦfacebook.com/dreamhostelwarsaw; map page 58. Superbly located hostel occupying four floors of a renovated town house, *Dream* comes with modern furnishings and well-equipped social areas, and never seems too crowded or frantic. The loft rooms are particularly

cute. Breakfast extra 15zł per person. Dorms 50zł, doubles 210zł

Hostel Helvetia ul. Sewerynów 7 30 ☎ 22 826 7108, ⓦhostel-helvetia.pl; map page 58. Dead central yet in a quiet street, this nicely furnished hostel has plenty of showers, a women's dorm and a separate apartment. They also offer swish doubles and apartments in *Helvetia Plus*, a couple of minutes' walk away (reception at the *Helvetia*). Breakfast extra 17zł per person. Dorms 45zł, doubles 170zł

New World Street Hostel ul. Nowy Świat 27 ☎ 22 828 1282, ⓦnws-hostel.pl; map page 58. Friendly staff and a cosy common room (complete with board games and books) make this the pick of the hostels at the Śródmieście end of the city centre. While the in-hostel atmosphere is calming, neighbouring streets are packed with bars. Breakfast extra 5zł per person. Dorms 55zł, doubles 160zł

Oki Doki Old Town Hostel Długa 6 ☎ 22 635 0763, ⓦokidoki.pl; map page 58. Bright decor, a jumble of different furnishings, lively social areas and an excellent Old Town location make this one of the most reliable hostels if you're after a mixture of comfort and friendly in-house atmosphere. Breakfast extra 20zł per person. Dorms 65zł, doubles 195zł

APARTMENTS

Pragapartments ☎ 792 217 313, ⓦpragapartments.com.pl; map page 54. A superb option if you're aiming to stay on the up-and-coming east bank of the River Vistula, offering a mixture of smartly-furnished, two-person studios and one- and two-room apartments in different locations in the Praga district. Studio 280zł, one-room apartment 340zł

★ **SleepWell Apartments** Nowy Świat 62 & Ordynacka 14 ☎ 600 300 749, ⓦsleepwell-warsaw.pl; map page 58. Superbly located just off Warsaw's main café strip, *SleepWell* offers fairly small rooms (they're very cute en-suite doubles rather than "apartments" in the real sense of the word), decked out in bold, kitschy colours. There are two locations but they are almost next door to each other (indeed the Nowy Świat address is in the courtyard behind the Ordynacka address). There's an electric kettle in the rooms and optional breakfast (served at the Ordynacka branch). 570zł

CAMPSITES

Majawa Camping 123 ul. Bitwy Warszawskiej 1920, nr 15/17 ☎ 22 822 9121, ⓦmajawa.pl; map page 54. Closest campsite to the centre, about 600m south of the Warszawa Zachodnia bus and train station, with some bungalows. Open May–Sept. Camping 100zł, bungalows 150zł

Wok ul. Odrębna 16 ☎ 22 612 7951, ⓦcampingwok.warszawa.pl; bus #146 from Warszawa Wschodna; map page 54. Small family campsite with tent pitches and two-person en-suite cabins underneath the pines, 10km southeast of the city. Open year round. Camping 100zł, cabins 200zł

1

WARSAW FOOD MARKETS

The last few years have seen the rise of a new breed of **market** in Warsaw, where fresh food and niche deli products are available alongside drinks, snacks and street food, enabling visitors to eat, drink and socialize as well as fill their shopping bags.

Biobazar Norblin Factory, ul. Żelazna 51/53, map page 58; Soho Factory, ul. Mińska 25, Praga, map page 54; ⊛biobazar.org.pl. Warsaw's most popular source of ecological produce (most of the things sold here are certified organic – look for the EU green-leaf logo), selling the whole gamut of Polish and imported food and drink. There are plenty of snacks on sale, including some nigh-irresistible sweets and cakes. Norblin Factory Wed 10am–6pm, Fri 4–8pm, Sat 8am–4pm; Soho Factory Sat 9am–4pm.

Targ Śniadaniowy al. Wojska Polskiego, Żoliborz, map page 54; Park Skaryszewski, Praga, map page 54; ⊛targsniadaniowy.pl. Literally "Breakfast Market" (although it lasts all day), this vastly popular weekend event is almost like a mini-festival, with rows of stands serving hot food, snacks, cakes, soft drinks and juices – many made by small-scale local producers, and much of it organic. Events are frequently themed, and there is often musical entertainment and a kids' play area. For other locations – including an indoor winter location – check ⊛facebook.com/targsniadaniowy. Wojska Polskiego mid-May to Sept Sat 9am–4pm; Park Skaryszewski mid-May to Sept every second Sat 9am–4pm.

EATING

Warsaw's **restaurants** have undergone something of a culinary revolution in recent years, with a burgeoning interest in modern Polish cuisine dovetailing nicely with a growing fascination with Mediterranean, Far Eastern and fusion food. **Cafés** range from the old-fashioned to modern minimalist, frequently serving salads and quiche as well as cakes, pastries and other sweet-tooth nibbles. Bear in mind that the distinction between Warsaw's eating and drinking venues is inevitably blurred, with many of the latter offering both snacks and full meals as well as booze, so be sure to check the "Bars" listings too (see page 87).

CAFÉS

Warsaw can boast a vivacious café life, with establishments ranging from classic patisseries serving cakes, coffee and hot chocolate to modern places offering an international menu of bistro food.

CENTRAL WARSAW

Blikle Café ul. Nowy Świat 35 ☎669 609 706; map page 58. Open since 1869, this is the oldest cake shop in the city and an elegant place in which to enjoy coffee and desserts. Famous for its doughnuts (*pączki*), it also does excellent but pricey breakfasts (30–60zł). Daily 9am–8pm.

★ **Kafka** ul. Oboźna 3 ☎22 826 0822, ⊛kawiarnia-kafka.pl; map page 58. One of Warsaw's most attractive destinations for tea and nibbles, with a bright, light-flooded interior. There is outdoor seating on the pavement outside, or you can take one of *Kafka*'s deckchairs and plonk it on the sloping bit of lawn across the street. Sandwiches, salads, pancakes, chunky soups of the day (from 9zł), plus wholesome and filling pasta dishes for around 18–25zł. Mon–Fri 9am–10pm, Sat & Sun 10am–10pm.

Labour Café and Deli ul. Tamka 49 ☎22 416 9150; map page 58. Conveniently situated a few strides away from the Chopin Museum, *Labour* is typical of the non-chain coffee shops that are springing up throughout Warsaw. Sourced coffee selected by a local roasting firm, scrambled-egg breakfasts, daily lunch menus, laid-back music and a good range of cakes; no wonder its become a second home for young locals with laptops. Mon–Fri 8.30am–9pm, Sat & Sun 10am–8pm.

Próżna ul. Próżna 12 ☎22 620 3257; map page 58. Charming, modern café in a crumbling tenement building on Warsaw's last intact street. Photos of Warsaw decorate the walls, and *pierogi*, salads, soups and fresh juice feature on the menu. Two-course set lunches are 20zł. Mon–Thurs & Sun 10am–11pm, Fri & Sat 10am–midnight.

★ **SAM** ul. Lipowa 7a ☎600 806 084; map page 58. Outstanding bakery-cum-deli that consistently gives the Warsaw café-crowd what they want: deli sandwiches (12–18zł), filling soups-of-the-day (15zł), intriguing savoury dips, and light, Middle Eastern-to-Asian mains (25–30zł) – all served with a variety of delicious fresh breads. There's also coffee, fruit smoothies and Polish craft beer. Head to the shop downstairs to pick up some take-out loaves and pies. Mon–Fri 8am–10pm, Sat & Sun 9am–10pm.

Vincent Nowy Świat 64 ☎22 828 0115, map page 58; ul. Chmielna 21 ☎22 270 2309, map page 58. Avoid the bland international coffee franchises currently choking the life out of Warsaw's pavements and seek out instead this small French-themed café-cum-bakery, serving reliably robust cappuccinos and cafés au lait. The croissants and quiches are first class – and the fresh baguettes are perfect for picnics. Daily 6am–11pm.

Wedel ul. Szpitalna 8 ☎22 827 2916, ⊛wedelpijalnie. pl; map page 58. Poland's top chocolaterie, with a stunning range of cocoa products served up in an old-style, high-ceilinged café with crocheted doilies on the tables. Try the hot chocolate *ekstra gorzka* (extra bitter). There's a second branch in Praga (see below). Mon–Fri 8am–10pm, Sat 9am–10pm, Sun 9am–9pm.

Wrzenie Świata ul. Gałczyńskiego 7 ☎ 22 828 4998; map page 58. In a courtyard behind Nowy Świat, this order-at-the-counter bookshop-café (the title of which is taken from a Ryszard Kapuściński collection and means something like "Boiling World") serves up croissants, sandwiches and tortilla wraps in bookish surroundings. The bookshop specializes in factual writing and reportage, organizing regular readings by Poland's main practitioners of the genre. Daily 9am–10pm.

PRAGA

Café Melon ul. Inżynierska 1, Praga ☎ 501 075 214; Metro Dworzec Wileński; map page 54. A bare-floorboard and even-barer-walls type place that still succeeds in being cosy, with solid rustic-looking tables, board games on the sideboard and a shelf or two of art-and-design books. Good croissants, cakes and sandwiches. Mon–Fri 10am–7pm, Sat & Sun 10am–11am.

Mucha nie siada ul. Ząbkowska 38, Praga ☎ 501 620 669; Metro Dworzec Wileński; map page 54. One of Praga's most comfy and welcoming nooks, offering toasted sandwiches, pancakes, bruschetta and salads. It's an easy place to settle in to, with stylish black floorboards, homely brick walls and bright fabrics – including funky cushions. Daily 10.30am–10pm.

Wedel ul. Zamoyskiego 36, Praga ☎ 22 619 5010, ⓦ wedel pijalnie.pl; tram #3, #8, #26 or #28 to ul. Lubelska; map page 54. The Praga branch of Poland's top chocolaterie (see page 84). Mon–Sat 9am–7pm, Sun 11am–6pm.

SASKA KĘPA

Café Rue de Paris ul. Francuska 11, Saska Kępa ☎ 22 617 8773; tram #7, #8, #9, #21, #24 or #25 to Rondo Waszyngtona; map page 54. This French-style café has a solid local following among those who know a thing or two about the correct texture of a croissant. There's also a sizeable menu of wholemeal crepes, and a small but seductive selection of quiches and gateaux. The interior,

with bench seating well padded with cushions, is pleasantly Pop-Arty. Mon–Fri 6.30am–9pm, Sat & Sun 8am–10pm.

RESTAURANTS

Warsaw has become something of a foodie city in recent years, with everything from hipster bistros to fine-dining establishments springing up all over town. Restaurants in the tourist-trodden Old Town tend towards the bland, and the best culinary hunting grounds are to be found in Śródmieście or beyond. A number of the famously cheap milk bars – canteen-style places doling out filling Polish staples for well under 10zł a head – still survive; otherwise, the price of a main course and drink at a proper restaurant can range from 35 to 45zł in casual establishments to 100zł or more at the more upmarket ones.

CENTRAL WARSAW

Butchery & Wine ul. Żurawia 22 ☎ 22 502 3118, ⓦ butcheryandwine.pl; map page 58. *B&W*'s menu concentrates on steaks (tenderloin, rib-eye, bavette) and burgers accompanied by French fries, although there's a scattering of seafood to keep things balanced. Mains cost upwards of 60zł depending on the dish (a Black Angus rib-eye will set you back 170zł), and with plenty of fine wines to wash it down with your overall spend could be much higher. Mon–Sat noon–10pm, Sun noon–8pm.

★ **Ę Rybę** ul. Jana Pawła II 18 ☎ 572 930 003, ⓦ erybe. pl; map page 58. Fish-and-chips Polish style, with deftly-battered hunks of halibut and hake served up with chips and salad. Cod burgers and tuna steaks also crop up an a menu that changes according to what's fresh (mains 20–30zł). It's a simple order-at-the-counter set-up but the food rarely disappoints. Daily 10am–9pm.

Kieliszki na Hożej ul. Hoża 41 ☎ 22 404 2109, ⓦ kieliszkinahozej.pl; map page 54. This high-ceilinged, tiled-walled place serves up Polish food with European finesses; mains (60–80zł) always include something in the fish, chicken or vegetarian line, and are based on fresh local ingredients. The impressive wine list is backed up by a tempting menu of Polish tapas-style nibbles (fried herring, marinated vegetables and so on). Mon–Wed noon–10pm, Thurs & Fri noon–11pm, Sat 2–11pm.

WARSAW ICE-CREAM PARLOURS

Ice cream has taken off in a big way in Warsaw, with an increasing number of places scooping out their own-recipe flavours.

Lodziarnia Akwarium ul. Francuska 50, Saska Kępa ☎ 22 616 2459; tram #7, #8, #9, #21, #24 or #25 to Rondo Waszyngtona; map page 54. Artisanal ice-cream parlour mixing traditional recipes with plenty of exotic alternatives (maracuya and hibiscus to name but two), and the occasional trial-and-error exercise in

seasonal flavours. Daily 10am–9pm.

Na Końcu Tęczy al. Wyzwolenia 15; map page 54. Ice-cream parlour that's also a sit-down café, serving imaginative ices made from natural ingredients. Expect a lot of seasonal-fruit flavours and plenty of surprises (rhubarb, cashew nut and more). Daily 10am–9pm.

1

Mleczarnia Jerozolimska al. Jerozolimskie 32 ☎ 22 826 1383; map page 58. Breathing new life into Warsaw's milk-bar business, *Mleczarnia* offers traditional dishes cheaply priced, served in friendly style in a neat, bright environment. Soups cost as little as 5zł, mains not much more. Mon–Fri 9am–8pm, Sat noon–6pm, Sun noon–5pm.

★ **Nienażarty** ul. Solec 97 ☎ 22 625 5026; map page 58. Intimate little place with low-key lighting and an imaginative, eclectic menu that features a lot of seafood, with shellfish and scampi to the fore. Signature dishes include mussels in wine sauce (39zł) and baked fish with lentils (39zł). Breakfast fry-ups are served until 1pm (2pm on weekends), while a good cocktail list makes it a popular place for a drink. Daily 9am–10pm.

Nolita ul. Wilcza 46 ☎ 22 292 0424, ☜ nolita.pl; map page 54. The interior of *Nolita* is smart but relatively minimalistic; the main focus is the creative food, which mixes French and Polish tradition with the odd contemporary exercise in surprise. A three-course lunch costs under 100zł, while mains on the evening menu are around 90–100zł, and the six-course tasting menu accompanied by appropriate wines clocks in at over 410zł. Mon–Fri noon–3pm & 6–10.30pm, Sat 5–11pm.

Radio Café ul. Nowogrodzka 56 ☎ 22 625 2784, ☜ radio cafe.pl; map page 58. Cushion-strewn café-restaurant serving mainstream Polish fare with a clutch of Mediterranean alternatives. It's got the kind of interior that has your eyes wandering around the walls, thanks to a scattering of artworks and a profusion of photographs documenting the work of Radio Free Europe (the American-funded, Munich-based station that broadcast Polish-language programmes during the Cold War). Cooked or continental breakfasts are 28zł; three-course lunches cost 30zł. Daily 7am–11pm.

★ **Solec 44** ul. Solec 44, Powiśle ☎ 798 363 996, ☜ solec. waw.pl; map page 58. Former industrial space with concrete floor, minimal decoration and wooden tables. The food style is Polish-European, with grills a speciality; the regularly changing menu usually includes at least one veggie, fish, game and steak item (mains 40–65zł, or 130zł for the best Black Angus steak). The predominantly Polish wine list adds an element of intrigue, while the range of craft beers and cocktails ensures that a lot of people come here just for the drinks. Mon–Thurs 4pm–2/3am, Fri–Sun noon–2/3am.

Sushi Zushi ul. Żurawia 6/12 ☎ 22 420 3373, ☜ sushizushi.pl; map page 58. In a city full of sushi outlets this delivers most in term of quality and style. Well-crafted sushi comes in both familiar and creative in-house fusion variations, while the central circular bar allows you to observe the chefs at work. The cool interior design and jazzy background sounds make *Sushi Zushi* a seriously hip place, and it can be very popular, even on weekday nights. Mon–Thurs noon–11pm, Fri & Sat noon–3am, Sun 1–10pm.

★ **Tel Aviv** ul. Poznańska 11 ☎ 22 621 1128; map page 54. Combining rough-hewn rusticity with contemporary design, vegan restaurant *Tel Aviv* serves up hummus in various flavours as well as a variety of Middle Eastern-flavoured soya cutlets. Most mains come under the 30zł mark and there's a respectable wine list. Daily 10am–midnight.

U Fukiera Rynek Starego Miasta 27 ☎ 22 831 1013, ☜ ufukiera.pl; map page 58. Long the flagship restaurant of culinary entrepreneur Magda Gessler – leading proponent of the idea that traditional Polish nosh and haute cuisine can go together – *U Fukiera* has slightly more quality and class than anywhere else on the Rynek. The menu rounds up a handful of classic fish and meat dishes, including leg of lamb (98zł) and saddle of venison (105zł). Extravagant fabrics and flower arrangements add an air of luxury to the interior. Daily noon–midnight.

Viaduct Pizza Bar al. 3 Maja 16/18a, Powiśle ☎ 505 370 977; map page 58. Tucked into an archway beneath the Poniatowski bridge, and with a scattering of outdoor tables, this is a great source of tasty thin-crust pizzas, with a menu mixing Italian standards (Quatro [sic] Formaggi; 29zł) and a few they've made up themselves. Cheerfully minimalist, they don't offer you knives and forks – but you do at least get a paper napkin. Wash your pizza down with craft beer or home-made lemonade. Daily noon–10pm.

Żurawina ul. Żurawia 32/34 ☎ 22 521 0666, ☜ zurawina.eu; map page 58. Large multifunctional place serving as café, restaurant and lounge bar, depending on what time you arrive. It's primarily a place to eat, however, with an international repertoire that's particularly strong on fish, steaks and game (mains 60–90zł). There's a good choice of quality breakfasts, and the two-course lunchtime specials (Mon–Fri) are a steal at 20zł. Good wine list and cocktail menu, and live jazz at least once a week. Mon–Sat 8am–midnight, Sun 8am–10pm.

SOUTH OF THE CENTRE

Amber Room al. Ujazdowskie 13 ☎ 22 523 6664, ☜ kprb.pl/amber; Metro Politechnika, or bus #116, #180 or #E2 to pl. na Rozdrożu; map page 54. Located in the Sobański Palace, currently the HQ of the Polish Business Association, this is something of a favourite among Warsaw wheeler-dealers but has a sound gastronomic reputation too. The menu limits itself to a handful of delectably prepared classic dishes (roast duck, rack of lamb, steak and a few fishy choices). A full meal with drinks will set you back well in excess of 160zł (there's also a nine-course tasting menu with wines for 520zł), but the three-course business lunch on weekdays (noon–3pm; 95zł) allows you to sample haute-cuisine, Warsaw-style, at an affordable price. Mon–Sat noon–11pm, Sun noon–9pm.

Belvedere New Orangerie, Łazienki Park ☎ 22 558 6701, ☜ belvedere.com.pl; bus #116, #180 or #E2 to pl. na Rozdrożu; map page 75. One of Warsaw's best and most expensive eateries – popular with the city's smart set – located in an orangery at the southern end of Łazienki Park. Fresh seafood, Mediterranean-Asian fusion and Polish meat-and-poultry classics share space on the menu. Reservations are advisable. Mon–Sat noon–4pm & 6–11pm, Sun noon–8pm.

Qchnia Artystyczna ul. Jazdów 2 ☎ 22 625 7627, Ⓦ qchnia.pl; Metro Politechnika, or bus #116, #180 or #E2 to pl. na Rozdrożu; map page 54. Wonderful location on the east-facing side of Ujazdowski Castle (see page 74), with excellent views towards the river from the outdoor terrace. A well-balanced Polish-international menu offers some creative salads and meat and fish mains (55–70zł); the potato pancakes are a cut above what you usually get in the average Polish restaurant. Mon–Wed & Sun noon–10pm, Thurs–Sat noon–11pm.

Restauracja Polska Różana ul. Chocimska 7 ☎ 22 848 1225, Ⓦ restauracjarozana.com.pl; tram #4, #18 or #35 to Rakowiecka; map page 54. One of the most attractive places to eat in Warsaw, located in a suburban villa southwest of Łazienki Park, with dining rooms straight out of an English country house and a beautiful garden to boot. Expect traditional food beautifully presented, with liver, tenderloin steaks, roast duck, freshwater fish and game dominating the menu (mains 45–82zł). The meringue desserts are a treat. Daily noon–midnight.

PRAGA

Centrum Zarządzania Światem ul. Okrzei 26, Praga ☎ 22 618 2197 Ⓦ centrumswiata.com; Metro Dworzec Wileński; map page 58. Loft-style space with industrial lighting, exposed brick and ventilation pipes, and a bistro menu of burgers, hummus dips, soups and sandwiches. The signature dish is Tarte Flambée ("Placek Alzacki" in Polish), a French cross between quiche and pizza, which comes in the classic cheese-and-ham version and with a variety of other toppings (20–25zł). Two-course set

lunches are available on weekdays (18zł). There's a long bar, and frequent DJ- or live music events. Mon–Thurs & Sun noon–midnight, Fri & Sat noon–2am.

★ **Skamiejka** ul. Ząbkowska 37, Praga (entrance on ul. Nieporęczka) ☎ 512 123 967; Metro Dworzec Wileński; map page 54. Full of odd domestic details, mismatched furniture and vinyl records, *Skamiejka* ("The Bench") is one of those absolutely charming restaurants that feels like you've been invited into someone's living room. It serves Russian food and more besides, with Slav classics like *Solanka* (chunky soup; 14zł) and beef stroganoff (23zł) joining forces with Ukrainian borsch and Georgian *Chinkali* (pasta pockets filled with juicy meat). Vodka is a must, although you might also consider a glass of Georgian tarragon-flavoured lemonade. Mon 5–10pm, Tues–Sun noon–10pm.

Warszawa Wschodnia Soho Factory, ul. Mińska 25, Praga ☎ 22 870 2918, Ⓦ mateuszgessler.com.pl; tram #3, #6 or #22 to Gocławska; map page 54. Headed up by leading Polish chef Mateusz Gessler, this elegant but not over-formal restaurant occupies what looks like the mother-of-all loft conversions: a large bright space with an open kitchen inside a red-brick former factory hall. As for the cooking, it's a winning blend of classic Polish and classic French cuisine, with lamb, duck, venison and rabbit to the fore (mains 70–80zł). Desserts are superb, and the wine list is up to the standard of the food. Daily 11am–11pm.

SASKA KĘPA

Dom Polski ul. Francuska 11, Saska Kępa ☎ 22 616 2432, Ⓦ restauracjadompolski.pl; tram #7, #8, #9, #21, #24 or #25 to Rondo Waszyngtona; map page 54. Moderately upscale restaurant serving Polish-European cuisine to a loyal Polish expat clientele. Roast duck with apples (60zł) is the signature dish, although game dishes such as pheasant, wild boar and venison (70–100zł) are equally tempting. Mon–Sat noon–11pm, Sun noon–10pm.

DRINKING AND NIGHTLIFE

Warsaw's drinking venues range from the flashy bars to well-hidden bohemian pubs. Most bars are concentrated in the **modern centre** well south of the Old Town, where areas such as Nowy Świat, ul. Poznańska and pl. Zbawiciela offer a varied array of drinking joints. Outside the centre, the **Praga** suburb is home to a growing alternative nightlife scene, and the **west bank of the Vistula** comes into its own as an alfresco drinking venue in summer. The **cost** of drinks in Warsaw is significantly higher than elsewhere in Poland and is now near Western European levels.

BARS

CENTRAL WARSAW

Bar Studio pl. Defilad 1 ☎ 603 300 835; map page 58. In the foyer of the Teatr Studio on the eastern side

of the Palace of Culture and Sciences, this big friendly bar does food in the daytime and becomes a popular nightspot later on, featuring DJs, screenings of classical music and live jazz. Daily 9am–3am.

Beirut Hummus and Music Bar ul. Poznańska 12; map page 54. Is it a café? Is it a bar? *Beirut* serves up fresh organic hummus with pitta bread plus a range of other Mediterranean snacks in a Lebanon-themed interior, while DJs or live music events draw in a posse of evening drinkers. Daily noon–2am.

Café Kulturalna pl. Defilad 1 ☎ 22 656 6281, Ⓦ kulturalna.pl; map page 58. An arty student hangout in the southeast wing of the Palace of Culture and Sciences, accessed through the lobby of the Teatr Dramatyczny. With 1950s-style furnishings, a small stage for gigs and DJs and an L-shaped balustraded terrace looking out onto pl. Defilad,

1

FESTIVALS AND EVENTS

Warsaw has a busy year-round programme of festivals. The tourist office (see page 82) will have details of these and other upcoming cultural events.

Easter Beethoven Festival Easter week ⓦ beethoven.org.pl. Works by Beethoven and other classical composers, frequently with a sacral theme.

Warsaw Theatre Meetings (Warszawskie Spotkania Teatralne) April ⓦ warszawskie.org. Innovative productions from leading theatres all over Poland.

Chopin Concerts Mid-May to Sept ⓦ lazienki-krolewskie.pl. Open-air recitals beside the Chopin statue in Łazienki Park (every Sun at noon & 4pm).

Orange Warsaw Festival Early June ⓦ orangewarsawfestival.pl. Rock-pop weekender attracting some big international names (Kings of Leon, Muse, Beyoncé), held at the Sluzewiec racetrack.

Mozart Festival Mid-June to late July ⓦ operakameralna.pl. All of the boy-wonder's operas (and many other works too), performed in Łazienki Park, Wilanów and other evocative venues.

Warsaw Summer Jazz Days Mid-late June ⓦ warsawsummerjazzdays.pl. A good mixture of avant-garde and ear-friendly jazz, with international names aplenty; recent guests have included Jeff Beck, Cassandra Wilson and Kamasi Washington. Venues throughout the city.

Jazz in the Old Town (Jazz na Starówce) July & Aug ⓦ jazznastarowce.pl. Summer-long season of free concerts on the Rynek Starego Miasta (every Sat at 7pm).

Singer Festival Late Aug-early Sept ⓦ festiwalsingera.pl. Ulica Próżna hosts a week of concerts, film screenings and markets in celebration of Warsaw's Jewish heritage.

Warsaw Autumn Mid-late Sept ⓦ warszawska-jesien.art.pl. Already boasting a sixty-year tradition, this is the world's leading festival of contemporary classical music, attracting the cream of international composers.

Warsaw Film Festival Mid-Oct ⓦ wff.pl. Quality new feature films from Europe and beyond, with projections in the Kinoteka and Multikino cinemas.

Warsaw International Jewish Film Festival Nov ⓦ wjff.pl. New features, documentaries and archive classics, all with a Jewish theme.

---

this is the kind of place that only Warsaw could come up with. Mon–Sat noon–last guest, Sun 3pm–last guest.

Czeszka Baszta ul. Solec/Most Poniatowskiego, Powiśle; map page 58. Certainly one of the most strangely located bars you are likely to visit in Poland, the "Czech Keep" is located inside one of the towers of the Poniatowski bridge – walk up the steps from ul. Solec to get there. The snug, bare-stone pub is probably the best place in Warsaw to drink Czech beer, served on tap or in a multitude of small-brewery bottles. Tues–Thurs 4–11pm, Fri & Sat 4pm–midnight, Sun 4pm–10pm.

Grizzly Gin Bar ul. Wilcza 46; map page 54. Gin-themed bar stacked with more brands of the juniper-based spirit than you ever knew existed; there's a long list of gin-based long drinks, alongside a full range of other alcohol. Lots of exposed brick and moody lighting make it a good place to spend an evening; occasional live gigs involve a lot of classy jazz and world music. Daily 4pm–4am.

★ **Między Nami** ul. Bracka 20 ☏ 22 828 5417, ⓦ miedzynamicafe.com; map page 58. Relaxing place hidden behind a large white awning, catering to an easygoing gay-straight-whatever crowd, with two levels of seating in an art gallery-style interior, and a scattering of streetside tables outside. Three-course lunch menus pull in a faithful crowd of daytime regulars, while DJs spin discs some evenings. Mon–Thurs 9am–11pm, Fri & Sat 10am–midnight, Sun 2–11pm.

★ **Plac Zabaw** bul. Grzymały-Siedlieckiego ⓦ facebook.com/placzabawnadwisla; map page 58. Located on the west bank of the river just south of the Świętokrzyskie bridge, the "Playpark" spreads its deckchairs over a grassy part of the riverbank and organizes alfresco gigs and open-air film screenings throughout the summer. May–Sept daily 11am–11pm.

Same Krafty ul. Nowomiejska 11/13; map page 58. Something of a godsend in the tourist-tramped Old Town, "Those Crafts" is a small and welcoming pub with a mind-boggling selection of Polish craft beers (on tap and bottles), plus inexpensive pizzas and burgers for those in need of refuelling. Knowledgeable staff will advise you on which brew to try next. Daily 2–11pm.

★ **Warszawa-Powiśle** ul. Kruczkowskiego 3B, Powiśle ☏ 22 474 4084; map page 58. This "kiosk for wódka and culture" (as the owners call it) is located in the UFO-shaped former ticket hall of the Warszawa-Powiśle station, and still proudly displays its red-neon station sign. Summer evenings bring out the best in the place, when crowds of good-natured revellers spill across the pavement out front. Daily 10am–3am.

SOUTH OF THE CENTRE

Charlotte: chleb i wino al. Wyzwolenia 18 (entrance on pl. Zbawiciela) ☏ 662 204 555; Metro Politechnika; map page 54. Chic and spacious café-bar with outdoor seating beneath pl. Zbawiciela's famous colonnades. It dishes out coffee-and-croissants during the daytime, and wine accompanied by cheese platters at night. Mon–Thurs 7am–midnight, Fri 7am–1am, Sat 9am–1am, Sun 9am–10pm.

Chmielarnia ul. Marszalkowska 10/16 ☎782 288 889; Metro Politechnika; map page 54. This bustling multi-tap beer pub has one of the best choices of ale in the city, from Polish boutique brews to international craft favourites. Punters also flock here for the irresistible Nepalese food: daily specials (served 11am–4pm; 19–26zł) always include at least one vegetarian choice. Daily 11am–midnight.

★ **Cud nad Wisłą** bul. Flotilly Wiślanej 1 ☎790 670 300; map page 54. In many ways the defining destination of the Warsaw riverbank scene, "Miracle on the Vistula" is a sprawling open-air hangout north of the Piłsudski bridge offing drinks, bar snacks and something different every day of the week: live music, an open-air cinema, stand-up comedy, weekend food markets or DJ events. June–Sept daily noon–midnight.

Plan B al. Wyzwolenia 18 (entrance on pl. Zbawiciela); Metro Politechnika; map page 54. The graffiti-covered wall next to the staircase makes this first-floor bar, with low-key lighting, red sofas and rickety wooden chairs, look slightly more grungy than it really is; while it does indeed specialize in alternative music, *Plan B* has a hippest-bar-in-the-neighbourhood reputation that pulls in a much wider crowd. Mon–Sat 1pm–3am, Sun 4pm–2am.

Pomost 511 ul. Flotilly Wiślanej 1 ☻facebook.com/Pomost511; map page 54. On the same riverside stretch as *Cud nad Wisłą* (see page 89) and with a similar mixture of culture, music and cold beers, *Pomost* offers open-air theatre as well as film shows and crowd-pulling DJs. May–Sept Mon–Wed & Sun noon–midnight, Thurs–Sat noon–3am.

PRAGA

Łysy Pingwin ul. Ząbkowska 11, Praga; Metro Dworzec Wileński; map page 54. A popular 1970s-style lounge with beer, snacks and good music, the "Bald Penguin" is a good starting point for a Praga bar crawl. Daily 3pm–1am, Fri & Sat 3pm–2am.

Skląd Butelek ul. 11 listopada 22, Praga; Metro Dworzec Wileński; map page 54. Winningly eccentric Praga bar decked out in Kraków-Kazimieirz style, with candles on the tables, lampstands in the corner and what looks like granny's bedroom dressing table behind the bar. There's more than one floor to the place, with private booths and a live-performance room towards the back. Tues–Sun 4pm–3am.

★ **W Oparach Absurdu** ul. Ząbkowska 6, Praga; Metro Dworzec Wileński; map page 54. One of the first bars to bring life to the Praga suburb, and still going strong. Inside there are several creaky levels of second-hand furniture, nooks, crannies and misplaced antiques – and there's still space for live music on Wed and Sat. Unmissable. Mon–Thurs & Sun 11am–2am, Fri & Sat 11am–4am.

CLUBS AND GIG VENUES

There's a reasonable range of clubbing opportunities in Warsaw, with new venues opening all the time. In addition, many of the establishments listed under "Bars" (see page 87) have late opening hours and in-house DJs. A number of clubs put on regular live music – check out their facebook pages or look out for fly posters. Established bands (whether Polish or foreign) play in larger multi-purpose venues (see ticket agencies ☻eventim.pl and ☻ticketpro.pl for news of big gigs on the horizon). Admission to gigs and club nights costs between 15zł and 50zł depending on the prestige of the club and the night of the week.

BarKa bul. Grzymały-Siedlieckiego ☻facebook.com/placzabawnadwisla; map page 58. Moored in front of the *Plac Zabaw* riverside bar (see page 88), this floating pontoon hosts themed DJ parties (frequently concentrating on retro genres such as 1960s soul or classical Polish pop) on summer evenings. Well worth checking out if the weather is warm. Mid-May to mid-Sept daily 11am–late.

Hydrozagadka ul. 11 Listopada 22 ☻hydrozagadka.waw.pl; Metro Dworzec Wileński; map page 54. Courtyard bar-cum-nightclub featuring a bare-bones interior with the odd sofa strewn around. Expect to hear leftfield DJs, and the kind of visiting indie bands that attract an informed alternative audience. Doors open 8–9pm.

Jazz Club Akwarium Krakowskie Przedmiescie 60A ☎664 063 050, ☻facebook.com/jazzclubakwarium; map page 58. Latest incarnation of a legendary jazz club, now located in a pavilion-like structure near the entrance to the Old Town, hosting soul-funk DJs and gigs by top-level jazz performers. Events usually kick off at 8pm.

Luztro al. Jerozolimskie 6 ☻luztro.pl; map page 58. This is what clubs are supposed to be like, with cutting-edge techno and electro music, a frenetic but friendly crowd and discounted beer for students. Weekends often have visiting DJs and neverending after parties. Tues–Thurs 10pm–8am, Fri & Sat 11pm–2pm, Sun 11pm–8am.

Opera Club pl. Teatralny 1; map page 58. Dancefloors and semi-private rooms scattered throughout the cavernous chambers beneath the Grand Theatre, making for a novel night out. Cocktails 19–25zł. Fri & Sat 10pm–5am.

Pogłos ul. Burakowska 12 ☎501 729 606, ☻facebook.com/klubpoglos; tram #21 to Rondo Radoslawa; map page 54. Alternative-leaning venue hosting indie/niche discos and all manner of live bands, with no genre left unexplored. There's a semi-covered yard that's open on summer weekends from 5pm. Doors open 7pm for gigs, 9pm for club nights.

Stodoła ul. Batorego 10 ☎22 825 6031, ☻stodola.pl; Metro Pole Mokotowskie; map page 54. Still the leading venue for medium-sized rock-pop bands, *Stodoła* was founded as a student club in the 1950s and has been at the centre of pretty much everything that the Polish music scene has had to offer, from the jazz boom of the early 1960s onwards. Doors usually open 6–7pm.

1

Tygmont ul. Mazowiecka 6/8 ⓦ tygmont.com.pl; map page 58. Once the city's top jazz venue, this is now a general music club, with themed DJ nights covering most danceable genres, plus occasional live gigs. Good menu of classic shots and cocktails. Tues–Sun from 10pm.

ENTERTAINMENT

Opera is a big favourite in Warsaw, and classical concerts, especially piano music, tend to attract big audiences. Despite this, concerts are rarely sold out and are fairly inexpensive. Tickets for many concerts are available from Eventim, at al. Jerozolimskie 25, just east of Centrum metro station (Mon–Fri 11am–6.30pm; ☎ 590 616 915, ⓦ eventim.pl) or Ticketpro (outlets in most Empik stores; ⓦ ticketpro.pl). Warsaw's cinemas offer a mixture of mainstream Western pictures, global art-house movies and homegrown hits, with most of the old, small cinemas now replaced by multiplexes. Film titles may often be translated, but films are shown in the original language with Polish subtitles – only children's films are dubbed. Cinema tickets cost about 12–20zł, usually with reductions on Mondays.

CLASSICAL MUSIC, BALLET AND OPERA

Evangelical Church (Kościół Ewangelicko-Augsburgski) pl. Małachowskiego 3. Focuses on organ and choral music, often with visiting choirs. Excellent acoustics.

Filharmonia ul. Jasna 5 ☎ 22 551 7127, ⓦ filharmonia.pl. The main concert venue, with regular performances by the excellent National Philharmonic as well as visiting ensembles. Students with ISIC cards and pensioners get 24 percent discount on most concerts (but probably not those by visiting international stars). Box office (entrance from ul. Sienkiewicza) Mon–Sat 11am–2pm & 3–7pm, Sun (concert days only) 4–7pm.

Łazienki Park ⓦ lazienki-krolewskie.pl. Varied summer programme of orchestral, choral and chamber concerts, held at weekends in the park (see page 88), often beside the Chopin monument, in the Orangery or inside the Palace.

National Theatre (Teatr Wielki) pl. Teatralny 1 ☎ 22 826 5019, ⓦ teatrwielki.pl. The venue for big opera, ballet and musical performances – everything from Mozart to contemporary Polish composers – in suitably grandiose surroundings. Box office Mon–Sat 9am–7pm, Sun 10am–7pm.

Opera Kameralna al. Solidarności 76b ☎ 22 831 2240, ⓦ operakameralna.pl. Chamber opera performances in a magnificent white-and-gold stucco auditorium. Box office Mon–Fri 11am–7pm or on the day of performance from 4pm.

Sinfonia Varsovia ☎ 22 582 7082, ⓦ sinfoniavarsovia.org. Contemporary composer Krzysztof Penderecki's home orchestra, a prestige outfit performing at home and abroad, and at various venues throughout the city.

Uniwersytet Muzyczny Fryderyka Chopina ul. Okólnik 2 ☎ 22 827 7241, ⓦ chopin.edu.pl. Regular free concerts by talented students.

Warsaw Music Society (Towarzystwo Muzyczne Warszawskie) ul. Morskie Oko 2 ☎ 22 849 6856, ⓦ wtm.org.pl. Frequent piano and guitar recitals in the neo-Gothic Pałac Szustra. Also hosts performances by the Ars Nova period instrument orchestra. Box office Mon–Fri 10am–3pm.

CINEMAS

Iluzjon ul. Narbutta 50A ☎ 22 462 7270, ⓦ iluzjon.fn.org.pl. National Film Archives venue, screening cinema classics from all over the world. There's a lovely neon sign over the rotunda-shaped entrance hall, and a convenient café.

Kino Muranów ul. Gen Andersa 5 ☎ 22 635 3078, ⓦ kinomuranow.pl. Old-style two-screen picture house with one of the city centre's best programmes of current European and art-house movies.

Kinoteka Palace of Culture and Sciences ☎ 22 551 7070, ⓦ kinoteka.pl. Multiple screens showing commercial films in this extraordinary Stalinist building (see page 67).

u-jazdowski Kino ul. Jazdów 2 ☎ 22 628 1271, ⓦ u-jazdowski.pl/kino. Art movies and assorted cinematic weirdness in the Contemporary Art Centre (Ujazdowski Castle).

FOOTBALL

By far the best-supported football team in the capital is Legia Warsaw (Legia Warszawa; ⓦ legia.com), who have won the national league twelve times and appeared regularly in European competitions. They play at the Legia Stadium, near the River Vistula, 3km southeast of the centre (bus #107 from Centrum or a 25min walk). International matches are played at the National Stadium (see page 79).

SHOPPING

SPECIALIST SHOPS

Atlas al. Jana Pawła II 26 ☎ 22 620 3639; map page 58. Gloomy but hugely useful travel bookshop. If you need a street plan of a Polish city or a hiking map of one of its national parks, you'll probably find it here. Mon–Fri 10am–7pm, Sat 10am–5pm.

Bolesławiec ul. Emilii Plater 47 ☎ 22 624 2426, ⓦ ceramikaboleslawiec.com; map page 58. Poland's favourite stoneware: bowls, mugs and the like with distinctive blue-and-white patterns. Mon–Fri 10am–7pm, Sat 10am–4pm.

Empik ul. Nowy Świat 15/17 (corner of al. Jerozo-

1

limskie), map page 58; Złote Tarasy shopping centre, map page 58; ⓦempik.com. Multimedia store with lots of books in Polish and English, DVDs and CDs, and a good selection of foreign press. Nowy Świat branch Mon–Sat 9am–10pm, Sun 11am–7pm; Złote Tarasy branch Mon–Sat 9am–10pm, Sun 9am–9pm.

Krakowski Kredens ul. Nowy Świat 22 ☎22 826 4001; map page 58. Jars of traditional-recipe jam, fruit preserves and horseradish sauce, as well as Polish sausage and smoked meats. Mon–Fri 10am–7pm, Sat 10am–4pm, Sun 10am–2pm.

Las Rąk ul. Chmielna 9 ☎501 248 765, ⓦlrlr.pl; map page 58. The "Forest of Hands" stocks locally-made folk-style souvenirs alongside contemporary-looking homeware and accessories by local designers. Daily 11.15am–7.45pm.

Muzant ul. Warecka 4/6 (entrance from Świętokrzyska) ☎022 826 1216, ⓦmuzant.pl; map page 58. Rack after rack of Polish vinyl, including many of the key jazz and big-beat names from the 1960s. Also a few posters and vintage magazines. Mon–Fri 11am–7pm, Sat 10am–2pm.

Pan tu nie stał ul. Koszykowa 34/50 ☎887 887 772, ⓦpantuniestal.pl; Metro Politechnika; map page 54. Warsaw outlet of the Łódź-based design team responsible for turning out some of the most creative, wearable and witty T-shirts, bags and accessories in Poland, including plenty of T-shirt options in kids' sizes. The name means "you were never standing here!" – a humorous reference to communist-era queue-jumping. Daily 4pm–4am.

PolArt – Dom Sztuki Ludowej Rynek Starego Miasta 10 ☎022 831 1805, ⓦepolart.pl; map page 58. Two floors of woodcarving, ceramics, Lowicz paper cuts, embroidered tablecloths and shawls. Mon–Fri 10am–6pm, Sat 10am–2pm.

Polish Poster Gallery ul. Dobra 56/66 ☎503 341 328, ⓦposter.pl; Metro Centrum Nauki Kopernik; map page 58. This stall in the atrium of the University Library (see page 65) sells Polish theatre and film posters, including many vintage items, plus a selection of equally collectable designer postcards. Mon–Fri 10am–5am.

SHOPPING MALL

Złote Tarasy Next to Warszawa Centralna train station ⓦzlotetarasy.pl; map page 58. Resembling an enormous glass-covered bubble emerging from the backside of the main train station, this is the biggest of the central shopping malls. Mon–Sat 9am–10pm, Sun 9am–9pm.

MARKETS AND BAZAARS

For details of Biobazar and Targ Śniadaniowy, Warsaw's popular food and street food markets, see the "Warsaw food markets" box (see page 84).

Hala Koszyki ul. Koszykowa 8; map page 54. Art Nouveau market hall beautifully restored and reopened in 2016, and filled with upmarket shops and stalls selling delicatessen goods and artisanal sweets. Also full of food and drink outlets, it fills up with revellers come the evening. Daily 8am–1am.

Hala Mirowska pl. Mirowski 1; map page 58. The two Art Nouveau market halls contain grim supermarkets, but the surrounding outdoor stalls are excellent for fresh produce, meats and flowers. Daily 7am–5pm.

Koło Bazar ul. Obozowa, Wola; tram #12, #13 or #24 to Koło; map page 54. This is the main antiques and bric-a-brac market, with everything from old postcards and militaria to vintage clothing, old samovars and furniture. There's a lot here for the serious collector providing you arrive early. Sat & Sun 7am–2pm.

DIRECTORY

Embassies Australia, ul. Nowogrodzka 11 ☎022 521 3444, ⓦaustralia.pl; Belarus, ul. Wiertnicza 58 ☎022 742 0990, ⓦpoland.mfa.bov.by; Canada, ul. Matejki 1/5 ☎022 584 3100, ⓦcanada.pl; Ireland, ul. Mysia 5 ☎022 849 6633, ⓦdfa.ie/irish-embassu/poland; New Zealand, al. Ujazdowskie 51 ☎022 521 0500, ⓦmfat.govt.nz; South Africa, ul. Koszykowa 54 ☎22 622 1031, ⓦdirco.gov.sa; UK, ul. Kawalerii 12 ☎022 311 0000, ⓦgov.uk/government/world/Poland; Ukraine, al. Szucha 7 ☎22 629 3446, ⓦpoland.mfa.gov.ua; USA, al. Ujazdowskie 29/31 ☎22 504 2000, ⓦpoland.usembassy.gov.

Hospital and clinics Warsaw's hospital, Centralny Szpital Kliniczny MSW, is at ul. Woloska 137 (☎22 508 1510, ⓦcskmswia.pl). The emergency ambulance number is ☎112. Damian, ul. Foksal 3/5 (Mon–Fri 7.30am–8pm, Sat 8am–3pm; ☎22 566 2253, ⓦdamian.pl), is a private medical clinic.

Left luggage There are 24hr-luggage lockers at Warszawa Centralna train station (see page 79).

Lost property If you've lost something on a municipal bus call ☎22 663 3297; on a tram ☎22 663 3297; on the metro ☎22 655 4242; or on a SKM train ☎22 699 7195.

Pharmacies There are 24hr aptekas on the top floor of Warszawa Centralna train station, at al. Jana Pawla 52/54, and at al. Solidarności 149.

Police Report crimes at the police office at Warszawa Centralna train station (☎022 603 7224), or at ul. Wilcza 21 (☎022 603 6411).

Post offices The main office is at ul. Świętokrzyska 31/33. It handles fax and poste restante (postcode 00-001) and is open 24hr. There are also post offices at Rynek Starego Miasta 15 (Mon–Fri 8am–8pm, June–Sept also Sat 9am–4pm), and Warszawa Centralna station main hall (Mon–Fri 8am–8pm, Sat 8am–2pm).

Łódź and central Poland

APARTMENTS IN A RESTORED TEXTILE FACTORY

Łódź and central Poland

Erstwhile powerhouse of the nineteenth-century textile industry, Łódź is one of the most changed cities in Poland, trading its gritty mill-town image for a new identity as an art-and-nightlife centre whose red-brick factories now serve as shopping malls and heritage zones. Only two hours by train from Warsaw, Łódź is both an appealing city-break destination in its own right and a handy base from which to visit both the Polish capital and the green plains that make up the centre of the country. Much of this central area consists of the region of Mazovia, a historical duchy sprinkled with attractive towns.

Midway between Łódź and Warsaw are a handful of day-trip destinations: the market town of **Łowicz**, an important centre of folk crafts and a convenient jumping-off point for the nearby aristocratic estates of **Arkadia** and **Nieborów**; **Żyrardów**, an almost perfectly-preserved nineteenth-century mill town; and the village of **Żelazowa Wola**, home to the delightful country house where composer Chopin was born. Northeast of Warsaw, the former concentration camp at **Treblinka** is marked by solemn memorials and a small museum.

Łódź

Mention **ŁÓDŹ** (pronounced "Woodge") to many Poles and all you'll get is a grimace, but this former textile town 110km southwest of Warsaw is a fascinating place, a creation of the Industrial Revolution that is rapidly reinventing itself as a forward-looking city of culture, commerce and style. Much of the city's nineteenth-century core has survived, with fortress-like red-brick factories rubbing shoulders with nineteenth-century apartment blocks and flamboyant urban villas. It is a landscape immortalized in Andrzej Wajda's Oscar-nominated film *The Promised Land*, based on the mill-town saga penned by Nobel laureate Władysław Reymont.

Today, Łódź's industrial buildings form the backdrop to a post-industrial civilization of shopping, dining and going out: the Manufaktura shopping mall, OFF Piotrkowska nightlife district and EC1 Planetarium are outstanding examples of what can be done with a bunch of old factories and a bit of imagination.

Łódź has long been a major player in Polish culture: the city boasts one of the best **orchestras** in the country, a **modern art** scene that dates back to the 1920s, and a renowned **cinema** school that produced the cream of the Polish film industry – Jerzy Skolimowski, Krzysztof Kieślowski, Andrzej Wajda and Roman Polański included.

Brief history

Łódź was an obscure village until the 1820s, when imperial Russia earmarked the area for industrial development. The city, on the westernmost edge of the Empire, used Western European skills to supply the vast Russian and Chinese markets with cheap fabrics. People poured in by the thousand: Russian civil servants, German factory technicians and a largely Polish workforce. Łódź's Jewish community produced a host of prominent

ARKADIA PARK

Highlights

① Łódź Art Museum Spread over two branches, this is the best modern art collection in Poland, full of insights into the avant-garde side of the nation's culture. See page 97

② Łódź EC1 Planetarium Gaze upon the wonders of the universe at this state-of-the-art planetarium in a former power station. See page 99

③ OFF Piotrkowska, Łódź There are few better illustrations of Poland's urban regeneration than this former industrial space containing a cluster of offbeat cafés, bars and shops. See page 102

④ Arkadia and Nieborów The landscaped gardens laid out for the Radziwiłł family are among the best-preserved aristocratic parks in the country. See page 105

⑤ Żyrardów The red-brick factories of this small Mazovian town are a must for lovers of nineteenth-century industrial architecture. See page 106

⑥ Żelazowa Wola Chopin's birthplace and nowadays a national shrine; there's a museum dedicated to the composer and you can attend summertime piano recitals in the surrounding park. See page 108

HIGHLIGHTS ARE MARKED ON THE MAPS ON PAGES 96 AND 98

figures, textile magnate Izrael Poznański, pianist Arthur Rubinstein, poet Julian Tuwim and cosmetics pioneer Max Factor (Maksymilian Faktorowicz) among them.

Łódź's prosperity declined following World War I when the city lost its privileged access to Russian markets. With the onset of World War II, Łódź was incorporated into the German Reich and renamed "Litzmannstadt" in honour of a World War I general. The Nazis established the first of their Jewish ghettos in Łódź (see page 100), and almost all of the city's Jews were murdered in the ensuing Holocaust. After the war, Łódź remained a textile-producing powerhouse right up until the economic changes of the 1990s, when most of the city's mills went bust. With former factories now transformed into shopping centres, art galleries and designer lofts, twenty-first century Łódź has become a leading example of post-industrial regeneration.

Ulica Piotrkowska

Running straight as an arrow through the centre of Łódź is the largely pedestrianized **ulica Piotrkowska**, a 3km-long boulevard that bustles with activity day and night. The street is lined with the mansions of the city's former *haute bourgeoisie*, many of the buildings peeling

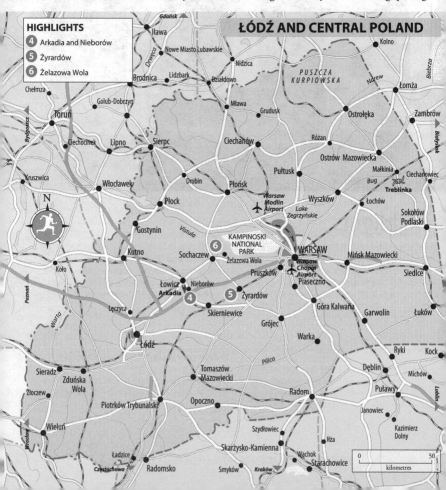

HIGHLIGHTS
④ Arkadia and Nieborów
⑤ Żyrardów
⑥ Żelazowa Wola

ŁÓDŹ AND CENTRAL POLAND

ŁÓDŹ ART CITY

Warsaw aside, Łódź is arguably the **contemporary art** capital of modern Poland – whatever the likes of Kraków or Poznań might say to the contrary. For those who want to find out what's happening on the cultural boundaries, we've listed five places below to start looking. In addition to these, don't miss the **Łódź Art Museum** (see below); the renovation of this museum and the construction of a new branch at the Manufaktura has given Łódź the prestige venues it needs to attract the international touring exhibitions, bringing in an increasing number of big names from the contemporary European scene.

Atlas Sztuki ul. Piotrkowska 116 ⓦatlassztuki. pl. This is the Polish art community's favourite private gallery, consistently showcasing the best in both domestic and international art. Housed in a pre-World War I Jewish theatre (and subsequently kosher meat market), it's worth visiting for the building alone. Mon–Fri 4–8pm, Sat 11am–5pm.

Leopold Kindermann Villa ul. Wólczańska 31 ⓦ mgs lodz.pl. This lovingly restored Art Nouveau villa houses the main branch of the City Art Gallery, with temporary exhibitions by contemporary artists from Poland and abroad. Tues–Fri 11am–6pm, Sat & Sun 11am–5pm.

Łódź Art Center ul. Tymienieckiego 3 ⓦlodzartc enter.com, ⓦfabrykasztuki.com. Contemporary art exhibitions in a renovated factory. The venue is run by umbrella organization Fabryka Sztuki (ⓦfabrykasztuki.

org), who also organize theatre, concert and club events. Mon–Wed & Fri noon–5pm, Thurs noon–7pm.

Łódź Kaliska ⓦlodzkaliska.pl. A five-member collective formed in 1979, Łódź Kaliska pioneered performance art and Dadaist provocation throughout the dark days of martial law. Their photographs of theatrically staged tableaux line the walls of the *Łódź Kaliska* pub (see page 103), the ultimate shrine to their work.

Manhattan Transfer ul. Piotrkowska 8 ⓦ pos.lodz. pl. This is the contemporary incarnation of the legendary Manhattan Gallery, originally housed in the basement of a block of flats (a block nicknamed the "Łódź Manhattan" on account of its sky-scraping pretentions). The new Manhattan is not as edgy, underground and agenda-setting as it used to be, but still makes essential viewing. Mon–Fri 11am–6pm.

with age, others restored to their former splendour. A scattered collection of modern statues recalls famous Łódź folk of the past – you'll see locals and tourists alike pausing for photo opportunities at **Rubinstein's Piano**, near the junction with ulica Moniuszki, or the **Three Industrialists** (portraying mill owners Poznański, Grohmann and Scheiber lolling around a dinner table), at the crossroads of Piotrkowska and Jaracza. Near the *Hotel Grand*, hall-of-fame-style plaques embedded in the pavement honour luminaries of the Łódź Film School – Roman Polański, Andrzej Wajda and Krzystow Kieślowski among them.

Łódź Art Museum: ms¹ and ms²

ms¹ ul. Więckowskiego 36 • Tues–Sun 10am–5pm • **ms²** Ogrodowa 19 • Tues 10am–6pm, Wed–Sun 11am–7pm • Ticket for one museum 12zł, combined ticket for both ms¹ and ms² 16zł • ⓦ msl.org.pl

Thanks to the shrewd acquisitions of the a.r. group, an art association founded in the 1920s by painter Władysław Strzemiński and sculptor Katarzyna Kobro, Łódź can boast the best modern art collection in the whole of Poland. The pioneering couple snapped up modernist works by some of Europe's biggest avant-garde names, donating the whole lot to the city in 1931. The collection is now spread over the two sites of the **Łódź Art Museum**: ms¹ and ms². Generally speaking, the best of the permanent collection is in ms², while the best of the temporary exhibitions is in ms¹.

Occupying a wing of the Poznański factory on the south side of the Manufaktura shopping centre (see page 99), **ms²** offers a wonderful blend of nineteenth-century red brick and modern white-wall gallery space. Inside, canvases by Max Ernst and Fernand Léger hang side-by-side with Polish works from the same period – deranged portraits by Witkacy here, cucumber-cool sculptures by Katarzyna Kobro there. The present-day crop of Polish artists is also well represented, with chin-strokingly enigmatic creations by Wilhelm Sasnal and Mirosław Bałka well to the fore. There's a whole floor devoted to temporary exhibitions, a café and a well-stocked art bookshop.

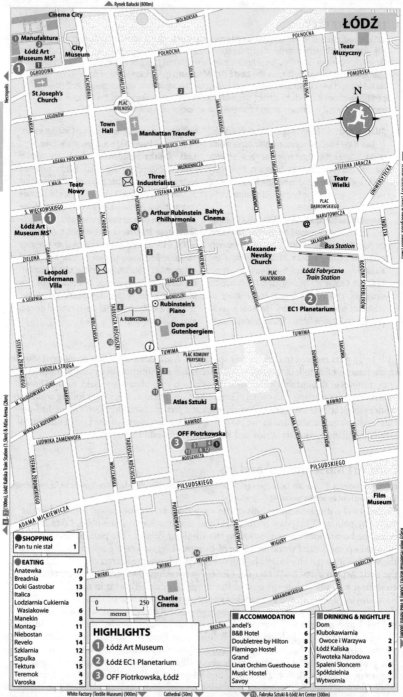

Rynek Bałucki (800m)

ŁÓDŹ

Necropolis

Jewish Cemetery (3km) & Radogoszcz Station (4km)

Bus Station

Łódź Kaliska Train Station (1.5km) & Atlas Arena (2km)

Księży Młyn residential district (300m) & Willa Herbst (600m)

White Factory (Textile Museum) (900m) · Cathedral (50m) · 15, Fabryka Sztuki & Łódź Art Center (300m)

● SHOPPING

Pan tu nie stał	1

● EATING

Anatewka	1/7
Breadnia	9
Doki Gastrobar	13
Italica	10
Lodziarnia Cukiernia Wasiakowie	6
Manekin	8
Montag	11
Niebostan	3
Revelo	14
Szklarnia	12
Szpulka	2
Tektura	15
Teremok	4
Varoska	5

HIGHLIGHTS

1 Łódź Art Museum

2 Łódź EC1 Planetarium

3 OFF Piotrkowska, Łódź

◼ ACCOMMODATION

andel's	1
B&B Hotel	6
Doubletree by Hilton	8
Flamingo Hostel	7
Grand	5
Linat Orchim Guesthouse	2
Music Hostel	3
Savoy	4

◼ DRINKING & NIGHTLIFE

Dom	5
Klubokawiarnia Owoce i Warzywa	2
Łódź Kaliska	3
Piwoteka Narodowa	1
Spaleni Słońcem	6
Spółdzielnia	4
Wytwornia	7

0 — 250 metres

The older branch of the museum, **ms¹**, is housed in a mock-Renaissance palace that once belonged to the factory-owning Poznański clan. One highlight of ms¹ is the so-called **Neoplastic Room**, a space designed by Strzemiński in the 1940s for the display of abstract works; looking like a 3-D recreation of a painting by Mondrian or Malevich, the room is the perfect place in which to hang works that draw similar inspiration.

Manufaktura

ul. Ogrodowa • Ⓦ manufaktura.lodz.pl

Nothing symbolizes Łódź's post-industrial transformation more spectacularly than the **Manufaktura**, a vast shopping and leisure complex that occupies a handsome ensemble of red-brick factory halls. Founded by Izrael Poznański, the nineteenth-century Jewish shopkeeper who rose to become one of the biggest textile magnates in the Russian Empire, the factory finally ceased production in 1997 – only to be reborn as a temple to post-industrial consumer culture. As well as the attractions listed below, Manufaktura is also home to ms2, the new branch of the Łódź Art Museum (see page 97).

Eksperymentarium

Mon–Sat 10am–10pm, Sun 10am–9pm • 17zł • ☎ 42 633 5262, Ⓦ experymentarium.pl

Manufaktura's daytime attractions include the **Eksperymentarium**, a hands-on science museum where children can learn some basic scientific principles by playing with plasma balls, gyroscopes, mirrors, magnets and so forth.

Factory Museum

Tues–Fri 9am–7pm, Sat & Sun 11am–7pm • 6zł • ☎ 42 636 2825, Ⓦ muzeumfabryki.com.pl

On the north side of the Manufaktura complex, beside the entrance to the Cinema City multiplex, the **Factory Museum** (Muzeum Fabryki) tells the history of the Poznański factory in accessible audio-visual style – staff will switch on some of the antiquated cloth-weaving machines if you show an interest.

City Museum

ul. Ogrodowa 15 • Mon, Tues & Thurs 10am–4pm, Wed, Sat & Sun noon–6pm • 12zł; free on Wed • ☎ 42 254 9000, Ⓦ muzeum-lodz.pl

Next door to the Manufaktura, on the corner of Ogrodowa and Zachodnia, the ostentatiously palatial building built by Izrael Poznański as a family home now serves as the **City Museum** (Muzeum Miasta Łodzi). The building features a lavish mixture of styles both inside and out: it is said that Poznański didn't understand what terms like neo-Gothic, neo-Renaissance or neo-Baroque actually meant, so simply ordered all of them from his architects. Downstairs are temporary exhibitions of modern art and photography, while up the grand staircase are the showpiece chambers, the dining room and the ballroom, filled with elaborately carved doorframes, stained glass and stucco nymphs.

The museum houses an extensive collection of memorabilia of **Arthur Rubinstein**, one of the greatest pianists of the last century, and a quintessential hedonist. He was particularly celebrated for his performances of Chopin, and his recordings remain the interpretive touchstone for the composer. One wing of the museum is given over to the **Gallery of Polish Masters** (Galeria Mistrzów Polskich), a collection strong on late-nineteenth and early-twentieth-century art. It contains a sprinkling of major works by Henryk Siemiradzki, Wojciech Gerson and Wojciech Kossak, but otherwise runs out of steam halfway round.

EC1 Planetarium

ul. Targowa 1/3 • Tues–Fri 8.30am–7pm, Sat & Sun 9.30am–7pm; the programme changes regularly so it's best to turn up and see what's on offer • 17zł • ☎ 539 997 693, Ⓦ planetariumec1.pl

With its combination of industrial red-brick and shiny modern glass, the **EC1** is another of Łódź's keynote transformational projects: an early twentieth-century power station currently being reinvented as a science, technology and cultural centre. Several visitor attractions are planned, including sections devoted to the history of cinema and the study of comics and computer games; the planetarium is the first to open its doors.

The **EC1 Planetarium** presentations don't just cover the night sky, but also involve filmic excursions to the surface of the moon, the history of space travel and even the voyages of Charles Darwin. The place is popular with school parties, so it's best to visit at weekends or on weekdays after 2pm. English-language provision is patchy but the spectacular visuals are more than worthwhile – entering the hollowed-out former-industrial building and approaching the metallic spherical projection space is an experience in itself.

Textile Museum

ul. Piotrkowska 282 • Tues, Wed & Sun 9am–5pm, Thurs–Sat noon–7pm • 12zł; free on Thurs • ☎ 42 683 2684, ⓦ muzeumwlokiennictwa.pl

Łódź's showcase **Textile Museum** (Muzeum Włókiennictwa) occupies the huge **Biała Fabryka** (White Factory), the oldest mechanically operated mill in the city, built by Berlin-born industrialist Ludwik Geyer in 1835. An extensive display with plenty of audio-visual content features a thrilling array of historic looms, documentary material on how workers and their masters lived, and some gorgeous examples of textile design throughout the ages. A **skanzen** outside the main building contains a handful of nineteenth-century workers' houses – you can peek inside the tiny interiors and marvel at how neat and homely they are.

Księży Młyn

The main eastern end of ulica Tymienieckiego is dominated by **Księży Młyn**, an extensive complex of manufacturing and residential buildings developed by German magnate Karl Scheiber in the mid-nineteenth century. The mills have long since been shut down, but the area remains a fascinating place to explore: most of the gorgeous red-brick buildings survive, including rows of terraced houses built for the workers.

Herbst Palace

ul. Przędzalniana 72, at the corner of Tymienieckiego • Tues–Sun 11am–5pm • 10zł • ☎ 42 674 9698, ⓦ palac-herbsta.org.pl

Standing in stark contrast to the dwellings of Księży Młyn's proletarians is the **Herbst Palace** (Pałac Herbsta), built for Scheiber's son-in-law Edward Herbst in 1875 on the model of a Palladian villa. Its lovingly restored interiors – with the grand public rooms downstairs, the intimate family ones above – betray influences ranging from ancient Rome via the Orient to Art Nouveau.

THE ŁÓDŹ GHETTO

The fate of the **Jews** of Łódź is one of the most poignant and tragic episodes of World War II. One month after the German occupation of the city on September 8, 1939, former velvet manufacturer **Chaim Rumkowski** was selected by the Nazis as the head of the Jewish Council of Elders, giving him absolute power over the community. When the Nazis created a Jewish ghetto in the northern suburb of **Bałuty**, Rumkowski soon made it a highly profitable enterprise, ruling his domain as a **despot**, and selecting those who had to make up the regular quotas demanded by the Nazis for deportation to the concentration camps. He cultivated the oratorical style of Hitler for his frequent addresses to the community. The most notorious of these was his "Give me your children" speech of 1942, in which he made an emotional appeal to his subjects to send their children to the camps, in order that able-bodied adults could be spared.

The ghetto was **liquidated** in the autumn of 1944. Rumkowski voluntarily chose to go with the others to Auschwitz, albeit armed with an official letter confirming his special status. He died there soon afterwards, most probably beaten to death by fellow Jews. An estimated 877 people survived the Łódź ghetto, many of them hidden by local Poles.

Film Museum

pl. Zwycięstwa 1 • Tues 10am–5pm, Wed & Fri 9am–4pm, Thurs, Sat & Sun 11am–6pm • 10zł; free on Tues • ⓦ kinomuzeum.pl

Industrialist Karl Scheiber's palatial former home now serves as the **Film Museum** (Muzeum Kinematografii), celebrating Łódź's status as one of Europe's major film schools. All of Poland's film greats get a look in, plus there's a fascinating selection of old cameras and projectors, and some absorbing temporary exhibitions delving deep into global cinema culture. Arguably the biggest star of the museum is the building itself, with its wood-panelled rooms, stuccoed ceilings and huge, ceramic-tiled ovens.

2

North of the centre: Jewish Łódź

Until World War II Łódź was home to an estimated quarter of a million Jews. The bulk of them lived in the area around **Rynek Bałucki**, 1km north of plac Wolności, although Jewish heritage sites and Holocaust memorials are scattered throughout the city's northern suburbs. Although Rynek Bałucki was at the heart of the wartime ghetto (see page 100), there are few reminders of that period now, and you're more likely to visit the square for its chaotic outdoor **market** than for any sense of historical resonance. The *Trail of Litzmannstadt Ghetto* **map**, available from the tourist office, is a thorough guide to the area.

Jewish Cemetery

ul. Zmienna • May–Sept Mon–Thurs & Sun 9am–5pm, Fri 9am–3pm; Oct–April Mon–Fri & Sun 8am–3pm • 6zł; skullcaps provided • Tram #6 to the Strykowska terminus

Dating from 1892, Łódź's **Jewish Cemetery** (Cmentarz żydowski) is the largest Jewish cemetery in Europe, with some 180,000 tombstones (and twice as many graves). Providing a spectacular centrepiece is the domed mausoleum of Izrael Poznański (who died in 1900), with fine Art Nouveau mosaics inside. At the south end of the cemetery is the so-called "ghetto field", full of small plaques remembering Łódź residents who passed through the ghetto before being murdered in camps elsewhere.

Radogoszcz Station

al. Pamięci Ofiar Litzmannstadt Getto 12 • Museum: Mon & Tues 9am–5pm, Wed & Thurs 10am–6pm, Sat & Sun 10am–4pm • Free • Bus #70 from Śmigłego Rydza to Inflancka

Under its German-language name of Radegast, **Radogoszcz Station** (Przystanek Radogoszcz) was where ghetto inhabitants – over 140,000 Jews all told, as well as five thousand Gypsies – boarded trains to the Chełmno and Auschwitz death camps. The restored station building now holds a small **museum** display, while examples of the kind of cattle trucks in which victims were transported stand beside the platform. A monument to those deported, in the form of a soaring red-brick column, rises solemnly beyond the western end of the platform.

ARRIVAL AND DEPARTURE	**ŁÓDŹ**

By plane Łódź's airport (ⓘ 42 683 5255, ⓦ airport.lodz.pl) is 6km southwest of the centre. From here, bus #88A goes to Łódź Fabryczna train station (2–4 hourly 4am–10pm; 35min), calling at Łódź Kaliska train station on the way. A taxi into the centre will set you back 40–50zł.

By train Łódź Fabryczna station is located on the eastern side of the town centre and predominantly handles eastbound services. Łódź Kaliska, 2km east of the centre (tram #12 to ul. Piotrkowska) handles trains to northern, western and southern destinations.

Destinations (from Łódź Fabryczna) Warsaw (Mon–Fri hourly, Sat & Sun every 2hr; 1hr 30min–2hr 30min);

Częstochowa (5 daily; 2hr 30min); Łowicz (Mon–Fri hourly, Sat & Sun every 2hr; 2hr; change at Łódź Widzew); Kraków (2 daily; 2hr 40min; change at Łódź Widzew).

Destinations (from Łódź Kaliska) Bydgoszcz (4 daily; 3hr–3hr 30min); Katowice (2 daily; 3hr 20min); Poznań (4 daily; 4hr); Toruń (1 daily; 2hr 30min); Wrocław (2 daily; 4hr 30min).

By bus The main bus stations are right outside the main train stations, Łódź Fabryczna and Łódź Kaliska.

Destinations (from Łódź Fabryczna) Gdańsk (3 daily; 5hr); Kraków (4 daily; 4–5hr); Toruń (1 daily; 3hr 20min).

Destinations (from Łódź Kaliska) Bydgoszcz (2 daily; 4hr); Toruń (3 daily; 3–4hr).

2

GETTING AROUND

By rickshaw The best way to get around the ul. Piotrkowska area is by rickshaw; they'll whisk you from one end to the other for a few złotys.

By tram For less central destinations there's a good tram network. Tickets cost 2.60zł (20min), 3.40zł (40min) or 4.40zł (1hr), or 12zł for a 24hr pass.

INFORMATION

Tourist information The helpful office at ul. Piotrkowska 87 (May–Sept Mon–Fri 9am–7pm, Sat & Sun 10am–4pm; Oct–April Mon–Fri 9am–6pm, Sat 10am–2pm; ☎ 42 638 5955, ⓦ cit.lodz.pl) has an excellent range of free maps and publications.

ACCOMMODATION

HOTELS

★ **andel's** ul. Ogrodowa 17 ☎ 42 279 1000, ⓦ vienna house.com; map page 98. Occupying a large chunk of the former factory that makes up the Manufaktura complex (see page 99), *andel's* is something of a monument to post-industrial regeneration, with plenty of exposed brick, swanky designer rooms, a top-floor swimming pool and a panoramic bar. Definitely the top place to stay in town if you can stump up the cash. Breakfast extra 50zł per person. **380zł**

B&B Hotel al. Kościuszki 16 ☎ 42 207 0040, ⓦ hotelbb. pl; map page 98. A "budget" hotel that actually provides all the creature comforts, *B&B* offers crisp, contemporary en-suite rooms, bright social areas and a modicum of functionality – drinks and snacks are dispensed by a vending machine rather than a white shirt behind a bar. Breakfast extra 25zł per person. **140zł**

Doubletree by Hilton ul. Łąkowa 29 ☎ 42 208 8000, ⓦ doubletreelodz.pl; map page 98. A bit more suave than the other new-build hotels in town, the *Doubletree* offers smart, tastefully-furnished rooms with plenty of light, and good cross-town views. There's a tenth-floor spa centre, a small pool, and (quite possibly uniquely in Poland) a row of beehives on the roof – a joint project with local naturalists. Breakfast extra 60zł per person. **370zł**

Grand ul. Piotrkowska 72 ☎ 42 633 9920, ⓦ grand.hotel. com.pl; map page 98. Grand indeed if you are a connoisseur of faded glories, this is a *belle époque* establishment that just about lives up to its name. Expect high-ceilinged rooms, a sweeping central staircase and potted plants the size of small trees. The corridors are filled with pictures of actors who have stayed here over the years; suite 205 is where David Lynch shot scenes for his 2006 film *Inland Empire*. **230zł**

Linat Orchim Guesthouse ul. Pomorska 18 ☎ 42 632 4661, ⓦ linatorchim.pl; map page 98. Guesthouse in the Jewish community centre featuring small but cosy en suites with bunk beds – which can serve as anything from singles to quads depending on requirements. **120zł**

Savoy ul. Traugutta 6 ☎ 42 632 93 60, ⓦ savoy.centrum hotele.pl; map page 98. Opened in 1911 and formerly home to the city's bohemian set, this dowdy, creaky-corridor building was immortalized in Joseph Roth's eponymous novel of post-World War I paranoia (see page 476), though today the cramped en-suite rooms are a bit on the brown side. **120zł**

HOSTELS

Flamingo Hostel ul. Sienkiewicza 67 ☎ 42 661 1888, ⓦ lodz.flamingo-hostel.com; map page 98. Łódź branch of the popular Kraków hostel, boasting a comfy common room and mix of bunk-bed dorms and private rooms. Dorms **35zł**, doubles **99zł**

Music Hostel ul. Piotrkowska 60 ☎ 533 533 263, ⓦ music-hostel.pl; map page 98. Neat and tidy hostel on the main street offering two six-bed dorms (one male, one female), as well as a private double, plus a well-equipped kitchen. Dorms **45zł**, doubles **120zł**

EATING

Łódź's restaurant and café scene can compete with almost any city in Poland. Ul. Piotrkowska is the heart of the action, with a concentration of eating and drinking venues in **OFF Piotrkowska**, a former factory courtyard at no. 138/140. There's another cluster of places around the **Manufaktura** (see page 99).

CAFÉS

Breadnia ul. Piotrkowska 86; map page 98. Bread and cakes baked on the premises, plus a big choice of breakfasts. Lunch-or-later eats include bagels with a variety of fillings (15zł), and a solid selection of pizzas. Mon–Sat 9am–10pm, Sun 9am–9pm.

Lodziarnia Cukiernia Wasiakowie ul. Traugutta 2 ☎ 42 649 7160, ⓦ facebook.com/CukierniaWasiakowieLodz; map page 98. One of the best places in town for own-make ice cream, *Wasiakowe* also produce cakes, tarts and meringues with a variety of fruit-and-berry flavours, and good strong coffee. The interior is Pop Art-meets-patisserie chintz. Mon–Fri 10am–8pm, Sat 10am–9pm, Sun noon–8pm.

Montag ul. Piotrkowska 107 ☎ 608 632 532, ⓦ facebook. com/montag; map page 98. Lovely little bakery in an off-street courtyard selling artisan breads, slices of quiche and delicious cakes. There's seating for about ten people. A cheese-and-ham sandwich made with lovely crusty bread is a steal at 6zł. Mon–Fri 7am–8pm, Sat 7am–4pm.

Niebostan ul. Piotrkowska 17 ☎501 120 766, ⓦ facebook.com/niebostan; map page 98. Deliciously offbeat café-bar with a big choice of leaf teas, an imaginative menu of sandwiches, pastas and cakes, plus a well-stocked fridge full of beers. It's located on the first floor and reached via a cast-iron stairway; in summer, the courtyard hosts weekend DJ events and gigs. Daily noon–1am.

Tektura Tymienieckiego 3 ☎721 186 056; map page 98. Inside Łódź Art Center (see page 97) is this high-ceilinged former factory space with minimalist decor and a jumble of furniture from different eras. Espresso, drip and aeropress coffees are on offer, alongside egg-and-bacon breakfasts, *owsianka* (oat porridge with various fruity flavours) and ciabatta sandwiches. Tues–Sat 9am–8pm, Sun 9am–5.30pm.

RESTAURANTS

Anatewka ul. 6 Sierpna 2/4 ☎42 630 3635; at Manufaktura ☎42 633 2277; ⓦ anatewka.pl; map page 98. High-quality Jewish-themed restaurant popular with locals and tourists alike, featuring crocheted tablecloths, candles, old clocks and sideboards. The menu contains a lot that is broadly central-European, alongside lamb *cholent* (39zł), goose livers with almonds (39zł) and other traditional Jewish dishes. Both branches daily 11am–11pm.

Doki Gastrobar ul. Piotrkowska 138/140 (in OFF Piotrkowska) ☎42 307 3101; map page 98. Located in a cluster of shipping containers at the entrance to the OFF Piotrkowska complex, *Doki* serves steaks, seafood and burgers in a mellowly-lit interior – with open-air seating on the top deck. Mains range from 30zł to 70zł and there are some to-die-for two-course set lunches for around 22zł. Also a good place for a cocktail. Daily 10am–11pm.

Italica al. Kościuszki 33/35 ☎42 670 6204, ⓦ pizzeria italica.pl; map page 98. A reliable and friendly Italian restaurant that keeps things simple: excellent pizzas in the 25–32zł range, a handful of pasta-based alternatives, and a minimum of thematic overload (checked tablecloths and a few pictures of a boot-shaped country will do). Daily 1–10pm.

Manekin ul. 6 Sierpna 1 ☎42 671 0784; map page 98. Pancake bar with a huge menu of inexpensive but filling eats (14–18zł), sit-down restaurant service and a kitchen counter that looks like a vintage tramcar. It's very popular, but service and turnover is quick. Mon–Thurs & Sun 10am–10pm, Fri & Sat 10am–11pm.

Revelo ul. Wigury 4/6 ☎42 636 8686, ⓦ revelo. pl; map page 98. Atmospheric Art Deco restaurant serving a mix of Polish classics, steak and seafood, and some mouthwatering desserts. Mains cost 30–60zł, or there's a six-course tasting menu for 96zł. Reservations recommended. Daily noon–11pm.

Szklarnia ul. Piotrkowska 138/140 (in OFF Piotrkowska) ☎506 061 981; map page 98. The post-industrial setting and quality, well-presented cuisine at *Szklarnia* make for a good combination. Polish pork, chicken and freshwater fish dishes (most mains 30–40zł) are teamed up with gourmet burgers, Mediterranean salads, pastas and pizzas. Cocktails are served in jam jars and milk bottles. Mon–Thurs & Sun 11am–9pm, Fri & Sat 11am–10pm.

Szpulka ul. Ogrodowa (in Manufaktura) ☎42 634 2472; map page 98. A mixture of rustic-looking wood and modern design details give a welcoming aspect to this popular bistro, offering a well-balanced, something-for-everyone menu of soups, salads, steaks and burgers. Three-course set lunches are a bargain at 25–32zł; cooked breakfasts weigh in at 20zł. Daily 8am–11.45pm.

Teremok ul. Piotrkowska 36 ⓦ teremok.pl; map page 98. This order-at-the-counter *pierogi* bar in an off-street courtyard specializes in Russian *pelmeni* and Georgian *hinkali* (dough pockets with a spicy meat filling). Hardly anything costs over 15zł. Tues–Thurs & Sun 11am–6pm, Fri & Sat 11am–9pm.

Varoska ul. Traugutta 4 ☎42 632 4546, ⓦ varoska.pl; map page 98. Pleasant, mid-priced Hungarian place with a nice line in goulash served in traditional brass cauldrons – a simple *porkolt* (pork goulash) will set you back 29zł, while the lamb goulash with red beans and dumplings weighs in at 44zł. There's a good selection of Hungarian wines and spirits. Daily noon–11pm.

DRINKING AND NIGHTLIFE

BARS

Klubokawiarnia Owoce i Warzywa Traugutta 9 ⓦ owoce iwarzywa.com; map page 98. Retro café-bar with an interior that looks rather like a (Polish) design magazine from the late 1960s/early 70s, and an arty-but-approachable clientele that fits in perfectly with the surroundings. A cool place to enjoy a daytime coffee-and-cake or a longer beer-lubricated evening. Mon–Thurs 10am–midnight, Fri & Sat 10am–1am, Sun noon–midnight.

Łódź Kaliska ul. Piotrkowska 102 ⓦ klub.lodzkaliska. pl; map page 98. Hidden down an alley, a wonderful and very popular pub full of mirrors, curios and artworks by the Łódź Kaliska art collective (see page 97), with a rooftop section that's open in good weather. Mon–Thurs noon–2am, Fri & Sat noon–3am, Sun 4pm–3am.

Piwoteka Narodowa 6 Sierpna 1/3 ⓦ piwoteka narodowa.pl; map page 98. Another shining example of Poland's ongoing good-beer revolution, the "People's Beer-o-theque" foregoes the mass-market brews in favour of the draught beers produced by Poland's smaller breweries. Guest beers are chalked up on the board beside the bar – staff are more than happy to advise on what to try. Mon–Sat 2pm–midnight, Sun 2pm–11pm.

Spaleni Słońcem ul. Piotrkowska 138/140 (in OFF

2

ŁÓDŹ FESTIVAL CALENDAR

Łódź's importance as a cultural centre is reflected in the growing number of **festivals**, which cover traditional spheres such as ballet and classical music as well as more contemporary preoccupations such as design and new media.

Ballet Meetings (Łódzkie Spotkania Baletowe) May/June ⓦ operalodz.com. Top-notch performances, taking place every odd-numbered year.

Soundedit June ⓦ soundedit.pl. Electronica and avant-garde music festival involving leading Polish contemporary composers and international heroes of the experimental – previous guests have included The Residents, Brian Eno and Michael Nyman.

Four Cultures Festival (Festiwal Łódź Czterech

Kultur) Sept ⓦ 4kultury.pl. Two weeks of films, concerts, literary evenings and discussions of and between the city's traditional residents – Poles, Jews, Germans and Russians.

Łódź Design Festival Oct ⓦ lodzdesign.com. The biggest design event in Poland: ten days of exhibitions, events and seminars, attracting tens of thousands of visitors.

Rubinstein Piano Festival Oct ⓦ arturrubinstein.pl. The heritage of Łódź-born Rubinstein is celebrated with a series of concerts featuring the world's great soloists.

Piotrkowska) ⓦ facebook.com/spalenisloncem; map page 98. Arguably the most hipsterish bar in a hipsterish district, *Spaleni Słońcem* ("Burnt by the Sun") combines gritty bare-wall interiors with a welcoming range of beers, shots, cocktails and fresh lemonades. It comes into its own in summer when it spreads its deckchairs out into the open courtyard. Daily 3.30pm–midnight.

Spółdzielnia ul. Piotrkowska 138/140 (in OFF Piotrkowska) ☎ 786 258 555, ⓦ spoldzielnia-lodz.pl; map page 98. The ultimate all-purpose Łódź bar, with craft beers, whiskies and a menu of steaks, burgers, pizzas and two-course lunch deals. Plenty of outdoor seating and a kids' corner. Mon–

Thurs & Sun 10am–10pm, Fri & Sat 10am–2am.

CLUBS AND LIVE MUSIC

Dom ul. Piotrkowska 138/140 (in OFF Piotrkowska) ☎ 601 385 310, ⓦ facebook.com/klubDOM; map page 98. Punk and alt-rock gigs in a minimalist, post-industrial club space. Gigs usually start at 8pm, club nights kick off after 10pm.

Wytwornia ul. Łąkowa 29 ☎ 42 639 5555, ⓦ wytwornia. pl; map page 98. The city's best-equipped venue for medium-sized rock, jazz and blues, with gigs two or three times a week. Tickets from Empik stores or from ⓦ ticketpro.pl.

ENTERTAINMENT

THEATRE AND CONCERT VENUES

Arthur Rubinstein Philharmonic ul. Narutowicza 20–22 ☎ 42 664 7979, ⓦ filharmonia.lodz.pl. Performances by the local symphony orchestra and visiting soloists of international renown.

Atlas Arena al. Bandurskiego 7 ☎ 42 272 1507, ⓦ atlas arena.pl. Sports and concert hall 2km west of the centre (just beyond Łódź Kaliska station), with a 15,000 capacity; it's hosted the likes of Roger Waters, Depeche Mode, Rihanna and Shakira. Tickets from Empik stores or from ⓦ eventim.pl.

Fabryka Sztuki ul. Tymienieckiego 3 ⓦ fabrykasztuki. org. Former factory venue hosting alternative gigs, fringe theatre and performance art.

Teatr Muzyczny ul. Połnocna 47/51 ☎ 42 678 1968,

ⓦ teatr-muzyczny.lodz.pl. The main venue for operetta, musicals and music-and-dance shows.

Teatr Wielki pl. Dąbrowskiego 1 ☎ 42 633 3186, ⓦ operalodz.com. Prestigious venue for musicals, opera and ballet, with performances three or four times a week.

CINEMA

Charlie ul. Piotrkowska 203 ☎ 42 636 0092 ⓦ charlie.pl. Four-screen boutique cinema housed in a former communist party ideological school, showing the kind of intelligent non-Hollywood films that don't always make it the multiplexes.

SHOPPING

Pan tu nie stał ul. Piotrkowska 138/140 (in OFF Piotrkowska) ⓦ pantuniestal.com; map page 98. Poland's foremost designers of T-shirts, hoodies, hats and bags – each emblazoned with ironic references to Polish popular culture – are based in Łódź, and this is their flagship store. Check out the website to see whether it's your style. There's also a cute range of postcards, books and the odd children's toy. Mon–Fri 11am–7pm, Sat 11am–6pm, Sun noon–4pm.

ŁOWICZ FOLK FESTIVALS

The ideal time to visit Łowicz is at **Corpus Christi** (late May/early June), when the town's womenfolk turn out in beautiful handmade traditional costumes for the two-hour procession to the collegiate church, followed by neat lines of girls preparing for first Communion. **Jarmark Łowicki** (last or second-to-last weekend in June) is a seven-century-old fair featuring handicraft stalls, folk music and dancing.

Łowicz and around

At first sight **ŁOWICZ**, 35km northeast of Łódź, looks just like any other concrete-ridden Polish town, but this outwardly drab place is, in fact, a well-established centre of **folk art and crafts**. Locally produced *wycinanki*, coloured paper cutouts featuring floral motifs, have become something of a Polish trademark, popping up regularly in contemporary textile and stationery design. Łowicz's brilliantly coloured, broad-skirted costumes (*pasiaki*) are the town's other best-known product. Accessible from both Warsaw and Łódź by train, Łowicz is an easy day-trip wherever you are staying. The town is based around two market squares, with the broad, square-shaped **Stary Rynek** (overlooked by an impressive brick cathedral) and the even broader, triangular **Nowy Rynek** linked together by the lively shopping street of ulica Zduńska.

Łowicz Museum

Stary Rynek 5/7 • Tues–Sun 10am–4pm • 10zł • ☎ 46 837 3928

The **Łowicz Museum** (Muzeum Łowiczkie) is housed in a missionary college designed by Baroque master Tylman van Gameren. On the ground floor is the former seminary **chapel**, adorned with frescoes by Michelangelo Palloni, court painter to King Jan Sobieski. Upstairs lies an extensive collection of folk artefacts, including furniture, pottery, paper cut-outs and examples of the local costumes still worn on feast days. Round the back of the museum is a small *skanzen*, containing old cottages complete with their original furnishings.

Museum of the Łowicz Village

Maurzyce, 7km northwest of town on the Kutno road • Daily: April & Oct 9am–4pm; May–Sept 10am–6pm • 8zł • Regional trains from Łowicz Głowny to Kutno stop at the Niedźwiada Łowicka halt, a 20min walk from the skansen

For an in-depth look at local folk traditions, head out of town to the open-air **Museum of the Łowicz Village** (Skansen wsi łowickiej). It's an impressive ensemble of thatched-hut farmstead buildings, many decorated with *wycinanki* paper cut-outs hanging from ceiling beams. Cut-out artists – along with other local craftspeople – are usually on hand to demonstrate their skills.

ARRIVAL AND DEPARTURE   ŁOWICZ

By train Łowicz Głowny train station is a 10min walk east of the Rynek. There are direct trains from Warszawa Centralna (10 daily; 1hr–1hr 30min) and Łódź Fabryczna (Mon–Fri hourly, Sat & Sun every 2hr; 2hr; change at Łódź Widzew).

EATING

Bordo Stary Rynek 8. Of several cafés on the Rynek, *Bordo* is the best in terms of coffee, ice cream and own-baked cakes – including some seductive fruit-plus-meringue concoctions. Sink into the comfy seats inside or take a table on the square-side decking. Daily 10am–8pm.

Pizza House ul. 3-go Maja 8 ☎ 46 837 8351. Just off Stary Rynek, this place doles out decent pizzas (20–25zł) in an attractive back yard illuminated by quirky coloured lanterns, or in an interior featuring snug booths. Mon–Thurs & Sun noon–10pm, Fri & Sat noon–midnight.

Arkadia and Nieborów

A short distance southeast of Łowicz, the main Łowicz–Skierniewice road passes two sights redolent of the bygone Polish aristocracy: the landscaped park of **Arkadia**, and the seventeenth-century palace at **Nieborów**. Together they make an easy and enjoyable day trip from Warsaw or Łódź. If you're relying on public transport, you'll need to head for Łowicz first and take a bus from there.

Arkadia

8km southeast of Łowicz • Daily 10am–dusk • 12zł • ⓦ nieborow.art.pl

The eighteenth-century **Arkadia** park is as wistfully romantic a spot as you could wish for. Conceived by Princess Helen Radziwiłł as an "ancient monument to beautiful Greece", the classical park is dotted with lakes and walkways, a jumble of reproduction classical temples, a sphinx and a mock-Gothic building that wouldn't look out of place in a Hammer film production. Many of the pieces were collected by the princess on her exhaustive foreign travels, caught up in the cult of the Classical that swept through the Polish aristocracy in the latter half of the eighteenth century.

Nieborów

13km southeast of Łowicz • **Palace interior** March, April & Oct Tues–Sun 10am–4pm; May & June daily 10am–6pm; July–Sept Mon–Fri 10am–4pm, Sat & Sun 10am–6pm • 22zł; March, April & Oct free on Tues; May–Sept free on Mon • **Gardens** Daily 10am–dusk • 12zł • ☏ 46 838 5635, ⓦ nieborow.art.pl

Five kilometres southeast of Arkadia lies the village of **NIEBORÓW**, whose country **palace** was designed for Cardinal Michał Radziejowski by the ever-present Tylman van Gameren in the 1690s. In 1766 the palace was acquired by Polish-Lithuanian landowner Michał Ogiński, who set about redecorating the interior in Rococo style before selling the place to Michał Radziwiłł, who filled Nieborów with his fine collection of European paintings. Now a branch of Warsaw's National Museum, the palace is one of the best maintained in the country, surrounded by handsome landscaped grounds.

The **palace interior** is filled with Roman tombstones and sculptural fragments, most famous of which is the classical-era sculpture known as the **Nieborów Niobe**. The grandest apartments (including a library with a fine collection of globes) are on the first floor, reached by a staircase clad in finely decorated Delft tiles. Outside, the palace **gardens** mix formal flowerbeds and tree-lined avenues with extensive sections of landscaped park – including two lakes linked by embankment-lined canal.

ARRIVAL AND DEPARTURE | ARKADIA AND NIEBORÓW

By bus Regular Łowicz–Skierniewice buses depart from Łowicz bus station (next to the train station), stopping off at Arkadia (hourly; 20min) and Nieborów (hourly; 30min) en route.

ACCOMMODATION AND EATING

Biała Dama al. Legionów Polskich 2, Nieborów ☏ 510 060 922, ⓦ dworek-nieborow.pl. This place opposite the palace entrance dishes out a sizeable repertoire of Polish pork and poultry dishes, and rents out cosy en-suite rooms on the floor above. Restaurant Mon–Fri 10am–8pm, Sat & Sun 10am–10pm. <u>180zł</u>

Pod Złotym Prosiakiem Nieborów 175, signed off the road at the northern end of Nieborów ☏ 501 327 880, ⓦ zlotyprosiak.pl. A traditional-style partly timbered building, serving up local food. It also offers accommodation in one double room and a four-person apartment (240zł). Restaurant daily 8am–10pm. <u>120zł</u>

Żyrardów

One of the best-preserved examples of a nineteenth-century industrial settlement anywhere in Europe, the small town of **ŻYRARDÓW** is an easy half-day trip from either Warsaw or Łódź. Set in flax-growing country, it became a major centre of linen production, thanks in large part to French engineer Philippe de Girard, who arrived in 1833 to supervise construction of the mills – the town was renamed Żyrardów in his honour. The textile industry collapsed in the late 1990s, leaving empty factories to brood over the red-brick terraced houses of those they once employed. With many of the mills now being repurposed as museums or loft developments, Żyrardów is finally moving towards a new future as a pleasant dormitory town in the Warsaw commuter belt. Arranged in a grid around **plac Jana**

Pawla II, the nineteenth-century heart of Żyrardów comprises rows and rows of red-brick houses, punctuated by red-brick churches, red-brick hospitals, red-brick schools and red-brick kindergartens.

Museum of Western Mazovia

ul. Karola Dittricha 1 • Tues–Fri 8am–4pm, Sat & Sun 11am–5pm • 5zł; free on Sat • ☎ 46 854 8180, ⓦ muzeumzyrardow.pl

Housed in a parkside villa that once belonged to linen magnate Karl Dittrich (who bought the Żyrardów mills in 1857 and set about creating the model factory town we see today), the **Museum of Western Mazovia** (Muzeum Mazowsza Zachodniego) contains pictures of the town in its industrial heyday, plus several brooding depictions of the Mazovian landscape by local painter Józef Rapacki.

Linen Museum

ul. Karola Dittricha 18 • Tues–Sun 10am–3pm • 6zł

The complex known as the Bielnik ("The Bleach House"), a glorious cluster of red brick, contains the **Linen Museum** (Muzeum Lniarstwa). Here, the factory floors have

FRÉDÉRIC CHOPIN (1810–49)

Few Polish artists have enjoyed the levels of international recognition achieved by **Frédéric Chopin** – or Fryderyk Szopen as he was baptized. He is, to all intents and purposes, the national composer, a fact attested to in the wealth of festivals and piano competitions held in his name.

Born of mixed Polish-French parentage in the village of **Żelazowa Wola**, where his father was a tutor to local aristocracy, Frédéric spent his early years in Warsaw and Mazovia, soaking up the folk tunes that would later permeate his compositions. He gave his first concert performance at the age of eight, and after a couple of years' schooling in Warsaw was enrolled at the newly created Warsaw Music Conservatory.

Chopin made his official **public debut** in 1829, performing the virtuoso Second Piano Concerto (F Minor), its melancholic slow movement inspired by an (unrequited) love affair with a fellow student. In the autumn of 1830 he travelled to Vienna, only to hear news of the **November uprising** against the Russians at home. He was never to return to Poland, a fate shared by many of the fellow exiles. Settling in Paris, Chopin befriended a host of other young composers (including Berlioz, Bellini, Liszt and Mendelssohn). The elegantly dressed, artistically sensitive Chopin soon became a society favourite, earning his living teaching and giving the occasional recital. In the years that followed he produced the rhapsodic *Fantaisie-Impromptu*, a book of études and a stream of nationalistically inspired polonaises and mazurkas.

Chopin's life changed dramatically in 1836 following his encounter with the novelist **George Sand**, who promptly fell in love with him and suggested she become his mistress. Chopin's affair with Sand coincided with his worsening health due to tuberculosis. Periods of feverish creativity alternated with lengthy lay-offs when he did nothing at all. Sojourns at Sand's country house at **Nohant** did wonders for Chopin's health, and it was here that he produced some of his most powerful music, including the sublime *Polonaise Fantaisie*, the Third Sonata and several of the major ballades.

Ditched by Sand in 1847, a miserable and by now penniless Chopin accepted an invitation from admiring pupil Jane Stirling to visit **Britain**. Chopin gave numerous recitals in London, making friends with Carlyle, Dickens and other luminaries of English artistic life. Increasingly weak, and unable either to compose or return Stirling's devoted affections, a depressed Chopin returned to Paris in November 1848. He was dead within months. In accordance with his deathbed wish, Mozart's *Requiem* was sung at the funeral; Chopin's grave in the **Père-Lachaise Cemetery** was sprinkled with earth from his native Mazovia. For many Poles, Chopin expresses better than anyone the essence of the national psyche, alternating wistful romanticism with storms of turbulent protest – "guns hidden in flowerbeds", in fellow composer Schumann's memorable description.

been left in much the same state as they were on the day production ceased in 1999, with rows of machines and racks of bobbins left in silent witness to the working-class culture of Poland's past.

ARRIVAL AND INFORMATION

By train Żyrardów's train station is on the southeastern side of the centre, a 10min walk from pl. Jana Pawła II. Destinations Łódź Fabryczna (hourly; 1hr); Łowicz Główny (8 daily; change at Skierniewice; 1hr); Warsaw Centralna, Śródmieście, Powiśle (every 30min; 35min–1hr).

ŻYRARDÓW

Tourist information The tourist office is centrally located in the Resursa cultural centre at ul. 1 Maja 45 (Mon–Fri 9am–5pm, Sat 10am–2pm; ☏ 46 854 2828, ⓦ resursa.zyrardow.pl).

EATING

Kawiarnia Tygielek pl. Jana Pawła II 3 ☏ 46 855 6622. Relaxing little place on the main square with a part-covered veranda. There's excellent coffee from the espresso machine or from a Turkish-style copper beaker *(tygielek)*, a choice of pasta dishes (20zł), rather fine cakes and a good selection of bottled beers. Mon 10am–8pm, Tues–Sun 10am–10pm.

Telegraf Bistro & Cafe ul. 1 Maja 54 ☏ 882 190 767. Red-brick-meets-contemporary-design café serving a splendid selection of cakes, soups and main meals (mostly pastas and big salads in the 25–30zł range). There's a kids' section with small chairs, low tables and a scattering of toys. Tues–Sat 10am–10pm, Sun 10am–9pm.

Żelazowa Wola

An enjoyable day out from either Warsaw or Łódź, the little village of **ŻELAZOWA WOLA** is the birthplace of composer and national hero, **Frédéric Chopin**. It is just beyond the outskirts of **Sochaczew**, a dusty town that's the starting point for a scenic narrow-gauge railway trip (see page 109).

Chopin Museum

Żelazowa Wola 15 • Museum and park Tues–Sun: April–Sept 9am–7pm; Oct–March 9am–5pm • Museum and park 23zł; park only 7zł; audio guide 10zł; free on Wed • ☏ 46 863 3300, ⓦ chopin.museum

The house where Chopin was born is now the **Chopin Museum**, surrounded by a large, tranquil park. The Chopin family lived here for only a year after their son's birth in 1810, but young Frédéric returned frequently to what became his favourite place – not least because of the musical inspiration he drew from the folk traditions of Mazovia.

Visitors enter the park via a striking modern pavilion containing the ticket office, gift shop and multimedia room. An (optional) ten-minute film tells you more than you need to know about the history of Żelazowa Wola, although the piano-trills of the Chopin backing-track do help to get you in the mood. The **house** where Chopin was born is just beyond, a typical nineteenth-century country mansion mixing rustic architecture with mock-palatial pretentions. Restored to period perfection, the building contains a collection of family portraits and other Chopin memorabilia. Exhibits are small in number but powerfully evocative: a few framed pages of an original score, for example, or a nineteenth-century grand piano which the composer is believed to have played in Paris.

Back outside, the surrounding garden was transformed into a magnificent **botanical park** during the 1930s, the colour-charged floral arrangements supposedly inspired by Chopin's music.

CHOPIN PIANO RECITALS

Piano recitals in Żelazowa Wola take place on weekends throughout the summer (early May to late-Sept Sat & Sun noon & 3pm; free with museum ticket). Concerts take place in the museum's music room, although on fine days the audience sits outside, the music wafting through the open windows.

THE SOCHACZEW–WILCZ TUŁOWSKIE RAILWAY

Ten kilometres southwest of Żelazowa Wola, the town of **Sochaczew** (reached by train from Warsaw) is the starting point for steam-hauled **narrow-gauge railway** excursions to the village of Wilcz Tułowskie, a scenic, 18km-long journey which takes you through forests on the fringes of Kampinoski National Park. Services (29zł per person) run on Saturdays from late May to mid-September (plus Wed & Sun, July & August), departing at 10.30am and arriving just over an hour later, giving you time for a walk in the forest before returning to Sochaczew at 2pm. Further details are available from the **Narrow-Gauge Railway Museum** (Muzeum Kolei Wąskotorowej; ☎ 46 862 5976, ⓦ mkw.e-sochaczew.pl) inside Sochaczew station. The museum itself (Tues–Sun 9am–4.30pm; 12zł) features an impressive line-up of narrow-gauge rolling stock from all over Poland.

2

ARRIVAL AND DEPARTURE

By public transport Take a train from Warsaw (Centralna, Srodmieście or Zachodnia) to the town of Sochaczew, from where bus #6 from the station forecourt trundles (roughly

ŻELAZOWA WOLA

hourly; 20min) to Żelazowa Wola. Getting to Sochaczew from Łódź involves taking a train from Łódź to Łowicz Głowny and changing there.

EATING AND DRINKING

Polka Żelazowa Wola 14 ☎ 46 863 2168. Traditional Polish food in attractively chintzy surroundings – everything

from savoury pancakes with mushrooms (10zł) to roast duck with beetroot (35zł). Daily noon–10pm.

Treblinka

Kosów Lacki, just south of the main Warsaw–Białystok railway line • Daily 9am–7pm • 6zł • ☎ 25 781 1658, ⓦ treblinka-muzeum.eu • Trains run from Warszawa Centralna to Małkinia, 8km north of the camp (hourly; 1hr 10min); there are usually taxis waiting outside Małkinia station (50zł return to Treblinka)

Located in an isolated tract of forest 80km northeast of Warsaw, **TREBLINKA** concentration camp was second only to Auschwitz-Birkenau in the number of victims. However, visiting Treblinka today is a totally different experience from visiting Auschwitz; the Germans did their best to destroy all evidence of the camp's existence, leaving little but tranquil forest and meadow. With a small museum and a dignified collection of memorials, however, it is as profound and moving as any of Poland's World War II memorial sites.

Established in 1941, the **Treblinka I concentration camp** was initially earmarked for Polish and Polish-Jewish slave labour. More than half of the 20,000 held here between 1941 and 1944 were either shot or worked to death in the adjacent gravel pit. In April 1942, construction on the larger **Treblinka II** was started 2km to the east, an extermination camp nearly identical to the one in the Lublin suburb of Majdanek (see page 202). Somewhere between 700,000 and 900,000 people were murdered here between July 1942 and October 1943, the vast majority of whom were Polish Jews (including 250,000–300,000 from the Warsaw ghetto). Thousands of Jews from Greece, Slovakia and elsewhere were also sent here, as well as two thousand Gypsies.

The camp was wound down following an August 1943 **uprising** in which three hundred inmates escaped (forty of whom survived the war). Every trace of the camp's existence was erased – an enormous task that involved the exhumation and incineration of over three-quarters of a million bodies – at the conclusion of which one of the guards was settled on the site to pose as a farmer.

The small **museum** at the entrance to the site contains archive photographs, poignant references to Janusz Korczak, the orphanage director who chose to accompany his orphans to Treblinka rather than save himself, and a chilling scale model of what the camp would have looked like at its greatest extent. A series of **stone memorials** commemorates the murdered: the sea of rough-hewn stones marked with names of places from which the victims came is incredibly powerful. A path leads to Treblinka I, where there are more symbolic tombs in an eerie, barren landscape of overgrown gravel pits.

Gdańsk and the Vistula Delta

SOPOT BEACH

Gdańsk and the Vistula Delta

Even by Polish standards, the northern Tri-City (Trójmiasto) – the dominant conurbation in northern Poland, consisting of Gdańsk, Sopot and Gdynia – is a historical heavyweight, being the place where World War II started with a bang and where the communist dictatorship ended with a whimper fifty years later. But rather than lingering on the past, the region is thundering forward. Two decades of economic boom have ensured rising living standards, improved transport links and a rocketing tourist industry.

Historical heritage remains well to the fore. **Gdańsk**, carefully reconstructed after World War II devastation, is filled with red-brick monuments to its medieval mercantile heyday. Nearby **Sopot**, with its golden beach, has been a tourist magnet for generations and preserves a genteel resort-town feel. The industrial port city of **Gdynia** only appeared on the map in the 1920s, and remains something of an architectural monument to the robustly modernist interwar years. The Tri-City is a good base for exploring neighbouring **Kashubia**, with its rolling hills, lakeside forests and distinctive folk culture. To the north, the **Hel Peninsula** boasts the region's best sandy beaches, while on the other side of the Tri-City is the attractive lagoon-side town of **Frombork** – former home of astronomer Nicolaus Copernicus. South from Gdańsk, a collection of Teutonic castles dot the banks of the Vistula and its tributaries. Highlights include the huge fortress at **Malbork**, once the headquarters of the Teutonic Knights, and, further south, the spectacular medieval architecture of **Toruń**. Also in the south is **Bydgoszcz**, with a historical mill district now beautifully restored.

Gdańsk

To outsiders, **GDAŃSK** was probably, until a decade or two ago, the most familiar city in Poland. The home of Lech Wałęsa, Solidarity and the former Lenin Shipyards, its images flashed across news bulletins during the 1980s, and the harsh industrial landscape of the harbour area fulfils expectations. By contrast, the streets of the town centre are lined with tall, narrow merchants' houses dating back to Gdańsk's days as a key member of the Hanseatic League. Many of these historic buildings have been restored, and are steadily filling up with bars, restaurants and shops, giving the city an ebbulient, forward-looking feel.

Before 1945, Gdańsk (or **Danzig,** as it was then) was a primarily German-speaking place that enjoyed cultural contacts with the whole of northern Europe – indeed the city centre looks not unlike Amsterdam. The postwar years marked a radical demographic shift, with the Germans forced out and replaced with Poles from the east. Germans are returning in numbers now, chiefly as tourists and business people, making an important contribution to the city's rapid emergence as one of Poland's economic powerhouses.

THE ELBLĄG–OSTRÓDA CANAL

Highlights

❶ Main Town, Gdańsk An archetypal north European port, full of imposing Gothic architecture, fog-bound quays and buzzing nightlife. See page 117

❷ European Solidarity Centre, Gdańsk This inspiring museum is a temple to non-violent revolution. See page 122

❸ Gdynia The former ugly duckling of the Tri-City now boasts compelling museums, unsung beaches and several great places to drink. See page 132

❹ Hel This quaint fishing village provides easy access to pristine beaches. See page 136

❺ Kashubia The rolling countryside west of Gdańsk is dotted with lakes and picturesque

villages, and endowed with a distinct local culture. See page 138

❻ Elbląg–Ostróda Canal Go on a boat trip with a difference – boats are hauled uphill on an intricate railway, part of one of the most ingenious systems of locks and slipways in Europe. See page 140

❼ Malbork Castle For centuries the headquarters of the Teutonic Knights, this monumental thirteenth-century castle dominates the banks of the Vistula. See page 143

❽ Toruń The traditional home of Polish gingerbread, this cultured university town is packed with exquisite medieval buildings. See page 148

HIGHLIGHTS ARE MARKED ON THE MAP ON PAGE 114

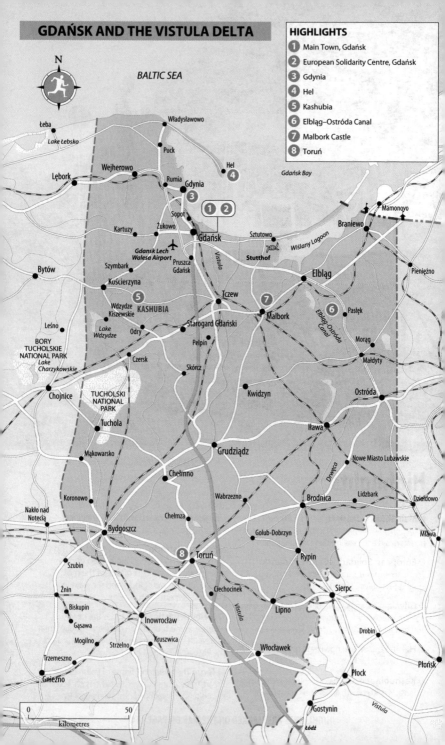

The historic **Main Town** holds most of the city's sights and is the obvious starting point for exploration; the **Old Town** (Stare Miasto), across the thin ribbon of the Raduna Canal, is the natural progression. The main focus for visitors to the third, southern quarter, the **Old Suburb** (Stare Przedmieście), is the National Museum. North along the Motława, **Westerplatte** – and its monument commemorating the outbreak of World War II – can be reached by boat from the central waterfront, a trip that allows good views of the famous **shipyards**. Moving north you'll hit the Oliwa suburb, whose cathedral is one of the city's most distinctive landmarks.

Brief history

The city's position near the meeting point of the River Vistula and the Baltic has long made Gdańsk an immense strategic asset: in the words of Frederick the Great, whoever controlled it could be considered "more master of Poland than any king ruling there". First settled in the **tenth century**, the city rose to prominence when the Teutonic Knights arrived in 1308, massacring the locals and installing a colony of German settlers in their place.

The city's economy flourished, and with the end of the knights' rule in the **mid-fifteenth century** – accompanied by the brick-by-brick dismantling of their castle by the city's inhabitants – Gdańsk (or Danzig as it was known to its predominantly German-speaking inhabitants) became to all intents and purposes an independent city-state. It had its own legislature, judiciary and trade monopolies, restricted only by the necessity of paying homage and taxes to the Polish monarch.

The Renaissance in Gdańsk

Gdańsk/Danzig's main period of development occurred between the **sixteenth century** and the Partitions of the **late eighteenth century**, as the burghers brought in Dutch and Flemish architects to design buildings that would express the city's self-confidence. A climate of religious tolerance allowed an influx of foreign merchants, notably Scottish Protestants fleeing religious persecution at home. The following century yielded two of the city's most famous sons: astronomer Jan Heweliusz (Johannes Hevelius), who spent most of his life here; and Daniel Fahrenheit, inventor of the mercury thermometer.

Annexation and the world wars

Prussian annexation of the city following the Partitions abruptly severed the connection with Poland and Gdańsk/Danzig's access to the lucrative Polish wheat market. Territorial status changed again after **World War I** and the recovery of Polish independence. The Treaty of Versailles created the semi-autonomous **Free City of Danzig**, squeezed between German-dominated West Prussia and the Polish port of Gdynia. This arrangement provided Hitler with one of his major propaganda themes in the 1930s and a pretext for attacking Poland: the German assault unleashed on the Polish garrison at Westerplatte on September 1, 1939 was the first engagement of **World War II**. It was not until March 1945 that Danzig was liberated, after massive Soviet bombardment.

Postwar Gdańsk

The **postwar era** brought communist rule, the expulsion of the ethnic German majority and a formal change of name from Danzig to Gdańsk. Parts of the centre were meticulously reconstructed and the shipbuilding industry revitalized. As the **communist era** began to crack at the edges, however, the shipyards became the harbingers of a new reality. Riots in Gdańsk and neighbouring Gdynia in 1970 were important precursors to the historic 1980 **Lenin Shipyards strike**, which led to the creation of **Solidarity** (see page 121). The shipyards remained at the centre of resistance to General Jaruzelski's government, the last major strike wave in January 1989 precipitating the Round Table negotiations that heralded the end of communist rule.

3

3

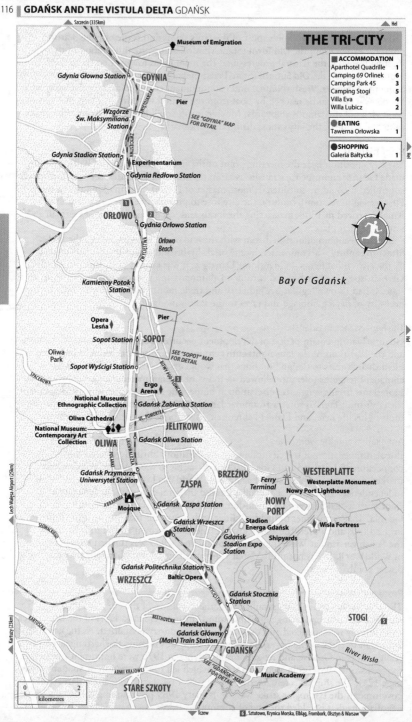

Szczecin (335km)

Hel

THE TRI-CITY

ACCOMMODATION

Aparthotel Quadrille	1
Camping 69 Orlinek	6
Camping Park 45	3
Camping Stogi	5
Villa Eva	4
Willa Lubicz	2

EATING

| Tawerna Orłowska | 1 |

SHOPPING

| Galeria Bałtycka | 1 |

Museum of Emigration

Gdynia Głowna Station

GDYNIA

Pier

SEE "GDYNIA" MAP FOR DETAIL

Wzgórze Św. Maksymiliana Station

Gdynia Stadion Station

Experimentarium

Gdynia Redłowo Station

ORŁOWO

Gydnia Orłowo Station

Orłowo Beach

Kamienny Potok Station

Bay of Gdańsk

Opera Leśna

Sopot Station

SOPOT

Pier

SEE "SOPOT" MAP FOR DETAIL

Oliwa Park

Sopot Wyścigi Station

Ergo Arena

National Museum: Ethnographic Collection

Gdańsk Żabianka Station

Oliwa Cathedral

JELITKOWO

National Museum: Contemporary Art Collection

OLIWA

Gdańsk Oliwa Station

Gdańsk Przymorze-Uniwersytet Station

ZASPA

BRZEŹNO

Ferry Terminal

WESTERPLATTE

Westerplatte Monument

Nowy Port Lighthouse

NOWY PORT

Mosque

Gdańsk Zaspa Station

Gdańsk Wrzeszcz Station

Stadion Energa Gdańsk

Wisła Fortress

Shipyards

Gdańsk Stadion Expo Station

Gdańsk Politechnika Station

WRZESZCZ

Baltic Opera

Gdańsk Stocznia Station

STOGI

Hewelanium

Gdańsk Główny (Main) Train Station

GDAŃSK

River Wisła

SEE "GDAŃSK" MAP FOR DETAIL

Music Academy

STARE SZKOTY

Tczew

Sztutowo, Krynica Morska, Elbląg, Frombork, Olsztyn & Warsaw

Lech Wałęsa Airport (25km)

Kartuzy (23km)

N

0   2
kilometres

Following the traumas of "shock therapy", the reform programme pursued with vigour in the **early 1990s**, Gdańsk blossomed economically, also profiting from the boom in **tourism** in the first decade of the twenty-first century. Such new-found economic optimism didn't extend to the famous shipyards, however, which have been denied state subsidies due to EU regulations and have cut their capacity drastically as a result. A much reduced shipbuilding industry still exists here, and the yards themselves have become the target of major regeneration schemes which will, in time, see the emergence of new residential and nightlife areas.

The Main Town

The largest of Gdańsk's historic quarters, the **Main Town** (Główne Miasto), preserves the appearance and atmosphere of a Hansa merchants' settlement. The layout, typical of a medieval port, comprises a tight network of streets, bounded on four sides by water and main roads – the Raduna Canal and River Motława to the north and east, Podwale Przedmiejskie and Wały Jagiellońskie to the south and west. Much of what you see today is a reconstruction; fighting between German and Russian forces in May 1945 destroyed ninety percent of Gdańsk's city centre and sixty percent of the suburbs.

Ulica Długa and Długi Targ

Ulica Długa, the main thoroughfare, and **Długi Targ**, the wide, open square to its east, create a natural focus of attention, with huge gateways guarding both entrances. The Upland Gate (see below) was the starting point of the "royal route" used by Polish monarchs on their annual state visits: they would pass from here through the richly decorated **Golden Gate** (Brama Złota) alongside **St George's Court** (Dwór św. Jerzego), a fine Gothic mansion with a statuette of St George and the Dragon on its roof. From here, ulica Długa leads down to the town hall, past several gabled facades worth studying in detail, including the sixteenth-century **Ferber Mansion** (Dom Ferberów; no. 28) and the imposing **Lion's Castle** (Lwi Zamek; no. 35), where King Władysław IV entertained local dignitaries.

Upland Gate and the Amber Museum

Targ Węglowy 26 • Amber Museum: Tues 10am–1pm, Wed & Fri–Sun 10am–4pm, Thurs 10am–6pm • 12zł • ☎ 58 573 3128, ⓦ mhmg.pl
Before the western entrance to Długa stands the outer **Upland Gate** (Brama Wyżynna), once the main entrance to Gdańsk; it was built in the late sixteenth century, when it spanned the city moat as part of the town's outer fortifications. The three coats of arms emblazoned across the archway – Poland, Prussia and Gdańsk – encapsulate the city's history. Exiting the gate, you walk through the attached Gothic **prison tower**, which once housed the city's torture chambers. Today it is home to the **Amber Museum** (Muzeum Bursztynu), which has a dazzling collection of amber – forty-million-year-old fossilized pine resin – and detailed information about the immense importance of the amber trade to the region. Some of the pieces have flies, mosquitoes, and in one case a small lizard, trapped inside.

Uphagen Mansion

ul. Długa 12 • Mon 10am–1pm, Tues–Sat 10am–6pm, Sun 11am–6pm • 10zł; free on Mon • ☎ 789 449 664, ⓦ mhmg.pl
One of the few houses open to the public along the bottom stretch of ulica Długa is the **Uphagen Mansion** (Dom Uphagena), former home of a leading Gdańsk merchant dynasty, which was rebuilt and refurnished in late eighteenth-century style after World War II. The reception rooms on the first floor are particularly elegant, each boasting original carved wooden panels on a different theme.

The Town Hall and the Historical Museum

ul. Długa 46 • Historical Museum: Mon 10am–1pm, Tues–Sat 10am–6pm, Sun 11am–6pm • 12zł; free on Mon • ☎ 58 573 3128, ⓦ mhmg.pl

Topped by a golden statue of King Sigismund August, the huge tower of the **town hall** (Ratusz Głównego Miasta) makes a powerful impact. Originally constructed in the late fourteenth century, with the tower and spire added later, the building was badly damaged during the last war, but the restoration was so skilful you'd hardly believe it. It now houses the **Historical Museum** (Muzeum Historyczne), but the lavish decoration almost upstages the exhibits on display. The highlight of the **Red Room** (Sala Czerwona), the main council chamber, is the central oval ceiling painting by Dutchman Isaac van den Block depicting *The Glorification of the Unity of Gdańsk with*

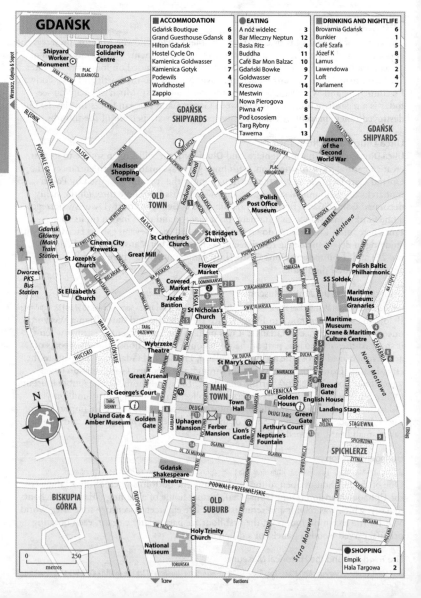

ACCOMMODATION			EATING			DRINKING AND NIGHTLIFE	
Gdańsk Boutique	6		A nóż widelec	3		Brovarnia Gdańsk	6
Grand Guesthouse Gdansk	8		Bar Mleczny Neptun	12		Bunkier	1
Hilton Gdańsk	2		Basia Ritz	4		Café Szafa	5
Hostel Cycle On	9		Buddha	11		Józef K	8
Kamienica Goldwasser	5		Café Bar Mon Balzac	10		Lamus	3
Kamienica Gotyk	7		Gdański Bowke	9		Lawendowa	2
Podewils	4		Goldwasser	7		Loft	4
Worldhostel	1		Kresowa	14		Parlament	7
Zappio	3		Mestwin	13			
			Nowa Pierogova	6			
			Piwna 47	8			
			Pod Łososiem	5			
			Targ Rybny	1			
			Tawerna	13			

GDAŃSK

SHOPPING	
Empik	1
Hala Targowa	2

Poland. Other rooms have haunting photographs of the city in 1945 after it had been almost completely flattened. The **upper floor** has reconstructions of shops and homes in the Free City of Danzig in the 1920s and '30s, and allows access to the **tower**, from where there are excellent views across the rooftops to the harbour.

Arthur's Court

Długi Targ 43/44 • Mon 10am–3pm, Tues–Sat 10am–6pm, Sun 11am–6pm • 10zł; free on Mon • ☏ 789 449 654, ⓦ mhmg.pl

Even in a street that's stuffed with fine mansions, **Arthur's Court** (Dwór Artusa) is a little bit special. The origins of the building date back to the fourteenth century, a period marked by a widespread interest in Arthurian legend. European merchants began establishing their own courts on the model of Camelot, entertaining in the chivalrous and egalitarian spirit of Arthur's knights. Founded in 1350, the Gdańsk court grew rapidly to become one of the most fabulous in Europe. An array of guild-based brotherhoods established their own benches in the main hall, becoming what was effectively northern Europe's first non-sectarian meeting place, combining the functions of guild house, civic hall, judicial court and reception centre for foreign guests. Mercifully, much of the court's rich interior was removed for safekeeping at the beginning of World War II: sections of the ceiling are original, as is the "Great Stove", a huge Renaissance ceramic oven.

Neptune Fountain and the Golden House

Immediately outside Arthur's Court is the wonderful **Neptune Fountain** (Fontanna Neptuna), with water trickling from the very tips of the god's trident. Continuing just to the south, you'll come to the **Golden House** (Złota Kamieniczka), an impressive Renaissance mansion named after the luminous gilding that covers its elegant four-storeyed facade.

The waterfront

At the eastern end of ulica Długa, the archways of the **Green Gate** (Brama Zielona), a former royal residence for the annual visit, open directly onto the **waterfront**. The adjacent bridge over the River Motława has good views looking north: to the right are the old granaries on **Spichlerze** island (there used to be over three hundred of them), and to the left is the old harbour quay, now a promenade.

Maritime Museum

Jan–June & Sept–Nov Tues–Sun 10am–4pm (Maritime Culture Centre till 6pm Sat & Sun); July & Aug daily 10am–6pm; Dec Tues–Sun 10am–3pm • Crane, Granaries and Sołdek each 8zł, or 18zł for all three (includes ferry ride across the Motława); People-Ports-Ships 8zł; Boats of the People of the World 6zł • ☏ 58 301 8611, ⓦ nmm.pl

The **Maritime Museum** (Muzeum Morskie) sprawls across both sides of the Motława. Forming part of the museum on the west bank is a massive and partly original fifteenth-century **crane** (Żuraw), the biggest in medieval Europe. Inside the crane, as well as the massive lifting gear used to unload goods at the harbourside, is an exhibition describing port life in the prosperous sixteenth to eighteenth centuries. Next to the crane, the **Maritime Culture Centre** houses two permanent exhibitions: **Boats of the People of the World**, featuring vessels from around the world; and **People-Ships-Ports**, covering storms and life at sea. The latter includes plenty of interactive elements, allowing you to sail remote-controlled model boats or take the wheel of a virtual ship.

Just across the Motława (connected by ferry; 1zł), another section of the museum is housed in three Renaissance **granaries**. Here there are extensive displays on Poland's history as a seafaring nation, sweeping right through from the earliest Slav settlements along the Vistula to the late twentieth century, taking in an exhibit on underwater archeology and astonishingly detailed models of ships along the way. Back out on the quayside you can explore the sturdy-looking **Sołdek**, the first steamship built in Gdańsk after World War II.

Ulica Mariacka

All the streets heading back into the town from the waterfront are worth exploring. **Ulica Mariacka** is a charmingly atmospheric and meticulously reconstructed street of spindly iron railings and dragon-faced gutter spouts, its gabled terraced houses now occupied by expensive amber jewellery shops and stylish cafés.

St Mary's Church

ul. Mariacka • **Church** Mon–Sat 8.30am–6.30pm, Sun 11am–noon & 1–6.30pm; Oct–April closes 5.30pm • 4zł • **Tower** Daily: April, May, Oct & Nov 9am–5.30pm; June–Sept 9am–8.30pm • 8zł

At the western end of ulica Mariacka stands the gigantic **St Mary's Church** (Kościół Mariacki), reputedly the biggest brick church in the world. Estimates that it could fit 20,000 people inside were substantiated during the early days of Martial Law, when huge crowds crammed the cold, whitewashed interior. The south aisle is dominated by a copy of the miraculous **Madonna of the Gates of Dawn** from Wilno (now Vilnius in Lithuania), many of whose Polish inhabitants ended up in Gdańsk in 1945, replacing the departing German population. The **high altar**, reconstructed after the war, is a powerful sixteenth-century triptych featuring a *Coronation of the Virgin*. Of the chapels scattered round the church, two of the most striking are the **Chapel of 11,000 Virgins**, with a tortured Gothic crucifix – the artist was said to have nailed his son-in-law to a cross as a model – and **St Anne's Chapel**, containing the wooden *Beautiful Madonna of Gdańsk* from around 1415. A curiosity is the reconstructed fifteenth-century **astronomical clock**, which tells not only the day, month and year but the whole saints' calendar and the phases of the moon; when completed in 1470 it was the world's tallest clock. If you're feeling fit, make sure you climb the 402 steps up to the rickety viewing platform on top of the church **tower**.

Polish Post Office Museum

ul. Obroncow Poczty Polskiej 1/2 • Tues 10am–1pm, Wed, Fri & Sat 10am–4pm, Thurs 10am–6pm, Sun 11am–4pm • 8zł • ☎ 58 301 7611, ⓦ mhmg.pl

Towards the northern end of the Main Town is the **old post office** building, immortalized by Günter Grass in *The Tin Drum*, and rebuilt after World War II. It was here, in September 1939, that a small contingent of employees of the Free City's Poczta Polska (Polish Post Office) battled it out with German forces. As at Westerplatte (see page 124), the Germans clearly weren't anticipating such spirited resistance; despite the overwhelmingly superior firepower ranged against them, the Poles held out for nine hours, finally surrendering when the Nazis sent in flame-throwers. The whole event is commemmorated by the small **Polish Post Office Museum** (Muzeum Poczty Polskiej w Gdańsku) inside the post office, with a stirring collection of photographs, and an absorbing section on the history of the postal service.

Museum of the Second World War

pl. W. Bartoszewskiego 1 • Tues–Sun 10am–7pm, last admission 5pm • 23zł • ☎ 58 323 7520, ⓦ muzeum1939.pl

A slanting structure that appears to be toppling into the Raduna Canal, the **Museum of the Second World War** (Muzeum II Wojny Światowej) is one of the most dramatic modern buildings in Europe, never mind Gdańsk. The upper, protruding stories are given over to offices and conference spaces, and visitors descend by lift or stairs to find the permanent exhibition, which stretches underground. It's not just the museum's architecture that has proved controversial: its permanent exhibition – designed to show the history of World War II from an international perspective (with a particular focus on civilians) – was considered insufficiently Polish by the government that came to power in 2015, and the curatorial team responsible for putting it together was dismissed. For the time being, the display continues to follow the narrative intended by its original creators. Using films, graphics, personal memories and dramatic use of exhibits (for instance a whole tank in a recreated city street), it's a tour-de-force of history-telling,

SOLIDARITY AND THE SHIPYARDS

It was in **August 1980** that a protest about sacked shipyard workers rapidly developed into a sit-in strike, leadership of which quickly fell to charismatic electrician **Lech Wałęsa**. The strikers won considerable concessions from the Polish government, most importantly the right to form the Soviet bloc's first ever independent trade union, **Solidarity** (Solidarność). The event had been preceded by riots in **1970**, when workers took to the streets in protest at price rises, setting fire to the Party headquarters after police opened fire; 45 people were killed. Riots erupted again in 1976, once more in protest at price rises on basic foodstuffs.

Even after the imposition of Martial Law in 1981, the Gdańsk workers remained in the vanguard of political protest: strikes here in 1988 and 1989 led to the Round Table Talks that culminated with the communists relinquishing absolute power.

in which almost every visitor can find something they can relate to – whether in the destroyed cities of mainland Europe or the London Blitz. The exhibition in its original form makes no bones about the cataclysmic impact of illiberal regimes on peaceful coexistence, human rights and civic society – which is probably why the right-wing radicals of today don't like it. What it might look like in a few years' time – and how much of the original exhibition might be retained – is something nobody knows.

The Old Town

Crossing the canal bridge brings you into the **Old Town** (Stare Miasto), altogether a patchier and less reconstructed area, characterized by a jumbled mix of old and new buildings. As you move further in from the Main Town, merchants' mansions increasingly give way to postwar housing.

The Great Mill
ul. Wielkie Młyny 16

Dominating the waterside is the seven-storey **Great Mill** (Wielki Młyn), the biggest mill in medieval Europe, built in the mid-fourteenth century by the Teutonic Knights. Its eighteen races milled corn for six hundred years; even in the 1930s it was still grinding out two hundred tons of flour a day. Previously a shopping mall, the mill has been earmarked as future exhibition space for the Amber Museum (see page 117).

Church of St Catherine
ul. Profesorska 3

Immediately opposite the Great Mill is the fourteenth-century brick **Church of St Catherine** (Kościół św. Katarzyny), the former parish church of the Old Town and one of the nicest in the city. The astronomer Johannes Hevelius and his family are buried here in a tomb in the choir.

The shipyards

Looming over the city from most angles you'll see the cranes of the famous **Gdańsk Shipyards** (Stocznia Gdańska), once known as the Lenin Shipyards. Along with the Nowa Huta steelworks outside Kraków, this was the crucible of the political struggles of the 1980s.

Monument to the Fallen Shipyard Workers

The square in front of the shipyard gates, plac Solidarności, is dominated by a set of towering steel crosses, a **monument** to workers killed during the shipyard riots of 1970 (see above). It was inaugurated in 1980 in the presence of Party, Church and opposition leaders.

European Solidarity Centre

pl. Solidarności 1 • Daily: May–Sept 10am–8pm; Oct–April 10am–6pm • 20zł • ☎ 58 772 4112, ⓦ ecs.gda.pl

The story of Solidarity's pivotal role in Poland's recent history is told in the **European Solidarity Centre** (Europejskie Centrum Solidarności), a bold contemporary building fashioned from rust-coloured corten steel that stands right beside the shipyard gates. The historical narrative is brought to life through a mixture of news clips, photographs, crackly recordings of strikers' songs and some telling historical relics – such as the bullet-perforated jacket of a participant in the 1970 strikes. The exhibition is not just constrained to Poland either: anti-communist uprisings in Berlin (1953) and Budapest (1956) also get fair coverage, and there's a comprehensive overview of the peaceful revolutions that swept across Eastern Europe in the late 1980s.

Hewelianum

ul. Gradowa 6; accessible via steps from behind the bus station • Most exhibitions Tues–Sun 10am–4pm; check website • Time Machine exhibition free; other exhibitions 15zł • ☎ 58 742 3352, ⓦ hewelianum.pl

Making much of the heritage of Gdańsk-born astronomer Johaness Hevelius (1611–87), the **Hewelianum** is an ambitious science-and-education attraction built into the dramatic red-brick environs of **Góra Gradowa**, a seventeenth-century hilltop fortress rising just behind the train and bus stations. Using hands-on exhibits and audio-visual displays to illustrate the laws of physics and the sweep of Earth's history, it also makes good use of the extensive complex of military buildings in which it is located, with different sections arranged around a central courtyard. Occupying the former mortar battery, **Time Machine** displays antique cannon alongside touch-screen displays allowing you to fire their virtual equivalents. Other sections include **Around the World**, which covers geology, volcanoes and the world's oceans with a feast of digital visuals; the **Energy Laboratory**, which introduces the world of machines and technologies; and the **Imagination Jungle**, which invites younger kids to construct environments of their own with an array of large blue building blocks. The fortress ramparts provide fantastic views of the city centre.

Old Suburb

Old Suburb (Stare Przedmieście), the lower part of old Gdańsk, was the limit of the original town, as testified by the ring of seventeenth-century bastions running east from plac Wałowy over the Motława. It's an unspectacular area of broad highways and blocky communist-era buildings; apart from the National Museum, there's little to keep you here.

National Museum in Gdańsk: Old Art Collection

ul. Toruńska 1 • May–Aug Tues, Wed & Fri–Sun 10am–5pm, Thurs noon–7pm; Sept Tues–Sun 10am–5pm; Oct–April Tues–Fri 9am–4pm, Sat & Sun 10am–5pm • 10zł; free on Fri • ☎ 58 301 7061, ⓦ mng.gda.pl

The main attraction of Old Suburb is the **National Museum in** Gdańsk: Old Art Collection (Muzeum Narodowe w Gdańsku: Oddział ztuki Dawnej), housed in a former Franciscan monastery. There's a wealth of Gothic art and sculpture here, all redolent of the town's former riches. The museum's most famous work is Hans Memling's colossal *Last Judgement* triptych (1471), depicting Jesus overseeing St Michael weighing souls, with the saved entering heaven and the damned being dragged to hell by demons. Look closely at St Michael's belt and you'll see the reflection of people viewing the painting – involving you in the scene too. The work has something of a chequered past: it was commissioned by the Medici family banker in Florence, then diverted to Gdańsk by pirates, looted by Napoleon, moved to Berlin, returned to Gdańsk, stolen by the Nazis and finally, after being discovered by the Red Army, hidden in the Thuringian hills, to be returned to Gdańsk by the Russians in 1956.

VIEW OF ULICA DŁUGA FROM THE GOLDEN GATE

TOUR BOATS TO WESTERPLATTE

The most fun way to get to Westerplatte is on one of the **tour boats** that leave from near the Green Gate (April–Nov: hourly 10am–4pm; 45zł return). Taking about thirty minutes each way, the trip provides an excellent view of the **shipyards** and the array of international vessels anchored there; en route it passes the sturdy, fifteenth-century **Wisła Fortress** (Twierdza Wisłoujście), later reinforced by Napoleon's forces. If you have children in tow, consider taking a cruise to Westerplatte on the *Lew* or Czarna *Perla* galleons (May–Oct: hourly 9am–7pm; 45zł return), which also depart from near the Green Gate.

Westerplatte and Nowy Port

It was at **Westerplatte**, the promontory guarding the harbour entrance, that the German battleship *Schleswig-Holstein* fired the first salvo of World War II on September 1, 1939. For a full week the garrison of 170 badly equipped Poles held off the combined assault of aircraft, heavy guns and over 3000 German troops, setting the tone for the Poles' response to the subsequent Nazi–Soviet invasion. Facing Westerplatte across the river is the suburb of **Nowy Port**, home to one of the Baltic's most graceful lighthouses.

Westerplatte Museum and Monument

Museum: May–Sept daily 10am–4pm • 5zł • ☎ 58 765 1844, ⓦ westerplatte.eu • Bus #106 from ul. Lakowa, water tram #5 (May–Sept) from Green Gate, or tour boat (see page 124)

The ruined army guardhouse and barracks of the Battle of Westerplatte still exist, and one of the surviving buildings houses a small **museum** chronicling the momentous events of September 1939. Beyond the museum it's a fifteen-minute walk to the main **Westerplatte Monument**, a grim 1960s slab whose symbolism conveys a tangible sense of history. The green surroundings of the exposed peninsula make for an enjoyable walk to the coast, with good views out onto the Baltic.

Nowy Port lighthouse

ul. Przemysłowa 6a • May–Aug daily 10am–7pm; Sept Sat & Sun 10am–5pm • 10zł • ☎ 601 150 251, ⓦ latarnia.gda.pl • Tram #5, or water tram #5 (May–Sept) from Green Gate

The elegant nineteenth-century **lighthouse** in Nowy Port, across the river from Westerplatte, is topped by a time ball that was dropped at noon every day to allow captains to reset their chronometers; now you can see it drop four times a day, at noon, 2pm, 4pm and 6pm. From the top there's a great view of Westerplatte and the Baltic and back over the shipyards to the city.

Oliwa

There are several good reasons to venture out to the modern suburb of **Oliwa**, the northernmost part of Gdańsk. One is its **cathedral**, one of the best-known buildings in the city. Forming part of the same complex are two branches of the National Museum, while surrounding it is the old palace **park**, an appealing spot with an enjoyable collection of exotic trees, hanging willows and a stream meandering through the middle.

Oliwa Cathedral

ul. Nowickiego 5 • **Cathedral** Mon–Sat 9am–6pm, Sun 2–6pm • Free • **Organ recitals** May, June & Sept Mon–Sat hourly 10am–1pm, Sun at 3pm & 4pm; July & Aug Mon–Fri hourly 10am–1pm & 3–5pm, Sat hourly 10am–3pm, Sun at 3pm, 4pm & 5pm; Oct–April Mon–Sat at noon, Sun at 3pm • Free • ☎ 58 552 4765, ⓦ archikatedraoliwa.pl

Unlike most of its surroundings, **Oliwa Cathedral** (Katedra Oliwska) miraculously came through the end of World War II largely unscathed, and today the restored complex is a remarkable sight. The towering main **facade** combines twin Gothic brick towers peaked with Renaissance spires and dazzling Rococo stuccowork to unusually striking effect. Originally part of the monastery founded by Danish Cistercians, the cathedral has seen its fair share of action over the years. The Teutonic Knights repeatedly ransacked the place in the 1240s and 1250s, a fire in the 1350s led to a major Gothic-style overhaul, and the Swedish army carried off much of the cathedral's sumptuous furnishings in 1626. The Oliwa Peace Treaty with Sweden (1660), signed in the abbey hall, was followed by lavish refurbishment of the building – notably the organ, begun in 1755. The Prussian Partition-era takeover of Gdańsk spelt the end of the abbey's glory days, the monastery finally being officially abolished in 1831.

The interior

The fine late seventeenth-century portal brings you into the lofty central **nave**, an exuberant structure topped by a star-spangled vaulted ceiling supported on arched pillars. The eye is drawn to the **high altar**, a sumptuous Baroque piece from the 1680s containing several pictures from the Gdańsk workshops of the period. Above it rises a deliciously over-the-top decorative ensemble, a swirling mass of cherubs being sucked into a heavenly whirlpool, with gilded sun rays breaking out in all directions.

The building's finest feature, however, is the exuberantly decorated eighteenth-century **organ**, which in its day was the largest instrument in Europe – seven men were needed to operate the bellows. The dark oak is ornamented with a mass of Rococo woodcarving, the whole instrument framing a stained-glass window of Mary and Child. With its sonorous tone and wealth of moving parts, including trumpet-blowing angels, it's a truly beautiful instrument – there are daily ribcage-rippling recitals to show it off.

National Museum in Gdańsk: Contemporary Art Collection

ul. Cystersów 18 • May–Sept Tues, Wed & Fri–Sun 10am–5pm, Thurs noon–7pm; Oct–April Tues–Fri 9am–4pm, Sat & Sun 10am–5pm • 10zł; free on Fri • ☎ 58 552 1271, ⓦ mng.gda.pl

Passing through the gateway down the lane alongside the cathedral brings you to the stately **Abbots' Palace**, which now houses the **National Museum in Gdańsk: Contemporary Art Collection** (Oddział Sztuki Nowoczesnej). Upstairs is an enjoyable gallery of twentieth-century Polish art, the centrepiece being a large selection of 1960s Pop Art and conceptual sculptures – a demonstration of how postwar Polish art escaped the ideological fetters of communist cultural policy.

National Museum in Gdańsk: Ethnographic Collection

ul. Cystersów 19 • May–Sept Tues, Wed & Fri–Sun 10am–5pm, Thurs noon–7pm; Oct–April Tues–Fri 9am–4pm, Sat & Sun 10am–5pm • 8zł; free on Fri • ☎ 58 552 1271, ⓦ mng.gda.pl

Across the courtyard from the Abbots' Palace, an old granary contains the **National Museum in Gdańsk: Ethnographic Collection** (Oddział Etnografii), a collection of furniture, handicrafts and fishing and farmyard tools from across the region. Emphasis is on the cultural minorities of Pomerania, Kashubia and surrounding areas, as well as on traditions imported by migrants from the eastern borderlands – now Ukraine, Belarus and Lithuania – after World War II.

ARRIVAL AND DEPARTURE   GDAŃSK

By plane Gdańsk Lech Wałęsa airport (information ☎ 525 673 531, ⓦ airport.gdansk.pl) is about 15km west of the city. The airport is connected to Gdańsk Główny train station by local SKM trains (5am–10.45pm roughly hourly; change at Gdańsk-Wrzesczc for Sopot and Gdynia Główna) or by bus #210 (5am–10.30pm; hourly Mon–Fri, twice hourly Sat & Sun); buy a bus ticket (3zł; valid for 45min from validation) from the news kiosk or the driver (exact change required) and punch it when you get on the bus. A taxi into town from the rank outside the airport costs around 70zł.

By train The main train station is Gdańsk Główny, a lovely red-brick pile 10min walk west of the old city.

Destinations Białystok (2 daily; 6hr 40min); Bydgoszcz (10 daily; 1hr 55min); Elbląg (hourly; 55min–1hr 30min); Hel (6 daily; 2hr 30min); Kartuzy (hourly; 1hr); Katowice (3 daily; 5hr 30min); Kraków (5 daily; 5hr 30min); Malbork (every 30min; 30–55min); Olsztyn (4 daily; 2hr 15min–2hr 50min); Poznań (4 daily; 3hr 45min–4hr); Szczecin (4 daily; 5hr); Toruń (6 daily; 3hr–3hr 30min); Warsaw (12 daily; 3hr 15min); Wrocław (3 daily; 6hr 20min).

By bus The dilapidated bus station, Dworzec Autobusowy (☎ 58 302 1532, ⓦ pks.gdansk.pl), is located on ul. 3 Maja, accessible via pedestrian subway from the train station.

Destinations Elbląg (12 daily; 1hr 30min); Kartuzy (hourly; 1hr); Sztutowo (hourly; 1hr 10min).

By boat Tourist boats (☎58 301 4926, ⊛zegluga.pl; 40zł) run from the Green Gate to Hel several times a day in summer, although they're often fully reserved well in advance. The Nowy Port ferry terminal, for boats to Sweden, is 6km north of the city centre; tram #7 runs to the bus station, right next to the train station.

Destinations Hel (May Sat & Sun only, June–Aug daily; 2hr); Nynäshamn (Sweden; 3 weekly; overnight; 18hr).

GETTING AROUND

By train The Tri-City's local train service, Szybka Kolej Miejska (SKM; ⊛skm.pkp.pl), connects Gdańsk Główny, Sopot (20min) and Gdynia (35min), with plenty of stops in between, including the suburb of Oliwa. Spurs of the network also run as far as Słupsk in the north (see page 448) and Gdańsk Airport to the west, although services on these stretches are not as frequent. Services on the main Gdańsk–Sopot–Gdynia stretch run roughly every 10min during the day, with services thinning out to once every hour or so in the early hours. Tickets, which must be validated before you get on the train, can be bought in the passage beneath the main station or from ticket machines on station platforms.

By tram, trolleybus and bus The municipal transport network (⊛ztm.gda.pl) consists of trams, running within all districts of Gdańsk; trolleybuses in Sopot and Gdynia; and buses across all three cities. Tickets can be bought from news kiosks, ticket machines near major stops or from the driver (exact change only), and must be validated upon entry. A full-fare ticket, valid for one journey, costs 3.20zł; a 3.80zł ticket, valid for a ride of up to 1hr, includes transfers. A 24hr ticket costs 13zł.

By water tram Water trams (⊛ztm.gda.pl) run on two routes in summer (May–Sept). The F5 sails from Żabi kruk to Nowy Port, calling at Green Gate, Targ Rybny and Westerplatte on the way; while F6 cruises from Targ Rybny to the National Sailing Centre in Stogi, east of the city. A single ticket costs 10zł. Current timetables are posted at landing stages.

By taxi Reliable taxi firms include Hello (☎58 301 5959, ⊛hallotaxi.gda.pl) and Neptun (☎58 511 1555, ⊛neptuntaxi.pl).

INFORMATION

Tourist information The city's tourist office at Długi Targ 28/29 (June & Aug daily 9am–7pm; Sept–May Mon–Sat 9am–5pm, Sun 9am–4pm; ☎505 877 021, ⊛visitgdansk.pl) has a good supply of maps and brochures and can make hotel reservations.

PROT (Pomorska Regionalna Organizacja Turystyczna) In the Upper Gate, ul. Wały Jagiellonskie 2a (☎58 732 7049); has a wealth of information on the Tri-City, Kashubia and the Baltic Coast.

ACCOMMODATION

HOTELS AND PENSIONS

Gdańsk Boutique ul. Szafarnia 9 ☎58 300 1717, ⊛hotelgdansk.com.pl; map page 118. Upmarket hotel housed in a seventeenth-century granary across the river from the Main Town, offering plush rooms filled with rich fabrics, exposed beams and old photos of Gdańsk. **750zł**

Grand Guesthouse Gdansk ul. Długa 4 ☎666 061 350, ⊛grandguesthouse.pl; map page 118. Bright, simple doubles (some en suite) and a small kitchen/social area in a restored townhouse right in the city centre. **230zł**

★ **Hilton Gdańsk** Targ Rybny 1 ☎58 778 7100, ⊛hiltongdansk.pl; map page 118. A suave riverside five-star that delivers the across-the-board comforts you would expect from the brand. Many rooms have fantastic views of the Motława (ask when booking), and there's a top-floor swimming pool. **800zł**

★ **Kamienica Goldwasser** ul. Długie Pobrzeże 22 ☎58 301 8878, ⊛goldwasser.pl; map page 118. A handful of lovely, antique-furnished apartments sleeping one to four people, near the crane and overlooking the Motława. Some are equipped with balconies, kitchenettes and fireplaces. **480zł**

Kamienica Gotyk ul. Mariacka 1 ☎58 301 8567, ⊛gotykhouse.eu; map page 118. Modest guesthouse in the reconstructed oldest house in Gdańsk, once home to Copernicus' housekeeper. The rooms are comfortable but comparatively plain, considering the building's history. **350zł**

Podewils ul. Szafarnia 2 ☎58 300 9560, ⊛podewils.pl; map page 118. A lovely old building with a lot of character right beside the Kamiński bridge, with lovingly restored interiors that retain a lot of their original features. **700zł**

★ **Villa Eva** ul. Batorego 28 ☎58 341 6785, ⊛villaeva.pl; map page 116. Upmarket bed and breakfast on a quiet suburban street, a 15min walk west from Gdańsk Wrzeszcz station, with large rooms and a pretty garden out back. It's enduringly popular with Polish cultural figures looking for a bit of intimacy and calm. **350zł**

HOSTELS

Hostel Cycle On ul. Spichrzowa 15 ☎531 153 700, ⊛hostelcycleon.com; map page 118. Small but colourful dorms and private rooms in an evocative red-brick building. There's a small common area, and bikes are available to rent (25zł/day). Dorms **70zł**, doubles **230zł**

Worldhostel ul. Brygidki 14 ☎504 973 953, ⊛worldhostel.pl; map page 118. Canal-side half-timbered house, featuring colourful rooms decorated with murals

representing world capitals. Dorms 75zł, doubles 260zł
Zappio ul. Świętojańska 49 ☎ 58 322 0174, ⓦzappio.pl;
map page 118. Budget hotel and youth hostel sprawled
over five floors of a beautiful prewar building, with big
windows, high ceilings and lots of period woodwork. Dorms
55zł, doubles 170zł

CAMPSITES
Camping 69 Orlinek ul. Lazurowa 5 ☎ 58 308 0739,

ⓦcamping69.com; bus #112 from train station; map
page 116. Some way out of town (about 15km east), this
campsite is in a lovely location on a lonely beach by the
woods. Open May–Sept. 46zł
Camping Stogi ul. Wydmy 9 ☎ 58 307 3915, ⓦcamping-
gdansk.pl; tram #8 from train station; map page 116.
Near Stogi beach, just 20min by tram from the centre, with
camping pitches and simple cabins sleeping two to five people.
Open May–Sept. Camping 60zł, two-person cabins 85zł

EATING

A nóż widelec ul. Pańska ☎ 721 797 026; map page
118. Boutique fish-fry hut outside the covered market
serving juicy cod and halibut fried in batter, served with
chips and salad. One of the best places for a quick fish-
and-chip lunch in Gdańsk, but a touch expensive at about
25–30zł for a decent-sized fillet. Daily 10am–6pm.
Bar Mleczny Neptun ul. Długa 33 ☎ 58 301 4988, ⓦbar
neptun.pl; map page 118. Reliable milk bar with a wide
range of cheap Polish meals on the menu. Prices rarely creep
above 12zł. Mon–Fri 7.30am–6pm, Sat & Sun 10am–5pm.
Basia Ritz ul. Szafarnia 6 ☎ 666 669 009, ⓦrestauracja-
ritz.pl; map page 118. Inventive Polish-Mediterranean
fusion with a pronounced accent on seafood and locally-
sourced, seasonal produce; this is one place where it's
worth shelling out on the five-course tasting menu (180zł).
Minimalistic decor, outdoor seating in spring and summer,
and fantastic waterfront views. Tues–Sun 1–9pm.
Buddha ul. Długa 18/21 ☎ 58 322 0044, ⓦbuddha
lounge.pl; map page 118. Thai food, including satays,
stir-fries and curries (mains around 28zł), served in fairly
tasteful Oriental surroundings. Daily noon–midnight.
Café Bar Mon Balzac ul. Piwna 36/39 ☎ 58 682 2525,
ⓦmonbalzac.pl; map page 118. A blend of bare brick,
antiques and designer furniture provide the setting for
some quality European cuisine with a pronounced seafood
accent – *moules* and scampi are among the favourites –
with delicious desserts to follow. Mains around 70zł. Live
music three times a week. Daily 7.30am–midnight.
Gdański Bowke ul. Długie Pobrzeże 11 ☎ 58 380 1111,
ⓦgdanskibowke.com; map page 118. Lively waterfront
restaurant serving traditional fish and meat dishes in big
portions (with few mains breaking the 50zł barrier); they
also brew their own unfiltered beer. Daily 9am–10pm.
Goldwasser ul. Długie Pobrzeże 22 ☎ 58 301 8878,
ⓦgoldwasser.pl; map page 118. A refined, fairly
expensive menu vaguely based on French cuisine, with
steaks for around 65zł. But the real draw is the opulent
interior, gleaming with polished wood, and the lovely ivy-
festooned terrace. Daily 10am–10pm.
★ **Kresowa** ul. Ogarna 12 ☎ 58 301 6653, ⓦfacebook.
com/restauracja.kresowa; map page 118. Waitresses
in period dress scurry around serving fabulous traditional
food from Lithuania, Ukraine and Russia, including

pelmeni, shashlik and *kwas*, a fermented grain drink. Mains
around 35zł. Daily 11am–10pm.
Mestwin ul. Straganiarska 20 ☎ 58 301 7882, ⓦface
book.com/Tawerna.Mestwin; map page 118. Delicious
traditional Kashubian peasant food – mainly variations
on meat, cabbage and potatoes – served in a restaurant
crammed with artwork from the region. You can eat well for
under 30zł. Mon 11am–6pm, Tues–Sun 11am–10pm.
Nowa Pierogova ul. Szafarnia 6. lok. 2. ☎ 516 414
200; map page 118. Cute seven-table café serving
Poland's traditional cheap staple (16–22zł per portion)
with a bit more pizzazz than usual. You can get trad-style
pierogi with meat, white cheese or cabbage, or there are
also a handful of more inventive fillings – Mexican chilli,
chicken curry, and spinach and feta among them. Daily
9am–10pm.
Piwna 47 ul. Piwna 47 ☎ 58 380 8880, ⓦpiwna47.
com; map page 118. Modish restaurant behind St
Mary's Church serving up a creative blend of Polish, North
European and Mediterranean fare, with a seasonal accent
on what's fresh from the market: grilled Mediterranean
and freshwater fish (45–65zł), beef, rabbit and fowl, and
some imaginative pastas (30–40zł). Great wine list, and
excellent desserts. Mon–Thurs 9am–10pm, Fri–Sun
9am–11pm.
★ **Pod Łososiem** ul. Szeroka 52/54 ☎ 58 301 7652,
ⓦpodlososiem.com.pl; map page 118. One of the most
luxurious restaurants in town, with prices to match (wild
boar with apples; 75zł). Specializing in game and seafood,
it's also known locally as the home of Goldwasser vodka
liqueur, a thick yellow concoction with flakes of real gold.
Reservations advised. Daily noon–10pm.
Targ Rybny Targ Rybny 6A ☎ 58 320 901; map page
118. Quality seafood restaurant that's relaxing rather
than formal, with plenty in the *moules* and lobster line,
although it also excels at local fried-fish dishes involving
cod and pike-perch. Mains are in the 50–80zł range. Mon–
Thurs & Sun noon–10pm, Fri & Sat noon–midnight.
Tawerna ul. Powroźnicza 19/20 ☎ 58 301 4114,
ⓦtawerna.pl; map page 118. Widely trumpeted as
Gdańsk's best seafood restaurant, with an imaginative and
luxurious menu that includes smoked eel (47zł), caviar and
salmon tartare. Daily 11am–11pm.

3

3

DRINKING AND NIGHTLIFE

Drinking in the city tends to centre on the bars and cafés on ul. Długa and parallel streets to the north. The **clubbing** scene in Gdańsk is very active, thanks in large part to the Tri-City's large student population, and several of the bars listed below also offer live music and/or dancing at weekends. Dedicated clubbers should note that there's also a good range of nightlife opportunities in Sopot (see page 129).

BARS AND PUBS

Browarnia Gdańsk ul. Szafarnia 9 ☎58 300 1717, ⓦbrowarnia.pl; map page 118. This upmarket brew-pub, housed in a seventeenth-century riverside granary, is a great place to sample locally produced lager, wheat and dark beers. It's also a restaurant, with a full menu of sophisticated Polish-European fare. Daily 1–11pm.

Café Szafa ul. Podmurze 2 ☎512 853 681, ⓦfacebook. com/cafeszafa; map page 118. Small, cramped but always animated, this park-side bar serves Lublin-brewed Perła on tap and a generous selection of shots and cocktails (16zł). DJs at weekends. Daily 4pm–3am.

Józef K ul. Piwna 1/2 ☎572 161 510, ⓦjozefk.pl; map page 118. A lively spot on two floors that's furnished with everything retro the owners could lay their hands on – old TVs, domestic junk, film projectors and a grandfather clock. There's a small street-facing terrace and an ample choice of drinks at the bar. Daily 10am–2am.

Lamus ul. Lawendowa 8 ☎58 691 9740, ⓦfacebook. com/CafeLamus; map page 118. Next door to *Lawendowa* (see below) and attracting a similarly laid-back, hipster crowd, *Lamus* cultivates an air of nonchalant cool with its Pop Art interior and jumble of retro furnishings. The selection of connoisseur beers is the main attraction, but they serve everything else alcoholic as well. Daily noon–1am.

Lawendowa ul. Lawendowa 8 ☎531 998 832; map page 118. Corner bar with a red-brick-meets-matt-black interior, a broad selection of trendy craft beers and craft ciders, and occasional live music. Daily noon–1am.

Loft ul. Młyńska 15 ☎604 927 879, ⓦfacebook.com/ loftpub.gdansk; map page 118. Relaxing, unpretentious haven for choosy drinkers, with a carefully curated selection of Czech, German and local craft beers on tap. Minimalist decor and a few artworks on the walls set the tone. Tues–Sun 1–9pm.

Vinifera ul. Wodopój 7 ☎512 762 799; map page 118. Legendary bar in a tiny, recently renovated canal-side house (the little doll's house referred to in Günter Grass's *The Call of the Toad*). It's a bit of a tight squeeze; action flows out onto a small courtyard in summer. Daily 4pm–midnight.

CLUBS

Bunkier ul. Olejrna 3 ☎531 711 207, ⓦbunkierclub. pl; map page 118. Former air-raid shelter housing a pub, a gallery and a club with two floors. Midweek events are usually free; weekend club nights cost from 10zł upwards. Daily 5pm–3am.

Gazeta Rock Café ul. Tkacka 7/8 ☎58 320 2423; map page 118. Friendly and fashionable basement bar decked out with pop memorabilia – it styles itself as the "Museum of Polish Rock" – with regular DJs and parties. Mon–Thurs & Sun 7pm–2am, Fri & Sat 7pm–4am.

Parlament ul. św. Ducha 2 (entrance on ul. Kołodziejska) ☎58 320 1365, ⓦparlament.com.pl; map page 118. Popular and unpretentious place for mainstream dance music. Wed–Sat 11pm–4am.

ENTERTAINMENT

CLASSICAL MUSIC, BALLET AND OPERA

Baltic Opera (Opera Bałtycka) al. Zwycięstwa 15 ☎58 763 4912, ⓦoperabaltycka.pl; Gdańsk-Politechnika station. One of the best classical venues in the country, with a varied programme of opera, operetta and dance.

Music Academy (Akademia Muzyczna) ul. Łąkowa 1/2 ☎58 300 9200, ⓦamuz.gda.pl. Hosts frequent chamber music recitals.

Polish Baltic Philharmonic ul. Olowianka 1 ☎58 320 6269, ⓦfilharmonia.gda.pl. Orchestral concerts in a stunningly converted Neo-gothic power station.

FOOTBALL

The main city football team, Lechia Gdańsk (ⓦlechia.pl), play at the 44,000-capacity Stadion Energa Gdańsk, a famously elegant amber-coloured oval that was built for the European Championships of 2012. It's 5km north of the centre in the suburb of Letnica – take tram #10 from Gdańsk Główny.

SHOPPING

The Tri-City's speciality is **amber**, which washes up on beaches along the Baltic coast, and in the summertime Gdańsk's Old Town is packed with peddlers selling amber jewellery. The thickest concentration of shops can be found on narrow ul. Mariacka, where amber glitters from practically every storefront, although you'll also find a few along ul. Długie Pobrzeże.

Empik ul. Podwale Grodzkie 8 ☎22 462 7250, ⓦempik.com; map page 118. Maps, guidebooks and English-language papers and periodicals. Mon–Sat 8am–9pm, Sun 11am–8pm.

GDAŃSK SHAKESPEARE THEATRE

Opened in 2014, the **Gdańsk Shakespeare Theatre**, ul. W. Bogusławskiego 1 (Gdański Teatr Szekspirowski; T 58 351 0101, W teatrszekspirowski.pl), is one of the best places on the planet in which to experience modern interpretations of the bard's work. The moodily enigmatic black-brick structure was built on the site of the Fencing School, where English plays are thought to have been performed in the seventeenth century, and its interior echoes Elizabethan theatre design, with two tiers of balconied boxes and a removable roof that allows for *plein-air* performances in summer. The repertoire includes a lot of Shakespeare, plenty of contemporary theatre by visiting troupes, and a fair amount of intelligent-rock and classical chamber concerts. It is also the main venue for the **Gdańsk Shakespeare Festival** (see below).

Galeria Bałtycka al. Grunwaldzka 141 T 58 521 8550, W galeriabaltycka.pl; map page 116. The largest shopping mall in town, next to Wrzeszcz station. Mon–Sat 9am–9pm, Sun 10am–8pm.

Hala Targowa (Covered Market) ul. Pańska; map page 118. Cheap clothes and bags on the ground floor; hams, cheeses and other deli products downstairs. The fruit and veg stalls are lined up outside. Mon–Fri 9am–6pm, Sat 9am–3pm.

3

LISTINGS

Hospital University Clinical Hospital (Uniwersiyteckie Centrum Kliniczne), ul. Dębinki 7 (T 58 727 0505).

Internet There are free wi-fi hotspots across the city centre. The *Jazz'n'Java* internet café is at ul. Tkacka 17/18 (daily 10am–10pm; T 58 305 3616).

Left luggage There are lockers at the train station (from 16zł per locker; exact change required; 24hr).

Pharmacy There's a 24hr pharmacy at the main train station.

Police The main city-centre station is at ul. Okopowa 32–35 (T 58 321 4622). In an emergency call T 997.

Post office There is a 24hr post office at ul. Długa 23/28.

Sopot

One-time stamping ground for the rich and famous, who came from all over the world to sample its casinos and high life in the 1920s and '30s, the beach resort of **SOPOT** remains the country's only really convincing riviera town. Boasting a glorious sandy beach, an iconic pier and a fashionable strolling strip in the shape of **ulica Bohaterów Monte Cassino**, it's the place where everyone comes to see and be seen. The town's position slap in the middle of the Tri-City makes it a year-round nightlife centre servicing both Gdynia and Gdańsk, as well as a growing business centre and an enduringly fashionable place to live.

FESTIVALS AND EVENTS IN THE TRI-CITY

In the summer months the Tri-City becomes the festival capital of Poland, boasting everything from Shakespeare to globally huge rock acts.

St Dominic's Fair (Jarmark św. Dominika) Late July to mid-Aug. The biggest show in town, with craft stalls, music and street theatre taking over over the city centre for three weeks.

Euro Chamber Music Festival Late June–late July W eurochambermusicfestival.com. Big international names perform in churches and concert halls.

Festival of Organ Music Late June–late Aug W filharmonia.gda.pl. Recitals on Oliwa Cathedral's magnificent organ (see page 124).

Open'er Festival Early July W opener.pl. An airfield just outside Gdynia is the scene of this four-day music event, bringing the top names of rock and pop to a 100,000-strong crowd.

Gdańsk Shakespeare Festival Late July–early Aug W festiwalszekspirowski.pl. Performances of recent Shakespeare productions from around the world.

Gdynia Film Festival Sept W festiwalgdynia.pl. Showcases the best Polish films of the year, many of them subtitled in English.

The seafront

Sopot's famous **pier** (*molo*; daily 24hr; May–Sept 8zł, Oct–April free) was originally constructed in 1928. At just over 500m it's by far the longest in the whole Baltic area, and a walk to the café at the end is considered an essential part of the Sopot experience. Adjacent to the pier is a **lighthouse** (daily 10am–10pm; 5zł), from the top of which you can get a good view of town.

Long sandy **beaches** stretch away on both sides of the pier. In the northern section you'll find ranks of bathing huts, some with marvellous wicker beach chairs for rent. A foot- and bike path leads all the way to the northern suburbs of Gdańsk and north to Gdynia, passing endless **fried-fish stalls** on the way – heading in either direction makes for a relaxing bike ride or one-hour stroll.

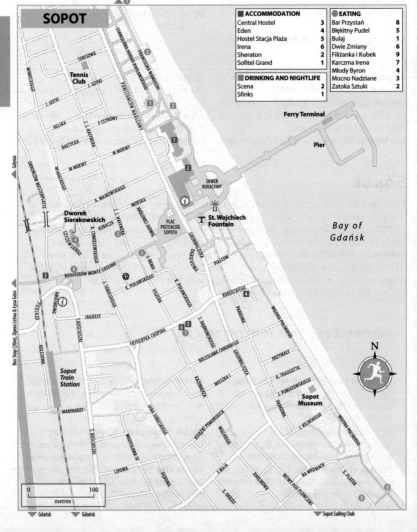

■ ACCOMMODATION	
Central Hostel	3
Eden	4
Hostel Stacja Plaża	5
Irena	6
Sheraton	2
Sofitel Grand	1

■ DRINKING AND NIGHTLIFE	
Scena	2
Sfinks	1

● EATING	
Bar Przystań	8
Błękitny Pudel	5
Bulaj	1
Dwie Zmiany	6
Filiżanka i Kubek	9
Karczma Irena	7
Młody Byron	4
Mocno Nadziane	3
Zatoka Sztuki	2

Sopot Museum

ul. Poniatowskiego 8 • Tues–Sun: June–Sept 10am–6pm; Oct–May 10am–4pm • 5zł; free on Sun • ☎ 58 551 2266, ⓦ muzeumsopotu.pl

Housed in a lovely 1904 villa set back from the seaside path, the **Sopot Museum** (Muzeum Sopotu) has several reconstructed period rooms reflecting the affluent bourgeois taste of the time, while documenting the fortunes of a typical Gdańsk merchant family in the twentieth century.

ARRIVAL AND INFORMATION
SOPOT

By train Sopot train station is just south of the top end of ul. Bohaterów Monte Cassino, a 10min walk from the pier. Sopot is served by regular SKM trains from Gdańsk (20min); mainline Warsaw–Gdynia trains also stop here.

By bus Municipal buses drops passengers off where al. Niepodległosci, the main north–south road, meets ul. Bohaterów Monte Cassino, just northwest of the train station.

Tourist information There are tourist offices (ⓦ sts. sopot.pl) at ul. Dworcowa 4, in the booth diagonally opposite the train station (May–Oct daily 10am–6pm; ☎ 733 535 205), and near the pier at pl. Zdrojowy 2 (daily 10am–6pm; ☎ 790 280 884). The branch at ul. Dworcowa can help book private rooms, pensions and hotels.

Bike hire Sopocki Rower, Skwer Kuracyjny, opposite the pier (May–Sept; 20zł/hr, 60zł/day; ☎ 518 518 458, ⓦ sopockirower.pl).

ACCOMMODATION

HOTELS AND PENSIONS

Eden ul. Kordeckiego 4/6 ☎ 58 551 1503, ⓦ hotel-eden.pl; map page 130. Pension in a stately villa built in 1908, nicely located in a park just south of the pier. The rooms themselves are unexceptional, but many have balconies and original parquet floors. <u>190zł</u>

Irena ul. Fryderyka Chopina 36 ☎ 58 551 2073, ⓦ pens jonat-irena.com; map page 130. Small, reasonably priced and well-kept pension a short way down the hill from Sopot station. All rooms are en suite, and there's a congenial restaurant in the basement (see page 132). <u>280zł</u>

Sheraton ul. Powstańców Warszawy 10 ☎ 58 767 1000, ⓦ sheraton.com; map page 130. The newest luxury hotel in town overlooks the pier and beach, and has large rooms, a club floor, spa and excellent marine-themed bar and restaurants. Check for discounts in off-season. <u>1025zł</u>

Sofitel Grand ul. Powstańców Warszawy 12/14 ☎ 58 551 0041, ⓦ sofitel.com; map page 130. Built in the 1920s in regal period style, Sopot's beachside *grande-dame* has been refurbished to suit modern tastes. The rooms at the front overlook a private section of beach. <u>880zł</u>

HOSTELS

Central Hostel ul. Bohaterów Monte Casino 15 ☎ 530 858 717, ⓦ centralsopot.pl; map page 130. Bang in the centre of town, this hostel is sparsely furnished but has a lively party atmosphere and sunny rooms. Dorms <u>60zł</u>, doubles <u>250zł</u>

Hostel Stacja Plaża ul. Fryderyka Chopina 38 ☎ 399 277 300, ⓦ stacjaplaza.pl; map page 130. A good mix of dorms, family room and doubles in a quiet residential street a short walk from the beach. There's also a nice common room and basic tea- and coffee-making facilities, although no breakfast. Dorms <u>60zł</u>, doubles <u>130zł</u>

CAMPSITE

Camping Park 45 ul. Bitwy pod Plowcami 73–79 ☎ 690 273 810, ⓦ park45.pl; bus #143 from train station to Hestii; map page 116. Partly wooded campsite near the beach, 3km south of the centre on the Sopot-Gdańsk border. There's a restaurant on site, and bike hire is available. Camping <u>67zł</u>, two-person bungalows <u>500zł</u>

EATING

★ **Bar Przystań** al. Wojska Polskiego 11 ☎ 58 550 0241, ⓦ barprzystan.pl; map page 130. Sopot's finest seafood café, in a lovely spot 1.5km south along the beach. The self-service fish dishes are great value, though expect queues at the weekend. The legendary *Zupa Rybacka* (Fisherman's Soup; 16zł) is a meal in itself. Daily 11am–11pm.

Błękitny Pudel ul. Bohaterów Monte Cassino 44 ☎ 58 551 1672, ⓦ blekitnypudel.pl; map page 130. Kitsch but cosy café-pub which also does fusion dishes, *pierogi* (with goose and plum; 25zł) and a tasty herring in cream. Hearty breakfasts, fancy burgers and plenty of fish and beef flesh out the menu. Mon–Thurs & Sun 10am–11pm, Fri & Sat 10am–2am.

★ **Bulaj** al. Franciszka Mamuszki 22 ☎ 58 551 5129, ⓦ bulaj.pl; map page 130. One of the best places in Sopot to eat quality fish, with fresh fillets of cod, halibut and pike-perch, frequently served with an imaginative and unusual selection of accompanying vegetables. The fishy theme extends to seafood-stuffed versions of Polish classics like *goląbki* and *pierogi*, although there are always some steak, rabbit and duck options on the menu too. The checked-tablecloth interior is nicely intimate, and there's open-air seating beside the wooden boardwalk leading to the beach. Mains hover around 45–55zł. Daily 11am–10pm.

Dwie Zmiany ul. Bohaterów Monte Cassino 31 ☎ 58 380 2127, ⓦ dwiezmiany.com; map page 130. Arty bistro-pub serving breakfasts, salads and a few more vegetarian choices than usual (mains 25–35zł). There's also a great selection of beers. Daily 9am–midnight.

★ **Filiżanka i Kubek** ul. Emilii Plater 12 ☎732 920 518; map page 130. Mellow café-restaurant in a suburban house near the beach, with tables spread across the garden lawn in summer. Lovely cakes, and a kids' corner with books and toys. Daily: May–Sept 10am–10pm; Oct–April 11am–8pm.

Karczma Irena ul. Fryderyka Chopina 36 ☎512 516 910, ⊚pensjonat-irena.com; map page 130. A fusion of traditional Polish and French cuisine dished up in a cosy antique-store interior, with mains such as roast duck, beef bourgignon and pike-perch cooked in wine weighing in at around 30–40zł. For dessert there are homemade puddings and pies. May–Sept daily 1pm–11pm; Oct–April Tues–Sun 8am–5pm.

Młody Byron ul. Czyżewskiego 12 ☎796 277 628; map page 130. This refined café in the Dworek Sierakowskich

gallery is the best place in town for tea, cakes and homemade lemonade. There are occasional concerts (see page 132) and cabaret, too. Daily noon–11pm.

Mocno Nadziane ul. Haffnera 7/9 ☎58 355 1515; map page 130. Contemporary-style *pierogi* bar serving several variations on the pastry-pocket theme, including some intriguing local fish-flavoured options (mains 10–20zł). It's also a good place to drink spirits and cocktails come the evening. Daily 11am–9pm.

Zatoka Sztuki al. Franciszka Mamuszki 14 ☎785 881 390, ⊚zatokasztuki.pl; map page 130. Restaurant and lounge bar with tables in a large, bright building full of odd bits of art and design; in summer, diners and drinkers spread out onto the beach. The seasonally changing menu always has a few meat, fish and pasta options, with mains ranging from 38zł for a fried cod fillet to 90zł for a steak. The cooked breakfasts (16zł) are worth making an early start for. Daily 9am–10pm.

DRINKING AND NIGHTLIFE

Scena al. Mamuszki 2 ☎601 208 435, ⊚scenaklub. pl; map page 130. Biggest of the club spaces along the seafront, with four floors hosting DJs, pop-rock and hip-hop concerts. Open Fri & Sat (more often in summer); events start at 9pm.

Sfinks ul. Powstańców Warszawy 18 ☎696 889 540; map page 130. Superbly atmospheric art gallery/bar/club that's a magnet for bohemians and arty types. Regular live gigs. Thurs–Sat 4pm–4am.

ENTERTAINMENT

Dworek Sierakowskich ul. Czyżewskiego 12 (off ul. Bohaterów Monte Cassino) ☎58 551 0756, ⊚tps-dworek.pl. This café/gallery hosts chamber music concerts every Thursday at 6pm in a room where Chopin is said to have played.

Opera Leśna ul. Stanisława Moniuszki 12 ☎58 555 8411, ⊚operalesna.sopot.pl. In the peaceful hilly park in the west of Sopot, the open-air Opera Leśna hosts large-scale productions throughout the summer; for tickets and programmes, check with the tourist office (see page 131).

Gdynia

Originally a small Kashubian village, **GDYNIA** went through a boom period in the 1920s and '30s thanks to its status as Poland's (then) only outlet to the sea. A large port was built, and the rapidly emerging city filled with fine-looking examples of Art Deco architecture. Today's Gdynia has a rather prosaic business-like appearance compared to resort-town Sopot and history-soaked Gdańsk, but it still boasts a lively seafront strip and some heavyweight attractions, most notably the **aquarium** and the **Museum of Emigration**. Recent years have seen the city centre undergo a significant facelift, and the futuristic 140m-high **Sea Towers**, built in 2008, have confirmed Gdynia's position at the forefront of the country's economic transformation.

Gdynia's **seafront** lies directly east across town from the main station. From the main pier, join the locals on a stroll along the main promenading ground, **Bulwar Nadmorski**.

Błyskawica and Dar Pomorza

al. Jana Pawła • **Błyskawica** May, June & Sept–Nov Tues–Sun 10am–12.30pm & 2–5pm; July & Aug Tues–Sun 10am–5pm; Dec–April closed • 14zł • ☎58 620 1381, ⊚muzeummw.pl • **Dar Pomorza** Jan–June Fri–Sun 10am–4pm; July & Aug daily 9am–6pm; Sept–Nov Tues–Sun 10am–4pm; Dec closed • 8zł • ☎58 620 2371, ⊚nmm.pl

The **Błyskawica**, a World War II destroyer, is moored on the northern side of Gdynia's pier. Visitors get to explore the inner workings of the battleship, along with a cross-section of a torpedo, various scale models and uniforms. A deck-top plaque commemorates the vessel's year-long wartime sojourn in Cowes on the Isle of Wight, where it helped to defend the port against a major German attack in May 1942. Further along the pier is another proudly Polish vessel, the three-masted frigate **Dar Pomorza**, built in Hamburg in 1909 and used as a Polish Navy training ship during the 1930s and again after World War II.

The aquarium

al. Jana Pawła II 1 • April, May & Sept daily 9am–7pm; June–Aug daily 9am–8pm; Oct & March daily 10am–5pm; Nov–Feb Tues–Sun 10am–5pm • 24zł • ☎ 572 504 608, ⓦ aquarium.gdynia.pl

At the end of the pier, the **aquarium** is home to around 250 species of sea life, including piranhas, lungfish and turtles. The aquarium's exhibits replicate conditions ranging from the Baltic Sea to the Amazon jungle and coral reefs, as well as providing a model of the whole Baltic Sea region. Close to the aquarium is a lumpy monument to Polish seafarer and novelist Joseph Conrad.

City Museum

ul. Zawiszy Czarnego 1 • Tues, Wed & Fri 10am–6pm, Thurs noon–8pm, Sat & Sun 10am–5pm • 10zł; free on Fri • ☎ 58 662 0910, ⓦ muzeumgdynia.pl

The **City Museum** (Museum Miasta Gdyni), a short walk through the park south of the pier, documents Gdynia's development from a humble farming village and holiday resort to a booming city, with imaginative use of photos, postcards and period items to illustrate the rate of progress.

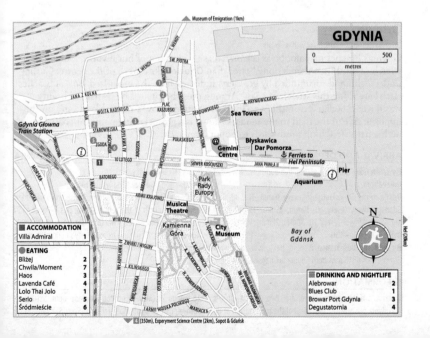

Experyment Science Centre

al. Zwycięstwa 96/98 • Tues–Fri 10am–6pm, Sat & Sun 10am–7pm • 20zł • ☎ 58 500 4994, ⓦ experyment.gdynia.pl • Trolleybus #21, #24, #26, #27 or #29 or bus #119, #133 or #137 from train station

Three kilometres south of the centre, just off the main road to Sopot, the **Experyment Science Centre** (Centrum Nauki Experyment) is an interactive science centre with a certain emphasis on computers and digital technologies. Sections include Waterworld (Hydroświat), where visitors (especially younger ones) can learn how water can power all kinds of things, and Tree of Life (Drzewo Życia), which takes a robustly Darwinian approach to evolution while also looking at the ways in which different animals see, hear and feel their surroundings.

Museum of Emigration

ul. Polska 1 • Tues noon–8pm, Wed–Sun 10am–6pm; last entrance 1hr before closing • 10zł; free on Wed • ☎ 58 623 3179, ⓦ polska1.pl • Bus #119, #133 or #137 from train station

Boasting the highly symbolic address of Polska 1 ("Number One, Poland Street"), 2km northwest of the centre, the **Museum of Emigration** (Muzeum Emigracji) occupies Gdynia's wonderfully restored Art Deco **Ship Terminal** (Dworzec Morski), which served as Poland's maritime window on the world during the interwar years. Inside is a state-of-the-art exhibition that examines the many ways in which the Polish nation has been shaped by migration – from the intellectual and political emigration of the nineteenth century to the EU-enabled population movements of the twenty-first. Archive film, photos and personal stories draw out the main narrative themes – the great pre-World War I migrations to North America are recalled through the eyes of a Polish family from a small village near Rzeszów. Particularly poignant is the section devoted to the forced resettlements that took place after World War II, when Poles from eastern territories grabbed by the Soviet Union were transported (very often in cramped cattle trucks) to new homes in the west. Outside the building is a short pier that looks out on Gdynia's modern-day port, still busy with cargo vessels and naval patrol ships.

Orłowo

Get off at Orłowo SKM station and walk downhill

Gdynia's beaches may not be as celebrated as those of Sopot but if you're looking for a stretch of sand then there's none better than **Orłowo**, 5km south of the centre. Curling under a cliff and surrounded by greenery, it doesn't have the urbanized look of beaches elsewhere along this stretch of coast. Among those bewitched by its natural beauty was novelist Stefan Żeromski, who lived in a cottage (now a rather bland café) on the opposite side of the road to the sands. Orłowo is a great starting point for coastal walks, with a path stretching southwards to Sopot 6km away.

ARRIVAL AND DEPARTURE   GDYNIA

By train Gdynia Główna station is a 20min walk west of the seafront.

Destinations Gdańsk airport (every 30min–1hr; 30min); Gdańsk Główny (every 10–30min; 35min); Hel (9 daily; 1hr 45min); Sopot (every 10–30min; 20min); Warsaw (12 daily; 3hr 20min–4hr).

By bus The bus station is right next door to Gdynia Głowna. Bus #510 runs from Gdynia to Gdańsk Lech Wałęsa airport six times daily.

Destinations Kartuzy (7 daily; 1hr 10min).

By ferry Stena Line ferries from Karlskrona in Sweden dock to the north of the centre – take bus #105 or #150 to get into town. Boats to Hel (May Sat & Sun only, June–Aug daily; 1hr; 40zł) leave from the city's main pier, where there's also a ticket office.

INFORMATION

Tourist information There are two tourist offices (ⓦ gdynia.pl): one just southeast of the train station at ul.

10 Lutego 24 (May–Sept Mon–Fri 9am–6pm, Sat & Sun 9am–4pm; Oct–April Mon–Fri 9am–5pm, Sat 9am–3pm;

☎ 58 622 3766), the other at the end of the pier (May–Sept Mon–Fri 9am–6pm, Sat 10am–5pm, Sun 10am–4pm; ☎ 58 620 7711). Both hand out free maps for walking and

cycling trips in and around town, and can also help with booking private rooms.

ACCOMMODATION

GDYNIA
Villa Admiral ul. 10 Lutego 29a ☎ 58 661 2038, ⓦ admiralvilla.com.pl; map page 133. This lovely old villa hidden away in a courtyard is a more intimate alternative to the big business hotels in town. Rooms are small but modern and well-furnished. **270zł**

ORŁOWO
★ **Aparthotel Quadrille** ul. Folwarczna 2 ☎ 58 351 0300, ⓦ quadrille.pl; Gdynia Orłowo station; map page

116. Lovely boutique hotel in Orłowo, with suites themed around famous authors and their works. Stylish furnishings throughout, and concientious service. Over 16s only. **430zł**
★ **Willa Lubicz** ul. Orlowska 43 ☎ 58 668 4740, ⓦ willalubicz.pl; 10min walk from Gdynia Orłowo station; map page 116. Charmingly old-fashioned 1930s villa just 5min from the beach in the southern suburb of Orłowo, with spacious, sunny rooms decked out with period detailing. **430zł**

EATING

GDYNIA
Bliżej pl. Kaszubski 1a ☎ 530 988 888, ⓦ blizej.gdynia. pl; map page 133. First-floor café-bar occupying a glass-and-concrete box on a fountain-splashed square, serving breakfasts, burgers, excellent cakes and good coffee. Daily 8am–10pm.
Chwila/Moment ul. Świętojańska 8 ☎ 58 623 3469, ⓦ chwilamoment.com.pl; map page 133. Bright glassy building overlooking a central crossroads, with a café (*Chwila*) on the ground floor, serving all-day breakfasts and tempting soup-and-sandwich deals, and upstairs an inspired, eclectic restaurant (*Moment*), offering everything from vegan curry (28zł) to big-hitting carnivorous dishes such as rib-eye steak (69zł). Chwila: Mon–Fri 7.30am–6pm, Sat & Sun 8.30am–6pm; Moment: Mon–Thurs 4–11pm, Fri 4pm–1am, Sat 1pm–1am, Sun 1–8pm.
Haos ul. Starowiejska 14 ☎ 536 277 977, ⓦ haos.menu; map page 133. Bright, colourful bistro serving Asian-themed food with a tempting range of Thai, Indonesian, Chinese and Japanese dishes. Popular favourites include dim sum dumplings (14zł) and red and green Thai curries (27zł). Mon–Thurs noon–11pm, Fri & Sat noon–midnight, Sun noon–11pm.
Lavenda Café ul. Starowiejska 11 ☎ 512 644 412, ⓦ lavendacafe.pl; map page 133. Choose from baguette sandwiches, inventive salads (such as scampi with chorizo and paprika; 39zł) and pasta dishes at this central café, or stop by for a slice of (excellent) cake and

homemade lemonade (including lavender flavour; 12zł). Mon–Sat 10–8pm, Sun noon–7pm.
★ **Lolo Thai Jolo** ul. Jana z Kolna 2 ☎ 58 351 0330, ⓦ thaijolo.pl; map page 133. Cute and cosy Asian bistro formed from a pair of sheds knocked together. It's a good bet for green curries and satay dishes, with mains clocking in at under 30zł. Mon–Sat 11.30am–9pm, Sun 11.30am–7pm.
Serio ul. 3 Maja 21 ☎ 534 588 388, ⓦ pizzaserio.com; map page 133. Excellent pizzas (25–35zł) and pastas served up in a stylish interior that blends post-industrial brutalism with homely woody touches. Convenient downtown location, too. Daily noon–11pm.
Śródmieście ul. Mściwoja 9 ☎ 600 488 761, ⓦ bistro srodmiescie.pl; map page 133. One of the Tri-City's top hipster bistros serves up gourmet burgers (25zł-ish), pork and beef sandwiches and hummus dips, with the predictable but welcome addition of craft beers and artisan lemonades. Daily 11am–midnight.

ORŁOWO
★ **Tawerna Orłowska** ul. Orłowska 3 ☎ 58 622 2220, ⓦ tawernaorlowska.pl; map page 116. Roomy restaurant filled with nautical knick-knacks in an old house right on the beach, with plenty of fishy specialities (baked turbot 40zł), a broad choice of shellfish, shrimps and scampi, and a persuasive list of cocktails. Daily: June–Aug 11am–midnight; Sept–May 11am–11pm.

DRINKING AND NIGHTLIFE

Alebrowar ul. Starowiejska 40 ☎ 535 207 067, ⓦ ale browar.pl; map page 133. The outdoor terrace of this animated pub, serving boutique beers from all over Poland, is the place to be on summer nights. You can order food from the *Czerwony Piec* pizzeria next door, and bring it to *Alebrowar* to consume. Daily 2pm–midnight.
Blues Club ul. Portowa 1 ☎ 58 621 0943, ⓦ bluesclub.

pl; map page 133. A front room with a well-stocked bar (including a big variety of whisky) leads to an exposed-brick inner sanctum lined with album covers, concert posters and gig photos. There's quality live music here once or twice a week, plus blues and jazz jam sessions (Tues and Wed respectively). A handy menu of tortillas and burgers is available. Entry on gig nights 15–30zł. Daily 2pm–midnight.

3

★ **Browar Port Gdynia** ul. Bulwar Nadmorski 2 ☎733 000 355, ⓦbrowarportgdynia.pl; map page 133. Lively pub on the seafront promenade serving beers brewed on the premises and a broad food menu that stretches from burgers to pizzas, ribs and fried fish. Mon– Wed 1–11pm, Thurs 11am–11pm, Fri 11am–1am, Sat 10am–1am, Sun 10am–11pm.

Degustatornia ul. Świętojańska 130 (entrance on ul. Władysława IV) ☎888 345 678, ⓦdegustatornia.pl; map page 133. Choose from hundreds of brews at this central pub, fittingly decked out with beer memorabilia and freaky furniture. Mon–Thurs 3pm–midnight, Fri & Sat 3pm–1am, Sun 3–10pm.

Hel

A long thin strip of woods and sand dunes sticking out into the Baltic Sea, the **Hel Peninsula** is very much a day-tripper's favourite. Marking the tip of the peninsula, just 25km north of Gdańsk by boat but over 100km by land, **HEL** is a small fishing port that preserves a handsome gaggle of nineteenth-century fishermen's cottages. The pristine strip of white-sand beach just east of the village ensures its enduring status as one of the Baltic's most alluring holiday spots.

Fishing Museum

bul. Nadmorski 2 • July & Aug daily 10am–6pm; Sept–June Tues–Sun 10am–4pm (till 3pm in Dec) • 10zł • ☎58 675 0522, ⓦnmm.pl

A good place to start your exploration of the village is Hel's **Fishing Museum** (Muzeum Rybołówstwa), housed in the Gothic fifteenth-century St Peter's Church (Kościół św. Piotra). Inside are model ships and plenty of fishing tackle, as well as some local folk art. The people of the peninsula are predominantly Kashubian, as evidenced in the local dialect and the distinctive **embroidery** styles on show in the museum.

Fokarium

ul. Morska 2 • Daily 9.30am–7pm • 5zł • ☎58 675 0836, ⓦfokarium.pl

A firm favourite with visitors to Hel is the **Fokarium** or seal enclosure, about 50m west of the Fishing Museum along the seashore. Here five or six seals spend their days eating (feeding times 11am & 2pm), swimming and lazing about – much like the average human visitor to Hel. There's a strong emphasis on conservation, with lots of information on sea life posted alongside the tanks.

The beach

At the southern end of ulica Wiejska, walk along ulica Leśna eastwards for fifteen min-utes through the woods to reach Hel's biggest attraction, the **beach** – a luxuriously wide, semolina-coloured ribbon of sand that extends as far as the eye can see, backed by wind-swept dunes. If you fancy a bit of sunbathing, this is the perfect place to escape the crowds.

Coastal Defence Museum

ul. Helska 16; the access road is 1km northeast of Hel train station • Daily: April & Oct 10am–4pm; May & Sept 10am–5pm; June 10am–6pm; July & Aug 10am–7pm • 12zł; English audio guides free; return trip on narrow-gauge railway 10zł • ☎697 888 583, ⓦhelmuzeum.pl

Located in the forests northwest of Hel village, the **Coastal Defence Museum** (Muzeum obrony wybrzeża) occupies the artillery bunkers built during the German occupation in World War II. The area was also fortified by the Polish military between 1918 and 1939, and the heroic defence of Hel against German forces in September 1939 is one of the main themes of the exhibition. It's a scattered site: the main display is located at the artillery bunker known as "**B-2 Bruno**", 400m off the Hel–Jurata road;

exhibits reveal the isolated life of the local garrison, and there's a display of artillery pieces outside. About 1.5km north is the former ammunition dump, now home to the **Museum of the Hel Railway** (same ticket), whish preserves rolling stock used on the narrow-gauge line constructed by the Polish military in the interwar years.

ARRIVAL AND INFORMATION HEL

By train The train station, with regular services to Gdynia (9 daily; 1hr 45min), is on ul. Dworska, a few minutes' walk from ul. Wiejska, the pedestrianized main street.

By ferry Tourist **boats** (May Sat & Sun only, June–Aug daily; ☎ 58 301 4926, ⓦ zegluga.pl; 40zł) run between Hel and the Green Gate in Gdańsk via Gdynia several times a day in summer, although they're often fully reserved well in advance.

Tourist information The tourist office is on the way to the beach at ul. Kuracyjna 26 (May–Sept daily 10am–6pm; ☎ 666 871 622).

ACCOMMODATION AND EATING

There are numerous **private rooms** (80–100zł) in Hel; the area around ul. Sikorskiego (at the northwestern end of ul. Wiejska) is the place to look for *wolne pokoje* signs. There are also **campsites** tucked away under the trees all along the peninsula, many of them offering bungalows for 60–120zł per person.

Captain Morgan ul. Wiejska 21 ☎ 58 675 0091, ⓦ captainmorgan.cypel.pl. A family-run hotel above a convivial, candlelit pub crammed with antiques and maritime junk. The cosy, modern en-suite rooms come with TVs and fridges. Pub daily 11am–1am. <u>120zł</u>

Helkamp ul. Kuracyjna 1 ☎ 606 388 184, ⓦ helkamp. com. Grassy campsite just east of Hel village on the way to the beach, offering a small shop, bar and kids' playground. Camping <u>55zł</u>, two-person chalets <u>350zł</u>

★ **Kutter Port: Smażalnia Ryb Bałtyckich** ul.

Żeglarska ☎ 58 675 0480, ⓦ kutter.pl. A big fish-fry shack with outdoor tables, this is the seasonal, port-side branch of the *Kutter* restaurant (a few steps away at ul. Wiejska 87). It's one of the best local places to enjoy succulent fillets of cod and halibut, lightly battered and priced by weight; a decent-sized fillet will set you back 25–30zł. May–Sept daily 11am–8pm.

Maszoperia ul. Wiejska 110 ☎ 58 675 0297, ⓦ masz operia.net. Intimate, candlelit restaurant in a nineteenth-century fisherman's hut, offering a full menu of fish and meat dishes, with mains mostly in the 30–40zł range. Daily 10am–10pm.

Willa Helios ul. Lipowa 2 ☎ 603 359 120, ⓦ helios. freehost.pl. Small *pensjonat* near the Fokarium with a plant-filled patio and bright, modern double rooms, as well as four- to five-person apartments for families. A kitchen is available for guests, and there are bicycles to rent. <u>150zł</u>

Kashubia

The expanse of lakes and hills stretching west of Gdańsk – **Kashubia** (Kaszuby) – is the homeland of one of Poland's lesser-known ethnic minorities, the **Kashubians**. A western Slav people linked closely to the Poles, the Kashubians were subjected to a German cultural onslaught during the Partition period, a process that was resisted fiercely. Nowadays you can hear the distinctive Kashubian language spoken all over the region, particularly by older people, and many villages still produce Kashubian handicrafts such as embroidered cloths and tapestries.

The highlight of Kashubia is the lakeside resort of **Chmielno**, set in rolling countryside that's perfect for hiking and cycling. The open-air museum at **Wdzydze Kiszewskie** is the place to aim for if you're interested in Kashubian folk culture, while the *skansen* at **Szymbark** offers folk culture and a little bit more besides.

Chmielno

Just west of regional capital Kartuzy, the village of **CHMIELNO** is set in idyllic surroundings, squeezed between three lakes – Białe, Rekowo and Kłodno. It's perfect hiking and boating country, and the waterside is dotted with holiday homes and *pensjonaty*. Chmielno is a centre of traditional Kashubian ceramics, and the **Museum of Kashubian Ceramics** on ulica Gryfa Pomorskiego (Muzeum Ceramiki Kaszubskiej: Mon– Sat 9am–6pm; 8zł; ☎ 505 134 724, ⓦ necel.pl) is also a working pottery workshop.

ARRIVAL AND INFORMATION

By public transport From Gdańsk catch a bus (hourly; 1hr) or train (hourly; 1hr 10min) to regional capital Kartuzy, from where there are regular buses to Chmielno (8 daily; 18min).

CHMIELNO

Tourist information The tourist office is at ul. Gryfa Pomorskiego 28a (Tues–Fri 10am–4pm, Sat & Sun 10am–2pm; ☎ 58 684 3091); it can help find **private rooms**.

ACCOMMODATION AND EATING

Chëcz u Kaszëbë ul. Gryfa Pomorskiego 28b ☎ 609 885 031. Lakeside restaurant in a cute thatched building which doubles as the local bar. Grilled trout and meat dishes are around 30zł. Mon–Sat noon–10pm, Sun 11am–9pm.

Krystian ul. Grzędzickiego 20 ☎ 607 041 534, ⓦ pen sjonatkrystian.pl. Modern pension on a quiet street leading down to Lake Kłodno, offering en-suite rooms with balconies. There's also a small bar out back, and boats to rent. **90zł**

Szymbark: CEPR

ul. Szymbarskich Zakładników 12 • May to mid-Sept Mon–Sat 9am–7pm, Sun 9am–10am; mid-Sept to April Mon–Sat 9am–4pm, Sun 10am–4pm • 20zł • ☎ 605 570 637, ⓦ cepr.pl

Set amid rolling hills 20km south of Chmielno, the tranquil village of **SZYMBARK** has over the last few years become one of the most visited spots in northern Poland, thanks to a privately-owned theme park-cum-*skansen known* as the **Regional Education and Promotion Centre** (Centrum Edukacji I Promocji Regionu w Szymbarku), or **CEPR**. Just south of the village, CEPR combines traditional Kashubian dwellings with a headline-grabbing collection of other attractions, best-known of which is the **Topsy-Turvy House** (Dom do góry nogami), a large wooden two-storey house that is positioned upside-down. Inside, communist-era interiors have been recreated in impressive detail – the overall message being that, for citizen of communist Poland, life really was topsy-turvy. There is also a "Siberian House", illustrating the hardships of Polish exiles sent to live in Irkutsk, and a beautiful half-timbered manor house from Salino near Gdynia.

3

ARRIVAL AND DEPARTURE

By train Trains run from Gdańsk-Wreszcz (5 daily; 55min) to the Szymbark-Wieżica halt, 4km north of CEPR on the far side of Wiezica hill.

SZYMBARK

By bus Buses from Gdańsk main bus station (5 daily; 1hr) stop on Szymbark's main street.

ACCOMMODATION AND EATING

Browar Kaszubska Korona ul. Szymbarskich Zakład-ników 12 ⓦ cepr.pl. In the middle of the CEPR complex, this boutique brewery and bar-restaurant sells half a dozen beers ranging from pils to porter, with plenty of fruit- and honey-flavoured brews in between. Open same hours as skansen.

Hotel Szymbark ul. Szymbarskich Zakładników 12 ☎ 58 736 6240, ⓦ hotelszymbark.pl. Neat en-suite rooms in a large, modern building inside the CEPR that combines contemporary comforts with folksy touches like wooden pillars and a shingle roof. **220zł**

Wdzydze Kiszewskie: the Kaszubian Ethnographic Park

ul. T I I Gulgowskich 68 • April, Sept & Oct Tues–Sun 9am–4pm; May & June Tues–Fri 9am–4pm, Sat & Sun 10am–6pm; July & Aug Tues–Sun 10am–6pm; Nov–March Mon–Fri 10am–3pm • 16zł • ☎ 58 686 1130, ⓦ muzeum-wdzydze.gda.pl • There's no direct transport from Gdańsk, although you can take one of the frequent buses from Gdańsk to Kościerzyna, and change there for a bus to Wdzydze Kiszewskie (4 daily; 30min)

Located at the eastern end of **WDZYDZE KISZEWSKIE**, 30km southwest of Szymbark, the **Kaszubian Ethnographic Park** (Kaszubski Park Etnograficzny) is one of the best *skansens* of its kind, bringing together a large collection of traditional Kashubian wooden buildings spread over a field overlooking Lake Goluń. The panoply of buildings, taken from villages across the region, range from old peasant cottages to barns, furnaces, a pigsty and a working sawmill. The early eighteenth-century **wooden church** is a treat: topped by a traditional wood-shingled roof, the interior is covered with regional folk-baroque designs and biblical motifs. The thatched cottage interiors are immaculately restored with original beds and furniture to reflect the typical domestic setup of the mostly extremely poor Kashubian peasantry of a century ago.

THE ELBLĄG–OSTRÓDA CANAL

The 81km-long **Elbląg–Ostróda Canal** (Kanał Ostródzko–Elblaski) was constructed in the mid-nineteenth century as part of the Prussian scheme to improve the region's economic infrastructure, but building it presented significant technical difficulties, due in particular to the large difference in water level (over 100m) between the beginning and end points. To deal with this problem, Prussian engineers devised an intricate and often ingenious system of locks, choke-points and **slipways**. These slipways, the canal's best-known feature, are serviced by large rail-bound carriages that haul the boats overland. Five of these amazing constructions operate over a 10km-long stretch of the northern section of the canal, located roughly halfway between Elbląg and Małdyty.

If you're travelling by car and want to view the slipways, turn west off the main road at **Marzewo**, a few kilometres north of Małdyty, and you'll meet the canal 5km down the road; follow a rough track running north along the canal to reach the slipways themselves.

BOAT TRIPS

Day-trips along the **Elbląg–Buczyniec** stretch of the canal operate in summer (July & Aug 5 daily; May, June & Sept Sat & Sun only; 4hr 40min; 120zł). Tickets should be booked online, well in advance, through Zegluga Ostródzko-Elbląska (☎89 670 9227, ⓦzegluga.com.pl). A bus back to Elbląg is available at the end of the trip; reserve a place in the bus (9zł) at the same time as you buy your ticket.

In addition, there are **two-hour trips** along the **Ostroda–Miłomłyn** stretch of the canal (departing at 10am; July & Aug 1 daily; May, June & Sept Sat & Sun only; 50zł) – there are no slipways on this route, but the beautiful canalside scenery makes it well worthwhile.

East of Gdańsk

East from Gdańsk, a short stretch of Baltic coastline leads up to the Russian border and beyond to the city of Kaliningrad. Midway along, the chilling **Stutthof** concentration camp lies just outside the village of Sztutowo, which marks the western end of the beach-lined Wiślana Peninsula. Inland, the lush rural terrain, well watered by tributaries of the River Vistula, boasts a host of quiet old Prussian villages. This is the region most closely associated with astronomer **Nicolaus Copernicus**, and several towns, notably the medieval centre of **Frombork**, bear his imprint. Nearby **Elbląg** is a major former Prussian centre which has lost much of its old character, but remains an important transport hub.

Stutthof concentration camp

May our fate be a warning to you – not a legend. Should man grow silent, the very stones will scream.
Franciszek Fenikowski, *Requiem Mass*, quoted in camp guidebook

Daily: May–Sept 8am–6pm; Oct–April 8am–3pm • Free; audio guides 15zł; cinema 3zł • ☎ 55 247 8353, ⓦstutthof.org • Regular Gdańsk–Krynica Morska (7 daily; 2hr 20min) and Elbląg–Krynica Morska buses (8 daily; 1hr 10) pass by the short access road to the camp – ask to be set down at Sztutowo Muzeum

Two kilometres west of the village of Sztutowo, a monument marks the entrance to the Nazi concentration camp site at **Stutthof** – a rude awakening after passing through so much idyllic countryside. The camp was initially built to intern Poles from the Free City of Danzig but eventually became a Nazi extermination centre for all of northern Europe. The decision to transform Stutthof into an international camp came in 1942, and in 1944 the camp was incorporated into the Nazi scheme for the "Final Solution", the whole place being considerably enlarged and gas ovens installed. Although not on the same scale as some other death camps, the toll in human lives speaks for itself: an estimated 85,000 people died here before the Red Army liberated the camp in May 1945.

In a large forest clearing surrounded by a wire fence and watchtowers, the peaceful, isolated setting of the camp makes the whole idea of what went on here seem unreal at first. Once through the entrance gate you'll see rows of stark wooden barrack blocks interspersed with empty plots of nothing but the foundations – much of the camp was torn down in 1945 and used as firewood. A **museum** housed in the barracks details life and death in the camp, with crude wooden bunks and threadbare mats indicating the living conditions the inmates had to endure. A harrowing gallery of photographs of gaunt-looking inmates brings home the human reality of what happened here: name, date of birth, country of origin and "offence" are listed below each of the faces; the victims, of 25 different nationalities, included political prisoners, communists and gays. In the far corner of the camp stand the gas ovens and crematoria. During the summer, the museum cinema provides further evidence of the atrocities.

Elbląg

The ancient settlement of **ELBLĄG**, the region's most important town after Gdańsk, was almost totally flattened during the bitter fighting that followed the Nazi retreat in 1945. Only recently has Elbląg's Old Town began to be properly reconstructed, and nowadays approximates the general appearance if not the precise architectural details of the city's pre-war architecture. The town is the starting point for fun boat trips on the **Elbląg-Ostroda canal** (see page 140), but otherwise doesn't merit a visit of any great length.

The Old Town and around

Rising dramatically out of the old marketplace, the **cathedral**, rebuilt after the war, is a massive brick Gothic structure, its huge tower the biggest in the region. Aside from a couple of fine original Gothic triptychs and statues, the interior is mostly rather vapid postwar decoration, leaving the place feeling sad and empty. Not far from the cathedral on ulica Kuśnierska is the Gothic St Mary's Church; no longer consecrated, the building houses **EL Gallery** (Tues–Sat 10am–6pm, Sun 10am–5pm; 8zł; ☎55 625 6784, ⓦgaleria-el.pl), an atmospheric space offering a revolving programme of contemporary art exhibitions. Just south of the Old Town along the river, off ulica Sluzebna, the local **Archaeology and History Museum**, bul. Zygmunta Augusta 11 (Muzeum Archeologiczno-Historyczne: Tues–Sun: May–Sept 9am–5pm; Oct–April 8am–4pm; 10zł, free on Sun; ⓦmuzeum.elblag.pl), includes exhibits from Truso, the eighth- to tenth-century trading post on the shores of Lake Druzno founded by the Vikings.

ARRIVAL AND INFORMATION   ELBLĄG

By train Elbląg's train station is a 15min walk east of the Old Town or a short ride on trams #1 or #2. Trains run from here to Olsztyn (hourly; 1hr 30min) and Gdansk (6 daily; 1hr 40min).
By bus Elbląg's bus station is next to the train station. There

are regular buses to Frombork (every 20–30min; 40min).
Tourist information The tourist office is at Stary Rynek 25 (May–Sept daily 10am–6pm; Oct–April Mon–Fri 8.30am–4.30pm; ☎55 239 3377, ⓦturystyka.elblag.eu).

ACCOMMODATION AND EATING

Kawiarnia Wyspa Skarbów Stary Rynek 10 ☎500 100 661, ⓦwyspa-skarbow.com.pl. Characterful café on the main square that mixes an old-fashioned living-room look with arty photos stuck to walls and ceilings. Good coffee and exquisite cakes. Mon–Thurs & Sun 10am–8pm, Fri & Sat 10am–9pm.
★**Pensjonat MF** ul. św. Ducha 26 ☎55 641 2610, ⓦpensjonatmf.pl. The best place to stay in Elbląg is this classy pension in an old townhouse, whose stylishly designed, good-value rooms come kitted out with flatscreen TVs and thick shag carpets. **250zł**

Pod Kogutem ul. Wigilijna 8–9 ☎55 641 2882. City-centre restaurant with a bright two-level interior and a traditional menu taking in *pierogi*, potato pancakes, roast pork knuckle and fish (fillet of perch 30zł). Daily 10am–10pm.
PTTK Campsite ul. Panienska 14 ☎55 641 8666, ⓦcamping61.com.pl. Just south of the Old Town, pleasantly located on the water, this campsite has pitches and guest rooms that sleep two to four people. Kayaks, bicycles and fishing rods are available to rent. Camping **32zł**, doubles **100zł**

3

NICOLAUS COPERNICUS

Nicolaus Copernicus – Mikołaj Kopernik as he's known to Poles – was born in **Toruń** in 1473. The son of a wealthy merchant family, he entered Kraków University in 1491 and subsequently joined the priesthood. Like most educated Poles of his time, he travelled abroad to continue his studies, spending time at the universities of Bologna and Padua.

On his return home in 1497 he became administrator for the bishopric of Warmia, working as a doctor, lawyer, architect and soldier (he supervised the defence of Olsztyn against the Teutonic Knights) – the archetypal Renaissance man. He spent some fifteen years as canon of the Frombork chapterhouse and constructed an observatory here, where he undertook the research that provided the substance for the *De Revolutionibus Orbium Caelestium*, whose revolutionary contention was that the sun, not the Earth, was at the centre of the planetary system. The work was published by church authorities in Nuremberg in 1543, the year of Copernicus's death; it was later banned by the papacy.

Frombork

A little seaside town 90km east along the Baltic coast from Gdańsk, **FROMBORK** was the home of **Nicolaus Copernicus** (see page 142), the Renaissance astronomer whose ideas overturned the church-approved, earth-centred model of the universe. Most of the research for his famous *De Revolutionibus* was carried out around this town, and it was here that he died and was buried in 1543. Just over a century later, Frombork was badly mauled by marauding Swedes who carted off most of Copernicus's belongings, including his library.

Cathedral Hill

The only part of Frombork to escape unscathed from World War II was the **Cathedral Hill** (Wzgórze Katedralne), a compact unit surrounded by high defensive walls, up from the old market square in the centre of town.

The Cathedral

Mon–Sat: May–Sept 9am–4.30pm; Oct–April 9am–3.30pm • 6zł

The Cathedral Hill's main element is the dramatic fourteenth-century Gothic **Cathedral**, inside which lofty expanses of brick rise above a series of lavish Baroque altars. The seventeenth-century Baroque **organ** towering over the nave is one of the best in the country, and the Sunday afternoon and occasional weekday recitals in summer are an established feature.

Copernicus Tower and Belfry Tower

Copernicus Tower July & Aug Tues–Sun 9.30am–5pm • 6zł • **Belfry Tower** Daily: May–Aug 9.30am–5pm; Sept–April 9am–4pm • 6zł

West of the cathedral, the **Copernicus Tower** (Wieża Kopernika) – possibly the great man's workshop and observatory – is the oldest part of the Cathedral Hill complex, and nowadays contains a mock-up of the astronomer's study. The **Belfry Tower**, in the southwest corner of the walls, has a Foucault pendulum swinging to and fro, proving conclusively that the Earth rotates. There's an excellent view from the top of the tower of Wiślana Lagoon stretching 70km north towards Kaliningrad.

Copernicus Museum

Tues–Sun: May–Aug 9am–5pm; Sept–April 9am–4pm • 6zł; free on Sun

Across the tree-lined cathedral courtyard in the Warmia Bishops' Palace is the **Copernicus Museum** (Muzeum Kopernika). Exhibits include early editions of Copernicus's astronomical treatises, along with a number of his lesser-known works on medical, political and economic questions and a collection of astrolabes, sextants and other instruments.

By bus Frombork's bus station is near the seafront, although many buses and minibuses drop off near the town square along ul. Kopernika. There are regular buses to and from Elbląg (every 20–30min; 40min).

Tourist information The tourist office is at Młynarska 5a

(June Mon–Sat 8am–4pm; July & Aug Mon–Sat 8.30am–4.30pm; Sept–May Mon–Fri 7am–3pm; ☎ 55 244 0677, ⓦ frombork.pl). It can direct you towards the town's stock of private rooms.

ACCOMMODATION AND EATING

Akcent ul. Rybacka 4 ☎ 556 202 300, ⓦ restauracja-akcent.com. A comfy alternative to the more rough-and-ready fish-fry bars near the port, *Akcent* serves up reasonable fillets of cod and halibut alongside traditional Polish treats from *pierogi* (14zł) to roast duck (40zł). Daily 10am–10pm.

Kopernik ul. Kościelna 2 ☎ 55 243 7285, ⓦ hotel kopernik.com.pl. A friendly hotel that attracts tour groups, offering spic-and-span en-suite doubles with views up to the cathedral. There's also a restaurant serving Polish food. <u>190zł</u>

The Vistula delta

3

Following the **River Vistula** south from Gdańsk takes you into a flat plain of isolated villages, narrow roads and drained farmland, traversed by a wide, slow-moving river. This was once the heart of the territory ruled by the **Teutonic Knights**, the religio-militaristic order which controlled the lucrative medieval grain trade from a string of riverside fortress towns. **Malbork**, the knights' headquarters, is home to one of the largest fortresses of medieval Europe. Continuing downriver, a number of similarly fortified towns – notably **Kwidzyn** and **Chełmno** – lead to the lively regional centre of **Bydgoszcz** and the ancient city of **Toruń**.

Malbork

Few towns make as dramatic an immediate impression as **MALBORK**, with the luminous red-brick turrets of its massive castle reflected in the River Nogat as you arrive from the north. It long served as the headquarters of the **Teutonic Knights** (see page 144), who established themselves here in the late thirteenth century, and proceeded to turn a modest fortress into the labyrinthine monster you see today. The town returned to Polish control in 1457, and the Knights, in dire financial difficulties, were forced to sell the castle. Although the eastern wings of the fortress, including the main church, were badly damaged by the Soviet assault at the end of World War II, they have mostly been restored to their original state, and the UNESCO-protected site is now one of Poland's most visited attractions.

Malbork Castle

Grounds Daily: late-April to Sept 9am–8pm; Oct to late-April 10am–4pm • Free • **Castle interiors** Daily: late-April to Sept 9am–7pm; Oct to late-April 10am–3pm; ticket office closes 2hr before closing time • 39.50zł mid-April to Sept, 29.50zł Oct to mid-April; ticket includes English-language audio guide; free entry on Mon but hire of audioguide (8zł) mandatory • ☎ 55 647 0978, ⓦ zamek.malbork.pl

The approach to the main body of **Malbork Castle** (Zamek w Malborku) is through the old outer castle, which wasn't rebuilt after World War II. When you've finished looking

---

MALBORK SON-ET-LUMIÈRE AND THE SIEGE DAYS

On summer evenings a spectacular **son-et-lumière show** presents the history of Malbork, with spectators sitting beside the outer walls of the castle (late-April to mid-Sept Mon–Wed, Sat & Sun at 9 or 10pm; 22zł). It's also well worth visiting Malbork during the lively **Siege Days** (Oblężenie Malborka; ⓦ oblezenie.zamek.malbork.pl), held on the third weekend of July, when locals in period dress re-enact the siege of the fortress and there are jousting tournaments, crafts fairs and concerts – book a room well in advance if you plan to stay the night.

THE TEUTONIC KNIGHTS

Formed in 1190 by Crusaders in Palestine, the **Teutonic Knights** combined the ascetic ideals of monasticism with the military training of a knight. The Knights – the **Teutonic Order of the Hospital of St Mary**, to give them their full title – established their first base in Poland at Chełmno in 1225, following an appeal from Duke Konrad of Mazovia for protection against the pagan Lithuanians, Jacwingians and Prussians. The Knights proceeded to annihilate the Prussian population, establishing German colonies in their place.

Having lost their last base in Palestine in 1271, the Teutonic Knights started looking around for a European site for their headquarters. Three years later they began building Malbork Castle – **Marienburg**, "the fortress of Mary", as they named it – and in 1309 the Grand Master transferred here from Venice. Economically, the Knights' chief targets were control of the Hanseatic cities and the trade in Baltic amber, over which they gained a virtual monopoly. Politically, their main aim was territorial conquest, especially to the east. The Polish kings soon began to realize the mistake of inviting the Knights in.

The showdown with Poland came in 1410 at the **Battle of Grunwald**, one of the most momentous clashes of medieval Europe. Recognizing a common enemy, an allied force of Poles and Lithuanians inflicted the first decisive defeat on the Knights, yet allowed them to retreat to Malbork unchallenged. It wasn't until 1457 that they were driven out of their stronghold by King Kazimierz Jagiełło.

In 1525, the Grand Master, Albrecht von Hohenzollern, having converted to Lutheranism, decided to dissolve the Order and transform its holdings into a **secular duchy**, paying homage before Polish King Sigismund at Kraków.

around inside, head over the **footbridge** to the other side of the River Nogat, where the view allows you to appreciate what a Babylonian project the fortress must have seemed to medieval visitors.

Middle Castle

Passing over the moat and through the daunting main gate, you come to the **Middle Castle**, with the **Grand Master's Palace** on the right side of the courtyard. The fourteenth-century chambers are wonderfully elegant, especially the **Grand Refectory** with its slender pillars leading up to delicately traced vaulting; its ingenious central heating system used long channels to pipe hot air from cellar fireplaces. Leading off from the courtyard are a host of cavernous chambers housing exhibitions on the history of the castle and the Teutonic Knights.

High Castle

From the Middle Castle a drawbridge leads under a portcullis into the smaller courtyard of the **High Castle**, the oldest part of the fortress. At the centre of the courtyard is the castle well and all along one side are the kitchens, with an enormous chimney over the stove. The stairs just to the right as you enter the courtyard lead to a first-floor balcony, and from here you can enter the beautiful **Chapter House**, with palm-leaf vaulting and wall paintings of Grand Masters of the Order. A long, narrow corridor leads away from the courtyard to the **dansker** over the old moat. This tower served a dual purpose: in times of war it was the knights' final refuge, while in peacetime it functioned as the castle lavatory. From the drawbridge, a path leads round the outer walls of the High Castle to the **Chapel of St Anne**, where eleven former Grand Masters were buried, and the castle mill.

ARRIVAL AND INFORMATION   MALBORK

By train The handsome Neo-gothic train station, on the main Gdańsk–Warsaw line, is a 10min walk east of the castle. Destinations Elbląg (12 daily; 20–30min); Gdańsk (every 30min; 30–55min); Warsaw (10 daily; 2hr 25min).

Tourist information The tourist office is at ul. Kościuszki 54 (July & Aug Mon–Fri 8am–7pm, Sat & Sun 10am–3pm; Sept–June Mon–Fri 8am–4pm; ☎ 55 647 4747, ⊕ malbork.pl).

ACCOMMODATION AND EATING

Malbork is usually treated as a day-trip destination but its excellent train connections ensure that it makes a good base – especially if you're **camping**, thanks to the presence of a couple of pleasant riverside sites. As far as eating is concerned, there are plenty of cafés situated in the centre of town, and there is rarely any problem picking up pastries, sandwiches and coffee.

Bistro na Fali Kałdowo Wieś 10 ☎601 624 661, ⓦbistronafali.pl. On the west bank of the Nogat below the railway bridge, this large timber-beamed dining room serves up quality Polish cuisine, with a good mixture of soups, poultry roasts and game (mains in the 30–35zł region). There's a big garden with swings. Daily 9am–9pm.

Camping Nogat Nr 197 ul. Parkowa 3 ☎55 272 2413, ⓦcaw.malbork.pl. Set just back from the Nogat riverbank a 10min walk north of the fortress, this campsite has tent and caravan pitches as well as two- and three-person chalets in a partly shaded site with lots of sports facilities. 70zł

Gościniec w Malborku ul. Walowa 20a ☎600 336 231, ⓦgosciniecwmalborku.pl. Family-run pension on the opposite side of the river from the castle – of which you get some great views. En-suite rooms are neat and cosy, and family rooms come with cooking facilities. No breakfast, but there is a kitchen available for use. 140zł

Kemping Na Stawem ul. Solskiego 10 ☎501 406 740, ⓦmalbork-kemping.eu. On the western side of the River Nogat, with good views of the fortress, this is a well-maintained campsite with pitches grouped around an artificial lake popular with local anglers. There's not much shade, but otherwise it's very pleasant, and convenient for Malbork-Kałdowo train station (note however that express trains don't stop there). 50zł

Pychotka ul. Piastowska 1. ☎792 318 025. There are less than half a dozen tables in this dainty *pierogi* restaurant but it's well worth squeezing in: most mainstream *pierogi* tastes are catered for, plus there are a handful of more contemporary choices (feta and spinach, for example). Opt for a regular six-*pierogi* portion (13–20zł) or a ten-piece mix of different ones. Daily noon–7pm or until the pierogi run out.

Kwidzyn

Forty kilometres south of Malbork, **KWIDZYN** is a smallish fortified town ringed by a sprawling industrial belt. The first stronghold established by the Teutonic Knights in the 1230s (some forty years before the move to Malbork), its original fortress was rapidly joined by a bishop's residence and cathedral. Three hundred years on, the castle was pulled down and rebuilt but the cathedral and bishop's chapterhouse were left untouched. Unlike the rest of the Old Town, the entire complex survived 1945 unscathed.

Kwidzyn Castle

ul. Katedralna 1 • Tues–Sun: May–Sept 9am–5pm; Oct–April 9am–3pm • 10zł; audio guide 6zł • ☎55 646 3799, ⓦzamek.kwidzyn.pl

Most of **Kwidzyn Castle** is poised on a hilltop over the River Liwa, but the immediately striking feature is the *dansker* toilet and defence tower, stranded out in what used to be the riverbed and connected to the main building by means of a precarious roofed walkway. The castle houses a modest local **museum**. Adjacent to the castle, the large, moody **cathedral** retains several original Gothic features, the most noteworthy being a beautiful late fourteenth-century mosaic in the southern vestibule.

ARRIVAL AND DEPARTURE   KWIDZYN

By train The train station is a 10min walk east of the castle. There are regular trains to Malbork (7 daily; 45min).

By bus Buses from Gdansk (4 daily; 1hr 40min) pull in at the bus station, next to the train station.

Chełmno

Named the "city of lovers" because of the relics of St Valentine kept in the parish church, the hilltop town of **CHEŁMNO** is one of the historical gems of northern Poland, with a thirteenth-century layout, nearly 3km of town walls and a skyline punctuated by the Gothic towers of red-brick churches.

Although a Polish stronghold existed here as early as the eleventh century, Chełmno really came to life in 1225 with the arrival of the Teutonic Knights. They made the town their first political and administrative centre, which led to rapid and impressive development. An academy was founded in 1386 on the model of the famed University of Bologna and the town continued to thrive right up to the time of the Partitions, when it lapsed into provincial obscurity.

The Old Town

Best way to enter the Old Town is via the **Grudziądz Gate**, a well-proportioned fourteenth-century Gothic construction topped by fine Renaissance gables. This leads to the pedestrianized ulica Grudziądzka and on to the Prussian ensemble of the **Rynek** at the heart of the town. Gracing the centre of the square is the brilliant-white **town hall**, with an exuberantly decorated facade. Rebuilt in the 1560s on the basis of an earlier Gothic hall, its elegant exterior, decorated attic and soaring tower are one of the great examples of Polish Renaissance architecture. At the back of the town hall hangs the 4.35m-long "Chełmno rod", a measure employed for the original planning of the town and used up until the nineteenth century. The best of Chełmno's churches is the **parish church** standing just west of the Rynek, an imposing thirteenth-century building with a fine carved doorway. Fragments of St Valentine's skull are contained in a small silver reliquary near the main altar.

3

ARRIVAL AND INFORMATION CHEŁMNO

By bus The bus station is on ul. Dworcowa, a 15min walk from the Old Town. There are hourly services to Bydgoszcz (1hr 15min) and Toruń (1hr 40min).

Tourist information The tourist office is inside the town hall on the Rynek (Mon–Fri 8am–4pm, Sat 10am–4pm, Sun 11am–3pm; ☎ 56 686 2104, ⓦ chelmno.pl).

EATING

Karczma Chełmińska ul. 22 Stycznia 1b ☎ 56 679 0605, ⓦ karczmachelminska.pl. The best restaurant in town, serving hearty Polish dishes for under 30zł in a tastefully rustic interior. Mon–Sat 1–10pm, Sun 1–6pm.

Bydgoszcz

First impressions of **BYDGOSZCZ**, surrounded by industrial and retail sprawl, aren't good. But persist and you'll find the city has a charming centre, bisected by a river and adorned with the full range of Polish architectural styles. Throw in some student-fuelled nightlife and you've got a good reason to hop over from Toruń, or to linger for a day or two.

Originally developed around a fortified medieval settlement, Bydgoszcz only really took off at the end of the eighteenth century when, as the Prussian town of Bromberg, it became an important textile-producing centre. Many of the restored and repurposed industrial buildings are on **Mill Island**, immediately west of a compact **Old Town**. North of the River Brda, **ulica Cieszkowskiego** is Bydgoszcz's prettiest street, lined with dozens of elegant Art Nouveau apartment buildings.

Old Market Square and around

The focal point of the old centre is the **Old Market Square** (Stary Rynek) on the south bank of the Brda, a pleasant space with a clutch of Baroque and Neoclassical mansions. A communist-era **monument** to the victims of Nazism marks the spot where Nazi planners demolished one side of the square to make space for parades. Behind the monument looms the vast bulk of the **Jesuit college**. In a secluded corner just to the north of the Old Market Square is the fifteenth-century **cathedral**, its exterior graced by a fine Gothic gable. Inside, the highlight is the sixteenth-century high altar of *The Madonna with the Rose*.

Mill Island

The cathedral overlooks **Mill Island** (Wyspa Mlynska), situated at the point where the Brda separates into several little channels. Crossed by dainty bridges and overlooked by old half-timbered granaries and red-brick warehouses, these fast-flowing waterways make up an area fancifully styled as the "Bydgoszcz Venice".

Red Granary

ul. Mennica 8a • April–Oct Tues, Wed & Fri 10am–6pm, Thurs 10am–7pm, Sat & Sun 11am–6pm; Nov–March Tues, Wed & Fri 9am–4pm, Thurs 9am–6pm, Sat & Sun 10am–4pm • 5zł; free on Sat • ☎ 52 585 9903, ⓦ muzeum.bydgoszcz.pl

One of the warehouses tucked away at the northern end of Mill Island holds the newly renovated **Red Granary** (Czerwony Spichrz), one of six branches of the **district museum** (Muzeum Okręgowe). The collection here focuses on modern and contemporary art.

Brda Granaries

ul. Grodzka 7–11 • April–Oct Tues, Wed & Fri 10am–6pm, Thurs 10am–7pm, Sat & Sun 11am–6pm; Nov–March Tues, Wed & Fri 9am–4pm, Thurs 9am–6pm, Sat & Sun 10am–4pm • 5zł; free on Sat • ☎ 52 585 9907, ⓦ muzeum.bydgoszcz.pl

East of the main square stand three quaint half-timbered riverside granaries dating from 1793–1800; these house the new **Brda Granaries** (Spichrza nad Brdą), a branch of the district museum worth visiting for its eclectic collection of artefacts relating to the history of the city.

The Exploseum

ul. Alfreda Nobla 1, 7km southeast of the centre • April–Oct Tues, Wed, Fri, Sat & Sun 9am–5pm, Thurs 9am–7pm; Nov–March Tues–Sun 9am–3.30pm • 12zł; free on Sat • ☎ 883 366 056, ⓦ exploseum.pl

Hidden among a tangle of woodland and former industrial facilities on the outskirts of town is the semi-derelict site of **DAG Fabrik Bromberg**, a factory in which 40,000 POWs and slave workers helped produce nitroglycerine and other explosives for the German army during World War II. Part of the site is now open as the **Exploseum**, a new museum housed in a grim collection of factory buildings, dark corridors and test bunkers. Amongst the displays are recreated chemistry labs, a section on the history of modern explosive production from Alfred Nobel onwards, and information on the acts of resistance and sabotage carried out by the factory's workers.

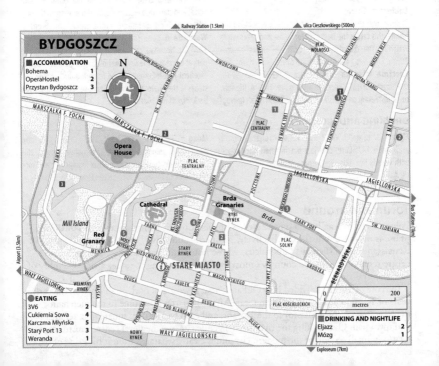

ARRIVAL AND INFORMATION

By plane Bydgoszcz's airport (t52 365 4700, Wplb.pl) is 3km south of town; to get to the centre, catch bus #80 (every 30min) to Rondo Jagiellonow, or take a taxi (around 20zł).

By train The train station is northwest of the city centre; a 15min walk down ul. Dworcowa (or bus #67) brings you to ul. Gdańska, from where it's a short hop over the river to the Rynek.

Destinations Gdańsk (10 daily; 1hr 55min); Kraków (1 daily; 7hr); Łódź Kaliska (2 daily; 4hr); Poznań (10 daily; 1hr 40min–2hr 30min); Toruń (hourly; 1hr); Warsaw (6 daily; 3hr 35min); Wrocław (5 daily; 4hr 20min).

By bus The bus station is 1km east of the centre along Jagiellońska; trams #1, #3, #5, #8 and #10 all head for the centre.

Destinations Chelmno (hourly; 1hr 15min); Toruń (every 30min; 1hr).

Tourist information The tourist office is just off the Stary Rynek at ul. Batorego 6 (Mon–Fri 9am–6pm, Sat & Sun 10am–4pm; ☎ 52 340 4550, ⓦ visitbydgoszcz.pl); it can help with booking private rooms.

ACCOMMODATION

★ **Bohema** ul. Konarskiego 9 ☎ 52 560 0602, ⓦ hotel bohema.pl; map page 147. This high-class hotel in an elegant town house is the best place to stay in Bydgoszcz, with large Art Nouveau-inspired rooms and smiling staff. In a quiet area just east of ul. Gdańska. **750zł**

OperaHostel ul. Focha 22 ☎ 53 645 2929, ⓦ opera hostel.com.pl; map page 147. Despite the name this is really an apart-hotel offering two- to four-person rooms in a restored townhouse overlooking the river. Rooms come with electric kettle and smart contemporary furnishings. Breakfast extra 25zł per person. **180zł**

Przystan Bydgoszcz ul. Tamka 2 ☎ 52 585 9601, ⓦ przystanbydgoszcz.pl; map page 147. Attractive contemporary hotel on Mill Island, overlooking the river. **240zł**

EATING

3V6 ul. 3 Maja 6 ☎ 52 325 2522, ⓦ 3v6.pl; map page 147. Excellent modern restaurant inside the *City Hotel* with plenty of game on the menu; try the boar with mushroom ragout (56zł) or venison with cognac sauce (45zł). Daily 6.30am–10pm.

Cukiernia Sowa ul. Mostowa 4 ☎ 52 566 3300, ⓦ sowa-restauracja.pl; map page 147. Overlooking the bridge, this café is the best spot for coffee and cakes while watching the crowds wander by. Mon–Thurs 11am–10pm, Fri & Sat 11am–midnight, Sun noon–10pm.

Karczma Młyńska ul. Mennica 1 ☎ 52 345 5786, ⓦ karczmamlynska.com.pl; map page 147. A friendly, rustic restaurant on Mill Island, good for Polish meals (*pierogi*

17–20zł, mains 30–40zł) and with lovely river views. Mon–Thurs & Sun noon–11pm, Fri & Sat noon–midnight.

Stary Port 13 ul. Stary Port 13 ☎ 52 321 6208, ⓦ staryport13.pl; map page 147. Excellent Polish food served in an over-the-top rustic interior complete with ponds and clattering watermills. Most mains are in the 40–60zł range. Mon–Sat noon–11pm, Sun noon–10pm.

Weranda ul. Konarskiego 9 ☎ 52 560 0600; map page 147. Art Nouveau café and restaurant overlooking the park at the rear of the *Bohema* hotel, with great service and excellent Polish-European food featuring duck, game and steaks – the Chateaubriand in Bernaise sauce will set you back 90zł. Daily 10am–11pm.

DRINKING AND NIGHTLIFE

Eljazz ul. Kręta 3 ☎ 52 322 1574, ⓦ eljazz.com.pl; map page 147. Cute, cool jazz bar in a red-brick space with weekly live gigs. Daily 4pm–2am, Fri till 3am, Sat till 4am.

Mózg ul. Parkowa 2 ☎ 52 345 5195, ⓦ mozg.pl; map page 147. Hangout for the alternative crowd, this rambling café-cum-music club hosts regular jazz and rock gigs. Daily 6pm–2am; July–Sept closed Sun–Wed.

Toruń and around

Poles are apt to wax lyrical on the glories of their historical cities, and with **TORUŃ** the praise is more than justified. This lively, prosperous university city was the birthplace of Renaissance man **Nicolaus Copernicus**, whose house still stands today, and its historic centre remains one of the country's most evocative, bringing together a rich assembly of architectural styles.

The core of Toruń is divided into Old and New Town areas, both established in the early years of Teutonic rule: the **Old Town** (Stare Miasto) quarter was home to the merchants, the **New Town** (Nowe Miasto) to the artisans, and each had its own square, market area and town hall. Overlooking the river from a gentle rise, the medieval centre constitutes a relatively small section of the modern city and is clearly separated from it by a ring of parks.

Brief history

Toruń's beginnings are similar to those of other towns along the northern Vistula. Starting out as a Polish settlement, it was overrun by Prussian tribes towards the end of the twelfth century, and soon afterwards the Teutonic Knights (see page 144) moved in. The Knights rapidly developed the town, thanks to its access to the river-borne grain trade, and its position was further consolidated upon entering the **Hanseatic League**. Disenchantment with the rule of the Knights led to the formation of the Toruń-based **Prussian Union** in 1440. In 1454, as war broke out between the Knights and Poland, the townspeople destroyed the Toruń castle; the 1466 **Treaty of Toruń** finally terminated the Knights' control of the area.

During the sixteenth and seventeeth centuries the town thrived on extensive royal privileges and increased access to goods from across Poland, but the Partitions in the eighteenth century were a decisive blow to Toruń's fortunes, when the town was annexed to Prussia and thus severed from its hinterlands. Like much of the region, Toruń was subjected to systematic Germanization, but a strongly Polish identity remained, and the twentieth century saw Toruń returned to Poland under the terms of the 1919 Versailles Treaty.

The Old Town

The **Old Town** area is the obvious place to start looking around, with the **Rynek Staromiejski**, in particular the town hall (see page 150), providing the focal point. Lining the square itself are stately mansions of Hansa merchants, many of whose facades are preserved intact. The finest houses flank the east side of the square. Off to

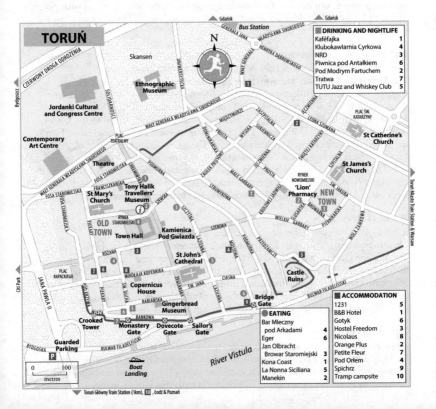

TORUŃ BOAT TRIPS

The view of the medieval city from the river is a memorable sight; you can admire it from the bridge leading to the train station, or, from May to September, you can take a forty-minute **boat trip** on the river itself (20zł). Boats depart on the hour between 9am and 7pm – head through the Monastery Gate down to the riverbank to reach the landing stage.

---

the west of the square stands **St Mary's Church** (Kościół Mariacki), a large fourteenth-century building with elements of its early decoration retained in the sombre interior.

The Town Hall and museum

Rynek Staromiejski 1 • Museum and tower: Tues–Sun: May–Sept 10am–6pm; Oct–April 10am–4pm • Museum 11zł; tower 11zł; combined ticket 17zł

Converted in the late fourteenth century from an older cloth hall, the **town hall** is a tremendous statement of civic pride – they don't come much bigger or more striking than this. A three-storey brick structure topped by a sturdy tower, its outer walls are punctuated by indented windows, framed by a rhythmic succession of high arches and complemented by graceful Renaissance turrets and gables.

The south entrance leads to an inner courtyard surrounded by fine brick doorways, the main one leading to the **town museum**, which now occupies much of the building. The ground floor contains a gorgeous collection of the **stained glass** for which the city was famed and some fine **sculptures**, especially the celebrated "Beautiful Madonnas" in which the Virgin is portrayed swooning in an S-shaped posture of grace. On the first floor **paintings** take over, the walls covered with portraits of Polish kings and wealthy Toruń citizens. For an additional few złoty you can climb the **tower** for the view of the city.

Tony Halik Travellers' Museum

ul. Franciszkańska 9/11 • Tues–Sun: May–Sept 10am–6pm; Oct–April 10am–4pm • 10zł • ⓦ muzeum.torun.pl

The **Tony Halik Travellers' Museum** (Muzeum Podróżników im. Tony'ego Halika) is small but fascinating collection honouring Toruń-born explorer and TV presenter Tony Halik (1921–98). A complex and colourful personality, Halik fought for the French Resistance after deserting from the Luftwaffe, then emigrated to the USA to work in the growing TV industry. His career-defining feat was to travel from Tierra del Fuego to Alaska by jeep with a young family in tow – the resulting book and TV film cemented his reputation. The museum (largely put together by Halik's second wife Elżbieta Dzikowska, who carried on travelling and collecting after Halik's death) contains a colourful array of costumes, headdresses and textiles from all over the world, with Latin American and Himalayan cultures particularly well represented.

St John's Cathedral

ul. Żeglarska 16 •Mon–Sat 8.30am–7.30pm, Sun 4.30–7.30pm; tower closed Nov–March • 3zł; tower 6zł

On atmospheric ulica Żeglarska sits **St John's Cathedral** (Katedra św. Jana), a large, magnificent Gothic structure, where Copernicus was baptized in 1473. The presbytery, the oldest part of the building, dates from the 1260s, but the main nave and aisles were not completed till the mid-fifteenth century. The **tower** houses a magnificent fifteenth-century *Tuba Dei*, the largest bell in Poland outside Kraków, which can be heard all over town; you can climb to the top of the tower for great views of the city.

Copernicus House

ul. Kopernika 15/17 • Tues–Sun: May–Sept 10am–6pm; Oct–April 10am–4pm • 12zł • ☎ 56 660 5683, ⓦ muzeum.torun.pl.

Halfway down ulica Kopernika you'll find the **Copernicus House** (Dom Kopernika), the high brick house where the great man (see page 142) was most probably born. Restored to something resembling its original layout, this Gothic mansion contains a studiously assembled collection of Copernicus artefacts: facsimiles of the momentous *De Revolutionibus*, models of astronomical instruments, original household furniture and early portraits.

Gingerbread Museum

ul. Rabiańska 9 • Daily: Jan–March 10am–6pm; April–Dec 9am–6pm; Polish-language sessions start hourly; English-language sessions at 1pm & 4pm must be reserved in advance on the museum's website • 15zł • ⓦ muzeumpiernika.pl.

You smell the **Gingerbread Museum** (Muzeum Piernika) before you see it. It's a delightful place to take children, where visitors get a hands-on cooking class as staff in period dress teach how gingerbread was made five hundred years ago – and you can eat the biscuits you make. The museum's gift shop is the best place in town to pick up gingerbread souvenirs.

The City Walls

Running along the southern perimeter of the Old Town is a stretch of defensive **walls** overlooking the river, all that remains of an extensive fortification system largely knocked down by nineteenth-century town planners. To the west, at the bottom of ulica Pod Krzywą Wieżą, stands the mid-fourteenth-century **Crooked Tower** (Krzywa Wieża), followed in quick succession by the **Monastery Gate** (Brama Klasztorna), **Dovecote Tower** (Baszta Gołębnik) and **Sailors' Gate** (Brama Żeglarska), all from the same period, the last originally leading to the main harbour.

The Castle

ul. Przedzamce 3 • Daily: March–Oct 10am–6pm; Nov–Feb 10am–3.45pm • 8zł • ☎ 660 061 352

Dominating the southeastern corner of the Old Town are the ruins of the Teutonic Knights' **castle**. While the castle here was nowhere near as massive as the later Malbork fortress, the scale of what's left is enough to leave you impressed by the Toruń citizenry's efforts in laying waste to it. The impressive Gdanisko outer tower and several basement rooms can be visited.

The New Town

Less grand than its mercantile neighbour, the **New Town** still boasts a number of illustrious commercial residences, most of them grouped around the **Rynek Nowomiejski**. On the west side of the square, the fifteenth-century Pod Modrym Fartuchem inn (no. 8) and at no. 13 the Gothic Pod Lwem ("Lion") pharmacy are particularly striking. Just off the eastern corner of the Rynek, the fourteenth-century **St James's Church** (Kościół św. Jakuba) completes the city's collection of Gothic churches. Inside, the Baroque decoration is relieved by occasional Gothic frescoes, panel paintings and sculpture – most notably a large fourteenth-century crucifix.

Ethnographic Museum

ul. Waly Sikorskiego 19 • Mid-April to June Tues & Thurs 9am–5pm, Wed & Fri 9am–4pm, Sat & Sun 10am–6pm; July–Sept Tues, Thurs, Sat & Sun 10am–6pm, Wed & Fri 9am–4pm; Oct to mid-April Tues–Fri 9am–4pm, Sat & Sun 10am–4pm • 14zł; free on Wed • ☎ 56 622 8091, ⓦ etnomuzeum.pl

Sitting in a park just north of the New Town, the old city arsenal houses the **Ethnographic Museum** (Muzeum Etnograficzne), which deal with the customs and crafts of northern Poland. Round the back of the building, a small *skansen* contains an enchanting collection of wooden buildings.

Jordanki Cultural and Congress Centre

al. Solidarności 1–3 • Ticket office Tues–Sat 1–7pm • ⓦ jordanki.torun.pl

Looking something like a gargantuan Cubist painting in three-dimensional form, the **Jordanki Cultural and Congress Centre** (Centrum Kulturalno-Kongresowe Jordanki) has quickly become an icon of contemporary Toruń, a modernist counterpoint to the red-brick Gothic glories on show elsewhere. Completed in 2016 to plans by Spanish architect Fernando Menis, it is home to the local symphony orchestra and is also the region's prime conference venue. Whether you have tickets for an event or not, the bold geometric shapes of the entrance lobby and the exterior are definitely worth a look.

Contemporary Art Centre

ul. Wały Sikorskiego 13 • July & Aug Tues–Sun noon–8pm; Sept–June Tues–Thurs 10am–6pm, Fri 10am–8pm, Sat & Sun noon–6pm • 8–12zł, depending on exhibition • ☎ 56 610 9718, ⓦ csw.torun.pl

Just northwest of the Old Town, the imposing **Centre of Contemporary Art** (Centrum Sztuki Współczesnej) hosts changing exhibitions of local and foreign modern art. The excellent museum shop sells art books and quirky Toruń souvenirs.

ARRIVAL AND INFORMATION

By train Toruń Główny, the main train station, is south of the river; it's a 2km walk to the city centre, or a short hop on bus #22, #25 or #27 (every 20min). Most trains also stop at the unstaffed Toruń Miasto station, about 1km east of the centre.

Destinations Bydgoszcz (hourly; 1hr); Gdańsk (6 daily; 3hr–3hr 30min); Kaliska (1 daily; 2hr 30min); Kraków (1 daily; 6hr 10min); Łódź Olsztyn (9 daily; 2hr 50min); Poznań (6 daily; 1hr 30min–2hr 15min); Warsaw (8 daily; 2hr 45min); Wrocław (1 daily; 4hr 10min).

By bus The station is on ul. Dąbrowskiego, a short walk north of the centre.

Destinations Bydgoszcz (every 30min; 1hr); Chelmno (hourly; 1hr 40min); Łódź (4 daily; 3hr 20min); Warsaw (8 daily; 4hr).

Tourist information The tourist office on Rynek Staromiejski 25 (Mon–Fri 9am–6pm, Sat & Sun 9am–10am; ☎56 621 0930, ⓦit.torun.pl) doles out free maps and can help book private accommodation and apartments.

ACCOMMODATION

HOTELS

★ **1231** ul. Przedzamcze 6 ☎56 619 0910, ⓦhotel 1231.pl; map page 149. Impressive boutique hotel inside the Teutonic Knights' thirteenth-century mill, with stylish rooms incorporating details of the original building, and an excellent restaurant downstairs. **450zł**

★ **B&B Hotel** ul. Szumana 8 ☎56 621 8100, ⓦhotel bb.pl; map page 149. Smart, stylish but still comfortingly inexpensive, the Toruń branch of the B&B chain delivers on all fronts, and is nicely situated within walking distance of the Old Town. **230zł**

Gotyk ul. Piekary 20 ☎56 658 4000, ⓦhotel-gotyk. com.pl; map page 149. Small hotel in the centre, with classically furnished en-suite roomsee pages painted in pastel tones and hung with heavy drapes; exposed wooden beams lend the place an air of antiquity. **250zł**

Nicolaus ul. Ducha Świętego 14–16 ☎56 470 8989, ⓦnicolaus.com.pl; map page 149. Boutique hotel in an old mansion, with comfy and rather chic rooms offering a mixture of exposed-brick authenticity and contemporary design. The top-floor rooms with attic ceilings are particularly cute. **360zł**

Petite Fleur ul. Piekary 25 ☎56 621 5100, ⓦpetite fleur.pl; map page 149. A stone's throw from the Rynek, this small hotel has an intimate feel. Rooms are simple and bright with pine floors and furnishings and modern bathrooms. **300zł**

Pod Orlem ul. Mostowa 17 ☎56 622 5024, ⓦpod orlemtorun.pl; map page 149. Well-located hotel that has been operating since the nineteenth century. The interior is a bit dark, but the simply furnished rooms are clean and comfortable. Cheaper on weekends. **360zł**

Spichrz ul. Mostowa 1 ☎56 657 1140, ⓦspichrz. pl; map page 149. Swish hotel in a monumental eighteenth-century granary beside the Mostowa city gate. Rooms have plenty of wooden beams and other original details, and there's a traditional restaurant attached. **350zł**

HOSTELS

Hostel Freedom Rynek Staromiejski 10 ☎731 218 415, ⓦfreedomtorun.pl; map page 149. Nicely decorated hostel in a creaky-floored apartment on the main square, with a small kitchen and neat bunk-bed dorms. Dorms **40zł**, doubles **100zł**

Orange Plus ul. Jeczmienna 11 19 ☎56 651 8457, ⓦhostelorange.pl; map page 149. A bright, cosy youth hostel at the eastern end of the Old Town, with friendly staff and comfortable, inexpensive rooms, plus free tea, coffee and internet. Dorms **35zł**, doubles **100zł**

CAMPSITE

Tramp ul. Kujawska 14 ☎666 359 924, ⓦcampingtramp. pl; map page 149. A short walk west of the train station, this campsite has a nice wooded setting near the river, though it suffers from traffic noise. Bungalows and rooms are available year-round. Camping **45zł**, bungalows **70zł**

EATING

Bar Mleczny pod Arkadami ul. Różana 1 ☎ 56 622 2428; map page 149. Traditional fast food, including filling *barszcz*, enormous omelettes and takeaway waffles (*gofry*), in contemporary surroundings. Mon–Fri 9am–7pm, Sat & Sun 10am–5pm.

Eger ul. Mostowa 3 ☎ 791 092 566, ⓦ egertorun. pl; map page 149. Smart, contemporary restaurant specializing in Hungarian food, serving up one of the best Hungarian fish soups (freshwater fish in a paprika-rich stew; 16zł) you're likely to find this far north. Mains are not too expensive (goulash with noodles weighs in at 28zł), and there's a good list of Hungarian wines. Mon–Thurs noon–10pm, Fri & Sat noon–11pm, Sun noon–9pm.

Jan Olbracht Browar Staromiejski ul. Szczytna 15 ☎ 797 903 333, ⓦ browar-olbracht.pl; map page 149. Pub-restaurant offering hearty mains such as *golonka* (pork knuckle), ribs and salmon steaks (all in the 30–40zł range), with a few local oddities (*pierogi* with goose filling; 20zł) thrown in. Two-course lunches (Mon–Fri noon–4pm) are a steal at 20zł. Microbrewery beers are the icing on the cake. Mon–Thurs & Sun 11am–

midnight, Fri & Sat 11am–1am.

Kona Coast ul. Chełmińska 18 ☎ 56 664 0049, ⓦ kona coastcafe.pl; map page 149. Something of a coffee-lover's café, offering drip and Chemex varieties as well as the espresso kind. The food menu extends to soups, pastas, tortilla wraps and great cheesecakes – all consumed to a trippy, jazzy, lounge-music soundtrack. Mon–Sat 8am–9pm, Sun 8am–8pm.

La Nonna Siciliana ul. Łazienna 24 ☎ 888 686 808, ⓦ lanonnasiciliana.pl; map page 149. Fine Sicilian restaurant with some exciting pasta dishes including chunky pockets of ravioli with spinach (23zł) and an exemplary spaghetti with prawns and garlic (30zł), as well as a dependable range of pizzas (30–35zł). Mon–Thurs & Sun noon–10pm, Fri & Sat noon–11pm.

Manekin Rynek Staromiejski 16 ☎ 56 621 0504, ⓦ manekin.pl; map page 149. The perfect place for pancake lovers, with a lengthy menu of innovative meat, veg and sweet fillings (try the salmon and camembert pancake for 19zł), plus soups and salads. It's popular, so be prepared to wait for a table. Daily 10am–11pm.

DRINKING AND NIGHTLIFE

Kaféfajka ul. Małe Garbary 1/3 ☎ 56 622 1017, ⓦ kafefajka.com; map page 149. This chilled-out place, filled with cushions, offers a huge range of colourful cocktails and shishas that bubble milk or gin instead of water. Mon–Wed 3pm–2am, Thurs–Sat 3pm–3am, Sun 2pm–2am.

Klubokawiarnia Cyrkowa Rynek Staromiejski 1 ☎ 698 832 129, ⓦ facebook.com/cyrkowatorun; map page 149. Circus-themed club in the basement of the town hall, with a mural-covered interior and outdoor seating on the square. Mon–Thurs & Sun 6pm–midnight, Fri & Sat 6pm–3am.

NRD ul. Browarna 6 ☎ 785 934 718; map page 149. A run-down but friendly centre of alternative culture, with regular art events, DJs and concerts. Daily 5pm–1am.

★ **Piwnica pod Antałkiem** ul. Ducha Świętego 1 ☎ 666 359 210, ⓦ facebook.com/piwnicapodantalkiem; map page 149. Cute pub and wine bar with retro furniture, historical photos on the wall and a semi-circular bar doling out excellent local Toruńskie beer, a good choice of wine, and

(this is Toruń after all) gingerbread-flavoured vodka. Daily 4pm–1am.

Pod Modrym Fartuchem Rynek Nowomiejski 8 ☎ 722 992 399, ⓦ krajina-piva.pl; map page 149. Homely pub furnished with an odd mixture of old and new, serving locally brewed (including gingerbread-flavoured) beer on tap and a host of bottles. The standard side order is *chleb ze smalcem* (bread and lard; 7zł), although there's also a solid menu of main-course food including pork chops, roast duck leg and pork knuckle cooked in beer (30zł). Daily 10am–midnight.

Tratwa ul. Flisacza 7; map page 149. Ramshackle alternative pub on two levels, with a leafy courtyard, cheap beer and a relatively young crowd. Punk/reggae/rock on the sound system, and occasional gigs or DJs. Daily 4pm–3am.

TUTU Jazz and Whiskey Club ul. Rabiańska 17 ☎ 56 676 8499, ⓦ kadr.torun.pl; map page 149. Brick-cellar drinking den decorated with pictures of jazz greats and album covers, and featuring a long bar backed by a wall of spirit bottles – with whiskys and whiskeys well represented. Regular jazz gigs during student term time. Daily 3pm–2am.

Mazuria and Podlasie

KAYAKING ON THE RIVER KRUTYNIA

Mazuria and Podlasie

Ask Poles to list the natural wonders of their country and they will automatically answer "lakes and forests" – things that the northeastern territories of Mazuria and Podlasie offer in rich abundance. These predominantly agricultural regions are famous for their clean waterways and surviving tracts of unspoiled wilderness; perfect terrain for walking, kayaking or simply communing with nature. There's plenty in the way of diverse cultural heritage too, with medieval towns, Teutonic fortresses and splendid churches dotting the landscape. Religious and ethnic diversity become increasingly evident the further east you go, with Poles, Lithuanians, Belarusians and even Tatars sharing the bucolic villages on Poland's eastern rim.

The so-called "land of a thousand lakes", **Mazuria** (Mazury) was formed by the last Ice Age, when retreating glaciers carved out the hollows now filled with water. A sparsely populated area of thick forests and innumerable lakes and rivers, Mazuria is one of the country's main holiday districts – a wonderful haunt for walkers, campers and watersports enthusiasts. The western fringes of Mazuria rub up against **Warmia**, a rich agricultural plain centred on **Olsztyn**, a pleasant small-scale city worth a short stay. From here bus and train links fan out towards the main lakeside resorts, with **Mikołajki** and **Wilkasy** offering the most in terms of activities and natural beauty.

East of Mazuria, little-visited **Suwalszczyzna** (named after its main town, **Suwałki**) offers an extraordinary wealth of rolling farmland, dense woods and reed-fringed lakes, of which those around the resort of **Augustów** offer most to the visitor. South of here stretches **Podlasie**, a land of open plains and primeval forest centred on the city of **Białystok**, ideal jumping-off point for heritage villages such as **Supraśl** and **Tykocin**, the latter the site of a beautifully preserved synagogue. Southeastern Podlasie is marked by the **Białowieża National Park**, continental Europe's last belt of virgin forest – the haunt of bison, elk and hundreds of varieties of flora and fauna.

Olsztyn

One of Poland's more laid-back regional capitals, **OLSZTYN** contains a compact and strollable Old Town as well as a suburban lake resort in the shape of Ukiel, just 1.5km from the city centre. Soviet troops burnt down much of the city in 1945 but an ample sprinkling of handsome brick buildings still remains, and the place has a markedly more relaxing atmosphere than some of Poland's more populous cities. Fans of Teutonic Order castles will be pleased to know that there's one in Olsztyn, and an even more impressive example in **Lidzbark Warmiński**, 50km to the north.

SUWAŁKI LANDSCAPE PARK

Highlights

❶ Krutynia Trail Spectacular kayaking on over a hundred kilometres of lakes and rivers winding through the heart of the Mazurian lake district. See page 163

❷ The Wolf's Lair Grimly compelling site of Hitler's secret command bunker, once the nerve centre of German military power. See page 166

❸ Suwałki Landscape Park Bewitching area of gently rolling farmland and forest, sprinkled with deep lakes and the odd rustic village. See page 177

❹ Supraśl Traditional, timber-built village near the Belarusian border, boasting a sumptuous museum collection of Orthodox icons. See page 183

❺ Tykocin Riverside town of cobbled alleys and one-storey houses, site of one of the most beautifully preserved synagogues in the country. See page 184

❻ Biebrża National Park Captivating lowland landscape of reeds and marshes, criss-crossed by accessible walking trails. See page 186

❼ Białowieża National Park Europe's largest surviving area of primeval forest, famous for its population of bison. See page 189

HIGHLIGHTS ARE MARKED ON THE MAP ON PAGE 158

Brief history

Long the administrative centre of Warmia, Olzsyn was fortified by the Teutonic Knights in the fourteenth century, only to be returned to the kingdom of Poland in 1466. Nicolaus Copernicus briefly served as the local administrator, helping to organize the defence of Olsztyn against the Knights in 1521. Coming under Prussian control after the First Partition of Poland, Olsztyn (known in German as **Allenstein**) remained part of East Prussia until 1945. The majority of the German-speaking population were expelled after World War II, replaced by Polish settlers from the eastern provinces annexed by the Soviet Union. Post-war development soon established Olsztyn as the region's major administrative and industrial centre, and it is now a prosperous and animated city of 175,000 people.

The Old Town

Olsztyn's **Old Town** (Stare Miasto) is entered via the fourteenth-century **High Gate** (Brama Wysoka), a solid chunk of red brick that serves as the city's visual trademark.

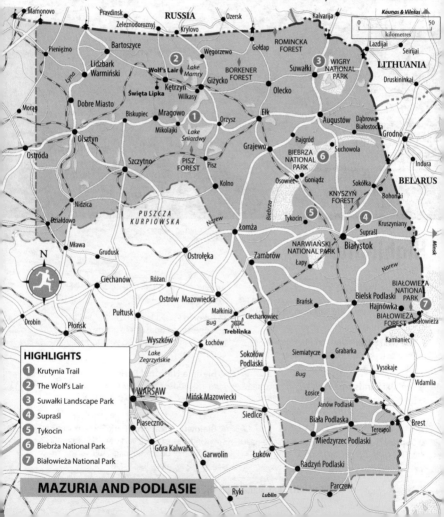

HIGHLIGHTS

1. Krutynia Trail
2. The Wolf's Lair
3. Suwałki Landscape Park
4. Supraśl
5. Tykocin
6. Biebrza National Park
7. Białowieża National Park

MAZURIA AND PODLASIE

PRUSSIA AND THE PRUSSIANS

Present-day Warmia and Mazuria make up the heartlands of what was known as **East Prussia** (Ostpreussen), the territory carved out by the **Teutonic Knights** (a semi-monastic crusading order) in the Middle Ages and subjected to various forms of German-speaking rule right up until 1945.

Despite competing German and Polish claims to the area, it was originally populated by neither: the indigenous inhabitants were Baltic tribes, most numerous of whom were the Borussians (later shortened to "**Prussians**"), a people closely related in language and culture to modern Lithuanians and Latvians. The Prussians were among the last of Europe's **pagans**, venerating sun, moon, trees and rivers. The job of **Christianizing** them was begun by Polish rulers as early as the tenth century, when Bolesław the Brave dispatched Bishop (and future Saint) **Adalbert** to the Baltic shores – the Prussians expressed their gratitude by having him chopped to pieces. The Prussian tribes were too disunited to offer resistance to the Teutonic Knights, who set about forcibly converting the locals to Christianity in the thirteenth century. The remaining Prussians were gradually assimilated by German-speaking colonizers, or fled east where they were absorbed into the Lithuanian nation.

Although the Prussians disappeared, their name lived on as a geographical label, and was ultimately adopted by the very people who had wiped them out. Following the secularization of the Teutonic Knights' lands in 1525, much of what is now northern Poland became the **Duchy of Prussia,** with Königsberg (now Kaliningrad in Russia) as its capital. The centre of power in Prussia gradually shifted westwards, and in 1701 Berlin emerged as the capital of a newly established **Kingdom of Prussia**. Prussia subsequently became the nucleus of the modern German state, which came into being in 1871.

From here ulica Staromiejska descends to the **Rynek**, which is surrounded by houses sporting an extraordinary variety of gables, taking the form of pediments, peaks and coronets. A few steps east of the Rynek looms the high brick tower of the early fifteenth-century **St James' Cathedral** (Bazylika św. Jakuba), containing an intricately patterned brick ceiling and a powerful Crucifixion triptych hanging over the high altar.

Olsztyn Castle and around

Museum: May, June & Sept Tues–Sat 9am–5pm, Sun 10am–6pm; July & Aug Tues–Sun 10am–6pm; Oct–April Tues–Sat 10am–4pm, Sun 10am–6pm • 10zł; free on Wed • ☎ 89 527 9596, ⓦ muzeum.olsztyn.pl

West of the Old Town sits **Olsztyn Castle**, fourteenth-century but extensively rebuilt, surveying the steep little valley of the River Łyna. The castle **museum** contains a good ethnographic section with a selection of folk costumes, art and furniture. The former living quarters of **Copernicus** can be found on the first floor of the southwest wing; along with a wistful portrait by Matejko and several of the astronomer's instruments, the rooms contain a sundial supposed to have been designed by Copernicus himself. It's also worth climbing the **castle tower** for a view over the town and surroundings. Coming out of the back of the castle you can stroll across the bridge over the gently coursing River Łyna to the park on the other side – an atmospheric spot, particularly at sunset.

Olsztyn Planetarium

al. Marszałka J. Piłsudskiego 38 • Six or seven shows daily 11am–6pm, usually commencing on the hour • 15zł • ☎ 89 650 0420, ⓦ planetarium.olsztyn.pl

A modernist white block with a silvery dome bulging from the top, **Olsztyn Planetarium** was digitalized in 2012 and has become a major regional attraction, offering projections of the night sky as well as visually captivating films (in Polish) about science, technology and natural history.

Lake Ukiel

1.5km west of town; walk west along Grunwaldzka, pass under the railway tracks and bear northwest at the roundabout onto Bałtycka • ⓦ ukiel.olsztyn.eu

One of the things that makes Olsztyn such a good introduction to the Mazurian Lake District is that it has a couple of nice lakes right on its own doorstep. A reasonably easy half-hour walk from the centre, the wood-fringed, four-square-kilometre expanse of **Lake Ukiel** is the city's favourite relaxation area, not least because of its recently redeveloped **beach** complete with leisure facilities and cafés.

ARRIVAL AND DEPARTURE OLSZTYN

By air Olsztyn-Mazury airport (☏ 89 544 3434, ⓦ mazuryairport.pl) is out in the countryside at Szymany, 58km south of Olsztyn. Trains run to Olsztyn train station (2–3 daily, timed to coincide with arrivals and departures; 45min). Minibuses operated by Markus Travel (ring to reserve; ☏ 507 077 250) run from the airport to Olsztyn train station (4–5 daily depending on airline timetable; 1hr).

By train The train station is northeast of the Old Town. It's a 20min walk into town; alternatively, take bus #1 or #7 down al. Partyzantów to pl. Jana Pawła II.

Destinations Elbląg (hourly; 1hr 30min); Gdańsk (4 daily; 2hr 25min–2hr 50min); Giżycko (7 daily; 1hr 30min–1hr 50min); Kraków (2 daily; 7hr 10min); Ruciane-Nida (2 daily; 1hr 40min); Toruń (9 daily; 2hr 50min); Warsaw (4 daily; 2hr 30min–3hr).

By bus The bus station is next to the train station. Some buses pick up and drop off on ul. Partyzantów, the main road directly in front of the train and bus stations.

Destinations from bus station Gdańsk (4 daily; 3hr);

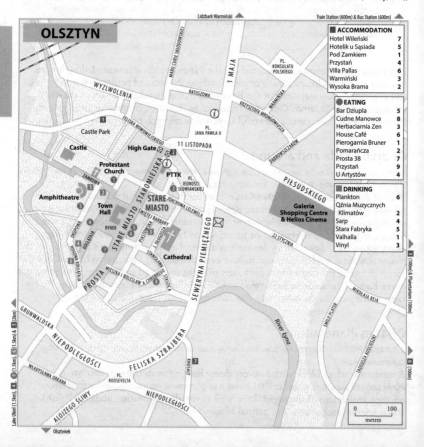

OLSZTYN

Lidzbark Warmiński ▲   Train Station (600m) & Bus Station (600m)

■ ACCOMMODATION
Hotel Wileński	7
Hotelik u Sąsiada	5
Pod Zamkiem	1
Przystań	4
Villa Pallas	6
Warmiński	3
Wysoka Brama	2

● EATING
Bar Dziupla	5
Cudne Manowce	8
Herbaciarnia Zen	3
House Café	6
Pierogarnia Bruner	1
Pomarańcza	2
Prosta 38	7
Przystań	9
U Artystów	4

■ DRINKING
Plankton	6
Qźnia Muzycznych Klimatów	2
Sarp	4
Stara Fabryka	5
Valhalla	1
Vinyl	3

Castle Park

Castle

High Gate

Protestant Church

Amphitheatre

Town Hall

PTTK

STARE MIASTO
STARE MIASTO

RYNEK

Cathedral

Galeria Shopping Centre & Helios Cinema

Olsztynek ▼

Mikolajki (2 daily; 1hr 50min); Ruciane-Nida (2 daily; 2hr); Vilnius (1 daily; 8hr); Warsaw (6 daily; 4hr 30min).

Destinations from ul. Partyzantów Kętrzyn (hourly; 2hr); Lidzbark Warmiński (every 30min; 50min).

INFORMATION

Tourist information There are two tourist offices in Olsztyn: the city tourist information centre in the new town hall at pl. Jana Pawla II 1 (June–Sept Mon–Fri 10am–6pm, Sat & Sun 10am–4pm; Oct–May Mon–Sat 10am–4pm; ☎ 89 521 0398, ⓦ visit.olsztyn.eu) will tell you what's going on in Olsztyn; while the regional tourist organization, beside the High Gate at Staromiejska 1

(Mon–Fri 10am–5pm, Sat 10am–3pm; ☎ 89 535 3565, ⓦ mazurytravel.com.pl), will fill you in on activities throughout Warmia and Mazuria.

PTTK Mazury In the same building as the regional tourist office, at Staromiejska 1 (Mon–Fri 8am–4pm; ☎ 89 527 3665, ⓦ mazury.pttk.pl); organizes boat rental and accommodation for the Krutynia kayaking route (see page 163).

ACCOMMODATION

Hotel Wilenski ul. Knosaly 5 ☎ 89 535 0122, ⓦ hotel wilenski.pl; map page 160. Elegant hotel in a renovated pre-war villa just minutes from the Old Town. The rooms come with some fancy touches, like handmade velvet wallpaper, and there's a charmingly old-fashioned restaurant on the ground floor. **29zł**

Hotelik u Sąsiada ul. Dębowa 6 ☎ 89 527 6891, ⓦ usasiada.olsztyn.pl; map page 160. Family-run pension just above the shores of Lake Ukiel, a 25min walk northwest of the centre. Simple en-suite rooms, a little garden and on-site parking. **150zł**

Pod Zamkiem ul. Nowowiejskiego 10 ☎ 89 535 1287, ⓦ hotel-olsztyn.com.pl; map page 160. Right under the castle walls, this is a small and welcoming place in a carefully renovated Art Nouveau villa filled with antiques and polished wood. Cute en suites come with TV. **220zł**

Przystań ul. Żeglarska 3 ☎ 89 535 0181, ⓦ hotel przystan.pl; map page 160. Smart contemporary rooms looking out on Lake Ukiel's yachting marina, with a spa

centre, bike hire (perfect for exploring the lakeside paths) and a noted restaurant (see page 162). **350zł**

Villa Pallas ul. Żołnierska 4 ☎ 89 535 0115, ⓦ villa pallas.pl; map page 160. Early twentieth-century villa set in leafy grounds within walking distance of the centre, offering tasteful rooms with modern bathrooms, plus an atmospherically old-school breakfast room/restaurant. Weekend discounts are available. **200zł**

Warmiński ul. Kołobrzeska 1 ☎ 89 522 1400, ⓦ hotel-warminski.com.pl; map page 160. Large, recently refurbished hotel gleaming with polished granite and glass, aimed at the business market and with correspondingly efficient service. **280zł**

Wysoka Brama ul. Staromiejska 1 ☎ 89 527 3675, ⓦ hotelwysokabrama.olsztyn.pl; map page 160. Simply decorated, no-frills doubles and dorms next to the High Gate; the rooms may have seen better days, but the location is hard to beat. Dorms **30zł**, doubles **75zł**

EATING

CAFÉS

Bar Dziupla ul. Stare Miasto 9/10 ☎ 89 527 5083, ⓦ dziupla.go3.pl; map page 160. Snack bar with a tasty selection of soups, potato pancakes, excellent *pierogi* (13.50zł) and inexpensive mains featuring plenty of fish and pork. Daily 8.30am–8pm.

Herbaciarnia Zen ul. Okopowa 23 ☎ 89 535 1559; map page 160. Speciality teahouse serving brews from around the world, decent coffee and good cakes. Mon–Thurs & Sun noon–10pm, Fri & Sat noon–11pm.

House Cafe ul. Stare Miasto 11/16 ☎ 881 349 388; map page 160. Done out to resemble a large open-plan living room, this café is the best place in Olsztyn for espressos, flat whites and muffins. Daily 8am–10pm.

Pomarańcza pl. Jedności Sł owianskiej 9 ☎ 721 157 362, ⓦ pomarancza.olsztyn.pl; map page 160. Colourful café serving sweet and savoury *nalesniki* (crepes; from 10zł), with dozens of fillings to choose from. Also sells soups, salads and alcoholic drinks. Daily noon–9.30pm.

RESTAURANTS

★ **Cudne Manowce** ul. Chrobrego 4 ☎ 89 535 0395, ⓦ cudnemanowce.pl; map page 160. With the homely, distressed look of a farmhouse kitchen, "Wonderful Backroads" serves up quality, inventive cuisine based on seasonal, locally-sourced products. *Pierogi* come with local fish or goats' cheese filling; other specialities include *czernina* (duck's blood soup) and *karmuszka* (local stew containing meat, beans, cabbage and other veg). Mains hover around 35–40zł, but daily specials are frequently cheaper. Wash it all down with Olsztyn-brewed Kormoran beer. Daily noon–10pm.

Pierogarnia Bruner ul. Stare Miasto 26/17 ☎ 89 521 0274, ⓦ pierogarniabruner.pl; map page 160. Traditional *pierogi* with a good choice of different stuffings (mushroom and cheese; 16zł), plus baked *pierogi* and sweet-fruit *pierogi*. They also do pancakes. Mon–Thurs & Sun noon–10pm, Fri & Sat noon–11pm.

Prosta 38 ul. Prosta 38 ☎ 698 447 788, ⓦ prosta38. pl; map page 160. Classy Polish-European dishes on a menu featuring plenty of seasonal variations; gourmet burgers are 30zł, fillet of pike 40zł. There's a more-than-respectable wine list, and some delicious desserts, too; the fruit-and-meringue *dacquoise* (12zł) is a great way to finish off a meal. Mon–Wed & Sun 10am–10pm, Thurs–Sat 10am–11pm.

★ **Przystań** ul. Żeglarska 3 ☎89 535 0181, ⓦrestauracje.olsztyn.pl; map page 160. A classy timber-and-glass pavilion on the shores of Lake Ukiel, a 20min walk northwest of the centre. The menu covers everything in the Polish culinary repertoire but it's the fresh fish that stands out, including pike perch from the lakes and tilapia from their own farm. A good fillet shouldn't set you back more than 35zł. Daily noon–10pm.

U Artystów Kołłątaja 20 ☎89 527 4321, ⓦfacebook. com/uartystowolsztyn; map page 160. Midway between restaurant and lounge bar, *U Artystów* offers a bit more in the way of salads and pasta dishes than the other places in town, as well as some rather fine Polish-European mains. Quality lunchtime specials range from 16zł to 27zł. Daily noon–9pm.

DRINKING AND NIGHTLIFE

Plankton ul. Żeglarska ☎89 333 5018, ⓦplankton-restauracja.pl; map page 160. Glassy pavilion on the Ukiel lakefront with seating out front, serving beer on tap and a food menu that stretches from breakfasts to fish soup and burgers. Daily 9am–9pm.

Qżnia Muzycznych Klimatów ul. Stare Miasto 29/32/1 ☎506 990 206, ⓦqzniapub.pl; map page 160. Lively pub with a small stage for live music and an interior scattered with instruments, band photos and other musical bric-a-brac. Good choice of bottled beer. Daily 11am–4am.

Sarp ul. Kołłątaja 14 ☎89 527 3357, ⓦfacebook.com/Klubsarp123; map page 160. Smart café-bar in the attic of a restored granary, with a good list of cocktails and outdoor riverside seating in summer. Daily 11am–2am.

Stara Fabryka ul. Kołłątaja 15 ☎732 987 408, ⓦstara fabrykapub.pl; map page 160. Raucous place above the river, popular with weekend hedonists, when it's a venue for DJs and karaoke. Daily 3pm–3am.

Valhalla ul. Okopowa 24A ☎570 501 666; map page 160. Friendly cubby-hole of a bar serving craft ales – which can be quaffed from one of the drinking horns behind the bar if you fancy a break from the usual glass. There's a heavy-metal pagan theme going on here, but it's not overdone. Daily noon–4am.

Vinyl ul. Piastowska 4 ☎666 247 218; map page 160. Roomy, comfortable pub in which the cult of the twelve-incher is celebrated with LP covers plastered to the walls, and a real record player behind the bar playing classic rock and new wave. There's a big choice of spirits, plus Czech beers from the Holba stable. Daily 2pm–2am.

Lidzbark Warmiński Castle

pl. Zamkowy 1 • Tues–Sun: mid-May to Aug 9am–5pm; Sept to mid-May 9am–4pm • 8zł • ⓦmuzeum.olsztyn.pl • Buses run from Olsztyn (every 30min; 50min), leaving from ul. Partyzanow in front of the station

Set amid open pastureland watered by the River Łyna, the town of **LIDZBARK WARMIŃSKI** was an important outpost of the Teutonic Knights, and their impressive **castle** ranks as one of the architectural gems of the region. Used as a fortified residence for the Warmian bishops, it echoes Frombork cathedral in its tiled roof, and Malbork fortress in the turreted towers rising from the corners. Much of the building is now occupied by the **Museum of Warmia and Mazury** (Muzeum Warmii i Mazur), which begins with portraits of Copernicus, who lived here briefly, before moving on to a display of Gothic sculpture in the Great Refectory. On the second floor is a collection of modern Polish art, as well as an exquisite exhibition of **icons**. The east wing of the castle was demolished in the mid eighteenth century to make way for a bishop's palace and gardens. The **winter garden** opposite the approach to the castle is the most attractive bit left, with a Neoclassical orangery that wouldn't be out of place in a royal residence.

The Mazurian lakes

East of Olsztyn, the central Mazurian lakeland opens out amid thickening forests. The biggest lakes – **Mamry** and **Śniardwy** – are real crowd-pullers, with all the advantages and disadvantages that brings: tourist facilities are fairly well developed, but accommodation can be hard to find on summer weekends. Commanding the

KAYAKING THE MAZURIAN LAKES

One of the best and most exciting ways of exploring the region is by water, and the vast complex of **lakes**, **rivers** and **waterways** means there are literally thousands of options to choose from. The key issue is getting hold of the necessary equipment, though it's becoming easier to turn up and rent yourself a kayak or canoe on the spot. Demand is increasingly high in season, so it pays to try to reserve a boat in advance.

A good resource is the **PTTK office** in Olsztyn (ul. Staromiejska 1; ☎89 527 3665, ⓦmazury. pttk.pl), which arranges kayak hire and advance accommodation bookings on some of the more popular routes. There are plenty of detailed **maps** of the region appropriate for kayakers: the most useful ones are the 1:120,000 *Wielkie Jezioro Mazurskie* and the Polish–English language 1:300,000 *Warmia and Mazuria*.

SORKWITY AND THE KRUTYNIA ROUTE

Sorkwity, 12km west of Mrągowo, is the starting point for the **Krutynia trail**, a beautiful and popular kayak run that ends 100km downstream at Ruciane-Nida. It's named after the river that makes up the last part of the journey. **Accommodation** along the route is provided by PTTK-run river stations (*stanice wodne*; usually open from mid-April to Sept) – basically kayak and canoe depots that also have bungalows and camping space.

Kayakers generally start from the *stanica wodna* at the edge of Sorkwity village. The route takes you through eighteen lakes, connected by narrow stretches of river that wind through dense forest, remote villages and idyllic countryside. The journey takes anything from five to ten days, though you can shorten the route to end at Krutyń. The Krutynia trail is very popular in high summer, so the best time to make the trip is either in spring or late summer. Overnight stops are generally in the following places:

Day one Bieńki (15km)
Day two Babięta (12km)
Day three Spychowo (12.5km)
Day four Zgon (10.5km)
Day five Krutyń (14km)
Day six Utka (18.5km), the first stop on the River Krutynia itself
Day seven Nowy Most (6.5km)
Day eight Kamień (10.5km) on Lake Bełdany
Day nine Ruciane-Nida (13.5km), the final destination (see page 171)

Olsztyn PTTK offers five- to ten-day kayak trips along the trail including overnight stops, priced between 650zł and 1,150zł. You will need to provide your own gear, including a sleeping bag. **Advance booking** is strongly recommended in summer.

approaches to Lake Śniardwy in the centre of the region, **Mikołajki** is the most pleasant and most attractively located of the major-league lakeside resorts. **Giżycko**, perched on the rim of Lake Mamry to the north, is the best base for public transport and lake cruises, although it is outdone by neighbouring **Wilkasy** when it comes to sheer lakeside charm. **Ruciane-Nida** provides access to the lakes and waterways of southern Mazuria, and has a pleasantly laid-back feel.

As well as lakeside pursuits, Mazuria also boast a wealth of historic churches and castles, including the famous monastery complex at **Święta Lipka**, and the Orthodox nunnery at **Wojnowo**. In addition, Mazuria hides one of the strangest and most chilling of all World War II relics, Hitler's wartime base at **Gierłoz**, a short bus ride away from the small town of **Kętrzyn**.

GETTING AROUND   THE MAZURIAN LAKES

By public transport Giżycko is the main transport hub, straddling the main Olsztyn–Kętrzyn–Ełk–Białystok railway line and offering onward bus connections to Mikolajki and the smaller resorts. A less frequently used railway line runs from Olsztyn to Ełk via Ruciane-Nida, although this is less useful as a stepping stone for onward travel. Travelling between Mazuria and Augustów, change at Ełk.

Giżycko

Squeezed between Lake Niegocin and the marshy backwaters of Lake Mamry, **GIŻYCKO** is one of the main lakeland centres. If greyish holiday-resort architecture lowers your spirits, however, don't plan to stay for long before heading out for the lakes. Wilkasy (see page 166) is a more pleasant base.

The modern town centre is set a few blocks inland around plac Grunwaldzki, but the liveliest part of Giżycko is the attractive waterside area south of the centre on the shores of Lake Niegocin. This is where you'll find the passenger jetty for **boat trips** operated by Żegluga Mazurska (see page 165) and a swanky yachting marina.

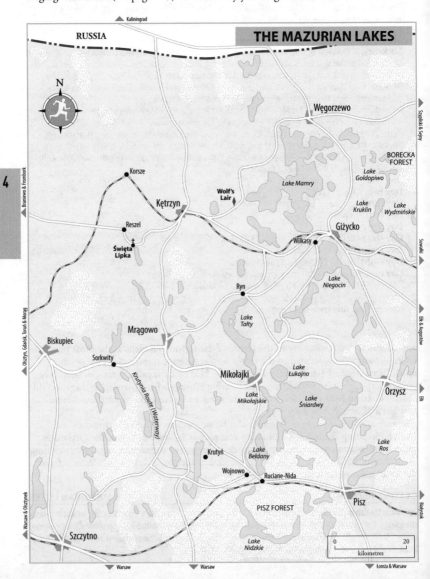

THE MAZURIAN LAKES

BOAT TRIPS ON THE MAIN MAZURIAN LAKES

From mid-April to October the **Żegluga Mazurska** boat company (ⓦzeglugamazurska.pl) runs regular **ferry services** on the main Mazurian lakes. Numerous itineraries are on offer, ranging from short circuits to longer trips linking Mazuria's main towns. They're intended as tourist excursions rather than as a means of public transport, but they represent a scenic and leisurely way of getting around. Some of the more important routes include: Giżycko–Mikołajki (3hr); Mikołajki–Ruciane (2hr); and Giżycko–Węgorzewo (2hr 30min).

There are several departures daily, although boats can be packed in peak season. **Tickets** are purchased at the passenger jetties at each stop. Prices start at 30zł per person for the shorter trips, rising to about 80zł per person for a long trip (eg Giżycko–Mikołajki). **Timetables** (*rozkłady*) for departures are posted by the jetties at all the major lakeside stop-off points, and are available from the tourist offices in both Mikołajki and Giżycko. Otherwise, contact Żegluga Mazurska's main office in Giżycko at al. Wojska Polskiego 8 (ⓣ87 428 5332).

Boyen Fortress

ul. Turystyczna 1 • Daily: May, June & Sept 9am–6pm; July & Aug 9am–8pm; Oct–April 9am–5pm • 12zł • ⓣ87 428 8393, ⓦboyen.gizycko.pl

One of Mazuria's most rewarding historical attractions, **Boyen Fortress** (Twierdza Boyen) is an enormous star-shaped affair built by the Prussians in the mid-nineteenth century to shore up their defences against the tsarist empire. A walking trail takes you all the way around the ramparts (allow at least thirty minutes for the full circuit), allowing excellent views of red-brick barrack blocks, gun emplacements and defensive ditches. Numerous exhibition areas contain displays of uniforms, weapons and horse-drawn artillery carriages, and volunteers dress up as Prussian soldiers during the summer season.

Pressure Tower

ul. Warszawska 37 • Daily: May & Sept 10am–6pm; June 10am–8pm; July & Aug 10am–10pm • 10zł • ⓣ87 428 5170, ⓦwieza-gizycko.pl

Looming above the eastern end of town is the sturdy red-brick **Pressure Tower** (Wieża Ciśnień), built in 1900. A popular local attraction, this water tower comes complete with a panoramic viewing deck and a small café at its summit, as well as a modest museum exhibiting old photographs of the town.

ARRIVAL AND INFORMATION
GIŻYCKO

By train The train station is at the eastern end of the Niegocin lakefront, a 10min walk from the town centre. Destinations Białystok (2 daily; 2hr 10min); Ełk (7 daily; 50min); Kętrzyn (7 daily; 30min); Olsztyn (7 daily; 1hr 30min–1hr 50min).

By bus Buses pick up and drop off in front of the train station.

Destinations Mikołajki (6 daily; 45min); Olsztyn (12 daily; 1hr 55min); Wilkasy (every 30min; 15min).

Tourist information The tourist office, ul. Wyzwolenia 2 (July & Aug Mon–Fri 9am–6pm, Sat & Sun 10am–4pm; Sept–June Mon–Fri 9am–5pm, Sat & Sun 10am–2pm; ⓣ87 428 5265, ⓦgizycko.turystyka.pl), is very helpful, with lots of information on activities in the area.

ACCOMMODATION AND EATING

Cesarski pl. Grunwaldzki 8 ⓣ87 732 7670, ⓦcesarski. eu. Mid-size hotel offering simple, tidy rooms on the main street, a 10min walk from the lakefront. The ground-floor restaurant serves everything from sushi to pizza, while the purple-themed *Café Lavenda* does a great line in meringues and fruit-cocktail drinks. Restaurant daily 8am–10pm. **285zł**

Hotel St Bruno ul. św. Brunona 1 ⓣ87 732 6500, ⓦhotelstbruno.pl. Warmly decorated rooms in a much-restored castle, complete with spa centre, mini-sized pool and bowling alley. The smart restaurant offers a highly polished repertoire of local specialities such as pike-perch,

rabbit and *woszta* (goose and bacon sausage), with mains hovering around 50–70zł. Restaurant daily 1–10pm. **350zł**

Pokoje u Mietka ul. Bohaterow Westerplatte 5 ⓣ660 024 565. A family-run guesthouse in a lovely old wooden house built in 1915, surrounded by a carefully tended garden. Rooms come with TVs and access to a kitchen. **120zł**

Siwa Czapla ul. Nadbrzeżna 11 ⓣ87 428 3440, ⓦsiwa czapla.pl. One of the better restaurants in town for local fish and Polish staples (mains 30–40zł), with a homely woody interior and an outdoor terrace facing the water. Daily noon–10pm.

4

Wilkasy

Some 5km west of Giżycko, **WILKASY** is a pleasingly laid-back holiday resort sprawled along the western shores of Lake Niegocin. With its assortment of lakeside homes and holiday cabins, it's a slightly more peaceful base than Giżycko. There are some nice enclosed swimming areas by the lakes, a plethora of fish-fry stalls and plenty of places renting out **canoes** and **kayaks**.

ARRIVAL AND DEPARTURE   WILKASY

By train Most trains on the Olsztyn–Giżycko line (4–5 daily) stop at Niegocin halt on the northern fringes of Wilkasy, 1km north of the centre.

By bus Wilkasy is served by regular local buses from Giżycko (every 30min; 15min), leaving from pl. Grunwaldzki, as well as by Giżycko–Mikołajki buses (6 daily; 15min).

ACCOMMODATION AND EATING

Osródek AZS ul. Niegocińska 5 ☎ 87 428 0700, ⓦ azs-wilkasy.com.pl. The best place to stay for an activity-based holiday, with a sizeable settlement of simple chalets and a well-appointed hotel complete with tennis courts, spa, gym and equipment rental (kayaks 50zł/day; mountain bikes 50zł/day). Hotel 250zł, chalets 70zł
Tajty ul. Przemysłowa 17 ☎ 87 428 0194, ⓦ hoteltajty.

pl. A medium-sized, family-oriented hotel with a peaceful location right on the lakefront, offering respectable en-suite rooms and a broad wooden deck overlooking the water. A sandy beach, high-wire park and boat rental (canoes 30zł/day) are nearby. The hotel restaurant serves Polish specialities and lots of seafood, including crab, sushi and eel soup. Restaurant daily noon–10pm. 300zł

Gierłoz: the Wolf's Lair

Daily 8am–dusk • 15zł; parking 5zł; 50zł for an English-speaking guide • ⓦ wolfsschanze.pl • Take a train to Kętrzyn from either Olsztyn (7 daily; 1hr–1hr 20min) or Giżycko (7 daily; 30min), then take municipal bus #1 (June–Sept only; 15min) or a Kętrzyn–Węgorzewo bus, some (but not all) of which pass the site; be careful to check return times, and allow 2hr to look around

It was among the forests just north of **GIERŁOZ**, 30km west of Giżycko, that Hitler built his **Wolf's Lair** (Wilczy Szaniec in Polish, Wolfsschanze in German), a huge underground command centre responsible for the entire Eastern Front. Private bunkers encased in several metres of concrete were built for Bormann, Göring, Himmler and **Hitler** himself, alongside offices, SS quarters and operation rooms. The 27-acre site was camouflaged by a suspended screen of vegetation changed to match the seasons. In 1945 the retreating **Germans** attempted to blow the whole place up but succeeded in only cracking the bunkers, ensuring the Wolf's Lair's survival as one of Mazuria's most popular – and most sobering – tourist attractions.

Peering into the cavernous underground bunkers today is an eerie experience. You can see the place, for example, where the assassination attempt on Hitler failed in July 1944 (see page 168), the SS living quarters, the staff cinema and other ancillaries of domestic Nazi life. The **airstrip** from which von Stauffenberg departed after his abortive assassination attempt is a couple of kilometres east from the main site, a lone runway in the middle of heathland – you'll need a guide to show you the way.

ACCOMMODATION AND EATING   THE WOLF'S LAIR

Wilczy Szaniec ☎ 89 741 0031, ✉ wilczyszaniec@ olsztyn.lasy.gov.pl. There's a simple **hotel** at the bunker

site with a reasonable restaurant. You can pitch a tent or park a trailer in the grounds. 100zł

Święta Lipka

Church Daily: April, Oct & Nov 6.30am–6pm; May–Sept 6.30am–8pm; Dec–March 9.30am–5.30pm • **Organ performances** April & Oct Mon–Sat 10am, noon & 2pm, Sun 10am, 12.30pm, 1.30pm & 3pm; May–Sept Mon–Sat hourly 9.30–11.30am & 1.30–5.30pm, Sun 10am, 12.30pm, 1.30pm, 3.30pm & 4.30pm; Nov–March Mon–Sat 10am & 2pm, Sun 10am, noon & 3pm • ⓦ swlipka.pl • Buses run from Olsztyn to Święta Lipka (5 daily; 1hr 40min); from Giżycko, take a train to Kętrzyn (7 daily; 30min) and then change to a bus to Święta Lipka (every 30min; 25min)

THE JULY BOMB PLOT

In the summer of 1944, the Wolf's Lair was the scene of the **assassination attempt** on Adolf Hitler that came closest to success – the **July Bomb Plot**. Its leader, **Count Claus Schenk von Stauffenberg**, an aristocratic officer and member of the General Staff, had gained the support of several high-ranking members of the German army. Sickened by atrocities on the Eastern Front, and rapidly realizing that the Wehrmacht was fighting a war that could not possibly be won, von Stauffenberg and his fellow conspirators decided to kill the Führer, seize control of army headquarters in Berlin and sue for peace with the Allies. Germany was on the brink of total destruction by the Allies and the Soviet Army: only such a desperate act, reasoned the plotters, could save the Fatherland.

THE BOMB

On July 20, Stauffenberg was summoned to the Wolf's Lair to brief Hitler on troop movements on the Eastern Front. In his **briefcase** was a small bomb, packed with high explosive: once triggered, it would explode in under ten minutes. As Stauffenberg approached the specially built conference hut, he triggered the device. Taking his place a few feet from Hitler, Stauffenberg positioned the briefcase under the table, leaning it against one of the table's stout legs no more than six feet away from the Führer.

Five minutes before the bomb exploded, Stauffenberg slipped from the room unnoticed by the generals and advisers, who were listening to a report on the central Russian front. One of the officers moved to get a better look at the campaign maps and, finding the briefcase in his way, picked it up and moved it to the other side of the table leg. Now, the table leg lay between the briefcase and Hitler. At 12.42 the bomb went off. Stauffenberg, watching from a few hundred yards away, was shocked by the force of the **explosion**. It was, he said, as if the hut had been hit by a 155mm shell; he had no doubt that the Führer, along with everyone else in the room, was dead. Stauffenberg hurried off to a waiting plane and made his way to Berlin to join the other conspirators. Meanwhile, Hitler and the survivors staggered out into the daylight: four people had been killed. Hitler himself, despite being badly shaken, suffered no more than a **perforated eardrum** and minor injuries.

The church at **ŚWIĘTA LIPKA**, some 45km west of Giżycko, is probably the country's most famous Baroque shrine. Lodged on a thin strip of land between two lakes, this magnificent **church** is in the middle of nowhere but – as all the souvenir stalls suggest – its location doesn't stop the tourists turning up in droves. The church is jammed with pilgrims during religious festivals, creating an intense atmosphere of Catholic devotion.

The name Święta Lipka – literally "holy lime tree" – derives from a local medieval legend according to which a Prussian leader, released from imprisonment by the Teutonic Knights, placed a statue of the Virgin in a lime tree as a token of thanks. Within a few years healing **miracles** were being reported at the place, and the Knights built a chapel on the site in 1320. Following their conversion to Lutheranism, the Knights destroyed the chapel in 1526. The present basilica was begun in 1687 under the direction of Vilnius architect Jerzy Ertly; to anyone familiar with Lithuanian churches, the "Eastern" Baroque of Święta Lipka will come as no surprise.

The church

In a country with a major predilection for Baroque richness, Święta Lipka is one of the most exuberant of them all. The tapering twin towers of the church facade and plain yellow and white stucco covering the exterior are quintessential Polish Baroque, and entrance to the complex is through a magnificent early eighteenth-century wrought-iron gate.

Inside, much of the ceiling is covered by superb **frescoes** depicting themes ranging from the lives of Christ and Mary to the Marian cult of Święta Lipka itself. The lofty main **altarpiece**, an imposing wooden structure completed in 1714, has three levels: the upper two contain pictures on biblical themes; the lowest a seventeenth-century icon of the Madonna and Child based on an original kept in Rome. Imitating the original medieval shrine, a rather grubby-looking eighteenth-century lime tree stands to the left of the altar, topped by a silver statue of the Virgin and Child, the base smothered in pennants pinned there by devout pilgrims.

THE AFTERMATH

It did not take long to work out what had happened, and the **hunt** for Stauffenberg was soon on. Hitler issued orders to the SS in Berlin to summarily execute anyone who was slightly suspect, and dispatched Himmler to the city to quell the rebellion. A few hours later the Supreme Command HQ was surrounded by SS troops, and the coup was over. The conspirators were gathered together, taken to the courtyard of the HQ and, under the orders of **General Fromm**, shot by firing squad. Stauffenberg's last words were "Long live our sacred Germany!" Fromm had known about the plot almost from the beginning, but had refused to join it. By executing the leaders he hoped to save his own skin – and, it must be added, knowingly saved them from the torturers of the SS.

Hitler's **ruthless revenge** on the conspirators was without parallel even in the bloody annals of the Third Reich. All the colleagues, friends and immediate relatives of Stauffenberg and the other conspirators were rounded up, tortured and taken before the "People's Court", where they were humiliated and given more-or-less automatic **death sentences**. Many of those executed knew nothing of the plot and were found guilty merely by association. As the bloodlust grew, the Nazi Party used the plot as a pretext for settling old scores, and eradicated anyone who had the slightest hint of anything less than total dedication to the Führer. General Fromm, who had ordered the execution of the conspirators, was among those tried, found guilty of cowardice and shot by firing squad. Those whose names were blurted out under torture were quickly arrested, the most notable being **Field Marshal Rommel**, who, because of his popularity, was given the choice of a trial in the People's Court or suicide and a state funeral. He opted for the state funeral.

The July Bomb Plot caused the deaths of at least **five thousand people**, including some of Germany's most brilliant military thinkers and almost all of those who would have been best qualified to run the post-war German government. Within six months the country lay in **ruins** as the Allies and Soviet Army advanced; had events been only a little different, the entire course of the war – and European history – would have been altered incalculably.

Filling virtually the entire west end of the building is the church's famous Baroque **organ** – a huge, fantastically ornate creation, decked with two layers of blue gilded turrets topped by figures of the saints, built in 1720 by Johann Mozengel, a Jew from Königsberg. The whole instrument appears to come alive when played, with gyrating angels strumming mandolins, cherubs blowing horns and cymbals crashing – an extraordinary sight and sound.

Mikołajki

Hyped in the brochures as the Mazurian Venice, **MIKOŁAJKI** is unquestionably the most attractive of the Mazurian resorts. Straddling the meeting point of two small lakes (Tałty and Mikołajskie), the small town has long provided a base for yachting enthusiasts. Despite being the most popular resort in Mazuria, it has succeeded in retaining its low-rise, **fishing village** appearance, with the new buildings managing more or less to blend in with their surroundings.

Most activity centres on the waterfront, where you'll find an extensive **marina** and a generous collection of outdoor **cafés** and **bars**. Just west of here is the passenger jetty used by the excursion boats operated by Żegluga Mazurska (see page 165). An attractive footbridge, colourfully illuminated at night, leads to the opposite bank and a **beach** area consisting of a grassy lawn and a couple of wooden piers.

Holy Trinity Church

Museum: April–Oct daily 9am–5pm • Free • ☏ 87 421 6810, ⓦ mikolajkiluteranie.pl

Unusually for modern Poland, the main church in town is the Protestant **Holy Trinity Church** (Kościół św. Trójcy), overlooking the shores of Lake Tałty. Designed by German architect Franz Schinkel, this solid-looking nineteenth-century structure is the centre of worship for the region's Protestant community. The neighbouring parish house contains the small **museum**, with a fascinating collection of old bibles.

Lake Łukajno

Four kilometres east of town, the nature reserve round **Lake Łukajno** is home to one of Europe's largest colonies of **wild swans**. It's an easy walk across rolling countryside, following the signed road which heads uphill from Mikołajki's central bus stop. The best viewing point is the **look-out tower** (*wieża widokowa*) at the lake's edge, signposted off the road, though whether you get to see the birds is a matter of luck and timing. The best months are July and August, when the swans moult; from a distance, the surface of the lake can look like a downy feather bed.

ARRIVAL AND INFORMATION
MIKOŁAJKI

By bus The bus stop lies just west of the centre; a 5min walk down ul. 3 Maja will bring you to the main square, pl. Wolności. There are six daily buses to Giżycko (45min).

Tourist information The tourist office at pl. Wolności 7 (April–June & Sept Mon–Fri 10am–5pm, Sat & Sun 10am–2pm; July & Aug daily 10am–6pm; Oct–March Mon–Fri 8am–4pm; ☎87 421 6850, ⓦmikolajki.eu) has information about kayak and boat rental. Most of the lakeside hotels also have their own stock of canoes and bicycles for use by guests.

ACCOMMODATION

HOTELS AND PENSIONS

Gołębiewski ul. Mrągowska 34 ☎87 429 0700, ⓦgolebiewski.pl; map page 170. This mammoth 600-room hotel northwest of town is a resort in itself, fully equipped for family holidays, with indoor pools, ice rink, riding stables, golf course and tennis courts. 690zł

Hotel Mikołajki al. Spacerowa 11 ☎87 420 6000, ⓦhotelmikolajki.pl; map page 170. A remarkable concrete-and-glass construction, built on an island opposite the marina and reached by 100m-long causeway.

The five-star amenities include soothing rooms with great views; spa, restaurant and bar facilities; and mooring facilities for guests' swanky boats. 900zł

Król Sielaw ul. Kajki 5 ☎87 421 6323, ⓦkrolsielaw.mazury.info; map page 170. Small and intimate B&B with neat en suites, including some cosy mansard-roofed rooms on the top floor. There's also one triple room (250zł) and a four-person apartment (350zł). 180zł

Pensjonat Mikołajki ul. Kajki 18 ☎87 421 6437, ⓦpensjonatmikolajki.pl; map page 170. Attractive

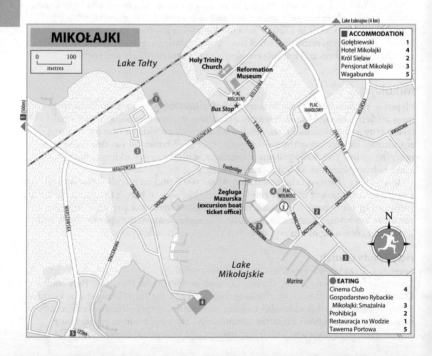

Lake Łukajno (4 km)

MIKOŁAJKI

Lake Tałty

0 — 100 metres

500m

Holy Trinity Church

Reformation Museum

PLAC KOŚCIELNY

Bus Stop

PLAC HANDLOWY

J.R. DĄBROWSKIEGO

KOLUZNA

MRĄGOWSKA

ŻEGLARSKA

3 MAJA

JANA PAWŁA II

WOLSKA

KWIATOWA

MRĄGOWSKA

Footbridge

ORZESZKOWEJ

OKRĘŻNA

OKRĘŻNA

Żegluga Mazurska (excursion boat ticket office)

PLAC WOLNOŚCI

ⓘ

KRÓLA JANA

ORZESZKOWEJ

DŁUGOSZOWA

WARSZAWSKA

SPACEROWA

Lake Mikołajskie

Marina

LEŚNA

N

ACCOMMODATION
Gołębiewski	1
Hotel Mikołajki	4
Król Sielaw	2
Pensjonat Mikołajki	3
Wagabunda	5

EATING
Cinema Club	4
Gospodarstwo Rybackie Mikołajki: Smażalnia	3
Prohibicja	2
Restauracja na Wodzie	1
Tawerna Portowa	5

4

pension offering en suites in a creaky but comfortable house that backs right onto the lakeside promenade. Bicycles and other sports equipment are available to rent. 250zł

CAMPSITE

In-season, numerous private gardens across the footbridge from the town centre accept tent-campers (look for *pole namiotowe* signs).

Wagabunda ul. Leśna 2 ☎ 87 421 6018, ⓦ wagabunda-mikolajki.pl; map page 170. A large, tree-shaded site perched on a hill above town, offering bungalows and plenty of space for tents and caravans. Camping 60zł, two-person bungalow 170zł

EATING

Along with the restaurants below, any number of cheap **fried-fish stalls** pop up along the lakefront in the summer months. Note that opening hours are prone to sudden changes, with establishments closing early (especially outside high season) if there are insufficient tourists in town. **Cinema Club** pl. Wolności 10 ☎ 690 316 942, ⓦ facebook. com/CinemaClubMikolajki; map page 170. Good-quality meat and fish dishes (including eel in dill sauce; 36zł) served in a movie-themed interior, or on the terrace, from which you can observe goings-on on the square. Live music and DJs in summer. Daily 11am–10pm, later in high season.
Gospodarstwo Rybackie Mikołajki: Smażalnia ul. Mrągowska 14; map page 170. Arguably the best fish-fry place in town, with fresh pike and pike-perch provided by the local fishing cooperative. A 250g fillet of fish with chips and salad will set you back around 40zł. June–Sept daily 11am–7pm; Oct–May Fri–Sun 11am–6pm.

Prohibicja pl. Handlowy 13 ☎ 87 421 9919, ⓦ prohibicja mikolajki.pl; map page 170. Part-pub, part-piano bar, with a decent choice of cocktails and regular live music. Daily: May–Sept 10am–1am; Oct–April noon–11pm.
Restauracja na Wodzie ul. Mrągowska 14 ☎ 690 316 942, ⓦ restauracjanawodzie.pl; map page 170. Big bar-restaurant occupying a pavilion right on the waterfront, serving freshwater fish, pan-fried or baked in wood-fired ovens (20zł), as well as fish-and-camembert stuffed *pierogi*, trout chowder, and burgers and pizzas. Daily noon–10pm.
Tawerna Portowa al. Kasztanowa 6 ☎ 87 421 5722, ⓦ tawernaportowa.eu; map page 170. One of the more reliable of the waterside restaurants, just downhill from the main square, serving up a popular mix of fish and chips (26–36zł) and steaks (50zł), with seating on an open veranda or glass-enclosed porch. Daily 9am–10pm.

Ruciane-Nida and the Pisz Forest

South of Mikołajki along a scenic forest road is the lakeside resort of **RUCIANE-NIDA**, actually two towns connected by a short stretch of road. Ruciane, the resort end of town, provides the main focus of interest; Nida is home to some postwar concrete housing blocks and little else. The jetty with the sign marked *Żegluga Mazurska* is the boarding point for **boat trips** (see page 165).

South of town lies the **Pisz Forest** (Puszcza Piska), a huge tangle of crystal-clear lakes, lazy winding rivers and dense forest thickets – mainly pine, with some magnificent pockets of mixed oak, beech and spruce in between. It's the largest forest in the region, one of the surviving remnants of the primeval forest that once covered much of northeastern Europe, and is a favourite with both walkers and kayakers – the Krutynia River (see page 163) runs through the middle of the forest.

ARRIVAL AND INFORMATION RUCIANE-NIDA

By train Trains run from Olsztyn (2 daily; 1hr 40min) to Ruciane-Nida train station, a 10min walk northwest of the waterfront.
By bus Buses from Olsztyn (2 daily; 2hr) pick up and drop off outside the train station.

Tourist information The tourist office in Ruciane at ul. Dworcowa 14 (April–Sept daily 9am–9pm; Oct–March Tues–Fri 7am–4pm; ☎ 87 423 1989, ⓦ ruciane-nida.pl) can help find private rooms.

ACCOMMODATION

Hotel Nidzki ul. Nadbrzeżna 1 ☎ 87 423 6401, ⓦ hotel nidzki.pl. Modern lakeside hotel offering comfortable, simply furnished rooms. There are lovely lake views from

the terrace, spa facilities and a smart restaurant with local food, plus boats and bicycles available for rent. 320zł

4

> ## THE OLD BELIEVERS
>
> The origins of the **Old Believers** (*Staroobrzędowcy*, or *Staroviertsii* in Russian) lie in the liturgical reforms introduced into the Russian Orthodox Church in the mid-seventeenth-century. Priests who opposed the reforms were removed from office, but many of their congregations persisted with the old practices and were dubbed "Old Believers" by a church hierarchy eager to see them marginalized. Peter the Great was particularly keen to get rid of them and it was under his rule that groups of Old Believers moved to the western fringes of the empire – in the hope that here at least they would be left alone to practise their religion as they wished. In liturgical matters, the Old Believers are egalitarian, choosing clergy from among the local community rather than relying on a priesthood. Services are conducted in **Old Church Slavonic** – the medieval tongue into which the scriptures were originally translated – rather than in modern Russian.
>
> There are only about five hundred active Old Believers left in Poland, although the number of people claiming descent from or kinship with these people is far larger – ensuring the survival of several Old Believer churches in rural pockets of the northeast.

Wojnowo

Six kilometres west of Ruciane-Nida, **WOJNOWO** is an attractively bucolic village of low wooden houses set among lush meadows. It was founded in the nineteenth century by **Old Believers** (see above), a traditionalist Orthodox Russian sect that had rebelled against the reforms of 1651 and been forced into exile as a result. Old Believers are still found in rural areas of Estonia, Latvia and eastern Poland, although their numbers are dwindling. There are no buses to Wojnowo so you'll need your own transport.

The nunnery

Daily 9am–6pm · Donation requested · ☎ 87 425 7030, ⓦ klasztor.info

Picturesquely situated on the shores of Lake Duś at the southern end of the village, the former Old Believer **nunnery** (Klasztor Starowiercow) is a simple wooden building that began life as a monastery in 1847, was refounded as a nunnery in 1885, and is now a private house. Inside, you can see a very impressive collection of old **icons**, while the monastery cemetery is filled with crosses with Cyrillic inscriptions.

Orthodox parish church

Mon–Sat 9am–2pm & 3–5pm, Sun 3–5pm · Donation requested

Clearly visible on the other side of the village is the charming **Orthodox parish church**, made of white-painted wood and crowned with a blue onion dome; if the church is locked, go down the path past the cemetery and through the flower garden to the house and ask for the key.

The Suwalszczyzna

Named after the administrative centre of **Suwałki**, the **Suwalszczyzna** is one of the least visited parts of Poland; even for Poles, anything beyond Mazuria is still pretty much *terra incognita*. Visually the area isn't that different from Mazuria: a pleasing landscape of rolling hills and fields interspersed with small, crystal-clear lakes, often extremely deep.

The main centre of southern Suwalszczyzna is the lake resort of **Augustów**, east of which stretches the **Augustów Forest** (Puszcza Augustowska) – what remains of a vast primeval forest that once extended well into Lithuania. The combination of wild forest, lakes and winding rivers has made the area a favourite with kayakers, walkers and cyclists.

In the north around Suwałki itself, the spectacular forest and lakescape of the **Wigry National Park** and the picture-postcard lakes and hillocks of the **Suwałki Landscape Park** provide the main natural highlights. Wandering through the fields and woodland thickets you'll find storks, swallows, brilliantly coloured butterflies and wild flowers in abundance, while in the villages modern life often seems to have made only modest incursions.

Augustów and around

On the edge of the Augustów Forest and close to lakes Necko and Białe, Augustów has long been associated with leisure, having been founded in 1557 by **King Sigismund August** to serve as his base for extended hunting expeditions in the woods. Further development followed the construction of the **Augustów Canal** in the nineteenth century, connecting the town to the River Niemen in the east and providing a convenient outlet for the region's most important natural commodity, wood. Still in use today, the canal offers the most convenient approach to the heart of the forest.

Lake Necko

As a town Augustów is nothing special, but it does allow immediate access to **Lake Necko**, immediately north of the centre; three blocks west of the Rynek, ulica Nadrzeczna leads north to a small beach and boat rental facilities. However, the best of the lakeside terrain lies northeast of the centre: head east from the Rynek and north across the bridge to the small tourist **port** on ulica 29 Listopada, the departure point for sightseeing **boats** in the summer (see page 175), and a pleasant spot from which to admire the swan- and duck-filled waterscapes of the lake. Beyond here, a network of woodland **walks** leads round the eastern shores of Lake Necko, passing several stretches of beach and a waterskiing centre.

4

ARRIVAL AND DEPARTURE **AUGUSTÓW**

By train The main station is 3km to the northeast; bus #2 runs into town.

Destinations Białystok (5 daily; 1hr 30min–1hr 50min); Suwałki (5 daily; 30min); Warsaw (2 daily; 4hr 20min).

By bus Augustów's bus station is right in the middle of town on Rynek Zygmunta Augusta.

Destinations Białystok (hourly; 1hr 40min); Ełk (hourly; 1hr 10min); Sejny (1 daily; 1hr); Suwałki (hourly; 30–55min); Warsaw (7 daily; 4hr 30min).

KAYAKING THE CZARNA HAŃCZA RIVER

Along with the Krutynia (see page 163) the **Czarna Hańcza River** is one of the most beautiful – and popular – **canoeing routes** in the northeast Polish lakelands. If you've ever had a hankering for a backwater canoeing expedition this is as good a chance as any to satisfy it. Rising in Belarus, the 140km-long river, a tributary of the Niemen, flows into the Augustów Forest, winding its way through the Wigry National Park up to **Lake Hańcza**, 15km northwest of **Suwałki**. On the usual kayaking route, the journey starts from **Augustów**, following the Augustów Canal east to the point where it meets the Czarna Hańcza; from there the route continues up the river to Suwałki, and beyond to Lake Hańcza.

An alternative route involves exploring **Lake Wigry** and the surrounding national park. This trip heads east from Augustów along the canal, turning north at **Swoboda** and continuing 12km into **Lake Serwy**, an attractive forest-bound tributary. From here the canoes are transported across land to the village of **Bryzgiel**, on the southern shores of Lake Wigry. Overnight camps are on the island of **Kamien**, one of several on the lake, and by the lakeside at **Stary Folwark** (see page 176), with a trip up to the monastery included. Leaving Wigry near the **Klasztorny peninsula**, kayakers re-enter the Czarna Hańcza, heading south through a spectacular forest-bound section of the river before rejoining the Augustów Canal and making their way back to Augustów.

Both trips can be organized through agencies in Augustów and take between six and twelve days, with accommodation – mostly in waterside campsites (*stanice wodne*) – and meals provided throughout: you'll need to provide your own sleeping bag and appropriate clothing. The current **cost** for either trip is around 130zł per person per day; in Augustów contact Szekla, ul. Nadrzeczna 70A (T 503 593 301, W szekla.pl), or Szot, ul. Konwaliowa 2 (T 87 644 6758, W szot.pl).

INFORMATION AND ACTIVITIES

Tourist information The tourist office is on the main square, at Rynek Zygmunta Augusta 8 (May, June & Sept Mon–Fri 8am–5pm, Sat & Sun 10am–3pm; July & Aug Mon–Fri 8am–8pm, Sat & Sun 9am–8pm; Oct–April Mon–Fri 8am–4pm; ☎ 511 181 848, ⓦ augustow.eu).

Boat rental and boat trips There are numerous agencies in Augustów renting out kayaks and canoes by the day; these outfits can also arrange longer trips down the Czarna

Hańcza river (see page 163). Boat trips down the Augustów Canal run in the summer months (see page 175).

Cycling The Augustów Forest makes for enticing cycling territory, with plenty of decent paths and roads, although they're not always clearly marked. The *Puszcza Augustowska* map (1:70,000) shows all the main routes through the forest, right up to the Belarusian border. Several places in town rent out bikes – ask the tourist office for details.

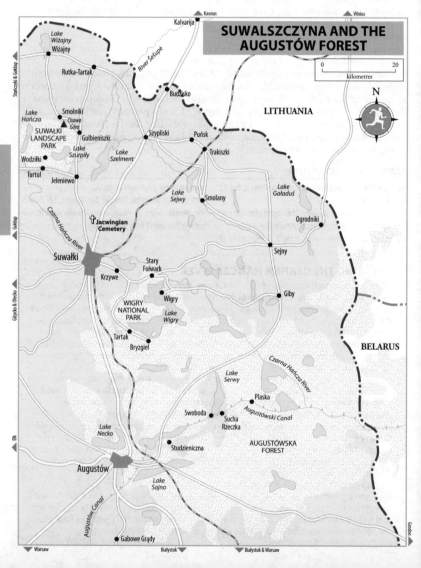

BOAT TRIPS ON THE AUGUSTÓW CANAL

The least strenuous way to explore the Augustów Forest is to take a **day-trip** from Augustów along the **Augustów Canal**. The shortest trips – a couple of hours – go east through the Necko, Białe and Studzieniczne lakes to Swoboda or Sucha Rzeczka, giving a taste of the beauty of the forest. Other boats go onward to Plaska and the lock at Perkuc, returning in the evening.

The forest is mainly coniferous, but with impressive sections of elm, larch, hornbeam and ancient oak creating a slightly sombre atmosphere, particularly along the alley-like section of the canal between Swoboda and Sucha Rzeczka, where the tallest trees blot out the sun, billowing reeds brush the boat and the silence is suddenly broken by echoing bird calls. Among the varied wildlife of the forest, cranes, grey herons and even the occasional beaver can be spotted on the banks of the canal, while deeper into the forest you might glimpse wild boar or elk.

Boats run in the summer, and leave from Augustów's tourist port on ulica 29 Listopada (May–Sept 8–10 trips daily; 30–50zł, depending on the route; ☎87 643 2881, ⓦzeglugaaugustowska.pl). Arrive early to queue for tickets, and it's also a good idea to take some food since restaurant stops on the way are unpredictable.

ACCOMMODATION AND EATING

Karczma Kaktusik ul. 29 Listopada 2 ☎697 720 033, ⓦkaktusik.augustow.pl. This restaurant-with-rooms offers traditional Polish food (mains 25–30zł) in faux-farmstead surroundings, with ponds and a play area outside. En-suite rooms above the restaurant are haphazardly furnished but cosy and charming with it. Restaurant daily 11am–10pm. **220zł**

Logos ul. 29 Listopada 9 ☎87 643 2021, ⓦaugustow-hotel.pl. A medium-sized hotel next to the tourist port offering neat and tidy en suites; the decor may be a bit dated, but the service is friendly and there's a restaurant and travel agency on site. **210zł**

Marina Borki ul. Narzeczna 147 ☎885 023 632. A large campsite just northwest of the centre on the shores of Lake Necko, with tent pitches beneath the trees and four- to six-person cabins. The on-site restaurant serves everything from *pierogi* to fried fish and has a terrace right by the lake.

Camping **50zł**, cabins **200zł**

Pod Jabłoniami ul. Rybacka 3 ☎516 025 606, ⓦpodjabloniami.pl. Small but bright en-suite rooms above an enjoyably casual restaurant on the banks of the Netta, just east of the main square. Outdoor seating is on a wooden deck floating on the canal, a great spot to nurse a beer; on the menu are pizzas (25zł), expertly aged steaks (69zł) and fresh fish priced by weight. Restaurant daily noon–midnight. **150zł**

Warszawa ul. Zdrojowa 1 ☎87 643 8500, ⓦhotel warszawa.pl. The most upscale option in town, with plush en suites in a prime location between the lake and dense woodland. There's a spa and gym on site, and plenty of facilities for small children. The hotel's *Pinarbo* restaurant is one of the fanciest in town, with a mixture of Polish and modern European cuisine. Restaurant daily 7am–1pm. **380zł**

Suwałki

The main market centre of Poland's rural northeast, **SUWAŁKI** is a rather formless place, consisting of a long central street and a scattering of grey suburbs. Although the main roads through town are choked with Poland-to-the-Baltics through traffic, few people actually stop off here, ensuring that Suwałki retains a modicum of provincial middle-of-nowhere charm. It's certainly a good place from which to explore the surrounding Suwalszczyzna, although accommodation in the nearby Wigry National Park (see page 176) may offer more in the way of rural seclusion.

Ulica Kościuszki

Suwałki's only real focal point is **ulica Kościuszki**, which runs straight through town on a north–south axis. Nearer its southern end is the stately Neoclassical **Parish Church of St Alexandra** on plac Piłsudskiego. About 400m further north, the **District Museum** at no. 81 (July & Aug Tues–Sun 9am–5pm; Sept–June Tues–Fri 8am–4pm, Sat & Sun 9am–5pm; 5zł; ☎87 566 5750, ⓦmuzeum.suwalki.pl) contains a fascinating display dedicated to local life over the last hundred years or so, enlivened by a jumble of family heirlooms and photographs.

The cemetery

On the corner of ul. Bakałarzewska and ul. Zarzecze

The jumbled ethnic mix that characterized Suwałki up until the outbreak of World War II is clearly illustrated in the **cemetery** on the west side of town, overlooking the Czarna Hańcza River. The cemetery is divided up into religious sections: Catholic, Orthodox, Protestant, Tatar and Jewish. The Orthodox section houses a special part for Old Believers (see page 172), while the Jewish cemetery was devastated by the Nazis – a lone memorial tablet now stands in the middle of the area.

ARRIVAL AND INFORMATION

By train The train station is a 15min walk east of the centre.
Destinations Augustów (5 daily; 30min); Warsaw (1 daily; 4hr 45min).

By bus The bus station is on ul. Utrata, a 10min walk east of the centre.
Destinations Stary Folwark (hourly; 20min); Warsaw (7 daily; 5hr).

SUWAŁKI

Tourist information The tourist office, ul. Hamerszmita 16 (June–Sept Mon–Fri 9am–6pm, Sat & Sun 9am–3pm; Oct–May Mon–Fri 8am–4pm; ☎87 566 2079, ⬧um. suwalki.pl), is keen on promoting eco-tourism in the region, and can book you into farmhouse B&Bs in the surrounding countryside – you'll need your own transport to get there, though.

ACCOMMODATION AND EATING

Karczma Polska ul. Kościuszki 101a (the far northern end of the street) ☎87 566 4860, ⬧karczmasuwalki. pl. Wooden furnishings and a traditional northeastern-Polish menu of *kartacze* (big potato dumplings stuffed with meat; 23zł), potato pancakes, pork cooked any number of ways and the odd freshwater fish. Mon–Thurs & Sun 10am–10pm, Fri & Sat 10am–midnight.

Loft 1898 ul. Pułaskiego 24k ☎87 739 5900, ⬧hotel loft.pl. A converted cavalry barracks 1.5km northeast of town provides the artfully gritty setting for a smart modern hotel; rooms combine exposed brick with all mod cons. There's a smart restaurant and nightclub on site. <u>250zł</u>

Logos ul. Kościuszki 120 ☎87 566 6900, ⬧suwalki. hotellogos.pl. This neat and welcoming affair right on the main street is one of the best hotels in town, with all the mod cons and an on-site restaurant and bar. <u>190zł</u>

Piwiarnia ul. Chlodna 2 ☎666 468 842, ⬧piwiarnia. suwalki.pl. Lively pub dominated by a long, narrow, stool-lined bar, serving various international beers and a range of Polish dishes. Mon–Thurs & Sun noon–midnight, Fri & Sat noon–2am.

Rozmarino ul. Kościuszki 75 ☎87 563 2400, ⬧rozmarino. pl. Pleasant pizzeria that also does a good range of pastas and salads; there's a separate winter garden in the courtyard out back. Pizzas cost around 25zł. Daily 10am–10pm.

Wigry National Park

Just 11km southeast of Suwałki, **Lake Wigry** forms the centre of the **Wigry National Park** (Wigiersky Park Narodowy), an unspoilt area of lakeland, river, forest and gently rolling fields. The lake in particular is a stunningly beautiful spot, a peaceful haven of creeks, marshes and woods, punctuated by the occasional village. More than twenty species of fish can be found in the lake, while the nearby woods harbour stag, wild boar, elk, martens and badgers. Wigry's most characteristic animal, however, is the **beaver**, and around the lake's southern and western shores you'll find plenty of evidence of their presence in the reservations set aside for them.

Krzywe and Stary Folwark

The park's headquarters (see page 177) are at the village of **KRZYWE**, 5km from Suwałki on the border of the park. A few kilometres east, **STARY FOLWARK** is a quiet spot on the lakeshore and the main base for accommodation in the park. You can **rent canoes** from a couple of outlets down by the water.

Wigry

A short drive or walk round the lake from Stary Folwark – or a quick paddle across it – is the tiny village of **WIGRY**, dwarfed by a former **Camadolese Monastery** (Pokamedulski Klasztor), founded here by King Władysław Waza in the 1660s.

WALKING AND CYCLING AROUND LAKE WIGRY

Wigry National Park is a rambler's paradise, with a good network of **marked trails** running through much of the area. For anyone tempted by the idea of exploring the region on foot, the *Wigierski Park Narodowy* **map** (1:46,000), which shows all the main trails, is a must. The longest route, marked green, takes you round the entire lake – nearly 50km in total – but there are also plenty of good shorter routes.

Cycling is a more challenging option: the trails take in narrow forest paths and sandy roads, which can make the going hard. Bike rental is possible from many guesthouses, or via the tourist office in Suwałki (see page 176).

Originally the monastery stood on an island but this is now linked to the shore. The monks were thrown out by the Prussians following the Third Partition, and their sizeable possessions – three hundred square kilometres of land and several dozen villages – sequestered. The church is a typical piece of Polish Baroque, with exuberant frescoes in the main church and monks' skeletons in the **catacombs** (May–Sept Mon–Sat 9am–6pm, Sun 1–6pm). The monastery itself has been turned into a popular conference centre and **hotel**.

ARRIVAL AND INFORMATION WIGRY NATIONAL PARK

By bus The park is easy to access, with buses on the Suwałki–Sejny route passing through Krzywe and Stary Folwark roughly every hour until about 5pm. The journey from Suwałki to Stary Folwark is about 20min.

Information The park's headquarters at Krzywe (Mon–Fri 7am–3pm, Sat & Sun 9am–4pm; Oct–April closed Sat & Sun; ⓦ wigry.org.pl) is the best source of detailed information and has a small natural history museum.

ACCOMMODATION AND EATING

Gospoda Pod Sieją Stary Folwark 48 ☎ 87 563 7010. A cute wooden pub with a fireplace, serving freshwater fish from the lake, *kartacze* dumplings, and other regional dishes; daily specials cost from 16zł. There's occasional live music, too. Daily noon–10pm.

Holiday Hotel Stary Folwark 106 ☎ 87 563 7120, ⓦ hotel-holiday.pl. Colourful modern building on the highway just west of the Stary Folwark turnoff, with some nice attic rooms and friendly staff; there's also a bar/restaurant out on the patio. Restaurant daily 7am–9pm. **180zł**

Nad Wigrami Stary Folwark 71 ☎ 87 563 7546, ⓦ nad wigrami.com. A family-run pension in a big house in Stary Folwark village, offering doubles, family rooms and a grassy garden. There are also bikes for hire, and a sauna on site. **120zł**

Suwałki Landscape Park

The Suwalszczyzna's trademark landscape of billowing grey-green hills and glittering lakes is at its most haunting in the **Suwałki Landscape Park** (Suwalski Park Krajobrazowy), a nature conservation area northwest of **Jeleniewo**, 10km out on the main road north from Suwałki.

Turtul and around

If you're driving then it's well worth aiming for **TURTUL**, 7km west of Jeleniowo, home of the park's tourist information office (see page 176). From here, a **red-marked trail** proceeds north through the heart of the park, reaching after 2km the settlement of **WODZIŁKI**, tucked away in a quiet wooded valley. The hamlet is home to a small community of Orthodox **Old Believers** (see page 172) whose original wooden *molenna*, or prayer house, is still in use, along with a nearby sauna (*bania*). Life in this rural village seems to have changed little since the first settlers moved here in the 1750s: the houses are simple, earth-floored buildings with few concessions to modernity, the old men grow long white beards, and the women don't appear to cut their hair. Most live surrounded by amazing collections of icons, rosaries, Bibles and other precious relics.

THE STAŃCZYKI VIADUCT

Just north of the hamlet of **Stańczyki**, west of Lake Hańcza, a huge, deserted twin **viaduct** straddles the Błędzianka River valley, seemingly lost out in the middle of nowhere. Before World War II Stańczyki was right on the East Prussian–Polish border: in 1910 the Germans built a mammoth double viaduct here as part of a new rail line, but the promised rail track never materialized. The viaduct has stood ever since, a towering monument to an architect and engineer's folly, no one apparently having the heart – or cash – to pull it down. These days a stroll on and around the viaduct is a favourite Sunday outing for local people.

Gulbieniszki

Directly north of Jeleniewo is **GULBIENISZKI**, the point of access for **Cisowa Góra** (258m), the hill known as the Polish Fujiyama. It was the site of pre-Christian religious rituals, and it's rumoured that rites connected with Perkunas, the Lithuanian fire god, are still observed here; the Lithuanians, who still make up a small percentage of the population of this region, were the last Europeans to be converted to Christianity, in the late fourteenth century.

Smolniki and Lake Hańcza

North of Gulbieniski the road divides; continuing west along the Wiżajny route, the next village is **SMOLNIKI**, just before which there's a wonderful **panorama** of the surrounding lakes. If you have a compass with you, don't be surprised if it starts to go haywire around here – the area has large deposits of iron-rich ore, as discovered by disorientated German pilots based at Luftwaffe installations here during World War II. Despite the obvious commercial potential, the seams haven't been exploited due to the high levels of uranium in the ore.

A couple of kilometres west of Smolniki, along a bumpy track through woods, lies clean, unspoilt **Lake Hańcza**, the deepest in Poland (108m). The Czarna Hańcza River (see page 163) joins the lake on its southern shore.

ARRIVAL AND INFORMATION   SUWAŁKI

By bus The best way to get to the park from Suwałki by public transport is to take a bus to Wiżajny (3–4 daily) and get off at either Gulbieniszki on the eastern side of the park, or Smolniki, the main entrance point on the northern side of the park.

Tourist information The park's tourist office is in Turtul (July & Aug Mon–Fri 8am–7pm, Sat 11am–6pm; Sept–June Mon–Fri 8am–3pm; ☎87 569 1801, ⓦspk.org.pl), where you can pick up maps of local walking trails.

Białystok

Uniquely among major Polish cities, the northeastern administrative centre of **BIAŁYSTOK** has retained the ethnic and religious mix – Poles, Belarusians and Ukrainians, Catholic and Orthodox – that characterized the country before the war. Only the Jews, who made up the majority of the inhabitants before being wiped out by the Nazis in 1943, are absent. Although ringed by factories and housing projects, the city contains a handsome and strollable centre, together with a modest handful of museums. However, its real value is as a touring base, with most of southern Podlasie within easy reach.

Brief history

According to legend, Białystok was founded in 1320 by the Lithuanian Grand Duke Gediminas (or **Gedymin** as he's known in Polish), but its emergence really began in the 1740s when local aristocrat Jan Branicki built a palace in the town centre. Partitioned off to Prussia and then to Russia, Białystok rapidly developed as a textile city, in competition with Łódź further west. Industrialization fostered the growth of a sizeable urban proletariat and a large **Jewish community**.

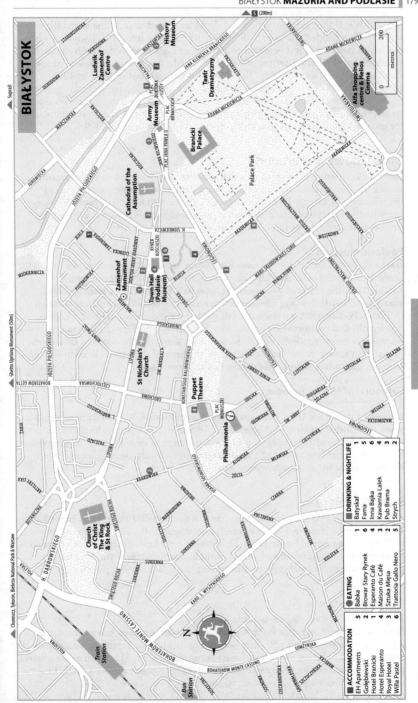

BIAŁYSTOK

◼ ACCOMMODATION	
EH Apartments	5
Gołębiewski	2
Hotel Branicki	1
Hotel Esperanto	4
Royal Hotel	3
Willa Pastel	6

● EATING	
Babka	1
Browar Stary Rynek	6
Esperanto Café	4
Maison du Café	2
Sztuka Mięsa	3
Trattoria Gallo Nero	5

◼ DRINKING & NIGHTLIFE	
Batyskaf	1
Fama	6
Inna Bajka	4
Kawiarnia Lalek	3
Pub Brama	2
Strych	5

5 (200m)

4

World War II brought destruction and slaughter to Białystok. Hitler seized the town in 1939, then handed it over to Stalin before reoccupying it in 1941 – which is when the Jewish population was herded into a ghetto and deported to the death camps. The heroic Białystok **Ghetto Uprising** of August 1943 (the first within the Reich) presaged the extinction of the city's Jewry. The killing was not confined to Jews: by 1945 more than half the city's population was dead, with three-quarters of the town centre destroyed. After the war, the authorities set about rebuilding the town, and from a strictly utilitarian point of view they succeeded: today Białystok is an economic centre for textiles, metals and timber, with a population of more than 250,000.

Ulica Lipowa and around

Białystok's central strolling ground is **ulica Lipowa**, an east–west boulevard constructed during the Tsarist epoch and featuring a smattering of Neoclassical mansions and churches along its route. Prominent among the latter is **St Nicholas' Church** (Cerkiew św. Mikołaja), a typically dark, icon-filled place of Orthodox devotion with ornate frescoes that are copies of those in the Orthodox cathedral in Kiev.

Podlasie Museum
Rynek Kosciuszki 10 • Tues–Sun 10am–5pm; closes 6pm on Fri May–Aug • 6zł • ☏ 85 742 1440, ⓦ muzeum.bialystok.pl

Towards its eastern end, ulica Lipowa opens out to form the triangular **Rynek Kościuszki**, at the centre of which sits the **town hall**. Reconstructed from scratch after World War II this cute colonnaded building now houses the **Podlasie Museum** (Muzeum Podlaskie). A good selection of works by some of Poland's better-known nineteenth- and twentieth-century artists – Malczewski, Witkiewicz, Krzyzanowski – is complemented by an enjoyable collection of local art, the portraits and landscapes displaying a strong feeling for the distinctive character of the region. In addition, the museum has an imaginative programme of temporary shows.

Cathedral of the Assumption
ul. Koscielna 2

Just east of the Rynek is the **Cathedral of the Assumption** (Katedra Wniebowźięcia), a vast neo-Gothic building with spaceship-like towers. According to local legend the tsarist authorities of 1900 only permitted construction of such a huge edifice because it was billed as an "extension" of a small seventeenth-century church that still stands – totally overshadowed – on its western flanks.

Branicki Palace

The most striking building in the town centre is the **Branicki Palace** (Pałac Branickich), destroyed by the Nazis in 1944 but rebuilt on the lines of the eighteenth-century building commissioned by Jan Branicki. It is now a medical academy, whose classical grandeur you can wander in and admire without much trouble if you look the student part. The **park** and formal gardens surrounding the palace are very pleasant.

Army Museum

ul. Kilińskiego 7 • Tues–Sun 9.30am–5pm • 7zł • ☏ 85 741 6449, ⓦ mwb.com.pl

North of the Branicki Palace is the **Army Museum** (Muzeum Wojska), an absorbing collection of uniforms and weaponry that also houses photos, newspapers and other documents from the wartime era of Soviet occupation (1939–41) as well as the original proclamation of the 1943 Białystok Ghetto Uprising. You can also see a Nazi "Enigma" code machine (see page 412).

LUDWIK ZAMENHOF AND THE ESPERANTO MOVEMENT

An artificial language invented as an instrument of international communication, **Esperanto** was the brainchild of **Ludwik Zamenhof** (1859–1917). The son of a Jewish language teacher, Zamenhof grew up in an environment coloured by the uneasy coexistence of Yiddish, Polish, Russian and German speakers. From an early stage Zamenhof, an eye doctor by training, dedicated himself to the cause of racial tolerance and understanding. He believed that the creation of a new, easily learnable **international language** would remove a key obstacle to communication and peaceable coexistence. Zamenhof set himself the task of inventing just such a language using root words common to European, and in particular Romance, languages. *Dr Esperanto's International Language* was published in 1887, but Zamenhof continued to develop his language by translating a whole range of major literary works. The new language rapidly gained international attention, and the world's first **Esperanto congress** was held in France in 1905. In the same year Zamenhof completed *Fundamento de Esperanto*, his main work, which soon became the basic Esperanto textbook and the one still most commonly in use today.

Historical Museum

ul. Warszawska 37 • Tues–Sun 9.30am–5pm • 6zł • ☎ 85 748 2119, ⓦ muzeum.bialystok.pl

Housed in an attractive nineteenth-century villa, the **Historical Museum** (Muzeum Historyczne) – a branch of the Podlasie Museum (see page 180) – reproduces the domestic interiors of nineteenth-century Bialystok with a lovely display of furnishings, crockery, drapes and costumes.

4

Ludwik Zamenhof Centre

ul. Warszawska 19 • Tues–Sun 10am–5pm • 10zł • ☎ 85 676 7367, ⓦ centrumzamenhofa.pl

The heritage of Białystok's best-known son is celebrated at the **Ludwik Zamenhof Centre** (Centrum im. Ludwika Zamenhofa), which is dedicated to international cultural exchange as well as nurturing knowledge of Esperanto (see above). On the ground floor is "The Białystok of Young Zamenhof", an exhibition employing music, film, photos and narration (mostly in Polish) to provide an evocative flavour of what the city looked – and sounded – like prior to World War I.

ARRIVAL AND INFORMATION   BIAŁYSTOK

By train The main train station is a 20min walk (or 5min bus ride on #2, #4 or #21) west of the city centre. Somewhat confusingly, the main exit faces away from the centre; turn right out of the front door then right again over the footbridge and you'll be heading in the right direction. Destinations Ełk (6 daily; 1hr 30min); Gdańsk (2 daily; 6hr 40min); Olsztyn (2 daily; 2hr 30min); Suwałki (5 daily; 1hr 50min–2hr 20min); Warsaw (8 daily; 2hr 30min).

By bus and minibus The bus station is across the footbridge from the train station at ul. Bohaterów Monte Cassino 20. Minibuses to Białowieża, Tykocin and Hajnówka leave from a stop just behind the station.

Destinations Białowieża (minibuses; 4 daily; 2hr); Hajnówka (buses and minibuses; hourly; 1hr–1hr 30min); Lublin (3 daily; 4hr 30min–5hr 30min); Olsztyn (3 daily; 5hr); Suwałki (15 daily; 2hr); Tykocin (buses and minibuses; hourly; 40min); Warsaw (8 daily; 3hr 15min).

Tourist information The tourist office is in the Philharmonia building at ul. Odeska 1 (Mon–Fri 9am–5pm, Sat & Sun from 10am; ☎ 503 356 482, ⓦ podlaskieit. pl), and doles out information on Białystok and on the Podlasie region as a whole.

ACCOMMODATION

EH Apartments ul. Lipowa 19/21 ☎ 515 493 370, ⓦ eh apartments.pl; map page 179. Neat, well-equipped tourist apartments, ranging from the roomy to the miniscule, mostly situated in residential buildings along ul. Lipowa but also elsewhere in central Białystok. Book online and then call in at their office to pick up the keys.

Two-person studios 180zł

Gołębiewski ul. Pałacowa 7 ☎ 85 678 2500, ⓦ gole biewski.pl; map page 179. A big, well-run place aimed at business travellers and upmarket tourists, with a good breakfast buffet and big weekend discounts. Located close to the Branicki Palace. 360zł

Hotel Branicki ul. Zamenhofa 25 ☎85 665 2500, ⓦhotelbranicki.com; map page 179. Elegant hotel meant to evoke the pre-war glamour of the *Białystok Ritz* (destroyed in 1944), with iron-railed balconies, a wooden elevator and various other antique touches. **375zł**

Hotel Esperanto ul. Legionowa 10 ☎85 740 9900, ⓦhotelesperanto.net; map page 179. Smart downtown hotel with an interior design style that isn't afraid to deploy loud colours. The attractive dining and drinking areas are sufficiently animated to attract a lot of non-resident nibblers and quaffers. **230zł**

Royal Hotel Rynek Kościuszki 11 ☎85 831 1801, ⓦroyal-hotel.pl; map page 179. Superbly situated hotel with plush, high-ceilinged rooms, a spa and beauty centre, and the (nowadays de-rigeur) boutique brewery-restaurant downstairs (see page 182). **280zł**

Willa Pastel ul. Waszyngtona 24a ☎85 748 6060, ⓦpastel.kasol.com.pl; map page 179. Smallish modern hotel within easy walking distance of the centre, offering friendly service and all the creature comforts, including a restaurant that does excellent game dishes. **320zł**

EATING

Babka ul. Lipowa 2 ☎690 273 707, ⓦfacebook.com/Babka.Bialystok; map page 179. Looking like a cross between a country cottage and a cocktail lounge, this popular restaurant represents a winning combination of folk motifs and contemporary design. The menu concentrates on the potato-heavy specialities of northeastern Poland: *babka* (tasty bricks of mashed-then-baked potato served with meat or mushroom sauce; 19zł) is the standard order. Mon–Thurs & Sun noon–10pm, Fri & Sat noon–midnight.

Browar Stary Rynek Rynek Kościuszki 11, in the Royal Hotel ☎85 831 1801, ⓦroyal-hotel.pl/browar; map page 179. Popular pub-restaurant serving imaginative, well-presented Mediterranean fare and four kinds of beer made on the premises. Two-course set lunches (Mon–Fri noon–4pm) are 22zł. Daily noon–midnight.

Esperanto Café Rynek Kościuszki 10 ☎85 742 6032, ⓦesperanto-cafe.pl; map page 179. Located in the town hall, this multi-purpose eating-and-drinking venue offers something to suit most tastes, with a menu that runs from traditional Polish through to pasta (mains 28–36zł) and ends with an excellent selection of cakes. The outdoor terrace is a popular place to drink. Mon–Thurs & Sun

10am–10pm, Fri & Sat 10am–midnight.

Maison du Café ul. Kilińskiego 10 ☎533 333 327, ⓦmaisonducafe.pl; map page 179. Café-patisserie on one of Białystok's prettiest streets, serving good coffee and gorgeous cakes. A small selection of lunchtime soups and salads draw inspiration from Mediterranean and Asian cuisine. Mon–Sat 7am–10pm, Sun 9am–10pm.

Sztuka Mięsa ul. Krakowska 11 ☎85 742 0740, ⓦfacebook.com/SztukaMiesa; map page 179. A play on words that means "piece of meat" or "the art of meat" depending on the context, this informal, semi-distressed-looking bistro is actually the source of some of the finest food in the city. The seasonally changing and eclectic menu (mains 35–70zł) ranges from burgers through to classic French soups, Mediterranean seafood and lovingly prepared entrecote steaks. Daily noon–11pm.

Trattoria Gallo Nero ul. Warszawska 30B ☎85 710 4444, ⓦgallonero.com.pl; map page 179. The place to go for decent Italian fare, with a long list of pasta and pizzas rounded off with some appetizing Mediterranean mains (cod in tangy Livornese sauce; 32zł). Tues–Thurs noon–9.30pm, Fri & Sat noon–10.30pm, Sun noon–9pm.

DRINKING AND NIGHTLIFE

Batyskaf ul. Pilsudskiego 29 ☎690 680 409, ⓦfacebook.com/bialystokbatyskaf; map page 179. The name of this pub means "bathyscape" and the interior looks a little bit like something out of a Jules Verne novel, with a mixture of retro and functional furnishings and lots of exposed piping. There's a long bar to crowd around, regular karaoke sessions and an outstanding choice of whiskies, rums and cocktails. Daily 5pm–1am.

Fama ul. Legionowa 5 ☎695 377 150; map page 179. Café in the municipal cultural centre that hosts jazz and rock gigs, occasional stand-up comedy and cabaret. Open 6pm–late.

Inna Bajka ul. Akademicka 10/1 ☎881 057 797; map page 179. Set in a large octagonal pavilion facing a lush park, with an extensive patio for outdoor seating, this lively bar-restaurant offers DJs at weekends and occasional live

music. Mon–Wed & Sun 9am–midnight, Thurs 9am–2am, Fri & Sat 9am–3am.

Kawiarnia Lalek ul. Kalinowskiego 1 ☎85 742 5031, ⓦbtl.bialystok.pl; map page 179. Inside the puppet theatre, this bar is a lively place for an evening drink and has an outdoor patio in summer. Mon–Sat 10am–2am, Sun 2pm–midnight.

Pub Brama Rynek Kościuszki 4 ☎505 239 192; map page 179. The perfect place for a summertime chill-out, this pub has a large garden courtyard slap bang in the centre of town, filled with wooden tables and benches. May–Sept daily 9am–6am.

Strych Rynek Kościuszki 22 ☎605 461 707, ⓦstrychpub.pl; map page 179. Atmospheric bar in the timber-beamed attic of a downtown apartment building, with a good choice of bottled beers from around eastern Europe, and a pool table. Daily 4pm–late.

4

Around Białystok

Białystok's greatest asset is that many of northern Poland's most rewarding destinations are right on its doorstep. Not far to the east, the charming village of **Supraśl** is home to a celebrated Orthodox monastery and is also the most convenient access point to the tranquil **Knyszyń Forest**. Further east are the old Tatar villages of **Kruszyniany** and **Bohoniki**, an intriguing ethnic component of Poland's eastern borderlands. West of Białystok, **Tykocin** is a former part-Jewish market town with a beautifully preserved synagogue; while the **Biebrza National Park** is a reedy rural idyll that's popular with bird-watchers.

Supraśl and the Knyszyń Forest

The village of **SUPRAŚL**, 16km northeast of Białystok, is a sleepy place made up largely of single-storey timber houses surrounded by neat gardens. Stretching either side of the village is the **Knyszyń Forest**, a dense swathe of sandy-soiled woodland that makes for beautifully tranquil walking terrain.

Basilian Monastery

At the northeastern edge of the village is the **Basilian Monastery**, a walled complex of buildings surrounding the impressive Orthodox **Church of the Annunciation** (Cerkiew Zwiastowania). An eye-catching structure featuring four corner towers and zestful zig-zagging **brickwork**, the church was built in the sixteenth century by the Grand Hetman of Lithuania, Aleksander Chodkiewicz, for the Orthodox order of St Basil. Destroyed by German shelling in 1944, it was reconstructed in the 1980s, and the famed Byzantine-style frescoes of the interior have been painstakingly repainted. The monastery buildings spent most of the communist period as a local school, but now they are once again occupied by Orthodox monks.

Icon Museum

May–Aug Mon–Thurs 10am–5pm, Fri 10am–6pm; Sept–April Tues–Sun 10am–5pm • 14zł; free on Thurs • ☎ 509 336 829, ⓦ muzeum.bialystok.pl

Fragments of the church's original frescoes can be seen in the extensive **Icon Museum** (Muzeum Ikon) in the monastery courtyard. The main aim of the museum is to explain the importance of the icon in Orthodox art, with reproductions of historical icons, English-language texts, and a sumptuous collection of church art from eastern Poland – all atmospherically lit and accompanied by ethereal background music. Particularly interesting are the locally produced brass icons, sufficiently durable to fit into someone's luggage – thus ensuring saintly protection during one's travels.

Knyszyń Forest

From the southern edge of Supraśl, a marked path takes you south through the lofty expanses of the **Knyszyń Forest** (Puszcza Knyszyńska) to the village of **Ciasne**, ending by the bus stop near **Grabówka** at the edge of the main road back into Białystok – a lovely 12km-long hike, in which the silence of the forest is broken at intervals by cackling crows overhead or startled deer breaking for cover.

ARRIVAL AND DEPARTURE   SUPRAŚL

By bus Hourly buses make the trip to Suprasl from Białystok (25min), dropping off at pl. Kosciuszki.

EATING

★ **Bar Jarzębinka** ul. 3 Maja 22 ☎ 884 008 043. A simple order-at-the-counter place that's famous for its *babka* – a delicious Belarusian-Lithuanian potato mush baked in square tins and covered in mushroom sauce. It also serves soups, stuffed *kartacze* dumplings, and (in summer) ice cream. Tues–Sun 11am–6pm.

The Tatar villages: Kruszyniany and Bohoniki

The old Tatar villages of **Kruszyniany** and **Bohoniki**, with their wooden mosques and Muslim graveyards, lie hard up against the Belarusian frontier, east of Białystok. The Tatars were given lands in eastern Poland by seventeenth-century King Jan Sobieski, in gratitude for their service in his military campaigns. They were by no means an exotic addition to the Polish-Lithuanian Commonwealth, the Lithuanian ruler Vytautas the Great having drafted Tatar units into his armies some three centuries before. Today some six thousand descendants of these first Muslim citizens of Poland are spread all over the country, particularly in the Szczecin, Gdańsk and Białystok areas.

Kruszyniany

Walking through **KRUSZYNIANY** is like time-travelling back a century or two: the painted wooden houses, cobbled road and wizened inhabitants seem like something out of Tolstoy. Surrounded by trees and set back from the road is the eighteenth-century **mosque** (May–Sept daily 9am–7pm; Oct–April by prior arrangement only; 5zł; ☎ 502 543 871, ⦿ kruszyniany.com.pl), a beautiful pea-green building recognizable by the Islamic crescents on its twin spires. Although the population is dwindling – currently the village musters only a handful of people for the monthly services conducted by the visiting imam from Białystok – the mosque's interior is well maintained. The building is divided into two sections, the smaller one for women, the larger one for men, containing the *mihrab*, the customary recess pointing in the direction of Mecca, and a *mimber* (pulpit) from which the prayers are directed by the imam.

Bohoniki

The **mosque** in more remote **BOHONIKI** is a similar, though smaller, building, a beautiful shade of coffee-brown on the outside, and stuffed with cosy-looking carpets within. You'll need to find the keyholder to let you in – the noticeboard will tell you where to go – and you should donate a few złoty for your visit.

The **Tatar cemetery** is hidden in a copse half a kilometre south of the village. Search through the undergrowth right at the back and you'll find older, tumbledown gravestones inscribed in Russian from the days when Bohoniki was an outpost of the tsarist empire. Tatars from all over Poland are still buried here, as they have been since Sobieski's time.

ARRIVAL AND DEPARTURE
KRUSZYNIANY AND BOHONIKI

By bus You'll need your own transport if you want to visit both mosques. Three direct buses a day run from Białystok to Kruszyniany (1hr 50min; last bus back from Kruszyniany is currently at 4pm). The only buses to Bohoniki are from Sokółka (an hour's train journey north of Białystok) and they do not run every day.

ACCOMMODATION AND EATING

Pod Lipami Kruszyniany 51 ☎ 85 722 7554, ⦿ dworek podlipami.pl. A comfortable pension with en-suite doubles, as well as family rooms with kitchenettes. The large garden outside has space for BBQs and evening bonfires. **160zł**

★ **Tatarska Jurta** Across the road from the Kruszniany mosque ☎ 85 749 4052, ⦿ kruszyniany.pl. Tasty traditional Tatar food such as *jeczpoczmaki* (samosa-like pastry parcels filled with potatoes, meat and veg; 23zł) and *kibiny* (pasties with meat or cabbage filling; 23zł). They also have neat and cosy en-suite rooms above the restaurant. Restaurant daily 11am–6pm. **200zł**

Tykocin

Set in the open countryside some 40km west of Białystok, **TYKOCIN**'s small size and unassuming nature belies its historical significance: as well as being the former site of the national arsenal, it also has one of the best-restored **synagogues** in Poland – a reminder that this was once home to an important Jewish community. Jews first came to Tykocin in 1522, and by 1900 a good fifty percent of the town was Jewish. But four hundred years of Jewish life came to a brutal end in 1941, when, over the course of two days, the town's entire Jewish population was rounded up by the Nazis and shot in the nearby woods.

Focus of the town is the enchanting **market square**, bordered by well-preserved nineteenth-century wooden houses.

The synagogue and museum

ul. Kozia 2 • Tues–Sun 10am–6pm • 10zł; free on Sat • ☎ 85 718 1613, ⓦ muzeum.bialystok.pl

Built in 1642, Tykocin's **Great Synagogue** (Wielka Synagoga) is one of the finest Baroque synagogues still in existence, extensively restored in two waves – the first in the 1970s, the second in 2015–16. It now serves as a beautiful **museum**, where recordings of Jewish music and prayers add to an evocative atmosphere. Beautifully illustrated Hebrew inscriptions, mostly prayers, adorn sections of the interior walls, as do some lively colourful **frescoes**. Most striking of all are the large Baroque bimah, and the ornate Aron Kodesh in the east wall. Valuable religious artefacts are on display, as well as historical documents relating to the town's now-lost Jewish community.

Over the square in the old Talmud house there's a well-kept local-history **museum** (same hours and ticket), featuring an intact apothecary's shop and a gallery of paintings by local artist Zygmunt Bujnowski (1895–1927).

Church of the Holy Trinity

The Baroque **Church of the Holy Trinity** (Kosciol Swietej Trojcy), commissioned by Białystok aristocrat Jan Branicki in 1741 and recently restored, has a beautiful polychrome ceiling, a finely ornamented side chapel of the Virgin and a functioning Baroque organ. The portraits of Branicki and his wife, Izabella Poniatowska, are by Silvester de Mirys, a Scot who became the resident artist at the Branicki palace in Białystok. Next to the church looking onto the river bridge is the **Alumnat**, a hospice for war veterans founded in 1633 – a world first.

The Jewish Cemetery

The **Jewish Cemetery** (Cmentarz Zydowski) on the edge of town, at the western end of ulica Holendry, is gradually blending into the surrounding meadow; as is often the case, there's no one able or willing to take care of it. Among the eroded, weather-beaten gravestones, however, a few preserve their fine original carvings.

ARRIVAL AND DEPARTURE **TYKOCIN**

By bus Tykocin is a 40min journey from the main bus station in Białystok; both bus and minibus services depart roughly hourly throughout the day.

ACCOMMODATION AND EATING

Kiermusy Kiermusy 12, 3km west of Tykocin ☎ 85 718 7079, ⓦ kiermusy.com.pl. Lavish rooms in a nineteenth-century manor house or nearby cottages, decorated in period style with rich fabrics and plenty of old-fashioned charm. The nearby *Rzym* restaurant, part of the same complex, is filled with rustic furniture and serves delicious, traditional Polish food – such as pork in mushroom sauce. Mains are around 30zł. Restaurant daily noon–10pm. **190zł**

Pod Czarnym Bocianem ul. Poświętna 16 ☎ 85 718 7408, ⓦ czarnybocian.prv.pl. A homely B&B on a cobbled street behind the parish church, run by a friendly local historian and enjoying a pleasant position on the river. **100zł**

Villa Regent ul. Sokolowska 3 ☎ 85 718 7476, ⓦ villa regent.eu. Hotel in a renovated old building across from the synagogue, offering attractive rooms, some with balconies. The restaurant mixes Polish classics with Jewish-influenced cuisine, from hummus dips to *czulent* and poultry-filled *kreplach* dumplings. Restaurant daily noon–8pm. **150zł**

4

> ## WILDLIFE IN BIEBRZA NATIONAL PARK
>
> The scenic river basin landscape of the **Biebrza National Park** is home to richly varied flora and fauna. Important residents include otters, a large beaver population, wild boar, wolves and several hundred elk. The **plant** community includes just about every kind of marshland and forest species to be found in the country, including a rich assortment of rare mosses. The park's **bird life** – of which more than 260 species have been recorded to date, many of them with local breeding habitats – is proving a major attraction with bird-watchers from all over Europe. **Spring** is the time to come, when floodwaters create an ideal habitat for waterfowl, including the pintail, shoveler and teal, as well as such rarities as the black tern and, most prized of all, the aquatic warbler.

Biebrza National Park

North and west of Tykocin lies one of Poland's unique natural paradises, an area of low-lying marshland that forms the **Biebrza National Park** (Biebrzański Park Narodowy); at around 600 square kilometres, it's the largest protected area in the country. Running through it is the River Biebrza, which has its source southeast of Augustów close to the Belarusian border. The river feeds a sizeable network of bogs and marshes that constitutes one of Europe's most extensive and unspoilt **wetlands**.

The park is divided into three sections, corresponding to portions of the river. The **Northern Basin**, the smallest and least easily accessible, lies in the upper part of the river, and is not much visited. The **Middle Basin** encompasses a scenic section of marshland and river forest, notably the **Red Marsh** (*Czerwone Bagno*) area, a stretch of strictly protected peat bog located some distance from the river valley floodlands, which is home to a large group of elk as well as smaller populations of golden and white-tailed eagles. The area is off-limits to anyone not accompanied by an official guide (see page 187). The **Southern Basin** consists of a combination of peat bogs and marshland, and is the most popular bird-watching territory on account of the large number of species found here. It's relatively easy to spot elk browsing among the shrubs from the viewing towers in this area.

Osowiec-Twierdza and the Southern Basin

The main entry point to the park is **OSOWIEC-TWIERDZA**, a drab village built to serve a massive tsarist-era fortress (*twierdza*) whose imposing grey walls can be seen stretching beside the railway tracks as you approach. The National Park Information Centre (see page 187) is a short walk from the train station.

The central part of the Southern Basin is within easy walking distance of Osowiec. After about 2km, the road north from the information centre will bring you to a bridge over the River Biebrza. Beyond here a pair of well-marked boardwalk trails take you across the soggy surface of the Biebrza's flood plain, providing access to a captivating landscape of tufted grasses and sedge. After another 2km the trail meets the main Białystok–Ełk road, where a **viewing tower** provides a wonderful panorama of the hypnotically desolate landscape of rush-filled swamp. Along the way you'll pass several remnants of the tsarist-era fortification system, as well as half-destroyed concrete bunkers built by the Germans during World War II. Many of these relics are used as nesting platforms by the park's bird population.

Alternatively, you can explore the park **by boat**, especially worthwhile if you want to head beyond the immediate vicinity of Osowiec. The most ambitious locally organized **excursion** takes you along the Biebrza and Narew rivers all the way from Rajgród in the north down to Łomza – a five- to seven-day trip involving stopovers at campsites and forester's lodges along the way. Check with the National Park Information Centre for current details.

ARRIVAL AND INFORMATION

By train Osowiec is 1hr by train from Białystok, and is served by seven daily trains on the Białystok–Ełk line.

National Park Information Centre The park's information centre is a short walk north of the train station (May–Sept daily 8am–5pm; Oct–April Mon–Fri 7.30am–3.30pm; ☎085 738 3035, ☜biebrza.org.pl).

BIEBRZA NATIONAL PARK

It sells entrance tickets to the park (6zł), offers advice on walking routes and has a small photographic display of the region's wildlife. The centre also arranges guides (150zł flat fee per group) for those eager to visit the restricted Red Marsh zone.

ACCOMMODATION AND EATING

Bartlowizna ul. Nadbiebrzańska 32, at the edge of Goniądz, 5km east of Osowiec-Twierdza ☎85 738 0630, ☜biebrza.com.pl. Almost a self-contained resort in its own right, this place offers a landscaped garden, tennis courts and stables. Its folk-style restaurant, *Bartla Inn*, serves up big portions of traditional Polish food (mains 25–35zł), including some more unusual offerings like

meat-stuffed *kartacz* (potato dumplings) and venison. Restaurant daily noon–10pm. <u>200zł</u>

Bóbr campsite Osowiec-Twierdza ☎724 754 528. Basic campsite 1.5km northwest of the train station, well poised for the main walking trails into the park. Wood for campfires is available to buy. <u>350zł</u>

The Białowieża Forest

The last major tract of primeval forest left in Europe, the ancient **Białowieża Forest** (Puszcza Białowieska) covers 1260 square kilometres, spreading over the border into Belarus. Most of the forest falls within the **Białowieża National Park** (Białowieski Park Narodowy), the first national park established in Poland and the only one currently numbered among UNESCO's World Natural Heritage sites. As well as being an area of inestimable beauty, the forest is also famous for harbouring a large population of **European bison**.

Nearly forty percent of the forest on the Polish side of the border belongs to a so-called **strictly protected area** (*obreb ochronny rezerwat*), a tightly controlled area that can only be visited accompanied by a guide. The rest of the national park is open to unaccompanied individuals, and there are plenty of marked paths and biking routes to enjoy – especially around the **Bison Reserve** west of **Białowieża village** and the **Royal Oaks Way** to the northwest. If you're spending any time in this part of the country, the extraordinary, primeval feel of the forest makes a visit here an experience not to be missed.

An obvious entry point to the Białowieża Forest is **Hajnówka**, a regional focus of Orthodox worship. Beyond the southern fringes of the forest, the extraordinary convent at **Grabarka** – the focal point of Orthodox pilgrimage in Poland – is also worth investigating.

Getting to Białowieża is straightforward, and if you start early in the day you can treat the forest as a day-trip from Białystok. However there's plenty of **accommodation** in Białowieża village, and the idea of a restful night or two in this beautiful landscape has undoubted appeal.

Brief history

For centuries Białowieża was a **private hunting ground** for a succession of Lithuanian and Belarusian aristocrats, Polish kings and Russian tsars, whose patronage ensured that the forest survived largely intact. Recognizing its environmental importance, the Polish government turned large sections of the forest into a national park in 1921, and sought to revive its **bison herds**, eaten to extinction by famished soldiers during World War I.

In 2016 the Polish government decided to triple the amount of **logging** in the forest, ostensibly in order to counter the spread of bark beetle. The decision has been opposed by Polish environmentalists, and faced legal challenges from both the EU and UNESCO, who listed the forest as a World Heritage site in 1979.

4

HAJNÓWKA FESTIVALS

There are two international festivals of Orthodox church music in Hajnówka, both of which take place in May. The **International Festival of Orthodox Choral Music** (ⓦfestival-hajnowka.pl) involves concerts in both Hajnówka and Białystok; while the **Hajnówka Days of Church Music** (ⓦfestiwal.cerkiew.pl) takes place in Hajnówka's Holy Trinity Church. Featuring choirs from Poland and its eastern neighbours, both offer a rare chance to hear haunting liturgical music of the highest quality.

Hajnówka

Some 70km southeast of Białystok, the sleepy settlement of **HAJNÓWKA** is an important centre for Poland's Belarusian minority, as evidenced by its magnificent Orthodox church. The town is an excellent jumping-off point to the Białowieża Forest, which stretches east of the town as far as the Belarusian border.

Holy Trinity Church

ul. Dziewiatowskiego 15 • Mon–Sat 10am–1pm & 2–5pm • ☎ 85 873 2971

An uncompromisingly modern structure consecrated in 1992, the Orthodox **Holy Trinity Church** (Cerkiew Świętej Trójcy) is one of the most beautiful sacral buildings in this part of Poland, its undulating roof and bulbous onion domes pitching it somewhere between ancient fairy-tale and the architectural avant-garde. The interior boasts a glittering iconostasis, a spectacular series of luminous frescoes, a unique stained-glass chandelier and a fine set of stained-glass windows.

The forest railway

Trips to Topiło depart at 10am on the following days: mid-May to June every Sat; July–Aug Tues, Thurs, Sat & Sun; Sept every Thurs & Sat • 30zł return • ☎ 85 682 2689

The easiest way to access the thick woodland around Hajnówka is to take a trip on the **forest railway** (*kolejka leśna*), the remainder of a dense network of narrow-gauge lines built by German occupying forces in 1916. The network was used by local logging companies until 1992, when it became more economical to transport the wood by truck. Departing from a tiny **station** on ulica Celna, twenty minutes' walk east of the centre, the line runs to the village of Topiło, 8km south of town. The train carries you through hauntingly dense forest, and halts for about 45 minutes in Topiło itself (where there's a small café) before returning to Hajnówka.

ARRIVAL AND INFORMATION HAJNÓWKA

By train The train station is in the centre of town but is only served by a handful of local services. With changes, you can get here from Białystok (change at Czeremcha; 2–3hr) and Warsaw (change at Siedlce; 4–5hr).

By bus The bus station is a 15min walk southwest of the town centre – although most services also pick up and drop off on the main ul. 3 Maja. Services to and from Białowieża only use the stops on ul. 3 Maja.

Destinations Białowieża (17 daily; 30–45min); Białystok (hourly; 1hr–1hr 30min).

Tourist information The tourist office at ul. 3 Maja 45 (May–Sept Mon–Sat 9am–5pm; Oct–April Mon–Fri 8am–4pm; ☎ 85 682 4381) sells maps of the Białowieża Forest and hands out bus timetables.

ACCOMMODATION AND EATING

Dom Nauczyciela ul. Piłsudskiego 6 ☎ 85 682 2585, ✉ bialistok@oupis.pl. A functional budget hotel with a mixture of spartan en suites and rooms with shared facilities – there's no breakfast, but you might get an electric kettle in the room. **85zł**

Leśny Dworek 3 Maja 42, in the same building as the town museum ☎ 85 682 5161. Small restaurant offering Belarusian dishes (mains 20–25zł), such as pork chops stuffed with ham and peas. Daily 11am–10pm.

Zajazd Bartnik ul. Parkowa 8 ☎ 606 141 987, ⓦhote bartnik.pl. Peaceful place beside a park with unfussy en-suite rooms, and a restaurant serving local fare such as potato pancakes, *kartacze* (potato dumplings) and *kiszka* (potato sausage). Few mains break the 30zł barrier. Restaurant noon–10pm. **160zł**

Białowieża and around

BIAŁOWIEŻA, a mere 2km from the Belarusian border, is a pretty agricultural village full of the single-storey wooden farmhouses that characterize Poland's eastern borderlands; colour-washed in a variety of ochres, maroons and greens, they're a picture of domestic tidiness. As the sprinkling of satellite dishes and gleaming new red roofs shows, tourism has made the village relatively prosperous compared with other parts of Podlasie.

The Palace Park

The **Palace Park** (Park Pałacowy) was laid out in the 1890s to accompany a neo-Gothic palace built to serve as the hunting lodge of the Russian tsars. The palace itself was damaged in World War II and demolished in the 1960s, but there's still much in the park to enjoy, including a brace of ornamental lakes and tree-lined avenues.

National Park Centre and Nature and Forest Museum

Museum: mid-April to mid-Oct: Mon–Fri 9am–4.30pm, Sat & Sun 9am–5pm; mid-Oct to mid-April Tues–Sun 9am–4pm • 12zł • ☎ 85 682 9700, ⊛ bpn.com.pl

At the centre of the Palace Park rises the gleaming new National Park Centre, which contains a guesthouse (see page 191), restaurant and the state-of-the-art **Nature and Forest Museum** (Muzeum Przyrodniczo-Leśne). The impressively detailed and well-presented display serves as a thorough introduction to the forest, including examples of the amazingly diverse flora and fauna. An observation tower provides expansive views over park and forest.

The Strictly Protected Area

Guided walking tours 258zł per group, plus 6zł entrance fee per person • **Horse-drawn cart rides** 270zł per four-person cart, including guide, plus 6zł entrance fee per person • Book ahead in summer

The most dramatic stretches of deep forest lie within the **Strictly Protected Area** (Obręb Ochronny Rezerwat) north of the village, which can only be visited with an **official**

4

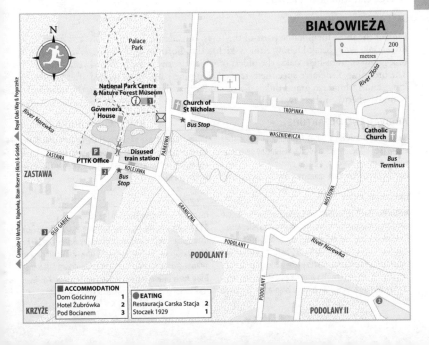

guide. Either the National Park Centre or the PTTK office (see below) can fix you up with a three-hour guided **walking tour**, and the PTTK can also arrange for three-hour tours by **horse-drawn cart**.

However you decide to enter the reserve, it's likely to be a magical experience. At times the serenity of the forest's seemingly endless depths is exhilarating, the trunks of oak, spruce and hornbeam swelling to a dense canopy, momentarily pierced by shafts of sunlight that sparkle briefly before subsiding into gloom. Along with larger animals, such as wolves, elk and beavers, the forest supports an astounding profusion of **flora and fauna**, including over twenty species of tree, thirteen varieties of bat, 228 species of birds and around 8000 different insect species.

European Bison Show Reserve

On the Hajnówka–Białowieża road • Mid-April to mid-Oct daily 9am–5pm; mid-Oct to mid-April Tues–Sun 8am–4pm • 8zł

Some 4km west of the village, the **Bison Reserve** (Rezerwat Pokazowy Zwierząt) is a large fenced area where some of the most impressive species living in the forest are on display. You can walk there in fifty minutes by following the **Żebra Żubra path**, a fascinating forest trail which leaves the Białowieża–Pogorzelce road just northwest of the village. A raised boardwalk takes you above the squelchy, fern-and-moss-covered forest floor, with a bewildering diversity of deciduous trees crowding in on either side – information boards along the way will help you to tell your ash from your alder.

The reserve itself contains several representatives of the forest's 250-strong population of bison. Don't be fooled by their docile demeanour: when threatened, the bison – *żubr* in Polish – can charge at over 50km an hour, which makes for a force to be reckoned considering that the largest weigh over 1000kg. The stout, sandy-coloured horses with a dark stripe on their backs that are also on show are **tarpans**, relations of the original steppe horses that died out in the last century. The tarpans are gradually being bred back to their original genetic stock after centuries of interbreeding with village horses. In other enclosures round the reserve you can see wolves, elk, wild boar and lynx.

The Royal Oaks Way

One of the most memorable parts of the forest outside the Strictly Protected Area is the **Royal Oaks Way** (Szlak Dębów Królewskich), 4km north of the bison reserve. It consists of a group of 40m-high oaks, the oldest of which are over four hundred years old. The brooding, venerable specimens ranged along the path are all named after Polish kings and Lithuanian grand dukes – a reminder that the forest lies along the historical boundary between these two realms.

ARRIVAL AND DEPARTURE

BIAŁOWIEŻA AND AROUND

By bus and minibus Buses terminate at the eastern end of the village, although you'll save time by getting off either at the southern or eastern entrance to the Palace Park. There are four daily minibuses from Białystok to the village (2hr); if you miss one of these, take one of the (roughly hourly) buses to Hajnówka, where you can pick up one of the frequent buses to Białowieża from the main street (see page 187).

INFORMATION

National Park Information Centre Inside the Nature and Forest Museum building (mid-April to mid-Oct Mon–Fri 9am–4.30pm, Sat & Sun 9am–5pm; mid-Oct to mid-April Tues–Sun 9am–4pm; ☎ 85 681 2901, ⓦ bpn.com.pl); the centre sells entrance tickets to the national park (6zł), as well as maps, and can also arrange guided walking tours of the Strictly Protected Area. They keep a list of private rooms (40–60zł per person) in the village.

PTTK office At the southern entrance to the Palace Park (daily: June–Sept 8am–6pm; Oct–May 8am–4pm; ☎ 85 681 2295, ⓦ pttk.bialowieza.pl), the PTTK office can arrange guided walking tours and horse-drawn cart tours.

Bike hire Bialowieskie Centrum Sportu on ul. Kolejowa (☎ 733 587 583, ⓦ cs.bialowieza.pl) hires out bikes.

ACCOMMODATION

Dom Gościnny In the National Park Centre building ☎85 682 9729, ⓦnoclegi.bpn.com.pl; map page 189. Guesthouse offering smart en-suite doubles and triples in a sleek, ultra-modern building right in the Palace Park. **160zł**

Hotel Żubrówka ul. Olgi Gabiec 6 ☎85 682 9400, ⓦhotel-zubrowka.pl; map page 189. The plushest option in town, built in the style of a luxurious hunting lodge and filled with wooden beams and rich tapestries. There's a spa and pool on site. **350zł**

Pod Bocianem ul. Olgi Gabiec 14 ☎85 681 2681, ⓦnoclegibialowieza.pl; map page 189. Charming family-run guesthouse near the park entrance, with snug en-suite rooms in traditional farmhouse buildings, and cabins grouped around a lawn, some with fireplaces and kitchens. **120zł**

EATING

Restauracja Carska Stacja Towarowa 4 ☎602 243 228, ⓦrestauracjacarska.pl; map page 189. Enchanting little restaurant set in a former railway station about 2km southeast of the village, with opulent decor reminiscent of the Tsarist period, and a menu brimming with delicious Russian dishes like *pielmieni* and partridges in apricot-fig sauce (mains 65–70zł). Daily 11am–last customer.

Stoczek 1929 ul. Waszkiewicza 79 ☎85 730 3209, ⓦstoczek1929.pl; map page 189. Traditional Polish fare done with style, with a menu that runs from *kartacze* dumplings stuffed with game (40zł) through pork, duck and game. A wooden building behind the restaurant holds a handful of two-room apartments and snug doubles under the attic roof. Restaurant daily noon–10pm. **250zł**

Grabarka

Hidden away in the woods 60km southwest of Hajnówka, the **convent** near the village of **GRABARKA** is the most important pilgrimage site in the country for Orthodox Poles. Although it's been the site of a chapel since medieval times, Grabarka didn't become a convent until 1947, when several groups of Orthodox nuns (some from eastern territories recently occupied by the Soviet Union) chose this isolated spot as the site of a new community. It quickly became the country's most venerated Orthodox spiritual centre, and the site of major pilgrimages on the main holy days. The largest takes place during the **Feast of the Transfiguration** (Przemienienie Pańskie) on August 19, when thousands of faithful from around the country flock to Grabarka, many by foot.

Church of the Transfiguration and the Holy Mount

Approached by a quiet forest road, the convent **Church of the Transfiguration** stands at the top of a small wooded hill. The dainty timber structure is crowded with brightly painted saintly icons, while outside the church is a striking thicket of thousands of **wooden crosses known as the Holy Mount** (Święta Góra). The oldest of these crosses – a gesture of piety carried by pilgrims – date back to the early eighteenth century, when pilgrims drawn by reports of miracles during a cholera epidemic began packing the slopes below the church.

ARRIVAL AND DEPARTURE   GRABARKA

By train If you're coming by public transport it's likely to be a long day out, so be sure to get an early start. You can take a train to the village of Sycze from Białystok (2 daily, changing at Czeremcha; 2hr 15min) or Hajnówka (3 daily, 1 of which involves changing at Czeremcha; 1hr 10min), then walk 1km through the woods up to the convent.

By bus Buses run to Grabarka village (roughly 500m from the convent) two or three times a day from the market town of Siemiatycze, which can be reached by regular bus from Białystok or Lublin.

Lublin and the east

RED SALON, ZAMOYSKI PALACE

5 Lublin and the east

Stretching from the River Vistula to the Belarusian and Ukrainian borders, the Lublin region is one of agricultural plains punctuated by backwoods villages and sleepy towns. This is historically one of Europe's main grain-producing areas, with local aristocrats amassing huge riches by shipping their produce down the river to the markets of Gdańsk. The palaces of these feudal landowners still dot the countryside, alongside market towns endowed by the magnates with fine public buildings and churches.

The main city of the region is bustling, self-confident **Lublin**, an economic and intellectual centre that also boasts one of Poland's most magical Old Towns. The smaller towns, particularly the old trading centres of **Kazimierz Dolny** and **Sandomierz** along the River Vistula, are among the country's most beautiful, long favoured by artists and retaining fine historic centres. A cherished weekend retreat of the Warsaw artistic set, Kazimierz in particular is one of the liveliest summertime destinations that Poland has to offer. Over to the east, **Zamość** has a superb Renaissance centre, miraculously preserved through wars and well worth a detour. All of these places had significant **Jewish populations** before World War II, and the well-preserved synagogue at **Włodawa** provides some insight into what the whole of eastern Poland must have looked like before 1939. Lublin in particular was one of the most important Jewish centres in Poland, which probably explains why its suburb **Majdanek** was chosen by the Nazis as the site of one of their most notorious death camps – a chilling place that demands to be visited.

Lublin

The city of **LUBLIN**, the largest in eastern Poland, is one of the most alluring urban centres in the whole country, thanks in large part to the evocative hive of alleys that constitute its magnificent Old Town. The fabric of this old quarter came through World War II relatively undamaged, and recent restoration has made the city centre ripe for tourism, though Lublin sees nothing like the crowds flowing into Kraków, Warsaw or Gdańsk. Lublin's increasingly vibrant festival scene (see page 204) has led to an explosion in the number of Polish visitors, lending the city a palpable air of excitement in the summer months.

Most of Lublin's medieval splendours are located in the **Old Town**, a compact, pedestrianized area connected by footbridge to the adjacent **castle hill**. The administrative centre of the city lies along **Krakowskie Przedmeście**, west of the Old Town, a strip which still retains many of its *belle-époque* facades. Also outside the Old Town lie numerous reminders of Lublin's once-thriving **Jewish community**, a population exterminated in the Nazi concentration camp at **Majdanek**, 6km from the city centre.

The Jews of Lublin p.201
Lublin festivals p.204
Walks around Kazimierz: the *wąwozy* p.210

The Festival of Folk Bands and Singers p.212
Zamość festivals p.220

KAZIMIERZ DOLNY

Highlights

❶ Lublin Youthful and vibrant city with a wonderfully atmospheric old centre, plentiful restaurants and a great folk museum. See page 194

❷ Majdanek Former Nazi extermination camp, preserved as a stark warning to future generations. Possibly the most moving of all Holocaust reminders in Poland: harrowing but necessary. See page 202

❸ Zamoyski Palace, Kozłówka A stunning Baroque palace with lavish interiors, some of which have been given over to a mesmerizing museum of communist-era art and propaganda. See page 205

❹ Kazimierz Dolny Beautifully preserved medieval town, long the favoured weekend destination for arty Warsaw folk. See page 208

❺ Sandomierz Historic Vistula valley trading town with many of its medieval and Renaissance buildings still standing. See page 212

❻ Krzyżtopór Castle One of Poland's most magnificent and haunting ruins, an adventure playground for kids and adults alike. See page 216

❼ Zamość Sixteenth-century model town, built as a showcase for Renaissance ideals and with a pronounced Italianate feel. See page 216

❽ Roztoczański National Park A bucolic paradise with low-lying hills, forests, lakes and tarpan ponies. See page 220

HIGHLIGHTS ARE MARKED ON THE MAP ON PAGE 196

5

Brief history

Lublin started as a **medieval** trade settlement controlling the route linking the Baltic ports with Kiev and the Black Sea. With the informal union of Lithuania and Poland that followed the marriage of Grand Duke Jogaila to Queen Jadwiga in 1386, Lublin became an important centre of economic and political contact between the two countries. It was no surprise that the city was chosen to host the signing of the **Union of Lublin** in 1569, when the nobility of both nations agreed to establish the **Polish-Lithuanian Commonwealth** – at the time the largest mainland state in Europe. Over a century of prosperity followed, during which the arts flourished and many fine buildings were erected. The **Partitions** rudely interrupted this process, leaving Lublin to languish on the edge of the Russian-ruled Duchy of Warsaw.

Following World War I, a **Catholic university** (the only one in Eastern Europe) was established, which grew to become a cradle of the Polish Catholic intelligentsia, most notably during the communist era. Today the city is home to two universities and a large student population and, with its burgeoning summer cultural scene, is a city of

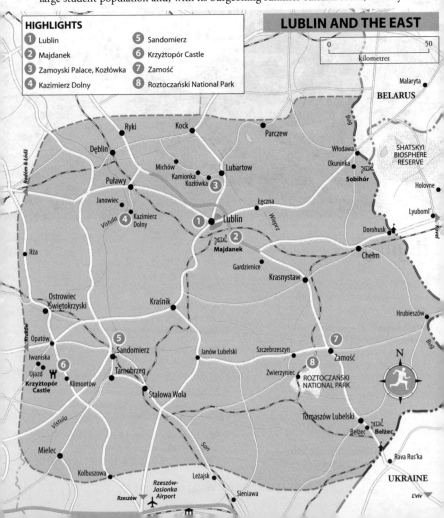

HIGHLIGHTS

1. Lublin
2. Majdanek
3. Zamoyski Palace, Kozłówka
4. Kazimierz Dolny
5. Sandomierz
6. Krzyżtopór Castle
7. Zamość
8. Roztoczański National Park

LUBLIN AND THE EAST

0 ——— 50
kilometres

huge creative potential – the kind of up-and-coming place that deserves to be watched in the future.

The Old Town

The fourteenth-century **Kraków Gate** (Brama Krakowska) is the main entrance to the **Old Town** (Stare Miasto), a largely pedestrianized web of cobbled streets broken up by arcaded squares. Largest of these is the **Rynek** (Market Square), dominated by the outsized **Old Town Hall** (Stary Ratusz). Of the surrounding burghers' houses, the **Konopnica House** (no. 12) – where Charles XII of Sweden and Peter the Great were both guests – has Renaissance sculptures and medallions of the original owners decorating its facade. The **Cholewiński House** (no. 9), on the northeast corner of the square, features further lively Renaissance decoration, with a faded but fierce-looking pair of lions.

The Cathedral

ul. Jezuicka 1/3 • Treasury, whispering room and crypt Tues–Sun 10am–4pm • Treasury and whispering room 4zł; crypt 4zł • ☎ 81 532 4412

To the south of the Rynek stands the **Cathedral**, a large sixteenth-century basilica with an entrance framed by ornate Neoclassical pillars. A doorway at the rear of the nave leads to the **treasury**, whose display cabinets are filled with lavishly embroidered vestments, chalices and crosiers. Adjoining the treasury is the **Whispering Room**, so called because its acoustic properties allow you to hear even the quietest voices perfectly from the other side of the chamber. Its ceiling is covered with ebullient frescoes by Joseph Meyer depicting the "triumph of faith over heresy".

Steps descend to the **crypt** where several seventeenth- and eighteenth-century bishops, nobles and townsfolk are buried. An open coffin holds the mummified remains of one Bishop Jan Michał de la Mars (died 1725), his fine boots and gloves hanging surreally from the ends of his withered limbs.

Lublin Underground Trail

Old Town Hall, Rynek 1 • Guided tours (45min): April–Sept Tues–Fri at 10am, noon, 2pm & 4pm, Sat & Sun at noon, 1pm, 2pm, 4pm & 5pm; Oct–March Sat & Sun at noon, 1pm, 2pm & 4pm • 10zł • ☎ 81 534 6570

Cellars underneath the Old Town Hall now house the **Lublin Underground Trail** (Lubelski podzemia), where guided tours take you through the history of the city, with the aid of scale models. A cupboard-sized tableau (aided by lights and music) tells the story of the fire of Lublin of 1719 – when friars from the Dominican monastery allegedly saved the Old Town from the flames by parading through the streets holding holy images aloft.

Fortuna Cellar

Rynek 8 • Daily: April–Oct 11am–7pm; Nov–March 11am–5pm • 9zł • ☎ 81 444 5555

A suite of barrel-vaulted chambers accessed by a steep flight of steps, the **Fortuna Cellar** (Piwnica pod Fortuną) houses a display telling the history of Lublin, with the aid of touch-screen computers, background music and sound – and yes, there is a torture room complete with the sound of a screaming victim. Piece de résistance however is the Fortuna Cellar itself, a sixteenth-century VIP drinking club where the wine-merchant owner would have entertained his guests with his best vintages. The beautifully-restored frescoes are a bit racy, with a semi-nude allegory of Fortune and a tenderly erotic portrayal of Cupid and Psyche.

Dominican Church and Monastery

ul. Złota 9 • Daily 8am–7pm, except during Mass

East of the Rynek stands the fine **Dominican Church and Monastery** (Kosciół Ojców Dominikanów), founded in the fourteenth century and reconstructed in the

5

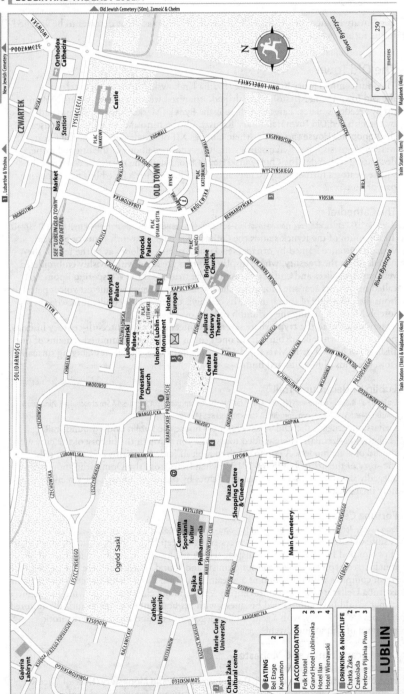

▲ Old Jewish Cemetery (50m), Zamość & Chełm

◀ New Jewish Cemetery

◀ Lubartów & Yeshiva

Train Station (1km) & Majdanek ▶
Train Station (1km) & Majdanek (4km) ▶
Majdanek (4km) ▶

River Bystrzyca

Orthodox Cathedral

PODZAMCZE

CZWARTEK

Bus Station

Castle

Market

OLD TOWN

RYNEK

SEE "LUBLIN OLD TOWN" MAP FOR DETAIL

Potocki Palace

Czartoryski Palace

Brigittine Church

Hotel Europa

Lubomirski Palace

Union of Lublin Monument

Juliusz Osterwy Theatre

Protestant Church

Central Theatre

KRAKOWSKIE PRZEDMIEŚCIE

Plaza Shopping Centre & Cinema

Main Cemetery

Centrum Spotkania Kultur

Philharmonia

Bajka Cinema

Catholic University

Marie Curie University

Chatta Żaka Cultural centre

Galeria Labirynt

Ogród Saski

◀ Village Museum, Puławy & Warsaw

N

0 ——— 250 metres

● **EATING**
| Bel Etage | 2 |
| Kardamon | 1 |

■ **ACCOMMODATION**
Folk Hostel	2
Grand Hotel Lublinianka	3
Hotel Ilan	1
Hotel Wieniawski	4

■ **DRINKING & NIGHTLIFE**
Chatka Żaka	2
Czekolada	1
Perłowa Pijalnia Piwa	3

LUBLIN

seventeenth. The church suffers from the familiar Baroque additions, but don't let that deflect you from the Renaissance Firlej chapel at the end of the southern aisle, built for one of Lublin's leading aristocratic families.

Grodzka Gate

ul. Grodzka 21 • Mon–Fri entrance by guided tour at 9.30am, 11am, 12.30pm & 2pm • Polish-language tour 8zł; English-language tour 12zł • ☎ 81 532 5867, ⓦ teatrnn.pl

Traditionally the main northern entrance to the Old Town and for centuries the symbolic divide between Christian and Jewish Lublin, the **Grodzka Gate** (Brama Grodzka) now houses an innovative exhibition and study centre devoted to the largely disappeared Lublin of the Jews. Conceived by the Teatr NN drama company (who also have offices and an auditorium here), the centre attempts to document Jewish Lublin by amassing as much information as possible about each individual inhabitant of the pre-World War II community and storing it in folders and boxes that visitors are invited to examine. There are also exhibits that you would expect from a traditional museum – photos, films, music and maps of the area as it used to be. The result is highly evocative and profoundly moving.

The Castle

On a hill just north of the Grodzka Gate (and connected to it by red-brick footbridge), Lublin's **castle** (*zamek*) is an offbeat 1820s neo-Gothic edifice built on the site of Kazimierz the Great's fourteenth-century fortress. One of the highlights of any trip to Lublin is a visit to the frescoes at its **Holy Trinity Chapel**.

Castle Museum

ul. Zamkowa 9 • Tues–Sun: May–Sept 10am–6pm; Oct–April 9am–5pm • 30zł combined ticket with Holy Trinity Chapel • ⓦ muzeumlubelskie.pl

The high points of the sizeable **Casle Museum** are the **ethnography** section, including a delightful collection of contemporary folk art and woodcarving, and the **art gallery**, where Jan Matejko's monumental *Union of Lublin* occupies a whole wall. Showing King Sigismund II August presiding over Polish–Lithuanian unification talks in 1569, it's actually quite a restrained picture by the painter's customarily florid standards.

Holy Trinity Chapel

Entry at 30min intervals: May–Sept daily 10am–5.30pm; Oct–April Tues–Sun 9am–4.30pm • 30zł combined ticket with Castle Museum • ⓦ muzeumlubelskie.pl

An elegant two-storey Gothic structure, the **Holy Trinity Chapel** (Kaplica św. Trójcy) is located at the back of the castle complex. The reason for its status as one of Lublin's finest draws is its stunning set of **medieval frescoes**, painted in Byzantine style by Orthodox artists commissioned by King Władysław II Jagiełło – who as Grand Duke of Lithuania (and son of an Russian princess) had been surrounded by Orthodox culture since birth. Entrance is limited to 25 viewers at a time, and the chapel is closed for ten minutes in every hour to ensure that the climate-control system does its job.

The frescoes are composed of panels, each painted in a single day. These begin with depictions of God the Father and move on through the cosmic hierarchy to scenes from the life of Jesus and the saints, ending with the risen Christ. Highlights include the vivid scenes from the life of Christ and the Virgin Mary covering the upper section of the nave and choir, in particular a powerful Passion cycle, along with an intriguing pair of frescoes involving Jagiełło himself.

Podzamcze and Jewish Lublin

Just below the castle is the oval-shaped **plac Zamkowy**, where a plaque on a raised pedestal shows a detailed plan of the surrounding **Podzamcze** district, the main Jewish

5

quarter destroyed by the Nazis in 1942 (see page 201). Occupying the high ground to the north is the part of town known as **Czwartek** ("Thursday"), in honour of the huge Thursday market that used to be held here from the late Middle Ages onwards.

The old Jewish cemetery

ul. Kalinowszczyzna • For access, contact the reception of Hotel Ilan, ul. Lubartowska 85 (☎ 81 745 0347, ⓦ hotelilan.pl) • No set fee but contributions welcome

Despite the Nazis' best efforts to destroy it, the **old Jewish cemetery** (Stary cmentarz żydowski) still contains abundant evidence of the full stylistic variety of Jewish monumental art. The oldest section, with tombstones from as early as 1541, houses the graves of many famous Jews, among them the charismatic Hassidic leader **Yaakov Yitzchak Horovitz** – one of several graves here regularly covered with pilgrims' candles – and **Shalom Shachna**, the renowned sixteenth-century master of the Lublin *Yeshiva*. Climbing to the top of the cemetery hill gives you a fine view back over the Old Town.

The new Jewish cemetery

ul. Walecznych, 500m north of the old Jewish cemetery • The mausoleum is open unpredictable hours (entry by donation) so check at the tourist office

Established in 1829, the **new Jewish cemetery** (Nowy cmentarz żydowski) was plundered by the Nazis, who also used it for mass executions. What you see today covers a fragment of the original plot. Most of the few remaining graves date from the

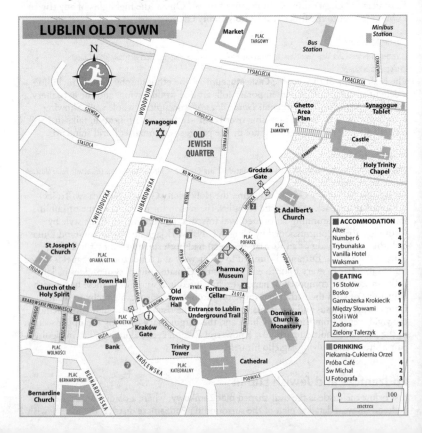

THE JEWS OF LUBLIN

Along with Kraków and Warsaw, Lublin ranked as one of the major Jewish centres in Poland. Dating from the mid-fourteenth century, the Jewish settlement took root in the **Podzamcze** district, located below the castle walls. The first brick **synagogue** and **yeshiva** (Talmudic school) were built in the mid-sixteenth century: from then on synagogues and other religious buildings proliferated – by the 1930s there were more than a hundred synagogues in the city.

In the 1790s Lublin emerged as an important centre of **Hassidism**, the ecstatic revivalist movement that swept through Eastern Jewry in the latter part of the eighteenth century. From 1862 onwards Jews were permitted to settle in the Old Town and in the streets around ulica Lubartowska, which became the centre of their community.

By the time of the Nazi conquest in September 1939 there were 40,000 Jews in the city. An official **ghetto area** was established, west of the castle, in March 1941, and the construction of **Majdanek concentration camp** commenced four months later. The ghetto was cleared in spring 1942, its inhabitants either shot in nearby forests or sent to **Bełżec camp** (see page 220). At the end of the war several thousand Jewish refugees resettled in Lublin. Many of these emigrated, however, in the wake of **anti-Semitic outbreaks** in Poland in 1945–46 and again in 1968. A tiny and largely elderly Jewish community remains in Lublin today.

late nineteenth century and the postwar years, and there are also a number of collective graves for Nazi wartime victims. The domed **mausoleum**, recently erected behind the cemetery entrance, houses a small but engrossing exhibition detailing the history of the Lublin Jewry.

The Yeshiva

Hotel Ilan, ul. Lubartowska 85 • Synagogue daily 8am–7pm (may be closed for prayers on Fri)

A palatial-looking yellow building at the top of ulica Lubartowska, the **Yeshiva** – or School of the Sages of Lublin as it was once known – was built in the late 1920s to serve as an international school to train rabbis and other community functionaries. It functioned until 1939, when the Nazis closed it down and publicly burned the contents of its huge library. Now run by the Warsaw Jewish Community, it contains a hotel – the *Ilan* (see page 203) – a restaurant and a functioning synagogue on the first floor which is open to visitors.

Krakowskie Przedmieście and around

West of the Old Town stretches **Krakowskie Przedmieście**, a partly-pedestrianized street lined with handsome Neoclassical buildings. A ten-minute walk along it brings you to **plac Litewski**, a flagstoned square centering on a fountain-splashed pool that is atmospherically illuminated at night. Occupying the southeastern corner of the square is the **Europa**, Lublin's oldest hotel. It was here that Nazi and Soviet officers held a celebratory dinner that Russian historians would prefer to forget, toasting the success of their joint invasion of Poland in September 1939.

Ogród Saski

Just beyond Krakowskie Przedmieście's western end lie the **Ogród Saski** ("Saxon Gardens"), so named because they were inspired by August III of Saxony's gardens in Warsaw. They make up Lublin's principal open space, with fastidiously tended flowerbeds sloping down towards wilder, densely wooded sections in the park's northern reaches.

Galeria Labirynt

ul. Ks. J. Popieluszki 5 • Tues–Sun noon–7pm • Free • ☎ 81 466 5921, ⓦ labirynt.com

5

Northwest of the Ogród Saski, housed in a one-storey pavilion that from a distance looks a bit like an elongated garden shed, **Galeria Labirynt** has been at the cutting-edge of Polish art ever since its foundation in 1956. Most of the leading names of the local contemporary art scene have exhibited here at some stage in their careers, and Labirynt's changing exhibitions remain essential viewing.

The Village Museum

al. Warszawka 96 • April & Oct daily 9am–5pm; May–Sept daily 9am–6pm; Nov–March Tues–Sun 9am–3pm • 12zł • ☎ 81 533 8513, ⓦ skansen.lublin.pl • Bus #18 or #20 from al. Racławickie or bus #18 from ul. 3 Maja

Lublin's extensive **Village Museum** (Muzeum Wsi Lubelskiej), 3km northwest of the Ogród Saski, presents an attractive jumble of rural buildings from surrounding villages. The entrance is marked by a massive, 1939 windmill from the village of Zygmuntów, while other highlights include a gate from Łańcuchów, carved in the Zakopane style by Stanisław Witkiewicz, and a church from Tarnoszyna, which sports an exotic trio of bulbous domes.

Majdanek

Droga Męczenników Majdanka • **Grounds** Daily 9am–dusk • Free • **Museum** Tues–Sun: April–Oct 9am–5pm; Nov–March 9am–4pm • Free; documentary 3zł (minimum 5 viewers); guided tours in Polish 70zł, tours in English 150zł • ☎ 81 710 2833, ⓦ majdanek.eu • Bus #23 or trolleybus #156 from ul. Królewska, or trolleybuses #153 or #158 from ul. Lipowa

The proximity of **Majdanek concentration camp**, 4km southeast of the city centre, is something of a shock. Established on Himmler's orders in October 1941, this was no semi-hidden location that local people could long be ignorant of – a plea more debatable at Auschwitz and Treblinka.

Standing beside the main entrance is an angular grey monument, erected in 1969 on the 25th anniversary of the camp's liberation by the Red Army. To the left of the monument, a modern pavilion has a **cinema** showing a short documentary about Majdanek as well as a well-stocked bookshop. From here a path slants across the fields to the main **museum** part of the site, where barracks and watchtowers have been reconstructed to give visitors some idea of what the camp looked like. An estimated 78,000 people, of which 75 percent were Jewish, were murdered here – more than half through hunger, disease or exhaustion and the rest by execution or in gas chambers. Immediately following the war, Majdanek was used by the Soviet NKVD (secret police) to hold captured Polish resistance fighters before they were shipped to Siberian gulags.

At the end of the main path through the site, a domed mausoleum contains the ashes of many of those murdered here. Below the mausoleum are the gas chambers and crematoria, blown up by the Nazis as they retreated but reconstructed afterwards to serve as a chilling lesson to future generations.

ARRIVAL AND DEPARTURE   LUBLIN

By train The train station is 2km to the south of the centre; from here bus #1 will take you to the edge of the Old Town, while bus #13 and trolleybus #150 both run to Krakowskie Przedmieście, just west of the centre.
Destinations Kiev (1 daily; overnight; 12hr); Warsaw (6 daily; 3hr).
By bus The bus station is just beyond the castle at the northern end of the Old Town.

Destinations Białystok (4 daily; 4hr 30min); Kiev (6 daily; 13hr); Przemyśl (1 daily; 5hr); Sandomierz (3 daily; 2hr).
By minibus Next door to the bus station is a separate minibus station, where minibuses from local towns arrive.
Destinations Kazimierz Dolny (14 daily; 1hr 40min); Puławy (every 30min; 1hr 30min–2hr); Włodawa (20 daily; 1hr 20min); Zamość (every 30min; 2hr).

INFORMATION

Tourist information The tourist office in the Old Town, at ul. Jezuicka 1/3 (daily: April–Oct 9am–7pm; Nov–March 9am–5pm; ☎ 81 532 4412, ⓦ lublintravel.pl), has helpful,

English-speaking staff, comprehensive accommodation listings and a big choice of maps for sale.

ACCOMMODATION

Alter ul. Grodzka 30 ☎ 81 516 9090, ⓦ hotelalter. pl; map page 200. Boutique hotel in an elegant house in the Old Town, featuring smart, cosy rooms and a small swimming pool. **600zł**

Folk Hostel Krakowskie Przedmieście 23 ☎ 887 223 887, ⓦ folkhostel.pl; map page 198. Conveniently located hostel with a nice mix of dorms and private doubles decorated in soothing pastels. Social areas are not large, but you get access to a basic kitchen, and all-day tea and coffee. Dorms **45zł**, doubles **100zł**

Grand Hotel Lublinianka Krakowskie Przedmieście 56 ☎ 81 446 6100, ⓦ lublinianka.com; map page 198. Recently renovated luxury hotel in a stately *belle époque* pile, with polished service, Turkish bath, a good restaurant (see page 203) and a first-floor terrace. **300zł**

Hotel Ilan ul. Lubartowa 85 ☎ 81 745 0347, ⓦ hotelilan. pl; map page 198. In the former Yeshiva (see page 201), complete with restored synagogue and mikveh on site, this hotel offers comfortable rooms with electric kettles. Kosher meals are available if you give them a few days' notice. **250zł**

Hotel Wienawski ul. Sądowa 6 ☎ 81 459 9200, ⓦ hotel wienawski.pl; map page 198. A smart businesslike place that's convenient for the Krakowskie Przedmieście

area. Rooms are neat and contemporary, and good service is a strong point. **300zł**

Number 6 ul. Złota 6 ☎ 669 289 900, ⓦ numer6.pl; map page 200. A decent option slap-bang in the centre, this sixteenth-century Burgher's house contains competitively priced self-catering apartments with kitchenettes and en-suite bathrooms. Two-person apartments **200zł**

Trybunalska ul. Rynek 4 ☎ 81 532 4065, ⓦ trybunalska. pl; map page 200. Smart rooms on the top floor of a combined bakery, café and restaurant. Some don't have windows but measure up style-wise in most respects, with neat en-suite bathrooms, matt-black surfaces and a bit of exposed brick. **250zł**

Vanilla Hotel Krakowskie Przedmieście 12 ☎ 81 536 6720, ⓦ vanilla-hotel.pl; map page 200. Design-conscious hotel in a great location, offering rooms with a challenging but not over-loud mixture of bold fabrics and primary colours. **315zł**

★ **Waksman** ul. Grodzka 19 ☎ 081 532 5454, ⓦ waks man.pl; map page 200. Upmarket but good-value retro pension in the heart of the Old Town, with four doubles and two suites (from 270zł) furnished with faux antiques in styles ranging from Louis XVI to Victorian-era. **230zł**

EATING

The main concentration of eating and drinking establishments is in the Old Town, although there's a string of places along the eastern, pedestrianized portion of Krakowskie Przedmieście too. Two culinary treats particular to the Lublin region are **cebularz**, an onion-scattered bread bun, and **forszmak**, a goulash flavoured with gherkins and other cottage-garden vegetables.

CAFÉS, ICE CREAM AND SNACKS

Bosko Krakowskie Przedmieście 4 ☎ 535 212 844; map page 200. Ice-cream parlour serving up plenty of unusual flavours (rosemary, fig and so on) as well as the Polish seasonal repertoire of fruits and berries – all made from natural ingredients. Daily 10am–9pm.

★ **Między Słowami** ul. Rybna 4 ☎ 508 217 014, ⓦ miedzy-slowami.com.pl; map page 200. A mellow café and independent bookshop in one, "Between the Lines" offers a global range of coffees and leaf teas, artisan soft drinks and the inevitable Polish craft beer. The small selection of secondhand English books is worth a browse. Daily noon–10pm.

Piekarnia-Cukiernia Orzel ul. Lubartowska 15 ☎ 158 858 887; map page 200. Family-run bakery full of delicious loaves and rolls of all types; it's one of best places in Lublin to pick up *cebularz*. Mon–Fri 6.30am–6pm, Sat 7am–5pm, Sun 9am–4pm.

RESTAURANTS

★ **16 Stołów** Rynek 16 ☎ 81 534 3040, ⓦ 16stolow.

pl; map page 200. Elegant, understated restaurant serving quality food at mid-range prices, with an accent on Polish cuisine reinterpreted in a contemporary European style. Veal, duck and pike-perch feature on the menu (most mains 40–50zł), and there's a globe-spanning wine list and conscientious service. Mon–Sat 1–11pm, Sun noon–6pm.

Bel Etage Krakowskie Przedmieście 56 ☎ 81 446 6263, ⓦ lublinianka.com; map page 198. Old-fashioned and a bit formal, but not over-expensive, this restaurant inside the *Grand Hotel Lublinianka* (see above) serves fine Polish-Central European cuisine, with mains in the 40–60zł range. There are some very reasonable lunchtime specials on weekdays. Daily 7am–11pm.

Garmażerka Krokieciek ul. Lubartowska 17 ☎ 81 532 3753, ⓦ facebook.com/garmazerka.krokieciek; map page 200. Order-at-the-counter canteen done out in colourful folksy decor and serving up dependable food, with chunky soups at 5–8zł, *pierogi wiejskie* (with buckwheat and cheese) at 7zł, and meat and potato mains from 12zł. Mon–Fri 10am–6pm, Sat 10am–3pm.

Kardamon Krakowskie Przemieście 41 ☎ 81 448 0257, ⓦ kardamon.eu; map page 198. Suave basement restaurant with glitzy Art Deco decor and a quality menu of French-Mediterranean fare (pork, steak, veal and excellent fish; 40–60zł), plus an extensive wine list. Mon–Sat noon–11pm, Sun noon–10pm.

5

LUBLIN FESTIVALS

Recent years have seen Lublin reinvent itself as a city of the arts, a metamorphosis that manifests itself most prominently in its increasingly popular summer street festivals.

Different Sounds (Inne Brzmienia) Early July ⓦ innebrzmienia.pl. Music and arts festival with events taking place throughout town and in the park outside Grodzka Gate. Highly rated for its intelligently curated mix of ethnic, alternative and experimental music (recent editions have featured performers as diverse as Einstürzende Neubauten, Tony Allen and Tortoise), this is one of the most refreshingly ear-bending events in Poland.

Carnival of Magicians (Carnaval Sztukmistrzów) Late July ⓦ en.sztukmistrze.eu. Named in sly reference to Isaac Bashevis Singer's novel *The Magician*

of Lublin, this festival features not just top international magicians but also jugglers, acrobats, buskers, clowns and all manner of street-performing talent.

Jagiellonian Fair (Jarmark Jagielloński) Mid-Aug ⓦ jarmarkjagiellonski.pl. Four-day celebration of craftsmanship and traditions, with stalls throughout the Old Town, drawing together artisans from the territories over which the Jagiellonians (at one time or another) once ruled: Lithuania, Poland, Belarus, Ukraine, Slovakia and Hungary. Also features open-air concerts with a folk-ethnic flavour.

Stół i Wół ul. Bramowa 2-6 ☎ 81 565 5555, ⓦ stoliwol.pl; map page 200. Roomy bare-brick pub-restaurant that specializes in grilled meat. The menu begins with burgers (from 29zł) and extends to T-bone and fillet steaks (from 70zł upwards depending on weight); unpasteurized Tyskie beer is served from the tank. Mon–Thurs & Sun noon–midnight, Fri & Sat noon–2am.

Zadora Rynek 8 ☎ 081 534 5534, ⓦ zadora.com.pl; map page 200. Small and excellent *crêperie*, good for a quick and cheap meal in the Old Town; crêpes cost 10–20zł. Daily 10am–11pm.

Zielony Talerzyk ul. Królewska 3 ☎ 500 068 241, ⓦ facebook.com/ZielonyTalerzyk; map page 200. Informal café-restaurant serving vegetarian and vegan food ranging from bread-and-hummus snacks to soups, vegetable curries and quiche, with mains hovering below the 25zł mark. Occasional live jazz. Daily 8am–midnight.

DRINKING AND NIGHTLIFE

BARS

★ **Perłowa Pijalnia Piwa** ul. Bernardyńska 15 ☎ 81 710 1205, ⓦ perla.pl; map page 198. With its huge oval bar, this brewpub looks more like an indoor drinking stadium than your average pub. Regular beers from the Perła Brewery are accompanied by a few seasonal specials – all at brewery prices. There's a range of snacks including *pierogi* and sausage. Mon–Thurs & Sun 2pm–midnight, Fri & Sat 2pm–2am.

Próba Café ul. Grodzka 5A ☎ 535 651 123; map page 200. Bright and colourful Old Town pub with a secluded summertime patio and an assortment of craft beers, bagels and cakes. Occasional concerts. Daily 9am–11pm.

Św Michał ul. Grodzka 16 ☎ 789 057 658, ⓦ pub regionalny.pl; map page 200. Lublin's biggest multi-tap, this elegant pub-restaurant has a bewildering array of craft beers, plus an extensive menu of meaty grills and local stews (food available till 10pm) to wash it down with. Mon–Thurs noon–midnight, Fri–Sun noon–2am.

U Fotografa ul. Rybna 11 ☎ 81 532 3717, ⓦ ufotografa.pl; map page 200. Old Town bar with a great range of craft beers, backed up by a menu of burgers, pasta and salads (15–20zł). The place lives up to its name ("At the Photographer's"), featuring an array of antique cameras and photographic work from local artists. Daily 2pm–midnight.

CLUBS AND GIG VENUES

Chatka Żaka ul. Radziszewskiego 16 ☎ 81 533 5841, ⓦ ack.lublin.pl; map page 198. Student club, also housing a cinema, concert venue and student bar. Daily 8am–10pm.

Czekolada ul. Narutowicza 9 ☎ 531 067 013, ⓦ klubczekolada.pl; map page 198. Hosting some well-known DJs in a funky and modern downstairs club, this is where Lublin's glamourous young things shake their stuff. Music tends to be R&B, soul and funk. Dress code; entry 10–15zł. Thurs–Sun 4pm–3am.

ENTERTAINMENT

CONCERT VENUES

Centrum Spotkania Kultur pl. Teatralny 1 ☎ 81 441 5632, ⓦ spotkaniakultur.com. State-of-the-art concert venue featuring top-notch opera, dance, musicals and cabaret.

Lublin Philharmonia ul. Skłodowskiej 5 ☎ 081 531 5112, ⓦ filharmonialubelska.pl. Has a regular programme of high-quality classical concerts.

Around Lublin

North and east of Lublin lie broad expanses of open farmland interspersed with belts of thick forest, and a handful of destinations that make an entertaining half-day trip from the city. The Zamoyski Palace at **Kozłówka**, with its museum of socialist art, is the one unmissable sight in the region. Evidence of eastern Poland's multicultural past is provided by the ornate synagogue at **Włodawa**; while the palace and park at **Puławy** recall the great aristocratic clans of the eighteenth and nineteenth centuries.

Zamoyski Palace, Kozłówka

Tues–Sun: April & Sept 9am–4pm; May–Aug 10am–5pm; Oct–Dec 10am–3pm; guided tours of the palace interior usually run on the hour • Guided tours 22zł; English-language guides an extra 50zł (book in advance); Gallery of Socialist Art 7zł • ☎ 81 852 8310, ⓦ muzeumzamoyskich.pl • There is no direct public transport from Lublin to Kozłówka

The **Zamoyski Palace** (Pałac Zamojskich) at **KOZŁÓWKA**, 35km northwest of Lublin, is among the grandest in the region. Fully restored in the 1990s, the **palace** is the recipient of a good deal of tourist hype – hence the processions of day-tripper buses lined up outside the entrance gates.

Built in the 1740s by the Bieliński family, the original two-storey Baroque palace complex was expanded in the early 1900s by its longtime owner, Count Konstanty Zamoyski, whose family took over the property in 1799 and kept it up to the beginning of World War II. Zamoyski's remodelling retained the essentials of the original Baroque design, adding a number of fine outbuildings, the iron gateway, chapel and elegant porticoed terrace leading up to the entrance to the building.

The interior

The palace **interior** can only be visited by guided tour. Once inside, you're immediately enveloped in a riot of artistic decor: the whole place is positively dripping with pictures, mostly family portraits and copies of Rubens, Canaletto and the like, along with a profusion of sculptures and fine furniture. Upstairs, the tour takes you into **Count Konstanty's private rooms**, where the elaborate Czech porcelain toilet set in the bedroom suggests a man of fastidious personal hygiene. After the countess's bedroom, decked out with a handsome selection of nineteenth-century furniture, you are led into the **Red Salon**, with its mass of heavy velvet curtains. The **Exotic Room** houses a fine selection of chinoiserie, while the **dining room** is sumptuous, heavy Baroque with a mixture of Gdańsk and Venetian furniture and enough period trinkets to keep a horde of collectors happy.

Gallery of Socialist Art

Housed in the former palace theatre, the **Gallery of Socialist Art** (Galeria sztuki realizmu socjalistycznego) brings together a large collection of postwar Polish art and sculpture, much of which was on display in the palace itself during the 1960s. Alongside busts of Bolesław Bierut, Mao Zedong, Ho Chi Minh and others, there's a gallery of sturdy proletarian heroes building factories and joyously implementing Five-Year Plans, while playing in the background are important speeches by Stalin and others. More traditional themes are also given a Socialist-Realist twist, as in such paintings as Zygmunt Radricki's *Still Life with Party Journal* and *Chopin's Polonaise in A-flat Major Performed in the Kościuszko Ironworks* by Mieczysław Oracki-Serwin. There's also a selection of buttons, postcards and propagandistic matchboxes.

Włodawa and around

Hard up by the Belarusian border, 70km northeast of Lublin, the sleepy town of **WŁODAWA** sits on a low hill overlooking the River Bug. What makes the place

5

worth visiting is its wonderfully well-preserved synagogue, which serves as a graceful memorial to a Jewish community that formed a clear majority of the town population until World War II. Virtually all of Włodawa's Jews perished in the concentration camp at **Sobibór**, 10km southeast of town.

Włodawa synagogue and museum

ul. Czerwonego Krzyża 7 • May & June Mon–Fri 10am–4pm, Sat & Sun 10am–2pm; July–Sept Tues–Sun 10am–4pm; Oct–April Tues–Fri 10am–3pm • 12zł • ☎ 82 572 2178, ⓦ muzeumwlodawa.pl

Built in the 1760s on the site of an earlier wooden structure, the **Włodawa synagogue** (Synagoga we Włodawie) is a typically solid-looking late Baroque construction with a palatial main facade. Despite severe damage by the Nazis, and postwar conversion into a warehouse, the synagogue was thoroughly restored in the 1960s and has since functioned as a **museum**. The major surviving original feature is the restored **Aron ha Kodesh**, a colourful, triple-tiered neo-Gothic structure raised in the 1930s and covered with elaborate stucco decoration. Across the courtyard from the synagogue is a smaller, nineteenth-century house of worship housing a multimedia display evoking traditional life in a Jewish shtetl of the eastern borderlands.

Sobibór

10km southeast of Włodawa, well signed from the Włodawa–Chełm road • Sobibór Memorial Site and Museum ☎ 82 571 9867, ⓦ sobibor-memorial.eu • Taxi from Włodawa approximately 60–70zł with 1hr waiting time

Surrounded by tranquil forest, the village of **SOBIBÓR** was the site of a brutally efficient Nazi extermination camp, which – despite only being operational from May to October 1942 – accounted for the murder of an estimated 250,000 Jews from Poland, Ukraine and Holland. The camp was hurriedly dismantled following a revolt led by a Soviet Jewish POW officer in which an estimated 300 inmates escaped – 47 of whom survived the war. A new **memorial museum** is currently being built at the site, under the auspices of the museum in Majdanek (see page 202).

ARRIVAL AND INFORMATION	**WŁODAWA**
By bus Minibuses from Lublin (20 daily; 1hr 20min) pull in at Włodawa's bus station, a couple of blocks west of the town centre.	**Tourist office** The tourist information centre, just east of the synagogue at ul. Rynek 4 (Mon–Fri 8am–5pm, Sat 8am–noon), is well stocked with leaflets.

EATING

Kawiarnia Centrum Czworobok 42–44 ☎ 692 783 646. Centrally placed café serving up tea, coffee, homemade cakes and a small range of hot meals - *pierogi, barszcz, gołąbki* and *forszmak* (7–15zł). Daily 10am–10pm.

Puławy

Fifty kilometres northwest of Lublin, **PUŁAWY** is home to one of Poland's most symbolic aristocratic seats, the **palace and park** built by the Czartoryski family. From 1775 onwards **Prince Adam Czartoryski** (1734–1823) and his wife **Izabela** (1746–1835) transformed the place into Poland's leading intellectual centre, Izabela establishing the nucleus of a national museum. In 1830 the estate was confiscated and the family exiled after the failure of the November Uprising, in which Adam and Izabela's son **Adam Jerzy Czartoryski** participated. The estate is currently an agricultural school, although the palace retains a handful of showpiece interiors, and the surrounding park provides fascinating insights into the aristocratic tastes of the period.

Czartoryski Palace

ul. Czartoryskich 8 • Daily tours in Polish on the hour: May–Sept 9am–5pm; Oct–April 9am–4pm • 6zł • ☎ 81 888 4411, ⓦ muzeumnadwislanskie.pl

5

Approached from a wide courtyard just south of what passes for a town centre, the **Czartoryski Palace** (Pałac Czartoryskich) was built in the 1670s by indefatigable Dutch-Polish architect Tylman van Gameren, although the current Neoclassical exterior owes a great deal to subsequent rebuildings. Through the main entrance and up the cast-iron staircase, the **Music Hall** and arcaded **Gothic Hall** offer hints of former grandeur. The latter was originally the palace ballroom, although many of the fittings were sold off during the tsarist period.

The palace park

Park Daily: April–Sept 6am–10pm; Oct–March 7am–6pm • Free • **Gothic House and Temple of Sibyl** Both Tues–Sun 9am–5pm • 6zł • ☏ 81 888 4411, Ⓦ museumnadwislanskie.pl

Designed by the industrious Izabela over a twenty-year period (1790–1810), the rambling **palace park** (Park Czartoryski) is a wonderful example of Romantic-era garden design. Noted for its variety of trees, the grounds are also dotted with a hotchpotch of "historical" buildings and monuments in the manner popular with the Polish aristocracy of the period.

Southeast of the palace is the **Gothic House** (Dom Gotycki), a square, two-storey building with a graceful portico, now housing a display of period furnishings. The same entrance ticket is valid for the **Temple of Sibyl** (Świątynia Sybilli) just opposite, consciously echoing the temple of the same name in Tivoli, near Rome. The rest of the park contains other follies, including a Chinese pavilion and assorted imitation classical statuary.

ARRIVAL AND DEPARTURE   PUŁAWY

By bus Buses and minibuses stop either at the bus station, 500m northwest of the palace at the junction of ul. Lubelska and ul. Wojska Polskiego; or on ul. Lubelska, near the bus station.

Destinations Lublin (every 30min; 1hr 30min–2hr); Warsaw Centralna train station (hourly; 2hr 30min).

EATING

Sybilla al. Królewska 17 ☏ 82 888 5886. Restaurant of the *IUNG Hotel* near the palace, serving inexpensive Polish standards such as *barszcz*, *pierogi* and *żurek* (7–12zł). Also

a decent place to take a coffee-and-cake break. Daily 10am–10pm.

Kazimierz Dolny

Picturesquely set between two hills and possessing one of Poland's best-preserved town centres, **KAZIMIERZ DOLNY** ("Lower Kazimierz"), is one of Poland's favourite tourist destinations, a fact reflected in its wealth of pensions, restaurants and galleries. Artists have been drawn here since the nineteenth century, attracted by the effervescent light and ancient buildings, while in more recent decades Kazimierz has been used as a backdrop for TV costume dramas. Despite its year-round popularity the town retains a relaxed, bohemian feel, and though it suffers overcrowding in high summer it never has the feel of being oppressively over-touristed.

Some history

The town is closely associated with **Kazimierz the Great** (1333–70), who rescued Poland from dynastic chaos and transformed the country's landscape in the process. It is said of him that he "found a wooden Poland and left a Poland of stone", and Kazimierz Dolny is perhaps the best remaining example of his ambitious town-building programme. Thanks to the king's promotion of the River Vistula grain and timber trade, a minor village was transformed into a prosperous mercantile town, gaining the nickname "little Danzig" in the process, on account of the goods' ultimate destination. Much of the money that poured in was used to build the ornate burghers' houses that still line the main square.

It was during this period, too, that **Jews** began to settle in Kazimierz, grateful for the legal protection proclaimed for them throughout Poland by King Kazimierz, and for the next five centuries Jewish traders and shopkeepers were integral to the character of the town. Jews accounted for up to fifty percent of Kazimierz's population when World War II began, but only a handful survived the war, with the result that Kazimierz entered the postwar era as a half-empty shell. However, Warsaw's elite soon rediscovered its rural charm.

The Rynek and around

Arranged around a solid-looking wooden well, the **Rynek** is ringed by an engaging mixture of original buildings, the opulent townhouses of rich Kazimierz merchants rubbing shoulders with more folksy structures, many boasting first-floor verandas jutting out from underneath plunging, shingle-covered roofs. Most striking of the merchants' residences around the square are the **Houses of the Przybyła Brothers** (Kamienice Przybyłów), both on the southern edge. Built in 1615, they bear some striking Renaissance sculpture: tourist literature will tell you that the largest one shows St Christopher, but his tree trunk of a staff and zodiacal entourage suggest something more like a Polish version of the Green Giant. Next door is the former **Lustig House** (Kamienica Lustigowska), once home to a notable local Jewish mercantile dynasty.

Celejowski House: the Town Museum

ul. Senatorska 11 • Daily: April–Sept 10am–5pm; Oct–March 9am–4pm • 9zł • ☎ 81 881 0104

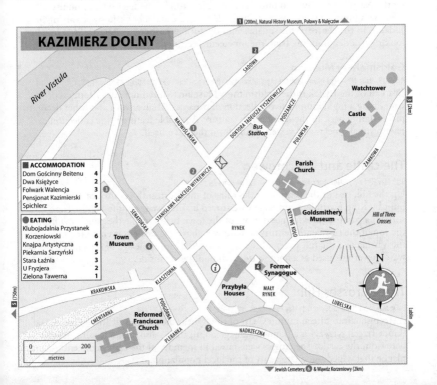

5

WALKS AROUND KAZIMIERZ: THE WĄWOZY

One of the characteristic features of the landscape around Kazimierz is the presence of so-called **wąwozy**, U-shaped gulleys that cut through the soft loamy soil. With their steep sides and overhanging vegetation, these tunnel-like *wąwozy* have the mystique of a set from a fantasy film, and provide the perfect excuse for local **walks**, winding from the outskirts of the town into the local countryside. Most famously picturesque of the *wąwozy* is **Wąwóz Korzeniowy**, located about 2.5km east of the centre and easily accessible by following ulica Nadrzeczna out of town.

Houses still carrying their Renaissance decorations can be seen on ulica Senatorska, which runs alongside the stream west of the square. Of these, the **Celejowski House** (Kamienica Celejowska) at no. 17 has a fabulous high attic storey, a balustrade filled with the carved figures of saints and an assortment of imaginary creatures, richly ornamented windows and a fine entrance portal and hallway. It houses the **Town Museum** (Muzeum Kazimierza Dolnego), which has a small exhibition on the town's history and a larger gallery of paintings of Kazimierz and its surroundings. The town was popular with Polish painters during the interwar years, particularly Polish-Jewish painters, who are well-represented here. The ground floor also houses temporary exhibitions.

Mały Rynek

Southeast of the main square, the **Mały Rynek** was the Jewish marketplace, and on its northern side you'll find the old **synagogue**. Dating from King Kazimierz's reign, the building you see today was reconstructed in the 1950s, following wartime damage by the Nazis, and converted into a cinema. Now run by the Jewish Community of Warsaw it houses a guesthouse (see page 211), a café and a bookshop speciaizing in Judaica. In the centre of the square stand the former **kosher butchers' stalls**, a rough-looking wooden building from the nineteenth century.

Goldsmithery Museum

Rynek 19 • Daily: May–Sept 10am–5pm; Oct–April 10am–4pm • 8zł; free on Tues • ☎ 81 881 0288, ⓦ mnkd.pl

Just east of the Rynek is the **Goldsmithery Museum** (Muzeum Sztuki Złotniczej), containing a highly impressive collection of ornamental silverwork and other decorative pieces dating back to the seventeenth century. A notable feature is the collection of Jewish ritual objects and vessels, many from the town itself.

The castle and watchtower

Both May–Oct daily 10am–6pm; Nov–April Fri–Sun 10am–3pm • 7zł

Up the hill, east of the centre, are the ruins of the fourteenth-century **castle** (zamek) built by King Kazimierz and largely destroyed by the Swedes in the 1650s. The surviving parapets provide good views of the town below, while the panorama from the top of the thirteenth-century **watchtower** above the castle is even better, taking in the Vistula and the full sweep of the countryside. During the age of the grain trade the watchtower was used as a lighthouse, with bonfires set inside.

Three Crosses Hill

Daily: May–Sept 10am–5.30pm; Oct–May 10am–dusk

A steepish climb fifteen minutes' east of the Rynek, the summit of **Three Crosses Hill** (Góra Trzech Krzyży) is a popular vantage point; there's also a path leading directly here from the castle. The crosses were raised in memory of the early eighteenth-century plague that wiped out a large part of the local population.

Jewish cemetery

ul. Czerniawa (1km out of town, east along ul. Nadreczna and then south on ul. Czerniawa)

The main **Jewish cemetery** stands in the Czerniawa Gorge, 1km out of town. Dating from at least the sixteenth century, the cemetery was destroyed by the Nazis, who ripped up the tombstones and used them to pave the courtyard of their headquarters in town. In the 1980s the tombstones were salvaged and re-assembled into a Wailing Wall-like monument – six hundred fragments in all – to moving and dramatic effect. A jagged split down the middle symbolizes the dismemberment of the local Jewish population, making this one of the most powerful Jewish memorials in the country. Wander up the hill behind the monument and you'll find decaying remnants of the former cemetery.

Natural History Museum

ul. Puławska 54 • Daily 9am–4pm; Oct–March closed Tues • 9zł • ☎ 81 881 0326, ⓦ mnkd.pl

Spread out alongside the main road to Puławy northeast of town lie several of Kazimierz's sixteenth- and seventeenth-century **granaries** (*spichlerze*) – sturdy affairs with Baroque gables that attest to the erstwhile prosperity of town merchants. One of these, a ten-minute walk from the centre, now houses the **Natural History Museum** (Muzeum Przyrodnicze), a didactic collection of stuffed animals from the region, while in front of the building stands the massive trunk of one of many poplar trees planted along the river around 1800 by Princess Izabela Czartoryski.

ARRIVAL AND INFORMATION

By bus Buses and minibuses arrive at Kazimierz's tiny bus station, a few steps north of the Rynek.

Destinations Lublin (14 daily; 1hr 40min); Puławy (20 daily; 30min); Warsaw Centralna train station (8 daily; 3hr).

Tourist information There's a helpful tourist office at Rynek 15 (April–Sept daily 9am–5pm; Oct–March Mon–Fri 8am–4pm; ☎ 81 881 0288), with good maps.

ACCOMMODATION

There's a wide range of accommodation in Kazimierz, although it's always advisable to book ahead, especially at weekends. Most local households rent out **private rooms** (40–60zł per person – look for "*noclegi*" signs or check the accommodation listings on ⓦ kazimierzdolny.pl).

Dom Gościnny Beitenu ul. Lubelska 4 ☎ 81 881 0894, ⓦ beitenu.pl; map page 209. Beautiful rooms in a former synagogue (see page 210) combining bare stone with warm textiles and wooden beams. There's a café and bookshop on site. 180zł

Dwa Księżyce ul. Sadowa 15 ☎ 81 881 0833, ⓦ dwa ksiezyce.com.pl; map page 209. Medium-sized hotel in a posh-looking house on a quiet street in the town centre, offering stylish en suites. Breakfast is in the swish restaurant downstairs. Ask for a room with a river view. 300zł

Folwark Walencja ul. Góry 16 ☎ 81 882 1165, ⓦ folwarkwalencja.pl; map page 209. In an eighteenth-century manor on the hill overlooking the town 2km to the east, this is a quiet pension with good rooms and an adjacent horse-riding school. 300zł

Pensjonat Kazimierski ul. Tyskiewicza 38 ☎ 81 881 0822, ⓦ pensjonatkazimierski.eu; map page 209. Smart rooms with creamy colour schemes in a modern building with a few traditional touches such as wooden balconies and a shingle roof. Sauna and jaccuzzi on site. 380zł

Spichlerz ul. Krakowska 59/61 ☎ 81 881 0036; map page 209. Occupying a large refurbished granary 1km from the town centre, the *Spichlerz* pension offers simple but decent rooms. Behind the pension is a peaceful, tree-shrouded campsite with excellent facilities and tennis courts. Doubles 250zł, camping 44zł

EATING

There are some excellent **restaurants** in Kazimierz, and your choices are not limited to Polish food. In addition to the places listed below, there are open-air bars by the river offering **fried fish** and beer. A produce **market** is held on the Rynek on Tuesday and Friday mornings.

★ **Klubojadalnia Przystanek Korzeniowa** ul. Doły 43 ☎ 502 722 432, ⓦ facebook.com/Korzeniowa; map

page 209. A wooden house near the entrance to Wąwóz Korzeniowy (see page 210), 2.5km east of the centre, serving an intriguing mix of simple home cooking and imaginative dishes based on seasonal ingredients (mains around 25–30zł). It's also a popular place to drink, and hosts live gigs and the occasional DJ event. Wed–Sun 11am–7pm; open later on gig nights.

5

Knajpa Artystyczna ul. Senatorska 7 ☎ 507 611 185, ⓦ facebook.com/KnajpaArtystyczna; map page 209. Polish food with a twist, melding local favourites like pork and salmon with Mediterranean vegetables and global spices. There are also good salads (25–30zł), and a fair amount for vegetarians too, with vegetarian *orzotto* (18zł) or Silesian *kopytka* dumplings with mushrooms (16zł) rounding out the menu. Mon 1–7pm, Tues–Thurs noon–7pm, Fri noon–9pm, Sat 10am–9pm, Sun 10am–8pm.

Piekarnia Sarzyński ul. Nadrzeczna 6 ☎ 081 881 0643, ⓦ sarzynski.com.pl; map page 209. Smart patisserie selling excellent cakes, gingerbread and ice cream to eat in or take away. It's also the best place to pick up *koguty* (bread buns baked in the form of a cockerel; different sizes from 6zł upwards) and local-favourite *cebularz* (bread bun with onion). Daily 6am–9pm.

Stara Łaźnia ul. Senatorska 21 ☎ 81 889 1350, ⓦ restauracjalaznia.pl; map page 209. Occupying a former bathhouse built in 1921 in extravagant, neo-Renaissance style, this stylish restaurant offers good food at reasonable prices. Dishes range from salad Nicoise (26zł)

to duck breast, pike perch and rack of lamb (35–50zł). It's a popular place with Warsaw film and media folks and, appropriately, there's an open-air cinema in the courtyard showing Polish classics on summer evenings. Daily 9am–10pm.

★ **U Fryzjera** ul. Witkiewicza 2 ☎ 081 881 0426, ⓦ restauracja-ufryzjera.pl; map page 209. One of Poland's best Jewish-themed restaurants, with wooden floorboards, distressed furniture and sepia photos of the Kazimierz of yore. Lots of duck, goose and lamb (mains 35–50zł), and good traditional dishes like *kugel* (a slab of baked potato mush) and *czulent* (barley stew), though out of season they won't have everything on the menu. Mon–Fri noon–midnight, Sat & Sun 9.30am–midnight.

★ **Zielona Tawerna** ul. Nadwiślańska 4 ☎ 081 881 0308; map page 209. Excellent but not overpriced restaurant with a relaxing, artfully decorated country-house interior and a delightful garden. The food is Mediterranean-influenced (mains 45–50zł), and the menu offers a wider range of vegetarian choices than anywhere else in this part of Poland. Daily noon–11pm.

Sandomierz and around

Eighty kilometres south from Kazimierz Dolny along the River Vistula, **SANDOMIERZ** is a fascinating old town with a well-preserved hilltop centre and a wealth of worthy monuments. Like other places in the southeast, Sandomierz rose to prominence through its position on the medieval trade route running from central Asia to central Europe. Following repeated sackings by Tatars and Lithuanians, the town was completely rebuilt by **Kazimierz the Great** in the mid-fourteenth century, gaining defensive walls and a cathedral which survive today. Sandomierz subsequently flourished by shipping local timber and corn down the River Vistula to Gdańsk, but suffered badly at the hands of the Swedes, who blew up the castle in 1656 – after which Sandomierz went into a long period of decline. Today it is one of Poland's prettiest provincial towns, and is also a good base from which to visit **Krzyżtopór Castle**, the semi-ruined Renaissance wonder 40km to the southwest.

The Rynek and around

Sandomierz's delightful, sloping **Rynek** stands at the centre of a relaxing jumble of cobbled alleyways. The Rynek is dominated by the fourteenth-century **town hall**, a Gothic building which had its decorative attic, hexagonal tower and belfry added in the seventeenth and eighteenth centuries. Many of the well-preserved **burghers' houses** positively shout their prosperity: nos. 5 and 10 are particularly fine Renaissance examples. Just north of the Rynek is the handsome red-brick **Opatów Gate** (Brama

Opatowska; daily: April–Oct 9am–7pm; Nov–March 10am–4pm; 4zł), a surviving part of King Kazimierz's fortification; climbing the gate's 154 steps is rewarded with great views over the town. Southwest from the Rynek along ulica Zamkowa is the **Eye of the Needle** (Ucho Igielne), a narrow passageway whose name refers to the Biblical proverb.

Underground Tourist Route

ul. Oleśnickich, just off the Rynek • Tours (40min; in Polish only) daily: April–Sept 9am–7pm; Oct–March 10am–5pm • 10zł • ☎ 15 832 3088

The **Underground Tourist Route** (Podziemna trasa) is a trip through the honeycomb of chambers beneath the Rynek where medieval merchants stored their food and wine. The guided tour takes you through thirty or so chilly Renaissance-era cellars, reaching a depth of 12m.

The Cathedral

ul. Katedralna 1 • Tues–Sat 10am–2pm & 3–5pm, Sun 3–5pm.

To the southern side of the Rynek you come to the murky **Cathedral**, constructed around 1360 on the site of an earlier Romanesque church but with substantial

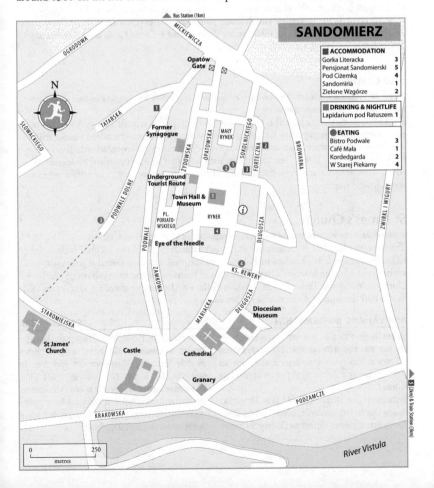

SANDOMIERZ

■ **ACCOMMODATION**
Gorka Literacka	3
Pensjonat Sandomierski	5
Pod Ciżemką	4
Sandomiria	1
Zielone Wzgórze	2

■ **DRINKING & NIGHTLIFE**
| Lapidarium pod Ratuszem | 1 |

● **EATING**
Bistro Podwale	3
Café Mała	1
Kordedgarda	2
W Starej Piekarny	4

Bus Station (1km)

MICKIEWICZA

OGRODOWA

Opatów Gate

N

TATARSKA

SŁOWACKIEGO

Former Synagogue

MAŁY RYNEK

ŻYDOWSKA

OPATOWSKA

SOKOLNICKIEGO

FORTECZNA

BROWARNA

Underground Tourist Route

PODWALE DOLNE

Town Hall & Museum

PL. PORIATO-WSKIEGO

RYNEK

PODWALE

Eye of the Needle

ZAMKOWA

DŁUGOSZA

ZWIRKI I WIGURY

KS. REWERY

MARIACKA

DŁUGOSZA

Diocesian Museum

STAROMIEJSKA

St James' Church

Castle

Cathedral

Granary

PODZAMCZE

KRAKOWSKA

5 (2km) & Train Station (3km)

River Vistula

0   250
metres

5

Baroque additions. Notable features include the set of early fifteenth-century Russo-Byzantine **murals** in the presbytery, probably by the same artist who painted the Holy Trinity Chapel in Lublin (see page 199). A gruesome series of eighteenth-century paintings surround the nave, charmingly entitled *The Torture Calendar* and depicting early church martyrs being skewered, decapitated and otherwise maimed in every conceivable way. As if this weren't enough, there's also a group of murals underneath the organ depicting violent scenes from the town's past, including Tatars enjoying a massacre of the local populace in 1259.

Diocesian Museum

ul. Długosza 9 • May–Sept Tues–Sat 9am–4.30pm, Sun 1.30–4.30pm; Oct–April Tues–Sat 9am–3.30pm, Sun 1.30–3.30pm • 6zł • ☎ 15 833 2670, ⓦ domdlugosza.sandomierz.org

Filled to bursting with a spectacular collection of arts and crafts, the **Diocesian Museum** (Muzeum Diecezjalne) is located in the so-called Długosz House, erstwhile home to the fifteenth-century chronicler Jan Długosz (1415–80). Highlights include an early seventeenth-century portable organ that still works, a collection of Renaissance locks and keys, and a set of seventeenth-century French playing cards illustrating the nations of the world. Among the artistic works there's a fine set of fifteenth- and sixteenth-century altarpieces, including the delicate *Three Saints* triptych from Kraków, as well as a Romanesque *Madonna and Child* stone carving and a *Christ Child with Madonna and St Catherine* by Lucas Cranach the Elder.

The castle

Museum: May–Sept Mon 1–3pm, Tues–Sun 10am–5pm; Oct–April Mon 1–3pm, Tues–Fri 9am–4pm, Sat & Sun 10am–4pm • 15zł; free on Mon • ☎ 698 637 893, ⓦ zamek-sandomierz.pl

Downhill from the cathedral is the **castle** (zamek), partly rebuilt by the Austrians in the nineteenth century after its destruction by the Swedes two hundred years earlier. The large open terrace, also used for open-air concerts in summer, affords good views back over the Old Town. The castle **museum** holds an undistinguished collection of silver, numismatics and regional folk art, although its temporary exhibitions are often more interesting.

St James's Church

al. Staromiejska 3 • Martyrs' Chapel: Mon–Sat 10am–5pm, Sun 10.30–11.30am & 1.30–3.30pm • ☎ 15 832 3774

The lime-shaded, late Romanesque **St James's Church** (Kościół św. Jakuba) is thought to be the earliest brick basilica in Poland – its restored entrance portal is particularly striking. Inside, the **Martyrs' Chapel** has a vivid painting of the martyrdom of local Dominicans by the Tatars in 1260, while in the northern nave there are glass cases said to contain the bones of the murdered monks.

ARRIVAL AND INFORMATION   SANDOMIERZ

By bus The bus station is 1.5km northwest of town; to get into town walk west to the end of ul. 11 Listopada and turn left onto ul. Mickiewicza. Many buses don't use the bus station, picking up and dropping off near the Opatów Gate instead.

Destinations (bus station) Lublin (2 daily; 2hr 10min); Opatów (hourly; 1hr); Warsaw Zachodnia (2 daily; 5–6hr).

Destinations (Opatów Gate) Krakow (20 daily; 3hr 10min);

Lublin (5 daily; 2hr 15min); Tarnobrzeg (10 daily; 30min).

Tourist information The tourist office at Rynek 20 (May–Sept daily 10am–6pm; Oct–April Mon–Fri 8am–4pm, Sat & Sun 9am–5pm; ☎ 15 644 6105, ⓦ sandomierz.travel) has a wealth of info on Sandomierz and the surrounding region. It also has a list of private rooms (50–70zł/person) and will help you find one if they're not too busy with other clients.

5

ACCOMMODATION

★ Gorka Literacka ul. Sokolniego 2/3 ☎ 668 762 654, ⓦ gorkaliteracka.sandomierz.org; map page 213. A wonderfully atmospheric place to stay, bang in the centre of town, this writers' retreat (open to non-scribblers too) has hosted the likes of Stanisław Lem, Czesław Milosz and Sławomir Mrozek in its time. It's decorated with antique furniture and has a decidedly retro communal kitchen. All rooms share bathrooms. <u>120zł</u>

Pensjonat Sandomierski ul. Ostrówek 17 ☎ 535 902 402, ⓦ pensjonatsandomierski.pl; map page 213. On the far side of the River Vistula, 2km southeast of the Rynek, this suburban house comes with chic contemporary rooms equipped with electric kettles and flat-screen TVs. Quiet location and nice garden. Breakfast extra 20zł per person. <u>130zł</u>

Pod Ciżemką Rynek 27 ☎ 15 832 0550, ⓦ hotel cizemka.pl; map page 213. Intimate hotel on the main square offering plush en-suite rooms in a sixteenth-century burgher's mansion. Rooms are neat if old-fashioned, and breakfasts are substantial. <u>270zł</u>

Sandomiria ul. Podwale Górne 10 ☎ 15 644 5244, ⓦ sandomiria.pl; map page 213. Spotless pension on the north edge of the town centre, with en-suite rooms, kitchen facilities, a café and parking. Breakfast extra 20zł per person. <u>180zł</u>

Zielone Wzgórze ul. Forteczna 6 ☎ 519 182 376; map page 213. This quiet house near the main square offers clean en-suite rooms with electric kettle, fridge and TV; many have outstanding balcony views. Parking is another plus. <u>150zł</u>

EATING

Bistro Podwale Podwale Dolne 8 ☎ 795 984 404, ⓦ bistropodwale.pl; map page 213. Chic, minimalist bistro in a barrel-vaulted, former apple-storage cellar, serving a handful of mains (ranging from chicken breasts to burgers; 24–29zł), with the focus on natural ingredients and locally-sourced products. It's also a laid-back place to drink in summer, with deckchairs spread across the lawn. Mon–Thurs & Sun 11am–10pm, Fri & Sat 11am–11pm.

Café Mała ul. Sokolnickiego 3 ☎ 602 102 225, ⓦ facebook.com/CafeMala; map page 213. The best place in town for coffee, just off the Rynek. Bright and cosy, it serves cakes, bruschetta sandwiches, ice cream and superb pancakes. Daily 9am–9pm.

Kordedgarda Rynek 12 ☎ 602 102 225, ⓦ facebook. com/kordegardasandomierz; map page 213. Mellow café in a former guardhouse with a popular outdoor terrace and relaxed vibe. There's a decent breakfast menu as well as toasted sandwiches and substantial salads (20zł). Daily 9am–11.30pm.

W Starej Piekarny ul. Ks Rewery ☎ 787 153 350, ⓦ bit. ly/WStarejPiekarny; map page 213. "The Old Bakery" serves soups, a few simple mains (12–20zł) and delicious bread on long communal tables. Daily 11am–7pm.

DRINKING AND NIGHTLIFE

Lapidarium pod Ratuszem Rynek 1 (beneath the town hall) ☎ 15 832 3355 ⓦ lapidariumpodratuszem. pl; map page 213. This cellar club is a great place to catch live rock and jazz. It also serves excellent burgers, steaks and salads. Mon–Thurs & Sun 6pm–midnight, Fri & Sat 6pm–2am.

Krzyżtopór Castle

Ujazd 73 • Daily: April–Oct 8am–8pm; Nov–March 8am–4pm • 10zł • ☎ 15 860 1133, ⓦ krzyztopor.org.pl • Ujazd is extremely difficult to reach by public transport, although it is theoretically possible to get there and back from Sandomierz in a day, changing buses at Opatów and Iwaniska en route; check the timetable (ⓦ e-podroznik.pl) carefully before setting off

Located in the village of Ujazd, 40km southwest of Sandomierz, **Krzyżtopór Castle** is one of the most spectacular ruins in Poland. Nothing in the surrounding landscape prepares you for the mammoth building that suddenly rears up over the skyline, and even then it's not until you're inside that you really begin to appreciate the sheer scale of the place. Built at enormous expense by Governor of Sandomierz, Krzysztof Ossoliński, the castle was completed in 1644, only a year before Ossoliński's death. It was thoroughly ransacked by the Swedes a decade later, a blow from which it never recovered.

The basic **layout** of the castle comprises a star-shaped set of fortifications surrounding a large inner courtyard and, within this, a smaller elliptical inner area. The design of the castle mimicked the calendar: there were four towers representing the seasons, twelve main walls for the months, 52 rooms, and 365 windows. There was even an additional window for leap years, kept bricked up when out of sync. Ossoliński's passion for

5

horses explains the network of 370 **stables** built underneath the castle, each equipped with its own mirror and marble manger. Carved on the entrance tower are a large cross (*krzyż*) and an axe (*topór*), a reference to the castle's name: the former is a symbol of the Catholic Church's Counter-Reformation, of which Ossoliński was a firm supporter, while the latter is part of the family coat of arms.

Zamość and around

Many of the old towns and palaces of southeast Poland have an Italian feel to them, nowhere more so than **ZAMOŚĆ**, around 100km southeast of Lublin. Somehow, Zamość managed to get through World War II unscathed, so what you see today is one of Europe's best-preserved Renaissance town centres, classified by UNESCO as an outstanding historical monument. With a grid-plan Old Town surrounded by star-shaped fortifications, it's a unique period piece and well worth making a special effort to see.

Southeast from Zamość, the road to the Ukrainian border passes through **Bełżec**, site of an infamous Nazi death camp whose victims are commemorated by a moving memorial.

Brief history

The brainchild of dynamic sixteenth-century chancellor **Jan Zamoyski**, Zamość is a remarkable demonstration of the way Poland's rulers looked towards Italy for ideas. In many ways the archetypal Renaissance man, Zamoyski based his model town on plans drawn up by Bernardo Morando of Padua – the city where he had earlier studied. Morando's plans produced a beautifully Italianate town complete with arcaded piazza and a state-of-the-art system of defensive bastions; Zamość was one of the few places to withstand the seventeenth-century "Swedish Deluge" that flattened so many other Polish towns. Strategically located on major **trade routes**, the town attracted an international array of merchants, notably the Armenians, who sold eastern fabrics to Polish aristocrats hungry for oriental style. The Partition era brought economic decline: early in the nineteenth century Zamość had sunk so far that even the Zamoyskis themselves had moved on. Today, however, Zamość is benefiting from European money and is well and truly on the rise as tourists flood back to its historic streets.

The Rynek

Ringed by a low arcade and the decorative former homes of Zamość merchants, the geometrically designed **Rynek Wielki** – exactly 100m in both width and length – is a superb example of Renaissance town planning. Dominating the northern side of the square is the **town hall**, a solid, three-storey structure topped by a soaring clock tower and spire. The sweeping, fan-shaped double stairway was added in the eighteenth century. East of the town hall, **ulica Ormiańska** features several of the finest houses on the square. Once inhabited by the Armenian merchants, the house facades are a whirl of rich, decorative ornamentation, with a noticeable intermesh of oriental motifs.

Zamość Museum

ul. Ormianska 30 • Tues–Sun 9am–4pm • 10zł • ☏ 84 638 6494, ⓦ muzeum-zamojskie.pl

A couple of exhuberantly decorated mansions house the **Zamość Museum** (Muzeum Zamojskie), focusing on the Zamoyskis and local history. There are copies of portraits of the town's founder, Jan, though these are outshone by a beautiful series of full-sized paintings, dating from the 1630s, of his son Tomasz Zamoyski and daughter-in-law

Katarzyna. Elsewhere, the archeological section contains ornate jewellery worn by the Goths who settled hereabouts, together with a display of mannequins wearing replica Goth robes – anyone seriously into hippy chic will find a wealth of inspiration here. Finally, there's a colourful assemblage of folk costumes, revealing the interplay of Polish and Ukrainian folk styles that's typical of the eastern borderlands.

The Cathedral

ul. Kolegiacka 1 • **Cathedral** Daily 6am–7pm • **Bell tower** May–Sept Mon–Fri 10am–4pm • 4zł

Southwest of the Rynek is the towering **Cathedral**, a magnificent Mannerist basilica designed by Morando to Zamoyski's exacting instructions and completed in 1600. The **presbytery** houses a finely wrought eighteenth-century Rococo silver tabernacle, as well as a series of paintings depicting the life of St Thomas attributed to Tintoretto. The grandest of the **chapels** is that of the Zamoyski family, which contains the marble tomb of Chancellor Jan and is topped with elegant Baroque stucco by the Italian architect Giovanni Battista Falconi. Adjoining the main building is a towering **bell tower**; the biggest of its bells, known as Jan, is over three centuries old.

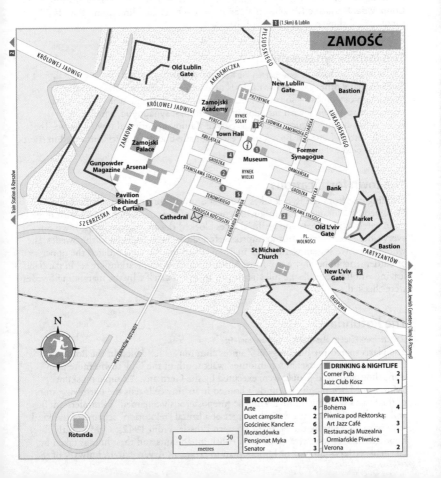

ACCOMMODATION	
Arte	4
Duet campsite	2
Gościniec Kanclerz	6
Morandówka	5
Pensjonat Myka	1
Senator	3

DRINKING & NIGHTLIFE	
Corner Pub	2
Jazz Club Kosz	1

EATING	
Bohema	4
Piwnica pod Rektorską:	
Art Jazz Café	3
Restauracja Muzealna	1
Ormiańskie Piwnice	
Verona	2

5

The Arsenal

ul. Zamkowa 2 • Tues–Sun: May–Sept 9am–5pm; Oct–April 9am–4pm • Entrance to all three exhibitions (Museum of Fortifications and Weapons, Pavilion Behind the Curtain and Gunpowder Magazine) 25zł; entrance to one exhibition 10zł • ☎ 84 638 6494, ⓦ muzeumarsenal.pl

Squeezed into the southwestern corner of the Old Town is an ensemble of buildings that played a key role in the military life of the town and which nowadays house the **Arsenal Museum of Fortifications and Weaponry** (Arsenał: Muzeum Fortyfikacji i Broni). The first is the Arsenal itself, a handsome Renaissance building built by Morando in the 1580s, and now crammed with cannons, sabres and pikes. There is plenty of multimedia content too: at one point, the history of Zamość is recalled by a hologram of a man clad in period knickerbockers.

On the opposite side of the road is the **Pavilion Behind the Curtain** (Pawilon pod Kurtyną), a modern structure tacked on to the curtain wall stretching west of the Szczebrzeska Gate. Dedicated to the history of the Polish army, the exhibition here begins with the defence of Zamość against invading Bolsheviks in 1920, and continues through World War II to the present day. Complete with archive film and sound effects, it's a gripping display. A multimedia card (10zł desposit) allows you to access additional touch-screen and video content. Tucked into the corner of the fortress is the **Gunpowder Magazine** (Prochownia), an imposing brick building from 1830. Inside there's a film show on the history of the town.

The former synagogue

ul. Pereca 14 • Tues–Sun: March–Oct 10am–6pm; Nov–Feb 10am–2pm • ☎ 84 639 0054 , ⓦ fodz.pl

As in so many other eastern towns, Jews made up a significant portion of the population of Zamość – some 45 percent on the eve of World War II. The most impressive surviving Jewish monument is the **former synagogue**, a fine early-seventeenth-century structure built as part of Zamoyski's original town scheme. The lovingly-restored interior boasts some exceptionally fine floral reliefs, arranged in frieze-form just below the ceiling.

The town fortifications

Heading east from the Rynek takes you over onto the former **town fortifications**. Designed by Morando, they originally consisted of a set of seven **bastions** with three main gates. Wide moats and artificial lakes blocked the approaches to the town on every side. After holding out so impressively against the Cossacks and the Swedes, the whole defensive system went under in 1866, when the Russians ordered the upper set of battlements to be blown up. Most of the remaining fortifications are set in parkland, leaving you free to walk the full circuit and see for yourself why the marauding Swedes were checked.

The Rotunda

ul. Męczenników Rotundy • May–Sept Tues–Sun 9am–8pm • Free

The Nazis spared the buildings of Zamość, but not its residents. In the **Rotunda**, a nineteenth-century arsenal ten minutes' walk south of the Old Town, more than eight thousand local people were executed by the Germans. A simple **museum** (Muzeum Martyrologii "Rotunda") housed in its tiny cells tells the harrowing story of the town's wartime trauma. Zamość (preposterously renamed "Himmlerstadt") and the surrounding area were the target of a brutal "relocation" scheme of the kind already carried out by the Nazis in Western Prussia. From 1942 to 1943 nearly three hundred villages were cleared of their Polish inhabitants and their houses taken by German settlers – all part of Hitler's plan to create an Aryan eastern bulwark of the

Third Reich. The remaining villages were left alone only because the SS lacked the manpower to clear them out. Three cells in the museum are dedicated to the Soviet wartime massacre of Polish army officers at Katyń (see page 73), and there's a sombre chapel in memory of local people deported to Siberia following the Soviet occupation of eastern Poland in 1939.

ARRIVAL AND DEPARTURE   ZAMOŚĆ

By train The train station is located 1km southwest of the centre off ul. Akademiczka. Note that most departures (except for Lublin) are very early in the morning.
Destinations Kraków (1 daily; 5hr 45min); Lublin (4 daily; 2hr 25min); Rzeszów (1 daily; 2hr 50min).
By bus The main bus station is 2km east of the town centre (local buses #10, #22, #44, #47 or #59 will drop you off in

the centre). Minibuses depart from one side of the road, main buses from the other – check timetables at both points for full information on all possible departures.
Destinations Kraków (3 daily; 5hr 45min); Lublin (hourly; 1hr 40min); Rzeszów (3 daily; 3hr); Zwierzyniec (Mon–Fri 10 daily, Sat & Sun 6 daily; 45min).

INFORMATION

Tourist information There are two tourist offices: in the town hall at Rynek 13 (May–Sept Mon–Fri 8am–6pm, Sat & Sun 9am–6pm; Oct–April Mon–Fri 8am–5pm, Sat & Sun 9am–5pm; ☎ 084 639 2292, ⓦ zci.zamosc.pl and

ⓦ travel.zamosc.pl); and in the Koszary Kozackie ("Cossack Barracks"), a red-brick fort at ul. Łukasińskiego 2E, adjoining the park north of the Old Town (daily 9am–5pm; ☎ 84 538 1733).

ACCOMMODATION

HOTELS AND PENSIONS
Arte Rynek 9 ☎ 84 639 3900, ⓦ artehotel.pl; map page 217. Boutique hotel right on the main square, with high-ceilinged rooms in a restored mansion. The decor has a subtle 1960s Pop Art touch that's not overdone, and there's a classy restaurant downstairs. 250zł
★ **Gościniec Kanclerz** ul. Partyzantów 6 ☎ 509 708 512, ⓦ goscinieckanclerz.pl; map page 217. Cosy rooms above a restaurant just outside the Old Town. Unassuming, intimate and friendly, and with a generous breakfast. 200zł
Morandówka ul. Staszica 25 ☎ 84 530 9900, ⓦ morandowka.pl; map page 217. Elegant mansion on the Rynek, with neat, comfortable rooms above a multi-purpose restaurant and café. In the summertime, breakfast on the outdoor terrace facing the town hall is a treat. 250zł

Pensjonat Myka ul. Starowiejska 25a ☎ 884 894 111, ⓦ noclegizamosc.pl; map page 217. This modern pension 1.5km north of the Old Town offers smart contemporary rooms and on-site parking. Breakfast extra 20zł per person. 180zł
Senator Rynek Solny 4 ☎ 084 638 9990, ⓦ senator hotel.pl; map page 217. Quality, intimate hotel with charming and tasteful rooms. Breakfast extra 25zł per person. 229zł

CAMPSITE
Duet campsite ul. Królowej Jadwigi ☎ 084 639 2499; map page 217. A 10min walk west of the centre, this unexciting campsite is acceptable for a night or two. Tennis courts on site. 90zł

EATING

Restaurant and bar life in the Old Town is flourishing, especially around the Rynek itself, where most places combine the roles of café and restaurant in a single establishment. However, outside the summer season you may be hard-pressed to find a meal after 8pm.
★ **Bohema** ul. Staszica 29 ☎ 84 627 1443, ⓦ bohem azamosc.pl; map page 217. Square-side patisserie serving scrumptious cakes – try the meringue with mascarpone and strawberry (8zł). There's a restaurant in the cellar, with a quality menu combining the best of Polish and European cuisine (mains 30–40zł). Daily 10am–midnight.
Piwnica pod Rektorską: Art Jazz Café Rynek 2 ☎ 84 530 1379; map page 217. Atmospheric basement bar-restaurant with check tablecloths, a horn section hanging

from the walls and occasional live jazz gigs. Food includes *gołąbki* with *kasza* (18zł), various *pierogi* and *barszcz* with cabbage and mushroom-filled dumplings (9zł). Daily noon–midnight.
Restauracja Muzealna Ormiańskie Piwnice Ormiańska 30 ☎ 84 638 7300 ⓦ muzealna.com.pl; map page 217. Cosy brick cellar that pays tribute to Zamość's cosmopolitan heritage with an Armenian-inspired menu that's heavy on grilled meats and kebabs (the shish kebab with lavash bread, at 25zł, is pretty much the standard order). Oriental carpets and cushions add to the atmosphere. Daily 10am–midnight.
Verona Rynek 5 ☎ 84 638 9031; map page 217. Italian-themed place divided into relaxing café-restaurant at ground level, and a hip, clubby, brick-lined resto-bar in

the cellar. Wherever you choose to sit expect reasonably authentic pizzas, refined pasta dishes and Mediterranean salads (mains 20–30zł), and some refreshing fruit-juice cocktails. Daily 10am–midnight.

DRINKING AND NIGHTLIFE

Corner Pub Żeromskiego 6 ☎ 84 627 0694, ⓦ corner pub.pl; map page 217. Upmarket Irish-style pub with reproduction posters and adverts on the walls, and a good range of beer, including Murphy's and Guinness on tap. The reasonable menu includes Irish breakfast (20zł) and fish and chips. Daily 11am–11pm.

★ **Jazz Club Kosz** ul. Szczebreska 3 ☎ 502 578 442, ⓦ kosz.zam.pl; map page 217. Legendary jazz bar currently housed in spacious quarters above the Szczebreszyn Gate, with DJs and dancing at weekends. *Kosz* also organizes the Jazz na Kresach festival (see page 220). Mon–Thurs & Sun noon–midnight, Fri & Sat noon–1am.

Bełżec

Grounds Daily: April–Oct 9am–6pm; Nov–March 9am–4pm • **Museum** Tues–Sun: April–Oct 9am–5pm; Nov–March 9am–4pm • Free • ☎ 84 665 2510, ⓦ belzec.eu • Bus from Zamość (12 daily; 1hr)

Forty kilometres southeast of Zamość, the unassuming village of **BEŁŻEC** is the site of one of Nazi Germany's most notorious extermination camps. Established on the southeastern fringes of the village in early 1942, the Bełżec camp was a key component of Operation Reinhard – the methodical annihilation of eastern Poland's entire Jewish population. Using six gas chambers to dispose of its victims at a rate of 1000 a time, the camp only accommodated a small number of long-term inmates, whose job it was to dispose of the bodies and process the victims' belongings. Only a handful of prisoners survived Bełżec, and with the Nazis razing the entire facility in spring 1943, the camp has remained one of the least documented of Poland's Holocaust sites. The site was largely abandoned to the weeds until 2004, when a new **memorial** was erected incorporating a huge open-air abstract sculpture comprising stark lumps of grey rubble. A state-of-the-art **museum** contains photos, films and English-language texts.

Roztoczański National Park

South of Zamość lies more of the open, sparsely populated countryside characteristic of much of the country's eastern borderlands. Arable land and pasture alternate with swathes of forest, the biggest of which is now protected by the **Roztoczański National Park** (Roztoczański Park Narodowy), a beautifully unspoiled area of rolling hills, forests and waterways covering an area of almost eighty square kilometres. Cutting across its heart is the beautiful and uncontaminated **River Wieprz**, which has its source just to the east. Most of the park is covered with pine, fir and towering beeches. Fauna includes **tarpans** – wild ponies brought back from the brink of extinction in the nineteenth century – as well as storks, cranes and beavers. The gateway to the park is **Zwierzyniec**, a mellow little place 32km southwest from Zamość.

ZAMOŚĆ FESTIVALS

If you happen to be in town at the right time there are several annual cultural happenings worth checking out. The **Jazz Na Kresach** festival ("Jazz on the Borderlands"; late May/early June), usually held in the last week of May or early June, is popular with Polish and other Slav jazzers. For the **Jarmark Hetmański** (second weekend in June) you'll find Polish and Ukrainian traditional music and a handmade-crafts market on the Rynek.

Zwierzyniec and around

ZWIERZYNIEC owes its existence to chancellor Jan Zamoyski, who purchased the surrounding forests in 1589 and built a palatial hunting lodge. Most of the complex was demolished in the 1830s, but a few important elements were spared, most notably the Zamoyski **chapel**, a delicate Baroque construction located on one of a series of islands in the willow-fringed palace lake.

National Park Museum

ul. Plażowa 3 • Tues–Sun: May–Oct 9am–5pm; Nov–April 9am–4pm • 4zł • ☎ 84 687 2286, ⓦ roztoczanskipn.pl • Buses from Zwierżyniec every 15min

A ten-minute walk south of central Zwierzyniec along ulica Browara brings you to the **National Park Museum** (Ośrodek Muzealny RPN), where you can pick up entrance tickets (4zł), maps and detailed information about walking routes in the park. The museum also contains a display on the park's flora and fauna.

Echo Lake and Bukowa Góra

Several short **walks** branch off from the National Park Museum. The easiest of these leads southeast through pine forest to the reed-shrouded **Echo Lake** (15min), the northern banks of which boast a wonderful, sloping sandy beach. From here, continue 200m along the road passing the lake and you'll come to an **observation deck**, from which you're likely to see grazing tarpans.

Another popular trail traces the old palace path southwest to **Bukowa Góra** (20min), an upland area of dense woodland where daylight is almost blotted out by the thick canopy of beech and firs. On the far side of Bukowa Góra lies an area of sandy-soiled heath with some fine views southwards: from here you can work your way eastwards towards Echo Lake in about twenty minutes.

ARRIVAL AND DEPARTURE   ZWIERZYNIEC

By bus The bus station is five minutes' north of the palace lake, on the far side of an unkempt town park. Destinations Kraków (3 daily; reserve on ☎ 84 639 8586, ⓦ busmax.pl); Zamość (Mon–Fri 10 daily, Sat & Sun 6 daily; 45min).

ACCOMMODATION, EATING AND DRINKING

Anna ul. Dębowa 1 ☎ 84 687 2590, ⓦ annazwierzyniec. pl. Just off the main road, this pension is a great central choice, offering cute en-suite rooms and a buffet breakfast. There's also bike rental here. <u>120zł</u>

Karczma Młyn ul. Wachniewskiej 1A ☎ 084 687 2527, ⓦ karczma-mlyn.pl. Colourful restaurant in a wooden building with surviving mill wheel outside, serving a reasonable selection of pizzas and meaty Polish favourites in an idyllic location near a lake. Daily noon–9pm.

Pijalnia Piwa ul. Browarna 7 ☎ 669 611 981. The local beer, a smooth, lager-style brew that's extremely difficult to find outside the region, is ideally savoured at the beer garden of the Zwierzyniec brewery itself, a grand nineteenth-century building. Mon–Thurs noon–8pm, Fri–Sun 10am–9pm.

Zacisze ul. Rudka 5B ☎ 84 687 2306, ⓦ zacisze. zwierzyniec.com. Popular but tranquil hotel in a medium-sized building surrounded by greenery, offering comfortable en-suite rooms and a good restaurant and bar. <u>120zł</u>

The Polish Carpathians

HIKING IN THE BIESZCZADY

The Polish Carpathians

Combining hanting natural beauty with diverse cultural traditions, the Polish Carpathians represent one of Eastern Europe's most richly rewarding areas of exploration. Rising in the Czech Republic, then running east along the Polish–Slovak border before arcing through Ukraine and Romania, the Carpathians form one of the continent's major mountain chains. The highest range of the Polish Carpathians is the Tatras, whose rugged alpine character is so distinctive that we've given them a chapter all to themselves (see page 324). Running east from the Tatras, Poland's remaining share of the Carpathians is relatively low in altitude and smooth in shape, but the deeply forested, sparsely populated valleys still exude a palpable sense of mystery.

The main ranges of southeastern Poland – the Beskid Sądecki, the Beskid Niski and the Bieszczady – make ideal hiking territory, and with few peaks over 1200m they're easily baggable by the moderately fit walker. Although tourism is on the increase, this corner of Poland is rarely swamped with visitors.

Traditionally, Carpathian Poland was one of the most culturally mixed areas in the country, and remains rich in contrasting folklores. Poles mingled with **Jews** in the market towns, while villages were inhabited by **Boykos** and **Lemkos** – highlanders who spoke dialects closer to Ukrainian than Polish. The majority of Boykos and Lemkos were deported following a bitter civil war in 1947 (see page 237), lending the highlands a half-abandoned aura that still pervades today. Many of the amazing **wooden churches** built by them do, however, remain, their pagoda-like domes and painted interiors making up some of the most spectacular folk architecture in Europe.

The main point of entry to the region is **Rzeszów**, a modestly sized city which has good transport links with the hills to the south. Just northeast of Rzeszów, the stately **Łańcut Palace** is one of Poland's most visited attractions, while the churches and museums of **Przemyśl** and **Sanok** shed light on the region's multicultural history. Southeast of Sanok, the **Bieszczady** are the most appealing Polish range after the Tatras, their stark bare summits rising above dark forests of pine and beech. To the west, nestling beneath the **Beskid Niski** range, the towns of **Gorlice** and **Krosno** were unlikely centres of a major oil-drilling boom in the mid-nineteenth century: local museums are full of oil memorabilia, including one in the village of **Bóbrka** devoted to oil-drilling. Further west still, the green **Beskid Sądecki** wrap themselves around the quaint spa resort of **Krynica** and the bustling regional centre of **Nowy Sącz**.

Rzeszów and around

The largest city in southeastern Poland and administrative capital of "Subcarpathia" (Podkarpackie), predominantly modern **RZESZÓW** may lack the kind of historical punch delivered by some of Poland's other regional centres but it still offers plenty to

SANOK SKANSEN

Highlights

❶ Łańcut Palace Sumptuous period rooms and well-kept gardens make this the most worthwhile of Poland's aristocratic seats outside Warsaw to visit. See page 229

❷ Przemyśl A quaint city of historic churches and narrow streets, with an outlying ring of nineteenth-century forts providing plenty of excuses for out-of-town excursions. See page 232

❸ Skansen, Sanok This treasure-trove of traditional architecture and folk art is also a monument to the cultural diversity of the region. See page 237

❹ The Bieszczady The bare-topped Bieszczady are arguably the most starkly beautiful highlands in Poland. See page 239

❺ The forest railway, Bieszczady Trundle at a leisurely pace through the western Bieszczady on this rare surviving relic of Poland's narrow-gauge railway network. See page 243

❻ Wooden church, Kwiatoń With its shingled exterior and trio of dainty domes, this is arguably the prettiest Lemko wooden church in Poland. See page 249

HIGHLIGHTS ARE MARKED ON THE MAP ON PAGE 226

enjoy, with a Rynek as lively as any in the country in summer. The area's best museums are a bus ride away, however, in **Łańcut** and Sanok, and southeastern Poland's main attraction – the mountains – lie well to the south.

The Rynek

Lined by imposing merchants' houses, Rzeszów's handsome **Rynek** bears witness to the city's long history as a local market centre. The square's star turn is the endearingly eccentric-looking **town hall, a** squat, sixteenth-century edifice remodelled just over a hundred years ago. Looking like a cross between a Disney castle and a Baroque church, it's profile features on much of the city's tourist literature.

Underground Tourist Route

Rynek 26 • Tours (50min) depart roughly hourly: May–Sept Tues–Fri 10am–7pm, Sat & Sun 11am–6pm; Oct–April Tues–Fri 10am–6pm, Sat & Sun 11am–5pm • 7zł • ☎ 17 875 4774, ⓦ trasa-podziemna.erzeszow.pl

Steps from the Rynek descend towards the entrance of the **Underground Tourist Route** (Podziemna Trasa Turystyczna) a series of passageways linking over twenty cellars where the city's merchants once stored their wares. Along the way you'll pass exhibits linked to the city's history, alongside costumed mannequins representing Rzeszów citizens of centuries past.

Regional Museum

ul. 3 Maja 19 • Tues, Wed & Fri 8.30am–3.30pm, Thurs 8.30am–5.30pm, Sat & Sun 2–6pm • 9zł • ☎ 17 853 5278, ⓦ muzeum.rzeszow.pl

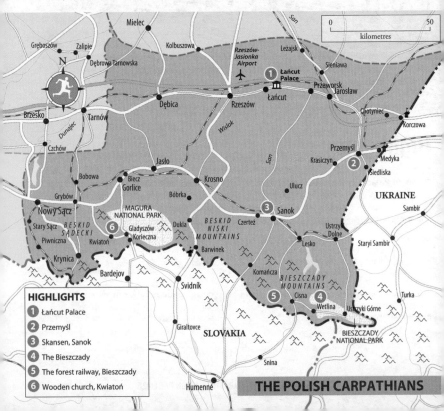

HIGHLIGHTS
1. Łańcut Palace
2. Przemyśl
3. Skansen, Sanok
4. The Bieszczady
5. The forest railway, Bieszczady
6. Wooden church, Kwiatoń

THE POLISH CARPATHIANS

Rzeszów's main pedestrianized thoroughfare, ulica 3 Maja, runs past the former Piarist monastery complex, where the **regional museum** (Muzeum Okręgowe w Rzeszowie) is ranged around the monastery courtyard. Aside from some undistinguished Polish and European paintings, the museum contains the biblical frescoes that once decorated the former cloister arcade, and also holds changing exhibitions focused on local history.

Museum of Bedtime Stories

Basement of the Maska Puppet Theatre, ul. Mickiewicza 13 • Tues–Fri 10am–4pm, Sat & Sun 10am–5pm • 7zł • ⓦ muzeumdobranocek.com.pl

Arguably Rzeszów's most memorable attraction is the **Museum of Bedtime Stories** (Muzeum Dobranocek), a colourful collection of puppets, toys, and illustrations devoted to the kind of childrens' programmes that used to be shown every evening on Polish TV. Based on the private collection of Wojciech Jama, the museum gives understandable pride of place to home-grown heroes such as **Bolek i Lolek**, the animated cartoon characters whose ten-minute adventures (made between 1963 and 1986) were full of old-school visual humour. What makes the museum so poignantly nostalgic is the fact that countries like Poland no longer make the kind of animated films they used to, edged out of global media markets by digital cartoon productions that are no longer hand-drawn or hand-modelled.

The New Synagogue: BMA Gallery

ul. Jana III Sobieskiego • Tues–Sun 10am–5pm • 6zł • ☎ 17 853 3811, ⓦ bwa.rzeszow.pl

East of the Rynek, a fine pair of former synagogues are all that remains of what was once the city's lively Jewish quarter. The so-called **New Synagogue** (Nowa Synagoga), a large seventeenth-century brick building designed by Italian architect Giovanni Bellotti, is now the **BWA Gallery**, with a changing display of exhibitions on two floors. Next door, the rebuilt **Old Synagogue** (Stara Synagoga), older by more than a century and gutted by the Nazis, houses the town archives.

ARRIVAL AND DEPARTURE   RZESZÓW

By air Rzeszów's airport (☎ 17 852 0081, ⓦ rzeszowairport. pl) is at Jasionka, 10km north of the city. Local buses #L and #51 (3zł) run into town, ending up near the train station.

By train The train station is a short walk north of the Rynek.

Destinations Jarosław (hourly; 35–50min); Łancut (hourly; 15min); Leżajsk (3 daily; change at Przeworsk; 1hr 30min); Kraków (8 daily; 2hr–2hr 40min); Przemyśl (12 daily; 1hr 15min–1hr 40min); Tarnów (hourly; 1hr–1hr 25min); Warsaw (4 daily; 5hr 40min–6hr 20min); Zamość (1 daily; 2hr 50min).

By bus The bus station is next to the train station.

Destinations Gorlice (8 daily; 2hr 15min); Krosno (4 daily; 1hr); Nowy Sącz (2 daily; 3hr 50min); Sanok (4 daily; 1hr 30min).

By minibus Minibuses run by Marcel Bus (ⓦ marcel-bus. pl) serve Krosno (every 30–45min; 1hr 30min), Lublin (7 daily; 4hr) and Sanok (every 30min-1hr; 2hr 10min), picking up and dropping off at the Europa shopping centre, one block south of the main bus station on ul. Piłsudskiego. Minibuses to Łańcut (every 30min–1hr; 25min) use pl. Wolnosci, just southeast of the train station. Minibuses to Leżajsk (hourly; 1hr 10min) and Zamość (3 daily; 3hr) pick up and drop off at ul. Sokoła, 200m west of the Rynek.

INFORMATION

Tourist information There's a tourist office (May–Sept Mon 9am–5pm, Tues–Fri 10am–7pm, Sat & Sun 11am–6pm; Oct–April Tues–Fri 10am–6pm, Sat & Sun 11am–6pm; ☎ 017 875 4774, ⓦ podkarpackie.travel) on the Rynek, inside the entrance to the Underground Tourist Route (see page 226); the staff have accommodation listings and loads of info about the whole region.

ACCOMMODATION

Ambasadorski Rynek 13 ☎ 17 250 2444, ⓦ ambasadorski.com; map page 228. Swish business-oriented hotel occupying a enviable square-side position, with deep-carpeted en suites, uniformed reception staff, and gym and sauna on site. **350zł**

Grand Hotel Boutique ul. Dymnickiego 1 ☎ 17 250

0000, ⓦgrand-hotel.pl; map page 228. Ranged around a galleried courtyard with a glass roof, this is a swish, design-conscious hotel with smart en-suite rooms – some with bathtub, some with state-of-the-art shower. **290zł**

Hotel Metropolitan ul. Slowackiego 16 ⓣ17 852 9770, ⓦhotelpodratuszem.pl; map page 228. Just round the corner from the main square, this is a rather exciting design choice on account of its bold carpets, unusual colour scemes and everything-just-right bathrooms. **270zł**

Pod Ratuszem ul. Matejki 8 ⓣ17 852 9770, ⓦhotel podratuszem.pl; map page 228. Just off the Rynek, and

with views of the town hall from some of the upper-storey rooms, this tall, narrow town house is an informal place with cosy en-suite rooms. Breakfast is delivered to your room on a tray. **185zł**

Va Bank Rynek 5 ⓣ17 852 7980, ⓦvabank.itl.pl; map page 228. Eleven-room B&B above the Rynek pub-restaurant of the same name, with a collection of singles, doubles and two-person apartments. Rooms are cheerfully decorated, and some doubles are attractively located at roof level under ceiling skylights. **180zł**

EATING

Bellanuna ul. Moniuszki 4 ⓣ515 516 500, ⓦbellanuna. pl; map page 228. Quality Italian restaurant in an attractive villa, serving classics like Milanese cutlets (30–

40zł) and a few pasta dishes (20–30zł), backed up by a good list of Italian wines. The house speciality is the Piedmont-sourced steak (75zł). Daily noon–10pm.

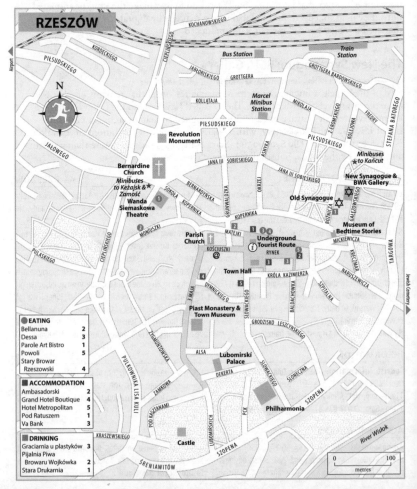

RZESZÓW

EATING
Bellanuna	2
Dessa	3
Parole Art Bistro	1
Powoli	5
Stary Browar Rzeszowski	4

ACCOMMODATION
Ambasadorski	2
Grand Hotel Boutique	4
Hotel Metropolitan	5
Pod Ratuszem	1
Va Bank	3

DRINKING
Graciarnia u plastyków	3
Pijalnia Piwa Browaru Wojkówka	2
Stara Drukarnia	1

Dessa ul. Matejki 2 ☎ 17 853 3857, ⓦ restauracjadessa. pl; map page 228. A combined restaurant/gallery/antique shop with a trinket-stuffed dining room and an outdoor terrace on the adjacent Rynek. The mixed menu of Polish and modern European fare (mains 35–45zł) includes some substantial salads and delicious desserts. Daily noon–11pm.

Parole Art Bistro ul. Sokoła 7 ☎ 511 131 019, ⓦ facebook.com/paroleartbistro; map page 228. Smart, chic cellar restaurant beneath the town theatre with French-Mediterranean cuisine (mains 40–55zł) featuring mussels, plenty of fish and extravagant desserts, plus an extensive wine list. Mon noon–9pm, Tues–Sun noon–11pm.

★ **Powoli** ul. Mickiewicza 4 ☎ 669 505 004, ⓦ facebook.com/powolicafe; map page 228. Just off the main square, this café offers own-recipe lemonades, a fine selection of cakes and (in summer) chilled coffee. It's bright, relaxing and slightly kooky. Mon–Fri 8am–10pm, Sat & Sun 9am–10pm.

Stary Browar Rzeszowski Rynek 20–23 ☎ 17 250 0015, ⓦ browar-rzeszow.pl; map page 228. Very large bar-restaurant complex with lots of wood and exposed brick, that serves up pizzas (25–35zł), steaks (70zł) and burgers (29zł) – and is pretty good at all of them. It also offers delicious ales brewed on the premises, with a pils, a pale ale and a porter to choose from. To cap it all, connecting doors lead to a next-door sushi restaurant from which you can cross-order. Mon–Wed & Sun noon–11pm, Thurs–Sat noon–1am.

DRINKING

Graciarnia u plastyków Rynek 10 ☎ 17 862 5647, ⓦ graty.itl.pl; map page 228. Labyrinthine cellar pub deep below the Rynek, crammed with artwork, posters, household junk and the odd coffin-shaped table. Mon–Thurs & Sun noon–midnight, Fri & Sat noon–3am.

Pijalnia Piwa Browaru Wojkówka ul. Kopernika 4 ☎ 533 346 087; map page 228. Bar serving on-tap beer from the Wojkówka brewery near Krosno. The decor is bland but the beer is great, and the food good value. Daily 3pm–1am.

Stara Drukarnia ul. Bożnicza 6a ☎ 790 798 905, ⓦ facebook.com/stara.drukarnia.5; map page 228. Combined pub and art gallery just off the Rynek, featuring distressed furniture, lots of exposed brickwork and an attention-grabbing collection of paintings on the walls. There's a huge selection of Polish craft beers on tap and by the bottle. Daily 4pm–2am.

Łańcut

Surrounded by immaculately kept gardens, the palace complex that dominates the centre of **ŁAŃCUT** (pronounced "Winesoot"), 17km east of Rzeszów, is one of the most visited attractions in the country. The palace itself is a treasure-trove of fine art and even finer interior decor, while the surrounding park offers large stretches of ornamental gardens and open parkland, dotted with various outbuildings – some of which house museums.

Brief history

The first building on the site, constructed by the Pilecki family in the second half of the fourteenth century, was burnt down in 1608 when royal troops ambushed its robber-baron owner **Stanisław Stadnicki**, known by his contemporaries as "The Devil of Łańcut". The estate was then bought by Stanisław Lubomirski, who set about building the basis of today's palace. Completed in 1641, it was surrounded by a pentagonal moat and outer ramparts, the outlines of which remain. The fortifications were dismantled in 1760 by **Izabela Czartoryska** (see page 206), wife of the last Lubomirski owner, who turned Łańcut into one of her artistic salons and laid out the surrounding park. Louis XVIII of France was among those entertained at Łańcut during this period, and the next owners, the **Potocki family**, carried on in the same manner, Kaiser Franz Joseph being one of their guests. Łańcut's last private owner, Count Alfred Potocki, evacuated the palace's most precious objects to Vienna as the Red Army advanced in 1944, hanging a Russian sign reading "Polish National Museum" on the gates. The Red Army left the place untouched, and it was opened as a museum later the same year.

The palace

Ticket office in the Manege (former stables) at the southwestern entrance to the park • Feb–May, Oct & Nov Mon noon–3.30pm, Tues–Sat 9am–4pm, Sun 9am–5pm; June–Sept Mon 11.30am–4pm, Tues–Fri 9am–4pm, Sat & Sun 10am–6pm; entry is on the hour; visitors can join a (Polish-language) guided tour or go round the exhibits on their own with an audio guide • 23zł; free on Mon; audio guide 4zł • ☎ 17 225 2008, ⓦ zamek-lancut.pl

6

Forty or so of the **palace**'s hundreds of rooms are open to the public and in summer they are crammed with visitors. The **corridors** are an art show in themselves: family portraits and busts, paintings by seventeenth-century Italian, Dutch and Flemish artists and copies of classical statues commissioned by Izabela. Adjacent to an opulent **ballroom** is the extraordinary eighty-seater **Łańcut theatre** commissioned by Izabela; as well as the ornate gallery and stalls, the romantic scenic backdrops are still there, as is the stage machinery to crank them up and down. Beyond lies the **old study**, decorated in frilliest Rococo style. The domed ceiling of the **Zodiac Room** still has its seventeenth-century Italian stucco, while the **Pompeii Hall** houses genuine Roman antiquities set in an amusing mock-ruin.

Orthodox Religious Art Museum

May–Sept Tues–Sat 10am–5pm, Sun 10am–6pm; Oct–April Tues–Sun 10am–4pm • 6zł

The old stables in Łańcut palace park now contain the **Orthodox Religious Art Museum** (Sztuka cerkiewna), housing a large and fabulous collection of icons and decorative art from Poland's Ukrainian, Boyko and Lemko communities. The bulk of the collection was removed from the Uniate and Orthodox churches of the surrounding region in the years following the notorious Operation Vistula of 1947 (see page 237). Among the choice items on show is a complete eighteenth-century iconostasis and a poignant, suffering *Christus Pantocrator*, reflecting the influences of Roman Catholic art on later Uniate and Orthodox iconography.

Orchid House

May–Sept Tues–Fri 10am–6pm, Sat & Sun 11am–7pm; Oct–April Tues–Sun 10am–4pm • 5zł

Due east of the palace is the **Orchid House** (Storczykarnia), established under the Potockis in the nineteenth century, and reopened in a state-of-the-art glasshouse in summer 2008. With jets of mist zapping the orchids every few seconds from pipes in the ceiling, it's a bit like going to the horticultural equivalent of a rock concert.

The Old Synagogue

pl. Jana III Sobieskiego 19 • May–Aug Mon–Wed, Fri & Sat 11am–6pm, Thurs 11am–4pm, Sun 2–6pm • ⓦ fodz.pl

Just outside the palace park, the newly-renovated **Old Synagogue** is a simple cream-coloured structure built in the 1760s on the site of an earlier wooden structure. The walls and ceiling are a mass of rich, colourful decoration including stucco bas-reliefs, frescoes, illustrated Hebrew prayers, zodiacal signs and false marble ornamentation. In the centre of the building stands the bimah, its cupola decorated with some striking frescoes of biblical tales and a memorable depiction of a leviathan consuming its own tail – a symbol for the coming of the Messiah – adorning the inner canopy.

ARRIVAL AND DEPARTURE	ŁAŃCUT
By train Łańcut's train station (hourly trains from Rzeszów; 15min) is a short taxi ride or a 2km walk north of the palace park entrance.	**By minibus** Rzeszów minibuses (every 30min–1hr; 25min) pick up and drop off on ul. Armii Krajowej, a 10min walk south of the palace park.

EATING

Zamkowa ul. Zamkowa 1 ☎ 17 225 2805. Old-school restaurant with loud wallpaper and starched napkins, occupying a wing of the palace and serving well-presented traditional Polish fish and pork dishes (mains 25–30zł).	Rosolis liqueurs, brewed by the local Polmos distillery (allegedly according to the Potocki family's old recipies) occupy pride of place on the drinks menu. Daily 11am–9pm.

Leżajsk

Thirty kilometres northeast of Rzeszów, the sleepy rural town of **LEŻAJSK** was once home to a sizeable Hassidic Jewish population, and the grave of Hassidic teacher Tzaddik Elimelech is today a major focus of pilgrimage. The town is also a Catholic spiritual centre of many centuries' standing, thanks to the presence of a Bernardine monastery on its northern outskirts.

Bernardine church and monastery

pl. Mariacki 8

The monumental **Bernardine church and monastery** (Sanktuarium i klasztor Bernardynów), 2km north of central Leżajsk, was built in the late 1670s to commemorate a celebrated series of miraculous appearances by the Virgin a century earlier. The cavernous church interior is a mass of Baroque decoration, with a huge gilded main altarpiece and a side altar (to the right) containing a miracle-working icon of the Madonna and Child. Pride of place, however, goes to the monster Baroque **organ** filling the back of the nave, one of the finest – and most famous – in Poland. With nearly six thousand pipes, and an organ case simply dripping with sculpted saints, angels and other fanciful creatures, the exquisitely decorated instrument produces a stunning sound more than capable of filling the building.

District Museum

ul. Mickiewicza 20A · May–Sept Mon, Wed & Fri 10am–4pm, Tues & Thurs 10am–6pm, Sat & Sun 1–7pm; Oct–April same times but closed Sat · 15zł · ☎ 17 240 2235, ⊕ muzeum-lezajsk.pl

Set back from Leżajsk's main street is the ochre **Staroszyński Palace**, where an extensive **district museum** (Muzeum Ziemi Leżajskiej) displays local archaeology, colourful wooden toys and a large multimedia display relating to the local brewing industry – the locally-made Leżajsk is one of Poland's tastiest beers, and it's well worth stocking up with a few bottles of the stuff at local shops before leaving.

Tzaddik Elimelech's tomb

Daily except Sat 8am–4pm; ring ☎ 604 536 914 if the gatekeeper isn't around.

Leżajsk was a major centre of the Hassidic movement, thanks in large part to local seventeenth-century teacher **Tzaddik Elimelech**, one of Hassidism's leading intellectual figures. The *tzaddik*'s tomb, enclosed by a cast-iron grille, lies in a whitewashed pavilion inside the Jewish cemetery, which spreads across a hillock just behind the Rynek. The tomb is regularly visited by Orthodox Jewish pilgrims, never more so than on Tzaddik Elimelech's anniversary which, according to the traditional Hebrew calendar, is on Adar 21 – a shifting date that usually falls in March.

ARRIVAL AND INFORMATION

LEŻAJSK

By train The train station is near the centre of town, midway between the monastery and the Rynek. There are three trains daily from Rzeszów (change at Przeworsk; 1hr 30min).
By bus Minibuses (hourly; 1hr 10min) from Rzeszów stop next to the train station.

Tourist information The Tourist and Cultural Information Centre is at ul. Mickiewicza 65 (Mon–Fri 9am–5pm; ☎ 17 785 1123, ⊕ citik.kultura.lezajsk.pl). It's well stocked with brochures and can help organize accommodation.

ACCOMMODATION AND EATING

U Braci Zygmuntów ul. Klasztorna 2e ☎ 17 242 0469, ⊕ hotel-lezajsk.pl. The most convenient place to stay, at the northern end of town near the monastery – small but quite comfortable. It also has a good restaurant serving everything from fried fish to *shashlik*-style skewer-kebabs. **140zł**

Jarosław

Fifty kilometres east of Rzeszów on the main road and rail line to the Ukrainian border, **JAROSŁAW** is one of the oldest towns in the country. Yaroslav the Wise, prince of Kiev, established a stronghold here some time in the eleventh century, and the town's position on major east–west trade routes led to its rapid development. Such was the importance of Jarosław's **Jewish population** that the Council of the Four Lands

(Polish Jewry's main consultative body) met regularly here during the seventeenth and eighteenth centuries. What remains of Jarosław's historic centre makes a half-day trip from Rzeszów or Przemyśl more than worthwhile.

The Rynek

Jarosław's focal point is the breezy, open central square where medieval fairs used to be held. The square is lined with the arcaded merchants' houses, most impressive of which is the **Orsetti Mansion** (Kamienica Orsettich) on the south side, built in the 1670s and featuring a beautifully decorated upper attic and a typically open, airy arcade. It's the home of the **town museum** (Muzeum Miasta; May–Sept Tues–Sat 9am–5pm, Sun 10am–5pm; Oct–Nov Tues–Fri 9am–3pm, Sat & Sun 10am–3pm; 7zł; ☎16 621 5437, ⓦmuzeum-jaroslaw.pl), which contains a substantial collection of Sarmatian portraits (see page 318), as well as weapons and period furniture.

Benedictine Abbey

ul. Benedyktyńska 5

Ten minutes' walk uphill to the north of Jarosław's town centre, the seventeenth-century **Benedictine Abbey** (Klasztor Sióstr Benedyktynek) centres on a skyline-defining twin-towered church, surrounded by red-brick fortifications that feature eight defensive towers. The church's so-called "Black Chapel" (Czarna kaplica) features a brick ceiling that looks like a mass of fused volcanic lava, the result of a fire started by retreating Germans in 1944.

ARRIVAL AND INFORMATION   JAROSŁAW

By bus and train The combined bus and train station, at the bottom of ul. Słowackiego, is a 15min walk southwest of the Rynek. Trains run hourly from Rzeszów (35–50min) and Przemyśl (30–45min), and there are also buses from Przemyśl (hourly; 55min).

Tourist information The tourist office at Rynek 5 (Mon, Sat & Sun 9am–5pm, Tues, Wed & Fri 8am–5pm, Thurs 8am–4pm; ☎16 624 8989, ⓦckip.jaroslaw.pl) has a wealth of information on the region.

EATING

Take Sushi Opolska 10 ☎533 533 544, ⓦtake-sushi. pl. A welcome change from the pork-and-potatoes fare on offer elsewhere, this place delivers accomplished oriental fare in casual-chic surroundings. Six-piece sets cost from 21zł. Mon–Sat 11am–10pm, Sun 2–10pm.

Przemyśl

Huddled on a hill above the River San, **PRZEMYŚL** is one of the most beguiling cities in eastern Poland. It served as both a key garrison town and an important spiritual centre in Habsburg times, and strolling through the church-filled old quarter can still feel like walking back through history to some far-flung corner of the Austro-Hungarian empire. Boasting an absorbing clutch of churches, museums and former military installations, the city is an ideal stop-off if you're heading towards Ukraine: the border is only 10km away.

Founded in the eighth century on the site of a prehistoric settlement, Przemyśl is the oldest city in southern Poland after Kraków, and an eternally important link in the trade routes from Poland to Ukraine. After the First Partition, Przemyśl became the third-biggest centre of the Austrian-ruled province of Galicia after Kraków and L'viv, a multi-faith city which was home to Catholic, Uniate and Orthodox bishops. After 1873 the Habsburgs turned Przemyśl into a major military strongpoint, building a huge ring of **fortifications** around the town – the crumbling remnants of which are increasingly popular as an offbeat tourist destination.

The Rynek

Przemyśl's Old Town centres on the busy, sloping **Rynek**, where the mid-eighteenth-century **Franciscan church** offers a florid demonstration of unbridled Baroque, including a wealth of sumptuous interior decoration and a fine columned facade.

Town Museum

Rynek 9 • Tues–Sat 9am–4pm, Sun noon–4pm • 10zł; free on Wed • ☎ 16 678 6501, ⓦ mnzp.pl

Occupying a sturdy town house, the **town museum** (Muzeum Historii Miasta Przemyśla) is something of a nostalgic tribute to nineteenth-century Przemyśl, with period interiors (complete with laboriously hand-painted Art Nouveau wall decorations), and a nice collection of Habsburg-era photographs.

National Museum of the Przemyśl Region

pl. Berka Joselewicza 1 • Tues–Sat 10am–4pm, Sun noon–3pm • 10zł; free on Thurs • ☎ 16 679 3000, ⓦ mnzp.pl

Slightly downhill from central Przemyśl, a boldly angular modern building provides an impressive new home to the **National Museum** of the Przemyśl Region (Muzeum Narodowe Ziemi Przemyskiej). The ground floor hosts a changing programme of themed exhibitions relating to regional or national history, while the upper storeys contain paintings by local artists and an assortment of antique furniture. There's an exhibit telling the story of Przemyśl Fortress, and a vibrant display of icons from the Carpathian region.

The Uniate Cathedral and Carmelite church

Uphill from the Rynek is Przemyśl's most evocative quarter, full of slanting streets overlooked by towering church belfries. Immediately behind the Franciscan church stands the seventeenth-century former Jesuit church, now the local **Uniate Cathedral**. Inside is a glittering iconostasis, displaying the full panoply of saints. Just up the hill is the **Carmelite church**, a fine late-Renaissance structure designed by Gelleazo Appiani in the early 1600s, with a sumptuous Baroque interior featuring an extraordinary pulpit shaped like a ship, complete with rigging.

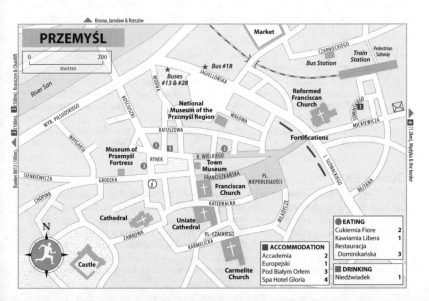

6

PRZEMYŚL FORTRESS

Beginning in the 1870s the Austrians set about turning Przemyśl into a major military strongpoint, constructing an inner ring of defensive positions in the immediate vicinity of the city, and an outer ring of 14 full-sized forts and 23 artillery bastions, pushing far out into the countryside. Accommodating a 150,000-strong garrison, the resulting **Przemyśl Fortress** (Twierdza Przemyśl) was intended to render Habsburg-ruled Galicia impregnable from Russian attack. With the outbreak of World War I, however, a relatively small Russian army simply surrounded Przemyśl and cut it off from supplies. Having eaten their way through their own cavalry horses, the fortress's defenders finally surrendered on March 22, 1915, due to lack of further food. The Austrians blew the forts up as they left, but enough of the system remains to make it a fascinating target for excursions. The _Twierdza Przemyśl_ **map**, available from the tourist office (see page 235), is a useful aid to exploration; otherwise pick up the 1:75,000 _Pogórze Przemyskie_ map from local bookshops.

One of the best-preserved installations is the **Salis Soglio** fort just outside the village of **Siedliska** (hourly minibus operated by Eurobus, from ulica Dworskiego in Przemyśl), 10km southeast of Przemyśl right by the Ukrainian border. A short walk east of the village, the fort's barrack blocks, powder magazines and ramparts are in good shape and are open to walkers. From Salis Soglio, you can follow a black-marked trail through rolling countryside to the remains of **Fort Borek**, 2km northeast, or **Fort Jaksmanice**, 4km west.

Another easily visited stretch of the fortress is near the village of **Bolestraszyce** (hourly bus from ulica Sportowa, one block north of Przemyśl bus station), 7km to Przemyśl's northwest, which is also the site of a major horticultural attraction. Buses drop off at **Bolestraszyce Arboretum** (May–Oct daily 10am–6pm; 10zł; ☎ 16 671 6425, ✺bolestraszyce.com.pl), an extensive botanical garden filled with trees and shrubs from around the world. Immediately to the east of the gardens, the ruins of **Fort San Rideau** provide ample opportunity to scramble around long-abandoned gun positions.

The Cathedral

Zamkowa 3 • Daily 10am–noon & 2–4pm

Roads twist their way up through Przemyśl's Old Town towards the **cathedral**, its sturdy 71m-high bell tower pointing the way. Remnants of the first twelfth-century rotunda can be seen in the crypt, and there's a fine Renaissance alabaster pietà to the right of the main altar, but Baroque dominates the interior, most notably in the Fredro family chapel.

The castle

Grounds open till sunset; tower Tues–Sun: April–Sept 10am–6pm; Oct–March 10am–4pm • 3zł

Up beyond the cathedral, a steeply climbing path leads through a park to the **castle**, the remains of the fourteenth-century construction built by King Kazimierz the Great and given a thorough Renaissance remodelling a century later. The castle's most striking architectural feature is the pair of newly renovated Renaissance towers, tubby cylinders topped with a ring of decidedly unmilitary-looking baubles. One of them can be scaled for a panoramic view.

Bunker 8813

ul. Piłsudskiego • Sat 2–6pm, Sun noon–6pm; other times by appointment • ☎ 505 077 838 or ☎ 530 068 480, ✺ projekt8813.pl

Set into the grassy riverbank just outside Przemyśl's _Accademia Hotel_, **Bunker 8813** is just one small surviving part of the **Molotov Line**, a series of fortifications stretching from the Baltic Sea to the Carpathians built by the Soviet Union following their occupation of eastern Poland in 1939. Restored by local enthusiasts, it is now a private museum containing a wealth of World-War II hardware. The bunker itself is an evocative place to ramble around, with concrete floors, iron doors and claustrophobic-looking living spaces.

ARRIVAL AND INFORMATION

PRZEMYŚL

By train Przemyśl's elegant Habsburg-era train station is a 10min walk northeast of the centre.
Destinations Jarosław (16 daily; 30–45min); Kiev, Ukraine (1 daily; 7hr 15min); Kraków (6 daily; 3hr 45min); L'viv, Ukraine (1 daily; 2hr); Rzeszów (12 daily; 1hr 15min–1hr 40min); Warsaw (1 daily; 7hr 20min).
By bus The bus station is on the far side of the tracks from the train station, to which it is linked by pedestrian underpass.

Destinations Jarosław (hourly; 55min); Lublin (1 daily; 4hr); L'viv, Ukraine (4 daily; 3hr–4hr 30min); Sanok (2 daily; 2hr).
Tourist information The tourist information office at ul. Grodzka 1 (mid-April to mid-Oct Mon–Fri 9am–5pm, Sat & Sun 10am–6pm; mid-Oct to mid-April Mon–Fri 9am–5pm, Sat 10am–2pm; ☏ 16 675 2163, ⓦ visit.przemysl.pl) is an excellent source of advice and has a good selection of local maps.

ACCOMMODATION

Accademia Wybrzeże J. Piłsudskiego 4 ☏ 16 676 1111, ⓦ hotelaccademia.pl; map page 233. Large, concrete lump on the riverbank just west of the centre, with bland but comfortable en suites. Small discount at weekends. 150zł
Europejski ul. Sowińskiego 4 ☏ 16 675 7100, ⓦ hotel-europejski.pl; map page 233. Small but acceptable en-suite rooms in a refurbished nineteenth-century building by the train station. 140zł
Pod Białym Orłem ul. Sanocka 13 ☏ 16 678 6107, ⓦ podbialymorlem.com.pl; bus #18; map page 233.

Medium-sized place occupying a futuristic (in a 1980s sort of way) villa, in a peaceful location 1.5km west along the river from the centre. The en-suite rooms are dated but tolerable, and the restaurant serves good home-cooked specialities. 130zł
Spa Hotel Gloria ul. Sybiraków 31 ☏ 16 675 0521, ⓦ hotelgloria.pl; map page 233. Part motel, part mock-castle, 1.5km east of the centre on the main road to L'viv. The en-suite rooms are plain but there's a decent breakfast spread, plus an on-site spa centre, small pool and sauna. 220zł

EATING AND DRINKING

★ **Cukiernia Fiore** ul. Kazimierza Wielkiego 17 B ☏ 16 675 1222, ⓦ cukierniafiore.pl; map page 233. Arguably the finest café in the Polish southeast, *Fiore* serves fantastic ice cream, an irresistible array of cakes and some pretty good coffee, too. Plonk yourself in the plush winter-garden-style interior, or opt for a table on the outdoor terrace. Daily 10am–8pm.
★ **Kawiarnia Libera** Rynek 26 ☏ 690 440 683, ⓦ face book.com/Kawiarnia.Libera; map page 233. Located in the back room of the Libera bookshop, this comfortable café is perfect for tea and coffee breaks as well as relaxing

evening beers. It features bare floorboards, old armchairs, bookcases and the kind of domestic bric-a-brac that might excite 1950s retro freaks, and there's a cute summer terrace overlooking a small patch of garden. Daily 10am–10pm.
Restauracja Dominikańska pl. Dominikański 3 ☏ 16 678 2075; map page 233. A consistently reliable venue for quality Polish cuisine, with excellently-presented dishes like pork fillets with mushrooms (28zł) or grilled pike perch (38zł). The interior is on the smart-but-sterile side, so grab one of the four square-side outdoor tables if you can. Daily 10am–10pm.

DRINKING

Niedźwiadek Rynek 1 ☏ 16 678 4994; map page 233. Jazz pub located in a suite of Baroque rooms in one wing of the town hall. Although primarily a drinking venue, there's a respectable menu of pork-chop and roast-chicken mains

(from around 22zł). In summer, there's a popular stretch of wooden-bench outdoor eating on the side of the Rynek. Daily 11am–midnight.

Sanok and around

The main routes south from Przemyśl and Rzeszów towards the Bieszczady head through a rustic landscape of wooded foothills to **SANOK**, a medium-sized provincial town perched on a hilltop above the San River. Best known within Poland for the Autosan vehicle factory (which sadly no longer makes the cutely old-fashioned cucumber-shaped buses it was famous for), Sanok is figuring ever larger as a tourist destination, not least because of its spectacular **skansen**. Extensive transport links make it a good base from which to explore Poland's far southeast, especially the extraordinary wooden church at **Ulucz** and the Jewish-heritage sites at nearby **Lesko**.

The Old Town

Sanok's historic centre revolves around the attractive hilltop Rynek. There are several fine chapels in the seventeenth-century **Franciscan Church** (Kościół Franciszkanów), on the edge of the Rynek, while just to the west on plac św. Michała is the original fourteenth-century **parish church** – destroyed in a fire in 1782 and rebuilt a century later – which hosted the wedding in 1417 of King Władysław Jagiełło and Elżbieta Granowska (his third, her fourth). A short way down the hill is the **Orthodox cathedral**, an imposing late eighteenth-century edifice with a fine iconostasis (open for Sunday services at 10.30am and 5pm, but at other times you can peer in through the vestibule).

The castle and Sanok Icon Museum

ul. Zamkowa 2 • April–Sept Mon 8am–noon, Tues–Sun 9am–5pm; Oct–May Mon 8am–noon, Tues & Wed 9am–5pm, Thurs–Sun 9am–3pm • 15zł • ☎ 13 463 0609, ⓦ muzeum.sanok.pl

Perched on a low hill north of the Rynek is the **castle**, a sixteenth-century construction built on the site of the original twelfth-century fortress, which guarded the main highway linking the southern Carpathians to the Baltic. Today the castle houses the fabulous **Sanok Icon Museum**, Poland's largest collection of Ukrainian, Boyk and Lemko icons. Though most of the pieces date from the sixteenth and seventeenth centuries, the oldest come from the mid-1300s. After the expected Madonnas, the most common subject is St Nicholas, always clad in luxuriant robes. On the top floor

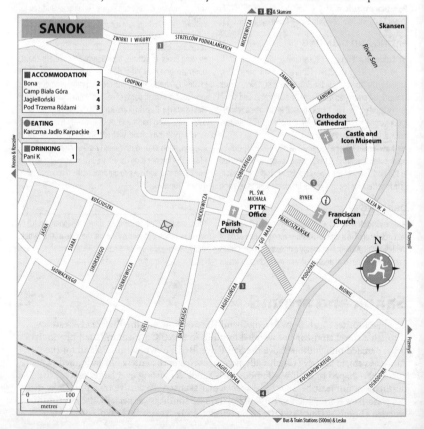

SANOK

■ ACCOMMODATION
Bona	2
Camp Biała Góra	1
Jagielloński	4
Pod Trzema Różami	3

● EATING
| Karczma Jadło Karpackie | 1 |

■ DRINKING
| Pani K | 1 |

Skansen

River San

Orthodox Cathedral

Castle and Icon Museum

PL. ŚW. MICHAŁA

PTTK Office

Parish Church

RYNEK

Franciscan Church

N

0   100
metres

Bus & Train Stations (500m) & Lesko

BOYKOS, LEMKOS AND OPERATION VISTULA

The Carpathian valleys of southeastern Poland form the traditional heartland of the **Boykos** (Бойко) and **Lemkos** (Лемко), both groups descended from nomadic shepherds who settled in the **Bieszczady** and **Beskid Niski** regions between the thirteenth and fifteenth centuries. Geographically speaking, the Boykos populated the eastern Bieszczady, while the Lemkos inhabited the western Bieszczady, the Beskid Niski and part of the Beskid Sądecki. Speaking dialects similar to modern Ukrainian, the Boykos and Lemkos led a life separate from that of the lowland Poles. Both groups belonged initially to the Orthodox faith, but many converted to the **Uniate (or "Greek Catholic") Church**, created in 1595 in order to place the non-Catholic communities of the southeast under firmer Polish control.

For centuries, these farming communities lived more or less peacefully. Their real troubles began towards the end of World War II, when units of the **Ukrainian Resistance Army (UPA)** were forced out of western Ukraine by the Red Army and took refuge in the hills of southeastern Poland. Like many anti-communist groups of the period, the UPA assumed that worsening relations between the Soviet Union and the West would ultimately lead to some kind of American-British invasion. Sustained by this forlorn hope, UPA guerrillas held out against Soviet-supported Polish forces for two years, famously assassinating the regional commander, General Karol Świerczewski, at Jabłonki in March 1947.

Suspecting that the UPA was sustained by Boyko and Lemko support, the Polish authorities decided to have the entire population of the Bieszczady and Beskid Niski deported. In a notorious operation codenamed **Operation Vistula** (Akcja Wisła), whole villages were emptied and their inhabitants resettled – either (in the case of many Lemkos) to the former German territories of the north and west, or (for most of the Boykos) to the Soviet Union. As a result, the Polish Carpathians have remained seriously depopulated to this day. Many villages evacuated in 1947 have simply disappeared, their crumbling buildings swallowed up by grass and shrubs. Nowadays Boykos and Lemkos are free to settle where they wish, but the sense of uprooted community still remains. Nowhere is this more evident than in the religious field: over 250 Uniate churches were taken away from the Lemkos in the wake of 1947, and given to the Catholic or Orthodox communities instead. Only a handful have since been returned.

6

of the castle is the **Beksiński Gallery**, displaying a selection of the imaginative canvases – part Dali-surrealist, part *Lord of the Rings* stage set – of the noted local artist, Zdzisław Beksiński (1929–2005).

Sanok Skansen

ul. Rybickiego 3, 2km north of central Sanok • Daily: April & Oct 9am–4pm; May–Sept 8am–6pm; Nov–March 8am–2pm • 15zł • ☎ 13 463 1672, ⓦ skansen.sanok.pl

Sanok's greatest draw is its **skansen**, spread along the northern bank of the River San. This open-air ethnographic museum, the largest and best in Poland, brings together examples of the different styles of all the region's main ethnic groups – Boykos, Lemkos, Dolinianie ("Inhabitants of the Valley") and Pogórzanie ("Uplanders").

Specimens of every kind of country building have been moved and reassembled here: smithies, inns, granaries, windmills, pigsties and churches, and for added verisimilitude you'll find storks, goats and other animals wandering about. A huge area near the entrance features a fabulous recreation of a nineteenth-century **market square**, with Jewish merchants' houses rescued from formerly bustling market towns like Ustrzyki Dolne and Jaćmierz. Up on the hillside in the **Boyko section** a couple of typical eighteenth-century wooden churches (one with a complete iconostasis) nestle peacefully in the shade of the trees. The neighbouring **Lemko section** has a good set of farmhouses, while the **Dolinianie area** features a quaint old fire station, complete with nineteenth-century fire engines, a church and a fine range of rural dwellings. In the **Pogórzanie section** there's a nineteenth-century school building holding some amazing old textbooks and report cards; note too the portrait of Kaiser Franz Joseph behind the teacher's desk.

ARRIVAL AND INFORMATION SANOK

By train The train station is a 15min walk southeast of the town centre. Trains run to Krosno (2 daily; 50min).

By bus The bus station is adjacent to the train station; most buses from here will take you up to the main square. Buses to/from Krosno pick up and drop off on ul. Dorcowa in front of the train station.

Destinations Cisna (July & Aug 8 daily, rest of year 3 daily; 2hr); Kraków (5 daily; 4hr 20min); Krosno (12 daily; 1hr);

Lesko (12 daily; 25min); Przemyśl (2 daily; 2hr); Rzeszów (4 daily; 1hr 30min); Ustrzyki Dolne (4 daily; 1hr 10min); Ustrzyki Górne (July & Aug 8 daily, Sept–June 3 daily; 2hr 30min); Wetlina (July & Aug 8 daily; Sept–June 3 daily; 2hr).

Tourist information The tourist office at Rynek 14 (Mon–Fri 9am–5pm; May–Sept also Sat & Sun 9am–1pm; ☎ 13 463 6060, ⓦ sanok.pl) has plentiful brochures and can help find accommodation throughout the area.

ACCOMMODATION

Bona ul. Białogórska 47 ☎ 13 464 6505, ⓦ bonasanok. pl; map page 236. Recently built hotel on the northern fringes of town, right opposite the *skansen*, that looks a bit like an oversized alpine chalet. Neat en suites come with TV, and some have balconies overlooking the San River. **200zł**

Camp Biała Góra ul. Ogrodowa 15/5 ☎ 13 463 2818, ⓦ campsanok.pl; map page 236. Campsite with pitches and A-frame bungalows on a hilltop overlooking the river, next to the *skansen*. Camping **45zł**, two-person bungalows **60zł**

Jagielloński ul. Jagiellońska 49 ☎ 13 463 1208,

ⓦ hoteljagiellonski.pl; map page 236. Comfortable, intimate hotel midway between the town centre and the station with spacious en suites with TV, and a restaurant serving excellent Polish fare. **180zł**

Pod Trzema Różami ul. Jagiellońska 13 ☎ 13 463 0922, ⓦ podtrzemarozami.pl; map page 236. Plain but adequate en suites in a good central position – a useful mid-priced fallback if the *Jagielloński* is full. A handful of triples and quads will suit families or groups. The hotel's restaurant does passable pizzas. **160zł**

EATING

Karczma Jadło Karpackie Rynek 12 ☎ 13 464 6700, ⓦ karczmasanok.pl; map page 236. Folksy restaurant decked out in wooden benches and sheepskins, offering Carpathian treats such as *hreczanyki* (pork-and-buckwheat

burgers; 26zł) and delicious *fuczki* (pancakes made from grated potato, sauerkraut and carrot), washed down with draught Leżajsk beer. Daily 10am–10pm.

DRINKING AND NIGHTLIFE

Pani K ul. Strzelców Podhalańskich 1 ☎ 501 580 252, ⓦ facebook.com/klub.panik; map page 236. Mildly

arty cellar bar which organizes occasional gigs, DJ events and film projections. Often takes a break in Aug.

Ulucz

If you have your own transport, the wooden church in **ULUCZ**, a tiny village 20km north of Sanok on the River San, is worth seeking out. Built in 1510, it's the oldest, and among the finest, of the Boyko *cerkwie* (as Orthodox and Uniate churches are called) located within Polish territory; others of similar vintage are all in Ukraine. A graceful, well-proportioned building poised on a hilltop, it has a large bulbous dome, a fine Baroque iconostasis and mural paintings of the Passion and Crucifixion. The key is kept in a house marked by a sign at the village entrance.

Lesko

A tranquil town in the northern foothills of the Bieszczady **LESKO** was an important centre of **Jewish culture** before World War II and still harbours a compelling handful of Jewish-related sights.

The former synagogue

ul. Berka Joselewicza 16 • Tues–Sun 10am–5pm • 5zł • ☎ 13 469 6649, ⓦ bit.ly/LeskoFormerSynagogue

Just north of Lesko's Rynek stands the **former synagogue**, a solid-looking Renaissance structure that was originally part of the town's defensive system. The vivacious, finely sculptured facade is emblazoned with a quotation from the Torah. Damaged in wartime, the building was reconstructed in the early 1960s, and is now an **art gallery**.

A small display in the entrance hall has some prewar photos of the synagogue, records of local families murdered by the Nazis and a detailed list of the location and size of Jewish communities throughout southeastern Poland.

Jewish cemetery

Immediately downhill from Lesko's town centre, the **Jewish cemetery** is one of the most beautiful and evocative in the whole country. Hidden from a distance by the trees, the steps up from the roadside (the Star of David on the rust-coloured gate tells you you're at the right entrance) take you up through a tangled knot of tree trunks and sprawling undergrowth to the hilltop cemetery site, around which are scattered about two thousand gravestones, the oldest dating back to the early 1500s. As in other major surviving cemeteries there's a wealth of architectural styles in evidence: note particularly the numerous ornately decorated Baroque tablets, featuring seven-branched candelabra, animal motifs and often a pair of hands reaching up in prayer from the top of the stone. It's the setting as much as the stones that makes this cemetery so memorable, a powerful testimony to centuries of rural Jewish presence.

6

ARRIVAL AND INFORMATION   LESKO

By bus Lesko's bus station is on the Sanok road, about 1km downhill from the main Rynek. There are regular buses to and from Sanok (12 daily; 25min).

Tourist information Situated beside the town hall, the tourist office (Mon–Sat 8am–5pm; ☎ 13 469 6695,

☺ bcit@lesko.pl) has a wealth of leaflets on the region and details of private rooms in farmhouses (*agroturystyka*) in nearby villages – although you'll need your own transport to get to these.

The Bieszczady

Of all the ranges that make up the Polish Carpathians, the **Bieszczady** are undeniably the most beautiful. Tucked into the far southeastern corner of the country, they are characterized by the mountaintop meadows known as **połoniny**, where grasses can grow beyond waist height. The *połoniny* often take the form of long undulating ridges, with exhilarating views opening up on either side. Seriously depopulated as a result of Operation Vistula in 1947 (see page 237), the Bieszczady have retained their unspoilt nature, with the diverse fauna including **black storks**, far rarer than their ubiquitous white relatives, and fifty-odd **brown bears**, as well as numerous **raptors, wolves, lynx** and even **bison**, which were reintroduced here in the 1960s. Much of the area is in the **Bieszczady National Park**.

The highest peaks in the region, at around 1300m, won't present many **hiking** problems as long as you're well equipped. Like all mountain regions, however, **weather** changes quickly, particularly on the exposed *połoniny*, where terrific storms can come at a moment's notice throughout the year. The best **map** for hikers is the green *Bieszczady Mapa Turystczyna* (1:65,000), published by *euromapa* and available throughout the region.

The best bases to aim for are the valley-bottom settlements of **Uztrzyki Górne** and **Wetlina**, both of which offer access to Połonina Caryńska and Połonina Wetlińska, two of the most starkly beautiful summits in the region. In the more densely wooded western Bieszczady, the village of **Cisna** is known for both its cosy B&Bs and the chance to ride on the Bieszczady **forest railway**.

GETTING AROUND

By bus Getting around the Bieszczady is easy enough in July and August, with several buses a day plying a circuit that takes in Sanok, Ustrzyki Górne, Wetlina and Cisna. Outside

this period there may be only one or two buses linking the Ustrzyki Górne–Wetlina–Cisna parts of the route, and you'll have to plan your itinerary carefully as a result.

INFORMATION

USTRZYKI DOLNE
Tourist office Rynek 16 (Mon–Fri 8am–4pm; ☎ 13 471 1130, ⓦ cit.ustrzyki-dolne.pl).
National Park Information Centre & Museum ul. Bełska 7 (Mon–Fri 8am–4pm; ☎ 13 461 1091, ⓦ bdpn.pl).

LUTOWISKA
National Park Information Centre Lutowiska 2 (May–Sept Mon–Fri 7am–5pm, Sat 9am–3pm; Oct–April Mon–Fri 7am–3pm; ☎ 13 461 0350, ⓦ bdpn.pl).

Lutowiska

On the way into the park at the old market town of **LUTOWISKA** you'll see makeshift barracks and drilling rigs, signs of the oil industry that has developed here sporadically since the last century. Up until 1939, more than half the residents of this remote area were Jews, and the abandoned **Jewish cemetery** east of the main road contains several hundred tombstones from the nineteenth and twentieth centuries. Near the village church a **monument** commemorates the more than six hundred local Jews shot here by the Nazis in June 1942.

Ustrzyki Górne

Spread out along the bottom of a peaceful river valley and surrounded by the peaks of the Bieszczady, **USTRZYKI GÓRNE** has an end-of-the-world feel to it. The final destination for most buses heading into the Bieszczady, it's little more than a bus stop girdled by snack bars and holiday villas, and there's nothing to do here but **hike**: luckily, well-marked trails start right next to the bus stop, getting you up onto the forest-carpeted hillsides within a matter of minutes (see page 241).

BIESZCZADY REGION

WALKS ON POŁONINA CARYŃSKA AND POŁONINA WETLIŃSKA

Usztryki Górne is the perfect point from which to launch yourself onto the Bieszczady's famous *połoniny*, with the **Połonina Carynska**, a two-hour climb to the west, offering an immediate taste of the Bieszczady's unique landscape. Once above the treeline and onto the grassy shoulders of the *połonina*, marvellous views open up on either side.

From the summit of Caryńska you can follow the ridge west, descending to meet the Ustrzyki–Wetlina road before ascending again onto the **Połonina Wetlińska**, another long ridge offering great views. On the eastern shoulder of the *połonina* is the **Chatka Puchatka mountain hut** (☎ 502 472 893, ⓦ bieszczady.net.pl/chatkapuchatka), a legendary refreshments stop with fantastic views, which sells cold and hot drinks as well as snacks of the crisps-and-chocolate-bar type; there are twenty beds if you want to stay the night (16zł; bring your own sleeping bag) – there's no electricity or running water but the ambience is wonderful and there's great home-cooked food.

From the hut the ridge-top walk heads westward to the summit of the Połonina Wetlińska, the 1256m-high **Roh**. Here you can savour yet more amazing vistas before descending to Wetlina village (see page 242), where you can book yourself into a hotel or catch a bus back to Ustrzyki Górne (3 daily; 30min).

Approaching Połonina Wetlińska **from Wetlina** is fairly simple, with a marked path behind the *Chata Wędrowca* restaurant (see page 242) leading up to the Przełecz Orlowicza saddle (1099m) in about two hours – the *Chatka Puchatka* hut (see above) is a further two hours to the east.

6

ARRIVAL AND DEPARTURE — USTRZYKI GÓRNE

By bus Ustrzyki Górne is served by summer-only buses from Kraków (July–Sept 4 daily; 7hr) and by buses on the Sanok–Cisna–Wetlina–Ustrzyki Górne–Lutowiska– Ustrzyki Dolne–Sanok loop (July & Aug 8 daily, Sept–June 3 daily). Ustrzyki Górne is 1hr 30min from Sanok, 30min from Wetlina.

ACCOMMODATION AND EATING

Accommodation choices in Ustrzyki Górne are limited, and there's a better range of **places to stay** on the far side of the park in Wetlina (see page 242) and Cisna (see page 242). There's a huddle of **restaurants** near the bus stop, all basically similar setups, specializing in the local trout and with outdoor seating. Ustrzyki Górne village shop has a basic range of food but attracts a devoted band of idlers with its plentiful supplies of Leżajsk beer.

Hotel Górski and Campsite ☎ 13 461 0604, ⓦ hotel-pttk.pl. Gloomy but comfortable PTTK-run hotel in a good riverside location at the north end of the village, with sparsely furnished en suites and amenities such as a sauna and a swimming pool. The campsite offers two- and four-person chalets as well as tent space. Hotel doubles 190zł, camping 40zł, two-person chalets 100zł

Wołostate and around

Seven kilometres south of Ustrzyki Górne, **WOŁOSTATE** is an important trail-head for hikes to the east, and the starting point for ascents of **Tarnica** (1346m), a typically grass-topped *połonina* standing a two-hour walk to the east. From here there's a mouth-watering range of up-and-down *połonina*-top hikes, with **Krzemien** (1335m) and the long ridge of the **Bukowe Berdo** (1213) lying to the northeast; and **Halicz** (1333m) and **Rozsypaniec** (1280m) to the southeast. Either would make a feasible day's hike from Wołosate; the really fit could do an outing from Ustrzyki to Krzemien and back in a day.

The Hucul Horse Centre

Wielka pętla bieszczadzka 2 • Daily 9am–5pm • ☎ 13 461 0650, ✉ zhkh@bdpn.pl

Wołosate is home to the **Bieszczady National Park Hucul Horse Centre** (Zachowawcza Hodowla Konia Huculskiego or ZHKH), a major breeding centre for the *hucul*, a stocky thick-necked horse hailing from the eastern Carpathians. There's a full menu of *hucul*-riding excursions: book in advance to enjoy anything from a 45-minute ride on a *hucul* in the paddock (30zł) to a day-long excursion in the surrounding hills (minimum 4 people; 200zł each).

Wetlina

Sixteen kilometres west of Ustrzyki Górne, the long, roadside-hugging village of **WETLINA** is one of the best places to stay in the region, with easy acccess to *połonina* walks (see page 241) and a good range of accommodation. It's also the culinary capital of the Bieszczady, with two adjacent restaurants vying with the countryside for your attention.

ARRIVAL AND DEPARTURE WETLINA

By bus Summer-only buses from Kraków to Ustrzykli Górne (July–Sept 4 daily; 7hr) pass through Wetlina on the way. Wetlina is also served by buses on the Sanok– Cisna–Wetlina–Ustrzyki Górne–Lutowiska–Ustrzyki Dolne–Sanok loop (July & Aug 8 daily, Sept–June 3 daily). **Wetlina is** 2hr from Sanok, 30min from **Ustrzyki Górne**.

ACCOMMODATION

Chaty w starym Siole Smerek 12 ☎ 664 273 776, ⓦ chatywsiole.pl. Five timber buildings set around the *W starym Siole* restaurant (see below) at the western end of Wetlina, each with traditional furnishings and modern conveniences. Can be rented by two to seven people, depending on availability. Two-person cabin 200zł

Cudne Manowce ☎ 501 536 599, ⓦ cudnemanowce. com.pl. Lovely timber house in meadow territory uphill from the main road and well-placed for walking up onto the *połonina*. Two- to four-person apartments come with timber balconies and great views. 220zł

Leśny Dwór ☎ 13 468 4654, ⓦ lesnydwor.bieszczady. pl/wetlina. This family-run hotel uphill from the main road (well-signed from the western end of the village) is one of the best places to stay in the Bieszczady, with carefully furnished rooms, good home cooking and a small library of local-interest books. Half board. 320zł

EATING AND DRINKING

★ **Baza Ludzi z Mgły** Wetlina 82. Thirsty hikers tend to congregate in the "Basecamp for the People of the Fog", a legendary offbeat bar in the middle of the village. With a roomy, timbered interior, a fantastic range of bottled beers and occasional live gigs in summer, this is a hard place to pull yourself away from. Usually open from 6pm.

★ **Chata Wędrowca** Wetlina. Set back slightly from the main road at the western end of Wetlina, the "Wayfarer's Cabin" is renowned for a local-meets-global menu that draws on local lamb, mountain trout and marinated meats. The *Chata's naleśnik gigant z jagodami* (gigantic blueberry pancake) has become something of a local trademark, and there is a wide range of bottled Slovak beers on offer, too. May–Oct daily noon–10pm.

W Starym Siole Wetlina ☎ 503 124 654, ⓦ staresiolo. com. Occupying a historic nineteenth-century building right beside the *Chata Wędrowca*, W Starym Siole is widely known for its own-recipe lentil- and bean-filled *pierogi*, although grilled sausages, lamb and steak are also excellent. There is a good range of bottled beers, and what must be the best wine list east of Kraków. May to mid-Oct daily 1–10pm.

Cisna and around

West of Wetlina the main road winds its way over the Przysłup pass before descending to **CISNA**, an engagingly rustic village with a burgeoning B&B industry. Largely emptied by the deportations of 1947, the village re-emerged fifty years later as a major beneficiary of the Bieszczady tourist boom. A large graffiti-covered monument near the main T-junction commemorates Cisna's role in the 1945–47 civil war, when the UPA (see page 237) had one of their main bases nearby. Cisna is the starting point for several easy-going **hikes**: the three-hour southbound ascent to the border-hugging **Okrąglik** (1101m) is the pick of the bunch, offering fine views of the rippling Slovak Carpathians as you approach the summit.

THE FOREST RAILWAY

Three kilometres west of Cisna, **Majdan** is the main boarding point for the **Bieszczady forest railway** (*kolejka leśna*; ☏ 13 468 6335, ⓦ kolejka.bieszczady.pl), a narrow-gauge line originally built for the local logging industry and nowadays one of the most popular tourist attractions in the region. The diesel-powered train, accompanied by a string of open-sided carriages, operates two short stretches of track from Majdan: one running 20km east to the mountain pass of **Przysłup**, calling at Cisna on the way (May, June & Sept Sat & Sun 9.30am; July & Aug daily 9.30am & 1.30pm); the other running about 30km west to **Balnica** (May, June & Sept Sat & Sun 1pm; July & Aug daily 10am, 1pm & 3.30pm). **Tickets** cost 24–26zł return, and **steam trains** run on some services in summer (July & Aug Tues & Fri). Much of the route is through hillside forests filled with a gloriously rich and diverse flora, the beautiful views over the valleys adding a touch of mountain thrill to the experience.

6

ARRIVAL AND INFORMATION   CISNA

By bus Cisna is served by Kraków–Ustrzyki Górne buses (July–Sept 4 daily; 6hr) and by most Sanok–Ustrzyki Górne buses (July & Aug 8 daily, Sept–June 3 daily; 1hr 30min).

Tourist information The tourist office, in the centre of town (June–Aug Mon–Fri 8am–8pm, Sat 8am–6pm, Sun 9am–5pm; Sept–May Mon–Fri 8am–6pm, Sat 8am–4pm; ☏ 13 468 6465), has information on B&B options, as does the town website (ⓦ cisna.pl; under "Noclegi").

Bike hire There's a summer-only bike-hire outlet in Cisna (40zł per day) near the main T-junction.

ACCOMMODATION

Przystanek Cisna Cisna 59 ☏ 696 038 595, ⓦ przystanek cisna.pl. Cosy pension in a traditional wooden house a short distance uphill from the tourist office, run by an English-speaking family and serving good vegetarian-only meals. Half-board. **250zł**

Tramp Cisna 118 ☏ 507 947 840, ⓦ bieszczadytramp. pl. Campsite right in the centre of the village, beside the stream. Tent and bike rental available. **30zł**

Troll Cisna 86 ☏ 792 015 254, ⓦ bieszczadytroll.pl.

Timber-built twelve-room pension in the centre of the village, owned by a Polish family who lived in Norway and brought back a Scandinavian taste for bright, clean rooms with lots of wood. **150zł**

Wołosan Cisna 87 ☏ 13 468 6373, ⓦ wolosan.pl. A thirty-room hotel and congress centre located amid meadows at the northern end of the village, offering bland but comfortable en suites with TV. **170zł**

EATING AND DRINKING

Karczma Lemkowyna ☏ 696 062 589, ⓦ lemkowyna. pl. Occupying a log-built house set back slightly from Cisna's main T-junction, this melodramatically folksy place with folk-attired wait-staff does a decent job of serving up Polish staples, with plenty of local variations of *pierogi*. Daily 10am–9pm.

★ **Siekierezada** Cisna 92 ☏ 13 468 6466, ⓦ siekiere zada.pl. Named after Edward Stachura's novel about

hard-living, hard-drinking forest folk, this bar decorated with wood-carved demons and iron chains is something of a cult destination. Providing you can avoid the camera-toting trippers on summer weekends, it's a fine place to sink a few beers after a hard day in the hills. Jazz, rock and blues concerts take place throughout the summer season. Daily 10am–11pm.

The Beskid Niski

West from Sanok the main road, closely tracked by the slow rail line, heads towards the provincial capital of **Gorlice** through the Wisłok valley, a pleasant pastoral route, with a succession of wooden villages in the hills of the **Beskid Niski** to the south. The main stops on the way to Gorlice are the medieval centres of **Krosno** and **Biecz**.

Krosno and around

At the heart of the country's richest oil reserves, **KROSNO** is the **petroleum** centre of Poland and also a major glassware producer. Prior to the discovery of oil, which

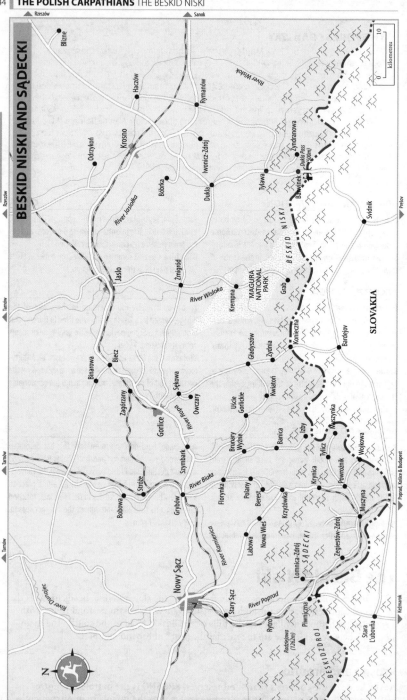

helped the town grow wealthy in the late 1800s, Krosno had quite a record of mercantile prosperity: a favourable position on medieval trade routes meant it rapidly became one of the wealthiest Renaissance-era towns in the country, as evidenced by the Italiananate merchants' houses lining the Rynek. With a brace of worthwhile museums and a café-lined main square, Krosno makes a pleasantly laid-back touring base for this part of Poland.

The area around Krosno holds a number of worthy diversions, including a museum devoted to the local oil industry in **Bóbrka**, and a *skansen* focusing on Lemko architecture in **Zyndranowa**.

6

Glass Heritage Centre

ul. Blich 2 (entrance on the northeastern corner of the Rynek) • Obligatory guided tours start on the hour every hour: July & Aug Mon–Sat 10am–7pm, Sun 11am–pm; Sept–June Mon–Sat 9am–5pm, Sun 11am–5pm; last admission 2hr before closing • 12zł, or 19zł including Threshold Cellars • ☎ 13 444 0031, ⊛ miastoszkla.pl

Glassmaking in Krosno goes back to the sixteenth century, although it was the construction of a modern (and still highly successful) factory in 1920 that really transformed Krosno into the capital of Polish glass. It's a status celebrated by the **Glass Heritage Centre** (Centrum Dziedzictwa Szkła), which offers a highly colourful display of glassmaking through the ages (including some great examples of classy Polish design), and a tour of the glass workshops, where you can observe the production of glass in real time. For a few extra złoty you can also visit the so-called "**Threshold Cellars**" underneath the town square, which contain an audio-visual display devoted to the history of glassmaking.

The Franciscan church

ul. Franciszkańska • Mon–Sat 9am–5pm, Sun 2–5pm

Just off Krosno's Rynek is the brick-facaded late Gothic **Franciscan church** (Kościół Franciszkanów), where the town's most famous monument, the Baroque **Oświęcim family chapel** occupies the north aisle. A sumptuously ornate piece, the chapel was designed by Italian architect Falconi in 1647–48 following the death of Anna of Oświęcim, whose full-sized portrait hangs on the wall, next to that of her half-brother Stanisław. Their placement together is more befitting husband and wife than half-siblings, a fact that helped fuel a tale of incestuous love between the pair. According to legend, Stanisław's boyish affection for Anna grew into a mature passion, leading him to abandon his position as courtier in Warsaw to petition the pope for a dispensation. When he returned, his request granted, Anna, overwhelmed with joy, expired, and Stanisław soon followed, dying of sorrow. In fact, there was no trip to Rome, and Stanisław returned to court soon after his beautiful half-sister succumbed to fever, from where he made arrangements for the raising of the chapel, "for worship and glory of God and, along with that, my beloved sister".

The parish church and around

ul. Piłsudskiego

Just off Krosno's Rynek to the north, the Gothic **parish church** is almost overflowing with treasures and curiosities. Note especially the fine, late Gothic crucifix above the spirited Baroque altar, the ceiling polychromy, the richly carved choir stalls, the massive incense burner and, to the right of the altar, an exquisite fifteenth-century *Coronation of Our Lady* from Kraków. Outside the church is a statue of **Robert Portius** (c.1600–61), a native of Dalkieth in Scotland, who made a fortune in the Krosno wine trade and also led the town's defence against an invasion by Transylvanians and Cossacks in 1657.

Subcarpathian Museum

ul. Piłsudskiego 16 • Tues–Fri 9am–4pm, Sat & Sun 10am–5pm; Nov–April closes 3pm • 10zł • ☎ 13 432 1376, ⓦ muzeum.krosno.pl

Housed in the sixteenth-century former bishops' palace, the highlight of the **Subcarpathian Museum** (Muzeum Podkarpacie) is a large and lovingly polished display of early kerosene lamps, the revolutionary device invented by Ignacy Łukasiewicz, the local pharmacist who sank what's claimed to be the world's first oil well in the village of Bóbrka, 10km south of town (see page 224). There's also a collection of paintings, with a series of attractive studies of Krosno by Matejko pupil Seweryn Bieszczad (1852–1923).

Handicraft Museum

ul. Piłsudskiego 19 • May–Oct Mon–Fri 9am–8pm, Sat & Sun10am–4pm; Nov–April Mon–Fri 8am–3.30pm, Sat 10am–2pm • 5zł; free on Sat • ☎ 13 474 8201, ⓦ muzeumrzemiosla.pl

Across the street from the Subcarpathian Museum, Krosno's excellent **Handicraft Museum** (Muzeum Rzemiosła) is full of surprises, including an intact barber shop from the 1920s, still in use until a few years ago. Also here is a seventeenth-century iron chest that the staff will let you open, and a wealth of old lathes, looms and other tools.

ARRIVAL AND INFORMATION   KROSNO

By train The train station, 1.5km west of the town centre, only receives a handful of services – including from Sanok (2 daily; 50min) – and the building is frequently closed. To get to the hilltop Old Town, head down ul. Kolejowa and turn right onto the main ul. Piłsudskiego.

By bus and minibus The bus station is adjacent to the train station.

Destinations Barwinek (6 daily; 50min); Dukla (every 15–

30min; 30min); Haczów (hourly; 30min); Kraków (hourly; 3–4hr); Rzeszów (every 30–45min; 1hr 30min); Sanok (12 daily; 1hr); Ustrzyki Górne (July & Aug 2 daily; 3hr).

Tourist information Krosno's helpful tourist office is at Rynek 5 (May–Oct Mon–Fri 9am–6pm, Sat & Sun 9am–4pm; Nov–April Mon–Fri 9am–4pm, Sat 10am–2pm; ☎ 13 432 7707, ⓦ krosno.pl).

ACCOMMODATION, EATING AND DRINKING

Hotel Portius ul. Bursaki 29a ☎ 13 474 8080, ⓦ hotel portius.pl. Modern three-star next to the Portius shopping centre, a short walk east of the Old Town, offering small but smart en suites and plenty of parking space. **210zł**

Hotel Śnieżka ul. Lewakowskiego 22 ☎ 13 432 3449, ⓦ hotelsniezka.pl. Intimate, civilized hotel in a characterful nineteenth-century old villa a couple of minutes' walk southeast of the bus station. The cute wood-panelled restaurant serves solid Polish staples, with daily specials clocking in at 15–18zł. Restaurant noon–10pm. **170zł**

★ **Klubokawiarnia Ferment** ul. Portiusa 4 ☎ 13 420 3242. Welcoming café-bar mixing chic comforts and

grungey-underground stylings in equal measure. There's a small but tempting menu of sandwiches, pastas and quiches, plus local-brewed Wojkowka beer and several other craft ales. Mon–Thurs & Sun 10am–11pm, Fri & Sat 10am–midnight.

Posmakuj Rynek 24 ☎ 533 540 175, ⓦ posmakujkrosno. pl. Good food served up in an evocative brick cellar – or on the square-side terrace in the summer months. Popular favourites include burgers (26zł) and decent pizzas (25–28zł), although there's also plenty in the way of Polish soups, *pierogi* and trout. Mon–Thurs & Sun noon–10pm, Fri & Sat noon–11pm.

Haczów Church

Daily 8am–4pm • Donation requested • ☎ 13 439 10 12, ⓦ parafiahaczow.pl • Minibus from Krosno (hourly; 30min)

At **HACZÓW**, 12km east of Krosno, the beautiful mid-fifteenth-century Gothic **church** is thought to be the oldest wooden structure in Poland, and the largest wooden-framed building left from its era in all Europe; it was added to UNESCO's World Heritage list in 2003. The nave is decorated with a fine sequence of scenes of the Passion of Christ and the lives of the Virgin Mary and the saints, arranged in several layers, while in a side chapel there's an early fifteenth-century wood pietà thought to be miraculous.

The Oil Industry Museum at Bóbrka

Bóbrka Kopalniana 35 • Tues–Sun: April & Oct 8am–4pm; May–Sept 9am–5pm; Nov–March 7am–3pm • 12zł; audio guide 10zł • ☎ 13 433 3478, ⓦ bobrka.pl • No public transport – although you can get a Krosno–Dukla minibus as far as Rogi/Rowne (every 15–30min; 20min) then walk 3km to the site

Historic sites of the petroleum industry may not rank high on most people's must-see lists, but the intriguing **Oil Industry Museum** (Muzeum Przemysłu Naftowego) at **BÓBRKA**, a tiny village 10km south of Krosno, makes a strong bid for the non-specialist's interest. Its chief claim to fame rests on the presence of what's widely reckoned to be the world's first proper oil well, sunk here in 1854 by local pioneer Ignacy Łukasiewicz. Highlight of the site is the enjoyable collection of early drilling derricks and rigs; at "Franek", the oldest specimen, built in 1860, you can see the crude oil bubbling away at the bottom of its well.

At the far end of the area, which takes a good hour to walk around, is a set of old workshops along with Łukasiewicz's former offices, which have been converted into an informative **museum**. Amongst the exhibits are a chart of the first oil field, complete with the locations of the first drill shafts, and a fine collection of kerosene lamps, including Łukasiewicz's prototype, made in 1853.

Zyndranowa Skansen

Zyndranowa 1 • Tues–Sun: May–Sept 9am–4pm; Oct–April 10.30am–3.30pm • 5zł • ☎ 13 4330712, ⓦ zyndranowa.org/pl • There is no public transport to Zyndranowa itself, although you can catch a minibus from Krosno to Barwinek (6 daily; 50min) and then walk the remaning 2.5km

Thirty-five kilometres south of Krosno, off the road to Barwinek and the Slovak border, the village of **ZYNDRANOWA** – really no more than a collection of farmhouses – is the location of a **skansen** devoted to local **Lemko culture**. Occupying a set of wooden farm buildings that are typical of Lemko rural architecture, it contains a vivid collection of religious art and traditional costumes, and a display detailing the results of Operation Vistula (see page 237). Two hundred metres down the road from the main collection, a renovated **Jewish village house** (*chata*) contains a small but well-presented exhibition about rural Jewish life and culture.

Biecz and around

BIECZ is one of the oldest towns in Poland and, thanks to a royal charter, was the conduit for nearly all the wine exported north from Hungary in medieval times. This trade thrived until the middle of the seventeenth century, when the Swedish invasion flattened the economy. Much of the town, fortunately, survived, and these days it's a placid and little-known rural backwater. A visit to Biecz and nearby **Binarowa** is an easy day-trip from Gorlice.

The town hall

Tower: May, June, Sept & Oct daily 9am–5pm; July & Aug daily 10am–7pm; Nov–April Mon–Fri 8am–4pm • 5zł

Biecz's Rynek is dominated by the 50m-high tower of the late Renaissance **town hall**, smartly renovated over the last few years. The steep climb up the tower steps is rewarded with a fine view over the Subcarpathian countryside.

Corpus Christi Church

Kromera 16a • June–Sept Mon–Sat 10am–1pm & 30min before mass • Donation requested

Biecz's main parish church, **Corpus Christi** (Kościół Bożego Ciała), is a massive Gothic brick structure complete with a 40m-high fortified bell tower, containing a fine collection of Renaissance tombs and Gothic pews. The arch of the choir is bridged by a dramatic seventeenth-century crucifix, flanked by wooden effigies of Mary and a Roman soldier wielding a long spear.

Regional Museum

ul. Węgierska 1 • May–Sept Tues–Fri 8am–5pm, Sat & Sun 9am–5pm; Oct–April Tues–Sun 8am–4pm • 4zł

Housed in an early sixteenth-century burgher's mansion that was once part of the town fortifications (hence the building's name, *Dom z bastą* or "House with a Bastion"), the eclectic **regional museum** (Muzeum ziemi Beckiej) is a real treat. Among the exhibits are the entire contents of an old pharmacy – sixteenth-century medical books, herbs and prescriptions included – and an extraordinary collection of musical instruments, notably a sixteenth-century *dudy* (Carpathian bagpipe), several old hurdy-gurdys and a colourful organ handmade in 1902 by "illiterate peasant" Andrzej Wojtanowski.

Marcin Kromer House

ul. Kromera 1 • May–Sept Tues–Fri 8am–5pm, Sat & Sun 9am–5pm; Oct–April Tues–Sun 8am–4pm • 4zł

Just outside the parish church, the **Marcin Kromer House** is a museum devoted to the eponymous Polish historian, who was born in this building in 1512. Royal secretary to kings Sigismund the Old and Sigismund Augustus, and later Prince-Bishop of Warmia, based in Lidzbark Warmiński (see page 162), Kromer was one of the leading Catholic churchmen of the age. His 1555 book *On the Origins and Deeds of the Poles*, early editions of which are proudly displayed here, was one of the first systematic histories of the Polish nation.

ARRIVAL AND DEPARTURE   BIECZ

By bus Frequent buses and minibuses from Tarnów (7 daily; 1hr 5min) and Gorlice (every 30min; 20min) drop you off right on the Rynek.

EATING

U Becza Rynek 2 • 733 612 616, w restauracjaubecza. pl. Café-restaurant on the main square with a two-prong strategy of serving pizzas and Polish favourites from *barszcz* to *pierogi*, none of which are too expensive; two-course daily specials weigh in at just 13zł. Daily 2–9pm.

Binarowa Church

May–Oct Wed 9am–5pm, Thurs–Sat 9am–6pm, Sun noon–5pm; in other months phone ahead • Donation requested • 692 385 244, w binarowa.wiara.org.pl • Binarowa is an intermediate stop for most (but not all) Biecz–Tarnów buses

Several villages in this area have beautiful wooden churches but the finest is at **BINAROWA**, 5km northwest of Biecz. Constructed around 1500 and added to the UNESCO World Heritage list in 2003, the church interior features some outstanding wall paintings. The marvellous *Passion* series near the altar dates from the seventeenth century; note the devils with huge eyes and long noses cowering in the background at the Resurrection. The harrowing *Last Judgement* scenes on the north wall date from the same period, while the exquisite floral motifs on the ceiling are older, painted soon after the church was built. Just as interesting is the furniture, mostly Baroque, including ornamented pews and painted confessionals from the 1600s.

Gorlice and around

Just 12km southwest of Biecz along the main road, the smallish industrial city of **GORLICE** has, like Krosno, been for a century associated with the oil industry, Ignacy Łukasiewicz having set up the world's first refinery here in 1853. The city was smashed up in World War I and restored in fits and starts throughout the ensuing decades, giving it a somewhat cobbled-together appearance. Decent facilities ensure that it's a good base for excursions into the surrounding countryside, with the synagogue at **Bobowa** and the gorgeous wooden churches at **Sękowa** and **Kwiatoń** the main out-of-town targets.

Regional Museum

ul. Wąska • Tues–Fri 9am–4pm, Sat & Sun 10am–2pm • 5zł

The **regional museum** (Muzeum regionalne), just south of the battered hilltop Rynek, is devoted to the bloody World War I battle of spring 1915, when the Russians were routed by a combined German and Austro-Hungarian force. As well as uniforms and weaponry, the display focuses on the social impact of the war and the privations faced by Gorlice's citizens.

Magdalena Skansen

ul. Lipowa, 2km southwest of the city centre along ul. Krakowska • May–Sept Mon–Fri 9am–2pm & 4–7pm, Sat 9am–2pm • 5zł • ☎ 600 491 470, ⓦ skansenmagdalena.cba.pl

Just outside the city centre, the **Magdalena Skansen** (Skansen Przemyslu Nafotwego Magdalena) is a former oil-drilling site with a variety of pumps and drilling towers preserved in situ. Surrounded by orchards and fields, it's a strangely incongruous-looking piece of heavy-industrial history.

ARRIVAL AND INFORMATION

GORLICE

By train The train station is at Gorlice Zagórzany, 4km northeast of the city centre, and is too infrequently served to be useful as an entry point.

By bus The bus station is close to the centre on the northern side of the city, although many services pick up and drop off on the main ul. Legionów, just downhill from the Rynek.

Destinations Biecz (every 30min; 20min); Bobowa (every 30min; 40min); Kraków (hourly; 3hr); Nowy Sącz (hourly; 1hr 10min); Tarnów (6 daily; 1hr 20min).

Tourist information The tourist office at Rynek 2 (May–Oct Mon 8am–6pm, Tues–Fri 7.30am–3.30pm; Nov–April Mon–Fri 8am–3.30pm; ☎ 18 355 1280, ⓦ gorlice.pl), has books, maps and information on accommodation.

ACCOMMODATION AND EATING

★ **Cukiernia Italia** ul. Mickiewicza 4 ☎ 513 403 055. Small and intimate patisserie with a handful of tables, serving awesomely good cakes, including meringues, cheesecake, croissants and *babeczki*. Mon–Fri 7.30am–7pm, Sat 8am–7pm, Sun 9am–7pm.

Dark Pub ul. Wąska 11 ☎ 18 352 0231. Despite the name, this is actually a bright and welcoming spot with a glitzy bar at street level and a slightly more staid pub-restaurant (complete with red British telephone box) down below, offering a competent range of meat-and-potato

staples for under 30zł. A garden patio adds to the appeal. Mon–Sat 10am–11pm, Sun 1–10pm.

Hotelik ul. Wąska 11 ☎ 018 352 0232, ⓦ darkpub. pl. Situated just off the Rynek above the *Dark* pub and restaurant, this pension offers neat en-suite rooms with crisp contemporary design features. 190zł

Margot ul. Sportowa 11 ☎ 018 352 3095, ⓦ hotel gorlice.pl. Spacious 29-room hotel with contemporary en suites with TV and desk space, next to a sports ground and a large indoor swimming pool. 190zł

Sękowa Church

Mass times: Mon–Sat 7am & 6pm, Sun 7am, 9am, 10.30am & 4pm • Buses run to Sękowa village from Gorlice (hourly; 15min)

Seven kilometres south of Gorlice, the UNESCO-listed Roman Catholic **church** at **SĘKOWA** straddles the historic borderline between the ethnic Polish and Lemko populations. A graceful structure with an extraordinary, two-tiered sloping roof that forms a rounded arcade, the church was a favourite subject of Polish artists from the Młoda Polska movement (see page 270). What you see today dates from the 1520s but was added on to – and in the case of World War I Austro-Hungarian soldiers who pillaged it for firewood, taken away from – several times in subsequent centuries. The building is usually locked outside Mass times, but the exterior is spectacular enough to merit a visit.

Kwiatoń Church

Wed 9am–1pm & 1.30–5pm, Thurs–Sat 9am–1pm & 1.30–6pm, Sun noon–5pm • ☎ 18 351 6187 & ☎ 660 105 342 • No public transport

Often described as the best-preserved Lemko church in Poland, the **Church of Our Lady** in **KWIATOŃ** (formerly the Uniate Church of St Paraskeva, but now used by a Catholic congregation) was built around 1700 from stout beams covered in thousands of wooden shingles — it's the trio of domes emerging from the delicately tiered roofs that give the church its famously fairy-tale aspect. The interior is as vivacious as they come, with an early twentieth-century iconostasis studded with saintly images, and vegetal designs from the same period covering the walls.

6

ZDYNIA'S LEMKO VATRA FESTIVAL

Twenty-five kilometres southeast of Gorlice on the road to Konieczna, the straggling hamlet of **Zdynia** hosts the annual **Lemko Vatra** ("Lemko Bonfire"), a three-day celebration of traditional culture that attracts Lemkos – and fans of Carpathian culture in general – from all over Poland and beyond. Taking place on the second-to-last weekend in July, the *Vatra* is one of the friendliest and most musically varied festivals you're likely to come across in Poland, providing a showcase for music from all over the Carpathian region, with village musicians, folklore societies and folk-rock acts from southern Poland, Slovakia and Ukraine among the guests. Bearing in mind the fact that Zdynia lies at the heart of the Lemko territories forcibly depopulated by the Polish government in 1947 (see page 237), the festival is a highly symbolic occasion.

Day tickets rarely exceed the 20zł barrier, plentiful food and drink is available from stallholders, and **camping** is possible (for a symbolic 5zł fee) on the hillsides overlooking the site. With **buses** from Gorlice only running to Zdynia on weekdays, if you're travelling via public transport it's a good idea to arrive with a tent on the Friday and stay until Monday if you can. Otherwise, try hitching a lift with other festival-goers, or pick up a taxi from Gorlice bus station (120zł each way).

Bobowa

Located in the hills between Gorlice and Nowy Sącz, the small town of **BOBOWA** (Bobover in Yiddish) was an important centre of Hassidism in the nineteenth century, when the Nowy Sącz *tzaddik* Shlomo Halberstam moved his yeshiva here. His son Ben Zion carried on the tradition, establishing schools throughout Małopolska. During World War II he helped other Jews, including his son Solomon, flee the Nazis before being murdered in L'viv in 1942. After the war Solomon refounded the yeshiva in Brooklyn, and by his death in 2000 the Bobover community had spread to London, Toronto and elsewhere.

The synagogue

Off the northeast side of the Rynek • Mon–Fri 10am–5pm; ask the barber (fryzjer) next door to unlock the building for you • 10zł per individual or group

Old photos of the Halberstam-dynasty rabbis hang in the entrance of the Bobowa **synagogue**, one of the best preserved in Poland. Built in 1756, the building was damaged by the Nazis, then restored and used as a vocational school from 1955 to 1994, when it was given to the Kraków Jewish community. Like many synagogues, this is a "nine fields" building, with four pillars dividing the main room into nine equal sections, at the front of which stands the vivid blue **Aron ha Kodesh**, a triumph of folk Baroque.

ARRIVAL AND DEPARTURE   **BOBOWA**

By train Trains from Tarnów and Nowy Sącz (both 6–7 daily; 1hr) stop at the Bobowa-Miasto station 100m west of the Rynek.

By bus Buses from Gorlice (every 30min; 40min) will drop you off on the Rynek.

The Beskid Sądecki

Southwest of Gorlice the hills continue with a range known as the **Beskid Sądecki**, another picturesque stretch of low-lying slopes. In addition to small market towns, scattered villages and traditional peasant farms, there's a sizeable Lemko population here and a wealth of old wooden churches. **Nowy Sącz**, the regional capital, makes an agreeable base, although you may find a better choice of tourist facilities in **Krynica**, a spa town further south. The *Beskid Sądecki: Mapa Turystyczna* (1:75,000) is widely available and particularly helpful when searching out the numerous wooden churches scattered in and around the hills.

Nowy Sącz

Perched above the confluence of the Dunajec and Kamienica rivers, **NOWY SĄCZ** was one of Poland's principal market towns in the Middle Ages, when it was the site of a royal residence and home to an important school of painters. The town is nowadays a rather workaday service centre and transport hub, although it does have a couple of worthwhile **museums** and a fine **skansen**, and the hills of the Beskid Sądecki are just a short bus or train ride to the south.

Nowy Sącz's spacious **Rynek** is dominated by its incongruous neo-Gothic **town hall**, ringed in summer by a collection of open-air cafés and beer gardens. Just off the square to the east, the Gothic **St Margaret's Church** (Kościół św. Małgorzata) has been fully modernized inside, but you'll find fragments of Renaissance-era polychromy to the left of the altar.

6

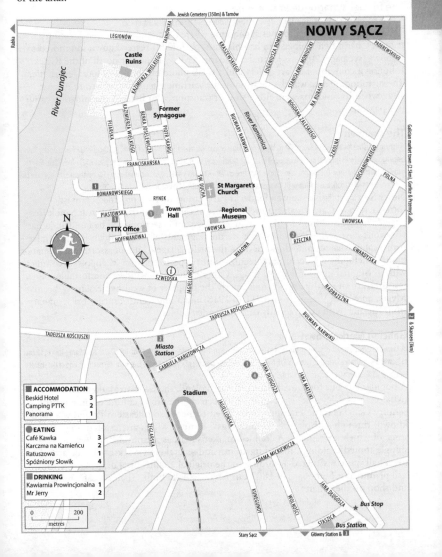

NOWY SĄCZ

ACCOMMODATION
Beskid Hotel — 3
Camping PTTK — 2
Panorama — 1

EATING
Café Kawka — 3
Karczma na Kamieńcu — 2
Ratuszowa — 1
Spóźniony Słowik — 4

DRINKING
Kawiarnia Prowincjonalna — 1
Mr Jerry — 2

0   200
metres

6

Regional Museum

ul. Lwowska 3 • Tues–Thurs 9.30am–3pm, Fri 9am–5pm, Sat–Sun 9am–4pm • 8zł; free on Sat • ☎ 18 443 7708, ⓦ muzeum.sacz.pl

Housed in the sixteenth-century Canonical House, Nowy Sącz's **regional museum** (Muzeum Okręgowe) contains a first-rate display of icons gathered from village churches throughout the region. The collection is not as extensive as that in Sanok (see page 235) but amply demonstrates the distinctive regional style of icon painting, and includes some wonderful examples of the *Hodigitria* (Holy Virgin and Child) theme popular in Uniate iconography, as well as a seventeenth-century composite iconostasis assembled from different village churches. There's plenty of folk art on show, too, including some *Christus Frasobliwy* sculptures, showing a seated Christ propping his mournful face on one hand.

The former synagogue and around

ul. Berka Joselewicza 12 • Wed & Thurs 10am–3pm, Fri 10am–5.30pm, Sat & Sun 9am–2.30pm • 5zł

The seventeenth-century **former synagogue** where the popular nineteenth-century *tzaddik* Chaim Ben Halberstam had his base – before his better-known son moved to Bobowa (see page 248) – is located in the former Jewish quarter north of the Rynek. It houses a contemporary art gallery and a small photo exhibition of local Jewish life. The surrounding area was the location of the wartime ghetto, liquidated in August 1942 when its residents were either shot or transported to Bełżec extermination camp (see page 220).

The skansen

Northern entrance for individual tourists at ul. Wienawy-Długoszewskiego, about 3.5km east of town; southern entrance for hourly Polish-language guided tours (price of guide is included in regular ticket price) via the Galician Market Town (see page 252) • Tues–Sun: May to mid-Oct 10am–6pm; mid-Oct to April 9am–3pm • 14zł; free on Sat • ☎ 18 441 4412, ⓦ muzeum.sacz.pl • For northern entrance take bus #14 from the train station, bus station or ul. Lwowska, or walk from the centre (45min) or take a taxi (15–20zł)

Nowy Sącz's extensive **skansen** (Sądecki Park Etnograficzny) provides a fantastic introduction to Carpathian culture. If you've already visited the *skansen* at Sanok (see page 237), the buildings in the Lemko and Pogórzanie sections will be familiar. What you won't have seen before, however, are the fragments of a Carpathian Roma hamlet – realistically situated some distance from the main village – and an assortment of manor houses, including a graceful seventeenth-century specimen from Małopolska, complete with its original interior wall paintings. Other highlights include a comfortable farmstead from nearby Zagorzyn, formerly the property of wealthy peasant Wincenty Myjak, an MP in Vienna from 1911 to 1918; and a nineteenth-century brick granary from Kicznia, with extravagantly carved wooden gables.

Galician Market Town

ul. Lwówska 226, 3km east of town on the road to Gorlice • Tues–Sun: May to mid-Oct 10am–6pm; mid-Oct to April 9am–4pm • Entrance to "town" free; entrance including interiors 7zł; free on Sat • ⓦ muzeum.sacz.pl • Accessible on foot from the northern end of the skansen (see page 252); otherwise catch bus #25 or #27

A popular day out for tourists from all over Poland, the **Galician Market Town** (Miasteczko Galicyjskie) is an attempt to recreate the urban culture of nineteenth-century Galicia (as the Habsburg-controlled corner of southeastern Poland was then known) through a display of old buildings – some of which are restored originals, some of which are replicas. A cobbled market square is surrounded by low-rise shingle-roofed buildings, including an inn and several craft workshops. The arcaded town hall was constructed according to the original architectural drawings for a town hall planned for Stary Sącz in 1807 but never actually built. There's a café, restaurant and shop on the square.

ARRIVAL AND INFORMATION

NOWY SĄCZ

By train There are two train stations: the more central Miasto station handles only a few local trains, while all others use the Główny station, 2km south of town. Local buses shuttle from here to the town centre, via the bus station. Destinations Kraków (6 daily; 2hr 50min); Krynica (4 daily; 1hr 40min); Tarnów (6–7 daily; 2hr).

By bus The bus station is located a 10min walk south of the centre. Buses to Krynica run from ul. Kolejowa, midway between the bus and train stations.

Destinations Gorlice (hourly; 1hr 10min); Kraków (every 30min–1hr; 2hr 10min); Krynica (every 30min; 1hr); Rzeszów (2 daily; 3hr 50min); Stary Sacz (every 30min; 20min); Zakopane (8 daily; 2hr 30min).

Tourist information The main tourist office is at ul. Szwedzka 2 (Mon–Sat 9am–5pm; ☎ 18 444 2422, ⓦ ziemiasadecka.info).

ACCOMMODATION

Beskid Hotel ul. Limanowskiego 1 ☎ 18 440 4000, ⓦ hotelbeskid.pl; map page 251. Seven-storey concrete affair near the train station, with smart but brownish rooms, a decent breakfast spread and a spa centre offering beauty treatments. 275zł

Camping PTTK ul. Nadbrzeżna 40 ☎ 18 441 5012; buses #5, #6 or #7; map page 251. Two kilometres east of the centre, this campsite offers grassy pitches and a neighbouring accommodation block with simply-decorated en-suite doubles, triples and quads. Camping 35zł, doubles 120zł

Panorama ul. Romanowskiego 4a ☎ 18 443 7110, ⓦ hotelpanoramanowysacz.pl; map page 251. Town-centre hotel offering thirty crisply-decorated en-suite doubles with TV – although some of the colour scemes are a bit '70s/'80s. 185zł

EATING

Café Kawka ul. J. Długosza 8 ☎ 18 448 8830, ⓦ cafe-kawka.pl; map page 251. An attractive wooden pavilion in the town park serving pizzas, salads, ciabatta sandwiches and a choice of savoury and sweet pancakes (9–12zł). *Kawka* also has a strong claim to be the best place in town for coffee and cakes, especially when the sun is shining and tables are spread outside. Daily 9am–10pm.

Karczma na Kamieńcu ul. Rzeczna 5 ☎ 18 414 4396, ⓦ naszakarczma.pl; map page 251. Farmstead-style timber building on the opposite side of the river from the Old Town, offering two floors of wooden-bench seating and a tasty menu of chops, steaks, freshwater fish and a good spread of lamb dishes (roast lamb with veg 40zł, grilled hunk of lamb chop 55zł). Daily 11am–11pm.

Ratuszowa Rynek 1 ☎ 18 443 5615; map page 251. Pretty much everything in the Polish culinary repertoire is on the menu at this place, which occupies pleasant rooms underneath the town hall, but it's the various varieties of *pierogi* (including a local lamb-stuffed version) that stand out. Daily 10am–10pm.

★ **Spóźniony Słowik** ul. J. Długosza 10 ☎ 513 949 818; map page 251. Occupying a pavilion in the town park, with an outdoor terrace in summer, the "Late Nightingale" (the title of a poem by Julian Tuwim) is a characterful café strewn with 1950s furniture, sundry *objets d'art* and the odd antique. It's a good spot for tea, coffee and cakes, plus there's a small menu of main meals. Occasional blues and acoustic gigs. Mon–Thurs & Sun 10am–10pm, Fri & Sat 10am–11pm.

DRINKING

★ **Kawiarnia Prowincjonalna** Corner of ul. Pijarska and ul. Piastowska ☎ 608 499 585, ⓦ prow incionalna.com; map page 251. A piece of bohemian Kraków plonked down in the Beskids, this homely, candlelit hangout features a winningly eccentric mix of lived-in furniture, ancient radiograms, piles of old magazines and a funky collection of paintings and graphic art on the walls. There are occasional concerts by top rock/jazz personalities, when there may be an entrance fee. Mon–Fri 9am–midnight, Sat & Sun 5pm–midnight or later.

Mr Jerry ul. Kościuszki 18 ☎ 536 464 536 ⓦ facebook. com/mrjerry.pizza.pub; map page 251. Bar-restaurant with lounge bar-themed furnishings and a decent selection of craft beers and cocktails, supplemented by a broad-based menu of global fast-food cuisine – think burgers (spicy chilli burger 20zł) and pizzas (23–27zł). Mon–Thurs 11am–11pm, Fri & Sat 9am–2am, Sun 2–10pm.

Stary Sącz

Sitting between the Dunajec and Poprad rivers 10km south of Nowy Sącz, **STARY SĄCZ** is the oldest urban centre of the region. It grew up around the convent founded by **St Kinga**, thirteenth-century daughter of King Bela IV of Hungary and wife of Bolesław the Chaste of Poland – Bolesław got his nickname from the fact he vowed

6

never to have sex with his spiritually minded spouse. Entering the convent herself after Bolesław's death, Kinga soon became the centre of a local cult, and was declared a saint by John Paul II in 1999.

Stary Sącz's ancient cobbled **Rynek** is one of the best-preserved market squares in southern Poland, lined by one- and two-storey houses, mostly from the eighteenth century. A particularly fine seventeenth-century mansion houses the **town museum** (May, June & Sept Tues–Sat 10am–3pm, Sun 10am–1pm; July & Aug Tues–Sat 10am–5pm, Sun 10am–3pm; Oct–April Tues–Sun 10am–1pm; 6zł; ☎18 446 0094, ⓦmuzeum.stary.sacz.pl), a low-key but pleasant diversion into local history.

The tiny town also has two noteworthy thirteenth-century churches: an imposing fortified Gothic **parish church** south of the square, subjected to the full Baroque treatment and with lovely pews and a fine organ from 1679; and the convent **Church of the Poor Clares**, to the east, its nave decorated by sixteenth-century murals depicting the life of St Kinga, its founder.

ARRIVAL AND DEPARTURE

STARY SĄCZ

By bus Buses #11 and #43 head to Stary Sącz from Nowy Sącz (every 30min; 20min); pick them up from ul. Jagiellońska beside the town park, or from the local bus station diagonally opposite the train station.

ACCOMMODATION AND EATING

Restauracja Marysieńka Rynek 2 ☎18 446 0072, ⓦrestauracja-marysienka.com.pl. Welcoming first-floor restaurant with moderately priced Polish dishes and good views onto the square from the window-side tables. Daily 10am–9pm.

Zajazd u Misia Rynek 2 ☎ 18 446 2451, ⓦzajazdu misia.pl. A friendly little pension with a handful of en-suite doubles, triples and quads. It also has an order-at-the-counter buffet serving *pierogi*, *bigos* and other staples. **120zł**

Krynica and around

If you only ever make it to one spa town in Poland, it should be **KRYNICA**. Redolent of *fin de siècle* central Europe, its combination of woodland setting, traditional timber architecture and health-restoring waters have made it a popular resort for over two centuries. In winter the ski slopes (and a large skating rink) keep the holiday trade coming in. The pedestrianized, flowerbedded strip between **Bulwary Dietla** and **aleja Nowotarskiego** forms the resort's centre; running along it is a market where you can pick up local specialities such as *oscypek* (smoked cheese).

Pump Room

al. Nowotarskiego 9 • Daily 6am–6pm

Krynica's main **Pump Room** (Pijalnia Wód Mineralnych) is a modern pavilion with trickling fountains and huge indoor plants. Hand over a few groszy at the desk before heading for the taps, where the purply-brown Zuber is reckoned to be the most concentrated mineral water in Europe – it's certainly one of the worst-smelling. Upstairs there's a concert hall that sees plenty of action during the summer season.

Nikifor Museum

bul. Dietla 19 • Tues–Sat 10am–1pm & 2–5pm, Sun 10am–3pm • 12zł • ☎18 471 5303, ⓦmuzeum.sacz.pl

Diagonally opposite the pump room is a row of handsome-looking wooden houses and pensions. One of them, the bright-blue Romanówka, houses the **Nikifor Museum** (Muzeum Nikifora), devoted to Lemko painter Nikifor (1895–1968), a legend in Polish folk art, whose style and spidery handwriting will be familiar if you've visited the *Camelot* café in Kraków (see page 301). In a style reminiscent of Lowry's scenes of industrial northern England, Nikifor painted Beskid landscapes and wooden churches but is perhaps best known for imagining extravagant, Habsburg-style train stations in paintings of villages that were actually far from the railway line.

Krynica funicular

al. Nowotarskiego 1 • Daily every 20–30min: May–July 9.30am–7pm; Aug 9.30am–6pm; Sept 10am–6pm; Oct–April 10am–4pm • 8zł one way, 12zł return

At the northern end of the pedestrianized strip, a **funicular train** (*kolej linowa*) ascends the nearby **Góra Parkowa** (741m) and drops you at the top for an enjoyable overview of town. A number of paths also lead up the hill.

Jaworzyna gondola

Daily: May–Sept & Dec–March 9am–5pm • 24zł return • ⓦ jaworzynakrynicka.pl • Accessible via the green-marked path from the town centre or on bus #2 from the centre

Three kilometres northwest of Krynica lies the nascent ski resort of **Carny Potok**, where the **Jaworzyna gondola** whisks you up to the 1114m-high summit of Jaworzyna. Here you can soak up the views or explore the network of paths on its wooded slopes.

ARRIVAL AND INFORMATION

KRYNICA

By train The train station is at the southern end of town; from here, ul. Ebersa heads towards the centre. Trains from Nowy Sącz (4 daily; 1hr 40min) take a scenic route through the deep, winding Poprad valley.

By bus The bus station is by the train station. Most Nowy Sącz–Krynica buses (every 30min; 1hr) bypass the Poprad valley entirely, taking the more direct Kamienica valley route to the north.

Tourist information The tourist office, at ul. Zdrojowa 4 (Mon–Fri 9am–5pm, Sat 10am–3pm; July & Aug also Sun 9am–1pm; ☎ 18 472 5588, ⓦ krynica-zdroj.pl), has loads of local info and can help you find private rooms.

ACCOMMODATION

Małopolanka Bulwary Dietla 13 ☎ 18 471 5896, ⓦ malopolanka.eu. Lovely olde-worlde pension with antique furnishings in the lobby and an on-site spa centre offering a full range of massages, mud baths and the like. **220zł**

Osrodek Wczasowy Paradise ul. Pulaskiego 49 ☎ 18 471 0000, ⓦ paradisekrynica.pl. Neat and comfy en-suite rooms in a modern interwar building that doesn't look up to much from the outside, but which has been very well done-up. The hotel's on-site sauna is a boon if you've spent the day walking or skiing. **220zł**

Witołdówka Bulwary Dietla 10 ☎ 18 471 5577, ⓦ witoldowka-krynica.pl. Grand old wooden building that looks like a haunted house from the outside but an elegant country hotel on the inside. Comfortable en suites come with TV. **220zł**

EATING AND DRINKING

Karczma Cichy Kącik ul. Sądecka 2 ☎ 18 471 2319, ⓦ cichykacik.com.pl. Decked out like a highland cottage, this restaurant is 1.5km north of the town centre on the road to Grybów, but is worth the trip for its local cuisine, with grilled lamb sausages (21zł) and lamb *pierogi* (25zł) among the specialities. With staff in Carpathian-highland garb and live music at weekends, it's a tourist trap, but a stomach-pleasing one at that. Daily 10am–10pm.

★ **Koncertowa** ul. Pilsudskiego 76/2 ☎ 18 471 5353, ⓦ restauracjakoncertowa.pl. Quality food beautifully presented in elegant surroundings – a good place for a special night out. The menu doesn't take too many risks (mains at 60–100zł include all the usual pork, steak and fowl suspects) but the way in which it is all cooked is on a par with the top Warsaw restaurants, and the desserts are delicious. Reservations advised. Daily noon–10pm.

Lilianka ul. Piłsudskiego 9 ☎ 18 471 5460. An old-fashioned, simply decorated café that serves up some of the best pastries, cakes and doughnuts in town. Decent coffee and a range of alcoholic drinks round out the menu. Daily 9am–10pm.

6

Kraków and Małopolska

THE SUKIENNICE, RYNEK GŁÓWNY

Kraków and Małopolska

The Kraków region attracts more visitors – Polish and foreign – than any other in the country. The main attraction is of course Kraków itself, a city that ranks with Prague and Vienna as one of the architectural gems of Central Europe. Poland's ancient royal capital, its streets are a cavalcade of churches and aristocratic palaces, while at its heart is one of the grandest of European public spaces, the Rynek Główny or main market square. Kraków is also home to Poland's oldest university, and has been home to many of the nation's greatest writers and artists. Until the last war, it was also a major Jewish centre, whose fabric remains clear in the quarters of Kazimierz and Podgórze, and whose culmination is starkly enshrined at the Nazi death camps of Auschwitz-Birkenau, west of Kraków.

7

As a major transport hub Kraków serves as an ideal base from which to visit **Małopolska** ("Little Poland"), an area of gently rolling lowlands which historically served as one of the heartlands of the Polish state. Among the places that can be treated as easy day-trips from Kraków are the pilgrimage site of **Kalwaria Zebrzydowska**, the rustic village architecture of **Lanckorona** and the birthplace of Pope John Paul II at **Wadowice**. The region's most handsome historic town after Kraków itself is **Tarnów**, a centuries-old market centre that stands in close proximity to one of Małopolska's most renowned folkloric sights: the village of **Zalipie** with its painted houses.

Kraków

KRAKÓW, former capital of Poland and the residence of its kings for centuries, was the only major city in the country to come through World War II undamaged. The city is indeed a visual treat, with the Wawel one of the most striking royal residences in Europe, and the old centre a mass of flamboyant monuments. It's a surprisingly Italianate city for this part of Europe, thanks largely to the Renaissance tastes of Poland's sixteenth-century rulers, who repeatedly lured top Italian architects north of the Alps with promises of huge bags of cash.

The heart of the city centre is the **Old Town**, bordered by the tree-shaded city park known as the Planty. The **Rynek Główny** is the focal point, with almost everything within half an hour's walk of it. A broad network of streets stretches south from here to the edge of **Wawel Hill**, with its royal residence, and beyond to the Jewish quarter of **Kazimierz**. Across the River Vistula, the suburb of **Podgórze** was the site of the wartime ghetto, and is within striking distance of the concentration camp at Płaszów. Further out to the west, the green cone of the **Kościuszko Mound** (Kopiec Kościuszki)

WAWEL CATHEDRAL

Highlights

❶ Kraków's Old Town One of the most wonderfully preserved old-town complexes in Europe. See page 261

❷ The Wawel Kraków's hilltop castle and cathedral was for centuries the political heart of the nation. See page 276

❸ Kazimierz The old Jewish quarter of Kraków, now the centre of a burgeoning bar scene, buzzes with visitors day and night. See page 282

❹ Podgórze This former industrial suburb south of the Vistula is Kraków's latest visitor hot spot, thanks to a clutch of fascinating attractions – the

Schindler Factory and the MOCAK Museum of Modern Art among them. See page 289

❺ Auschwitz-Birkenau The infamous Nazi death camp, on the outskirts of Oświęcim, is a compelling memorial to man's inhumanity. See page 309

❻ Kalwaria Zebrzydowska A unique landscape of rolling hills and Baroque chapels that's ideal for low-key hikes. See page 313

❼ Ojców National Park This beautiful valley of limestone crags and medieval castles makes for a great day out from Kraków. See page 315

HIGHLIGHTS ARE MARKED ON THE MAPS ON PAGES 260 AND 262

and the attractive woodland of **Las Wolski** provide the targets for strollers and cyclists. Connoisseurs of megalomaniac urban planning will not want to miss **Nowa Huta**, the Stalinist model suburb 7km to the northeast.

As a year-round city-break destination, Kraków doesn't really have a tourist season, although the place is at its prettiest in spring, summer and the depths of winter. You'll need a good two to three days to do justice to the historical centre and the Wawel, much longer if you're keen to explore the city in depth.

Brief history

According to the *Polish Chronicle* penned by Wincenty Kadłubek in 1202, Kraków was founded by local strongman **Krak,** who killed the dragon of Wawel Hill by offering it animal skins stuffed with sulphur – which it duly and fatally devoured. In reality, **Slavic peoples** settled here as early as the eighth century, forming a major trading centre by the tenth. The emerging city was incorporated into the growing kingdom of the **Piasts,** who made Kraków the capital of the country in 1038. Sacked by the Tatars in 1241, Kraków was rebuilt by **Prince Bolesław the Shy**, and the geometric street plan he bequeathed to the city has remained pretty much unchanged to this day.

Kazimierz the Great (1333–70) founded a **university** here in 1364 – the oldest in Central Europe after Prague – and removed restrictions on Jewish settlement, paving

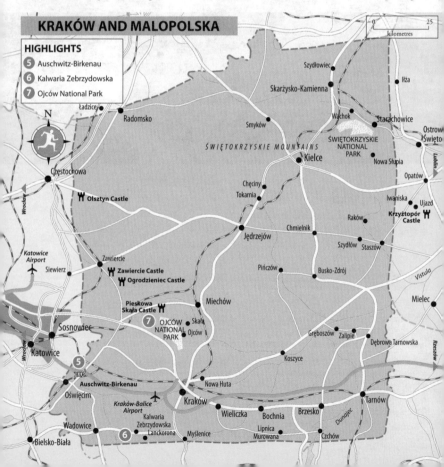

KRAKÓW AND MALOPOLSKA

HIGHLIGHTS
5 Auschwitz-Birkenau
6 Kalwaria Zebrzydowska
7 Ojców National Park

the way for the growth of a thriving **Jewish community**. The Renaissance heralded Kraków's emergence as an important European centre of learning, its most famous student (at least, according to local claims) being the young **Nicolaus Copernicus**. King Sigismund III Waza's decision to move the capital to Warsaw in 1596 was a major blow. Although royal coronations (and burials) continued to take place on Wawel for some time, Kraków went into decline, a process accelerated by plague in 1652 and Swedish occupation in 1655–57.

From the Partitions to World War I

Following the **Partitions**, and a brief period as an independent city state, Kraków was eventually incorporated into the **Austrian** province of Galicia. Habsburg rule was comparatively liberal, and Kraków (in contrast to Russian-dominated Warsaw) enjoyed considerable intellectual freedom. The city became a hotbed of political activity: **Józef Piłsudski** began recruiting the patriotic Polish Legion here prior to World War I, and from 1912 to 1914 Kraków was **Lenin**'s base for directing the international communist movement. Kraków also became a major centre of the arts. Painter **Jan Matejko** produced many of his stirring paeans to Polishness during his residency as art professor at the Jagiellonian University, and the city was the centre of **Młoda Polska** (Young Poland) – the modernist art movement (see page 270) that drew in virtually every creative spirit who happened to be around town at the time.

7

World World II and postwar Kraków

The brief interlude of independence following World War I ended for Kraków in September 1939 when the **Nazis** designated it the city capital of the so-called General Government, which covered all those Polish territories not directly annexed to the Reich. Governor Hans Frank exercised a reign of unbridled terror, presaged by the arrest and deportation of professors from the Jagiellonian University in November 1939. The elimination of Kraków's Jewish community, most of whom perished in the death camps, soon followed.

The main event of the immediate postwar years was the construction of the vast **Nowa Huta steelworks** to the east of the city, a daunting symbol of the communist determination to replace Kraków's Catholic, intellectually oriented past with a bright new industrial future. The plan did not succeed: the peasant population pulled in to work in the steel mills never became the loyal proletariat that the communist party hoped for. Kraków's reputation as a centre of Catholicism was enhanced by the election of **Pope John Paul II** in 1978, who until then had been archbishop of Kraków. Nowa Huta also had an unforseen environmental impact on the city, with atmospheric **pollution** wreaking havoc on the fine old facades of the centre. A thorough clean-up operation in the 1990s reduced air pollution to negligible levels. Since the fall of communism in 1989, the city has been transformed by the rapid rise of consumer culture, an increase in tourist numbers and a huge influx of foreign students – all lending the place the youthful, energetic and self-confident air one sees today.

The Old Town

The compact grid of medieval streets that makes up Kraków's **Old Town** (Stare Miasto) is centred on the set-piece square of **Rynek Główny**, ringed by magnificent houses and towering spires. Long the social hub of the city, it's an immediate introduction to Kraków's grandeur, and the stately network of passageways and Italianate courtyards leading off the square is riddled with shops, cafés and bars. Architecturally the square boasts as fine a collection of period buildings as any in Central Europe. This, combined with echoes of the events played out here, such as the Prussian Prince Albrecht of Hohenzollern's act of homage to Sigismund the Old in 1525 or Kościuszko's

KRAKÓW

7

HIGHLIGHTS

1. Kraków's Old Town
2. The Wawel
3. Kazimierz
4. Podgórze

ACCOMMODATION

Krakowianka campsite	3
Smok campsite	2
Vienna House	1
Easy Cracow	1

DRINKING AND NIGHTLIFE

Studio	1
Zaczek	2

EATING

Stylowa	1

SEE "KRAKÓW-CITY CENTRE" MAP FOR DETAIL

SEE "KAZIMIERZ & PODGÓRZE" MAP FOR DETAIL

N

Nowa Huta Steelworks
Josif Stalin 2 tank
Museum of Nowa Huta
Ark of the Lord
River Długa
Cistercian Abbey
Museum of Poland under the Communist Regime
St Bartholomew's Church
Maximilian Kolbe Church
Polish Air Museum
Stanisław Lem Garden of Experiments
Park Wodny
Museum of the Home Army
Kraków Opera
OLD TOWN
Train Station
Wawel
KAZIMIERZ
PODGÓRZE
Pomorska Street Museum
Groteska Theatre
National Museum
STU Theatre
Cracovia Stadium
Wisła Stadium
Salwator Church
Norbertine Church
Kościuszko Mound
Sanctuary of God's Mercy
Płaszów
Dębiusz Park
Las Wolski
Piłsudski Mound
Zoo
Tyniec Abbey
Balice Airport

NOWA HUTA
BIEŃCZYCE
MOGIŁA
MISTRZEJOWICE
PŁASZÓW
ŁAGIEWNIKI
PODGÓRZE
ZWIERZYNIEC
PRZEGORZAŁY
BRONOWICE
BIELANY
TYNIEC

Sandomierz
Tarnów
Zakopane
Kalwaria Zebrzydowska
Oświęcim (Auschwitz)
Katowice & Częstochowa
Kielce

0 2 kilometres

impassioned rallying call to the defence of national independence in 1794, provides an endlessly renewable source of inspiration.

The Sukiennice

Dominating Rynek Główny from its central position, the medieval **Sukiennice** is one of the most distinctive sights in the country – a vast cloth hall built in the fourteenth century and remodelled in the 1550s, when a roof-level parade of gargoyles was added by Florentine stonemason Santi Gucci (c.1530–1600). Its commercial traditions are perpetuated by a **covered market**, which bustles with tourists throughout the year. The colonnades on either side were added in the late-nineteenth century in an attempt to smarten up the Rynek and provide a home for a brace of elegant terrace cafés, most famous of which is the **Noworolski** on the Sukiennice's eastern side. The centre of Kraków social life in the years before World War I (Lenin was one of the more famous regulars), the café boasted a series of sumptuously decorated Art Nouveau salons, of which one – with a separate entrance from the rest – was a ladies'-only tearoom. Many of the *belle époque* interiors were renovated in the 1990s, making it well worth a visit (see page 301) – although the locals who used to idle away the afternoon over tea and *sernik* have been almost entirely replaced by tourists.

The Sukiennice: Gallery

Rynek Główny 3; entrance from the eastern side of the Sukiennice • Tues, Wed, Fri & Sat 10am–6pm, Thurs 10am–8pm, Sun 10am–4pm • 16zł • ☎ 12 433 5400, ⓦ mnk.pl

Occupying the upper floors of the Sukiennice is the newly-restored **Sukiennice: Gallery of Nineteenth-Century Polish Art** (Galeria Sztuki Polskiej XIX Wieku), a no-holds-barred collection of national heavyweights which carries a strong patriotic punch. Nowhere is this more evident than in *Torches of Nero*, the canvas donated by painter **Henryk Siemiradzki** to start off the collection in 1879. Showing early Christians being burned at the stake for the entertainment of the Roman Emperor, it was always understood by contemporaries to be a metaphor for Polish suffering under foreign rulers.

National themes are even more explicit in the canvases of **Jan Matejko**: occupying a large stretch of one wall is his *Kościuszko at Racławice*, a hysterically over-dramatized portrayal of the Polish rebel army's victory over the Russians in 1794. Elsewhere in the gallery, Tadeusz Ajdukiewicz's luminous portrait of actress Helena Modrzejewska (1880) is one of the most alluring pictures in Polish art, although the flame-haired nude on horseback that forms the subject matter of Władysław Podkowiński's *Ecstasy* (1895) has her fair share of admirers.

The gallery's first-floor terrace (complete with coffee-shop franchise) provides the ideal vantage point from which to observe the milling crowds on the Rynek.

Rynek Underground

Rynek Główny 1; entered from the eastern side of the Sukiennice • April–Oct Mon 10am–8pm, Tues 10am–4pm, Wed–Sun 10am–10pm; Nov–March: Mon & Wed–Sun 10am–8pm, Tues 10am–4pm; closed second Mon of month • 19zł; free on Tues • ☎ 12 426 5060, ⓦ podziemiarynku.com

Central Kraków's newest and busiest tourist attraction is the **Rynek Underground** (Podziemia Rynku), an extensive subterranean museum that stretches beneath the market square. Featuring an imaginative mix of raw history and multimedia innovation, it is based around the archeological excavation that took place when the Rynek was being repaved during 2005–08. Such was the excitement caused by the medieval-to-modern range of archeological finds that the idea of an in-situ display documenting the history of Kraków as a market centre was born. Opened September 2010, the Rynek Underground receives an average of over 30,000 visitors a month – there's usually a queue at the ticket desk so be prepared to wait.

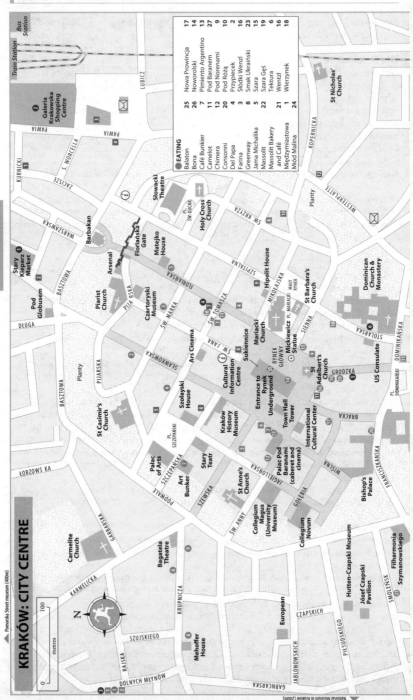

KRAKÓW: CITY CENTRE

EATING			
Balaton	25	Nowa Prowincja	17
Bona	26	Noworolski	14
Café Bunkier	7	Pimiento Argentino	13
Camelot	11	Pod Baranem	27
Chimera	12	Pod Norenami	9
Consonni	20	Pod Róża	10
Del Papa	4	Przypiecek	2
Farina	3	Słodki Wenzl	16
Greenway	8	Smak Ukraiński	23
Jama Michalika	22	Szara	15
Massolit	5	Szara Gęś	19
Massolit Bakery		Tektura	6
and Café	21	Wenzl	16
Międzymiastowa	1	Wierzynek	18
Miód Malina	24		

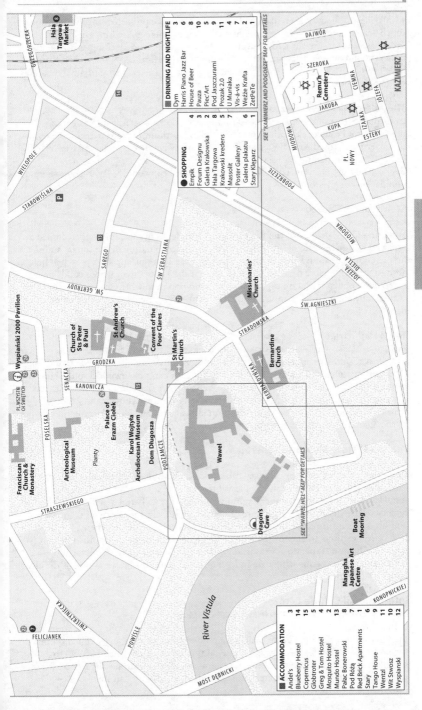

7

■ DRINKING AND NIGHTLIFE

Dym	3
Harris Piano Jazz Bar	6
House of Beer	8
Pauza	10
Piec'Art	5
Pod Jaszczzurami	11
Prozak 2.0	9
U Muniaka	7
Vis-à-vis	4
Weźże Krafta	2
ZetPeTe	1

● SHOPPING

Empik	4
Forum Designu	3
Galeria Krakowska	2
Hala Targowa	8
Krakowski kredens	5
Massolit	7
Poster Gallery/	
Galeria plakatu	6
Stary Kleparz	1

Hala Targowa Market

Wyspiański 2000 Pavilion

DAJWÓR

SZEROKA

KAZIMIERZ

Remu'h Cemetery

CIEMNA

JÓZEFA

JAKUBA

KUPA

IZAAKA

ESTERY

PL. NOWY

MIODOWA

PODBRZEZIE

JÓZEFA DIETLA

MIODOWA

ŚW. AGNIESZKI

SEE "KAZIMIERZ AND PODGÓRZE" MAP FOR DETAILS

Missionaries' Church

STRADOMSKA

Bernardine Church

BERNARDYŃSKA

WIELOPOLE

STAROWIŚLNA

SAREGO

ŚW. SEBASTIANA

ŚW. GERTRUDY

Church of Sts Peter & Paul

St Andrew's Church

Convent of the Poor Clares

St Martin's Church

GRODZKA

SENACKA

KANONICZA

Palace of Erazm Ciołek

Karol Wojtyła Archdiocesan Museum

Dom Długosza

PODZAMCZE

Franciscan Church & Monastery

POSELSKA

Archeological Museum

Planty

PL. WSZYSTKICH ŚWIĘTYCH

STRASZEWSKIEGO

Wawel

SEE "WAWEL HILL" MAP FOR DETAILS

Dragon's Cave

ZWIERZYNIECKA

FELICJANEK

River Vistuła

Boat Mooring

Manggha Japanese Art Centre

KONOPNICKIEJ

MOST DĘBNICKI

POWIŚLE

■ ACCOMMODATION

Andel's	3
Blueberry Hostel	14
Copernicus	15
Globtroter	5
Greg & Tom Hostel	4
Mosquito Hostel	2
Mundo Hostel	13
Pałac Bonerowski	8
Pod Różą	7
Red Brick Apartments	1
Stary	6
Tango House	9
Wentzl	11
Wit Stwosz	10
Wyspiański	12

Entering through a screen of fog onto which images are projected, the display features touch-screen computers, recreated thatched wooden huts representing the market square as it was in the eleventh century, and videos of actors dressed up as medieval traders acting out everyday situations. Original finds unearthed by the archeologists have been left in situ, while glass-bottomed walkways take you above original medieval storehouse floors and stretches of cobbled street.

The Adam Mickiewicz Statue

Immediately east of the Sukiennice is a statue of national poet **Adam Mickiewicz**, unveiled amid much celebration in 1898. The romantic author and patriotic symbol never actually visited Kraków, although his remains were transported here from Paris in 1890 to be buried in Wawel Cathedral (see page 276). The original statue was destroyed by the Nazis in 1940, although the faithful copy on display today remains a popular meeting point.

St Adalbert's Church

Rynek Główny • Mon–Sat 9am–2pm & 3–5pm, Sun 1–5pm

Squatting in the shadow of the Rynek's much grander buildings, the copper-domed **St Adalbert's Church** (Kościół św. Wojciecha) is the oldest building in the square and the first church to be founded in Kraków. The saint was a Slav bishop who preached here around 995 AD before heading north to convert the Prussians, at whose hands he was martyred. Popular with city-centre shoppers who pop in to whisper a quick prayer, the church's intimate, snug interior is filled with exuberant frescoes illustrating scenes from the saint's life.

Town Hall Tower

Rynek Główny • Daily: May–Oct 10.30am–6pm; Nov–March noon–6pm; closed first Tues of month • 9zł • ☎ 12 426 4334

Just off the southwestern corner of the Sukiennice, the onion-domed **Town Hall Tower** (Wieża Ratuszowa) is all that remains of a fourteenth-century town hall, pulled down in the 1820s by a city government eager to free up more space in the square. Reached by a steep, twisting staircase, the 70m-high viewing platform provides an excellent panorama of the city centre – and a close-up look at the gargoyles adorning the parapet of the Sukiennice immediately opposite.

Kraków History Museum: Cyberteka

Rynek Główny 35 • Tues–Sun 10am–5.30pm • 12zł; free on Tues • ☎ 12 619 2335

Occupying the Krzysztofory Palace (Pałac pod Krzysztofory), the **Kraków History Museum** (Muzeum Historyczne Krakowa) reopened in 2014 after a long period of renovation with a new permanent exhibition called the Cyberteka, which tells the history of the city through a mixture of dioramas, models, touch-screen computers and films. It's informative and entertaining up to a point, although there's a relative lack of real exhibits to anchor the whole thing down. During Advent, the museum basement hosts a stupendous exhibition of **szopki**, the amazingly colourful and detailed Christmas cribs which are indigenous to Kraków and serve as one of the city's visual trademarks.

International Culture Centre

Rynek Główny 25 • Tues–Sun 11am–7pm • 12zł • ☎ 12 424 2800, ⓦ mck.krakow.pl

Some of the more compelling cultural history exhibitions in Kraków can be found at the **International Culture Centre** (Międzynarodowe Centrum Kultury), which occupies the pod Kruki ("Under the Raven") house on the Rynek. Established in 1990 to stimulate intellectual dialogue between eastern and western Europe, the Centre hosts exhibitions focusing on recent trends in art and contemporary culture.

THE HEJNAŁ BUGLE CALL

Legend has it that in the thirteenth century a watchman at the top of the Mariacki Church's northern tower saw Tatar invaders approaching and took up his trumpet to raise the alarm. His warning was cut short by an arrow through the throat. The legend lives on, and every hour, on the hour, a lone **trumpeter** plays the sombre *hejnał* (bugle call) melody four times, from four different windows, on each occasion halting abruptly at the precise point the watchman was hit. National radio broadcasts the *hejnał* at noon every day and Polish writers are still apt to wax lyrical on the symbolism of the trumpet's warning.

Mariacki Church

pl. Mariacki 5 • Mon–Sat 11.15am–5.45pm, Sun 11.15am–2pm • 10zł; tickets from the ticket office opposite the south door

Presiding haughtily over the northeastern corner of the square, the twin-towered St Mary's or **Mariacki Church** (Kościół Mariacki) is one of the finest medieval structures in the country, and easily qualifies as Kraków's most instantly identifiable building. Dating from the 1220s, the Mariacki was for centuries the church of German merchants who lived around the Rynek, and it was they who endowed the place with altars and chapels. It was a late-thirteenth-century spurt of reconstruction that resulted in the two Romanesque **towers**, the northern one growing taller than the other because it was adapted to serve as the lookout post of the town watchman. This tower's prong-like spire, encircled by eight bauble-capped turrets, was finally finished off in 1478.

The tourist entrance to the church is through the south door – the square-side west door having been set aside for the local faithful. Iluminated by light streaming in through stained-glass windows, the walls of the **nave** are decorated with richly-coloured friezes by nineteenth-century artist Jan Matejko. Otherwise the main focal point is the huge stone **crucifix** attributed to the Nuremberg master craftsman Veit Stoss, hanging in the archway to the presbytery.

The Mariacki altar

The biggest crowds are drawn by the majestic **high altar** at the eastern end of the church. Carved by German master **Veit Stoss** (c.1440–1533) between 1477 and 1489, this huge winged polyptych is one of the finest examples of late Gothic art in Europe. It triumphantly displays every facet of late Gothic sculpture, from the huge figures in the central shrine to the tiny figurines and decoration in the borders. Subtle use is made of a whole gamut of technical devices, from three different depths of relief to a graded degree of gilding according to the importance of the scene. The altar is opened at 11.50am (Sundays and saints' days excluded) by a nun wielding a huge pole, revealing inner panels decorated with reliefs of the Annunciation, Nativity, Adoration of the Magi, Resurrection, Ascension and Pentecost; for a good view, arrive a good ten minutes before the opening. These superb scenes are a fitting backdrop to the central panel – an exquisite **Dormition of the Virgin** in which the graceful figure of Mary is shown reclining into the arms of the watchful Apostles.

St Barbara's Church

Mały Rynek 8 • Mon–Sat 9am–6pm, Sun 2–5pm

Standing in the shadows of St Mary's Church is the fourteenth-century **St Barbara's Church** (Kościół św. Barbary), famous for the remarkable late-Gothic pietà, sculpted in stone and attributed to the anonymous local artist known as "Master of the Beautiful Madonnas". Initially St Barbara's was a Polish-speaking church at a time when St Mary's was dominated by German-speaking merchants – a state of affairs reversed by decree of King Sigismund I in 1537.

The Hipolit House

pl. Mariacki 3 • April–Oct Wed–Sun 10am–5.30pm; Nov–March Wed & Fri–Sun 9am–4pm, Thurs noon–7pm • 9zł • ☎ 12 422 4219, ⓦ mhk.pl/branches/hipolit-house

The **Hipolit House** (Kamienica Hipolitów) is a beautifully restored example of a late-medieval merchant's house, named after a family of cloth traders who lived here in the seventeenth century. The richly stuccoed rooms provide the perfect home for a collection of domestic interiors through the ages: highlights include an over-the-top Rococo bedroom, and a nineteenth-century bourgeois parlour which, scattered with domestic knick-knacks, looks as if the owners have just popped out and will be back any minute.

Ulica Floriańska

Of the three streets leading north off the Rynek, **ulica Floriańska** is the most animated. Part of the so-called "Royal Route" (Droga Krolewska), it was via Floriańska that the Kings of Poland would enter town before continuing towards their residence on Wawel Hill (see page 277).

The Matejko House

ul. Floriańska 41 • Tues–Sat 10am–6pm, Sun 10am–4pm • 8zł; free on Sun

Halfway up ulica Floriańska is the sixteenth-century **Matejko House** (Dom Matejki), home of painter Jan Matejko until his death in 1893. Famous for his colour-charged depictions of key events in Polish history, Matejko was out of step with an art establishment that saw him as a hysterical romantic, but was venerated as a visionary by the wider, gallery-going public. In an age before the invention of cinema, a Matejko painting was the blockbuster of the day. The artist's former home is a delightful piece of domestic history – some of the rooms are like a sourcebook of nineteenth-century interior design, retaining the oriental furniture that Matejko chose himself. There's also a rousing collection of old costumes, armour and other props the artist used as inspiration, including a stuffed horse mounted on wheels that served him well when painting equestrian scenes.

Floriańska Gate

ul. Floriańska • City walls: April–Oct daily 10.30am–6pm; closed second Thurs of month • 8zł combined ticket with Barbican

Presiding over the northern end of ulica Floriańska, the **Floriańska Gate** (Brama Floriańska) originally served as the main northern entrance to Kraków, and is still busy with the constant flow of tourists and townsfolk. A stocky fourteenth-century structure, it is decorated on its south side with an animated relief of a water-pouring St Florian, patron saint of firefighters. In summer you can walk the short stretch of surviving **city walls** (*mury obronne*) on either side of the gate, where there's a small display illustrating what Kraków's defences looked like before they were demolished in the nineteenth century. Comprising 3km of wall nearly 3m thick, interspersed with 47 towers and bastions, they must have been an impressive sight.

The Barbican

ul. Basztowa • May–Oct daily 10am–6pm; closed second Mon of month • 8zł combined ticket with city walls

Just outside the Floriańska Gate, the **Barbican** (Barbakan) looks from a distance like the kind of castle that children should be bouncing around in, but is on closer inspection a formidable addition to Kraków's medieval defences. Boasting seven spiky turrets, it was built in 1498 as an extension of the city's northern defensive wall, although the covered passage linking the Barbakan to the Brama Floriańska has long since disappeared.

Czartoryski Museum

ul. św Jana 19 • Currently closed for renovation • ⓦ mnk.pl

Traditionally considered Kraków's finest art collection, the **Czartoryski Museum** (Muzeum Czartoryskich) is currently closed for long-term renovation and is unlikely to reopen its doors any time soon. Founded by Izabela Czartoryska (1746–1835) and initially based at the family's estate in Puławy, the collection was purchased by the Polish State in 2016, and will reopen as a branch of the National Museum in Kraków when renovations are complete. In the meantime, the collection's most famous painting, Leonardo da Vinci's extraordinary *Lady with an Ermine*, will be displayed in the National Museum's main building (see page 275).

Plac Szczepański

One of Kraków's most impressive set-pieces of early twentieth-century architecture is **plac Szczepański**, a broad square lined with sturdy apartment blocks and Art Nouveau mansions. The ugly parking lot that used to cover much of the square was replaced with a neatly paved plaza complete with illuminated fountains in 2010.

Szołayski House

pl. Szczepański 9 • Tues–Sat 10am–6pm, Sun 10am–4pm • 14zł • ☎ 12 433 5450, ⓦ mnk.pl

Occupying a handsome town house of fifteenth-century origins, the **Szołayski House** (Kamienica Szołayskich) is one of the city's prime venues for touring art exhibitions, frequently with international content. The house has, in the recent past, exhibited important collections connected with the artist and playwright Stanislaw Wyspiański and the critic and collector of Japanese art Feliks Manggha Jasieński (1861–1929), although it's not known how much of their works will be displayed permanently in the Szołayski House in future.

Palace of Arts

pl. Szczepański 4 • Mon–Fri 8.15am–6pm, Sat & Sun 10am–6pm • 9zł • ☎ 12 422 6616, ⓦ palac-sztuki.krakow.pl

Dominating the western end of plac Szczepański is the **Palace of Arts** (Pałac Sztuki), a stately structure built in 1901 to serve as the headquarters of Kraków's Fine Arts Society. A typical Art Nouveau building inspired by everything from Greek temples to Baroque mansions, the palace's facade is adorned with reliefs by Jacek Malczewski and busts of Matejko, Witkiewicz and other local artists. Nowadays it hosts high-profile art exhibitions, often featuring major international works on loan from abroad.

The Art Bunker

pl. Szczepański 3a • Tues–Sun 11am–6pm • Admission price varies • ⓦ bunkier.art.pl

Standing in modernist contrast to almost everything else connected with Kraków's Old Town is the **Art Bunker** (Bunkier Sztuki), a brooding grey masterpiece of 1960s brutalism whose concrete walls stretch along one side of Planty Park. The minimalist interior is the city's main venue for large-scale contemporary art shows. It also houses a well-stocked art bookshop, and the perennially popular *Café Bunkier* (see page 300).

Collegium Maius: the University Museum

ul. Jagiellońska 15 • **Courtyard** Dawn–dusk • Free • **University Museum Standard Exhibition** Tours depart approx. every 20min April–Oct Mon, Wed & Fri 10am–2.20pm, Tues & Thurs 10am–5.20pm, Sat 10am–1.30pm; Nov–March Mon–Fri 10am–2.20pm, Sat 10am–1.30pm • 12zł • **University Museum Full Exhibition** Tours depart Mon–Fri 1pm • 16zł • ☎ 12 663 1501, ⓦ maius.uj.edu.pl

The historic heart of Kraków's renowned Jagiellonian University is the **Collegium Maius** ("Grand College"), a Gothic house donated by King Władysław II Jagiełło in 1400 and expanded in the centuries that followed. Initially the place where professors lived and taught their students, it subsequently served as the university library before being turned into a museum. The building's arcaded **courtyard** is one of the most magical spots in Kraków, a tranquil cloister surrounded by stone staircases and overhanging oriel windows. One recent addition (dating from 1999) is the **mechanical clock** on the south wall, from which carved figures of Władysław Jagiełło, Queen Jadwiga and university rectors emerge five times a day (9am, 11am, 1pm, 3pm & 5pm).

MŁODA POLSKA

Like Art Nouveau in France and Jugendstil in Germany, **Młoda Polska** ("Young Poland") administered an invigorating dose of modernity and style to Polish culture in the decades prior to World War I. Młoda Polska was much wider in scope than its French and German counterparts, however, revitalizing painting, poetry and music as well as architecture and design. It was also unique in that most of its protagonists shared a sense of cultural mission: Poland was a country under foreign occupation at the time, and it was only natural that artists saw creative activity as a patriotic as well as a personal duty.

EXPLORING THE UNCONSCIOUS

Młoda Polska was never an organized movement; the term was first coined in 1899 to describe a new generation of culturally active Poles who were united by their rejection of mainstream bourgeois taste. The cultural scene in Kraków contained plenty that was worth rebelling against, dominated as it was by the so-called Positivists, who advocated a sober realistic approach to the arts, or by romantic souls like Jan Matejko, the backward-looking painter of epic historical events. Matejko's former students at Kraków's art academy – Józef Mehoffer and Stanisław Wyspiański among them – were far more interested in exploring an alternative world of the unconscious, spiritual and symbolic. The new mood of rebellion also meant the cultivation of decadent, bohemian behaviour at the expense of good manners, and the replacement of cheery optimism with dreamy melancholia. It was a mind-set eloquently summed up by Młoda Polska poet **Kazimierz Tetmajer** in his most famous piece of verse *Nie wierzę w nic* ("I believe in nothing"), the kind of poem that finds a receptive audience among stroppy students to this day.

"LIFE"

Kraków's position in the Austrian Empire made it an incubator of new ideas: news of cultural innovations arrived here quickly from Vienna, and the Austrian authorities were in any case fairly liberal when it came to cultural politics. Considerations like these certainly persuaded publicist

The museum

Several first-floor rooms of the building play host to the **University Museum** (Muzeum Uniwerzytecki), which offers a choice of tour: the Standard Exhibition Tour takes in most of the university's history, while the longer Full Exhibition Tour packs in more detail. The **Standard Tour** begins with a series of elaborately decorated assembly halls and lecture rooms, several of which retain the mathematical and geographical murals once used for teaching, as well as an impressive library of old books. The most valued possession in the **Treasury** (actually a glass cabinet behind an iron grille) is a tiny copper globe, constructed around 1520 as the centrepiece of a clock and featuring the earliest known illustration of America – labelled "a newly discovered land" but placed in the wrong hemisphere. The **Aula** or grand assembly hall has a Renaissance ceiling adorned with portraits of Polish royalty and professors; its portal carries the inscription *Plus Ratio Quam Vis* – "Wisdom rather than Strength". Those who opt for the **Full Tour** will be treated to a display of antique scientific instruments and the university's valuable collection of Gothic and Renaissance paintings.

St Anne's Church

ul. św Anny • Tues, Thurs & Sat 1–7pm, Sun 2–7pm

The university **St Anne's Church** (Kościół św. Anny) was designed by Tylman van Gameren (1632–1706), the Dutch-born architect who spent much of his professional life in Poland. A monumental Baroque extravaganza, built on a Latin cross plan with a high central dome, it's widely regarded as Gameren's most mature work, the classicism of his design neatly counterpoised by rich stucco decoration added by the Italian sculptor Baldassare Fontana.

Collegium Novum

ul. Gołębia 24

Stanisław Przybyszewski to launch the periodical *Życie* ("Life") here in 1898, harnessing the young creative talent of the city and providing a focus for the anti-establishment scene. Przybyszewski held court in the (no longer standing) *Turliński* café on ulica Szczepańska, which soon became the unofficial headquarters of the south Polish arts world. When the landlord of the *Turliński* moved to Lwów, everyone decamped to the newly opened *Jama Michalika* on Floriańska. It was here that the Młoda Polska set initiated the **Zielony Balonik cabaret** in 1905 – many of Kraków's brightest talents were either performing on stage or being satirized in the sketches. The *Jama Michalika* still exists (see page 301), although it's nowadays the territory of tourists rather than trendsetters.

ZAKOPANE

Młoda Polska's key players also included **Tadeusz Boy Żeleńsky**, one of the main sketch-writers for Zielony Balonik, and **Feliks "Manngha" Jasieński**, the authority on Japanese art who introduced the younger generation of painters to Oriental styles. An even bigger creative impulse came from a rediscovery of Poland's indigenous folk traditions. Many Młoda Polska luminaries – notably Tetmajer, fellow poet **Jan Kasprowicz**, and architect **Stanisław Witkiewicz** – lived for much of the year in the mountain village of Zakopane (see page 327), drawing inspiration from both the natural beauty of the scenery and the age-old styles of music, dress and handicrafts cultivated by the local inhabitants. Central to the spirit of the age was the belief that Polish culture could be regenerated through renewed contact with its village roots.

After 1914 the effects of war and social upheaval opened the door to a more extreme set of aesthetics, and surviving members of the Młoda Polska generation went their separate ways. However, the era left Poland with a huge cultural legacy, exemplified more than anything by the all-embracing oeuvre of painter, dramatist and designer **Stanisław Wyspiański**. His plays, rich in national symbolism and collective soul-searching, are considered classics of Polish literature, while his work in the visual arts – above all the stained-glass windows in the Franciscan church (see page 272) – has helped form the visual identity of both Kraków and the country at large.

One of Kraków's most splendid neo-Gothic buildings is the **Collegium Novum**, completed in 1887 to serve as the Jagiellonian University's administrative headquarters, with an interior modelled on the Collegium Maius. Standing in front of the building is the **Copernicus statue**, commemorating the university's most famous supposed student – although the only evidence that he ever studied in Kraków is a payment-book entry referring to one "Mikołaj son of Mikołaj from Toruń".

The Dominican church and monastery

ul. Stolarska 12 • Mon–Sat 9am–8pm

Dominating the Old Town southeast of Rynek Główny is the large brickwork basilica of the thirteenth-century **Dominican church and monastery**. The original Gothic building was seriously devastated by fire in 1850, but much of the sumptuous interior decoration survives. Today it's one of Kraków's most popular churches, with Masses held hourly every morning of the week.

Inside, the nave is lined with a succession of chapels. Reached via a flight of steps at the end of the north aisle, **St Hyacinth's chapel** has some rich stuccowork by Baldassare Fontana on the dome above the freestanding tomb, and paintings portraying the life of the saint by Thomas Dolabella. The Baroque **Myszkowski family chapel**, in the southern aisle, is a fine creation from the workshop of Florentine mason Santi Gucci, the exuberantly ornamented exterior contrasting with the austere, marble-faced interior, with busts of the Myszkowski family lining the chapel dome. Similarly noteworthy is the **Rosary chapel**, built as a thanks offering for Sobieski's victory over the Turks at Vienna in 1683, and housing a supposedly miracle-producing image of Our Lady of the Rosary. A fine series of **tombstones** survives in the chancel, notably those of the early thirteenth-century prince of Kraków, Leszek Czarny (the Black), and an impressive bronze tablet of the Italian Renaissance scholar Filippo Buonaccorsi, built to a design by Veit Stoss and cast at the Nuremberg Vischer works.

TOP 5 ART NOUVEAU KRAKÓW
Palace of Arts see page 269
The Franciscan Church see page 272
Wyspiański 2000 Pavilion see page 272
Mehoffer House see page 274
Jama Michalika café see page 301

The Franciscan church and monastery

pl.Wszystkich Świętych • Mon–Sat 9.45am–4.15pm, Sun 1.15–4.15pm

Standing roughly opposite the Dominican Monastery on the western side of plac Wszystkich Świętych, the **Franciscan church and monastery** is home to the Dominicans' long-standing rivals in the tussle for the city's religious affections. One of Kraków's major churches, it has witnessed some important events in the nation's history, notably the baptism in 1385 of the pagan Grand Duke Jogaila of Lithuania (who adopted the Polonized name Władysław Jagiełło for the occasion), prior to his assumption of the Polish throne. The church's most striking feature is its celebrated series of Art Nouveau **murals** and **stained-glass windows**, designed by Stanisław Wyspiański in 1895–1905 following the gutting of the church by fire fifty years earlier. An exuberant outburst of floral and geometric mural motifs extol the naturalist creed of St Francis, culminating in the magnificent stained-glass depiction of God the Creator in the west window, the elements of the scene seemingly merging into each other in a hazy swirl of colour. The Gothic **cloisters**, reached from the southern side of the church, contain a memorable set of portraits of Kraków bishops dating back to the fifteenth century and continuing up to the present day.

Wyspiański 2000 Pavilion

pl. Wsystkich Świętych • Daily 9am–7pm • Free

Those who can't get enough of Art Nouveau artist Stanisław Wyspiański should on no account miss the **Wyspiański 2000 Pavilion** (Pawilon Wyspiański 2000). A slab-like structure erected (despite the name) in 2007, the pavilion contains contemporary stained-glass windows made from Wyspiański designs originally intended for the Franciscan church but never completed at the time. It's clear to see why the Franciscans thought twice before putting these particular Wyspiański sketches into effect: the windows depict three great figures from Polish history – St Stanisław, King Henry the Pious and King Kazimierz the Great – but portray them in unabashedly modern and unsettling style. Kazimierz in particular appears as a skeletal spectre, symbolizing (for Wyspiański at least) the ghost of Poland's past glory.

Archeological Museum

ul. Poselska 3 • July & Aug Mon–Fri 11am–5pm, Sun 10am–3pm; Sept–June Mon, Wed & Fri 9am–3pm, Tues & Thurs 9–6pm, Sun 11am–4pm • 10zł; audio guide 5zł; underground cellars 4zł • 📞 12 422 7560, 🌐 ma.krakow.pl

Heading south through the Planty from the Franciscan church brings you swiftly to the **Archeological Museum** (Muzeum Archeologiczne), housed in a medieval monastery that subsequently served as a prison. Ancient Egypt is represented by a colourful array of painted sarcophagi, and there's a fascinating collection of pre-conquest ceramics from Peru collected by local archaeologist Władysław Kruger. One exhibit the locals are extremely proud of is a carved pillar bearing the head of **Światowit**, chief god in the pagan Slav pantheon. Thought to date from the ninth century, the pillar has three layers of decoration, with Światowit at the top representing the heavens, human forms in the middle symbolizing the earth, and ugly faces at the bottom to signify the underworld. Światowit himself has a face on each side of the pillar – one for each of the winds, it is thought.

Outside in the garden, a plain-looking doorway leads to the **underground cellars** (*podziemia*), used as a prison by the Habsburgs and subsequently pressed into service by both the Gestapo and postwar communist secret police as a place of torture and execution. A caption or two runs briefly through the stories of those incarcerated here; the bare cells speak for themselves.

Ulica Grodzka

Heading south from plac Wszystkich Świętych towards Wawel Hill, **ulica Grodzka** is one of Kraków's most handsome streets. Many of its houses bear quirky decorative details, most notably the gilded stone lion above the **Kamienica Podelwie** ("House Under the Lion") at no. 32, the oldest such stone emblem in the city.

Church of Sts Peter and Paul

ul. Grodzka • April–Oct Tues–Sat 9am–5pm, Sun 1.30–5.30pm; Nov–March Tues–Sat 11am–3pm, Sun 1.30–5.30pm

Halfway down ulica Grodzka, the austere twin-domed **Church of Sts Peter and Paul** (Kościół św. Piotra i Pawła) is fronted by imposing statues of the twelve apostles, actually copies of the pollution-scarred originals, now kept elsewhere for preservation's sake. Modelled on the Gesù in Rome, the church is the earliest Baroque building in the city, commissioned by the Jesuit preacher **Piotr Skarga** when he came to Kraków in the 1590s to quell Protestant agitation. Nestling under a broad dome, the interior is relatively bare – clearly intended to invoke spiritual awe rather than delight the congregation with decorative detail.

Currently undergoing renovation., the church **crypt** holds the the tombs of both Skarga and surrealist playwright Sławomir Mrożek (buried here in 2013). The intention is that other eminent cultural figures will be laid to rest here in future.

St Andrew's Church

ul. Grodzka • Daily 8am–5pm

Sporting an eye-catching pair of octagonal towers, **St Andrew's Church** (Kościół św. Andrzeja) is the only Romanesque structure in Kraków to have survived in anything like its original form, having withstood the Tatar raids of 1241 thanks to its partially fortified exterior. The interior was given a thorough Baroque makeover in the eighteenth century, with master of swirling stuccowork Baldassare Fontana doing his best to turn nave and choir into the ecclesiastical equivalent of an extravagantly iced cake. Positioned beside the organ is a Rococo pulpit in the shape of a sailing boat, agile cherubs swinging playfully from the rigging.

Ulica Kanonicza

Running roughly parallel to ulica Grodzka is the atmospheric **ulica Kanonicza**, a quiet, cobbled alley lined with beautifully restored Gothic town houses. It was here that the Kraków Catholic hierarchy lived during the Middle Ages, hence the place's name – "canons' street".

Palace of Erazm Ciołek

ul. Kanonicza 17 • Tues–Sat 10am–6pm, Sun 10am–4pm • 9zł; free on Sun • ☎ 12 433 5920, ⓦ mnk.pl

Kraków's most rewarding museum of religious art is housed in the wonderfully restored former **Palace of Erazm Ciołek** (Pałac Erazma Ciołka), the fifteenth-century pied-à-terre of a Kraków-born commoner who rose to become royal confidant and Bishop of the town of Płock. The collection kicks off with a stream of show-stopping Gothic highlights, first of which is the Virgin and Child of Krużlowa, a sensuous fourteenth-century statue of a swooning Madonna holding a jauntily mischevious toddler. This is followed by several spectacular altarpieces: Nicolaus Haberschrack's Augustinian Church Altar of 1460 features wonderfully animated crowd scenes alongside an anguished and bloody *Mocking of Christ*. A roomful of Renaissance marble follows, including heavenly bas-reliefs of angels executed by Gianmaria Mosca Padovano, one of the Italian masters invited to Kraków by Poland's style-hungry sixteenth-century monarchs. No less compelling is the room labelled the "Hall of Death", which commemorates Polish funerary practices of the past with a row of so-called "coffin portraits" – images of the deceased which were stuck on the end of the sarcophagus.

7

> **TOP 5 MUSEUMS**
>
> **Józef Czapski Pavilion** see page 275
> **The National Museum** see page 275
> **Museum of the Home Army** see page 276
> **Oskar Schindler's Emalia Factory** see page 290
> **Polish Air Museum** see page 294

On the opposite side of the courtyard from the ticket office, a section devoted to **Orthodox religious art** (*sztuka cerkiewna*) contains a rich hoard of icons recovered from the decaying village churches of eastern Poland. A beautifully carved eighteenth-century iconostasis from the village of Lipowec displays the ordered hierarchy of saintly images displayed in Orthodox churches the world over from the Byzantine era onwards, with a calm-faced Jesus on the right, an aura-emanating Madonna on the left, and the patron of the church (in this case the white-bearded St Nicholas) at her side.

Karol Wojtyła Archdiocesan Museum

Kanonicza 21 • Tues–Fri 10am–4pm, Sat & Sun 10am–3pm • 5zł • ☎ 12 421 8963, ⊛ muzeumkra.diecezja.pl

Almost at the bottom of ulica Kanonicza, housed in an impressive pair of recently renovated late fourteenth-century mansions belonging to the archbishop of Kraków, is the **Karol Wojtyła Archdiocesan Museum** (Muzeum Archdiecezjalne im. Karola Wojtyły), with a wealth of religious art plucked from the churches of the surrounding Małopolska region. The highlight of the collection in the first gallery is a set of Gothic sculptures, including a wonderful sequence of Madonnas and female saints, and an exquisite relief of the Adoration of the Magi dating from the 1460s. Elsewhere, look out for a delightful sixteenth-century triptych from Racławice Olkuskie in which the Virgin Mary and St Anne appear to be bouncing the Christ Child from lap to lap. Rounding off the exhibitions are several rooms filled with photos, vestments and other memorabilia relating to Karol Wojtyła (Pope John Paul II), who lived in this building when a humble priest in Kraków.

North and west of the Old Town

When it comes to big-hitting history museums and art galleries, many of Kraków's core sights are just outside the Old Town, a short walk beyond the Planty Park.

Mehoffer House

ul. Krupnicza 26 • Tues–Sat 10am–6pm, Sun 10am–4pm • 9zł; free on Sun • ☎ 12 433 5880, ⊛ mnk.pl

Standing almost unnoticed at the wetern end of café- and restaurant-filled ulica Krupnicza, the **Mehoffer House** (Dom Mehoffera) is an essential stop on any Art Nouveau tour of Kraków. Occupying the house where painter Józef Mehoffer (1869–1946) lived and worked, it's stuffed with *belle époque* furnishings, pictures of old Kraków and Mehoffer's own artworks. Mehoffer was heavily involved in renovating and re-styling Kraków's historic churches, and many of his fresco designs – such as the heavenly children's faces of *Angels with Stars*, produced for Wawel Cathedral in 1901 – are given full exposure here.

It was as a stained-glass artist that Mehoffer was most in demand, fashioning pieces that were intended to serve as windows or room partitions in bourgeois homes. Positioned at the top of the main staircase here is an outstanding example of the genre in the shape of *Vita somnium breve* (1904) – an allegory of the immortality of art in which smiling muses hover fairy-like above a dying maiden. Mehoffer was also a keen horticulturalist, and his carefully designed **garden** at the back of the house has been returned to its original, glorious state – with restorers using Mehoffer's own watercolours as a guide.

The Europeum

pl. Sikorskiego 6 • Tues–Sat 10am–6pm, Sun 10am–4pm • 9zł; free on Sun • ☎ 12 433 5760, ⊛ mnk.pl

The National Museum in Kraków's collection of foreign art from medieval times to the nineteenth century is displayed in the **Europeum**, in a beautifully adapted seventeenth-century granary. It's a small collection of very high quality. Tick-box highlights include Bertel Thorvaldson's marble statue *Mercury Before Killing Argus*, Lucas Cranach the Elder's fraught *Suicide of Lucrecia* and a Paolo Veneziano *Crucifixion*. Take time however to pause in front of the lesser-known names: the gaggle of Renaissance beauties depicted in the *Rape of Europe* – painted by the anonymous painter known to art historians as the Master of King Ladislas of Durazzo – is the kind of low-key crowd scene you might miss when wandering round a bigger museum.

Józef Czapski Pavilion and the Hutten-Czapski Museum

Both museums at ul. Piłsudskiego 12 • Tues–Sat 10am–6pm, Sun 10am–4pm • **Józef Czapski Pavilion** 9zł; Hutten-Czapski Museum 9zł; both free on Sun • ☎ 12 433 5840, ⓦ mnk.pl

A chic white cube opened in 2016, the **Józef Czapski Pavilion** (Pawilon Józefa Czapskiego) is a wonderful museum dedicated to the kind of compelling local personality who deserves to be more widely known. A graduate of Kraków art academy, the painter, writer and activist Czapski (1896–1993) is celebrated above all for his role in unearthing the truth about the 1940 Katyń massacres of Polish officers by the Soviet secret police (see page 73). He himself had been taken captive by the Soviets in 1939, and did a lot of the spade work in finding out how his compatriots were murdered. Exiled in Paris after the war, he continued to propagate the truth about the killings, in the face of continuing Soviet denials. Czapski's story is warmly told through old photographs and archive film, alongside examples of the fascinating diaries he maintained throughout his life – the neatly written-up entries accompanied by ebullient sketches and pasted-in photographs. Many of his postimpressionistic paintings brighten the walls.

Józef Czapski was a grandson of Count Emeryk Hutten-Czapski, whose palatial town house stands in front of the Czapski Pavilion and is now home to the **Hutten-Czapski Museum** (Muzeum im. Emeryka Hutten-Czapskiego). This huge collection of coins, prints and old books is worth visiting for the well-preserved pre-World War I display halls.

National Museum in Kraków

al. 3 Maja 1 • Tues–Sat 10am–6pm, Sun 10am–4pm • 11zł; free on Sun • ☎ 12 433 5500, ⓦ mnk.pl

Ten minutes west of the Old Town along ulica Piłsudskiego, a tawny-coloured lump of interwar architecture serves as the main building of the **National Museum in Kraków** (Muzeum Narodowe w Krakowie), an impressive hoard of objects and artworks that fully merits a few hours of your sightseeing time. The first-floor starts off with a **weapons gallery** packed with the shining breastplates and eagle-feather wings that made the Polish hussars such a fearsome sight on the seventeenth-century battlefields of Europe. A sizeable collection of **military uniforms** takes the story up to the twentieth century – the sober grey tunic of interwar leader Marshal Piłsudski standing in contrast to the flamboyant traditional uniforms of the Polish *uhlans* serving with the Austro-Hungarian cavalry.

Highlights of the **Gallery of Decorative Art** include brightly enamelled Romanesque crosses from Limoges and stunning stained glass from Kraków's medieval churches. Look out too for the display of silky robes and sashes worn by local noblemen in the seventeenth and eighteenth centuries, when the belief that the Polish aristocracy was descended from an ancient eastern tribe known as the Sarmatians (see page 318) sparked a craze for all things oriental.

On the second floor, the **Gallery of Twentieth-Century Polish Art** begins with major works from artists involved in the Młoda Polska movement (see page 270), before moving on to the big names of the post-World War II era: look out in particular for Maria Jarema's jazzy abstract paintings of the 1950s, and the colour-charged canvases of the subtly primitivist Jerzy Nowosielski.

VISITING THE WAWEL

"Doing" the Wawel can take all day, but with the judicious use of coffee breaks it's hugely rewarding, and by no means as tiring as you might expect. The outer courtyard is open to all-comers but all other attractions require separate tickets; there is no combined ticket covering all the exhibitions.

Tickets for **Wawel Cathedral** (covering the Royal Tombs, Sigismund Tower and the Cathedral Museum) are sold from a separate office opposite the cathedral's main portal. **Tickets for the museum attractions** in the royal castle – the State Rooms, the Private Royal Apartments, the Treasury and Armoury, the Oriental Art Exhibition and the Lost Wawel – can be purchased from the **Visitors' Centre** at the back of the outer courtyard (April Mon 9–11.45am, Tues–Fri 9am–3.45pm, Sat & Sun 9.30am–3.45pm; May & June daily 9am–5.45pm; July & Aug daily 9am–6.45pm; Sept & Oct daily 9am–4.45pm; Nov–March Tues–Sun 9am–2.45pm; ☎ 12 422 1697, ⓦ wawel-krakow.pl).

Note that from April to October, tickets for visiting the main attractions on that day are only on sale until 11.45am on Mondays, and until 3.45pm on all other days. Entry to the State Rooms, Private Apartments and Treasury is staggered to prevent overcrowding, and your ticket will be valid for a particular **time slot** – on summer weekends all the available tickets for these attractions sell out quickly, so it's a good idea to arrive early. Entrance to the museum attractions is **free** one day a week, either Monday (April–Oct; last entry noon) or Sunday (Nov–March; last entry 3pm).

English-speaking **guides** for small groups and individuals are available from the Visitors' Centre, and cost 90zł for one attraction, 140zł for two, or 390zł for all of them excluding the cathedral and Cathedral Museum. If there's one place where it would be worth coughing up for your own guide, this is it.

Pomorska Street: People of Kraków in Times of Terror

ul. Pomorska 2 • April–Oct Tues–Sun 10am–5.30pm; Nov–March Tues, Wed & Fri 9am–4pm, Thurs noon–7pm, Sat & Sun 10am–5pm • Entrance to Gestapo cells free; exhibition hall 7zł; free on Tues • ⓦ mhk.pl

Number Two Pomorska Street is an address which still sends a shudder down Cracovian spines. Built in the 1930s to provide hostel accommodation for students, the bulding was turned into an interrogation centre by the Gestapo during the Nazi occupation, and today hosts **Pomorska Street: People of Kraków in Times of Terror** (Ulica Pomorska: Krakowianie wobec terroru), a museum devoted not just to World War II but also its Stalinist aftermath. The cells where Polish prisoners were tortured by the Gestapo are preserved pretty much as they were, together with the graffiti scratched by the inmates. An adjacent hall tells the history of Kraków from 1939 to 1956, with a fascinating collection of documentary photographs that draws together the horrors of the Nazi period and the grim years of hardline communism that followed. One picture shows Plaszów concentration camp chief Amon Goeth parading for the photographer on his white horse – an image that may be familiar to those who have seen the film *Schindler's List*.

Museum of the Home Army

ul. Wita Stwosza 12; it's best reached by walking through the train station to the far side of the tracks • Tues–Sun 11am–6pm • 13zł; free on Sun • ☎ 12 410 0770, ⓦ muzeum-ak.pl

The story of organized resistance to the Nazi occupation during World War II is one of the most inspiring narratives of Polish modern history, and finally seems to have got the museum it deserves in the shape of the gripping **Museum of the Home Army** (Muzeum Armii Krajowej). Housed in a stunningly renovated Austrian military HQ, it combines military hardware and personal stories with plenty of hands-on technology – visitors are given a media card which triggers video displays as they rove around the exhibition.

Polish resistance to the occupiers was active right from the start, although it wasn't until 1942 that the Home Army was established as the armed wing of a complex underground state. Resistance involved a huge proportion of the population, and the museum records innumerable uplifting stories: one such is the role played by the **Szare Szeregi** ("Grey Ranks"), boy- and girl-scouts who volunteered to undertake reconnaissance and courier duties (and in the case of older scouts, sabotage missions).

The Home Army was thrown into open battle with **Operation Storm** in 1944, when Polish units cooperated with the Red Army in the liberation of Vilnius and L'viv – many of the Home Army officers who took part in these operations were subsequently arrested by a Soviet security establishment that put as much effort into persecuting their anti-Nazi allies as in chasing down the Nazis themselves. Operation Storm ended with the Warsaw Uprising of August 1944 (see page 70), a heroic effort deliberately sabotaged by the Soviets, who refused to lend any assistance to the insurgents despite being on the opposite bank of the River Vistula at the time.

Wawel Hill

For over five hundred years, Poland was ruled from **Wawel Hill**, site of both the royal castle where kings resided, and the cathedral where they were crowned and buried. Even after the capital moved to Warsaw, Polish monarchs continued to be buried in the cathedral, as were many of the nation's venerated poets and heroes. Today, both cathedral and castle serve as a three-dimensional textbook of Polish history, making Wawel a near-obligatory pilgrimage for locals and tourists alike.

Waza Gate and the outer courtyard

Courtyard open daily: March & Oct 6am–6pm; April & Sept 6am–7pm; May & Aug 6am–8pm; June & July 6am–9pm; Nov–Feb 6am–5pm • Free

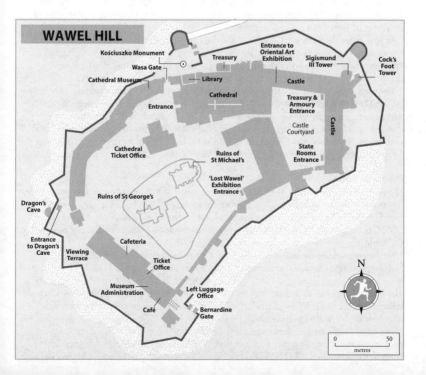

Entrance to the Wawel is via a cobbled path that leaves ulica Podzamcze just opposite the junction with Kanonicza. At the top of the path, a typically dramatic statue of Tadeusz Kościuszko – a copy of one destroyed by the Nazis – stands before the sixteenth-century **Waza Gate** (Brama Wazowska), protected by two huge red-brick bastions. As you emerge into the Wawel precinct the cathedral rears up to the left, with the castle and its outbuildings and courtyards beyond. Directly ahead is a huge, open **square**, once the site of a Wawel township, but cleared by the Austrians in the early nineteenth century to create a parade ground. In the middle of the square, alongside a well-tended garden, lie the remains of two Gothic churches, **St Michael's** (Kościół św. Michala) and **St George's** (Kościół św. Jerzego), both raised in the fourteenth century only to be demolished by the Austrians. Beyond the ruins, it's worth taking in the view over the river from the terrace at the western edge of the hill.

Wawel Cathedral

April–Oct Mon–Sat 9am–5pm, Sun 12.30–5pm; Nov–March Mon–Sat 9am–4pm, Sun 12.30–4pm • Cathedral free; Royal Tombs and Sigismund Bell 12zł; audio guide 7zł; ticket includes entrance to Cathedral Museum (see page 279) • ☎ 12 429 9516, ⓦ katedra-wawelska.pl

"The sanctuary of the nation … cannot be entered without an inner trembling, without an awe, for here – as in few cathedrals of the world – is contained a vast greatness which speaks to us of the history of Poland, of all our past." So was **Wawel Cathedral** evoked by former Archbishop Karol Wojtyła of Kraków. As with Westminster Abbey in London or St Peter's in Rome, the moment you enter Wawel, you know you're in a place resonant with national history. The first cathedral was built here around 1020 when King Bolesław the Brave established the Kraków bishopric. However the present brick and sandstone basilica is essentially Gothic, dating from the reigns of Władysław the Short (1306–33) and Kazimierz the Great (1333–70). All bar four of Poland's 45 monarchs are buried here, and the royal tombs are a directory of six centuries of European art and sculpture.

As you enter the cathedral, look out for the bizarre collection of **prehistoric animal bones** near the entrance, supposedly the remains of the Kraków dragon (see page 281), but actually a mammoth's shinbone, a whale's rib and the skull of a hairy rhinoceros. As long as they remain, so legend maintains, the cathedral will too.

The view down the nave of the cathedral, with its arched Gothic vaulting, is blocked by the **Mausoleum of St Stanisław** (Mauzoleum św. Stanisława), a seventeenth-century silver sarcophagus by the Gdańsk smith Peter van der Rennen. It commemorates the bishop murdered by King Bolesław at Skałka in 1079 for his opposition to royal ambitions. Stanisław was canonized in 1253 and his remains were moved to Wawel the following year, quickly becoming the focus of pilgrims.

The Royal Tombs

Kicking off the tour of the **Royal Tombs** is the tomb of **King Władysław Jagiełło**, to the right of the shrine to St Stanislaw. Dating from the mid-1400s, it's a beautiful marble creation with a fine Renaissance canopy added by the king's grandson, Sigismund the Old. On either side, an outstanding array of **side chapels** punctuate the entire length of the building.

To the right of the cathedral entrance, the Gothic **Holy Cross Chapel** (Kaplica Świętokrzyska) is the burial chamber of King Kazimierz IV Jagiełło (1447–92), his marble effigy the characteristically expressive work of the great Veit Stoss (see page 267). The bold, Byzantine-style paintings on the walls and ceiling were completed by Orthodox artists from the eastern fringes of the Polish-Lithuanian Commonwealth – a pointed reference to the multi-faith communities over which the Jagiellonian monarchs ruled.

The most celebrated of the chapels is the **Sigismund Chapel** (Kaplica Zygmuntowska) on the south side of the nave, a masterpiece of Renaissance sculpture designed for King Sigismund the Old (1506–48) by the Italian architect Bartolomeo Berrecci. The work was overseen by Sigismund's wife Bona, who as a member of the Milanese Sforza family clearly knew a thing or two about Italian style. Under a dome studded with stucco rosettes lie a series of niches containing effigies of King Sigismund the Old and his nearest family (spouse Queen Bona, daughter Anna Jagiellońka, and fork-bearded son King Sigismund August), all depicted in reclining pose as if lounging around in the wake of some regal banquet. The richly detailed walls of the chapel include reliefs of saints alongside distinctly non-Christian subject matter taken from classical myth – nymphs, griffons and sphinxes among them. Opposite the chapel is the modern **tomb of Queen Jadwiga**, wife of King Władysław Jagiełło and one of the country's most loved monarchs – in reality, her remains are buried nearby beneath her own favourite crucifix.

The marble and sandstone **tomb of King Kazimierz the Great**, immediately to the right of the high altar, is a dignified tribute to the revered monarch, during whose reign the cathedral was consecrated. The fourteenth-century **St Mary's Chapel** (Kaplica Mariacka), directly behind the altar, was remodelled in the 1590s by Santi Gucci to accommodate the austere black marble **tomb of King Stefan Batory** (1576–86). The **tomb of King Władysław the Short** (1306–33), on the left-hand side of the altar, is the oldest in the cathedral, completed soon after his death; the reclining, coronation-robed figure lies on a white sandstone tomb edged with expressive mourning figures.

Accessed from the left aisle, the **crypt** houses the remains of numerous Polish kings and queens, many encased in pewter sarcophagi, notably the Sigismunds and Stefan Batory. Also buried here are the poets Adam Mickiewicz and Juliusz Słowacki, and national heroes Prince Józef Poniatowski, Tadeusz Kościuszko and Józef Piłsudski. Standing with the crowds filing past this pantheon, you catch the passionate intensity of Polish attachment to everything connected with past resistance and independent nationhood.

Sigismund Tower

The ascent of the fourteenth-century **Sigismund Tower** (Wieża Zygmuntowska) is rewarded with an expansive panorama over the city and close-up views of the five medieval bells. The largest, an eight-tonne monster known as "Zygmunt", cast in 1520 from melted-down Russian cannon captured at the Battle of Orsza, is 2.5m in diameter, 8m in circumference, and famed for its deep, sonorous tone, which according to local legend scatters rain clouds and brings out the sun. These days it doesn't get too many chances to perform, as it's only rung on Easter Sunday, Christmas Eve and New Year's Eve.

Cathedral Museum

Wawela 3 • Mon–Sat: April–Oct 9am–5pm; Nov–March 9am–4pm • 12zł including entrance to Royal Tombs and Sigismund Tower

In a separate building opposite the main entrance, the **Cathedral Museum** (Muzeum Katedralne) displays the lavish collection of chalices, monstrances and devotional objects amassed by the cathedral over the centuries. Several of the exhibits radiate a powerful sense of historical significance, notably the Spear of St Maurice, presented to King Bolesław the Brave by Emperor Otto III when they met at Gniezno in 1000 AD, and a delicately embroidered mitre believed to have been worn by St Stanisław.

Wawel Castle

Entering the tiered courtyard of **Wawel Castle**, which occupies the eastern half of the Wawel complex, you might imagine that you'd stumbled on an opulent Italian palazzo. This is exactly the effect Sigismund the Old intended when he entrusted the conversion of King Kazimierz's Gothic castle to Florentine architect Bartolomeo Berrecci (c.1480–1537) in the early 1500s. The major difference from its Italian models lies in the response to climate: the window openings are enlarged to maximize the available light, while the overhanging wooden roof – held up by an unusually sensual set of bulbous columns – is sturdier to withstand snow.

The State Rooms

April–Oct Tues–Fri 9.30am–5pm, Sat & Sun 10am–5pm; Nov–March Tues–Sat 9.30am–4pm, Sun 10am–4pm • 18zł • ⓦ wawel.krakow.pl

Entered from the southeastern corner of Wawel Castle courtyard, the **State Rooms** (Reprezantacyjne Komnaty Królewskie) begin with the ground-floor apartments of the castle governor, liberally scattered with furnishings through the ages – not all of which are directly associated with Wawel Castle. An ensemble of large royal reception rooms await upstairs, beginning with the **Tournament Room** where people would wait before being admitted to the king's presence – it gets its name from the frieze of jousting knights painted by Hans Dürer, brother of the more famous Albrecht. The next-door **Military Room** contains another animated Dürer frieze, this time showing King Sigismund the Old reviewing his armies.

A glance upwards at the carved ceiling of the **Audience Hall** at the southern end of the wing will tell you why it's nicknamed the "Heads Room". Created for Sigismund the Old in the 1530s by Sebastian Tauerbach of Wrocław and Jan Snycerz, only thirty of its original 194 heads remain, but they are all remarkably detailed and lifelike artworks in their own right – most are believed to be portraits of Kraków locals. Running around the walls, another frieze by Hans Dürer illustrates *The Life of Man* with a procession of richly costumed figures symbolizing the progression from youth to old age. Hanging on the walls both here and in the adjoining corridors are some of King Sigismund August's splendid assembly of **Flanders tapestries**, many of which came from the Brussels workshop of the "Flemish Raphael", Michiel von Coxie. The tapestries were evacuated to Britain, then Canada on the outbreak of World War II – they didn't return to Kraków until 1961.

Next come a suite of rooms furnished by the seventeenth-century Waza dynasty, most of them featuring lavish Cordoba wall-coverings fashioned from tooled leather. Highlights include the **Bird Room** (named after the wooden birds that used to hang from the ceiling), dominated by a Rubens portrait of Prince Władysław Waza; the large, tapestry-adorned **Senators' Hall,** used for formal meetings of the Senate in the days when Kraków was still the capital; and numerous connecting vestibules filled with imposing portraits of the Polish royal family.

The Private Royal Apartments

April–Oct Tues–Fri 9.30am–5pm, Sat & Sun 10am–5pm; Nov–March Tues–Sat 9.30am–4pm • 25zł • ⓦ wawel.krakow.pl

The lavish interior design tastes of Poland's monarchs are given thorough exposure in Wawel Castle's **Private Royal Apartments** (Prywatne Apartamenty Królewskie) which basically consist of the reconstructed living quarters of Renaissance monarch Sigismund the Old – the last Polish king to regard the Wawel as his full-time home. Much of the period furniture on display has been collected from various sources by curators keen to convey a sense of how a sixteenth-century monarch might have lived, the king's own possessions having long since disappeared. One surviving item of original decor is the *Story of the Swan Knight*, a mid-fifteenth-century French tapestry adorning one wall of Sigismund's bedchamber.

The Treasury and Armoury

April–Oct Mon 9.30am–1pm, Tues–Fri 9.30am–5pm, Sat & Sun 10am–5pm; Nov–March Tues–Sat 9.30am–4pm • 25zł • ⓦ wawel. krakow.pl

Wawel Castle's combined **Treasury and Armoury** (Skarbiec i Zbrojownia) is located in the Gothic vaults of the Łokietek tower, one of the oldest parts of the castle. Although the Treasury's collection is short on crown jewels (most of these were plundered by the Prussians in 1795), there's a wealth of fascinating historical detail here – notably the dainty coronation slippers of Sigismund August (he was ten years old at the time), and a fifth-century ring inscribed with the name "MARTINVS", found near Kraków. Prize exhibits are the solemnly displayed Szczerbiec, a thirteenth-century copy of the weapon used by Bolesław the Brave during his triumphal capture of Kiev in 1018, used from then on in the coronation of Polish monarchs; and the early sixteenth-century Sword of Justice, belonging to Sigismund the Old.

The adjacent Armoury has spiky medieval halberds, primitive artillery pieces, and the exquisitely engraved suits of ceremonial armour made by the master metalworkers of Nuremberg. There are several examples of the eagle-feather wings which were strapped to the backs of seventeenth-century Polish hussars, a characteristically Polish piece of fancy dress which lent the wearer a fearsome, angel-of-death appearance.

> **TOP 5 KRAKÓW FOR KIDS**
> **Rynek Underground** see page 263
> **Dragon's Cave** see page 281
> **Kościuszko Mound** see page 291
> **The Stanisław Lem Garden of Experiments** see page 294
> **Puppet shows at Groteska Theatre** see page 306

The Oriental Art Exhibition

April–Oct Tues–Fri 9.30am–5pm, Sat & Sun 10am–5pm; Nov–March Tues–Sat entrance only at 11am & 2pm • 8zł • ⓦ wawel.krakow.pl

Housed in the west wing of Wawel Castle, the **Oriental Art Exhibition** (Sztuka Wschodu) was founded in 1920 to display the war loot collected by King Jan Sobieski in the wake of his victory over the Ottoman Turks outside Vienna in 1683. Pride of place goes to the tents of the Ottoman commanders, each vivaciously patterned with intertwined tulip, thistle and leaf forms. Exposure to such examples of eastern design had a profound impact on the Polish aristocracy, who remained addicted to oriental-styled textiles and clothes for the best part of a century. The visual feast continues with Iranian carpets, illuminated manuscripts, and a collection of Chinese and Japanese porcelain.

The Lost Wawel

April–Oct Mon 9.30am–1pm, Tues–Fri 9.30am–5pm, Sat & Sun 10am–5pm; Nov–March Tues–Sat 9.30am–4pm, Sun 10am–4pm • 10zł • ⓦ wawel.krakow.pl

Entered from the outer courtyard of Wawel Castle, the **Lost Wawel** exhibition (Wawel Zaginiony) consists of a subterranean walking route that takes in many of the medieval remains found underneath the current castle, most notably the well-preserved walls and towers of the tenth-century **Rotunda of Sts Felix and Adauctus** (Rotunda św. Feliksa i Adaukta), the oldest known church in Poland. A diverse collection of medieval archeological finds rounds off the display.

The Dragon's Cave and the riverfront

Daily: May & June 10am–6pm; July & Aug 10am–7pm; Sept & Oct 10am–5pm • 3zł

Accessible by narrow staircase from the Wawel Castle courtyard (and exited on the Vistula riverbank), the **Dragon's Cave** (Smocza Jama) is the legendary haunt of a fire-breathing beast who terrorized the local population until killed by a certain Krak – who tricked the dragon into eating an animal skin stuffed with sulphur. There's not a great deal to see inside, but kids may well enjoy the story. Outside the mouth of the cave, on the riverfront promenade, an effete-looking **bronze dragon** (the work of local sculptor Bronisław Chromy) entertains tourists by belching a brief blast of fire every couple of minutes. From the Dragon's Cave, a walk west along the bend of the river towards the **Dębnicki bridge** is rewarded by an excellent view back over the castle.

Manggha Japanese Art Centre

Konopnickiej 26 • Tues–Sun 10am–6pm • 20zł • ☎ 12 267 2703, ⓦ manggha.krakow.pl

From Wawel Hill, crossing either the Dębnicki bridge to the west or the Grunwaldzki bridge to the south will place you within five minutes' walking distance of the **Manggha Japanese Art Centre** (Centrum Sztuki i Techniki Japońskiej Manggha), a cool slab of modernist architecture designed by Arata Isozaki. The centre displays the extensive collection of Japanese art amassed by Feliks "Manggha" Jasieński, a leading

7

THE JEWS OF KRAKÓW

(The) Jews are gone. One can only try to preserve, maintain and fix the memory of them – not only of their struggle and death (as in Warsaw and Auschwitz), but of their life, of the values that guided their yearnings, of the international life and their unique culture. Cracow was one of the places where that life was most rich, most beautiful, most varied, and the most evidence of it has survived here.

Henryk Halkowski, a surviving Kraków Jew. Extracted from Upon the Doorposts of Thy House *by Ruth Ellen Gruber (Wiley)*

The Jews of Kraków occupy a significant place not just in the history of the city but in that of Poland as a whole. The first Jews settled in Kraków in the second half of the **thirteenth century**, a small community establishing itself on ulica św. Anny, then known as ulica Żydowska (Jewish Street), in the Old Town. In the **fifteenth century** the community was enlarged by an influx of Jews fleeing persecution and discrimination from countries all over Europe. Significant numbers of Jews were by now setting up home south of the Old Town in Kazimierz, where they built their own marketplace and a synagogue (the predecessor of the Stara Synagoga that you can still see standing today). The community's gradual shift to Kazimierz was a process completed in 1495, when a serious fire in the city was blamed on the Jews, provoking their expulsion from the Old Town.

The **sixteenth century** was a time of significant growth for the city, a development in which Jews participated actively as goldsmiths, publishers, furriers and, especially, butchers. It was something of a golden age for Jewish culture too, with Kraków's Talmudic scholars enjoying high international prestige. Rabbis and elders of the Kraków community were chosen to represent Małopolska on the Council of the Four Lands when it met for the first time in Lublin in 1581. The area of Jewish settlement was expanded in 1583, and again in 1603, with a wall along ulica Józefa separating it from other parts of Kazimierz.

Under the terms of a **nineteenth-century** statute promulgated in the wake of the establishment of the Free City of Kraków (1815–46), the walls separating Jewish and Christian communities were torn down. Jews were now permitted to live anywhere in Kazimierz; Jewish merchants and craftsmen could, with special permits, reside throughout the city. The period following the end of **World War I** was one of intense population growth in Jewish Kraków, the community rising from 45,000 people in 1921 to more than 64,000 on the eve of the Nazi invasion. Most, but by no means all, of Kraków's Jews lived in Kazimierz. The mostly poor

---

nineteenth-century Japanologist who wrote a much admired book about Eastern aesthetics entitled *Manggha* (his transliteration of the Japanese term "manga", or sketch), and subsequently adopted the term as his own literary pseudonym. Among the exhibits are ceramics, silks, samurai armour and one of the finest collections of late eighteenth- to early nineteenth-century woodcuts you're likely to see in Europe. A terrace café offers a good view onto the river and Wawel Hill.

Kazimierz

Kazimierz is a 10min walk south of the Wawel along ul. Stradomska and its continuation, ul. Krakowska; alternatively, take tram #6, #8 or #10

South from Wawel Hill lies the suburb of **Kazimierz**, originally a distinct town named in honour of King Kazimierz, who founded the settlement in 1335. The king's intention was to break the power of Kraków's German-dominated merchant class by establishing a rival market centre, and the granting of royal privileges to the new settlement led to its rapid development – as attested to by its large Rynek and impressive collection of churches. Initially settled by Poles, the ethnic make-up of Kazimierz began to change with King Jan Olbracht's decision to move Kraków's significant **Jewish population** into the area from the Old Town in 1495.

In tandem with Warsaw, where a **ghetto** was created around the same time, Kazimierz grew to become one of the main cultural centres of Polish Jewry. Jews were initially

Hassidim dominated the synagogues, prayer houses and Talmudic schools of the quarter, while the more upwardly mobile sections of the community moved to other districts, and increasingly adopted the manners of their Gentile neighbours. This was a period of rich cultural activity, notably in the **Jewish Theatre**, established in 1926 in southern Kazimierz, the biggest star being the legendary Ida Kamińska, still remembered today as one of the great prewar Polish actresses.

WORLD WAR II

Following the **Nazi invasion** of Poland in September 1939, Jews were increasingly subjected to discriminatory legislation. In March 1941, an official **ghetto** area was established in the **Podgórze** district. Jews from the area surrounding Kraków were herded into the ghetto, and from June 1942 onwards, mass deportations to Bełżec extermination camp began. A new forced labour camp was set up in November 1942 at **Płaszów**, just south of the ghetto (see page 289).

A major SS operation on March 14, 1943 removed or murdered the remains of the ghetto population. Those not killed in cold blood on the streets were either marched out to Płaszów or transported to the gas chambers of Auschwitz. Thus were nearly seven hundred years of Jewish presence in Kraków uprooted and effectively destroyed. Under the ruthless rule of its notorious commander **Amon Goeth**, Płaszów was transformed into a murderous work camp where those who didn't die from hunger, disease and exhaustion were regularly finished off at whim by the twisted Goeth himself, who was later tried and executed in Kraków in September 1946. In January 1945, with Soviet forces rapidly advancing west, many of the surviving camp inmates were moved to Auschwitz (the workers at Oskar Schindler's factory excepted), and the site dynamited by the camp guards.

POSTWAR JEWISH KRAKÓW

After World War II roughly six thousand Jewish survivors returned to the city, about a third of whom had lived there before the war. Subsequent waves of **emigration to Israel and the USA** went in step with the ups and downs of domestic and international politics, the largest occurring after the anti-Semitic campaigns unleashed in Poland in 1968–69, leaving an increasingly introverted and elderly community hanging on by the 1980s. Since the fall of communism there has been an upsurge in interest in the city's Jewish past, symbolized by the increasingly popular summer **Jewish Festival** (see page 308), and a determined drive to renovate Kazimierz's architectural glories. The city's Jewish population can never be fully reconstituted, but the effort to ensure that their culture and memory receive due recognition continues today.

limited to an area around modern-day ulica Szeroka and ulica Miodowa, and it was only in the nineteenth century that they began to spread into other parts of Kazimierz. By this time there were ghettoes all over the country, but descriptions of Kazimierz in Polish art and literature make it clear that there was something special about the headily oriental atmosphere of this place.

The prewar soul of the area was to perish in the gas chambers of Bełżec, but many of the buildings, synagogues included, have survived. The past two decades have seen a **revival** of activity in Kazimierz. Long-neglected buildings have been renovated, and the area has seen a marked increase in visitors – in part due to Steven Spielberg's 1993 film *Schindler's List*, much of which was filmed in and around Kazimierz (see page 290). Modern Kazimierz is an invigorating mixture of gentrified tourist suburb and bohemian inner-city area: cafés, bars and clubs patronized by sassy young Cracovians have successfully colonized Kazimierz's old tenement houses, making it Kraków's number one area for nightlife outside the Old Town. Above all, today's Kazimierz is a place to enjoy, as well as to ponder the more profound aspects of Poland's Jewish heritage.

Ulica Józefa

The obvious route into the formerly Jewish parts of Kazimierz is along **ulica Józefa**, so named following Joseph II's visit to the area to celebrate southern Poland's annexation by the Habsburg Empire at the end of the eighteenth century. Now home to a string

7

KAZIMIERZ AND PODGÓRZE

● EATING

Galeria Tortów Artystycznych	9
Good Good	13
Horai	11
Jadłodajnia Wczoraj i Dziś	16
Karakter	1
Kawiarna Literacka	15
Kolory	4
Lody na Starowiślnej	7
Marchewka z groszkiem	14
Nolio	10
Pierogi u Vincenta	6
Polakowski	2
Rękawka	18
Studio Qulinarne	12
Szalom Falafel	5
Szara Kazimierz	3
Zakładka	17
Zazie	8

■ ACCOMMODATION

Alef	3
Klezmer-Hois	1
Kolory	2
Secret Garden Hostel	4

■ SHOPPING

Antykwariat na Kazimierzu	2
Austeria	3
Ideafix	6
Lokator	7
Mapaya	4
MOCAK	8
Pan Tu Nie Stał	9
Plac Nowy	1
Produkty Benedyktyńskie	5

■ DRINKING & NIGHTLIFE

Alchemia	1
Don Chichote	4
Drukarnia	7
Eszeweria	6
Forum Przestrzenie	8
Mleczarnia	2
Piękny Pies	3
Singer	5

Galeria Kazimierz Shopping Centre

New Cemetery

Oskar Schindler Emalia Factory

MOCAK Museum of Contemporary Art

KRAKÓW-ZABŁOCIE

PRZEMYSŁÓW

TRAUGUTTA

JANOWA WOLA

Kraków-Zabłocie Station

KĄCIK

Płaszów Concentration Camp (1.5km)

PODGÓRSKA

DASZYŃSKIEGO

HALICKA

STAROWIŚLNA

Galicia Jewish Museum

Old Synagogue

DAJWÓR

Municipal Engineering Museum

KAZIMIERZ

DAJWÓR

Pałac Jordanów

Mikveh

Remuh Synagogue

SZEROKA

Remu Cemetery

CIENIA

Isaac Synagogue

High Synagogue

WĄSKA

JAKUBA

KUPA

ESTERY

IZAAKA

Tempel Synagogue

Kupa Synagogue

MIODOWA

PODBRZEZIE

MASZKOWA

PL. NOWY

Market Hall

Judaica Foundation

BOŻEGO CIAŁA

JÓZEFA

Corpus Christi Church

ŚW. WAWRZYŃCA

GAZOWA

MOSTOWA

BOHATERÓW
GETTA

PL.

SOLNY

River Vistula

PODGÓRSKA

Cricoteka

JÓZEFIŃSKA

Pharmacy Under the Eagle

MOST POWSTAŃCÓW

LIMANOWSKIEGO

PODGÓRZE

Galicia Starmach

WĘGIERSKA

RYNEK PODGÓRSKI

BRODZIŃSKIEGO

FATHER BERNATEK BRIDGE

BERNARDYŃSKA

JÓZEFA DIETLA

Misjonarzy' Church

STRADOMSKA

Bernardine Church

ŚW. AGNIESZKI

SKAŁKA

Pauline Church

St Catherine's Church

PAULIŃSKA

PIEKARSKA

SKAWIŃSKA

SKAŁECZNA

AUGUSTIAŃSKA

KRAKOWSKA

WĘGŁOWA

MESKA

MIODOWA

SKAWIŃSKA

BOCHEŃSKA

BONFRATERSKA

TRYNITARSKA

PL. WOLNICA

Ethnographic Museum

BOŻEGO CIAŁA

MOST PIŁSUDSKIEGO

Planty

LEGIONÓW

N

0   100
metres

Ethnographic Museum

of hipster bars, craft shops and boutiques, Józefa is an appropriate introduction to the mildly zany ebullience of today's Kazimierz.

High Synagogue

ul. Józefa 38 • Mon–Fri & Sun 9am–6pm • 12zł • ☎ 12 430 6889

Presiding over the eastern end of ulica Jozefa is the buttressed **High Synagogue** (Synagoga Wysoka), built in the late 1550s and so named because the prayer hall was located on the first floor of the building, the ground floor being occupied by shops. Devastated by the Nazis, the building was renovated in the 1960s and turned into a conservation workshop. Nowadays it hosts exhibitions on Jewish history in the restored prayer hall, where the fragmentary remains of Hebrew inscriptions can still be seen on the walls. The Judaica-oriented Austeria bookshop (see page 307) occupies the ground floor.

Isaac Synagogue

ul. Kupa 16 • Mon–Thurs & Sun 9am–6pm, Fri 9am–2pm • 10zł • ☎ 12 430 2222

One of Kazimierz's most prominent prayer houses, the **Isaac Synagogue** (Synagoga Izaaka) is a graceful Baroque structure named after the wealthy local merchant, Isaac Jakubowicz (in Yiddish, Reb Ajzyk), who financed its construction in the 1630s. Getting the building started proved more of a challenge than the merchant anticipated: despite securing permission from King Władysław IV, Jakubowicz's plans were forcefully opposed by the parish priest of Corpus Christi, who protested to the bishop of Kraków that it would result in priests carrying the sacraments having to pass in front of, and thus presumably be contaminated by, a synagogue. Thankfully, the bishop proved rather more enlightened than his ecclesiastical inferior, and building went ahead. Ransacked by the Nazis, the surviving hull of the building was fully restored in the 1990s. The lofty interior boasts an ornate stuccoed ceiling, sizeable chunks of Hebrew inscriptions on the walls, and a reconstructed Aron Ha Kodesh. Nowadays it serves as a social centre run by the Chabad-Lubavich branch of Orthodox Jewry.

Old Synagogue

ul. Szeroka 24 • April–Oct Mon 10am–2pm, Tues–Sun 9am–5pm; Nov–March Mon 10am–2pm, Tues–Thurs, Sat & Sun 9am–4pm, Fri 10am–5pm • 10zł; free on Mon • ☎ 12 422 0962, ⓦ mhk.pl

The grandest of all the Kazimierz synagogues and the earliest surviving Jewish religious building in Poland, the **Old Synagogue** (Stara Synagoga) overlooks **ulica Szeroka** ("Wide Street"), a broad open space whose numerous synagogues constituted the focus of religious life in Jewish Kraków. Modelled on the great European synagogues of Worms, Prague and Regensburg, the present Renaissance building was completed by Mateo Gucci in the 1570s, replacing an earlier brick building destroyed, like much of the surrounding area, by a fire in 1557.

The synagogue's story is closely entwined with the country's history. It was here that Kościuszko came to rally Kraków Jews in 1794 in support of armed resistance to the Partitions, a precedent followed by the Kazimierz rabbi Ber Meissels during the uprisings of 1831 and 1863. President Ignacy Mościcki made a symbolically important state visit to the synagogue in 1931, a move designed to demonstrate official amity with the country's Jewish population. Predictably, the Nazis did a thorough job of destroying the place. Following the war, the painstakingly rebuilt synagogue was converted into a **museum** of the history and culture of Kraków Jewry. There's a powerfully evocative set of photos illustrating life in the ghetto before World War II, and a superb wrought-iron bimah produced by a sixteenth-century Kraków workshop.

Remu'h Synagogue and cemetery

ul. Szeroka 40 • Mon–Fri: May–Sept 9am–6pm; Oct–April 9am–4pm • 10zł • ☎ 12 429 5735

On the western side of ulica Szeroka, the tiny **Remu'h Synagogue** (Synagoga Remu) is very much a functioning prayer house and a popular place of pilgrimage. It was founded in 1557 by King Sigismund August's banker, Izrael Isserlis Auerbach, probably in memory of family members felled by the plague of 1552. However, it gets its name from the founder's son Rabbi Moses Isserlis (1525–72; "Remu'h" is a shortened form of "Rabbi Moses"), whose Talmudic school was renowned throughout Europe. The interior includes an impressive cast-iron grille surrounding the central bimah, and an ancient-looking armchair (said to have belonged to Remu'h) to the right of the Aron Ha Kodesh.

Behind the synagogue is the Remu'h **cemetery**, established twenty or so years earlier, and in use until the end of the eighteenth century, after which it was supplanted by the New Cemetery (see below). Many of the gravestones were unearthed in the 1950s, having been covered with a layer of earth in the interwar years – a saving grace, as the rest of the cemetery was smashed up by the Nazis during the occupation. One of the finest stones is that of Rabbi Remu'h, its stele luxuriously ornamented with plant motifs. Just inside the entrance, tombstones torn up by the Nazis have been collaged together to form a high, powerful Wailing Wall.

Galicia Jewish Museum

ul. Dajwór 18 • Daily 10am–6pm • 16zł • ☎ 12 421 6842, ⓦ galiciajewishmuseum.org

Lodged in a wonderfully restored brick warehouse on the eastern fringes of Kazimierz, the **Galicia Jewish Museum** (Żydowskie Muzeum Galicja) was founded by photographer Chris Schwartz (1948–2007) to commemorate the now-disappeared Jewish communities of the former Habsburg Province of Galicia – a multi-ethic patchwork of territories which once stretched from Kraków in the west to well beyond L'viv (nowadays part of Ukraine) in the east. Centrepiece of the display is *Traces of Memory*, an evocative series of photographs by Schwarz himself illustrating the (frequently abandoned and derelict) synagogues and graveyards of southeastern Poland. The museum also hosts themed exhibitions relating to Jewish heritage, and there is a media room where you can watch 1930s documentary films illustrating Jewish life in Kraków, Vilnius and elsewhere.

New Cemetery

ul. Miodowa 55 • Mon–Fri & Sun 9am–4pm

At the eastern edge of Kazimierz, on the far side of a tunnel underneath the railway tracks, the **New Cemetery** (Nowy Cmentarz) succeeded the Remu'h as the main Jewish burial site in the early 1800s. A quiet, meditative place of overgrown walkways and ivy-covered tombstones, the cemetery is among the most evocative testaments to Jewish life in the district. The New Cemetery was full by the early twentieth century and a new burial ground was established in Plaszów to the south. With the latter location destroyed by the Nazis, however, attention was re-focused on the New Cemetery as a place for post-Holocaust remembrance – and it's here that you'll find modern family memorials scattered in between the nineteenth-century gravestones.

Tempel Synagogue

ul. Miodowa 24 • Mon–Fri & Sun 10am–5pm • 10zł • ☎ 12 430 5411

The **Tempel Synagogue** (Synagoga Templu) is a magnificent, neo-Renaissance construction founded in 1862 by the local Association of Progressive Jews, with whose modernist, reforming theology it was long identified. The stunning interior presents an intoxicating blend of Moorish and Gothic influences, the large central hall surrounded by the women's gallery, erected on decorated iron supports, and graced by ornate wall decorations and lavish stuccowork on the ceiling. In the centre sits the bimah, and beyond it the white marble altar, separated from the main body of the interior by a decorated screen wall. Illuminating the whole building is a glowing set of

36 stained-glass windows, featuring geometrical motifs alongside characteristic floral and plant designs.

Kupa Synagogue
ul. Miodowa 27 • Daily except Sat 10am–5pm 9.30am–5pm • 5zł • ☎ 12 429 5735

The **Kupa Synagogue** (Synagoga Kupa) was built in the 1640s with funds collected from the local community. Extensively restored in the 2000s, it preserves a beautiful painted celiing featuring a mixture of oriental and Art Nouveau motifs, and a zodiac frieze around the walls. An outdoor stairway leads to the latticed gallery where the female half of the congregation used to pray.

Plac Nowy
Much in contemporary Kazimierz revolves around **Plac Nowy**, the district's main marketplace in the nineteenth century and nowadays the focus of its frenetic nightlife. Focus of the square is the centrally placed **Okrąglak** ("log"), a dodecahedron-shaped red-brick building, which served as a kosher slaughterhouse before World War II.

The stately ochre building on the corner of plac Nowy and ulica Meiselsa was the nineteenth-century site of the Bet-ha midrash, a prayer house and study hall. Fully restored in the 1990s, the midrash is now home to the **Judaica Foundation** (Mon–Fri 10am–6pm, Sat & Sun 10am–2pm; ☎ 12 430 6449, ⓦ judaica.pl), a Jewish cultural centre that hosts regular concerts and exhibitions – it's always worth looking in to see what's going on.

Municipal Engineering Museum
ul. św Wawrzyńca 15 • Tues 9am–4pm, Wed–Fri 9am–8pm, Sat & Sun 10am–8pm • 10zł; free on Tues • ☎ 12 428 6600, ⓦ mim.krakow.pl

The former tram depot in southern Kazimierz provides the suitably post-industrial setting for the **Municipal Engineering Museum** (Muzeum Inżynierii Miejskiej), home to a fabulous collection of vintage tramcars, buses and municipal machines – including several antique printing presses. The extensive and fascinating collection of motor vehicles starts with the swanky saloon cars made by the Warsaw Automobile Works in the 1950s. Unfortunately, the same models were still being churned out in the 1970s, which helps explain why Polish consumers turned their backs on domestic-designed cars and went instead for automobiles like the Polski Fiat (popularly known as the Malucha or "tiddler"), made under license in Poland until 2000. One Polish model which somehow never made it as an icon of mass-consumerism was the Smyk mini-car (made in Szczecin in 1957), which did away with the need for doors – both driver and passengers climbed in through a large hinged bonnet.

Corpus Christi Church
ul. Bożego Ciała 26 • Mon–Sat 9am–noon & 1.30–7pm

As the presence of several churches indicates, the western part of Kazimierz represents the heart of the original Christian settlement. Despite its Baroque overlay, which includes some ornately carved choir stalls and a boat-shaped pulpit complete with rigging, the interior of the **Corpus Christi Church** (Kościół Bożego Ciała) retains a high Gothic nave complete with stained-glass windows installed around 1420. Tomasso Dolabella's high-altar painting of *The Descent from the Cross* looks down on a choir lined with ornate seventeenth-century choir stalls, backed by a row of paintings illustrating scenes from the Passion. Hidden away in St Anne's chapel is the grave plaque of Italian architect **Bartolomeo Berrecci**, creator of the castle courtyard on Wawel Hill, who liked Kraków so much he settled down here – until killed in a drunken brawl in 1537.

Ethnographic Museum
pl. Wolnica 1 • Tues–Sun 10am–7pm • 13zł; free on Sun • ☎ 12 430 5575, ⓦ etnomuzeum.eu

On **plac Wolnica**, the old market square of Kazimierz, the much-rebuilt fourteenth-century town hall now houses the **Ethnographic Museum** (Muzeum Etnograficzny). This highly enjoyable treasure-trove of ethnic artefacts begins with a series of re-created peasant interiors from around Kraków. The exquisitely painted furniture in the Lower Silesian room will probably have you jotting down ideas for your dream cottage. Particularly stunning is the cottage from Małopolska, flamboyantly decorated with floral motifs – houses like this can nowadays only be seen in the village of Zalipie (see page 320). A stunningly colourful collection of costumes awaits upstairs, alongside some intriguing insights into the often bizarre world of Polish folk culture – note the goat, stork and death's-head masks worn by Christmas carollers, and the alarming straw effigies burned at Shrovetide to mark the departure of winter.

St Catherine's Church

ul. Augustiańska 17 • Mon–Fri 10am–4pm, Sat 11am–2pm

Arguably Kazimerz's finest Christian edifice, **St Catherine's Church** (Kościół św. Katarzyny) was founded by fourteenth-century monarch Kazimierz the Great for Augustine monks brought from Prague. The large basilican structure is a well-preserved example of Kraków Gothic, despite suffering everything from earthquakes to the installation of an Austrian arsenal. The interior is something of an artistic treasure trove, with an impressively gilded main altar, a gripping sixteenth-century Wheel of Death just above the main entrance door, and a statuette-encrusted tombstone of Laurence Spytek Jordan (died 1568) on the southern wall. The adjoining cloisters contain a wealth of late-Gothic murals, notably the serene, blue-robed Holy Mother of Consolation overlooking the chapel of the same name.

Pauline Church at Skałka

ul. Skałeczna 15 • Church daily 7am–7pm ; Vault of the Meritorious April–Oct daily 9am–5pm • 5zł • ☎ 12 619 0900, ⓦ skalka-paulini.pls

Looming over the Vistula riverbank in western Kazimierz are the twin Baroque towers of the **Pauline Church**, traditionally known as **Skałka** (the Rock) due to the raised site it occupies. It is believed to be the place where St Stanisław, patron saint of Poland, was killed by agents of King Bolesław the Bold in 1079, and the church is very much his shrine. The main focus for pilgrims is the St Stanisław altar in the left aisle, where a piece of rock encased in glass is supposedly part of the block on which he was beheaded.

In the church's crypt, the **Vault of the Meritorious** (Krypta Zasłużonych) is a national pantheon containing the remains of many who have made a major contribution to Polish culture. Among the artistic heavyweights laid to rest here are painters Stanisław Wyspiański and Jacek Małczewski and composer Karol Szymanowski. The most recent inductee to the Skałka hall of fame was Nobel Prize-winning poet Czesław Milosz (1911–2004), whose stark, unadorned casket provides something of a modern counterpoint to the more ornate affairs belonging to his nineteenth-century neighbours.

Centrepiece of the church's forecourt is the **Spring of St Stanisław** (Sadzawka św Stanisława), a balustraded pool fed by natural springs. The healing qualities of the waters here are traditionally attributed to the miraculous powers of St Stanisław himself. A Baroque statue of the saint healing a sick man rises on a pillar from the centre of the pool.

Father Bernatek Bridge

Nothing better expresses Kazimierz's re-emergence as a go-ahead stylish suburb than the **Father Bernatek Bridge** (Kładka Ojca Bernatka), the footbridge that curves its way across the Vistula River towards Podgórze on the opposite bank. Opened in 2010, it's a graceful structure made up of three curving limbs – one for pedestrians, one for cyclists and one for the suspension arch above them. Spectacularly illuminated at night, it's a magnet for smoochy strollers, its railings encrusted with padlocks bearing the names of the lovers that left them here.

Podgórze and Płaszów

You can walk to Podgórze from Kazimierz by crossing the Father Bernatek footbridge at the southern end of Mostowa; alternatively, trams #3 and #24 run from the Old Town to pl. Bohaterów Getta

Immediately south of Kazimierz, road and rail bridges reach across the Vistula to **Podgórze**, a formerly workaday suburb that is currently one of the fastest-changing parts of the city. Former industrial buildings are giving way to smartly contemporary housing blocks, while a brace of important new museums have radically altered the region's cultural profile.

Long an area of mixed Polish and Jewish settlement, Podgórze owes its notoriety to the creation in March 1941 of a **ghetto** (centred on the suburb's main market square, today's plac Bohaterów Getta), into which the entire Jewish population of the city was forcibly resettled. In December 1942 the ghetto was divided into Ghetto A for those physically fit for work, and Ghetto B for the rest. In March 1943 Ghetto A was relocated to the forced labour camp at Plaszów, while the inhabitants of Ghetto B were either murdered on the spot or sent to the extermination camps.

Cricoteka

ul. Nadwiślańska 2-4 • Tues–Sun 11am–7pm • 10zł; free on Tues • ☎ 12 442 7770, ⓦ news.cricoteka.pl

A haughty oblong pod mounted on pillars above a nineteenth-century power station, the **Cricoteka** (or Cricoteka Centre for the Documentation of the Art of Tadeusz Kantor, to give it its full name) opened in 2014, and is a building every bit as avant-garde as the plays Tadeusz Kantor directed. Artist and theatre director Kantor (1915–90) founded the Cricot 2 drama group in 1955, going on to mount a series of groundbreakingly absurdist performances – which frequently took place in the kind of intimate cellar spaces that gave the cultural scene of the 1950s and '60s its particular underground flavour. An enthusiastic popularizer of the unclassifiably odd Polish dramatist Witkacy (see page 328), Kantor exerted a huge influence on fringe theatre across Europe, frequently employing movement, stagecraft and setting to create work that was both humorous and disturbing in equal measure.

Visitors enter the building at ground level before ascending by lift to a display which does its best to introduce Kantor's wide-ranging and complex oeuvre: there are plenty of video recordings of Kantor plays for those who want to take time to absorb his take on theatre. The top-floor café offers panoramic views back across the river towards Kazimierz.

Plac Bohaterów Getta

Centre of Kraków's wartime ghetto, the broad expanse of **plac Bohaterów Getta** is home to one of the more unusual **memorials** to Kraków's Jewish community. Conceived by local architects Piotr Lewicki and Kazimierz Łatak in 2005, it comprises metal chairs of various heights scattered across the square. Inspiration for the memorial came from the memoirs of ghetto pharmacist Tadeusz Pankiewicz, who witnessed the ransacking of Jewish homes during the final clearing of the ghetto in March 1943. Furniture was deliberately thrown around and smashed by the German guards, as if to symbolize the final destruction of the Jewish community in Kraków.

Pharmacy under the Eagle

pl. Bohaterów Getta 18 • Mon 10am–2pm, Tues–Sun 9am–5pm; closed second Tues of month • 10zł; free on Mon • ☎ 12 656 5625, ⓦ mhk.pl

Sited on the southwest corner of Podgórze's plac Bohaterów Getta is the **Pharmacy under the Eagle** (Apteka Pod Orłem), the former ghetto pharmacy run by Dr Tadeusz

---

SCHINDLER'S LIST

The story of Podgórze's wartime ghetto shot to international prominence due to the 1993 film **Schindler's List**, which recounted the wartime exploits of German industrialist **Oskar Schindler**, who saved the lives of over a thousand ghetto inhabitants by employing them in his Emalia enamel factory (see page 290). Film director **Steven Spielberg** shot the majority of the film in and around the area, sometimes using the original buildings, as in the case of Schindler's factory, and in other cases, building locations from scratch – a prime example being the Płaszów concentration camp, re-created in an old quarry not far from the original site.

Pankiewicz (1908–93) and his three assistants – the only Gentiles permitted to live in the ghetto, and the prime point of contact between Jews and the world outside. Inside lies an intimate and affecting portrayal of wartime pharmacy life, with archaic jars, a traditional till and a Bakelite telephone providing bags of period atmosphere. Wooden drawers and lidded cabinets contain potted biographies of Poles who helped their Jewish neighbours; touch-screen computers offer more detail on the individual fates of ghetto inhabitants.

Oskar Schindler's Emalia Factory

ul. Lipowa 4 • April–Oct Mon 10am–4pm (closes 2pm first Mon of month), Tues–Sun 9am–8pm; Nov–March Mon 10am–2pm, Tues–Sun 10am–6pm; last admission 90min before closing time • Entrance is restricted at busy times; you can book a time slot in advance at ⓦ bilety.mhk.pl • 21zł; combined ticket with MOCAK 24zł • ☎ 12 257 1017, ⓦ mhk.pl

Ten minutes' walk east of plac Bohaterów Getta, in the former industrial district of Zablocie, **Oskar Schindler's Emalia Factory** (Fabryka Emalia Oskara Schindlera) still stands. It was here that the German industrialist employed hundreds of Kraków Jews in order to keep them off the Nazi deportation lists – a story brought to worldwide attention in the film *Schindler's List* (see above). The building served as an electronics factory from 1945 until 2004, after which it was redeveloped as a major cultural heritage site. Reopened as a museum in 2010, the factory has fast become one of Kraków's most visited sites.

A superbly arranged permanent exhibition entitled **Kraków Under Nazi Occupation** tells the story of wartime Kraków and the fates of the peoples who lived there – with special reference to Schindler and others who risked their lives to protect Jews. The display itself is a tour-de-force, beginning with photographs of urban life in the pre-1939 period and moving through the war years with a series of moving tableaux – all illustrated with original artefacts, newsreel footage, filmed interviews with survivors, and well-chosen sound effects (the distant chuffing of steam locomotives eloquently sums up the constant fear of deportation). In one room, Schindler's recreated office desk stands opposite a contemporary sculpture bearing the names of the Jews he saved. Temporary exhibitions of historical interest are held on the ground floor, where there is also a simple café.

MOCAK Museum of Contemporary Art in Kraków

ul. Lipowa 4 • Tues–Sun 11am–7pm • 14zł; free on Tues; combined ticket with Oskar Schindler Emalia Factory 24zł • ⓦ mocak.pl

Opened in May 2011, the **MOCAK Museum of Contemporary Art** (Muzeum Sztuki Wspóczesnej w Krakowie) occupies several renovated buildings formerly belonging to Oskar Schindler's Emalia Factory, with a new building tacked on to the front to provide the main exhibition space. The cavernous white-and-grey interior is enlivened considerably by the regularly-changing menu of high-profile exhibitions (locally-curated group shows as well as international touring events). The museum's **permanent collection** is relatively small but contains a handful of post-1980 Polish greats. Look out for enigmatic films by Jozef Robakowski, sculptural installations by Mirosław Bałka, and Malgorzata Markiewicz's autobiographical photographs dealing with pregnancy and motherhood. Almost as absorbing as the exhibits themselves are the museum's café space (bearing the imprint of Italian architect Claudio Nardi) and shop (see page 307).

Płaszów concentration camp

ul. Jerozolimska • Take tram #3, #6, #9, #13, #23 or #24 to the Cmentarz Podgorski stop (trams #3 and #24 come direct from the Old Town, passing through Kazimierz on the way), then head down ul. Jerozolimska (marked by a sign reading "Podgórze: dawny obóz Płaszów") to find the camp entrance

As well as imprisoning people in the ghetto in Podgórze, the Nazis also relocated many Jews to the **labour camp at Płaszów**, built on the far side of an old Austrian hill fort 1.5km south of Podgórze in autumn 1942. Many of the inmates succumbed to overwork, malnourishment and the arbitrary cruelty of the guards, and the site was also used for mass executions of Jews from the Podgórze ghetto. Converted into a full-blown concentration camp in January 1944, Plaszów was wound down by January the following year when its remaining prisoners were transported to Auschwitz.

Levelled after the war, the Plaszów site is now an empty heath bordered by residential blocks. Standing at the entrance is the so-called **Grey House**, formerly the villa of camp commander Amon Goeth. Just behind the house is the site of a former Jewish **cemetery**, razed when the camp was built. There is a single recently-restored tombstone – that of Sarah Schenirer (1883–1935), founder of the Bais Yaakov network of schools for Jewish girls. From here a path leads southeast through the heart of the former camp. Overrun by wild grasses and shrubs, this gently rolling landscape, punctuated by limestone outcrops, has the tranquil and untended feel of an inner-city nature reserve. After ten minutes a left fork leads up onto a verdant hill and to a monolithic concrete **monument** to the victims of the camp, erected in the 1960s. In true communist style, the inscription on its side refers simply to the "martyrs" of Hitlerism without mentioning their ethnicity. A smaller plaque placed nearby by the city's Jewish community states unequivocally who the victims of Płaszów actually were.

The western suburbs and Las Wolski

Blessed with extensive patches of greenery and liberally sprinkled with low hills, Kraków's **western suburbs** offer an experience very different from the tourist-trodden streets of the city centre. The first of these green spaces is **Błonia**, a large triangular meadow that hosted huge open-air masses during Pope John Paul II's visits to Poland in 1979, 1983, 1987 and 2002. This last occasion attracted an estimated 2.2 million people, and is thought to be the biggest public gathering in Polish history.

Further west, the riverside quarter of Zwierzyniec is the starting point of the walk to the **Kościuszko Mound**, a strangely alluring man-made hill raised in tribute to a quintessentially Polish hero. Beyond the mound stretches **Las Wolski**, a huge wedge of forest which gives Cracovians a genuine piece of wild countryside right on their doorstep. Here, the **Piłsudski Mound** and the little-visited **Camadulensian Hermitage** provide ample focus for your wanderings. Further afield, the **Benedictine abbey** at **Tyniec** offers intriguing encounters with Kraków history in an out-of-town setting.

The area presents numerous opportunities for **cycling**: potential itineraries include the trip from Zwierzyniec past the Kościuszko Mound and into Las Wolski forest; or along the south bank of the Vistula towards Tyniec. The gravelly tracks of the Las Wolski itself are perfect for a burst of **mountain biking.**

Kościuszko Mound

al. Waszyngtona 1 • Daily 9am–dusk • 14zł • ☎ 12 425 1116, ⓦ kopieckosciuszki.pl • A 45min walk from the Old Town; or bus #101 from Rondo Grunwaldzkie

Rising above the eastern edges of the Las Wolski forest is the **Kościuszko Mound** (Kopiec Kościuszki), a 100m-high cone of soil erected in the 1820s in honour of

Poland's greatest revolutionary hero, **Tadeusz Kościuszko** (1746–1817). A veteran of the American War of Independence, Kościuszko returned to Poland to lead the resistance to the Partitions, swearing his famous **Oath of National Uprising** before a huge crowd assembled on Kraków's Rynek Główny in March 1794. Kościuszko's army, largely comprising scythe-bearing peasants, went on to win a famous victory over Russian forces at R**acławice** in April. Finally captured by the Russians five months later, Kościuszko went on to become the personification of Poland's tradition of resistance.

Kościuszko's Mound is the best-known example of a uniquely Cracovian phenomenon which dates back as far as the seventh century – when man-made mounds were raised to honour chieftains or provide a platform for sky-worship. The tradition was continued with the construction of the Piłsudski Mound in the 1930s (see below).

The final approaches to the mound are dominated by a huge red-brick fort built by the city's Austrian rulers in the 1850s. Work your way round to the back of the fort to gain access to the mound itself, which from this perspective looks like an enormous green pudding. An easily scaled spiral path winds its way to the top, where you can savour panoramic views back towards central Kraków, with the Wawel clearly visible in the foreground and the smokestacks of Nowa Huta further away to the northeast; the views even reach as far as the Tatra Mountains on really clear days.

Las Wolski

Bus #134 (every 20–30min) runs from the Cracovia Stadium near the National Museum to the zoo bus stop

A rippling succession of densely wooded hill, **Las Wolski** (Wolski Forest) lies 4km west of city's Old Town. Crisscrossed by marked paths, it's a popular area for picnics, hiking and mountain biking. Ideal starting point for exploration of the area is the parking lot and bus stop next to Kraków Zoo right in the centre of the forest.

Piłsudski Mound

An easy ten-minute stroll northwest of the zoo stands the **Piłsudski Mound** (Kopiec Piłsudski), raised in 1934 to mark the twentieth anniversary of the Polish Legion – a military outfit formed to fight for Polish independence under the auspices of the Habsburg Empire. When the Legion's founder Marshal Józef Piłsudski died a year later, the mound was re-dedicated to him. During World War II the German occupiers planted the mound with trees in an attempt to cover it up, while serious rains in 1997 eroded the mound to the point of obliteration. Subsequent renovation (with bags of soil ceremonially delivered from historically important sites all over Poland) has produced the lush green cone visible today. Paths spiral upwards to the 38m-high summit, where visitors can enjoy a sumptuous panorama of Las Wolski's forest canopy, with the church spires of central Kraków further over to the east.

Tyniec Abbey

ul. Benedyktyńska 37 • Museum Mon–Fri 9am–5pm, Sat & Sun 10am–6pm • 7zł • ☎ 12 688 5452, ⊛ kultura.benedyktyni.com • Bus #112 from Rondo Grunwaldzkie.

The village suburb of **Tyniec** is a popular excursion on summer weekends on account of its **abbey**, an eleventh-century foundation that was the Benedictines' first base in Poland. Perched on a white limestone cliff, the abbey makes an impressive sight from the riverbank paths. The original Romanesque abbey was rebuilt after the Tatars destroyed it during the 1240 invasion, and then completely remodelled in Gothic style in the fifteenth century, when the defensive walls were also added. Most of the church's interior furnishings date from the Baroque era; particularly charming are the pulpit in the form of a ship's prow, and choir stalls individually painted with scenes from the life of St Benedict. The **Abbey Museum** (Muzeum Opatctwa) displays church silver and medieval sculptures in a well-designed, atmospherically-lit display space.

Nowa Huta

Trams #4, #9, #15 or #22 (40min) run from the city centre to Nowa Huta's pl. Centralny

Raised from scratch in the late 1940s on the site of an old village, the vast steel-working and residential complex of **Nowa Huta** ("New Forge") now has a population of more than 200,000, making it by far Kraków's biggest suburb. Intended by the communists to function as a working-class counterweight to Catholic, conservative Kraków, Nowa Huta confounded its creators by becoming one of the epicentres of Solidarity-era opposition activity and all-round resistance to communist rule. The locals campaigned hard for the right to build churches in what was originally intended as an atheist proletarian paradise, and it is these churches – often featuring groundbreaking modern architecture – that constitute the main reason to visit Nowa Huta today.

Made up of broad avenues laid out on a geometric plan, Nowa Huta is a Stalinist-era re-working of Renaissance ideals – although the jury is still out on whether the settlement deserves to be studied as an important example of urban planning or simply consigned to the dustbin of architectural history. From the central plac Centralny, seemingly endless streets of residential blocks stretch out in all directions – a bigger contrast with Kraków's Old Town would be hard to imagine.

Plac Centralny

A huge hexagonal space ringed by typically grey slabs of Socialist Realist architecture, **plac Centralny** incorporates the arcading typical of a sixteenth-century market square into a monumental series of grim residential blocks. Originally named after Josef Stalin, the square was re-dedicated to Ronald Reagan after 1990 – although plac Centralny is the moniker that has stuck in the popular consciousness.

Museum of Poland under the Communist Regime

os. Centrum E1 • Tues–Sun 10am–5pm • 10zł; free on Tues • ☎ 12 446 7821, ☒ mprl.pl

Occupying the former Światowid cinema just east of Plac Centralny, the **Museum of Poland under the Communist Regime** (called Muzeum PRL-u or "Museum of the Peoples' Republic" in Polish) is very much a work in progress, offering a series of hugely worthwhile temporary exhibitions on life in the one-party state, while plans for a permanent exhibition are still being drawn up. A former bomb shelter and civil defence HQ beneath the cinema is also open to visitors, providing some idea of what the Third World War might have looked like had it actually kicked off.

Historical Museum of Nowa Huta

os. Słonecznie 16 • April–Oct Tues–Sun 9.30am–5pm; Nov–March Tues & Thurs–Sat 9am–4pm, Wed 10am–5pm • 6zł • ☎ 12 425 9775

A short distance north of plac Centralny, the **Historical Museum of Nowa Huta**, (Dzieje Nowej Huty) doesn't have a permanent collection, but does host frequently fascinating exhibitions about the settlement's history. It also functions as a **tourist information centre**, distributing free brochures and maps.

Josif Stalin 2 tank

The quietly residential ulica Ignacego Mościckiego, a ten-minute walk north of plac Centralny, is the site of one of the few surviving socialist-era monuments in Nowa Huta, the **Josif Stalin 2 tank**. Basically a late version of the Soviet-built T-34, tanks such as these were used by the Polish armies who fought under Soviet command towards the end of World War II, and although this particular model may never have seen actual combat, it nevertheless serves as a fitting tribute to former combatants.

The Ark of the Lord

ul. Obrońców Krzyża 1 • ☎ 12 644 0624, ☒ arkapana.pl • Tram #5 (from Basztowa in the Old Town or from pl. Centralny in Nowa Huta) to al. Kocmyrzowska, then walk north up ul. Obrońców Krzyża

The best-known symbol of Nowa Huta's rejection of state-sponsored atheism is the **Ark of the Lord** (Arka Pana), a boldly innovative church whose appearance on the settlement's skyline was greeted with grim resignation by the communist authorities. Designed by Wojciech Petrzyk in the late 1960s, the church's curvy Le Corbusier-influenced exterior was a clear demonstration of the Polish church's superiority to the communist party in the style stakes as well as the spiritual field. The Ark bears added significance for locals because of its close association with Karol Wojtyła (Pope John Paul II). He was the bishop who lobbied for its construction, personally laid the foundation stone in 1969, and (by now a cardinal) consecrated the church on May 15, 1977.

Officially dedicated to the Virgin Mary, the church got its name from its ark-like shape, with a concrete cross emerging mast-like from what looks like the prow of some huge ocean-going craft. The outer walls are encrusted with mountain pebbles, giving them an organic sensuous texture when seen close up. The **interior** is no less revolutionary – everything you would expect to see in a Catholic church is here, but seems to have been pulled out of place: instead of a high altar, Bronisław Chromy's bronze statue of Christ on the Cross is positioned halfway down the aisle, the Saviour seemingly poised to leap out Icarus-like over the congregation; while secondary chapels are placed at mezzanine level instead of to the right and left of the nave.

Maximilian Kolbe church

os. Tysiąclecia 86 • ⓦ mistrzejowice.net • Trams #1, #16 and #20 from plac Centralny all pass by the building

Nowa Huta's other great example of contemporary church architecture after the Ark of the Lord is the large **Maximilian Kolbe Church** (Kościół św. Maksymiliana Kolbego), in the Mistrzejowice district. Consecrated in 1983, it is dedicated to one of Catholic Poland's most important martyrs, a priest called Kolbe, who was sent to Auschwitz for giving refuge to Jews; in the camp, he took the place of a Jewish inmate in the gas chambers. Although not as striking as the Arka, the Kolbe church is another fine example of how the contemporary arts have been put to good use by the ecclesiastical authorities, with angular concrete ribbing adorning the ceiling, and an impressively anguished Crucifixion above the main altar.

Polish Air Museum

al. Jan Pawła II 39 • Tues–Sun 9am–5pm • 15zł; free on Tues • ⓦ muzeumlotnictwa .pl • Trams #4 and #15 run along al. Jana Pawła II, just south of the museum – get off at the AWF or Wieczysta stop

Despite being around since the 1960s, the **Polish Air Museum** (Muzeum Lotnictwa Polskiego) entered a new era of popularity in September 2010, when an ambitious new pavilion was opened to house its more dramatic exhibits. The pavilion contains 21 planes either parked on the floor or hanging from the ceiling; among the older machines is a German World War I Albatross of the kind used by Baron von Richthofen. Outside are several more hangars full of aircraft, including many of the Polish-made machines of the interwar years; particularly eye-catching is the PZP PIIc, an innovative gull-wing aircraft produced in 1935 whose design was much copied by rival manufacturers. Although Poland's fledgling air force made little impact in World War II, many of its pilots escaped to Britain to serve with the Polish Air Wing of the RAF – celebrated here with the inclusion of a Spitfire fighter aircraft. There's a row of Russian-built Cold War-era aircraft parked outside, with tube-shaped MIGs being upstaged by the sleek, silver-bodied Illyushin bombers.

Stanisław Lem Garden of Experiments

al. Pokoju 67 • Daily: April–Aug 8.30am–7pm; Sept 8.30am–5pm; Oct 8.30am–3pm • 10zł; children under 7 free; family ticket 30zł • ⓦ ogroddoswiadczen.pl • Tram #4 or #15 to the Park Lotników Polskich stop, then a 15min walk; or tram #22 to the M1 shopping centre, which is right opposite the garden's gate

Named after the popular science fiction writer and long-time Kraków resident Stanisąw Lem (1921–2006), the **Garden of Experiments** (Ogród Doswiadczeń im. Stanisława

Lema) occupies a large open-air site in the southeastern corner of Park Lotników Polskich – an attractively leafy area that's well worth a stroll in its own right. The main purpose of the garden is to encourage children of all ages to engage with science by playing around with various pieces of apparatus. Visitors can swing around on the end of a huge pendulum, bang away on an outlandish xylophone to test the resonance of different materials, or try balancing on wobbly boards to learn a thing or two about the nature of equilibrium. Each of the attractions is accompanied by English-language instruction plaques.

The Cistercian abbey of Mogiła

ul. Klasztorna 11 • ☎ 12 644 2331 • Tram #15 or #20 from pl. Centralny (the #15 runs direct from Basztowa in the Old Town) to ul. Klasztorna, then a 5min walk

Situated in the semi-rural suburb of Mogiła, 2km east of plac Centralny, the **Cistercian Abbey** (Opactwo Cystersów) was built around 1260 on the regular Cistercian plan of a triple-aisled basilica with a series of chapels in the transepts. The Abbey Church, one of the finest examples of early Gothic in the region, is a tranquil, meditative spot, the airy interior graced with a fine series of Renaissance murals. There's a serene Gothic statue of the Madonna and Child on the main altar, and some exuberant stained glass.

Wieliczka

Fifteen kilometres southeast of Kraków is the UNESCO-listed **salt mine** at **WIELICZKA** (Kopalnia Soli Wieliczka), a unique phenomenon described by one eighteenth-century visitor as being "as remarkable as the Pyramids and more useful". Salt deposits were discovered here as far back as the eleventh century, and from King Kazimierz's time onwards local mining rights, and hence income, were strictly controlled by the Crown. During World War II, the Germans manufactured aircraft parts in Wieliczka's subterranean chambers, using Poles and Jews as slave labour. Active mining ceased in 1997, although salt is still extracted from water seepages and much of the salt sold in Poland still comes from here. Profitability as a tourist attraction ensures that the mine remains a major employer: indeed, its popularity is such that you should be prepared for big crowds in summer.

The mine

Daily: April–Oct 7.30am–7.30pm; Nov–March 8am–5pm • Entrance to the mine is by 2hr guided tour only: Polish-language tours depart as soon as enough people have assembled; English-language tours depart every 30min from 9am onwards. Ticket-office queues are long, especially in summer and at weekends • English-language tour 84zł; Polish language tour 55zł • ⓦ kopalnia.pl • Trains run from Kraków Główny to Wieliczka-Rynek (every 30min; 25min), a short distance downhill from the mine

The result of almost ten centuries of continuous excavation, the **Wieliczka Salt Mine** (Kopalnia Soli Wieliczka) covers a much bigger area than the town itself. It consists of an estimated 300km of passageways on nine levels, the deepest of which is nearly 330m below ground. The 3.5km-long tourist route only takes in a fraction of this, descending through three levels to a depth of 125m – still sufficient to give you an impression of the mine's staggering scale. The temperature inside the mine is a constant 14°C, so remember to dress warmly.

The journey starts by walking down a long wooden staircase, escorted by guides wearing the smart green-and-black uniforms traditionally worn by miners on ceremonial occasions. Down below, visitors pass through a succession of chambers carved from the dark grey salt. For much of its history the mine was a virtual underground city where people worked, ate, kept horses and stored business archives. The only thing they didn't do here was sleep.

Undoubted highlight of the tour is **St Kinga's chapel** (Kaplica św Kingi), with staircases and chandeliers carved out of the salt by several generations of miners. Begun in 1895, the chapel features a pulpit in the form of Wawel Hill, and a statue of St

Kinga on the high altar. Daughter of King Bela IV of Hungary and wife of Bolesław the Chaste of Poland, Kinga allegedly lost her engagement ring somewhere south of Kraków, only to retrieve it some time later encased in a lump of Wieliczka salt – Kinga has been patron of Wieliczka's miners ever since. Work on the chapel is still going on, one of the most recent sculptural additions being a statue of Pope John Paul II. Down at the lowest level, the cavernous **Warsaw Hall** (Komora Warszawa) can hold a full symphony orchestra on its salt-carved stage. Nearby, a small **museum** reveals what a back-breaking job mining must have been – until the advent of mechanization, rock salt was laboriously crushed with hand-operated wooden machines.

The tour over, you can shop for salt-related souvenirs in the subterranean gift store, eat in the cafeteria, or send a card from the mine's post office, before returning to the surface via the noisily clanking lift.

ARRIVAL AND DEPARTURE   KRAKÓW

BY AIR
John Paul II airport (☎ 801 055 000, ⓦ krakowairport. pl) is at Balice, 15km west of the city, and handles both domestic and international flights.

Transport to the city Trains run from the airport (4am–11pm; every 30min; 9zł) to the main train station, Kraków Główny; buy tickets from machines in the station or from the conductor. If you are aiming for the western side of central Kraków, bus #252 goes from the airport forecourt to the Cracovia stop near the National Museum (5am–10.30pm; every 30min–1hr; 4zł); there are ticket machines at the bus top and inside the bus itself. Outside these hours, night bus #902 runs to the main train station (11.45pm–2.45am; every 90min; 4zł). Taxis cost 70–100zł depending on your bargaining skills and the time of day – fares rise by fifty percent between 11pm and 5am.

BY TRAIN
Kraków Główny The train station is on the northern fringes of the Old Town, within walking distance of central sights and hotels. There are no train station buildings above ground: access to the ticket hall and platforms is via an underground walkway which is also accessible from the Galeria Krakowska shopping centre. There are left-luggage lockers (from 6zł/24hr depending on size) near the ticket hall.

Destinations Białystok (1 daily; 5hr 40min); Częstochowa (4 daily; 1hr 40min); Gdańsk (5 daily; 5hr 30min); Katowice (4 daily; 2hr 20min); Krynica (2 daily; 4hr 30min); Łódź Widzew (2 daily; 2hr 40min); Nowy Sącz (6 daily; 2hr 50min); Oświęcim (10 daily, 2hr); Poznań (6 daily; 5hr–6hr); Przemyśl (6 daily; 3hr 45min); Rzeszów (8 daily; 2hr–2hr 40min); Szczecin (3 daily; 8hr); Tarnów (hourly; 1hr–1hr 20min); Warsaw (16 daily; 3hr 25min–3hr 45min); Wrocław (8 daily; 3hr 30min); Zakopane (7 daily; 3hr 10min–3hr 40min).

International destinations There are daily trains to Budapest Keleti (1 daily; overnight; 10hr 30min); Kiev (2 daily of which 1 overnight; 18hr; change at Przemyśl); Prague (1 daily; overnight; 8hr 30min); and Vienna (1 daily; overnight; 8hr 50min). International tickets have to be purchased from the designated international counters (*kasa międzynarodowa*) in the ticket hall – there are frequently long queues here in summer.

BY BUS
Dworzec Autobusowy The main bus station (☎ 703 403 340, ⓦ mda.malopolska.pl) is just east of the train station – to which it is connected by underground walkway. There is an ATM in the ticket hall and left-luggage lockers (daily 5am–11pm; 9–16zł depending on size). Note that long queues for tickets, especially at weekends and public holidays, are common. Buses depart from one of two storeys: the upper storey (marked as "G" or "górny" on signs and tickets) is on the same level as the ticket hall; the lower storey (marked as "D" or "dolny") is down the stairs.

Destinations Cieszyn (6 daily; 4hr); Kalwaria Zebrzydowska (every 15–30min; 50min); Katowice (every 15min; 1hr 40min); Nowy Sącz (every 30min; 2hr 30min); Oświęcim-Muzeum Auschwitz (every 30min; 1hr 30min); Tarnów (every 30min; 1hr 30min); Wadowice (every 30min; 1hr 20min); Zakopane (every 30min; 2hr 30min–3hr); Żywiec (hourly; 2hr 30min).

International destinations There are services to Lwów, Bratislava and most western European capitals.

BY MINIBUS
Private minibuses to small-town locations use a variety of different stops. Minibuses to Lanckorona use the Estradka parking lot on ul. Wita Stwosza; minibuses to Ojców National Park use the stop on Prądnicka opposite Nowy Kleparz market. Tickets are bought from the driver.

Destinations Lanckorona (Mon–Fri 8 daily; Sat & Sun 3 daily; 1hr 20min); Ojców National Park (Mon–Fri 8 daily, Sat & Sun 4 daily; 55min).

7

BY CAR

Arriving by car, major roads from all directions are well signposted, though once in the centre you'll need to cope with heavily enforced zonal parking restrictions, with the risk of wheel clamps on illegally parked vehicles. There's a conveniently placed guarded car park just behind Starowiślna 13, a 5min walk southeast of the centre, but it soon fills up.

GETTING AROUND

BY TRAM AND BUS

Central Kraków is compact enough to get around on foot, although the efficient municipal transport network (MPK), consisting of trams and buses, comes in handy if you're visiting attractions in the suburbs. Regular routes operate from about 5am until 11pm, after which night buses operate selected routes at hourly intervals.

Tickets You can buy tickets for daytime tram and bus services at kiosks and shops displaying the MPK symbol, or from ticket machines at bus and tram stops and inside the vehicles themselves. Regular single-journey tickets for Zone 1 (including everywhere you are likely to visit in Kraków except the airport) cost 3.80zł, although most journeys in the city centre will be covered by a 20min ticket (2.80zł). There are also tickets for 24hr (15zł), 48hr (24zł) and 72hr (36zł), as well as a weekend family ticket (two adults and two children under 16; valid on Sat & Sun; 16zł). Remember to punch your ticket on entering the bus or tram – if you're caught without a valid ticket, you'll be fined 240zł.

BY TAXI

Taxis cost around 7zł initial charge, followed by 2.50zł per kilometre. Remember to make sure that the driver turns on the meter, and note that from 11pm to 5am rates go up by fifty percent. There are ranks around the centre of town at pl. św. Ducha, Mały Rynek, pl. Dominikański, pl. Szczepański, pl. Wszystkich Świętych, ul. Sienna (roughly opposite the main post office) and on the roof of the main train station. Calling a radio taxi, such as Radio Taxi 919 (☎ 19191), Wawel Taxi (☎ 19666) or Barbakan (☎ 19661), can work out significantly cheaper. Partner Corporation operate a subsidized taxi service for people with disabilities, using minibuses adapted for wheelchair access (☎ 19688).

BY ELECTRIC GOLF CART

A fleet of four- to six-seater electric golf carts (*meleks*) is permanently lined up on the northeastern side of the main square, ready to take visitors on tours of the city, usually incorporating the Old Town, Kazimierz and Podgórze (120zł for 30min; 200zł for 1hr). They will also ferry passengers taxi-like to destinations around the city centre, although you will need to agree on a price beforehand.

BY BIKE

Cycling is a great way of getting around the Old Town, where heavy traffic is scarce. There is a network of bike rental points throughout the city operated by Wavelo (ⓦ wavelo.pl). You'll need to register online, enter credit card details and choose a payment plan – the "12hr per day" plan currently costs 29zł. There are other bike rental places around town: expect to pay 6–8zł/hr, or 40–70zł/day; weekend rates can be more expensive.

TOURS

Cracow Tours ul. Krupnicza 3 ☎ 12 430 0726, ⓦ cracow tours.pl. City tours as well as trips to Wieiczka and Auschwitz.

Free Walking Tour ☎ 513 875 814, ⓦ freewalkingtour. com. Free walking tours of the city.

Kraków Bike Tours Grodzka 2, south of Rynek Główny ☎ 12 430 2034, ⓦ krakowbiketour.com. Guided cycling tours in and around Kraków.

INFORMATION

Municipal tourist office (ⓦ infokrakow.pl) operates information booths at four central locations: in the Planty near the train station underpass at ul. Szpitalna 25 (daily: May–Oct 9am–7pm; Nov–April 9am–5pm; ☎ 12 354 2720); just north of Rynek Główny at ul. św. Jana 2 (daily 9am–7pm; ☎ 12 354 2725); south of Rynek Główny in the Wyspiański 2000 Pavilion, Wszystkich Świętych 2 (daily 9am–5pm); and in Kazimierz, at ul. Józefa 7 (daily 9am–5pm; ☎ 12 354 2728). It also has another information booth at the airport (daily 9am–7pm; ☎ 12 285 5341). Each has a stock of brochures listing accommodation and attractions or covering historical themes.

Listings The monthly booklet *Karnet* (ⓦ karnet.krakow. pl), published in a bilingual Polish/English edition by the Kraków Festival bureau and given free at tourist information centres and cultural institutions, is the best guide to city events, from classical music to theatre, gallery exhibitions and jazz and rock concerts.

ACCOMMODATION

There's an impressive choice of accommodation in Kraków, with many establishments occupying characterful old buildings in and around the Old Town. **Prices** are more expensive here than in most other Polish cities, with the majority of hotels of three-star-status and above charging 400zł a night and upwards. Cheaper rates are frequently available if you book online. Decent mid-range accommodation is provided by a growing number of guesthouses and B&Bs in central locations, with doubles costing 180–300zł. There is also a plethora of downtown hostels offering self-contained double rooms for 160–180zł as well as bunk-bed dorm accommodation for around 50–70zł per person.

HOTELS AND B&BS

THE OLD TOWN AND AROUND

★ **Andel's** ul. Pawia 3 ☎ 12 660 0100, ⓦ viennahouse. com; map page 264. Facing the Old Town from the plaza outside the train station, this elegant wedge of contemporary style is an eye-pleaser both inside and out, offering rooms with flat-screen TVs and big windows. There are plenty of lounge-style bar and restaurant areas to hang around in, plus a sauna and gym in the basement. 580zł

Copernicus ul. Kanonicza 16 ☎ 12 424 3400, ⓦ copernicus.hotel.com.pl; map page 264. Medium-sized luxury hotel occupying a carefully renovated historic building on a quaint, cobbled street. Spacious rooms and high standards of service – plus a small swimming pool in the basement. Not all rooms have bathtubs. 950zł

★ **Globtroter Guesthouse** pl. Szczepanski 7/15 ☎ 12 422 4123, ⓦ globtroter-krakow.com; map page 264. This characterful converted apartment building, with a jumble of furniture and balconies overlooking a secluded, beautifully maintained walled garden, is an increasingly rare find this close to the main square. No breakfast, but rooms do have electric kettles. 280zł

Pałac Bonerowski ul. Św. Jana 1 ☎ 12 374 1300, ⓦ palacbonerowski.pl; map page 264. Much-restored fifteenth-century town house that once belonged to the Boner family (Swiss merchants favoured by King Sigismund the Old) and now contains spacious rooms with swanky bathrooms and other creature comforts. Some of the smarter doubles and suites overlook the main square. The multi-tiered chandelier in the spiral staircase is a major feature – go to the top and look down for the full effect. Breakfast extra 65zł per person. 800zł

Pod Różą ul. Floriańska 14 ☎ 12 424 3300, ⓦ podroza. hotel.com.pl; map page 264. A hotel since the seventeenth century (and with a guest list that includes Balzac and Liszt), the much-renovated *Pod Różą* lives up to its pedigree with four floors of spacious rooms, each featuring swish bathrooms and leather furniture. There are several apartments (900–1600zł), including several swanky open-plan affairs with bathtubs. Breakfast extra 60zł per person. 550zł

Stary ul. Szczepańska 5 ☎ 12 384 0808, ⓦ stary.hotel. com.pl; map page 264. Fifteenth-century merchant's house, melding high-ceilinged rooms and original bare-stone features with resolutely modern furnishings such as sleek black armchairs and slinky designer bathrooms. As

well as a gym, saunas and a salt inhalation room, there's a small but spectacular swimming pool located in the brick-arched cellar. 950zł

Tango House ul. Szpitalna 4 ☎ 12 429 3114, ⓦ tango house.pl; map page 264. Hidden in a secluded courtyard just round the corner from the main square, *Tango* is a B&B of two halves: the old part has a spectacular nineteenth-century staircase and parquet-floored en suites; while the new part houses smart studios with kitchenettes. Breakfast extra 20zł per person. 320zł

Vienna House Easy Cracow Przy Rondzie 2 ☎ 12 299 0000, ⓦ viennahouse.com; map page 262. A solid mid-range choice that offers good rates because it's just outside the tourist-trodden routes, although it's still well-placed for the train station and Old Town. Cosy colourful rooms, helpful staff and a well-rounded buffet breakfast. 370zł

Wentzl Rynek Główny 19 ☎ 12 430 2664, ⓦ wentzl. pl; map page 264. Intimate, twelve-room hotel above a well-known restaurant (see page 301), offering spacious rooms with parquet floors, classy rugs and – in some cases – direct views onto the main square. 860zł

Wit Stwosz ul. Mikołajska 28 ☎ 12 429 6026, ⓦ hotelws.pl; map page 264. Bright, comfortable rooms in a historic house, just off the Mały Rynek. Good price for the quality and location. 490zł

★ **Wyspianski** ul. Westerplatte 15 ☎ 12 422 9566, ⓦ hotel-wyspianski.pl; map page 264. Viewed from the outside this grey lump doesn't look all that special, but it's an ideal mid-range choice, offering neat rooms and a buffet breakfast just big enough to make you feel slightly spoiled. Above all it's a convenient walking distance from almost everything (Old Town, Kazimierz and train station included), and it's got a big guarded car park at the back. 430zł

KAZIMIERZ AND PODGÓRZE

Alef ul. św Agnieszki 5 ☎ 12 424 3131, ⓦ alefhotel.pl; map page 284. With corridoors and stairwells packed with paintings, this is something of a temple to twentieth-century Polish art. Rooms themselves are more prosaic, featuring a strange mix of careworn furniture, adequate bathrooms and small TVs – although there are a couple of "high standard' doubles that mix antique furnishings with flat-screen TVs, a/c and modern bathrooms. 330zł

Klezmer-Hois ul. Szeroka 6 ☎ 12 411 1245, ⓦ klezmer. pl; map page 284. Characterful ten-room hotel in a rambling old house, furnished with some choice retro pieces from various past epochs. Rooms on the top floor feature sloping attic ceilings and the kind of stripy wallpaper you last saw in a costume drama. Some rooms have toilet and shower in the hallway, but don't let that put you off. 280zł

Kolory ul. Estery 10 ☎ 12 421 0465, ⓦ kolory.com. pl; map page 284. Bright en-suite rooms above the

7

Kolory café (see page 301), all with TV and folk-style design details. Some rooms overlook the lively pl. Nowy; marginally quieter rooms are at the back. 250zł

HOSTELS

Blueberry Hostel ul. Wrzesińska 5/5 ☎ 12 426 4664, ⓦ blueberryhostel.com; map page 264. Small, intimate hostel with a relaxing boutiquey feel in a beautifully decorated, parquet-floored flat near Kazimierz. Dorms 65zł, doubles 165zł

Greg & Tom Hostel ul. Pawia 12/7 ☎ 12 422 4100, ⓦ gregtomhostel.com; map page 264. Bright and cheerful apartment block opposite the train station offering backpacker accommodation without the rough edges. Expect modern six-bed dorms and parquet-floored doubles decked out in snazzy textiles. There's a gleaming communal kitchen, and as well as a buffet breakfast there's a free buffet "supper" in the early evening. Dorms 60zł, doubles 150zł

Mosquito Hostel Rynek Kleparski 4/6 ☎ 12 430 1461 and 660 926 190, ⓦ mosquitohostel.com; map page 264. Comfortable and sharply-decorated hostel just around the corner from the Stary Kleparz market, offering a mixture of dorms and private rooms. Informative staff, buffet breakfast and a cosy galley kitchen are the winning ingredients. Dorms 60zł, doubles 200zł

★ **Mundo** ul. Sarego 10 ☎ 12 422 6113, ⓦ mundo hostel.eu; map page 264. Tucked away in a calm courtyard midway between the Old Town and Kazimierz, this classy, comfortable hostel has twin rooms decked out with ethnic textiles, hardwood floors and bathroom facilities that look as if they've jumped straight out of a design magazine. The relaxing kitchen-cum-lounge features a free internet terminal, and there's a decent-sized breakfast. Doubles 180zł

Secret Garden ul. Skawińska 7, Kazimierz ☎ 12 430 5445 and 531 810 078, ⓦ thesecretgarden.pl; map page 284. This spacious, bright and cheerful hostel on a quiet street aims to provide hotel-like standards at hostel prices. There's a high proportion of double and triple rooms (although none of them are en-suite), a roomy kitchen and a front yard brightened up by pot plants. Breakfast extra 10zł per person. Doubles 160zł, triples 220zł

APARTMENTS

Red Brick Apartments ul. Kurniki 3 ☎ 12 628 6600, ⓦ redbrick.pl; map page 264. A handsome nineteenth-century building converted into holiday apartments in a range of shapes and sizes, with some wonderful split-level studios, and smart modern furnishings throughout. A brisk 10min walk from the Old Town proper, it's perfectly placed for the train station. Breakfast extra 25zł per person. Two-person apartments 340zł

CAMPSITES

There's a modest handful of suburban campsites in Kraków and, although they're several kilometres from the centre, all are well-served by public transport.

Krakowianka ul. Żywiecka Boczna 2 ☎ 12 268 1135, ⓦ krakowianka.com.pl; tram #8 from pl. Wszystkich Świętych; map page 262. Tranquil suburban site next to the wooded Solvay park, just off the Zakopane road 6km south of town. The Solvay shopping mall is a 5min walk away, but there's nothing else of sightseeing or recreational interest in this part of town. Open May–Sept. 65zł

Smok ul. Kamedulska 18 ☎ 12 429 8300, ⓦ smok. krakow.pl; buses #109, #209, #229, #239 and #249 from Salwator stop 100m east of the access road; map page 262. Privately run site 4km west of town in a pleasant suburban setting, with plenty of greenery, and within walking distance of both Las Wolski and Zwierzyniec. It's on the main Oświęcim road, well-signed in both directions. Open all year. 92zł

EATING

Wherever you eat in Kraków you'll find **prices** somewhat cheaper than in Western Europe, even in the smart establishments on and around the Rynek. Places can get crowded on busy summer weekends, when it's well worth reserving a table in advance if you've set your heart on somewhere in particular. You'll have no trouble picking up international **snack food** in the city centre. There are also numerous hole-in-the-wall joints doling out *zapiekanki* – baguette-sized slices of Polish bread topped with toasted cheese, tomato, mushrooms and a variety of other ingredients.

CAFÉS

There's a profusion of cafés in and around the city centre, many of which have outdoor terraces in summer. Those ringing the Rynek Główny make nice places in which to soak up the atmosphere, with the additional distraction of the assortment of roving buskers vying for the tourist złoty. Many cafés remain open well into the night and provide comfortable venues in which to indulge in more serious drinking.

THE OLD TOWN AND AROUND

Bona ul. Kanonicza 11; map page 264. Bookshop café with soothing jazzy music and a big range of leaf teas. Also serves sandwiches (12zł), a couple of hot-lunch pasta dishes (18zł) and a more-than-decent lemon meringue pie. Daily 11am–8pm.

Café Bunkier pl. Szczepański 3a; map page 264. Attached to the Bunkier Sztuki art gallery (see page 269), this café is a good place for a pot of tea and a cake during the daytime, *and* remains popular well into the evening. Its park-side terrace under a huge wrought-iron awning is a hugely popular meeting point and people-watching spot. Daily 9am–1am.

Camelot ul. św Tomasza 17; map page 264. Atmospheric café featuring rustic wooden tables, folk sculptures strewn around the place and original watercolours by self-taught naïve artist Nikifor. English-language newspapers are available, and delicious *szarlotka* (apple pie) is on the menu. The *Loch Camelot* cellar club (see page 306) frequently hosts concerts and cabaret. Daily 9am–midnight.

★ **Consonni** pl. Wszystkich Świętych 7 ☎ 12 426 4315; map page 264. Cute modern patisserie whose long glass counter-cabinet is absolutely stuffed with things that are very hard to refuse. Expect divine meringues, cream cakes, cheesecakes and all kinds of biscuits, plus good strong coffee, leaf teas, home-made lemonades and fruity smoothies. Mon–Sat 8am–8pm, Sun 8am–10am.

Jama Michalika ul. Floriańska 45; map page 264. Atmospheric old café, opened in 1895 and much patronized by artists of the Młoda Polska generation (see page 270). It's worth dropping in at least once to admire the lovingly preserved Art Nouveau interior, but the atmosphere of cultural ferment has long since departed. Mon–Thurs & Sun 9am–10pm, Fri & Sat 9am–11pm.

Massolit ul. Felicjanek 4 ⓦ massolit.com; map page 264. Canadian-owned bookshop-cum-café, with a huge selection of new and used English-language books spread throughout several rooms of a nineteenth-century apartment. With café tables plonked here and there between the shelves, it's a superbly soothing place in which to wind down over coffee – and the carrot cake is well worth a try too. Mon–Thurs 9am–9pm, Fri 9am–8pm, Sat & Sun 10am–8pm.

Massolit Bakery and Café ul. Smoleńsk 17 ⓦ facebook.com/MassolitBakeryCafe; map page 264. The recent offshoot of the *Massolit* (see above) doesn't have any books for sale, but it's a marvellous place to tuck into granola breakfasts, bagels (the salmon-and-cream-cheese variety clocks in at 13zł) and yummy cheesecake alongside your espresso, aeropress or drip. Mon–Fri 8am–7pm, Sat 10am–7pm.

Nowa Prowincja ul. Bracka 5; map page 264. Informal order-at-the-counter café with super-strong coffee, a good choice of snacks and salads, a fine *tarta cytrynowa* (lemon meringue pie; 9zł) and a charming array of distressed-looking benches and chairs to sprawl over. Daily 9am–11pm.

Noworolski Rynek Główny 1/3; map page 264. Elegant, ultra-traditional café occupying the arcaded eastern side of the Sukiennice, opened in 1910 and still boasting its original Art Nouveau interior. Once the favoured haunt of the Kraków cultural and political elite,

---

TOP 5 CAFÉS

Camelot see page 301
Nowa Prowincja see page 301
Tektura see page 301
Kawiarnia Literack see page 301
Kolory see page 301

---

it's nowadays patronized by older-generation Cracovians and tourists entranced by the historic setting. Daily 9am–midnight.

Słódki Wenzl Rynek Główny 19; map page 264. Square-side café combining bright modern decor with traditional standards with regard to cakes and pastries department. Definitely the place to linger over an extravagant ice cream while observing the flow of human traffic on the square. Daily 10am–11pm.

Tektura ul. Krupnicza 7 ☎ 501 855 260; map page 264. Hardcore coffee shop and café brewing up the black stuff from single-source, artisan-roasted beans. The cakes are excellent, and there are some good breakfast and lunchtime sandwich options too. It gets busy though. Daily 9am–9pm.

KAZIMIERZ AND PODGÓRZE

Galeria Tortów Artystycznych ul. Bożego Ciała 22, Kazimierz ☎ 604 055 530; map page 284. If cake is your priority then the "Gallery of Artistic Cakes" is hands-down your best option in Kazimierz, with a glass counter brimming with fruit-topped cheesecakes, rich chocolate confections and deliciously wobbly cream slices. Daily 9am–8pm.

Kawiarnia Literacka ul. Krakowska 41, Kazimierz ☎ 503 773 844, ⓦ kawiarnia-literacka.pl; map page 284. One of the best of Kraków's bookshop-cafés, with tables strewn among the bookshelves, and a small kids' play area. Excellent coffee and fruit cocktails, alongside a snack list that runs from croissants to hummus and salads. Good choice of alcohol too, embracing Argentinian wine and Bulgarian brandy. Daily 11am–11pm.

★ **Kolory** ul. Estery 10, Kazimierz ☎ 12 429 4270, ⓦ kolorycafe.pl; map page 284. Parisian-themed café with reproduction French posters plastering the walls and something of a shrine to wayward songwriting genius Serge Gainsbourg above the bar. Reassuringly strong coffee makes this a popular daytime hang-out, although it's just as popular in the evening when many Kazimierz bar-crawlers kick off their nocturnal journey with a drink or two here. Mon–Thurs & Sun 8am–midnight, Fri & Sat 8am–2am.

Rękawka ul. Brodzińskiego 4, Podgórze; map page 284. A supremely mellow spot featuring mildly distressed furniture and a sprinkling of houseplants, *Rękawka* serves up seriously strong coffee as well as sandwiches, fancy

7

7

KRAKÓW ICE-CREAM PARLOURS

You can find decent ice cream on almost every corner in Kraków, although a couple of parlours enjoy a particular measure of cult status.

Good Lood pl. Wolnica 11, Kazimierz ☎695 336 010; map page 284. Popular ice-cream parlour serving up signature ices such as creamy strawberry, alongside experimental one-offs, and sorbets for the dairy-conscious. Daily 11am–10pm.

Lody na Starowiślnej (Pracownia Cukiernicza Stanisław Sarga) ul. Starowiślna 83, Kazimierz; map page 284. A local favourite for over thirty years, this place was serving made-on-the-premises ice cream in a variety of own-recipe flavours, long before artisan ice cream became popular. Whether it still deserves its reputation as the best ice-cream shop in Kraków is very much a matter of taste, but it still draws huge queues. Note that it turns into a doughnut bakery in winter (Nov–Feb). Daily 9am–7pm.

Mediterranean salads and an exemplary *szarlotka* (apple pie). The perfect place to recharge your batteries if you've been looking round the Podgórze and Płaszów districts. Daily 9am–9pm.

RESTAURANTS

Mainstream restaurants concentrate on the pork, veal and poultry dishes traditional to Polish cuisine, usually with the addition of a few steaks and other international dishes. Mediterranean cuisine is common in the more style-conscious establishments, while Asian restaurants – some Arabic and Indian, but mostly Chinese and Vietnamese – are making their presence felt in and around the centre. Several restaurants in the Kazimierz district concentrate on the Jewish culinary tradition, with dishes like jellied carp and *czulent* (meat-and-barley stew) appearing on menus.

THE OLD TOWN AND AROUND

Balaton ul. Grodzka 37 ☎12 422 0469; map page 264. Cheap, unpretentious Hungarian-themed restaurant serving up paprika-rich stews and robust red wines, although you don't have to be a paprika fan to fit in here – the freshwater fish and roast fowl are also recommended. A simple but filling goulash soup will set you back 20zł, potato pancakes with goulash sauce 37zł. Daily noon–10pm.

★**Del Papa** ul. św. Tomasza 6 ☎12 421 8343, ⓦdelpapa.pl; map page 264. Cosy Italian restaurant with a restful garden patio, serving up some of the best fresh pasta in the city. There's plenty in the veal cutlet line (try the crispy-coated *cotoletta alla Milanese* for 35zł), plus freshwater and sea fish (pike perch with walnut and pear 40zł), and a good list of Italian wines. Daily 11.30am–11pm.

Farina ul. św Marka 16 ☎12 422 1680, ⓦfarina.com.pl; map page 264. Bare floorboards and floral tablecloths strike a note of homely domesticity for this Iberian-themed seafood restaurant. Opt for the baked sea bream (75zł) or sea bass (85zł) rather than the more prosaic fried or grilled fillets of fish. Daily noon–11pm.

Międzymiastowa ul. Dolnych Młynów 10/7a ☎577 304 450, ⓦmiastowa.com; map page 264. Post-industrial bar-restaurant offering up well-executed global bistro fare in a bustling atmosphere. Expect lots in the pizza, pasta and burger line, plus meat and fish mains in the 35–45zł range. Gin cocktails are a speciality, and the home-made lemonades are well worth a guzzle. Cooked breakfasts and two-course set lunches (Mon–Fri noon–5pm; 20zł) provide additional reasons to pop by. Mon–Sat 9am–midnight, Sun 10am–midnight.

★**Miód Malina** ul. Grodzka 40 ☎12 430 0411, ⓦmiodmalina.pl; map page 264. Candlelight, rustic furniture and a colour scheme based on the restaurant's name ("Honey Raspberry") make this one of the most popular places in the centre to enjoy good food in a warm, informal atmosphere. The Polish-international menu ploughs through the usual chicken, veal, lamb and duck territory – although dishes are prepared with a bit more pizzazz than elsewhere. Most mains hover in the 45–70zł range, although inexpensive staples like *pierogi* an *gołąbki* are well under half that amount. Lleave room for the *szarlotka* (apple pie) with vanilla sauce. Daily noon–midnight.

Pimiento Argentino Rynek Główny 30 ☎12 430 62856, ⓦpimiento.pl; map page 264. This popular spot on the main square has a reputation for being the best place in town to tear apart a hunk of grilled flesh. Inded the menu is mostly about steak (250g of meat will set you back 70–120zł depending on the cut), although you can also choose shank of lamb, pork ribs or fish. Daily noon–11pm.

Pod Baranem ul. św. Gertrudy 21 ☎12 429 4022; map page 264. Plain, unpretentious and reliable source of moderately priced Polish food. The small menu includes the inevitable pork-chop fare but also a couple of fish choices, as well as venison (35zł) and boar (40zł). Daily 11am–11pm.

Pod Norenami ul. Krupnicza 6 ☎661 219 289, ⓦpodnorenami.pl; map page 264. Oriental restaurant serving vegetarian and vegan food in a serene interior featuring semi-distressed wood furniture and a few

CANTEEN RESTAURANTS AND CHEAP EATS

As you might expect from a university city, Kraków is well supplied with buffet food bars and order-at-the-counter **canteens**. Many of these dish out filling and cheap portions of Polish standards such as *pierogi*, *barszcz* and *placki*, although there's a growing choice of vegetarian fare and international street food too.

THE OLD TOWN

Chimera ul. św. Anny 3 ☎12 292 1212; map page 264. Expansive buffet selection in a soothing courtyard, with attractively priced main courses, a salad bar and plenty of vegetarian choices. Daily 9am–10pm.

Greenway ul. Krupnicza 22; map page 264. Comfy vegetarian café-restaurant offering an excellent choice of cheap and healthy stews and savoury pancakes,

along with a good salad selection. Mon–Fri 9am–9pm, Sat & Sun 10am–8.30pm.

Przypiecek ul. Sławkowska 32; map page 264. Simple wooden-bench eatery that serves excellent *pierogi* made on the premises. Own-recipe specials include vegetarian *pierogi* with broccoli, and *pierogi kresowie* (*pierogi* stuffed with buckwheat and chopped liver). Open 24hr.

KAZIMIERZ AND PODGÓRZE

Jadłodajnia Wczoraj i Dziś pl. Bohaterów Getta 10 ☎12 656 2075; map page 284. Mellow, relaxing order-at-the-counter place that has been a family business for eighty years. Good *pierogi* from 8zł, plus dishes-of-the-day (check the blackboard) priced at around 18–20zł. Well placed for MOCAK and the Emalia Factory. Daily 10am–6pm.

Pierogi u Vincenta ul. Bożego Ciała 12 ☎506 806 304; map page 284. Lemon walls and a weird-shaped chandelier make this quite an arty place in which to wolf down a broad selection of own-recipe *pierogi* at 12–16zł per portion. The trademark minced-meat-and-lentil *pierogi* are well worth trying, and

there are also plenty of vegetarian options (such as *pierogi* with broccoli and feta). Only six tables. Daily 11am–9pm.

Polakowski ul. Miodowa 39 ☎12 421 1721; map page 284. Tasty Polish food served up in a country-kitchen interior, with soups weighing in at around 6–7zł, and mains from 12zł. Very popular, so be prepared to share a table. Daily 9am–10pm.

Szalom Falafel ul. Jakuba 21 ☎508 316 348; map page 284. Israeli takeaway serving falafel, hummus, *shakshuka* (eggs poached in spicy red sauce) and pizza – with genuinely kosher ingredients. Daily 9am–10pm.

discreet oriental touches. The red and green curries (28zł) are excellent, and there are large lists of Chinese dishes (with tofu or seitan substituting for chicken and pork) and sushi with vegetables or tofu. Mon–Thurs & Sun noon–10pm, Fri & Sat noon–11pm.

Pod Różą ul. Floriańska 34 ☎12 424 3300; map page 264. Perfectly prepared Polish-European cuisine in the glass-covered courtyard of the *Pod Różą* hotel. The menu limits itself to a handful of classic main courses (70–80zł), with game and fish well represented. Fabulous soufflés and semifreddos for dessert (25–30zł), and a long wine list. Daily noon–11pm.

Smak Ukraiński ul. Grodzka 21 ☎12 421 9294, ⊕ukrainska.pl; map page 264. Reasonably priced Ukrainian restaurant with tables squeezed into a folksy cellar, and more courtyard seating up top. Filling meaty favourites from Poland's eastern neighbour include *tarnopolskie zrazy* (flattened dumplings stuffed with mincemeat), *zakarpatski delikates* (a pork and bacon roll in sweet and sour sauce) and various grills – washed down with *kvass* (a traditional malt drink) or Obołoń lager. Daily 8am–11pm.

Szara Rynek Główny 6 ☎12 421 6669, ⊕szara.pl; map page 264. Modern European cuisine in an upscale but not over-formal environment, with lamb, game and fish dishes featuring heavily. Mains hover around the 70–90zł range, but cheaper daily specials are usually on offer as well. Be aware that portions are on the small side. Daily 11am–11pm.

Szara Gęś Rynek Główny 17 ☎12 430 6311, ⊕szarages.com; map page 264. Classic Polish cuisine in an elegant suite of barrel-vaulted rooms, with roast goose, venison and freshwater fish playing starring roles among the entrées (50–70zł). Finish off with one of the extravagant, set-piece desserts. Daily noon–11pm.

Wentzl Rynek Główny 19 ☎12 429 5299, ⊕restauracja wentzl.pl; map page 264. Top-quality international cuisine with a French accent, attentive service and seating by the main square. It's deservedly expensive, with main courses of goose, lamb, steak and fish weighing in at around 70–90zł. Daily noon–midnight.

Wierzynek Rynek Główny 15 ☎12 424 9600, ⊕wierzynek.pl; map page 264. Historic restaurant on several floors, with a refined interior and centuries of tradition, serving up the best in Polish pork and duck, as well as the kind of goat, venison and sturgeon dishes that you might not see so often elsewhere. With mains costing 90–150zł, it's not the cheapest place in town, but probably worth it. Booking is essential if you want a table inside in the evening: the outside terrace has a faster turnover and you may well be lucky. Daily noon–midnight.

KAZIMIERZ, PODGÓRZE AND AROUND

Horai pl. Wolnica 9 ☎ 12 430 0358, ⓦ horairestaurant. pl; map page 284. Popular oriental restaurant that goes for restrained modern decor rather than Far Eastern kitsch. There's a broad range of pan-Asian cuisine on the menu (mains 27–33zł), although it's the Thai dishes that stand out. Mon–Thurs & Sun noon–10pm, Fri & Sat noon–11pm.

Karakter ul. Brzozowa 17 ☎ 795 818 123, ⓦ facebook. com/karakter.restauracja; map page 284. A modern European menu of grill-steaks, roast duck and fish (mains 35–45zł) served up in a smart, post-industrial interior with graphic art on the walls. It's also a good place for wine and cocktails, with bread-and-pâté platters (23zł) an excellent accompaniment. Mon 5–11pm, Tues–Thurs & Sun noon–11pm, Fri & Sat noon–midnight.

Marchewka z groszkiem ul. Mostowa 2 ☎ 12 430 0795, ⓦ marchewkazgroszkiem.pl; map page 284. A typical Kazimierz interior of bare floorboards and antique-shop furnishings provides the homely setting for good-value, good-quality dining. There are some tasty soups, and hearty traditional mains such as pork knuckle, roast duck and *zrazy* (rolled beef stuffed with pickles), mostly for 30zł or under. Ukrainian brews Obołoń and Lvivskie count among the bottled beers. They also do cooked breakfasts for around 10zł. Daily 9am–10pm.

Nolio ul. Krakowska 27 ☎ 12 346 2449, ⓦ nolio.pl; map page 284. Smart, jazzy pizzeria, serving tasty pizzas with carefully sourced ingredients (the mozzarella comes from a farm in Italy). A simple Margherita wil set you back 21zł. Very popular, so book ahead. Daily 10am–11pm.

Studio Qulinarne ul. Gazowa 4 ☎ 12 430 6914, ⓦ studioqulinarne.com; map page 284. Located in a former bus garage (though you wouldn't know by looking at it), this stylish place has high ceilings and folding doors opening up onto the street. Order from the seasonally-changing menu of fish and meat, or opt for the three-course set menu (150zł) or the five-course menu with wine pairing (305zł). It's also a popular place for a drink, with a seductive list of cocktails and shots. Mon–Sat 6–10pm.

Szara Kazimierz ul. Szeroka 39 ☎ 12 429 1219, ⓦ szarakazimierz.pl; map page 284. Pretty much the same menu (and similarly high standards of presentation and service) as the Old Town branch of *Szara* on Rynek Główny (see page 303), but in a wonderful Kazimierz location. Steak, lamb, duck and fish mains cost 60–80zł, and there are two-course set lunches on weekdays for 35zł. In summer choose between pavement seating on the picturesque ul. Szeroka, or back-patio seating in a walled garden behind the Remu'h synagogue. Daily 11am–11pm.

ZaKładka ul. Józefińska 2 ☎ 12 442 7442, ⓦ zakladka bistro.pl; map page 284. Excellent and not-too-pricey French-inspired cuisine, from seafood to poultry and rabbit, with mains around 50zł; substantial salads cost 26–36zł. It's also a perfect place to stop for wine and a bite – baguette sandwiches and other snacks are chalked up on the board. Tues–Thurs noon–11pm, Fri & Sat noon–midnight, Sun noon–10pm.

Zazie ul. Józefa 34 ☎ 500 410 829, ⓦ zaziebistro.pl; map page 284. Checked tablecloths and an intimate atmosphere produce a French bistro vibe, ideal for tucking into quiches (15zł), potato gratin dishes (27zł) and traditional mains such as beef bourguignon (31zł). Superb desserts, and a marvellous list of French wines. Mon 5–11pm, Tues–Thurs & Sun noon–11pm, Fri & Sat noon–midnight.

NOWA HUTA

Stylowa os. Centrum bl. 3 ☎ 12 644 2619; map page 262. Opened in 1956 and long considered Nowa Huta's only upmarket address, *Stylowa* is nowadays a rather charming and old-fashioned place that offers an insight into what top restaurants were like in communist-era Poland. The menu is a standard *barszcz*-to-pork-chop journey through Polish cuisine, with the occasional racy foreign dish such as Chicken Kiev thrown in for good measure. Mains rarely exceed the 25zł mark. Daily 10am–10pm.

DRINKING AND NIGHTLIFE

The bulk of Kraków's **drinking** culture takes place in the innumerable bars of the Old Town and Kazimierz. The bar-filled **Tytano complex** (a former cigarette factory on ul. Dolnych Młynów, just west of the Old Town) is the one other location you need to take note of when planning an evening out. Many bars have DJs and dancing in the evening, and there isn't always a clear distinction between drinking venues and nightclubs.

BARS
THE OLD TOWN AND AROUND
Dym ul. św Tomasza 1; map page 264. Narrow coffee-bar-cum-drinking den with artfully distressed walls and a similar-looking clientele. Outdoor seating in the alleyway provides a Mediterranean vibe in summer. Daily 10am–

midnight.

House of Beer ul św. Tomasza 35 ☎794 222 136; map page 264. This roomy and convivial Old Town pub is the ideal place to plough your way through a selection of the increasingly excellent ales turned out by Poland's small breweries. There is always a handful of guest beers on tap, while the choice of bottled varieties runs into the hundreds. A menu of straightforward pub food makes it a handy place to catch a bite. Daily 2pm–2am.

Pauza ul. Stolarska 5/3 ☎608 601 522, ⓦpauza. pl; map page 264. Roomy first-floor hang-out with a crowded bar area and loungey spaces on either side. With art exhibitions on the walls, occasional DJs and a fridge full of craft beers, it's a typically Cracovian hangout. Daily 10am–2am.

Vis-à-vis Rynek Główny 29 ☎12 422 6961; map page 264. Functional, matt-black café-bar on the main square, long favoured by Polish artists and still something of a cult destination among older Cracovian drinkers. There's outdoor seating in spring and summer. The statue seated at a table beside the entrance is of actor and director Piotr Skrzynecki (1930–97), long associated with the Piwnica pod Baranami cabaret group (see page 306). Mon–Fri 8am–11pm, Sat 9am–11pm, Sun 10am–11pm.

★ **Weźże Krafta** ul. Dolnych Młynów 10/3 ☎12 307 4050; map page 264. Roomy, high-ceilinged post-industrial space in the courtyard of the Tytano complex, with a mind-boggling choice of beers from boutique breweries across Poland. Daily 2pm–2am.

KAZIMIERZ AND AROUND

Alchemia ul. Estery 5 ☎12 421 2200, ⓦalchemia. com.pl; map page 284. Darkly atmospheric, candlelit café-pub in the heart of Kazimierz. You'll see bohemians, fashionably arty types, local drunks and bemused tourists lolling around in its suite of four rooms. Top-quality live music (mostly jazz or alternative rock) in the basement. Daily 9am–4am.

★ **Don Chichote** ul. Krakowska 5; map page 284. Enjoyably cramped and intimate bar with a range of nooks and crannies on two levels, and Czech Holba beer on tap (and a bigger choice in bottles). It's a really great place to catch live music (from cover bands to top blues and jazz), if the musicians can get on to the tiny stage. Daily 4pm–3am.

Drukarnia Nadwiślańska 1 ☎12 656 6560, ⓦdrukarnia club.pl; map page 284. Roomy bar just over the river from Kazimierz, with several rooms decked out in different styles, from arty Parisian café to brash party pub. There's also a basement-level gig venue hosting regular rock and jazz. Mon–Sat 9am–3am, Sun 9am–1am.

Eszeweria ul. Jozefa 9 ☎12 292 0458, ⓦbit.ly/ Eszeweria; map page 284. Characteristically dimly-lit Kazimierz café bar that is sometimes so dark inside that

you can't even see the person behind the counter, never mind the range of drinks on offer. Once you've succeeded in choosing your tipple, sink into one of the salvage-chic armchairs indoors, or head for the small and intimate courtyard at the back. Mon–Thurs & Sun 9am–2am, Fri & Sat 9am–4am.

Forum Przestrzenie ul. Marii Konopniclej 28 ⓦforum przestrzenie.com; map page 284. Occupying the reception of the former *Forum Hotel*, this hugely popular café-bar extends out onto the riverbank in summer, offering deckchairs, film shows, food fairs and an indie-retro musical mix. A decent food menu (veggie curries 18zł) and fantastic views of the Wawel add to the list of attributes. Daily 11am–2am.

Mleczarnia ul. Meiselsa 20 ☎12 421 8532, ⓦbit.ly/ Mleczarnia; map page 284. Small, dark and smoky, *Mleczarnia* offers the archetypal lets-get-drunk-in-grandma's-living-room Kazimierz experience. Its beer garden (on the opposite sie of the road) is one of the most popular spots in Kraków come the summer. Daily 10am–2am.

Piękny Pies ul. Bożego Ciała 9 ⓦbit.ly/PieknyPies; map page 284. Something of a late-night haven for committed drinkers, decadent intellectuals and die-hard eccentrics, the "Beautiful Dog" gets the mixture of student scruffiness and Central European chic just right. Join the throng around the bar in the front room, slump into a dark sofa in the lounge area or descend to the basement to check out what the weekend DJs are playing. Mon–Sat 4pm–5am, Sun 4pm–2am.

Singer ul. Estery 22 ☎12 292 0622, ⓦbit.ly/Singer Krakow; map page 284. Classic Kazimierz café-bar whose retro style – nineteenth-century parlour furniture, lacy tablecloths and an old piano in the corner – has been mercilessly copied by its rivals. With a mixed clientele of laid-back locals and foreign interlopers, *Singer* comes into its own in the early hours when the bar area turns into an impromptu dancefloor. The name refers to the old tailors' sewing machines that serve as tables. Daily 9am–3am or later.

CLUBS AND GIG VENUES

We've listed dedicated clubs with a regular line-up of DJs or live bands below. As far as live music is concerned, jazz has a long tradition in Kraków and is generally easier to find than rock – although it's worth checking listings or looking out for posters on the off-chance that there's something going on.

THE OLD TOWN AND AROUND

Harris Piano Jazz Bar Rynek Główny 28 ⓦharris. krakow.pl; map page 264. Basement space right on the main square offering a regular programme of blues, funk and jazz. Jam sessions are usually free; gigs cost 10–30zł depending on who is playing. Performances usually start around 9.30pm. Daily noon–2am.

7

7

CABARET

Cabaret in Kraków dates back to the pre-World War I period, when artists associated with the Młoda Polska movement (see page 270) established the **Zielony Balonik** (Green Balloon) cabaret to provide a showcase for political satire, comedy sketches and song. The tradition was revived in communist times with the creation of the **Piwnica pod Baranami** in 1956, initially a student-run affair that endured to become Kraków's longest running and best-loved cabaret. The Piwnica pod Baranami, at Rynek Główny 27 (☎12 421 2500, ⓦpiwnicapodbaranami.pl), is still going strong today; its main rival is **Loch Camelot**, ul. św. Tomasza 17 (☎602 763 680, ⓦlochcamelot.art.pl) – the latter established in 1992 in order to revive the traditions of the original Zielony Balonik. Performances are usually at the weekend and tickets sell out fast, so it's best to book in advance.

Piec'Art ul. Szewska 12 ☎12 429 6425, ⓦpiecart.pl; map page 264. Two barrel-vaulted cellars, one with a small stage at the end, with jazz gigs and jam sessions a couple of times a week (and an entrance charge depending on who's playing). There's a full menu of nibbles and main meals if you want to make an evening of it. Daily 2pm–3am.

Pod Jaszczurami Rynek Główny 8 ⓦpodjaszczurami.pl; map page 264. Large student club under vaulted gothic ceilings, constantly busy as much for its cheap beer and laid-back atmosphere as for its packed programme of events – anything from karaoke and retro discos to literary readings. Mon–Thurs & Sun 11am–1am, Fri & Sat 11am–4am.

Prozak 2.0 pl. Dominikanski 6 ⓦprozakdwazero.pl; map page 264. Subterranean warren for serious fans of house, hip-hop, techno and other electronic-dance genres. Tues–Sun 11pm–5am.

U Muniaka ul. Floriańska 3 ☎12 423 1205, ⓦfacebook.com/umuniaka; map page 264. Founded by saxophonist Janusz Muniak (1941–2016), this tunnel-like live-music space offers live jazz every night of the week. The cute cubby-hole bar area is packed with antique-style clutter. Daily 7pm–2am.

ZetPeTe ul. Dolnych Młynów 10 ⓦfacebook.com/zetpete.krk; map page 264. Concert and club venue in the Tytano complex hosting indie bands, DJs of every genre from dub reggae to house, and regular theatre, film and art events. Daily 5pm–2am or later depending on event.

WEST OF THE OLD TOWN

Studio ul. Budryka 4 ☎12 617 4545, ⓦklubstudio.pl; map page 262. Located in the middle of a student campus, this is Kraków's leading venue for live music as well as a popular clubbing venue, hosting international touring acts, leading Polish bands and regular student discos. On non-event days it serves as a pub. Check the schedule before heading out. Daily noon–2am.

Żaczek al. 3 Maja 5 ⓦklubzaczek.pl; map page 262. Student bar-cum-club in a roomy glass-fronted pavilion on the ground floor of the Żaczek hall of residence – which ensures a regular supply of party-happy customers. During term time (roughly Oct–June) the bar is open for coffee and beers during the daytime, while gigs, DJ-driven events and karaoke nights kick off during the evenings. Daily noon–11.45pm or later, depending on event; closed July–Sept.

ENTERTAINMENT

There is a good deal happening on the cultural front, with a regular diet of classical music and opera and a long-established cabaret tradition. The tourist information centre at ul. św. Jana 2 (see page 298) handles information and tickets for many cultural events, and also holds copies of the free listings guide *Karnet* (ⓦkarnet.krakow.pl).

CONCERT VENUES

Capella Cracoviensis ⓦcapellacracoviensis.pl. The city's best-known choir gives fairly regular concert performances at churches and other venues around the city – check the website for details.

Filharmonia Szymanowskiego ul. Zwierzyniecka 1 ☎12 619 8733, ⓦfilharmonia.krakow.pl. Home of the Kraków Philharmonic, one of Poland's most highly regarded orchestras. Box office Mon–Fri 2–7pm, Sat from 1hr before concerts.

Kraków Opera ul. Lubicz 48 ☎12 296 6260, ⓦopera.krakow.pl. Occupying a state-of-the-art auditorium opened in 2008 (also the city's main venue for ballet), Kraków's

opera company mixes the classics with contemporary works. The season lasts from late Sept to mid-June.

PUPPET THEATRE

Groteska ul. Skarbowa 2 ☎12 633 4822, ⓦgroteska.pl. Innovative puppet theatre whose shows frequently feature a mixture of live actors and marionettes. Childrens' shows take place in the daytime, grown-up material in the evening.

CINEMAS

Films arrive in Kraków at around the same time as their release in Western Europe, and are usually shown in the original language with Polish subtitles.

Ars ul. św. Tomasza 11 ☎ 12 421 4199, ⓦ ars.pl. Five screens (the Aneks, Kiniarnia, Reduta, Salon and Sztuka) grouped together in one building in the heart of the Old Town, screening everything from commercial blockbusters to art films and cinema classics.

Kijów al. Krasińskiego 34 ☎ 12 433 0033, ⓦ kijow.pl. Elegant 1960s-era concrete-and-glass building, showing current box-office hits and the odd art film in a big auditorium just west of the Old Town.

Kino pod Baranami Rynek Główny 27 ☎ 12 423 0768, ⓦ kinopodbaranami.pl. Old-school cinema with original seats and fittings. Non-mainstream cinema from around the globe.

FOOTBALL

One of the most successful soccer clubs in the country, Wisła Kraków (ⓦ wisla.krakow.pl) were the dominant force in Polish football during the early 2000s. They play at Wisła Stadium on ul. Reymonta (a 25min walk from the Rynek; otherwise bus #144 passes close by). Kraków's other team is Cracovia (ⓦ en.cracovia.pl), the first soccer team to be formed in Poland (in 1906), and the favourite boyhood club of Pope John Paul II. Cracovia won the championship five times between 1921 and 1948, but have spent recent seasons struggling to survive in the top flight. Their stadium is just beyond the *Cracovia* hotel on al. Focha.

SHOPPING

Most of Kraków's mainstream fashion and household shops are concentrated in big shopping **malls**, leaving the Old Town to be colonized by an interesting mix of luxury-label clothes stores, craft shops and souvenir outlets. As you would expect from a university city, there are more second-hand **bookshops** (*antykwarjaty*) than you can shake a stick at, many of which are well worth a browse for vintage guidebooks, art albums and English-language novels.

BOOKSHOPS

Antykwariat na Kazimierzu ul. Meiselsa 17, Kazimierz ☎ 12 292 6153; map page 284. Antiquarian bookstore in the basement of the Judaica Foundation (see page 287), with a good selection of Judaica and history-related titles. Mon–Fri 10am–6pm, Sat & Sun 10am–2pm.

Austeria ul. Józefa 38, Kazimierz ☎ 12 430 6889; map page 284. Occupying the ground floor of the High Synagogue (see page 285), Austeria carries a large selection of books about Jewish Poland in most major languages, plus a selection of Klezmer CDs. Daily 10am–6pm.

Empik ul. Floriańska 14 ☎ 22 462 7250; map page 264. Multimedia store with plenty in the way of maps, tourist-oriented books, glossy international magazines and English-language literature. Also has a branch at the Galeria Krakowska mall (see page 308). Daily 9am–9pm.

Lokator ul. Mostowa 1, Kazimierz ⓦ lokatormedia.pl; map page 284. The books on sale here are mostly Polish-language, although the selection of small-press art books, and graphic art by local illustrators make this the kind of place where you may well pick up something stylish and unusual. There's a café too. Daily 10am–8pm.

Massolit ul. Felicjanek 4 ☎ 12 432 4150, ⓦ massolit.com; map page 264. Engagingly eccentric English-language bookstore, with a warren of stuffed shelf-lined rooms. Impressive collection of Polish literature in English translation, and titles concerning every aspect of Central European history and culture. It also houses a unique café (see page 301). Mon–Thurs & Sun 10am–8pm, Fri & Sat 10am–9pm.

FOOD AND DRINK

Krakowsi kredens ul. Grodzka 7 ☎ 12 423 8159; map page 264. Delicatessen serving quality local products, from fresh sausage and smoked hams to jars of horseradish sauce, preserved fruit and jams. Mon–Fri 10am–7pm, Sat 11am–7pm, Sun 11am–5pm.

Produkty Benedyktyńskie Krakowska 29, Kazimierz ☎ 12 422 0216; map page 284. Preserves, honeys, cheeses, marinated mushrooms and a host of other traditional delicatessen products, bearing the brand of the Benedictine Monastery of Tyniec. It's all high quality and mostly locally made – although little of it is produced by the Benedictines themselves (it's actually a clever franchising operation conceived by the business-savvy monks). Mon–Fri 9.30am–6pm, Sat 9.30am–2pm.

ART, DESIGN AND FASHION

Ideafix ul. Bocheńska 7, Kazimierz ☎ 12 422 1246; map page 284. Clothes, accessories, lampshades and other useful domestic items, all made by young Polish designers. Mon–Fri 11am–7pm, Sat 11am–5pm.

Forum Designu ul. Dolnych Młynów 10 ☎ 730 740 025, ⓦ forumdesignu.pl; map page 264. Located at the back of the Tytano ex-factory complex this is a large showroom bringing together a broad range of local fashion, accessory and household designers – essential browsing. Mon–Sat 11am–7pm, Sun 11am–5pm.

Mapaya ul. Józefa 3, Kazimierz ☎ 501 351 444, ⓦ mapaya.pl; map page 284. Elegant, arty, eclectic and above all wearable clothes from an established local designer. Mon–Sat 11am–6pm.

MOCAK ul. Lipowa 4; map page 284. The souvenir shop inside the MOCAK Museum of Contemporary Art sells more than just postcards and coffee-table books; you can pick up quality clothes, handbags, ties and soft furnishings made by local designers. Tues–Sun 11am–7pm.

7

KRAKÓW FESTIVALS AND EVENTS

Kraków offers a year-round diet of cultural events and folkloric happenings, many of which are well worth planning your holiday around.

SPRING–SUMMER

Misteria Paschalia Easter week ⓦ misteriapaschalia.com. Major festival of religious music through the ages, with performances in historic churches or in Kraków Filharmonia.

Kraków Film Festival (Krakowski festiwal filmowy) Late May–early June ⓦ kff.com.pl. Highly-regarded gathering of documentaries, animated films and shorts, with the coveted Złoty Smok ("Golden Dragon") awards going to the winners.

Dragon Parade (Parada smoków) First or second Sat in June ⓦ paradasmokow.pl. A fantastic, fun-for-all-the-family occasion organized by the Groteska puppet theatre, involving a parade of dragons (made by community groups and schools) around Kraków's main square. In the evening there's a son-et-lumière show with dragons battling each other below Wawel hill.

Midsummer's Eve (Wianki) June 23 or nearest weekend ⓦ biurofestiwalowe.pl. Traditionally celebrated by virgins throwing wreaths in the River Vistula while bonfires are lit on the water's edge, Wianki is nowadays the excuse for a huge outdoor pop concert and firework display.

Crossroads (Rozstaje) Early July ⓦ rozstaje.pl. World music from Poland and abroad, usually with a strong central European flavour. Open-air gigs in front of Kazimierz town hall.

Festival of Jewish Culture (Festiwal kultury żydowskiej) Late June to early July ⓦ jewishfestival.pl. Ten days of music, theatre, film and discussion, with events held in the synagogues and squares of the Kazimierz district. The festival closes with a huge open-air Klezmer concert on ul. Szeroka.

Live Festival Aug ⓦ livefestival.pl. Major rock festival attracting top international headliners, held in a field near the Polish Air Force Museum.

AUTUMN–WINTER

March of the Dachshunds (Marsz Jamników) First or second Sun in Sept. Sausage dogs wearing fancy dress are paraded through town to the main square, where prizes are awarded for the best outfits.

Sacrum Profanum Mid- to late Sept ⓦ sacrumprofanum.com. Open-ended festival of modern music featuring anything from Kraftwerk to Karlheinz Stockhausen. A high-quality event featuring top international performers.

Unsound Oct ⓦ unsound.pl. Week-long celebration of international electronica and avant-garde DJ activity in various venues across town.

Szopki competition (Konkurs szopek) Dec. Kraków craftsmen display their *szopki* (ornate Christmas cribs featuring model buildings and nativity figures) on the main square. The best examples are displayed in the Kraków History Museum.

Advent market (Targi Bożonarodzeniowe) Dec. Craft stalls selling jewellery, accessories, woodcarving, speciality foodstuffs, mulled wine and sausages fill the main square.

Pan Tu Nie Stał ul. Nadwiślańska 9, Podgórze ☎ 667 432 671; map page 284. Witty, individual and eminently affortable T-shirts, bags, socks and hats from the Łódź-based design team. Mon–Fri 11am–7pm, Sat 11am–5pm.

Poster Gallery/Galeria plakatu ul. Stolarska 8 ☎ 12 421 2640, ⓦ postergallery.art.pl; map page 264. Dedicated to the best of Polish poster art, with a rich collection of originals, reproductions and graphic art postcards. Mon–Fri 11am–6pm, Sat 11am–2pm.

SHOPPING MALL

Galeria Krakowska ul. Pawia 5 ⓦ galeria-krakowska.pl; map page 264. Central shopping mall next to the train station. Mon–Sat 9am–10pm, Sun 10am–9pm.

MARKETS

Hala Targowa Grzegórzecka; map page 264. Sizeable collectors' and bric-a-brac market held on Sunday mornings, an easy 5min trot east of the Old Town. Stamps, coins, badges, crafts, genuine antiques and pure junk. Sun 7am–2pm.

Plac Nowy Kazimierz; map page 284. Collectors' market most weekends, and a big clothes and accessories' market on Sundays. Sun 7am–2pm.

Stary Kleparz market map page 264. Bustling warren of stalls 5min north of the Old Town, with the best in fresh fruit and veg. It's also the ideal place to pick up fresh Carpathian sheep's cheeses such as *bundz* and *bryndza*, whole dried sunflowers and dried mushrooms. Mon–Sat till dusk.

Sukiennice Rynek Główny. Stalls running the length of the medieval cloth hall, selling amber jewellery, woollens, embroidery and a host of other souvenirs. A bit of a tourist trap, with prices to match. Daily 8am–dusk.

DIRECTORY

Consulates USA, ul. Stolarska 9 (☎12 424 5100, ⓦ pl. usembassy.gov).

Hospital and clinics University Hospital (Szpital Unywersytecki) is east of the Old Town at ul. Kopernika 50 (☎12 351 6601). The emergency ambulance number is ☎112. A reputable private clinic in a central location is Ars Medica, ul. Warszawska 17 (Mon–Fri 8am–7pm; ☎12 423 3834, ⓦ ars-medica.pl).

Internet access Garinet, ul. Floriańska 18 (daily 9am–10pm; ☎12 423 2233).

Laundry Frania Café, ul. Stradomska 19 (daily 9am–10pm; ☎783 945 021 ⓦ franiacafe.pl).

Left luggage There are lockers at both the train and bus stations (6–16zl/day).

Pharmacies Useful central pharmacies include Bobilewicz, ul. Grodzka 26 (Mon–Fri 8am–9pm, Sat 9am–6pm, Sun 10am–5pm) and Pod Złotym Tygrysem, cnr Rynek Główny and Szczepańska (Mon–Fri 8am–8pm, Sat 8am–3pm, Sun 10am–2pm). Pharmacies take it in turns to stay open 24hr according to a rota; check the information posted in their windows to find out which one is on duty.

Post offices The main post office is at ul. Westerplatte 20 (Mon–Fri 7.30am–8.30pm, Sat 8am–2pm, Sun 9–11am); it has a poste restante and offers phone and fax services. The branch just outside the train station has one counter open 24hr.

Małopolska

The area around Kraków presents an attractive landscape of rolling fields, quiet villages and market towns. It traditionally goes by the name of **Małopolska** (literally "Little Poland"), a territory which – together with Wielkopolska ("Great Poland"), formed the heartland of the medieval Polish state. It's a region marked by the progress of Polish history, from the medieval castles of the **Ojców National Park** to the Renaissance shrines of **Kalwaria Zeberzydowska** and the birthplace of the Polish pope, Karol Wotyła, at **Wadowice**. Most attractive of the Małopolska towns is **Tarnów**, a historic market centre whose dainty Rynek looks like a miniaturized version of the more famous main square in Kraków. The most visited destination in this part of Poland is also its most notorious, the **Auschwitz-Birkenau** concentration camp – preserved more or less as the Nazis left it – at Oświęcim, due west of Kraków.

All of the destinations covered in this section can be treated as day-trips from Kraków. Most places in Małopolska can be reached by bus from Kraków in a couple of hours, and there are express trains to Tarnów.

Oświęcim: Auschwitz-Birkenau

Seventy kilometres west of Kraków, **OŚWIĘCIM** is notorious throughout the world for being the site of Auschwitz-Birkenau, the Nazi prison, labour camp and extermination site in which an estimated 1.1 million people were murdered between 1940 and 1945. As many as 200,000 people passed through some part of the Auschwitz camp system and survived, however, providing a hugely important body of testimony on how the Nazi incarceration and extermination systems actually worked. Indeed the museum at the site was largely founded by former inmates – which helps to explain why Auschwitz is such a symbolic witness to history today. Of all the museums you are ever likely to visit in your life, this is arguably the most profound.

The Auschwitz **memorial museum** consists of two main parts: the **Auschwitz** concentration camp, 3km west of central Oświęcim, and the **Birkenau** extermination camp 3km further to the northwest. Auschwitz is visited by well over 1 million people every year and can get very busy; entrance is subject to time restrictions, and tickets must be reserved in advance online. The much larger Birkenau site is less likely to be swamped by visitors, and arguably offers more opportunities for contemplation.

Auschwitz

Daily: Feb 7.30am–4pm; March & Oct 7.30am–5pm; April, May & Sept 7.30am–6pm; June–Aug 7.30am–7pm; Nov & Jan 7.30am–3pm; Dec 7.30am–2pm • From April to Oct visitors to Auschwitz (not Birkenau) between 10am and 4pm must sign up for a guided tour (regular departures; 3hr); visitors wishing to visit the site independently can come outside those hours • Independent visitors free; guided tours in Polish 30zł, in English 45zł • All visitors, whether looking around the site independently or joining a guided tour, must book in advance on the museum website – unless they have signed up for one of the tours offered by travel agencies in Kraków (see page 298), in which case advance booking is not necessary • ⓦ auschwitz.org

Approaching the site from the visitors' car park, the **Auschwitz concentration camp** looks at first like an innocuous collection of warehouses or a semi-abandoned military barracks. It's only when you pass through the entrance gate bearing the notorious cast-iron inscription *Arbeit Macht Frei* ("Work brings freedom") that you begin to realize you are in a place of imprisonment, torture and death.

The site itself consists of the sturdy brown-brick **blocks** built by the Poles to house migrant workers in the 1930s and taken over by the Germans in 1939. Most of these blocks are devoted to "national exhibitions", containing memorial displays established by countries whose citizens suffered at Auschwitz Many of them – such as block 20, devoted to French and Belgian Jews; or block 21, covering Jews from the Netherlands – are beautifully presented, profoundly evocative and powerfully moving. Block 13 contains an account of Europe's Roma communities, together with Germany's Sinti – a Roma-related people who also fell victim to Nazi race policies. Other blocks contain more general displays covering the inner workings of the camp: numbers 5 and 6 are particularly harrowing, containing room after room of spectacles, prosthetic limbs, suitcases, clothes and shoes confiscated from inmates and abandoned here when the Germans retreated.

Between blocks 11 and 10 stands the flower-strewn **Death Wall**, where thousands of prisoners were summarily executed. **Block 11** itself is where the first experiments with Zyklon B gas were carried out on Soviet POWs and other inmates in September 1941. The prison blocks finish by a **gas chamber** and a pair of ovens where the bodies were incinerated.

Birkenau

Daily: Feb 7.30am–4pm; March & Oct 7.30am–5pm; April, May & Sept 7.30am–6pm; June–Aug 7.30am–7pm; Nov & Jan 7.30am–3pm; Dec 7.30am–2pm • Free • A free shuttle bus departs from the Auschwitz site to Birkenau every 15min • ⓦ auschwitz.org

Roughly 3km northwest of Auschwitz, the subsidiary camp of **Birkenau** was begun in autumn 1941 to accommodate Soviet POWs earmarked for use as slave labour. Most of the Soviet prisoners died of starvation that same winter, and Birkenau was adapted to suit a new and even more sinister purpose: the mass murder of Europe's Jews. Transports got under way by late 1942, with victims delivered to a railway platform right inside the camp before being marched to the gas chambers. Disposing of the murdered – and sorting through their stolen belongings – was a labour-intensive task requiring a huge population of (mostly) Jewish slave workers, who lived in appalling conditions in Birkenau's barracks.

It is along the former railway tracks that you enter the camp, passing through a red-brick archway before emerging into the numbingly huge, 170-hectare site. Most of the barrack blocks were razed in 1945 but a handful remain, empty but for examples of the wooden cots and meagre mattresses on which inmates slept.

At the northern end of the camp is a stark grey **monument** to the dead, rising above the twisted ruins of **gas chambers** dynamited by the Germans as they retreated. The monument was unveiled in April 1967, when up to 200,000 people (including many former inmates) converged on the camp to take part in what the authorities termed a "grand anti-fascist meeting". To the right of the monument, beyond a group of cylindrical sewage-treatment towers, is an area dubbed "**Canada**" by the inmates (due to its far-away position in the extreme north of the camp) where gas chambers and crematoria stood beside warehouses where the belongings of victims were processed. One of the few buildings still standing here is the so-called **Sauna**, where newly arrived prisoners were undressed, shaved and assigned camp clothes – a grim museum

7

AUSCHWITZ AND THE FINAL SOLUTION

Following the Nazi invasion of Poland in September 1939, Oświęcim and its surrounding region were incorporated into the domains of the Third Reich and the town's name changed to **Auschwitz**. The establishment of concentration camps in the newly conquered territory was a German priority right from the start – camps in Germany proper were already overcrowded with political prisoners, and the occupation of Poland dramatically increased the number of potential undesirables who would need to be interned. The unassuming town of Oświęcim made the perfect site – it already had a Polish-built camp for migrant workers, and the buildings were easily converted into prison blocks. The inmates made an ideal source of slave labour for Oświęcim's burgeoning chemical industry.

Work on the camp began in April 1940, and obedient Nazi functionary **Rudolf Höss** was appointed its commander. In June of that year the Gestapo delivered the first contingent of prisoners, mostly Polish students and schoolchildren arbitrarily rounded up to serve as a deterrent to others. Overworked, undernourished and subjected to beatings, the prisoners suffered from high mortality rates right from the beginning. Following Hitler's attack on the Soviet Union in 1941, Soviet POWs flooded into the camp, necessitating the construction of a huge subsidiary camp at nearby Birkenau, and conditions deteriorated further – deaths from starvation or arbitrary violence set standards of cruelty that were to worsen as the war progressed.

Auschwitz's role as an extermination camp for Jews grew out of the Wannsee Conference of January 1942, when the Nazis decided on the so-called **Final Solution** and began looking for locations where mass-murder could be conducted on an industrial scale. The technology of mass killing had already been perfected after experiments in the use of poison gas at Auschwitz and other locations, and **Auschwitz-Birkenau** was now chosen as one of the principal venues for the forthcoming genocide.

By the end of 1942, **Jews** were beginning to be transported to Auschwitz from all over Europe, many fully believing Nazi propaganda that they were on their way to a new life of work in German factories or farms. After a train journey of anything up to ten days in sealed goods wagons and cattle trucks, the dazed survivors were herded up the station ramp, lined up for inspection and divided into two categories by the SS: those deemed "fit" or "unfit" for work. People placed in the latter category, up to 75 percent of all new arrivals, were then ordered to undress, marched into the "shower room" and gassed with **Zyklon B** cyanide gas sprinkled through special ceiling attachments. In this way, up to two thousand people were killed at a time (the process took fifteen to thirty minutes), an efficient method of murdering people that continued relentlessly throughout the rest of the war. The greatest massacres occurred from 1944 onwards, after the special railway terminal had been installed at Birkenau to permit speedier "processing" of the victims to the gas chambers. Gold fillings, earrings, rings and even hair – subsequently used, amongst other things, for mattresses – were removed from the bodies before incinerating them. Cloth from their clothes was recycled into army uniforms, their watches given to troops in recognition of special achievements or bravery.

The precise numbers of those murdered in Auschwitz-Birkenau may never be known. According to most estimates, about 1,100,000 people died in the camp, the vast majority (90 percent) of whom were Jews, along with sizeable contingents of Romanies (Gypsies), Poles, Soviet POWs and a host of other European nationalities.

display takes you methodically through the process. Just beyond lie the remains of Crematorium IV, burned down in a desperate revolt by 450 Sonderkommando (the inmates who were forced to carry out body-disposal tasks) in October 1944. A few steps further on is the so-called **Grey Lake**, where human ashes were once deposited.

Oświęcim: the Auschwitz Jewish Centre

pl. Ks. Jana Skarbka 3 • Mon–Fri & Sun: April–Sept 10am–6pm; Oct–Nov 10am–5pm • 10zł • ☎ 33 844 7002, ⓦ ajcf.pl

The centre of Oświęcim itself lies 3km east of the Auschwitz camp on the opposite bank of the River Soła. Aside from an unassuming Rynek, ringed by cafés, and a red-brick Gothic church overlooking the river, the main focus of interest is the **Auschwitz Jewish Centre** (Centrum Żydowskie w Oświęcimiu) just off the Rynek, which occupies the former mansion of the Konreich family and incorporates the next-door synagogue. Jews lived in Oświęcim for over 400 years prior to World War II, calling the town Oshpitzin, and it's the rich private and social histories of the people of Oshpitzin that makes this museum a celebration of life rather than a meditation on horror. Photographs of pre-World War II life feature football matches, scouts and guides, school fetes, bathing trips to the River Soła and, perhaps most compellingly, images of local Christians and Jews together digging defensive ditches and tank traps on the eve of war in 1939. A connecting door leads to the synagogue, where a beautifully restored prayer hall centres on a handsomely balustraded bimah.

ARRIVAL AND INFORMATION

By bus Buses from Kraków (every 20–30min; 1hr 30min) drop off and pick up on ul. Wieźniów Oświęcima, 200m east of the entrance to the Auschwitz site. Ask the driver for "Auschwitz Muzeum" if you're unsure where to get off. Most of these buses terminate in central Oświęcim, 3km further east.
By train Arriving by train (10 daily, 2hr) is less convenient: Oświęcim train station lies 2km north of central Oświęcim, and 2km northeast of the Auschwitz site.

OŚWIĘCIM: AUSCHWITZ-BIRKENAU

By tour Several travel agencies in Kraków (see page 298) run tours to the site.
Tourist information There is a tourist information centre (May–Sept Mon–Fri 8am–6pm, Sat & Sun 8am–4pm; Oct–April daily 8am–4pm; ☎ 33 843 0091, ⊛ it.oswiecim.pl) in the shopping mall/restaurant complex opposite the entrance to Auschwitz camp.

EATING AND DRINKING

There is a canteen restaurant at the Auschwitz Museum entrance (open same times as the museum) serving order-at-the-counter snacks, drinks and hot meals. The shopping mall on the opposite side of the road also has a couple of snack and pizza places.
Café Bergson pl. Ks. Jana Skarbka 2 ☎ 573 086 436.

Coffee, cakes and bagels in the Kluger House, just behind the Jewish Centre in central Oświęcim. Also serving as the Jewish Centre's gift shop, it's a colourful and relaxing place, with homely furnishings and extra seating on the secluded mezzanine. Daily 11am–7pm.

Kalwaria Zebrzydowska, Lanckorona and Wadowice

Southwest of Kraków lies an enchanting landscape of rolling hills and sleepy country towns, two of which are of great significance to Poles: **Kalwaria Zebrzydowska**, a centre of pilgrimage second only to Częstochowa (see page 353), and **Wadowice**, birthplace of Karol Wojtyła, better known as Pope John Paul II. **Lanckorona**, a charming village of traditional wooden houses, is within walking distance of Kalwaria and can be visited in the same trip. Numerous local buses work the Kraków–Kalwaria–Wadowice route, ensuring that you can see all three places in the space of a long day.

Kalwaria Zebrzydowska and around

Nestled among hills some 30km southwest of Kraków, the town of **KALWARIA ZEBRZYDOWSKA** looks and feels like a footnote to its main attraction: a hilltop monastery whose Calvary route, linking various Baroque chapels in the neighbouring hills, is one of Poland's most compelling landscapes.

The Calvary came into being in the early seventeenth century, when Mikołaj Zebrzydowski, lord of nearby Lanckorona (see page 314), became convinced that the local countryside's similarity to the landscape outside Jerusalem gave it a special spiritual significance. Having decided to mark his discovery with the construction of a series of Calvary chapels, he sent an envoy to Jerusalem for drawings of the holy places – many of his buildings are modelled on those in the holy city. The place is particularly busy during the **Festival of the Assumption** (Aug 15) and at **Easter**, when the Passion Plays are performed on Maundy Thursday and Good Friday and the events of Holy Week are re-enacted outside the Calvary chapels. With local volunteers tied on crosses and onlookers dressed as Romans, it's a powerful spectacle.

The monastery and the Calvary chapels

Dominating the landscape from its perch, the Benedictine **monastery** is reached via a steep street which darts up from Kalwaria's undistinguished town centre. The towering main **Basilica of the Virgin** (Bazylika Matki Bożej) is a familiar Baroque effusion, with a silver-plated figure of the Virgin standing over the high altar. The object that inspires the greatest devotion, however, is the **painting** of the Virgin and Child in the Zebrzydowski chapel, said to have been shedding tears at regular intervals since the 1640s.

The starting point for the **Calvary** begins immediately outside the monastery. It's really made up of two interlocking routes, the main Via Dolorosa (marked as "Dróżki pana Jezusa" on signboards), and a sequence of Marian Stations ("Dróżki Matki Bożej"), each of which wends its way up and down hillocks, along tree-lined avenues, through forest and in and out of rustic villages. Every few hundred metres or so you'll come across a cluster of chapels – some of which resemble insignificant huts, others magnificent domed structures with the appearance of mini-cathedrals. There are regular processions of schoolkids and coach parties "doing" the chapels nearest the monastery, but the further reaches of the Calvary routes are relatively crowd-free, contemplative places.

Lanckorona

Five kilometres east of Kalwaria Zebrzydowska, and reached by a minor road off the Kraków–Bielsko-Biała highway, the hillside village of **LANCKORONA** has long been noted for its traditional folk architecture and unhurried rustic feel. At the centre of the village lies a spacious, sloping **Rynek**, lined with low, pastel-coloured houses, their broad shingle roofs hanging over wooden-pillared porches. Paths leave the upper end of the square towards Lanckorona's medieval **castle**, an evocative ruin shrouded in forest.

ARRIVAL AND INFORMATION   KALWARIA ZEBRZYDOWSKA

By bus Buses run from Kraków (every 15–30min; 50min) to Kalwaria Zebrzydowska **bus station**, a 20min walk east of the monastery.

By train The Kalwaria Zebrzydowska–Lanckorona **train station** (served less frequently by trains from Kraków to Bielsko-Biała, Sucha Beskidzka and Zakopane) is a further 10min walk from the bus station, in the same direction.

By minibus Lanckorona is served by regular minibus from

ul. Wita Stwosza in Kraków (Mon–Fri 8 daily; Sat & Sun 3 daily; 1hr 20min) although it makes sense to combine Lanckorona with a visit to Kalwaria – the easternmost point of the Calvary route (the Bernardine Church in Brody) is only a 45min walk over the hill.

Tourist information Kalwaria's tourist office is at ul. Mickiewicza 4 (Mon–Fri 8am–4pm; ☏ 33 873 3771, ⓦ it. ckstkalwaria.com).

ACCOMMODATION AND EATING

Pensjonat Lanckorona 114 ☏ 33 876 3401. Café-restaurant on Lanckorona's main square serving up everything from *pierogi* to tortillas in a rustic interior decked out with semi-antique knick-knacks. Mon–Thurs 10am–6pm, Fri–Sun 10am–7pm.

Restauracja Klasztorna In the monastery courtyard, Kalwaria Zebrzydowska ☏ 608 211 992. Cheap, filling Polish staples and a terrace with outstanding views. Daily 7am–8pm.

Wadowice: Birthplace of Pope John Paul II

ul. Kościelna 7 · Daily: April & Oct 9am–6pm; May–Sept 9am–7pm; Nov–March 9am–4pm; closed last Tues of month · Guided tours obligatory: Polish-language tour departs every 10min; English-language tour 2–3 daily (reserve online) · Polish tour 20zł; English tour 30zł; free on Tues · ☏ 33 823 3565, ⓦ domjp2.pl

Fourteen kilometres west of Kalwaria Zebrzydowska is the little town of **WADOWICE**, whose rural obscurity was shattered by the election of local boy **Karol Wojtyła** to the papacy in October 1978. Main point of reference here is the **Birthplace of Pope John Paul II** (Muzeum Dom Rodzinny Ojca Świętego Jana Pawła II), a few steps away from the onion-domed **parish church** where Karol Wojtyła was baptized in 1920. The simple two-room apartment where Wojtyła spent the first eighteen years of his life has been turned into a tasteful and restrained **museum**. It certainly succeeds in portraying the late pontiff as a rounded personality, with photographs of him skiing, hiking, playing in goal for the school team and taking part in student drama productions.

ARRIVAL AND INFORMATION

WADOWICE

By bus The bus station, with services to Kraków (every 30min; 1hr 20min) and Kalwaria Zebrzydowska (every 30min; 40min), is on the eastern side of the town, a 10min walk from the main square.

Tourist information The tourist office is at ul. Kościelna 4 (April–Oct Mon–Fri 9am–4pm, Sat & Sun 10am–4pm; Nov–March Mon–Fri 8am–4pm, Sat 10am–4pm; ☎33 873 2365, ⓦit.wadowice.pl).

EATING

Kawiarna Galicja ul. Kościelna 5 ☎33 823 3420. Right next to Pope John Paul II's birthplace, this is an ideal place to try *Kremówka Wadowicka*, the deliciously wobbly slice of custard that is thought to have been the former pontiff's favourite treat. Daily 9am–7pm.

Ojców National Park

Immediately northwest of Kraków, the limestone gorge of the **Ojców valley** has a unique microclimate and an astonishingly rich variety of plants and wildlife. Most of it is protected by the **Ojców National Park** (Ojcówski Park Narodowy: ⓦojcowskiparknarodowy.pl), one of the country's smallest and most memorable protected regions. With an attractive and varied landscape of scenic river valley, twisted rock formations and peaceful forests, the park is perfect for a day's walking or cycling. The *Ocjówski Park Narodowy* map (1:22,500), widely available both in Kraków and on arrival in Ojców, is a useful aid.

The valley also gives access to the most southerly of the **castles** built by King Kazimierz to defend the southwestern reaches – and, most importantly, the trade routes – of the country from the Bohemian rulers of Silesia. Known as the **Eagles' Nest Trail** (Szlak Orlich Gniazd), these mainly ruined fortresses are strung along the hilly ridge extending westwards from Ojców as far as Olsztyn.

Ojców and into the valley

The principal point of access to the river gorge is **OJCÓW**, 25km from Kraków, the national park's only village and in season filled to bursting with local school groups. Developed as a low-key health resort in the mid-nineteenth century, it's a delightful village, with wooden houses straggling along a valley floor framed by deciduous forest and craggy limestone cliffs.

Ojców Castle

April–Oct Tues–Sun 10am–4.45pm, stays open later at the height of summer • 3zł

Overlooking the village to the north is the ruined **Ojców Castle** (Zamek w Ojcowie), the southern extremity of the Eagles' Nest Trail and an evocative place in the twilight hours when it is circled by squadrons of bats. There's not much of the castle left, apart from two of the original fourteenth-century towers, the main gate entrance and the walls of the castle chapel, but there are excellent views over the winding valley.

Chapel on the Water

A few hundred metres north up the valley from Ojców Castle is the curious spectacle of the **Chapel on the Water** (Kaplica na Wodzie), straddling the river on brick piles. This odd site neatly circumvented a nineteenth-century tsarist edict forbidding religious structures to be built "on solid ground", part of a strategy to subdue the intransigently nationalist Catholic Church. These days, it's only open for visits between Masses on Sundays.

Kraków Gate and Shorty's Cave

Cave open daily: late April to Aug 9am–6.30m; Sept 9am–5.30pm; Oct 9am–4.30pm • 8zł • ⓦ grotalokietka.pl

Heading south from the village takes you through a small gorge lined with strange rock formations, most famous of which, about fifteen minutes out from the village, is the **Kraków Gate** (Krakowska Brama), a pair of rocks which seem to form a huge portal leading to a side valley. Before reaching the Kraków Gate you may well be enticed uphill to the west by a (black-waymarked) path to the **Shorty's Cave** (Grota Łokietka), some thirty minutes' distant, the largest of a sequence of chambers burrowing into the cliffs outside Ojców. According to legend, it was here that King Władysław the Short was hidden and protected by local peasants following King Wenceslas of Bohemia's invasion in the early fourteenth century. Around 250 m long, the rather featureless illuminated cave is a bit of a letdown if you've come expecting spectacular stone and ice formations. Individual travellers will have to wait to join a guided group before being allowed inside.

7 Pieskowa Skała Castle

Sułoszowa • **Courtyard** Daily 8am–dusk • Free • **Museum** May–Sept Tues–Thurs 9am–5pm, Fri 9am–1pm, Sat & Sun 10am–6pm; Oct Tues–Thurs, Sat & Sun 10am–4pm, Fri 10am–3pm; Nov–April Sat & Sun 9am–3pm (entry on the hour) • 18zł • ☎ 12 389 6004, ⓦ pieskowaskala.eu

Hugging the side of the valley 9km north of Ojców, **Pieskowa Skała** is the region's best-known and best-preserved castle. An elegant Renaissance rebuilding of a fourteenth-century original, complete with delicately arcaded courtyard, it rises up photogenically behind an 18m-high limestone pillar known locally as **Hercules' Club** (Maczuga Herkulesa).

The castle **museum** offers a breathtaking sweep through several centuries of art, beginning with some fine Gothic wood-carved Madonnas, St Barbaras and St Catherines, and an exquisitely rendered sculpture of St Mary of Egypt, her entire body covered by the long tresses of her hair. A spectacular bevy of altarpieces includes a grippingly gruesome *Martyrdom of St Stanisław* with his tormentor King Bolesław looking impassively on; another panel bears a bizarre scene of punishment in which the unfaithful wives of Kraków are forced to suckle puppies while their own children are put to the teat of a bitch. A sequence of Baroque rooms feature sumptuously decorated Flemish tapestries, the most notable among them depicting heroic scenes from the life of Alexander the Great, culminating in his triumphant entry into Babylon in a chariot.

ARRIVAL AND INFORMATION   OJCÓW NATIONAL PARK

By minibus Private minibuses run from Krakow, opposite Nowy Kleparz market (Mon–Fri 8 daily, Sat & Sun 4 daily; 55min).

Tourist information The PTTK information office (Mon–Fri 9am–3pm; ☎ 12 389 2010, ⓦ ojcow.pttk.pl) is next to the car park in the village of Ojców, and can help find accommodation if you want to stay over. A souvenir shop in the same building sells maps.

EATING

Bar Sąspówka Ojców 34 ☎ 602 366 337, ⓦ saspowka. pl. Located beside the car park beneath Ojców Castle, this simple café-restaurant has outdoor seating overlooking a fish pond. It serves decent *pierogi* and potato pancakes, and specializes in grilled trout (20zł). Daily 10am–7pm.

Restauracja Herbowa In Pieskowa Skała castle ☎ 501 573 415. Café-restaurant in the bare-stone surrounds of a medieval castle tower, serving a classy selection of Polish favourites, from *pierogi* (15zł) to beef cheeks braised in beer (28zł). You can enjoy coffee and cakes on the terrace at the top of the tower, offering fine views over the valley. May–Oct daily 10am–7pm.

Tarnów and around

Although somewhat in the shadow of its larger neighbour to the west, the regional centre of **TARNÓW**, 80km east of Kraków, is nonetheless a fascinating town in its own right. Long the seat of the wealthy Tarnowski family, Tarnów grew under their patronage to become an important Renaissance-era centre of learning, a branch of Kraków University being set up here in the mid-1500s. Later, wars and Partition brought the inevitable decline, and in the twentieth century Tarnów's long-standing Jewish population was a particular target for the Nazis. Frequent and fast rail connections make it an easy and attractive day-trip from Kraków, but Tarnów can also serve as a base for trips around the region, including north to the folk art centre of **Zalipie**.

The well-preserved Old Town retains all the essentials of its original medieval layout. Oval in shape, the chequerboard network of angular streets, cobbled alleyways and open squares is ringed by the roads built over the ruins of the sturdy defensive walls that were pulled down by the Austrians in the late nineteenth century.

The town hall

Rynek 1 • Tues & Thurs 9am–5pm, Wed & Fri 9am–3pm, Sat & Sun 9am–4pm • 8zł • ☎ 14 692 9000, ⓦ muzeum.tarnow.pl

Centrepiece of Tarnów's arcaded Rynek is the fifteenth-century **town hall**, a chunky, two-storey building whose parapet is topped by grotesque heads reminiscent of those adorning Kraków's Sukiennice. Inside is a branch of the **regional museum** (Muzeum

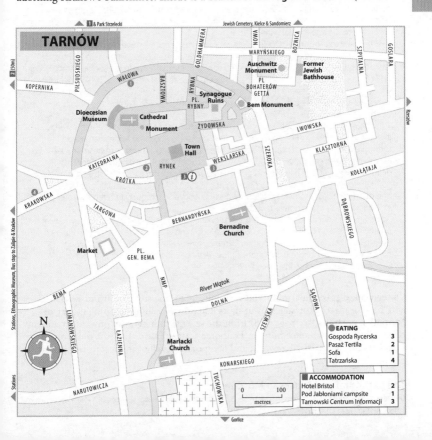

SARMATISM

A loose system of fashions, beliefs and values, the phenomenon known as **Sarmatism** defined Polish society in the seventeenth and early eighteenth centuries. Based on the erroneous belief that the Polish nobility was directly descended from the ancient **Sarmatians** – a tribe of Iranian origin who swarmed across eastern Europe between the first and fifth centuries AD – Sarmatism engendered a fascination with all things eastern.

The idea that Poles could be descended from Sarmatians seems to have sprung from a cartographical misunderstanding. Many Renaissance map-makers were unsure of what geographical label to apply to Eastern Europe, and scoured their classical history books in search of a suitable name: "Sarmatia" was what they came up with. Learned minds in Poland seized upon the beguiling idea that the Sarmatians had resided in Polish territory during antiquity, and were increasingly happy to adopt these mysterious horse-riding nomads as their ancestors. The idea that a Slav race like the Poles could claim descent from the Sarmatians was clearly absurd; however, intellectuals got round the obvious objections by arguing that it was merely the Polish aristocracy, not the common people, who were descended from the Sarmatians, and it was precisely this unique lineage that gave them the right to rule.

Polish high society knew very little about the Sarmatians, but assumed that they were similar in appearance to other Eastern races with whom they'd had more recent contact – especially the Turks and **Tatars**, who were a constant presence on Poland's southeastern borders. Under the influence of these neighbours, wealthy Poles developed a taste for luxuriant gowns and silken sashes, and this style of dress became universally adopted by a nobility eager to demonstrate its Sarmatian credentials. Armenian merchants did a roaring trade in caravanning exotic textiles into Poland from the East, and set up wholesale depots in Zamość and Kraków to deal with the demand.

Adherence to the Sarmatian ideal was not just a matter of fine clothes. The idea that the original Sarmatians were warlike conquerors was enthusiastically taken up by Polish aristocrats who were themselves expected to spend long months in the saddle campaigning on Poland's eastern borderlands. Sarmatism became a **moral code** which placed a higher value on action and bravery than on domestic pursuits, and which cultivated a brash disregard for social niceties. Hunting, feasting and drinking were extolled as the only activities worthy of a true Sarmatian lord.

By the middle of the eighteenth century, however, Poles in Kraków and Warsaw were increasingly adopting Western modes of dress and behaviour, and Sarmatism was left to the more conservative-minded aristocrats of eastern Poland. Indeed Sarmatism reached its apogee in the person of Polish-Lithuanian aristocrat **Karol Radziwiłł**, a man who deliberately played the hooligan in order to rile an increasingly etiquette-obsessed Warsaw court. He habitually subjected his peers to humiliating drinking marathons, once blew up one of his own castles in order to amuse party guests, and famously entered the royal palace in Warsaw in a carriage drawn by bears.

The Polish-Lithuanian state had ceased to exist by 1795, and what was left of Sarmatism quietly shuffled off with it. However the Sarmatist mindset has exerted a subtle influence over Polish society ever since. Whether in the boorish anti-Westernism of right-wing politicians, or the showy extravagance of the new rich, one has the feeling that the Sarmatians are yet to breathe their last.

Okręgowe), displaying armour and weapons, including some beautiful Persian and Turkish pieces. The spacious upstairs hall houses a show-stopping gallery of **Sarmatian portraits** (see page 318) from the seventeenth-century onwards, remnants of a collection which once hung in Podhorce Castle, east of L'viv. At the fore are members of the wealthy Rzewuski and Sanguszko families, in Eastern-influenced period dress.

The Cathedral and Diocesan Museum

Cathedral pl. Katedralny • Tues–Sat 10am–noon & 1–5pm, Sun 1–3pm • **Diocesan Museum** pl. Katedralny 6 • Tues–Sat 10am–noon & 1–3pm, Sun 9am–noon & 1–2pm • Free • ☎ 14 621 9993

Immediately west of the Rynek stands the **cathedral**, ostensibly dating from the fourteenth century but rebuilt in the nineteenth. A relatively uneventful interior is redeemed by a fine collection of Renaissance tombs near the altar, beginning with the grand sixteenth-century memorial to **Jan Tarnowski**, designed by Giovanni Maria Mosca and surrounded with friezes representing his military triumphs.

Behind the cathedral, a series of sixteenth-century tenements on a quiet, atmospheric side street house the **Diocesan Museum** (Muzeum Diecezjalne), one of the best collections of Gothic art in the country. The setting itself is splendid, with artworks hung gracefully in ancient rooms with original ceiling beams. Highlights include three large, fifteenth-century triptychs from St Leonard's Church in Lipnica Murowana, a lovely painting of a white-robed St Catherine of Alexandria, and an elegant set of fourteenth- and fifteenth-century wooden pietà.

The Jewish Quarter

East of the Rynek takes you into what used to be the **Jewish quarter** of the town, a fact recalled in the names of streets such as ulica Żydowska and Wekslarska ("moneylenders"). The first Jewish settlers arrived here in the mid-fifteenth century, and on the eve of World War II they constituted forty percent of Tarnów's population. In 1939 the Nazis established a **ghetto** to the east of the Old Town, filling it with local Jews as well as many transported in from elsewhere, and the population of the massively overcrowded area rose to forty thousand. Between June 1942 and September 1943, virtually all the ghetto's residents were shot or deported to death camps, principally Auschwitz, and most of the area was destroyed. A few Jewish monuments, however, remain.

Architecturally the narrow streets around ulica Żydowska, all of which escaped wartime destruction, remain essentially as they were before the war. The battered bimah, covered by a brick-pillared canopy that stands forlornly in the middle of a small square, is all that remains of the magnificent sixteenth-century **synagogue** that stood here until the Nazis gutted it in November 1939. Just northeast of here on the opposite side of plac Bohaterów Getta, the Moorish-looking **Jewish bathhouse** is now a shabby shopping arcade-cum-office block; it was from here that a group of 728 local people were transported to Auschwitz in June 1940 to become the first inmates of the camp, a fact commemorated by the monument just across the street.

Ethnographic Museum

ul. Krakowska 10 • Tues & Thurs 10am–5pm, Wed & Fri 9am–3pm, Sat & Sun 10am–4pm • 8zł • ☏ 14 622 0625

A ten-minute walk west of the Old Town along busy ulica Krakowska brings you to the outstanding **Ethnographic Museum** (Muzeum Etnograficzne), devoted in large part to the customs and culture of Poland's **Roma** (gypsy) community. An estimated twenty thousand Roma live in the country, the majority concentrated in eastern Małopolska and the Carpathians. There's a good collection of costumes, folk art and archival photographs, a sombre account of the Roma's treatment at the hands of the Nazis and, bravely, a section detailing contemporary prejudice against Roma in Polish society. To round things off, there are a group of four traditional painted Roma caravans displayed in the yard at the back of the museum. Each May a traditional Roma camp is re-created in the yard as part of the **Gypsy Summer Festival**.

Park Strzelecki

Ten minutes' walk north of the centre along ulica Piłsudskiego, **Park Strzelecki** is the town's main strolling ground, a tranquil kilometre-long stretch of flower beds and landscaped woodland. At its northern end stands the **mausoleum** of General Bem, an arresting Neoclassical monument standing on an island in the middle of a lake. It was built to house the relics of the hero, brought back to Poland from Aleppo in 1929 (see page 320).

7

> ## JÓZEF BEM (1784–1850)
>
> The Tarnów-born patriot and adventurer **Józef Bem** was a leading figure in the failed 1830–31 uprising against central Poland's tsarist rulers, a role for which he was widely celebrated. A prototype of the dashing military figures beloved of the Polish Romantic tradition, the swashbuckling general is almost equally celebrated in Hungary for his part in the 1848 uprising against Vienna. Following the failure of the Hungarian revolt, Bem travelled east to join Ottoman forces in their struggle with Russia, assuming the name Murat following a rapid (and tactically appropriate) conversion to Islam. Before having the chance to do much for the Ottomans, however, he died in Aleppo, Syria, his cult status among Poles already safely assured.

ARRIVAL AND INFORMATION   TARNÓW

By train The train station is situated on the southwest side of town, a 10min walk from the centre – buses #2, #9 or #41 will drop you on the edge of pl. Gen Bema at the southern side of the Old Town.
Destinations Kraków (hourly; 1hr–1hr 20min); Krynica (4 daily; 3hr 30min); Nowy Sącz (10 daily; 1hr 40min–2hr).
By bus The bus station is situated next to the train station.
Destinations Kraków (every 30min; 1hr 30min); Krynica

(5 daily; 2hr 45min); Nowy Sącz (16 daily; 1hr 45min); Zakopane (3 daily; 4hr); Zalipie (Mon–Fri hourly, Sat & Sun 5 daily; 40min).

Tourist information There is a tourist office at Rynek 7 (May–Sept Mon–Fri 8am–8pm, Sat & Sun 9am–5pm; Oct–April Mon–Fri 8am–6pm, Sat & Sun 9am–5pm; ☎ 14 688 9090, ⓦ it.tarnow.pl).

ACCOMMODATION

Hotel Bristol ul. Krakowska 9 ☎ 14 621 2279, ⓦ hotel bristol.com.pl; map page 317. Ideally situated between the train station and the Old Town, this once-grand hotel features serviceable rooms and heaps of pre-World War I atmosphere in the public areas. Breakfast is served in a charmingly olde-worlde dining room. 230zł
Pod Jabłoniami campsite Piłsudskiego 28A ☎ 14 621 5124, ⓦ camping.tarnow.pl; bus #30 from the train station; map page 317. Neat campsite a 15min

walk north of the centre, offering four-person cabins and tent and caravan pitches in an attractive apple orchard. Camping 65zł, cabins 165zł
Tarnowski Centrum Informacji Rynek 7 ☎ 14 688 9090, ⓦ it.tarnow.pl; map page 317. The tourist office has four guest rooms above the office – clean, modern and good-value en suites that should be booked ahead. No breakfast, but there are plenty of cafés in the vicinity. 100zł

EATING

Gospoda Rycerska ul. Wekslarska 1 ☎ 14 627 5980; map page 317. This unpretentious place just off the Rynek has pizza as well as grilled food and Polish standards such as *bigos* (a budget-busting 12zł) and *pierogi*, served up in a cosy wooden interior. Mon–Fri 11am–midnight, Sat & Sun 11am–noon.
Pasaż Tertila pl. Kazimierza Wielkiego 2 ☎ 14 627 8278, ⓦ pasaz-tarnow.pl; map page 317. Hidden away in a passageway just off the Rynek, this smart and welcoming restaurant is a good bet for Polish food. Mains range from *pierogi* through steaks to fish, with a sprinkling of globally-inspired dishes such as vegetarian *orzotto* (18zł) and chilli con carne (22zł). Daily noon–10pm.

Sofa ul. Wałowa 15 ☎ 535 700 408, ⓦ sofatarnow.pl; map page 317. Central café with a cosy living-room vibe and some gorgeous cakes. It's also a pretty useful place for breakfasts and light lunches in the salad-or-sandwich line (16–22zł). Mon–Fri 7am–8pm, Sat 8am–9pm, Sun 9am–9pm.
Tatrzańska ul. Krakowska 1 ☎ 14 622 4636; map page 317. Genteel café-restaurant patrolled by white-shirted wait-staff and stuffed full of house-plants, with an international menu and well-priced soups (8zł) and pastas (20zł). The place is also the local favourite for ice cream and cakes: to pass through Tarnów without trying *Tatrzańska*'s apple pie (*szarlotka*; 14zł) would be a crime. Daily 9am–10pm.

Zalipie

The sprawling village of **ZALIPIE**, 30km north of Tarnów, is a charming diversion into the folk traditions of rural Poland. Before the late nineteenth century, cottages here lacked chimneys, and village women used lime to whiten the soot-blackened outer walls of their houses. When chimneys were introduced the practice survived as a novel form of decoration, with women painting **geometric and floral motifs**, first inside their houses and later on outer walls. Word of the tradition spread, and Zalipie painters like Felicja Curyłowa (1904–74), were feted at Kraków ethnographic fairs of the 1930s. A first **house-painting competition** was organized in 1948, and since 1965 the event has been held annually on the weekend following Corpus Christi (May/June), with around twenty of Zalipie's houses receiving a fresh array of colourful patterns each year.

Felicja Curyłowa Museum

Zalipie 135 • Tues–Sun 10am–4pm • 4zł

Approaching Zalipie from the main Dąbrowa Tarnowska-Gręboszów road, signs point the way to the **Felicja Curyłowa Museum** (Muzeum Felicji Curyłowej), a century-old building, today cared for by descendants of Zalipie's most famous artist. Inside, the main living room or "black" room contains a massive stove, costumes, painted ceramics and heirlooms; while the "white" room, which was only used on Sundays and special occasions, holds the better furniture and embroideries.

Painter's House

Zalipie 128a • Mon–Fri 8am–4pm, Sat & Sun noon–6pm • Free

From the Felicja Curyłowa Museum, the loop road that runs around the village (roughly 3km in all) leads past more painted houses before reaching the **Painter's House** (Dom Malarek), the local cultural centre, where there is a display of photographs from past house-painting competitions as well as a gallery of oil paintings by local artists.

ARRIVAL AND DEPARTURE   **ZALIPIE**

By minibus Private minibuses operating the Tarnów–Gręboszów and Tarnów-Bieniaszowice routes pick up and drop off on the main road 1km south of Zalipie (roughly hourly Mon–Fri, 5 daily Sat & Sun); catch them from the stop on ul. Krakowska near Tarnow's bus station. The last minibus back to Tarnów passes through Zalipie around 6pm.

Podhale, the Tatras and the Pieniny

THE PEAKS OF TRZY KORONY

Podhale, the Tatras and the Pieniny

Forming the border with Slovakia, the Tatra Mountains are Poland's grandest and most beautiful, snowcapped for much of the year and markedly alpine in feel. Along with their foothills, the Podhale, and the neighbouring, more modest peaks of the Pieniny, they have been an established centre for hikers for the best part of a century. The region as a whole is perfect for low-key rambling, and there are few areas in Europe where you can get so authentic a mountain experience without having to be a committed climber. Other outdoor activities are well catered for, too, with raft rides down the Dunajec Gorge in summer and some fine winter skiing on the higher Tatra slopes.

Eighty kilometres long, with peaks rising to over 2500m, the Polish Tatras are actually a relatively small part of a range that stretches across the border into Slovakia. A two-hour bus ride south of Kraków, the bustling resort of **Zakopane** is the main holiday centre, conveniently placed for access to the highest Tatra peaks and with plenty of attractive folk architecture in the immediate surroundings. The mountain valleys running south from Zakopane provide easy-going hiking through spectacular scenery, while the peak-fringed **Morskie Oko** lake just to the southeast is one of Poland's most celebrated beauty spots.

The route to Zakopane runs through the **Podhale**, a rustic region of lush meadows, winding valleys and old wooden villages that starts to the south of **Nowy Targ**. To the east, the **Pieniny** range are lower than the Tatras but no less dramatic, steep slopes crowding above the **Dunajec River** to create a gorge. The best place from which to explore the Pieniny is the former spa resort of **Szczawnica**, a quaint little place enjoying a growing reputation as a summertime centre for walking and biking.

ARRIVAL AND GETTING AROUND

By public transport Both Zakopane and Szczawnica are easily reached by bus from Kraków. Once there, minibuses shuttle from the resort centres to the outlying attractions,

THE TATRAS AND THE PIENINY

depositing hikers at trail heads and ferrying them back to town before nightfall.

The Podhale

From Kraków, road and rail routes to Zakopane run south through the **Podhale**, the hilly farming terrain that forms the approach to the Tatra Mountains. It's a memorable landscape of undulating slopes and strip-farmed fields, many of which are still worked by stocky horses attached to a variety of carts and ploughs. Few Podhale towns merit an overnight stay in their own right but there are plenty of enticing mid-journey stop-offs if you're passing through.

Chabówka: Railway Museum

Chabówka, 3km west of Rabka · **Museum** Mon–Fri 8am–3pm, Sat & Sun 8am–6pm ·8zł · **Steam trains** July & Aug Sat & Sun, depart Chabówka at 9am · 30zł return · Ⓦ parowozy.pl

---

The *górale* p.327
Witkacy p.328
Karol Szymanowski p.330

Festivals in Zakopane p.333
Dunajec gorge Raft trips p.340

RAFTING ON MORSKIE OKO

Highlights

❶ Zakopane architecture The highland town of Zakopane has long been celebrated for its pointy-gabled, timber-built houses, a rustic style which is still practised in local building. See page 327

❷ Hiking in the Tatras Offering anything from easy-going valley-bottom strolls to calf-straining high-mountain scrambles, the Tatra range provides hikers with the most varied and beautiful terrain in the country. See page 334

❸ Morskie Oko A serene high-altitude lake surrounded by lofty peaks, the Morskie Oko

("Eye of the Sea") is one of the most popular targets for visitors to the Tatra Mountains. See page 336

❹ Niedzica Castle This medieval cluster of towers and bastions rears dramatically above the calm waters of the Czorstyn Reservoir. See page 338

❺ Rafting on the Dunajec Gorge Rafting down this twisting section of the River Dunajec, squeezed by cliffs, is one of Poland's classic journeys. See page 340

HIGHLIGHTS ARE MARKED ON THE MAP ON PAGE 326

The nondescript village of **CHABÓWKA** grew around an important nineteenth-century railway junction and, appropriately enough, is now the site of a fascinating open-air **Railway Museum** (Skansen taboru kolejowego). More than a hundred locos and wagons are lined up for inspection, including a cannon-bristling armoured train once used by the Polish army. Particularly eye-catching are the dainty pre-World War I steam engines, alongside the kind of elegant, wood-panelled passenger carriages you don't see much of nowadays. Several of the museum's steam locomotives are still working, regularly pulling trains from Chabówka to Kasina Wielka via Mszana Dolna in summer. There are a number of other summer-weekend specials, some going as far as Nowy Sącz – check the website for details.

Nowy Targ

Occupying a plateau crossed by the Czarny Dunajec River, **NOWY TARG** is the administrative capital of the Tatra region. Established in the thirteenth century, it was redeveloped as an industrial centre after World War II, and is now a dispiriting grey sprawl. It is however an important transport hub, offering bus connections to the Pieniny.

Nowy Targ Market
ul. Targowa • Thurs & Sat 6am–3pm, Sun 6am–2pm

Nowy Targ's one big attraction is the animated, thrice-weekly **market** (Nowotarski jarmark), held at the Nowa Targowica market grounds 1km northeast of the centre. Agricultural produce is sold alongside sack-loads of cheap clothes and shoes, and there's

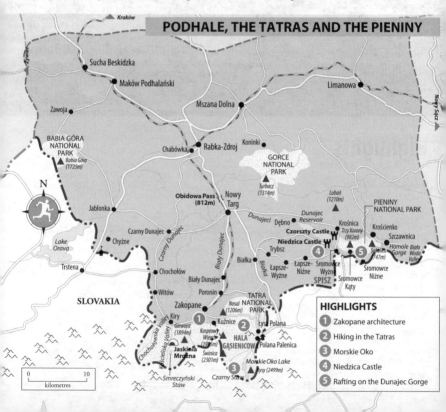

PODHALE, THE TATRAS AND THE PIENINY

HIGHLIGHTS
1. Zakopane architecture
2. Hiking in the Tatras
3. Morskie Oko
4. Niedzica Castle
5. Rafting on the Dunajec Gorge

THE GÓRALE

The inhabitants of the Tatra region, the **górale**, are known throughout Poland for preserving traditions that have died out elsewhere. The region was "discovered" by the Polish intelligentsia in the late nineteenth century, for whom the *górale* symbolized an authentic form of Polish culture unsullied by outside influence. However, this was also an economically backward region, the poverty of rural life leading thousands of górale to emigrate to the United States in the 1920s and 1930s.

Many *górale* still dress in **traditional costume** on Sundays and for other major community events – weddings, festivals and the like. The men's costume consists of tight-fitting woollen trousers decorated with coloured strips of embroidery (*parzenice*), decorated jackets and waistcoats and a feather-topped hat. The women wear thin woollen blouses, thickly pleated skirts festooned with flowers and brightly coloured headscarves. The *górale* are also the guardians of one of Poland's most vibrant **folk-music** traditions, retaining an appetite for the kind of rootsy, fiddle-driven dance music that has all but died out in the lowlands. Traditional bands regularly appear at local festivities and weddings (which are usually a high-profile component of any given Saturday), and also appear regularly in the restaurants of Zakopane.

a profusion of local crafts for sale: wooden kitchen utensils, wicker baskets, *kożuchy* (fur-lined jackets and coats) and *pantofle* (slippers). Sunday is the day for used cars.

ARRIVAL AND DEPARTURE   NOWY TARG

By train Nowy Targ train station, 1km southwest of the town centre, has connections to Kraków Plaszów (5 daily; 2hr 20min–2hr 50min) and Zakopane (5 daily; 20–30min).
By bus The bus station is 300m southeast of the main square.

Destinations Dębno (10 daily; 20min); Kraków (every 30min; 1hr 40min); Krościenko (10 daily; 40min); Szczawnica (2 daily; 1hr); Zakopane (every 30min; 30–50min).

Zakopane and around

Nestling in a bowl of pastureland between brittle grey peaks, **ZAKOPANE** is a major mountain resort, deluged with visitors throughout its summer **hiking** and winter **skiing** seasons. The main street, the pedestrianized **ulica Krupówki**, is an over-developed tourist trap given over to a garish assortment of folk-kitsch restaurants, fast-food joints and souvenir stalls selling plastic junk. On either side, however, lie leafy streets lined with *fin de siècle* **wooden villas**, a reminder that Zakopane was once the chosen resort of Poland's artistic elite. With hiking trails branching out from the suburbs, Zakopane remains the best possible place from which to access the most stunning scenery anywhere in Poland.

Brief history

Zakopane has been an established attraction for Poles since the 1870s, when the purity of the mountain air began to attract big-city doctors and their consumptive city patients. Within a few years, this highland village of sheep farmers was transformed into a health resort, with many Kraków-based artists and intellectuals living here for several months every year. One of them was **Stanisław Witkiewicz** (1851–1915), who developed the distinctive Zakopane architectural style based on traditional wooden building forms. The houses he built – all steep pointy roofs and jutting attic windows – went down a storm with a pre-World War I middle class who were crazy for all things rustic. In the years before World War I, Zakopane experienced a *belle époque* of arty hedonism, with all manner of poets, painters and composers descending on the place to get drunk, behave outrageously and steal each other's girlfriends. After World War I more mainstream forms of tourism took over, Zakopane becoming Poland's premier skiing centre – a status it retains today.

WITKACY

Painter, dramatist and hallucinogenic drug enthusiast Stanisław Ignacy Witkiewicz (1885–1939) – **Witkacy** as he's commonly known – was born the son of Stanisław Witkiewicz, the artist and critic who popularized the Zakopane Style of traditional architecture. Educated at home by a father who distrusted schools, Witkacy was surrounded from an early age by the artists and actors who made up the Polish cultural elite.

As a resort town attracting all kinds of free-thinkers, Zakopane functioned as an artistic and emotional playground for Witkacy, and his **private life** was rather complicated as a result. After a long affair with actress Irena Solska, ten years his senior, Witkacy got engaged to one of his mother's boarding house guests, Jadwiga Jaczewska, in 1914 – who duly shot herself on learning that her fiancé was still seeing both Solska and one other lover. Eager to leave this behind, Witkacy set off on a long expedition to New Guinea and Australia with celebrated anthropologist Bronisław Malinowski (with whom he also had an intimate relationship), returning home when **World War I** broke out. He signed up for the Russian army (an act of rebellion against his anti-Russian father), and fought with distinction on the Austrian front. Wounded near Voronezh, he was sent for rehabilitation in St Petersburg, then a wildly decadent city full of opportunities for a good party. It was here that Witkacy began to experiment with mind-altering **narcotics**.

After the war Witkacy re-established himself in Zakopane and in 1924 set up a commercial **portrait-painting** studio: intended as an ironic statement on the position of the artist in capitalist society, it turned out to be extraordinarily successful. Witkacy's portraits of well-heeled society figures were relatively sober and realistic, while those of his friends, painted while high on one substance or another, were wild and deranged in comparison; you'll see examples of both these styles hanging on the walls of Poland's museums and galleries. In the corner of each canvas Witkacy noted which narcotic he had been taking when painting. Witkacy believed that his intake of drugs while painting would reveal the true personality of the sitter. Most of his subjects are female, members of what he called his "metaphysical harem".

Witkacy also produced over twenty **plays**, most of which were premiered in Zakopane by his own theatre company. These absurdist dramas were cold-shouldered by uncomprehending 1920s Polish audiences, and were only rediscovered in the 1950s, when Tadeusz Kantor opened the legendary Cricot 2 Theatre with a performance of Witkacy's *Cuttlefish*. Witkacy's **prose works** tended towards the darkly surreal, his 1930 novel *Nienasycenie* ("Insatiability") revolving around an epic struggle between a Poland ruled by the dictator Kocmołuchowicz ("Slovenly") and communist hordes from China invading Europe from the east.

In a sense, reality fulfilled Witkacy's worst apocalyptic nightmares. Following the Nazi invasion of Poland in 1939, the artist fled east. On learning that the Soviets were also advancing into Poland, a devastated Witkacy committed suicide, a legendary act that ensured his place in the pantheon of Polish patriots.

Tatra Museum

ul. Krupówki 10 • Tues–Sat 9am–5pm, Sun 9am–3pm • 7zł • ☎ 18 201, ⓦ muzeumtatrzanskie.pl

The **Tatra Museum** (Muzeum Tatrzanskie) extolls the virtues of local folk culture through a sequence of recreated peasant house interiors and some stunning costumes – note the colourfully embroidered, strutting-peacock jackets traditionally worn by *górale* menfolk. Zakopane's emergence as a tourist resort is remembered with pictures of Tytus Chałubiński, the doctor who did more than anyone to promote the health-giving properties of the mountain air; Stanisław Witkiewicz; and the wealthy Dembowski family, who collected Podhale folk crafts and held high-society salons in their Zakopane villa.

Willa Oksza: Gallery of 20th Century Art

ul. Zamoyskiego 25 • Wed–Sat 10am–6pm, Sun 10am–4pm • 7zł • ⓦ muzeumtatrzanskie.pl

Occupying a beautifully restored timber house designed by Stanisław Witkiewicz in 1895, the **Willa Oksza** hosts themed exhibitions focusing on the artists who congregated in Zakopane in the years before and after World War I. Exhibits might include drawings by Witkiewicz, photographs and paintings by his son Witkacy (see above) or the snowscapes of skiing enthusiast Rafał Malczewski, but whatever's on display you can always enjoy the building itself.

St Clement's Church and graveyard

One of the oldest streets in Zakopane, ulica Kościeliska is liberally sprinkled with traditional buildings, kicking off with the wooden **St Clement's Church** (Kos'ciół św. Klemensa). The low-ceilinged interior holds several examples of a popular local form of folk art: devotional paintings on glass, in this case depicting the Stations of the Cross.

Outside in the **graveyard** lie the tombs of many of the town's best-known writers and artists, among them that of **Stanisław Witkiewicz** (1851–1915), godfather of the Zakopane architectural style. His grave is marked by a canopied shrine-pole from Samogitia, the

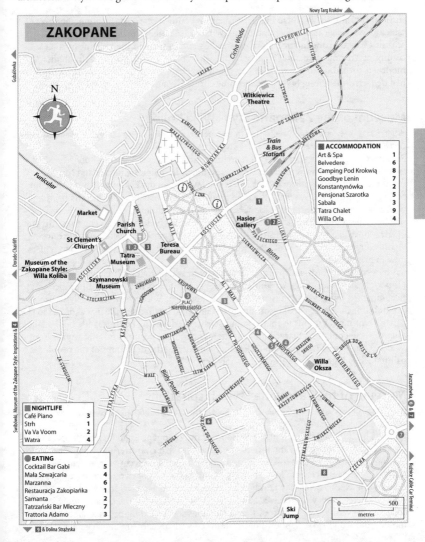

ZAKOPANE

0   500

metres

KAROL SZYMANOWSKI

After Chopin, **Karol Szymanowski** (1882–1937) is Poland's greatest composer, forging his own distinctive style in an exotic and highly charged mix of orientalism, opulence and native folk music. As a TB sufferer Szymanowski spent much time in Zakopane, becoming a devoted enthusiast of local folklore. Among Szymanowski's works directly influenced by Tatra music are the song cycle *Słopiewnie* (1921), the *Mazurkas for piano* (1924–25) and, above all, the ballet *Harnasie* (1931), which is stuffed full of outlaws and features a spectacular highland wedding. Alongside two violin concertos and his *Symphony Song of the Night*, Szymanowski's greatest work is the **Stabat Mater** (1926), a choral piece of stunningly austere beauty which draws on the traditions of old Polish church music. Szymanowski died in 1937, receiving an illustrious state funeral. The Obrochta family, one of the leading *górale* bands, played around his tomb in the Skałka Church in Kraków.

---

rustic area of Lithuania where the artist spent his youth. There's also a commemorative tablet to Witkiewicz's equally famous son, **Witkacy** (see page 328), whose body was returned to Zakopane in 1988 from its previous resting place in the Ukraine by a communist regime desperate to curry favour with Poland's intelligentsia. Fifty thousand mourners turned up to pay their respects, and only later was it revealed that the authorities had delivered the wrong body – the genuine corpse having proved impossible to locate.

Museum of the Zakopane Style: Willa Koliba

ul. Kościeliska 18 • Wed–Sat 9am–5pm, Sun 9am–3pm • 7zł; combined ticket with the Museum of the Zakopane Style: Inspirations 10zł • ☎ 18 201, ⓦ muzeumtatrzanskie.pl

A must for anyone interested in Polish architecture and design, the **Willa Koliba** (erected in 1892) was Stanisław Witkiewicz's first experiment in designing houses and furnishings based on traditional Podhale models. Now the **Museum of the Zakopane Style** (Muzeum Stylu Zakopańskiego), it starts off with a ground-floor display of the **folk crafts** from which Witkiewicz got his inspiration, before moving on to the kind of furniture that he set about designing – chunky chairs adorned with squiggly details in an engaging mixture of Art Nouveau and folkloric forms. There's also a **scale model** of Witkiewicz's greatest architectural creation, the Willa Pod Jedłami, an extraordinarily intricate wooden house now in private hands.

A biographical words-and-pictures display reveals what a rogue Witkiewicz was, using his poor health as an excuse to conduct a series of love affairs in the spas of Europe. Accompanied by long-time mistress Maria Dembowska, Witkiewicz eventually went to live full time in the Croatian resort of Lovran in 1907, leaving his wife in Zakopane to eke a living renting out rooms to the very tourists attracted here by her husband's books. The museum also contains a marvellous collection of deranged **portraits** by Witkiewicz's son, Witkacy (see page 328), including a lot of distorted, angular depictions of the people he painted while high on one substance or another.

Museum of the Zakopane Style: Inspirations

Droga do Rojów 6 • Wed–Sat 9am–5pm, Sun 9am–3pm • 7zł; combined ticket with the Museum of the Zakopane Style: Willa Koliba 10zł • ☎ 18 201, ⓦ muzeumtatrzanskie.pl

Opened in 2009, this branch of the **Museum of the Zakopane Style** (Muzeum Stylu Zakopańskiego) focuses on the love of craftsmanship that characterized local households, feeding the imagination of folk enthusiasts like Witkiewicz. Occupying a lovingly-restored nineteenth-century log cabin, the building consists of two main spaces: the so-called Black Room where the family ate and slept around a central stove; and the White Room, where guests were received. The latter contains many of the ethnographic items collected by Witkiewicz's mistress, Maria Dembowska, including painted chests, cheese moulds and wood-carved spoon-holders adorned with archaic sun and vegetal symbols.

Szymanowski Museum

ul. Kasprusie 18 • Tues–Sun 10am–5pm • 9zł • ☎ 18 202 0040, ⓦ mnk.pl

Nestling in a lush cottage garden on the west side of the town centre is the **Szymanowski Museum**, devoted to composer Karol Szymanowski (see page 330), who lived here in the 1930s. The display employs touch-screen audio-visual content to bring the period to life, although many of the exhibits speak for themselves: photographs of Szymanowski holidaying with pianist Arthur Rubinstein, portraits of the Obrochta family (the local folk musicians who inspired much of Szymanowski's music), and fantastic folk-based costumes that featured in the ballet *Harnasie*.

Hasior Gallery

ul. Jagiellońska 18b • Wed–Sat 11am–6pm, Sun 9am–3pm • 7zł • ☎ 18 201, ⓦ muzeumtatrzanskie.pl

East of the centre, a wooden building in a side alley houses the **Władysław Hasior Gallery** (Galeria Władysława Hasiora), presenting the work of one of the country's key postwar artists. Whether building installations from piles of junk or constructing pseudo-religious banners from pieces of metal, Hasior (1928–99) was typical of many Polish artists of the 1960s and '70s in developing an enigmatic and often subversive form of sculpture that had little to do with the ideological dictates of either church or state – although both institutions sponsored his work at different stages. Ranging from massive landscape installations to jokey throwaway pieces, Hasior's *oeuvre* will leave you uncertain as to whether he was a visionary or a charlatan, but the gallery is entertaining enough to make such confusion worthwhile.

Jaszczurówka Chapel

Out on the southeastern fringes of town, 3.5km from the centre, the wooden chapel at **Jaszczurówka** is one of Stanisław Witkiewicz's best-known creations. Built in 1904 on a grassy slope overlooking the road, it's a delicate structure featuring intricately carved portals and several tiers of steeply sloping roof. Inspired by Norwegian village churches as well as local Podhale buildings, it looks like something out of a Nordic fairy tale.

Gubałówka Hill

Funicular Northern end of ul. Krupówki • Daily: July & Aug 7am–9pm; Sept–June 8am–5pm • 21zł return • **Toboggan run** May–Sept daily 10am–5pm • 5zł • ⓦ pkl.pl

There's an excellent view of the Tatras from the top of **Gubałówka Hill** (1120m), just northwest of the centre and best reached by taking the **funicular**, although you can also walk (1hr). At the summit you'll find a string of souvenir stalls no less tacky than the ones clogging up the centre of Zakopane, but the panorama of jagged peaks to the south is splendid enough to more than justify the trip. Just below the summit, the dry **toboggan run** (*zjeżdżalnia*) is well worth a circuit or two.

ARRIVAL AND INFORMATION   ZAKOPANE

By train The train station is at the eastern end of town, a 15min walk from the main ul. Krupówki.

Destinations Gdańsk (1 daily; 16hr; overnight); Katowice (1 daily; 5hr 30min); Kraków (7 daily; 3hr 10min–3hr 40min); Nowy Targ (9 daily; 20min); Warsaw (1 daily; 9hr; overnight).

By bus The bus station is in the courtyard of the train station.

Destinations Katowice (1 daily; 3hr 40min); Kraków (every 30min; 2hr 30min–3hr); Krościenko (5 daily; 1hr 10min); Nowy Sącz (5 daily; 2hr 20min); Nowy Targ (every 30min;

40min); Polana Palenica (minibuses; depart when full; 45min); Tarnów (2 daily; 4hr); Warsaw (2 daily; 8–9hr).

By car If you have your own transport, note that parking can be a problem in the centre; your best bet is the big car park at the southern end of town near the ski jump.

Tourist office There are two tourist information centres: at ul. Kościuszki 17 (Mon–Sat 8am–8pm, Sun 9am–5pm; ☎ 18 201 2211, ⓦ zakopane.pl), and at ul. Kościeliska 7 (Mon–Sat 9am–5pm; ☎ 18 201 2004, ⓦ visitmalopolska.pl). Both are a helpful source of information on the whole area.

8

ACTIVITIES

Skiing The ski season traditionally runs from December to March. The most popular runs are on Nosal and Kasprowy Wierch, as these are the ones with ski lifts. Instructors at the slopes charge 60–70zł per hour for lessons. Ski rental costs about 35zł per day. Strama Ski School based at Nosal (ⓦ strama-szkola.pl) runs skiing and snowboarding courses for kids and adults and rents out gear.

Husky sledding Fun Dog (ⓣ 502 485 787, ⓦ fundog.pl) offer instruction and will let you take the reins, with prices starting at 100zł per person.

Mountain biking In summer, legions of enthusiastic bikers head for the designated cycle routes in the hills north of Zakopane (some 650km in total) and within the national park area. You can rent mountain bikes at a number of places around town. Bike Point at ul. Tetmajera 4 (daily 9am–7pm; ⓣ 884 310 035, ⓦ bike-point.pl) has a range of regular pushbikes and mountain bikes for 50–80zł/day.

Hiking Maciej Krupa (ⓣ 604 776 415, ⓔ maciej.krupa@ przewodnictwo.org) is an experienced mountain guide who can lead both advanced and casual hikers; he's also a local historian who can provide expert cultural tours of the town itself.

Bungee jumping There is a 90m-high bungee-jump crane near the Wielkia Krokiew ski-jumping grounds (May–Oct daily 11am–6pm; 130zł; ⓣ 505 472 113, ⓦ bungeezakopane.pl).

ACCOMMODATION

Zakopane is increasingly well served with a wide range of accommodation, although it's still worth **booking** rooms well in advance in midsummer or during the skiing season. The prices quoted below are peak midsummer prices – peak skiing-season prices may be 30–40 percent higher.

HOTELS AND PENSIONS

★ **Art & Spa** ul. Kościuszki 18 ⓣ 18 200 0670, ⓦ art andspa.pl; map page 329. A lovely old villa set in its own grounds, *Art & Spa* exudes a classy country-house feel, with plush spacious rooms, a well-equipped spa centre with small pool, and one of Zakopane's more expensive buffet breakfasts. **450zł**

Belvedere Droga do Białego 3 ⓣ 18 202 1200, ⓦ belve derehotel.pl; map page 329. Top-drawer hotel 2.5km from town, with high standards of service and smart, comfortable rooms – not all have bathtubs though, so ask when you book. Attic ceilings in the top-floor rooms add a bit of extra atmosphere. On-site swimming pool, gym and beauty centre make this the perfect place for a spa-style break. **450zł**

Konstantynówka ul. Jagiellońska 18 ⓣ 18 533 0363; map page 329. Rooms above the *Zakopiańska* restaurant (see page 333) in a beautifully restored Zakopane-style house – novelist Joseph Conrad stayed here during his last visit to Poland in August 1914. Rooms come with folksy textiles, lots of wood and modern bathrooms. And with breakfast served in what is one of Zakopane's finest restaurants, it's a very good option for this kind of price. **260zł**

★ **Pensjonat Szarotka** Małe Żywczańskie 16a ⓣ 18 206 4050, ⓦ szarotka.pl; map page 329. You can forgive the *Szarotka* its dim stairwell and creaky floorboards: this charming pointy-gabled suburban house is almost a museum of the era in which it was built, with hallways decorated with interwar tourist posters and sepia photographs of skiing champions, and a range of different shaped en-suite rooms with TV, many with quirky semi-antique furnishings. A grand breakfast is served in a bright room full of Art Deco objets d'art. **150zł**

★ **Sabała** ul. Krupówki 11 ⓣ 18 201 5092, ⓦ sabala-zakopane.pl; map page 329. Occupying a great position on the main strip, this modern building incorporates many traditional wooden features, especially in the restaurant. There's a small swimming pool in the timber-ceilinged attic. **480zł**

Tatra Chalet ul. Bogdańskiego 5 ⓣ 18 200 0175, ⓦ tatrachalet.pl; map page 329. Smart but welcoming new building on the fringes of town featuring an intimate handful of studio suites. The contemporary interiors feature a lot of whites and creams, flat-screen TVs, electric kettles, and small balconies with countryside views. On-site sauna and outdoor jacuzzi. **420zł**

Willa Orla ul. Kościeliska 50 ⓣ 18 201 2697, ⓦ orla.com. pl; map page 329. Ostentatiously-gabled Zakopane-style house on a street that's full of them, offering unpretentious but cosy rooms, many with sloping attic ceilings. The buffet breakfast is served up in a sunny room stuffed with vintage clocks. **165zł**

HOSTELS

Goodbye Lenin ul. Chłabowka 44 ⓣ 18 200 1330, ⓦ zakopane.goodbyelenin.pl; map page 329. Located in tranquil semi-rural suburbs some 3km east of the centre, this hostel is a traditional-style timber building with snug triples and doubles. It's initially difficult to find under your own steam so call in advance for directions. Doubles **120zł**, triples **150zł**

CAMPING

Camping Pod Krokwią ul. Żeromskiego ⓣ 18 201 2256, ⓦ pokrokwia.pl; map page 329. Large and well-appointed site with its own folk-style restaurant, located a 30min walk from the centre, across from the bottom of the ski jump at the south end of town. Camping **50zł**, chalets (two people) **120zł**

FESTIVALS IN ZAKOPANE

The biggest annual event is the **International Festival of Highland Folklore** (Międzynarodowy Festiwal Folkloru Ziem Górskich), a week-long celebration of traditional music taking place in mid- to late August. It attracts groups from highland regions around the world, as well as the top local acts – you're unlikely to get a better chance to sample the exuberance of a *górale* choir, whooping their way through a string of joyous mountain melodies. Other events of note include the biennial **Karol Szymanowski Music Days** in July, featuring classical recitals by Polish and foreign artists in and around the town.

EATING

Central Zakopane offers a surfeit of **restaurants** – many offering local food in faux-rustic surroundings to the accompaniment of live folk music. One local product well worth trying is *oscypek*, the bun-shaped **sheep's milk cheeses** offered by street vendors all over town; the smoked variety (easily identifiable by its tawny brown rind) is particularly delicious.

CAFÉS

Cocktail Bar Gabi ul. Zamoyskiego 10 ☎ 18 201 3721; map page 329. It's not a bar and it doesn't sell cocktails, but does qualify as one of the best cafés in town. There's a long glass cabinet filled with how-can-you-possibly-refuse cakes, and a big choice of ice cream to boot. Reliably good coffee also. Daily 10am–9pm.

Samanta ul. Krupówki 4a ☎ 18 201 4572; map page 329. Not quite as heavenly as *Gabi*, but still an ideal place in which to sink your spoon into a succulent slice of *szarlotka* (apple pie), accompanied by a reassuringly strong cup of coffee. The bakery counter is a good place to stock up on fresh bread and rolls. Daily 9am–9pm.

RESTAURANTS

Mała Szwajcaria ("Little Switzerland") ul. Zamoyskiego 11 ☎ 18 201 2076, ⓦ malaszwajcaria.pl; map page 329. If the Tatras and the Alps ever met, then this is what people would eat on the border: an imaginative fusion of Polish and Swiss cuisine – local lamb on one side, fondue and raclette on the other – that somehow manages to bring out the best in both. Prices are very reasonable, and the set lunch menu's a steal. Daily 11am–11pm.

★**Marzanna** ul. Balzera 17E ☎ 18 206 2461; map page 329. Down a side street opposite the Nosal ski slopes (and helpfully signposted by a huge knife, fork and spoon), *Marzanna* is highly rated for its soups and *pierogi*,

and also serves decent-sized and admirably inexpensive mains such as cod in batter (20zł) and breaded pork chop (20zł). The interior features all kinds of folksy knick-knacks stuck to the walls or hanging from the ceiling, and there are a few tables outside too. Daily noon–8pm.

Restauracja Zakopiańska ul. Jagiellońska 18 ☎ 18 533 0363, ⓦ restauracjazakopianska.pl; map page 329. An imaginative take on Polish cuisine involving fresh local ingredients and a bit of creative twist in the flavour combinations on offer: crispy *pierogi* with lamb (30zł), Polish pork chop with a shake of chilli (45zł) or no-nonsense Tatra classics like pan-fried trout (40zł). Stick around for the delicious house desserts. With everything presented and served with finesse, this is a fine place for a special meal. Daily noon–11pm.

Tatrzański Bar Mleczny Droga na Bystre 2; map page 329. Arguably the best of the order-at-the-counter canteens, the "Tatra Milk Bar" is a darn sight cheaper than most restaurants and serves reputable, filling Polish fare in clean and pleasant surroundings. Listening to the orders being called out and trying to work out which one is yours only adds to the fun. Daily 11am–7pm.

Trattoria Adamo pl. Niepodległości 1 ☎ 18 201 9250, ⓦ trattoria-adamo.pl; map page 329. Roomy Italian with a homely interior and seating out on the square, serving inexpensive but palatable pizzas from about 20zł upwards. They also do pastas and salads, and there's a children's corner too. Daily noon–10pm.

DRINKING

★**Café Piano** ul. Krupówki 63; map page 329. Contemporary design meets rustic chic at this bar, in a secluded alleyway off the main street, with swings instead of bar stools and a garden patio thick with shrubs and ferns. Daily noon–midnight.

★**Strh** ul. Krupówki 4a ☎ 18 200 1898, ⓦ strh.pl; map page 329. On the third, attic floor of a shop-and-office building, and with excellent views of the main street if you get the right seat, *Strh* is a chic, relaxingly living-room-like

space in which to linger over a couple of evening beers. Fried-egg breakfasts, healthy salads and refreshing fruit smoothies help make it a popular spot in the daytime, too. Daily 9am–midnight.

Va Va Voom ul. Kościuszki 10 ☎ 788 120 5752, ⓦ facebook.com/klubvavavoom; map page 329. Chic lounge bar-cum-dance club at the top of a spiral staircase, with a DJ repertoire which extends beyond top-forty pap. Wed–Sun from 9pm.

8

Watra ul. Zamojskiego 1 ☏512 351 744; map page 329. Pub-restaurant done up in predictably timber-folksy style and featuring a wide-ranging variety of live music (anything from folk to chanson to rock). The added attraction is that it's also a microbrewery, serving Watra beer – they do an excellent lager-style brew as well as wheat, Märzen and honey flavoured varieties. Daily 8am– midnight or later.

Tatra National Park

The **Tatra National Park** (Tatrzański park narodowy) begins right outside Zakopane's southern outskirts, where the wooded flanks of the Tatra Mountains rise dramatically above rustic suburban houses. They are as beautiful as any mountain landscape in northern Europe, the ascents taking you on boulder-strewn paths alongside woods and streams up to the ridges where grand, windswept peaks rise in brilliant alpine sunshine. The park receives over 2 million visitors a year, with large crowds thronging the hiking trails in spring and summer. The park also hosts large numbers of lynx, golden eagles and brown bear, although you're only likely to see them in remote, higher-altitude areas.

Though many of the peak and ridge climbs are for experienced climbers only, much is accessible to regular walkers and all paths are well marked. It is as well to remember that the Tatras are an alpine range and as such demand some respect and preparation. The most important rule is to stick to the marked paths, and to arm yourself in advance with a decent **map**. Remember never to leave the tree line (about 2000m) unless visibility is good, and when the clouds close in, start descending immediately.

ESSENTIALS   TATRA NATIONAL PARK

Entrance fee 5zł (collected at booths at main access points to the park).

Maps and equipment The best map is the *Tatrzański Park Narodowy/Tatra National Park* (1:30,000), which has all the paths accurately marked and is colour-coded. You should not venture out without waterproofs and sturdy boots, and it's sensible to have to supply of basic rations as well as water. Lastly, take a whistle – blow six times every minute if you need help.

Mountain rescue service Tatrzańskie Ochotnicze Pogotowie Ratunkowe or TOPR (☏985).

Weather The weather is always changeable; most rain falls in the summer, when there may also be thunderstorms and even hail- and snow-showers. Even on a warm summer's day in the valleys, it can be below freezing at the peaks. Set out early (the weather is always better in the morning), and tell someone when and where you're going.

Accommodation Overnighting is possible in the seven PTTK-run huts dotted across the mountains and clearly marked on the *Tatra National Park* map. Most huts are open during the spring-to-autumn hiking season, although it's best to ring and check first before setting out. The huts provide dorm beds (35–45zł per person), mattress space on the floor in busy periods, and basic canteen food. Camping isn't allowed in the national park area.

The Dolina Białego and Dolina Strążyska valleys

For some easy and accessible valley hiking, the **Dolina Białego** and **Dolina Strążyska** valleys each provide a relaxed long afternoon's walk from Zakopane; taken together they make an enjoyable and not overly strenuous day's outing. Leaving Zakopane to the south, along ulica Strążyska, you reach Dolina Strążyska after around an hour's walk. At the end of the valley (3hr) you can climb to the **Hala Strążyska**, a beautiful high mountain pasture (1303m); the **Siklawica waterfall** on the way makes an enjoyable rest point, a stream coursing down from the direction of Giewont. The views are excellent, too, with Mount Giewont (1894m) rearing up to the south, and to the north a wonderful panorama of Zakopane and the surrounding countryside. Walk east along the meadow to the top of Dolina Białego and you can descend the deep, stream-crossed valley, one of the gentlest and most beautiful in the region, continuing back to the outskirts of Zakopane (6–7hr in total).

Kasprowy Wierch

Cable car Daily: March, April & Oct 8am–5.30pm; May, June & Sept 8am–6.30pm; July & Aug 7am–9pm; Nov–Feb 8am–4pm • 47zł one way, 59zł return • It's essential to buy tickets in advance with a reserved time slot: they can be bought online (Ⓦ pkl.pl), from the ticket office at ul. Krupówki 48 in Zakopane (Mon–Fri 9am–5pm) or from vending machines outside the ticket office and at other points around town • Kuźnice is a 3km walk (or 3min minibus journey) south from Zakopane along the Dolina Bystrego

Tallest of the mountains that girdle Zakopane – although not the tallest in the Polish Tatras, as that honour goes to Rysy (see below) – is **Kasprowy Wierch** (1985m), a craggily rugged ridge that has since 1936 been accessible via cable car from the hamlet of Kuźnice, 3km south of Zakopane. The summit is just above the cable-car station, although high-summer crowds may mean that you have to queue up in order to get there.

From the summit, many day-trippers simply walk back down to Kuźnice via the high-altitude meadow known as the Hala Gąsienicowa (2hr). A longer alternative is to strike west (allow 3hr) to the summit of **Mount Giewont** (1894m), the "Sleeping Knight" that overlooks Zakopane. Watch out if it's been raining, however, as the paths here get pretty slippery and are very worn in places. The final bit of the ascent is rocky: secured chains aid your scramble to the top. From the summit, topped with a tall cross, the views can be spectacular on a good day. For the return, head down to Kuźnice through the Dolina Kondratowa past the *Hala Kondratowa* hut (🕿 18 201 9114, Ⓦ kondratowa.com); allow forty minutes to get to the hut, then a further hour to get to the village. This downward journey is fairly easy going and the whole trip is quite feasible in a day if you start out early.

East from Kasprowy Wierch: the Orła Perć

East of Kasprowy Wierch, the walking gets tougher. From **Świnica** (2301m), a strenuous ninety-minute walk from the summit, experienced hikers continue along the **Orła Perć** (Eagles' Path), a challenging, exposed ridge with spectacular views. The *Pięc Stawów* **hut** (🕿 781 055 555, Ⓦ piecstawow.pl), occupying a lovely lakeside position in the high valley of the same name, provides overnight shelter at the end (4hr). From the hut you can hike back down Dolina Roztoki to **Łysa Polana**, a border-crossing point with Slovakia in the valley (2hr). Here you can either catch a bus back to Zakopane, or head southwards towards Morskie Oko.

Morskie Oko

Minibuses from Zakopane bus station run to Polana Palenica (depart when full; 45min), the start of the walk to Morskie Oko

Encircled by spectacular sheer cliff faces and alpine forest, the large glacial lake of **Morskie Oko** ("Eye of the Sea"; 1399m) is one of the Tatras' big attractions, and one of the most popular day-trip destinations for tourists staying in Zakopane. It's frequently deluged by trippers, although the crowds thin out the further beyond Morskie Oko you go. Starting point for the gentle ascent to the lake is **Polana Palenica**, east of Zakopane, where there's a large car park surrounded by snack huts. A fairly obvious track leads past a national park booth (charging the 5zł entrance fee to the park) and climbs slowly through the trees towards Morskie Oko, which is some 9km (1hr 45min) uphill. Horse-drawn carts (65zł per person) are on hand to ferry those tourists who can't face the walk.

The *Morskie Oko* **hut** (🕿 602 260 757, Ⓦ schroniskomorskieoko.pl), a lovely Zakopane-style villa situated by the side of the lake, serves up decent grilled-sausage-type fare, and provides a convenient base for the ascent of **Rysy** (2499m), the highest peak in the Polish Tatras. Closer to hand, on the same red-marked route is **Czarny Staw** (1580m), a lake that, if anything, appears even chillier than Morskie Oko.

Dolina Kościeliska

Minibuses from Zakopane to Chochołów and Czarny Dunajec pass the entrances to the Dolina Kościeliska valley (12 daily; 25min)

Six kilometres west from Zakopane on the Czarny Dunajec road, the hamlet of **KIRY** marks the entrance to the **Dolina Kościeliska**, a deep verdant valley much in evidence on postcards of the region. For around 120zł a horse-drawn cart will run you down the first section of the valley to a point known as **Polana Pisana**, but from here on it's walkers only. A distinctive feature of Kościeliska is the **caves** in its limestone cliffs – once the haunts of robbers and bandits, legend has it. Take a detour off to the left from Polana Pisana – marked *jaskinia* (caves) – and you can visit various examples, including **Jaskinia Mroźna**, where the walls are permanently encased in ice. Beyond Polana Pisana, the narrow upper valley is a beautiful stretch of crags, gushing water, caves and greenery. The awe-inducing scenery so inspired Witkacy's fiancée Jadwiga Jaczewska (see page 328) that she chose this as the venue for her suicide.

About 45 minutes beyond the Polana Pisana is the *Hala Ornak* hut (☎695 530 813, ⊛schronisko-ornak.pl), a popular overnight stop for long-distance hikers with a **restaurant**; day walkers return back down the valley to take the bus back to Zakopane. There are two marked paths leading beyond the hut for those who want to continue. The eastern route takes you the short distance to **Smreczyński Staw** (1226m), a tiny mountain lake surrounded by forest; the western route follows a high ridge over to Dolina Chochołowska (see below) – a demanding walk and only for the fit.

Dolina Chochołowska

Served by minibuses from Zakopane (14 daily; 30min)

Two kilometres northwest of Kiry lies the entrance to the **Dolina Chochołowska**, a 10km-long defile following the course of a stream deep into the hills. From the car park at the head of the valley, it's a good hour's walk to the *Chochołowska* hut and **restaurant** (☎18 207 0510, ⊛chocholowska.com), beautifully situated overlooking the meadows, with the high western Tatras and the Czech border behind. A clandestine meeting between the pope and Lech Wałęsa took place here in 1983 and is commemorated by a tableau on the wall. The steep paths up the eastern side lead to ridges that separate the valley from Dolina Kościeliska (see page 336) – one path, from a little way beyond the car park, connects the two valleys, making the cross trip possible.

8

East of the Tatras

East of the Tatras, the mountains scale down to a succession of lower ranges stretching along the Slovak border. The walking here is excellent, though less dramatic than in the Tatras. Highlights of the region are the **Pieniny** mountains and the **Dunajec Gorge** far below, where you can go rafting. Routes towards the Pieniny pass through the rolling hills of the **Spisz** region, site of the postcard-pretty **Niedzica Castle**. The best base from which to explore the area is the spa town of **Szczawnica**, from where local buses provide access to the surrounding towns and villages.

The Spisz region

The road east from Nowy Targ to Szczawnica follows the broad valley of the Dunajec through the **Spisz**, a rural, backwoods region whose villages are renowned for their wooden houses, churches and folk art. Nowy Targ–Krościenko buses pass along the main road, but public transport elsewhere is meagre.

Dębno: Church of the Archangel Michael

ul. Koscielna 42, Dębno • Mon–Fri 9am–noon & 2–4.30pm, Sat 9am–noon; closed on rainy days due to humidity • Donation requested • ☎ 18 275 1797 • Nowy Targ–Krościenko buses (10 daily) pass by the church lane

Fourteen kilometres from Nowy Targ, the village of **DĘBNO** has one of the best-known wooden churches in the country, the **Church of the Archangel Michael** (Kościół św. Michała Archanioła), a shingled, steep-roofed larch building, put together without using nails and surrounded by a charming wicket fence, with a profile vaguely reminiscent of a snail. Inside, walls and ceiling are covered in exuberant, brilliantly preserved fifteenth-century polychromy and **woodcarving**. The subjects are an enchanting mix of folk, national and religious motifs, including some fine hunting scenes. In the centre of the building, fragments survive of the original rood screen, supporting a tree-like cross, while the original fifteenth-century altarpiece triptych features a militant-looking St Catherine.

Czorsztyn Castle

May–Sept daily 9am–6pm; Oct–April Tues–Sun 10am–3pm • 5zł • Nowy Targ–Krościenko buses pass through Krośnica, a 2km walk north of Czorsztyn; a taxi boat runs from Czorsztyn to Niedzica (see page 338) in summer (roughly hourly; 6zł)

Immediately east of Dębno lies the **Czorsztyn Reservoir**, a controversial hydroelectric project which was opposed by many environmentalists before the valley was finally subsumed by water in 1997. At the eastern end of the reservoir, by the village of **CZORSZTYN**, sits **Czorsztyn Castle** (Zamek Czorsztyn). It's largely a ruin – struck by a thunderbolt in the 1790s, it was abandoned after the resulting fire – although a couple of towers and battlements have been made safe for visitors. From its heights you get sweeping **views** south to the castle of Niedzica (see below) across the mouth of the Dunajec Gorge.

Niedzica Castle

Museum: May–Sept daily 9am–7pm; Oct–April Tues–Sun 9am–4pm • 14zł • ☎ 18 262 9489

Built in the fourteenth century to guard a strategic position on the Polish-Hungarian border, **Niedzica Castle** (Zamek w Niedzicy) is one of the most dramatically situated strongholds in the country, perched precariously above the waters of the Czorsztyn Reservoir. The sweeping concrete crescent of the reservoir's **dam**, immediately east of the castle, only adds to the setting.

Niedzica's castle **museum** is a limited affair consisting of a scale model of the castle, a few old prints, and the odd suit of chain-mail armour. It is the building itself that is the real star turn, offering a wonderfully evocative succession of stone chambers clad with animal skins and sweeping views from its towers. According to local folk wisdom, documents revealing the location of the lost treasure of the Incas are concealed somewhere in the castle – local magnate and adventurer Sebastian Berzeviczy married a descendent of the Inca royal house in the eighteenth century, reportedly acquiring sacred texts which were passed down to subsequent generations.

Just downhill from the castle gates, a footpath leads along the top of the **dam** (*zapora*), providing excellent views back across the reservoir, with the battlements of Czorstyn visible on the far side of the water.

ARRIVAL AND DEPARTURE   NIEDZICA CASTLE

By car Despite being just across the water from Czorsztyn, Niedzica is a fairly roundabout trip by road, involving heading back to Dębno, or southeast towards Sromowce Niżne.

By minibus Niedzica is served by summer-only minibus from Szczawnica (hourly; 35min).

By taxi boat In summer, taxi boats (roughly hourly; 6zł) cross the water between Czorsztyn and Niedzica, making it possible to visit both fortresses in the space of an afternoon.

ACCOMMODATION

Polana Sosny Niedzica 1.5k southeast of the castle ☎ 18 262 9403, ✉ polana.sosny@niedzica.pl. Cosy rooms in the Chata Spiska, a traditional farmhouse building moved here from the village of Łapszy Niżny, and transformed into a comfortable B&B with original wooden fittings. There's a well-appointed campsite next door (same contact details). Doubles 200zł, camping 45zł

The Pieniny

A short range of Jurassic limestone peaks, rearing above the spectacular Dunajec Gorge, the **Pieniny** offer some stiff hillwalking but require no serious climbing to reach the 1000m-high summits. Jagged outcrops are set off by abundant greenery, with the often humid mountain microclimate supporting a rich and varied flora. Like the Tatras, the Pieniny are a national park and have a network of controlled paths. The main range of mountains, a 10km-long stretch between Czorsztyn and Szczawnica, is the most popular hiking territory, with the peaks of **Trzy Korony** the big target. The detailed *Pieniński Park Narodowy* (1:22,500) **map** is useful and is available in most tourist offices and bookshops. The principal point of access to the park is the small town of **Krościenko**, although **Szczawnica**, 4km east, offers better accommodation possibilities.

Krościenko and the Trzy Korony

Pleasantly situated at the confluence of the Dunajec and Krośnica rivers, the otherwise bland little town of **KROŚCIENKO** is the main starting point for **hikes to the Trzy Korony** (Three Crowns; 982m). From the bus stop in the middle of Krościenko you can follow the signs – and in summer the packs of hikers – south on the yellow route. The path soon begins to climb through the mountainside woods, with plenty of meadows and lush clearings on the way. Around two hours from Krościenko, you'll reach **Okrąglica**, the highest peak of the Trzy Korony, via some chain-banistered steps. On a clear day there's an excellent view over the whole area: the high Tatras off to the west, the slopes of Slovakia to the south, and the Dunajec Gorge far below.

Many hikers take the same route back, but two alternatives are worth considering. One is to walk to Szczawnica (see below), a two- or three-hour hike. Head back along the route you came as far as Bajków Groń (679m), about three-quarters of the way down, and from there follow the blue path across the mountains south to Sokolica (747m). The other possibility, if you want to combine the walk with the Dunajec Gorge, is to descend the mountain southwest to Sromowce Kąty (3hr), starting point for the raft trip downriver (see page 340).

8

ARRIVAL AND DEPARTURE   KROŚCIENKO

By bus Buses run from Nowy Targ to Krościenko (10–12 daily; 40min).

ACCOMMODATION

Camping Cypel ul. Zdrojowa ☏ 18 262 3368, ⊚ cypel. pieniny.net. Busy but spacious campsite on a meadow beside the River Dunajec, equipped with pebbly beach, kids' playground, shop, bar, and kayak rental facilities. **17zł**

Szawnica

Set back from the confluence of the Dunajec and Grajcarek rivers, **SZCZAWNICA** is a quaint nineteenth-century spa resort which now serves as the main holiday base for the Pieniny region. There's plenty of accommodation in town, and – in summer at least – frequent minibus services to the region's main tourist draws, most notably the rafting embarkation point at Sromowce-Kąty (see page 340). Szczawnica's interwar reputation as an arty society resort owed much to the pulling power of Count Adam Stadnicki, who owned most of the village from 1909 until World War II. Many of Szczawnica's buildings were returned to Stadnicki's descendants after 1989, spurring a wave of renovation that has seen the village regain much of its former charm.

Plac Dietla

Tap Room pl. Dietla 1 • Mon–Fri 7.30am–5.30pm, Sat & Sun 9am–5pm • ☏ 18 540 0422 • **Museum** pl. Dietla 7 • Tues–Sun 10am–6pm • 6zł • ☏ 18 540 0433

In the old centre of the village on **plac Dietla**, a nineteenth-century **tap room** (*pijalnia*) serves up cups of Szczawnica's waters (1.80zł plus 0.50zł for a plastic cup, or 14zł for a ceramic beaker with drinking pipe). A gallery upstairs from the tap room hosts exhibitions of local or historical interest. Opposite the *pijalnia* there's a **museum**, with a small but engaging collection of Pieniny costumes, including the embroidered waistcoats for which the region is famous.

DUNAJEC GORGE RAFT TRIPS

Below the heights of the Pieniny, the fast-moving **River Dunajec** twists its way between a succession of craggy peaks. The river is a magnet for canoeists, who shoot fearlessly through the often powerful rapids; for the less intrepid, the two- to three-hour **raft trip** provides a gentler though thoroughly enjoyable version of the experience. Tourists have been rafting down the waters of the Dunajec since the 1830s, a tradition derived in turn from the ancient practice of floating logs downriver to the mills and ports.

Run by the Polskie Stowarzyszenie Flisaków Pienińskich (Association of Pieniny Raftsmen; ☎ 18 262 9721, ⓦ flisacy.pl), trips begin at the village of **Sromowce Kąty** (daily: April & Sept 9am–4pm; May–Aug 8.30am–5pm; early to mid-Oct 9am–3pm; mid- to end-Oct 9am–2pm). Rafts seat around a dozen people and leave as soon as they're full – although you might have to queue, especially at weekends. There is a choice of two trips: **to Szczawnica** (2hr 15min; 54zł) at the eastern end of the gorge; or **to Krościenko** a further 10km downstream (2hr 45min; 68zł). From either place a bus (10zł) can bring you back to Sromowce Kąty.

The rafts are sturdy log constructions, made of four pontoons held together with rope, and are punted downstream by two navigators (wearing traditional embroidered jackets), who usually commentate on the trip in impenetrable Pieniny dialect. Although the river has some fast-flowing stretches, the raft journey is for the most part a leisurely downstream drift, allowing plenty of time to enjoy the scenery – especially the sheer limestone crags that hover above the sharp turns of the river. The Dunajec here forms the border with Slovakia, and at several points Slovak villages face their Polish counterparts across the banks.

Sromowce Kąty is connected to Szczawnica by seasonal minibuses (hourly; 30min), and to Nowy Targ by bus (5 daily; 1hr).

8

Palenica

Chairlift: June–Aug & Dec–April 9am–8pm • 17zł return • ⓦ pkl.pl

You can get up onto an eastern spur of the Pieniny by taking the **chairlift**, just below the main street, to the 722m-high **Mount Palenica**, which provides excellent views of the valley. There's a short downhill run and a modest snowboard park here in winter, although it's nothing for the serious winter-sports enthusiast to get excited about.

The Dunajec Gorge path

The Palenica chairlift terminal is the starting point for the **Dunajec Gorge** (Przełom Dunajca) foot- and cycle-path, which runs westwards along the south bank of first the Grajcarek and then the Dunajec, crossing over into Slovakia after 3km, and continuing for another 9km along the banks of the gorge as far as Cerveny Kláštor, the Slovakian starting point for rafting trips. You should at least follow the path for the 2km it takes you to reach the end of Szczawnica village; here you get excellent **views** of the cliffs marking the eastern end of the Dunajec Gorge, from which the bobbing forms of rafts emerge.

ARRIVAL AND GETTING AROUND SZCZAWNICA

By bus The bus stop is on the main street just west of the centre.

Destinations Krościenko (every 30min; 10min); Kraków (hourly; 2hr 30min–3hr); Nowy Sącz (hourly; 1hr).

By minibus Summer-season minibuses run to and from Jaworki (hourly; 10min), Niedzica (hourly; 35min) and

Sromowce Kąty (hourly; 30min) from the bus stop on the main street.

By bike Bikes can be hired (20–25zł/day) from numerous outlets throughout Szczawnica, notably at the Palenica chairlift terminal.

INFORMATION

Tourist information The Pieniny Tourist Centre at ul. Główna 1 (daily 8am–7pm; ☎ 18 262 2332, ⓦ pieninskie

centrumturystyki.pl) sells hiking maps and can book tours throughout the Pieniny.

ACCOMMODATION

Batory Park Górny 13 ☎ 18 262 0207, ⓦ batory-hotel.pl. Smart en-suite rooms in a thoroughly renovated nineteenth-century building where novelist Henryk Sienkiewicz (see page 411) was once a guest. There's an on-site sauna and steam-bath. **460zł**

Orlica ul. Pienińska 12 ☎ 18 262 2245, ⓦ orlica.com. Former hostel that has been nicely done up to serve as a pension for families and groups, with en-suite doubles, triples and quads in a charming timber building. It's at the eastern end of the Dunajec Gorge, 2km west of central

Szczawnica. Breakfast is extra (choose from the restaurant menu). **150zł**

Modrzewie Park Hotel ul. Park Górny 2 ☎ 18 540 0404, ⓦ mparkhotel.com. Built in 1939 for the daughter of Count Adam Stadnicki, this elegant retreat in the woods above the centre offers chic rooms and spa facilities. **600zł**

Willa Marta il. Główna 30 ☎ 18 262 2270, ⓦ willa marta.pl. Historical pension once patronized by Poland's cultural elite, and still popular with artists and journalists. The en-suite rooms are smallish but comfortable. **200zł**

EATING

Bohema ul. Główna 30 ☎ 795 131 577, ⓦ willamarta. pl. Restaurant of the *Willa Marta* pension (see page 341) with a genteel dining room and attractive park-facing veranda. Opt for trusty stomach-fillers like *pierogi* with buckwheat (16zł), or splash out on the pan-fried trout (27zł). It's worth popping in for a scoop or two of Marta's own-brand ice cream. Mon–Thurs & Sun 11am–9pm, Fri & Sat 11am–10pm.

Café Helenka pl. Dietla 1 ☎ 18 540 0402, ⓦ cafe-helenka.pl. With a large terrace overlooking the village centre, this is the perfect place to soak in Szczawnica's spa-resort charms. It's a good spot for a light lunch, with a menu that includes French-influenced tarts and quiches (18zł) alongside stock Polish fare and some dreamy desserts. Mon–Thurs 10.30am–7.30pm, Fri–Sun 10am–8.30pm.

Jaworki and around

Six kilometres east of Szczawnica, the rustic village of **JAWORKI** is the starting point for several hikes in the pasture-covered uplands that make up the eastern Pieniny. Sitting above the centre of the village is a bulb-domed eighteenth-century **church**, built for the Lemko community before their expulsion to other parts of Poland during Operation Vistula (see page 237) in 1947. Although now belonging to the Catholic Church, the structure retains a beautiful, Orthodox-influenced altarpiece studded with saintly icons. High in the eaves nests Poland's biggest colony of horseshoe **bats**.

Homole Gorge and Biała Woda

A well-signed path at the western end of Jaworki heads south into the **Homole Gorge** (Wąwoz Homole), where a fast-flowing stream gurgles its way beneath jagged rock formations. Featuring steel bridges and staircases, the path zig-zags through the gorge for about thirty minutes before leading up into the surrounding pastures. A sign to the left leads to the *Szałas Bukowinki* **hut**, where you can enjoy basic refreshments in a meadow munched by cows and the odd horse. Alternatively, follow the road east out of Jaworki to access a longer but gentler walking route through the narrow **Biała Woda valley**, again bordered by rugged, rocky terrain.

ARRIVAL AND DEPARTURE   JAWORKI AND AROUND

By minibus Summer-season minibuses run to Jaworki (hourly; 10min) from Szczawnica's main street.

EATING AND DRINKING

Bacówka ul. Biała Woda 1 ☎ 603 974 614, ⓦ bacowka jaworki.nrs.pl. Located in a traditional wooden-beamed building, *Bacówka* ("the hut") makes good use of the locally-raised trout and lamb (the latter either roast or stewed in goulash), alongside a customary array of Polish pork-and-potato dishes. Daily 11am–10pm, although they will close early if it gets quiet.

Muzyczna Owczarnia ul. Biała Woda 13 ☎ 18 262 2266, ⓦ muzycznaowczarnia.pl. Somewhat incongruous for a remote village in the Carpathians, the *Muzyczna Owczarnia* ("musical sheep-pen") is a concert and club venue hosting fairly well-known Polish pop-rock acts as well as serious jazz and folk. Before you visit, check the website to see whether it's worth heading out.

Upper Silesia

KATOWICE

9 Upper Silesia

Long thought of as the heartland of Polish heavy industry, Upper Silesia remains an area of disarming contrasts. At its centre stands the Silesian Metropolis, a fourteen-city urban constellation centred on former coal-town Katowice. With two million inhabitants, this is the most densely populated part of the country. To the south, however, lies some of the most bewitching countryside in Poland, in the form of the fir-clad Silesian Beskid Mountains that make up the province's border with the Czech Republic. The once-mighty coal and steel industries of the Metropolis went into steep decline after 1989, but with factories becoming art galleries and mines being redeveloped as tourist attractions, there's plenty in the way of industrial heritage to enjoy.

Having both an international airport and a major international railway junction, **Katowice** is your most likely entry point to the region, a gritty post-industrial city that's slowly coming into its own as a major cultural centre. A train ride away lies **Częstochowa**, the site of mass pilgrimages inspired by the miracle-working icon known as the Black Madonna. South of Katowice, rolling farmland rises gently to meet the pine-cloaked **Beskids**, providing a surfeit of attractive hiking territory. Ranged around the foothills, the Baroque palace at **Pszczyna**, the delightful towns of **Cieszyn** and **Żywiec**, and the up-and-coming ski resort of **Szczyrk** are the main targets for travellers.

Katowice and around

Once considered the ugly duckling of Polish cities, 400,000-strong **KATOWICE** is slowly but inexorably climbing up the league table of urban cool. Katowice's centre was rebuilt in grey concrete style in the 1960s and '70s, lumping the city with a socialist-brutalist image that has proved difficult to shake off. However, the inner-city area preserves pockets of nineteenth-century grandeur, and the coal-mining suburbs are enjoying a new lease of life as industrial heritage attractions.

Spodek

al. Korfantego 35 • ⓦ spodekkatowice.pl

North of the Rynek you can't miss Katowice's most alluring structure, the futuristic sports hall known as the **Spodek** ("flying saucer"), a smooth, dark doughnut of a building that looks like the kind of battleship that Darth Vader might cruise around the universe in. Built between 1964 and 1971, it is the one remnant of Katowice's communist-era makeover that still enjoys popular affection – or indeed any lasting relevance. Rock concerts, trade exhibitions and sporting events are held here (see page 351).

Rondo Sztuki

Rondo Jerzego Ziętka • Tues–Fri 11am–7pm, Sat & Sun 10am–6pm • ⓦ rondosztuki.pl

A short history of Upper Silesia p.347   **Upper Silesia's show mines** p.352
Katowice festivals and events p.351   **The Black Madonna and Jasna Góra** p.354

GUIDO MINE, ZABRZE

Highlights

❶ Silesian Museum, Katowice A superbly-designed museum occupying a former coal-mining site, this is post-industrial regeneration at its most ambitious. See page 346

❷ Silesian Park, Katowice This mammoth-sized city park boasts fairground rides, rose gardens, a folk museum and more. See page 347

❸ Show mines Upper Silesia's industrial heritage has been put to good use at spectacular show mines such as the Guido coal mine at Zabrze and the Museum of Silver Mining at Tarnowskie Góry. See page 352

❹ Radio Mast, Gliwice One of the tallest wooden structures in the world, this 1930s technological relic is very much a Silesian icon. See page 353

❺ Cieszyn A charming historic market town straddling Poland's frontier with the Czech Republic. See page 356

❻ Pszczyna palace One of the finest palaces in the country, surrounded by bison-grazed parkland. See page 359

❼ The Silesian Beskids Rippling pine-covered hills criss-crossed by hiking trails, accessed from the mountain resort of Szczyrk. See page 355

HIGHLIGHTS ARE MARKED ON THE PAGE ON PAGE 346

9

Rising above the Rondo Jerzego Ziętka tram stop immediately in front of the Spodek is the **Rondo Sztuki** (Art Roundabout), a crescent-shaped glass pavilion housing ambitious contemporary art shows. With a super-sleek café-bar on the first floor, it's probably the coolest public transport interchange you'll ever encounter.

Silesian Museum

ul. Dobrowolskigo 1 • Tues–Sun 10am–8pm • 24zł • ☏ 32 213 0870, ⓦ muzeumslaskie.pl

Occupying the re-landscaped former site of the Ferdynand coal mine just northeast of the city centre, the **Silesian Museum** (Muzeum Śląskie) is one of the most innovative new museums in the country. The original pit-head tower and several red-brick buildings have been affectionately preserved, although the bulk of the exhibition space lies underground, beneath modern cube-like pavilions that look like a row of enormous light-boxes. The display runs through the whole **history of Silesia** (see page 347) in imaginative and emotionally engaging style, covering themes such as the region's mixed German-Polish heritage, mass economic migrations, working-class life under capitalism and communism, and the region's technological and cultural achievements. There's a very thorough collection of Polish **art**, including some fabulous local naïve art, much

UPPER SILESIA

HIGHLIGHTS

1. Silesian Museum, Katowice
2. Silesian Park, Katowice
3. Show mines
4. Radio Mast, Gliwice
5. Cieszyn
6. Pszczyna palace
7. The Silesian Beskids

A SHORT HISTORY OF UPPER SILESIA

Upper Silesia's rich mineral seams have been extensively mined since the Middle Ages but it wasn't until the nineteenth-century **Industrial Revolution** that the area became heavily urbanized. With a population composed equally of Germans and Poles (and with many of mixed blood), the fate of the area became a hot political issue after **World War I**, with both Poland and Germany laying claim to the territory. The Western powers at first favoured Poland, which would otherwise have been a poor agricultural country with no industrial base. Strong support for the Polish claim came from the French, who wished to weaken Germany and establish a strong ally to its east. This unnerved the British: Prime Minister Lloyd George went so far as to suggest that allocating Upper Silesia to Poland was like giving a clock to a monkey.

The international community decided that the issue be settled by **plebiscite**. Fearful of German manipulation, the Silesian Poles mounted **insurrections** in 1919 and 1920. Finally held in March 1921, the plebiscite was won by the Germans – a result discredited by the fact that large numbers of voters were shipped back into Silesia from elsewhere in Germany. The Poles responded by launching a third insurrection in May, this time winning control of many urban areas. Called upon to arbitrate, the League of Nations decided on **partition** of Upper Silesia, drawing a line right down the middle of the province. The Germans got the western half, while the Poles were granted Katowice and the majority of the mines. Polish Upper Silesia was given autonomy by the government in Warsaw in recognition of its unique status and multicultural heritage – it was the most technologically advanced and westernized part of the inter-war republic. Upper Silesia's borders were re-drawn once again in **1945**, when the whole of Silesia was awarded to Poland. Most of the German population left, and Polish settlers arrived to take their place.

Throughout the **communist period**, Upper Silesia's workers enjoyed a privileged position; mining wages were three times the national average income. However, Silesia's workers became strong supporters of the Solidarity movement in the 1980s. The massacre of nine striking miners at the **Wujek** coal mine in 1981 effectively ended any community of interest between the working class and the regime that claimed to represent them. Many of the less profitable factories closed in the 1990s, reducing Silesia's serious **pollution** problems but adding to the ranks of local unemployed. However, Upper Silesia's skilled workforce and excellent communications have made it an obvious target for foreign investment, and the aura of post-industrial decay is nowadays disappearing beneath a palpable sense of big-city bustle.

of which is devoted to the coal-mining life. With a couple of other spaces devoted to temporary exhibitions, and an above-ground garden laid out around the cube-like pavilions, it's an altogether enthralling museum.

NOSPR Concert Hall and International Conference Centre

Just west of the Silesian Museum, on the same former coal-mine site, stand two more striking pieces of architecture. The **NOSPR Concert Hall** (see page 351), opened in 2014, is an iconic tribute to the red-brick architectural style that gave Katowice its signature look. Even if you've not got a ticket to a performance it's possible to look round the social areas, including the smart café-restaurant at mezzanine level. Next door is the **International Conference Centre** (Międzynarodowe Centrum Kongresowe or MCK; ⓦ mck.katowice.eu), which opened the following year; follow paths over the undulating grass-covered roof to enjoy views back down towards the Spodek, whose curvaceous form seems in perfect harmony with its new architectural neighbour.

The Silesian Park

Southeastern entrance on ul. Chorzowska • **Elka Chairlift** Tues–Thurs 11am–7pm, Fri & Sun till 8pm, Sat till 9pm • 10zł one-way • **Happy Town** Daily 10am–7pm • 40zł • **Silesian High Wire Park** Daily: May & Sept 10am–6pm; June–Aug 10am–8pm; Oct–April 10am–4pm • 35zł • **Zoo** Daily: April & Oct 9am–6pm; May–Sept 9am–7pm; Nov–March 9am–4pm • 12zł • ⓦ parkslaski.pl • Trams #6, #11, #19, #23 and #33 from the Rynek (destination Chorzów) pass along the park's southern edge

9

Three kilometres northwest of the centre, on the administrative boundary between Katowice and the neighbouring city of Chorzów, the **Silesian Park** (Park Śląski) is very much the pride of the Upper Silesian conurbation – an enormous expanse of greenery conceived by socialist planners in the 1950s as an area of leisure, relaxation and escape for the metropolis's proletarian hordes. Running east–west above the park, the 2km-long **Elka Cableway** (Kolejka Elka) conveys passengers some 20m above the ground in either eight-person gondolas or four-person open chairs.

Marking the southeastern entrance to the park is **Happy Town** (Wesołe Miasteczko), Poland's largest amusement park offering a variety of rides. Next door is the **Silesian High Wire Park** (Śląski Park Linowy), offering three treetop routes of varying degrees of difficulty. From here a central avenue leads northwest through the heart of the park, passing a boating lake, a swimming pool, seven hectares of rose garden and a sizeable **zoo**. At the northwestern end of the avenue looms the huge bowl of the **Silesia Stadium** (Stadion Śląski), venue for international football matches and outdoor rock concerts. English fans may wish to forget that Katowice was the scene of a famous 2–0 defeat in June 1973 that helped to confirm England's decline as a footballing power. The Poles, meanwhile, went on to enjoy a golden decade of international success.

Upper Silesian Ethnographic Park

ul. Parkowa 25 • Daily: May–Sept 9am–7pm (till 9pm Sat & Sun); Oct 9am–5pm; Nov–April 9am–4pm • 8zł • ☎ 32 241 0718, ⓦ muzeumgpe-chorzow.pl • Tram #6, #11, #19 or #33 from Katowice Rynek to the Stadion Śląski stop

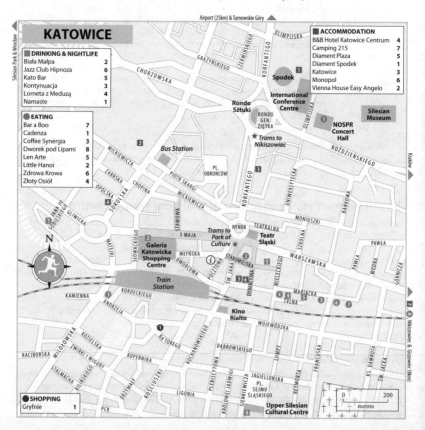

Located on the northwestern boundary of the Silesian Park, the **Upper Silesian Ethnographic Park** (Górnośląski Park Etnograficzny) presents a fascinating array of rural buildings ranged across an area of gently rolling meadowland. Jostling for attention are timber cottages from the Beskid Mountains, straw-thatched farmhouses from the Pszczyna region, and – most arrestingly of all – an eighteenth-century wooden church from the village of Nieboczów, with a wonderfully wavy shingle roof and a rash of pimply onion domes.

Nikiszowiec

Bus #30 (direction Giszowiec) from al. Korfantego

Arguably the most alluring part of Katowice's industrial heritage is **Nikiszowiec** (colloquially known as "Nikisz"), a model suburb 6km southeast of the centre, built in 1908–15 to house workers employed in the nearby Wieczorek coal mine. Designed by Berlin architects Georg and Emil Zillmann, the suburb comprises a series of red-brick quadrangular and triangular residential blocks, each punctuated with fortress-like gateways leading through to inner garden courtyards. Presiding over the whole ensemble is the similarly red-brick **St Anne's Church** (Kościół św. Anny), a neo-Baroque structure basking beneath a fat sensual dome. It's a fascinating place for a wander – and the proximity of the Wilson Pit Gallery provides plenty to build an excursion around.

Wilson Pit Gallery

ul. Oswobodzenia 1 • Daily 9am–7pm • Free • ⓦ szybwilson.org • Bus #30 (direction Giszowiec) from al. Korfantego

One kilometre east of Nikiszowiec back along the road to Katowice, the **Wilson Pit Gallery** (Galeria Szyb Wilson) occupies the above-ground machine halls of the former Wilson coal mine. Filling this vast space with changing exhibitions of quirky but accessible contemporary art, the gallery is a leading example of how Katowice's industrial heritage can be put to good use.

Giszowiec

Bus #30 from al. Korfantego

Lying some 8km south of central Katowice, just beyond Nikiszowiec, the suburb of **Giszowiec** looks like a piece of southern England pulled out of context and plonked in the midst of the Silesian coalfields. Designed in 1906 for the Giesche coal-mining company by the Zillmann cousins – who went on to plan Nikiszowiec (see above) – the model settlement of Giszowiec sprang from the same garden-city philosophy that inspired British urban planner Ebenezer Howard. The result is an extraordinary slice of suburban utopia, with rows of one- and two-storey semis and their neat little gardens arranged around a leafy central park. Amazingly, socialist planners nearly bulldozed the whole lot in the 1960s in order to extend a tower-block housing estate; in the event, underground mine workings made the terrain unsuitable for tall buildings, and the core of Giszowiec was spared.

ARRIVAL AND DEPARTURE   KATOWICE

By air Katowice's airport is at Pyrzowice, 25km northeast of the centre. PKM city buses (roughly hourly through the day with longer gaps between services throughout the night; 50min; 27zł; pay the driver) run from the airport to the train station. Minibuses to and from Kraków are run by Matuszek (☎32 236 1111, ⓦmatuszek.com.pl) and Pyrzowice Ekspres (☎603 966 598, ⓦpyrzowiceekspres. pl), but these are often booked far in advance – best to reserve a seat as soon as you know your travel plans.

By train Trains arrive at the modern, user-friendly station right in the centre on pl. Szewczyka.

Destinations Bielsko-Biała (every 30min; 1hr 20min); Częstochowa (hourly; 1hr 10min); Gliwice (every 30min; 30min); Kraków (4 daily; 2hr 20min); Łódź Widzew (3 daily; 2hr 45min); Poznań (5 daily; 4–6hr); Prague (1 daily; 5hr 10min); Pszczyna (every 30min; 1hr); Szczecin (2 daily; 8–9hr); Vienna (2 daily; 4hr 30min); Warsaw (9 daily; 3hr 20min–3hr 40min); Wrocław (5 daily; 2hr 20min); Żywiec (hourly; 2hr).

By bus The bus station is a 10min walk north of the train station on ul. Piotra Skargi. Buses run from here to Kraków (every 15min; 1hr 40min). Minibuses to Cieszyn run from

9

the parking lot on the south side of Katowice train station

(Mon–Sat 15 daily, Sun 10 daily; 1hr 30min).

INFORMATION

Tourist information The tourist office at ul. Rynek 13 (Mon–Fri 9am–7pm, Sat 9am–5pm, Sun 9am–1pm; ☏ 32 259 3808, ⓦ katowice.eu) offers free maps and bags of local advice.

ACCOMMODATION

HOTELS

B&B Hotel Katowice Centrum ul. Sokolska 4 ☏ 32 700 5088, ⓦ hotelbb.pl; map page 348. Contemporary design, bright social areas and decent-sized rooms make this an excellent choice for anyone looking for reliable level of comfort at a decent price. Breakfast 25zł per person extra. **160zł**

Diament Plaza ul. Dworcowa 9 ☏ 32 746 7000, ⓦ hotel diament.pl; map page 348. Dependable three-star right by the station, offering pastel-coloured en suites with desk space. Breakfast from 45zł per person extra. **210zł**

Diament Spodek al. Korfantego 35 ☏ 32 606 8585, ⓦ hoteldiament.pl; map page 348. With neat if uninspiring rooms, the main attraction of this hotel is its location inside Katowice's most famous example of forward-looking modernist architecture, and proximity to the Spodek's indoor swimming pool and fitness facilities. Breakfast 40zł per person extra. **150zł**

Katowice al. Korfantego 9 ☏ 32 258 8281, ⓦ hotel-katowice.com.pl; map page 348. This 1960s-era block offers plain but habitable en suites with TV. The upper floors have good views of downtown Katowice's grey, socialist-era cityscape. **320zł**

Monopol ul. Dworcowa 5 ☏ 32 782 8282, ⓦ monopol katowice.hotel.com.pl; map page 348. Beautifully renovated nineteenth-century building offering five-star comforts, with rooms decked out in modern materials with Art Deco touches. Guests can use the swimming pool, saunas and gym in the basement. Breakfast 70zł per person extra. **600zł**

Vienna House Easy Angelo ul. Sokolska 24 ☏ 32 783 8100, ⓦ angelo-katowice.pl; map page 348. Stylish four-star with a flair for contemporary design – the furnishings and light fittings in the social areas are all mood-enhancingly colourful, and the rooms are small but spankingly modern. Breakfast 60zł per person extra. **490zł**

CAMPSITE

Camping 215 ul. Trzech Stawów 23 ☏ 32 256 5939; bus #4 from al. Korfantego; map page 348. Camping in an industrial city like Katowice might sound paradoxical, but there's a well-tended, lakeside site south of the city in the Dolina Trzech Stawów ("Valley of the Three Lakes"), a popular outdoor recreation area. Tennis courts, swimming pool, sauna and beer garden feature among the facilities. Open mid-May to late Sept. **35zł**

EATING

Bar a Boo ul. Mariacka 37 ☏ 32 399 1526; map page 348. The main rival of *Len Arte* (see below) for the best-pizza-in-town crown – which place you prefer may very well depend on whether you can find a free table. With very good pizzas (20–25zł) and a lot of imaginative pasta dishes, it fills up quickly. Daily 11am–1am.

Cadenza pl. Wojciecha Kilara 1 ☏ 32 732 5347, ⓦ cadenza.pl; map page 348. Starched-napkin restaurant inside the NOSPR concert venue, offering smooth service and modern European classics such as stewed beef cheeks (40zł) and lamb shanks (52zł) plus a couple of vegetarian and fish options. Three-course business lunches (Tues–Fri; 35zł) are a great way to sample *Cadenza*'s output on a budget. Daily 10am–10pm.

★ **Coffee Synergia** ul. Andrzeja 29/2 ☏ 502 930 253; map page 348. The kind of coffee shop that earns superlatives for pretty much everything that it does: cakes, toasted sandwiches, lunchtime soups, and of course the coffee, which is taken very seriously indeed. Daily 8am–9pm.

Dworek pod Lipami Pod Lipami 1, Giszowiec; bus #30 to Giszowiec; map page 348. Situated in a smart villa overlooking Giszowiec's park, this is the place to come for traditional Silesian cooking – muscular meaty dishes accompanied by plenty of cabbage and potatoes. Beef roulade (a roll of meat stuffed with shredded pork and pickled vegetables; 35zł) is the standout, although standards are good here whatever you order. Daily 10am–11pm.

Len Arte ul. Mariacka 25 ☏ 32 308 8430; map page 348. Intimate place that's frequently full, thanks to their excellent thin-crust pizzas (25–35zł) featuring toppings thrown together from Italian-sourced ingredients. Mon–Thurs & Sun 1–10pm, Fri & Sat 1pm–midnight.

★ **Little Hanoi** ul. Staromiejska 4 ☏ 886 623 388; map page 348. An elegant and not overly expensive place to eat quality Vietnamese cuisine, with mains such as Hanoi Duck around the 40zł mark, although a bowl of noodles with vegetables (14zł) or a generous serving of pho soup (27zł) makes a perfectly respectable meal. The interior is nicely done, with minimalist modern furnishings placed beneath a cluster of colourful lanterns, and there is outdoor seating on the pedestrianized strip. Daily noon–10pm.

Zdrowa Krowa ul. Mariacka 33 ☏ 730 101 520; map page 348. Classy sit-down burger joint that has a wide range of options – fish and veggie versions included. With many burger-plus-fries options clocking in at under 30zł, it's popular. Mon–Thurs & Sun noon–10pm, Fri & Sat noon–3am.

KATOWICE FESTIVALS AND EVENTS

Katowice enjoys an increasingly high profile as a live-music city, with a lot of events organized under the aegis of municipal arts organization **Miasto Ogrodów** ("City of Gardens"; Ⓦ miasto-ogrodow.eu). The two festivals below have become pillars of the Polish alternative scene.

Off Festival Early Aug Ⓦ off-festival.pl. Brainchild of alt-rock star Artur Rojek, this is one of the biggest indie music events in Central Europe, attracting top international names.

Tauron Nowa Muzyka Late June/early July Ⓦ festiwalnowamuzyka.pl. Alternative dance music and the wilder fringes of DJ culture celebrated in a four-day block of events, most held in post-industrial spaces.

Złoty Osioł ul. Mariacka 1 ☎ 501 465 690; map page 348. You can eat well for under 15zł at this cult vegetarian restaurant that looks like a cross between a student bedsit and an oriental textile market. What's available will be on view at the counter – usually an inexpensive range of filling and frequently quite spicy stews and soups, with the odd lasagne and quiche thrown in. Mon–Sat 10am–10pm, Sun noon–10pm.

DRINKING AND NIGHTLIFE

Undisputed centre of Katowice's going-out scene is ul. Mariacka, pedestrianized in 2008 and colonized by pubs and bars soon afterwards. Outdoor gigs and DJ events are organized on ul. Mariacka most weekends from late April until mid October.

Biała Małpa ul. 3 Maja 38 ☎ 720 866 173, Ⓦ biala malpa.pl; map page 348. Dark and welcoming multi-tap beer pub with minimal furniture but a plethora of tempting brews chalked up on the board beside the bar. There's a big courtyard with makeshift sofas (futons on pallets), which is warmed in winter. Daily noon–midnight.

Jazz Club Hipnoza pl. Sejmu Śląskiego 2 ☎ 660 476 156, Ⓦ jazzclub.pl; map page 348. South of the train station on the second floor of the Upper Silesian Cultural Centre (Górnośląski Centrum Kultury), this laidback pub decked out in armchairs, sofas and lampstands is the city's most popular venue with the studenty, arty, young-professional crowd. There's a solid food menu too – with pizzas (15–20zł) and grilled steaks (30–35zł) predominating. Live jazz or blues about once a week. Daily noon–1am; closed July & Aug.

Kato Bar ul. Mariacka 13 Ⓦ bit.ly/KatoKatowice; map page 348. One of the first places to open on the Mariacka strip, Kato has become something of a cult destination among visitors in search of the new spirit of the city. The interior is loungy but unfussy; offbeat Czech and Polish beers are available by the bottle. Mon–Sat noon–late, Sun 3pm–late.

Kontynuacja ul. Staromiejski 8 ☎ 668 525 825; map page 348. Representing the civilized end of the multi-tap craft-beer spectrum, Kontynuacja is a cooly-designed, sit-down space rather than a stand-up bar, with lots of matt surfaces and exposed brick. The choice of great beers is impressive; indeed, no alcohol other than beer is served. Mon–Thurs & Sun 4pm–midnight, Fri & Sat 4pm–2am.

Lorneta z Meduzą ul. Mariacka 5 ☎ 32 200 0660, Ⓦ facebook.com/lornetazmeduza; map page 348. A Mariacka landmark, Lorneta mixes Art Deco design details with a similarly nostalgic menu of cheap food and drink – beer and wódka are reassuringly cheap, while food nibbles such as white sausage or marinated herring are all priced at 9.50zł. The name Lorneta z Meduzą translates as "binoculars with a jellyfish" – the jellyfish in this case is the seductively wobbly dish that is pig's trotters in aspic; the binoculars refer to the double vodka you wash it down with. In summer, drinkers spill out onto the pavement. Open 24hr.

Namaste ul. Jana III Sobieskiego 27 ☎ 503 451 704, Ⓦ namaste.katowice.pl; map page 348. This mellow bar has walls covered in inspiring photos of seriously togged-up people going up mountains, piles of old travel magazines lying around and a nice garden, plus frequent screenings of travel-related talks and film shows (in Polish). There's a good choice of beer, and they also do pizzas. Daily 3–11pm.

ENTERTAINMENT

NOSPR Concert Hall pl. Wojciecha Kilara 1 ☎ 32 732 5320, Ⓦ nospr.org.pl. Home to the Polish National Radio Symphony Orchestra (Narodowa Orkiestra Symfoniczna Polskiego Radia, or "NOSPR"). The wavy panels and curving surfaces of the 1800-capacity auditorium provide perfect acoustics. Ticket office open Tues–Sat 10am–8pm.

Spodek al. Korfantego 35 Ⓦ spodek.com.pl. Rock concerts and sporting events are held at this multipurpose arena.

SHOPPING

Gryfnie ul. Andrzeja 8 Ⓦ gryfnie.com; map page 348. Colourful T-shirts, hats, socks, childrenswear and more from the local Gryfnie ("byooutiful") label – all items feature Silesian visual themes or Silesian-dialect slogans. Gryfnie also stocks a few books and ironic (frequently coal-themed) souvenirs. Mon–Fri 10am–7pm, Sat 10am–3pm.

9

UPPER SILESIA'S SHOW MINES

Some of Upper Silesia's most spectacular industrial heritage sites are to be found in the former coal- and silver-mining regions, where a handful of disused pits have been opened to the public as **show mines**. As well as offering insights into mining history, each of the sites below involves visitors in a memorable underground journey, and is well worth a day-trip from Katowice to see.

Visits to the mines are by **guided tour**, which usually depart every half an hour or on the hour. Individual tourists can turn up and hope to join one of these, although it's advisable to **book in advance** on the telephone numbers provided below. Regular tours are in Polish, but this shouldn't detract too much from the experience; if you want an English-language guide ring a couple of days in advance and expect to stump up an extra 50–60zł.

TARNOWSKIE GÓRY

Twenty kilometres north of Katowice and accessible by regular train, **Tarnowskie Góry** has been a major silver- and lead-mining centre ever since the thirteenth century. There are two heritage sites here, beginning with the **Museum of Silver Mining**, 2.5km south of town at ul. Szczęść Boże 52 (Kopalnia Zabytkowa Rud Srebronosnych: daily 9am–3pm; June–Aug open till 5pm Sat & Sun; 45zł; ☎ 32 285 2981, ⓦ kopalniasrebra.pl). Dating back to medieval times, the mine was formerly worked for silver, lead and copper, and in the small museum you'll see models of how the mine was operated and water levels controlled. The highlight, though, is a motorboat trip along the flooded drainage tunnels that were excavated as needs arose; dozens of kilometres of passageways undermine the entire area. From Tarnowskie Góry train station, catch bus #151, #734 or #735 to the Kopalnia Zabytkowa stop.

Situated in the wooded Park Repecki 4km southwest of the centre, the **Black Trout Gallery** (Sztolnia Czarnego Pstrąga: April, May, Sept & Oct Sat & Sun 10am–4pm; June–Aug daily 10am–5pm; Nov–March Sat & Sun 11am–3pm; 24zł; ☎ 32 285 2981, ⓦ kopalniasrebra.pl) is a 600m-long drainage tunnel linking two mine shafts, Szyb Ewa and Szyb Sylwester. It takes its name from the eponymous fish which occasionally found their way into the tunnels from the rivers into which they drain. Entering via Szyb Ewa, the tour consists of a spooky journey by boat along the narrow rock-hewn gallery, during which associated legends are recounted; at one point any woman wanting to find a husband within the year is invited to rap on the wall. From Tarnowskie Góry train station, catch bus #1, #134, #614 or #780 to the end of the line.

ZABRZE

Just east of Gliwice and served by regular Katowice–Gliwice trains, **Zabrze** was one of Upper Silesia's most prolific coal-producing cities, and the local skyline is still studded with the skeletal pithead structures of the mines.

Located in the southern suburbs of Zabrze, the **Guido Mine** (Kopalnia Guido: July & Aug Tues–Sun 9am–7pm; Sept–June Tues–Fri 8.30am–3pm, Sat & Sun noon–5pm; 39zł; ☎ 32/271 4077, ⓦ kopalniaguido.pl) was founded by Count Guido von Donnersmarck in 1855, and more or less exhausted by the 1940s. Once you've descended in rattling cage-lifts to a depth of 170m, the 90-minute tour takes in displays of mining machinery through the ages, and a re-creation of the underground stables where pit ponies spent their working lives. The mine is a twenty-minute walk south of Zabrze train station or a brief trip on tram #3.

Gliwice

Only twenty minutes west of Katowice by train, **GLIWICE** was one of the original powerhouses of Upper Silesian industry, thanks in large part to the coke-fired blast furnaces established here by trailblazing Scottish engineer John Baildon in 1796. Evidence of Gliwice's erstwhile prosperity can be seen in the parade of fine nineteenth-century apartment blocks lining the main street, ulica Zwycięstwa.

The Palm House

ul. Fredry 6 • Tues–Fri 9am–6pm, Sat & Sun 10am–6pm • 7zł

Set in the park west of the train station, the modern glass pavilions of Gliwice's **Palm House** (Palmiarnia) provide an extensive home to exotic flora from around the world. Of particular interest is the Tropical Plants Pavilion, an indoor recreation of a tropical rainforest featuring lianas, bromelias, orchids and a small pond patrolled by the odd piranha.

Villa Caro
ul. Dolnych Wałów 8a • Tues 9am–3pm, Wed 9am–4pm, Thurs & Fri 10am–4pm, Sat 11am–5pm, Sun 11am–4pm • 8zł; free on Sat • ⓦ muzeum.gliwice.pl

Downtown Gliwice's star turn is the **Villa Caro**, which has the best-preserved nineteenth-century interiors in southern Poland. Built by German-Jewish magnate Oscar Caro in 1885, the villa is richly decorated with stucco ceilings, intricate wall panelling and all manner of fine furniture. Caro himself was an enthusiastic collector, with Renaissance paintings, seventeenth-century Samurai armour and Chinese opium pipes adding up to an eclectic personal museum.

Gliwice Radio Mast
ul. Tarnogórska 129 (a 20min walk north up ul. Tarnogórska from Gliwice train station) **Mast and park** Daily: May–Sept 6am–10pm; Oct–April 8am–8pm • Free • **Museum** Tues–Fri 10am–4pm, Sat & Sun 11am–4pm • 5zł • ⓦ muzeum.gliwice.pl

Two kilometres northeast of central Gliwice, the vintage 1930s **radio mast** (Radiostacja Gliwicka) is one of Poland's most powerfully alluring sights. Standing 111m tall, this gauntly elegant structure is reckoned to be the highest surviving wooden structure in the world. Locals remember it as the scene of a notorious provocation on the night of August 31, 1939, when the Germans – eager to start a war with Poland for which the Poles would be blamed – arranged for their agents to attack the station in the guise of Polish "insurgents": World War II kicked off the following day. At the foot of the mast is a modern landscaped park featuring ornamental shrubs and fountains. The former transmission station just east of the mast, filled with archaic pre-World War II control panels, now serves as a modest **museum**, although it's the bold geometrical thrust of the mast itself that's the real attraction.

ARRIVAL AND DEPARTURE
GLIWICE

By train Gliwice's train station is just off the northern end of ul. Zwycięstwa; the centre of town (with the main Rynek and the Villa Caro) is a 15min walk south from here. Trains run from Gliwice to Katowice (every 30min; 20min) and Strzelce Opolskie (hourly; 40min).

EATING AND DRINKING

Kafo ul. Wieczorka 14 ☎ 508 503 338, ⓦ kafo.info. Cult café-bar just west of the Villa Caro that was one of the first places in Upper Silesia to introduce punters to the delights of aeropress, Chemex and coffee from specific origins. Still bubbling up a good brew, it also serves excellent cakes, biscuits and toasts. Mon–Fri 7am–8pm, Sat & Sun 10am–8pm.

MoMo Rynek-Ratusz ☎ 570 170 080. Right in the middle of Gliwice's Rynek is this rather suave restaurant and bar serving elegantly turned-out steak, duck and seafood dishes in the 40–60zł range. With Tyskie beer from the tank and a tempting list of cocktails, it's also a popular place to drink. Mon–Thurs & Sun 10am–11pm, Fri & Sat 10am–1am.

Waga ul. Zwycięstwa 6 ☎ 536 935 030. Stylish buffet restaurant with fill-your-own-plate food priced by weight. Eat your way through Polish staples or opt for mildly spicy Asian options. Mon–Fri 8am–7pm, Sat 11am–4pm, Sun noon–5pm.

Częstochowa

When it comes to the central role played by Catholicism in contemporary Poland, there are few places more symbolic than **CZĘSTOCHOWA**. Home to the famous icon known as the **Black Madonna**, the city-centre monastery of **Jasna Góra** (Clear Mountain) is one of the world's greatest places of pilgrimage. Crowds are at their largest during the major Marian **festivals** – May 3, August 26, September 8, December 8 and most of all **August 15** (Assumption), when up to a million pilgrims converge. Many come on foot, with tens of thousands making the nine-day walk from Warsaw to

9

THE BLACK MADONNA AND JASNA GÓRA

Częstochowa grew up around the hilltop monastery of **Jasna Góra**, founded in 1382 by Duke Ladislaus II of Opole. Ladislaus donated the miraculous icon known as the **Black Madonna** a couple of years later, turning the monastery into a major focus for pilgrims. According to legend the Black Madonna was painted from life by Saint Luke, although it is more likely to be of early medieval Italian origin. The black refers to the heavy shading used by the artist, subsequently darkened by age. The image on show today may indeed be a copy made in the 1430s following the icon's first great "miracle", when thieves attempted to steal the painting only to find that it increased in weight and could not be carried. In frustration the thieves slashed the Virgin's face, which immediately started shedding blood.

The monastery was fortified in the early **seventeenth century**, enabling its defenders to hold out against a numerically superior army of Swedes in 1655 – inspiring a national fightback against a foe who had all but extinguished Polish independence. This dramatic turn of fortune was attributed to the miraculous power of the Black Madonna, although the image wasn't actually here at the time – it had been removed to southern Silesia for safekeeping. After **World War II** Jasna Góra became a major focus of opposition to the communist regime. The Church skilfully promoted the pilgrimage as a display of passive resistance, a campaign that received a huge boost in 1978 with the election of Karol Wojtyła, archbishop of Kraków and a central figure in its conception, as **Pope John Paul II**.

celebrate the occasion. Częstochowa is best visited as a day-trip from Katowice, Kraków or Łódź; once you've seen Jasna Góra there's not a lot else to detain you.

Jasna Góra

Information centre Daily: May to mid-Oct 8am–7pm; mid-Oct to April 8am–5pm • ⓦ bop.jasnagora.pl

Częstochowa's main street, aleja Najświętszej Maryi Panny (usually abbreviated as "NMP"), cuts through the modern heart of the city, terminating at the foot of the monastery of **Jasna Góra**. A swathe of public park covers the lower reaches of the hill,

above which protrude the monastery's seventeenth-century battlements. Visitors enter the complex via the south gate, beyond which lies a visitor information centre, run by nuns, and, usefully, complete with an ATM.

The Chapel of the Miraculous Image

Black Madonna viewings: Mon–Fri 6am–noon & 1.30–9pm, Sat & Sun 6am–1pm & 2–9pm

A separate church in its own right, the **Chapel of the Miraculous Image** (Kaplica Cudownego Obrazu) is the focal point of the monastery. It's also the only part to retain much of the original Gothic architecture, though its walls are so encrusted with votive offerings and discarded crutches and leg-braces that this is no longer obvious. Masses are said here almost constantly but you'll have to time it right if you want a view of the **Black Madonna**, a sight that should not be missed. Part of the time the icon is shrouded by a screen, each raising and lowering of which is accompanied by a solemn trumpet fanfare. When it's on view, only the faces and hands of the Madonna and Child are visible; the rest of their bodies are "dressed" in varying sets of jewel-encrusted robes that glitter impressively against the black walls.

The museums

Daily 9am–5pm

Jasna Góra's treasures are kept in three separate buildings. At the southwestern end of the monastery is the **Arsenał**, devoted to the military history of the fortress and containing a superb array of weapons, including Turkish war loot donated by King Jan Sobieski. Nearby, the **Treasury of National Memory** (Skarbiec Pamięci Narodu) contains a fascinating collection of Solidarity banners from the 1980s, and a diorama (complete with model soldiers) illustrating the Swedish siege of 1655.

A few doors up is the **Six Hundredth Anniversary Museum** (Muzeum Sześćsetlecia), which tells the monastery's story from a religious standpoint. Exhibits include votive offerings from famous Poles, prominent among which is Lech Wałęsa's 1983 Nobel Peace Prize certificate, along with the oversized pen he used to sign the landmark August 1980 Gdańsk Agreements (see page 466).

ARRIVAL AND INFORMATION CZĘSTOCHOWA

By train Częstochowa's train station lies just southeast of al. NMP (Najświętszej Maryi Panny).
Destinations Katowice (hourly; 1hr 15min); Kraków (4 daily; 1hr 40min); Łódź Widzew (4 daily; 1hr 30min); Warsaw (8 daily; 2hr 30min–2hr 50min).

Tourist information The well-stocked tourist information centre is at al. NMP 65 (Mon–Sat 9am–5pm; ☎ 34/368 2250, ⓦ czestochowa.pl).

EATING

Café Belg al. NMP 32 ☎ 34 361 1324; map page 354. Atmospheric little café with a jumble of armchairs spread over a parquet floor, renowned for its reliably strong coffee, huge choice of leaf teas and craft beers. Occasional live music and art exhibitions. Mon–Sat 9am–11pm, Sun 4–11pm.
Café Skrzynka ul. Dąbrowskiego 1 ☎ 34 324 3098;

map page 354. The place to go for respectably-sized sweet and savoury pancakes (18–20zł), alongside salads, sandwiches and cakes. Art exhibitions, occasional concerts and free wi-fi are *Skrzynka's* other major virtues. Mon–Thurs 8am–10pm, Fri 8am–midnight, Sat 10am–midnight, Sun noon–10pm.

The Silesian Beskids

Running along Silesia's border with the Czech Republic, the **Silesian Beskids** (Beskid Śląski) present an archetypal central European mountain landscape characterized by fir-clad slopes reaching up towards bald summits. It is a region of wooden churches, folk costumes and occasional castles. The industrial city of **Bielsko-Biała** is the main entry point to the Silesian Beskids, but the best base from which to tour the region is

9

the historic market town of **Cieszyn**. To its north is the outstanding palace museum in **Pszczyna**, while southeast lies **Szczyrk**, the main hiking and skiing resort. Further east, Żywiec is another attractive town famous for its beer-brewing heritage.

Bielsko-Biała

Located in the shadow of the Beskid Mountains, **BIELSKO-BIAŁA** is a useful transport hub. However, it's hardly one of Poland's most compelling cities, and is best treated as a place to change buses rather than somewhere to stick around.

ARRIVAL AND DEPARTURE
BIELSKO-BIAŁA

By train The main train station is right in the centre of town, on the border between Bielsko and Biała.

Destinations Katowice (every 30min; 1hr 30min–2hr 30min); Pszczyna (every 30min; 30–50min); Żywiec (hourly; 40min).

By bus The bus station is slightly uphill to the east of the train station.

Destinations Cieszyn (hourly; 1hr 10min); Kraków (12 daily; 3hr); Szczyrk (every 30min; 40min); Wisła (3 daily; 1hr 10min); Zakopane (3 daily; 3hr 30min).

Cieszyn

Straddling the Czech frontier 35km west of Bielsko-Biała, **CIESZYN** has the kind of attractive market squares, cobbled streets and well-preserved buildings that most other towns of Upper Silesia conspicuously lack. It's also fairly unusual in being a town that's shared between two countries: with both Czechoslovakia and Poland laying claim to Cieszyn in the wake of World War I, the town was split in two, with the River Olza forming the frontier. The medieval centre, complete with Rynek and castle, fell to the Poles, while the Czechs had to make do with the suburb (now known as Český Těšín) on the opposite side of the river. Nowadays, with both Poland and the Czech Republic belonging to the EU's Schengen zone, people are free to wander where they wish: you can sightsee on one side of the border, and eat and drink on the other. Cieszyn is also an excellent base for onward travel, with three daily trains running from the Czech side of town to Prague.

Cieszyn's central **Rynek**, with the eighteenth-century town hall, stands at the highest point of the central area. Just off its southwest corner is the Gothic **Church of St Mary Magdalene** (Kościół św. Marii Magdaleny), containing a mausoleum of Piast dukes who established an independent principality here in 1290.

Museum of the Cieszyn Region

ul. Regera 6 • Entry on the hour: March–Sept Tues, Thurs, Sat & Sun 10am–2pm, Wed & Fri noon–4pm; Oct–Feb Tues, Thurs–Sun 10am–2pm, Wed noon–4pm • 10zł • ☎ 33 851 2933, ⓦ muzeumcieszyn.pl

Heading east from the Rynek along Regera brings you to a handsome eighteenth-century mansion, former residence of the princes of Cieszyn and now home to the **Museum of the Cieszyn Region** (Muzeum Śląska Cieszyńskiego). Inside lies an attractively laid-out assemblage of art and furniture through the ages, with one room devoted to the museum's nineteenth-century founder, Jesuit priest Jan Leopold Szersznik, whose collection – including everything from Japanese clogs to mammoth's teeth – is displayed in the cabinet-of-curiosities style in which he left it. Among the lovingly restored period interiors are a ballroom decorated with Arcadian landscape paintings and plaster cherubs riding on goat-back, and a richly decorated stable built by horse-mad aristocrat Filip Saint-Genois d'Anneaucourt (who bought the mansion in 1831); the latter now serves as the museum café (see page 358).

Ulica Głęboka

Running west from the Rynek, Cieszyn's main street, **ulica Głęboka**, sweeps downhill towards the river, passing a sequence of imposing mansions on the way. If you head down ulica Sejmowa to the left and then take the first turning right, you'll find yourself on ulica Trzech Braci ("Street of the Three Brothers"). Here stands the **well** associated with the legend of the town's foundation. In the year 810, the three sons of King Leszko III met at this spring after a long spell wandering the country. They were so delighted to see each other again that they founded a town and named it "I'm happy" (*cieszym się*).

From the foot of ulica Głęboka, it's only a few paces along ulica Zamkowa to the **Most Przyjazni** (Friendship Bridge), which leads across the river to the Czech part of town.

Cieszyn Castle

ul. Zamkowa 3 • Daily 9am–5pm • Free • ☎ 33 851 0821, ⓦ zamekcieszyn.pl

Looming above ulica Zamkowa as it turns towards the river is **Cieszyn Castle** (Zamek Cieszyn), a former Habsburg hunting lodge now transformed into a cultural centre containing music school, artists' studios and an attractive gallery space hosting excellent exhibitions of contemporary Polish design.

Piast Tower

Daily: April 9am–5pm; May & Sept 9am–6pm; June–Aug 9am–7pm; Nov–March 9am–4pm • 6zł

Round the back of the castle, a small round hill is crowned by the fourteenth-century Gothic **Piast Tower** (Wieża Piastowska), the only surviving part of the Piast palace. From the top, there's a superb view over both sides of the town and the Beskidy beyond.

9

Chapel of St Nicholas

Alongside the Piast Tower stands one of the oldest surviving buildings in Silesia, the **Chapel of St Nicholas** (Kaplica św. Mikołaja), a handsome Romanesque rotunda dating back to the eleventh century, with the vestiges of a well from the same period in front of it.

ARRIVAL AND INFORMATION

CIESZYN

By train Cieszyn's train station is on the eastern side of town, a 10min walk downhill from the main Rynek. The Český Těšín station on the Czech side of town handles services to destinations in the Czech Republic.
Destinations (from Cieszyn) Katowice (change at Czechowice-Dziedzice; 8 daily; 2hr 30min–3hr 20min).
Destinations (from Český Těšín) Ostrava (hourly; 50min); Prague (3 daily; 4hr 45min).

By bus Cieszyn's bus station is next to the train station.
Destinations Bielsko-Biała (hourly; 1hr 10min); Katowice (Mon–Sat 15 daily, Sun 10 daily; 1hr 30min); Kraków (6 daily; 4hr).
Tourist information The well-organized tourist office is at Rynek 1 (Mon–Fri 8am–4pm, Sat 9am–1pm; ☎33 479 4249, ⓦ cieszyn.pl).

ACCOMMODATION

Dworek Cieszyński ul. Przykopa 14 ☎33 858 1178, ⓦ dworek-cieszynski.pl; map page 357. A handful of cosy rooms above the restaurant of the same name (see page 358), just below the town centre and near the riverbank. **160zł**
Gambit ul. Bucewicza 18 ☎33 852 0651, ⓦ hotel gambit.com.pl; map page 357. Concrete lump a 15min walk north of the bus station which is actually quite nice once you get inside. Simply furnished en suites, some with ravishing views of the surrounding hills. Buffet breakfast 20zł per person extra. **120zł**

Liburnia ul. Liburnia 10 ☎33 852 0531, ⓦ liburnia hotel.pl; map page 357. Functional but eminently comfortable three-star located in a retail park within easy walking distance of the old town. Three- and four-person apartments will suit families, and there's a restaurant/pizzeria on site. **205zł**
Olza al. Łyska 16 ☎33 445 9010, ⓦ camping-olza. xn.pl; map page 357. This campsite is attractively situated beside the river, a 25min walk south of the centre, and has an on-site restaurant and plenty of woodland walks on its doorstep. **40zł**

EATING

Café Muzeum ul. Tadeusza Regera 6 ☎502 315 875; map page 357. Refined spot in a dreamily elegant, rotunda-shaped former stable inside the grounds of Cieszyn Museum. Pots of tea, top-notch coffee and hot chocolate, and a good choice of cakes are all on offer. Mon–Sat 9am–6pm, Sun 10am–6pm.
Dworek Cieszyński ul. Przykopa 14 ☎33 858 1178, ⓦ dworek-cieszynski.pl; map page 357. A good place to tuck into traditional meat and fish dishes (25–35zł) in a suite of folksy wood-panelled dining rooms, with a roomy river-facing terrace. Daily 11am–10pm.
Kamienica Konczakowskich Rynek 19 ☎033 852 1896, ⓦ kamienica-konczakowskich.pl; map page 357. Neat, traditional restaurant on the main square, offering steaks, pastas and a handful of Mediterranean-inspired dishes, with mains in the 40–60zł bracket. With a

good choice of spirits and long drinks it's a popular place to drink, too. Mon–Thurs & Sun 11am–10pm, Fri & Sat 11am–midnight.
Klubokawiarnia Presso ul. Zamkowa ☎721 341 420, ⓦ facebook.com/KlubokawiarniaPresso; map page 357. Arty café next to the entrance porch of Cieszyn Castle, with designer couches, tea and coffee, the odd cake, and beer from the local Browar Zamkowy brewery. Some of the interior accessories are made by Polish designers and are for sale. Mon–Thurs & Sun 11am–8pm, Fri & Sat 11am–9pm.
Pizzeria La Nostra ul. Głęboka 20 ☎790 780 888, ⓦ pizzeria.lanostra.pl; map page 357. Pay-at-the-counter place with seating in a brick-vaulted basement, serving rather good thin-crust pizzas at reasonable prices (22–25zł). Mon–Sat 11am–10pm, Sun noon–10pm.

Pszczyna

About 40km south of Katowice, the small town of **PSZCZYNA** is dominated by the eighteenth-century **ducal palace** that stands in the town centre, occupying the western side of a handsome Rynek lined with fine mansions.

The palace

ul. Brama Wybrańców 1 • April–June, Sept & Oct Mon 11am–3pm, Tues 10am–3pm, Wed 9am–5pm, Thurs & Fri 9am–4pm, Sat 10am–4pm, Sun 10am–5pm; July & Aug Mon 11am–3pm, Tues 10am–3pm, Wed–Fri 9am–5pm, Sat 10am–5pm, Sun 10am–6pm; Nov–March Tues 11am–3pm, Wed 9am–4pm, Thurs & Fri 9am–3pm, Sat 10am–3pm, Sun 10am–4pm • 15zł • ⓦ zamek-pszczyna.pl

The **Pszczyna palace** originated as a Piast hunting lodge in the twelfth century. Sold to the Promnitz family in the sixteenth century, it was transformed into an aristocratic residence in the Renaissance style before undergoing a thorough Baroque rebuild following a fire. The palace was subsequently taken over by the Hochbergs, one of Germany's richest families, who expanded it and added the English-style park that extends behind. Stunningly refurbished, it now houses the **Palace Museum** (Muzeum Zamkowe), which features furniture and historic artefacts rescued from stately homes all over Silesia.

Much of the ground floor is taken up with the so-called **Royal Apartments** (Apartamenty Cezarskie), where Kaiser Wilhelm of Germany – together with much of his general staff – took up residence during World War I. His bedroom and office have been faithfully re-created, with photographs of Ludendorff and Hindenburg recalling the strategic brainstorming sessions that took place here.

Ascending the aptly named Grand Staircase you reach the apartments designed for Princess Daisy von Pless, an English lady from the Cornwallis-West family who married Prince Hans Heinrich Hochberg in 1891. There are some lovely portraits of Princess Daisy, and a room full of the antlers formerly belonging to beasts butchered by Heinrich himself, a keen hunter. The highlight, however, comes when you reach the stunning **Chamber of Mirrors**, where huge mirrors in gilded brass frames create an impression of a much larger room. Ornate balconies look down onto the chamber from the second-floor gallery, while murals depicting the four seasons and the signs of the zodiac are squeezed in between the stucco decoration.

The park, bison enclosure and skansen

Bison enclosure Daily: April–Aug 9am–7pm; March & Sept till 6pm; Feb & Oct till 5pm; Jan, Nov & Dec till 4pm • 10zł • **Skansen** Daily: April–Aug 9am–7pm; March till 6pm; Feb, Oct & Nov till 5pm; Dec & Jan till 4pm • 10zł

Behind the castle lies the extensive landscaped **park**, with small lakes spanned by a sequence of gracefully arching bridges. A special enclosure in the west of the park is grazed by a herd of **bison**, raised at the reserve of Jankowice 7km southeast of town. The enclosure also holds deer, mouflon and goats; feeding times for the beasts are posted at the entrance. Heading east through the park will bring you onto ulica Dworcowa and (eventually) back to the train and bus stations, but not before first passing a small **skansen** of reassembled rural buildings brought here from locations throughout the Beskids.

ARRIVAL AND INFORMATION

By train The train station (with the bus station next door) is a 10min walk from the Rynek.
Destinations Bielsko-Biała (every 30min; 30–50min); Katowice (every 30min; 1hr); Żywiec (hourly; 1hr).

Tourist information The helpful tourist office is just off the Rynek in the palace gateway (Mon–Fri 8am–4pm, Sat & Sun 10am–4pm; ☏ 32 212 9999, ⓦ pszczyna.info.pl).

ACCOMMODATION AND EATING

Café u Telemanna Brama Wybrańców 1 ☏ 32 449 1520, ⓦ utelemanna.pl. Tucked away in the palace gateway, this café is as cosy a place as any for a quick drink and slice of cheesecake; its name is a reminder that Baroque composer Georg Philipp Telemann was once *kapellmeister* at Pszczyna. Tues–Thurs & Sun 9am–7pm, Fri & Sat 9am–8pm.

Michalik ul. Dworcowa 11 ☏ 32 210 1388, ⓦ umichalika. com.pl. Hotel situated midway between the train station and the palace, offering small but bright rooms with contemporary furnishings, shower and TV. **180zł**

Pałac Bażantarnia Barbórki 47 ☏ 601 406 352, ⓦ palac bazantarnia.pl. Housed in a former hunting lodge that was once part of the palace estate, this boutique hotel 3km northwest of town has ten rooms, each themed around a historical style. The top-floor rooms with attic ceilings are particularly cute. There's a classy restaurant on site, too. **220zł**

9

Restauracja Frykówka ul. Rynek 3 ☎ 32 449 0020, ⓦ frykowka.pl. Roomy café-restaurant on the main square offering a well-balanced menu of light Mediterranean food (risottos and pastas in the 24–26zł range) mixed in with some real culinary treats, such as beef cheeks with green beans (40zł) and Silesian beef roulade with dumplings (40zł). Daily 10am–10pm.

Szczyrk

Fifteen kilometres southwest of Bielsko-Biała, the long, straggling village of **SZCZYRK** is the main resort of the Beskids, popular with hikers in summer and offering some pretty demanding **downhill skiing** in winter. If you're heading for the hills, the locally available Beskid Śląski i Żywiecki (1:75,000) **map** will come in very handy.

Skrzyczne

Chairlift: daily 8.30am–5.30pm • 16zł return

Fifteen minutes' walk southwest of the bus station, an all-year-round two-stage **chairlift** runs to the summit of **Skrzyczne** (1245m), the highest peak in the range, where there's the usual refuge and restaurant; opposite is the 1117m-high peak of Klinczok, with the conurbation of Bielsko-Biała beyond. The energetic alternative to the chairlift is to slog up either the blue or the green trail for a couple of hours from Szczyrk; the latter trail continues south to Barania Góra (1220m), the source of the **River Vistula**, Poland's greatest waterway, which winds a serpentine 1090km-long course through Kraków, Warsaw and Toruń before disgorging itself into the Baltic near Gdańsk.

ARRIVAL AND INFORMATION   SZCZYRK

By bus Szczyrk's bus station is roughly at the midpoint of its single street. Get off the bus here – otherwise you'll end up several kilometres away at the final stop, in the town's westernmost reaches.

Tourist information The tourist office, just up from the bus station at ul. Beskidzka 41 (Mon–Sat 9am–5pm, Sun 9am–1pm; ☎ 33 815 8388, ⓦ szczyrk.pl), sells local hiking maps, and can also direct you towards private rooms and pensions.

ACCOMMODATION AND EATING

Green Pub ul. Myśliwska 13 ☎ 33 817 9477. Combined pub and restaurant that has been a popular fixture on the Szczyrk scene for well over a decade, occupying a bright timber hut that looks a bit like a large-ish garden conservatory. The menu features a something-for-everybody mixture of Italian, Greek and Mexican dishes, although quality varies widely from one season to the next. Daily 11am–11pm.

Klimczok Poziomkowa 20 ☎ 33 826 0100, ⓦ klimczok. pl. Three kilometres west of the centre, *Klimczok* looks like a cross between an alpine chalet and a corporate headquarters, and is very much the winter resort hotel of choice, featuring a restaurant, pub, swimming pool and disco. Summer 490zł, winter 700zł

Pensjonat Koliba ul. Skośna 17 ☎ 33 817 9930, ⓦ pensjonatkolibaszczyrk.republika.pl. Right by the Skrzyczne chairlift, this is a good-value *pension*, with simple en suites with TV and breakfast. Summer 100zł, winter 150zł

Stara Karczma ul. Myśliwska 2 ☎ 33 817 8653. This restaurant offers filling meat-and-potato dishes in a folksy wooden-hut environment, complete with antlers, boar skins, wait-staff in traditional costume and occasional live music. Daily 11am–11pm.

Żywiec

Arguably the most attractive of Silesia's historic towns after Cieszyn, the former ducal seat of **ŻYWIEC** lies on a small plain surrounded by the green, pudding-shaped Beskid Żywiecki hills. Attractions include a handsome Rynek and a lush castle park, although the town's main claim to fame is the Żywiec brewery, founded in 1856 and still supplying just under thirty percent of the country's lager-swilling needs.

The Old Castle and Park

ul. Zamkowa 2 • **Museum** Mon–Fri 9am–5pm, Sat & Sun 10am–4pm • 18zł • **Park** Open all hours • Free • **Park of Miniatures** Daily 10am–6pm • 5zł • ☎ 33 861 2124, ⓦ muzeum-zywiec.pl

Beginning life as a medieval strongpoint, the **Old Castle** (Stary Zamek) was completely rebuilt as an aristocratic residence in the eighteenth and nineteenth centuries, hence the appealing mash-up of Neo-Gothic and Neo-Renaissance styles you see today. It was bought by Karl Ludwig von Habsburg in 1838 and much of the castle's **museum** is given over to portraits and mementoes of Karl Ludwig and his descendants. Sections on local history include a room devoted to the so-called Żywiec Bourgeois Dress, the nineteenth-century urban clothes that fell somewhere between traditional folk costume and modern town wear – bonnets, billowing skirts and tulle aprons rich in floral patterns. The palace courtyard contains additional sections on archaeology, natural history and ethnography.

Outside, the **park** was laid out in the early twentieth century to include a mixture of ornamental and "natural" elements, with rose garden, pond and hexagonal "Chinese Pavilion" (now a summer-only café) counterpointing long lines of lime trees and open expanses of grass. The park also contains the **Park of Miniatures** (Park Miniatur) containing models of famous Polish buildings.

Żywiec Brewery Museum

ul. Browarna 88, 2km southwest of centre • Tues–Sun 10am–6pm • Museum tour (1hr 30min) 30zł; museum and brewery tour (2hr 30min) 35zł • ☎ 33 861 9627, ⓦ muzeumbrowaru.pl

With its instantly identifiable logo and nationwide-distribution, Żywiec beer is an icon of Polish consumer culture, and it's no wonder that the entertaining and visually imaginative **Żywiec Brewery Museum** (Muzeum Browaru) has proved so popular. Individual visitors have to join a guided tour, which can get booked solid at peak times; making a reservation by telephone is the best way of ensuring you don't miss out. Multimedia displays and recreated pre-World War I street scenes guide you through the history of the brand, providing numerous insights into the social history of Poland on the way. Those who have chosen the longer of the two tours will also get a close-up look at how the beer is made. A spot of tasting, and a visit to the Żywiec shop, are how it all ends.

ARRIVAL AND INFORMATION
ŻYWIEC

By train Żywiec's train station is a 15min walk southwest of the centre on ul. Dworcowa.

Destinations Bielsko-Biała (hourly; 40min); Katowice (hourly; 2hr); Pszczyna (hourly; 1hr); Žilina/Slovakia (change at Zwardoń; 2 daily; 3hr 30min).

By bus There's a bus station behind the Tesco supermarket, opposite the train station, with services to Bielsko-Biała

(8 daily; 45min) and Kraków (hourly; 2hr 30min). Some buses use a stop on ul. Żeromskiego, just east of the Rynek, including the service to Zakopane (1 daily; 3hr).

Tourist information The tourist office at ul. Zamkowa 2 (daily 8am–4pm; ☎ 33 861 4310) is a good place to pick up information on the region and buy maps.

ACCOMMODATION AND EATING

Browar Krajcar ul. Świętokrzyska 8 ☎ 33 861 7777. Micro-brewery giving the local beer corporation a good run for its money, with pils, wheat beer and seasonal varieties (9zł/0.4l) backed up by a hearty menu of tortillas, burgers, pastas and grilled chicken. Mains 25–35zł. Daily 10am–midnight.

De Kaffee Stary Zamek. Barrel-vaulted palace outhouse serving coffee, ice cream, and excellent cakes – including some mesmerizing meringues. Mon–Fri 9am–9pm, Sat & Sun 10am–8pm.

Pokoje Gościnne u Meresa ul. Kościuszki 40 ☎ 33 861 0147, ⓦ restauracjaumeresa.pl. The en-suite guest

rooms in the courtyard of the U Meresa restaurant are small and simply furnished but have all the important details (wi-fi, breakfast, TV, a smile from the staff). The central location is a major plus. **280zł**

Żywiecki ul. Kępka 3, Przyłęków ☎ 33 506 5080, ⓦ hotel-zywiecki.pl. The one quality hotel in the region is 10km southeast of town in the middle of nowhere – the perfect location for doing a spot of hill walking, hiring one of the hotel's bicycles, or immersing yourself in the small but cleverly designed pool. Interiors feature an artful mix of contemporary style and rustic touches. **420zł**

Lower Silesia

CHURCH OF PEACE, ŚWIDNICA

10

Lower Silesia

In many ways Lower Silesia is Poland's answer to Yorkshire in the UK, a vast swathe of territory that embraces everything from post-industrial cities to stately homes and stark highlands – while at the same time retaining a strong sense of regional otherness. Lower Silesian capital Wrocław is one of the cultural powerhouses of the new Poland, an addictively cosmopolitan centre which combines the attractions of a medieval Old Town with state-of-the-art museums, modern architecture and good food. It's a great base from which to explore the varied attractions elsewhere in the province, from magnificent churches and monasteries to underground former-mine attractions and some of the best hillwalking terrain in the country.

Bang in the centre of the province, the old ducal capital of **Świdnica** contains a famously impressive UNESCO-protected church, while further west the former coal-mining centre of **Wałbrzych** has turned its industrial heritage to good use and is also the jumping-off point for the sumptuous palace at **Książ** and the secret Nazi tunnel-city of the **Riese** complex. For natural beauty, it's best to make a beeline for the mountains to the south and west, where the Sudety chain contains some of the most popular recreation areas in the country. Of these, the **Karkonosze National Park** is the easiest to reach from Wrocław, with the regional centre of **Jelenia Góra** providing access to the mountain resorts of **Karpacz** and **Szklarska Poręba**. Slightly further east, the **Kłodzko Region**'s outlying massifs provide plenty of easy-walking territory, with refined old health resorts such as **Kudowa-Zdrój**, **Lądek-Zdrój** and **Międzygórze** offering plenty of affordable accommodation.

Changing ownership several times over the centuries between Poland, Bohemia, Austria and Prussia, Lower Silesia was only definitely assigned to Poland in 1945. Largely German-speaking up till that point, most original inhabitants were expelled after the war, with the towns and villages repopulated by refugees originating from all corners of Poland, but especially from what is now western Ukraine, around L'viv. Although the original mix of cultures has now been replaced by the Polish monoculture, the region is economically vibrant, very beautiful in its southern reaches and delightfully easy to get around, thanks to the Prussians' penchant for building railways everywhere.

Wrocław

Poland has changed more than almost any other European country in the last ten years and the Lower Silesian capital **WROCŁAW** (pronounced "*Vrots*-waff") is one of its most transformed cities, a go-ahead place with a huge student population and a burgeoning arts scene. Indeed, Wrocław brings together pretty much everything that's good about contemporary Poland: a thoroughly modernized cross-section of attractions, a sack full of historical influences and an increasingly varied dining and nightlife scene.

RENAISSANCE CITY HALL, WROCŁAW

Highlights

❶ Main square, Wrocław The boisterous heart of this burgeoning city is a genuine Polish set-piece, complete with iconic town hall. See page 367

❷ Szczytnicki Park, Wrocław With fountains, gardens and some amazing modern architecture, this is one out-of-the-centre destination that fully merits the tram ride. See page 376

❸ Churches of Peace The beautiful UNESCO-listed timber-framed churches in Świdnica and Jawor are the largest of their kind. See page 385 page 386

❹ Książ One of the most evocative castles in the country, perched on a hilltop above the winding River Pełcznica. See page 388

❺ Riese Tens of thousands of prisoners toiled to build this mysterious underground complex for the Nazis. See page 388

❻ Jelenia Góra Gateway to the Karkonosze mountians and an enthralling small city in its own right. See page 389

❼ Karpacz This popular holiday village gives direct access to the hiking trails of the Karkonosze, and is also home to one of the most unusual churches in Poland. See page 393

❽ The Kłodzko Region An enchanting area of rolling hills and fir-clad mountains, dotted with laid-back spa resorts and bizarre rock formations. See page 395

HIGHLIGHTS ARE MARKED ON THE MAP ON PAGE 366

10

There are certainly a lot of cultural references to pack in: Wrocław has belonged to Poland, Czechia, Austria, Germany and then Poland again over the last thousand years, and its defining architectural styles range from Gothic through Baroque and Neoclassical to twentieth-century Modernism. Wrocław's tenure as European Capital of Culture in 2016 bestowed the city with a clutch of new museums and concert halls, and a renewed sense of arty attitude. All of this is on an easily digestible level: the city is nowhere near as big and overwhelming as Warsaw, and lacks the mega-touristed bustle of Kraków.

Wrocław's **central area**, centred on a typically spacious and elegant market square, is delineated by the **River Odra** to the north and by the bow-shaped **ulica Podwale** to the south – the latter following the former fortifications whose defensive moat, now bordered by a shady park, still largely survives. The Odra's progress through the city is broken by a number of peaceful islets, formerly sandbanks where the shallow river was once forded, and now linked to each other and to the mainland by quaint cast-iron **bridges** – which have together become something of a collective Wrocław trademark. The much larger island of **Ostrów Tumski**, further east, is the city's ecclesiastical heart, with half a dozen churches and its own distinctive buzz. Many of the city's key visitor highlights lie a short tram ride from the centre, with new headline attractions such as the Afrykarium, Hydropolis, the Zajezdnia History Centre and the Contemporary Art Museum serving as potent symbols of Wrocław's new city-break status.

Brief history

The earliest documentary evidence of Wrocław is a ninth-century record of a Slav market town called Wratislavia situated on a large island at the point where the River Odra was easily crossed. It was a spot that subsequently became known as Ostrów

Tumski (Cathedral Island) in honour of the bishopric founded here in 1000 AD by Bolesław the Brave. As the settlement developed, German merchants were encouraged to make their home on the southern bank of the river. They named the town **Breslau**, joined the **Hanseatic League**, and prospered.

In 1335 Breslau was annexed by the **Bohemian kings**. During two centuries of Bohemian rule a mixed population of Germans, Poles and Czechs lived in apparent harmony, and the city carried out the construction of its huge brick churches. Most of these were transferred to Protestant use at the Reformation, despite the Bohemian crown passing to the staunchly Catholic **Austrian Habsburgs** in 1526. During the Thirty Years' War, Breslau's economy was devastated and its population halved.

The years of Austrian rule saw Breslau become increasingly Germanized, a process accelerated when it finally fell to Frederick the Great's **Prussia** in 1763. Throughout the nineteenth and early twentieth centuries Breslau was one of Prussia's then Germany's leading cities, home to an important university and some impressive modern architecture.

World War II and modern Wrocław

Towards the end of **World War II** the retreating Germans decided that Breslau should be defended whatever the cost, turning the entire city into a fortress. It managed to hold out for four months against the Red Army, only capitulating on May 6, 1945, two days before Germany's unconditional surrender. However, street fighting left seventy percent of the city in ruins, with three-quarters of the civilian population having fled west. Rechristened with the modern Polish version of its original name, Wrocław, the city was subsequently returned to Poland. Most of the remaining German citizens were shunted westward, while the inhabitants of **Lwów** (now L'viv in Ukraine) were transferred here, bringing many of their institutions with them. Although a relatively modest amount of government aid was made available for its **restoration**, a distinctive and thoroughly Polish city emerged from the wreckage.

The city was hit by freak **floods** in July 1997, covering a third of the city in water and cutting electricity and water supplies. The clean-up operation was rapid and thorough, and the following two decades were largely marked by commercial optimism and economic boom. Nowadays Wrocław's confused German-Polish heritage is the source of fascination rather than ethnic angst, an attitude exemplified by the crime novels of the city's leading cultural export **Marek Krajewski**, in which the decidedly noir Breslau of the 1930s and '40s is convincingly revisited.

The Rynek and around

Magnificent main squares are something of a tradition in Poland, and Wrocław's **Rynek** is no exception. A spacious quadrangle of handsome merchants' houses surrounds a **town hall** bristling with turrets and an accompanying ensemble of municipal buildings. Skirted by shops, cafés and restaurants, the square is the perfect socializing space – and all the better for the fact that tourists are (for the time being at least) still outnumbered by locals.

Of the mansions lining the Rynek, those on the south and western sides are the most distinguished and colourful. Among several built in the self-confident style of the Flemish Renaissance, no. 2, the **Griffin House** (Pod Gryfami) is particularly notable. The most striking house is no. 8, mostly Baroque but preserving parts of its thirteenth-century predecessor; it's known as the **House of the Seven Elektors** (Pod Siedmioma Elektorami), a reference to the seven grandees superbly depicted on the facade who elected the Holy Roman emperor, Leopold I. A black Habsburg eagle cowers menacingly over the building's doorway.

The town hall

Symbol of the city for the last seven centuries, the magnificent **town hall** owes its present appearance to the fifteenth-century high point of local prosperity, when the

10

WROCŁAW

Poznań (160km) ▲ 1 (750m) ▲ 2 (150m) ●

STANISŁAWA DUBOIS

SKITOWA DOBNERA

BOLESŁAWA DOBNERA

ROMANA DMOWSKIEGO

MOST MIESZCZAŃSKI

MOST STANISŁAWA DUBOIS

WŁADYSŁAWA JAGIEŁŁY

NADODRZE

WOJCIECHA CYBULSKIEGO

RYBACKA

KS. WITOLDA

MOST POMORSKI PIERWSZY

2

GENERAŁA WŁADYSŁAWA SIKORSKIEGO

MOSTOWA

KS. WITOLDA

MOST POMORSKI POŁUDNIOWY

MOST UNIWERSYTECKI PÓŁNOCNY

River Odra

MOST SIKORSKIEGO

GRODZKA

PLAC UNIWERSYTECKI

MOST UNIWERSYTECKI POŁUDNIOWY

Collegium Maximum & University Museum

Church of the Blessed Name of Jesus

RYBACKA

DZIEWINA

SOKOLNICZA

Arsenał

CIESZYŃSKIEGO

NOWY ŚWIAT

ŁAZIENNA

MALARSKA

KUŹNICZA

UNIWERSYTECKA

NOŻOWNICZA

3

LEGNICKA

NABYCIŃSKA

PLAC JANA PAWŁA II

Św. Barbary

ŚW. MIKOŁAJA

ŚW. MIKOŁAJA

KIEŁBAŚNICZA

WIEŻIENNA

KOTLARSKA

SZEWSKA

LEGNICKA

A. ZELWEROWICZA

RUSKA

GRABARSKA

BIAŁOSKÓRNICZA

RZEŹNICZA

St Elizabeth's Church 6

RYNEK

PRZEJŚCIE GARNCARSKIE
PRZEJŚCIE ŻELAŹNICZE

WITA STWOSZA

BRANIBORSKA

MARTYŃSKA

SOKOLNICZA

Pan Tadeusz Museum 7

SUKIENNICE

RYNEK

St Mary Magdalene Church

ROBOTNICZA

ŚW. ANTONIEGO

PAWŁA WŁODKOWICA

KAZIMIERZA WIELKIEGO

PSIE BUDY

RUSKA

PLAC SOLNY

RYNEK

Town Hall

KURZY TARG

ŚW. MARII MAGDALENY

ŁACIARSKA

Kolejkowo

PLAC ORLĄT LWOWSKICH

White Stork Synagogue

KAROLA SZAJNOCHY

E. GEPPERTA

1

New University Library

OFIAR OŚWIĘCIMSKICH

ŚWIDNICKA

OŁAWSKA

SZEWSKA

OFIAR OŚWIĘCIMSKICH

Oława

BULWAR T. JASIŃSKIEGO

City Historical Museum

KAZIMIERZA WIELKIEGO

12

KAZIMIERZA WIELKIEGO

9

TĘCZOWA

PODWALE

KRUPNICZA

National Forum of Music

PLAC WOLNOŚCI

St Dorothy's Church

IWANA PAWŁOWA

ŚW. TRÓJCY

SADOWA

Opera Wrocławska

HELENY MODRZEJEWSKIEJ

WIDOK

MENNICZA

10

PROSTA

ŚWIEBODZKA

PODWALE

PROMENADA STAROMIEJSKA

11

Teatr Kameralny

PLAC TEATRALNY

TEATRALNA

GRABISZYŃSKA

PLAC LEGIONÓW

MUZEALNA

ŁĄKOWA

Corpus Christi Church

BOŻEGO CIAŁA

ŚWIDNICKA

PODWALE

PROSTA

JOACHIMA LELEWELA

TADEUSZA KOŚCIUSZKI

KOLEJOWA

PLAC TADEUSZA KOŚCIUSZKI

TADEUSZA KOŚCIUSZKI

JĘCZMIENNA

SWIDNICKA

13

PSZENNA

OWSIANA

MARSZAŁKA JÓZEFA PIŁSUDSKIEGO

STAWOWA

SKWIERZYŃSKA

WINCENTEGO STYSIA

SWOBODNA

WOJCIECHA BOGUSŁAWSKIEGO

NASYPOWA

ŚWIDNICKA

Teatr Muzyczny Capitol

PERONOWA

TADEUSZA ZIELIŃSKIEGO

GWIAŹDZISTA

SWOBODNA

WOJCIECHA BOGUSŁAWSKIEGO

POWSTAŃCÓW ŚLĄSKICH

KOMANDORSKA

BOROWSKA

0 ———— 250

metres

Contemporary Art Museum (850m), Airport (11km) & Zielona Góra (160km) ▲

Zajezdnia History Centre (2km), Jelenia Góra & Legnica ▲

Jewish Cemetery (1.3km) ▼   ▼ Bus Station (100m)

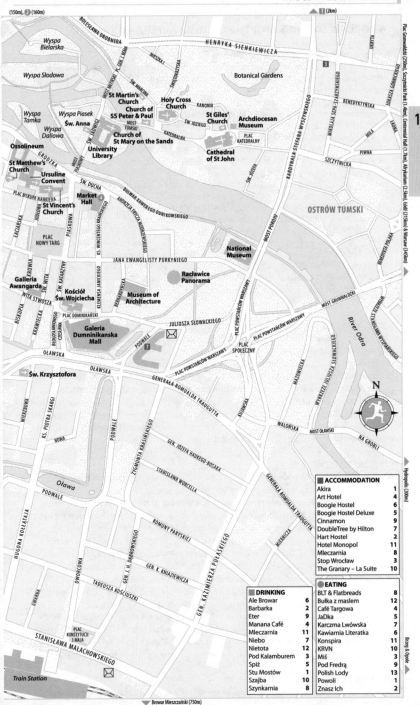

10

■ ACCOMMODATION

Akira	1
Art Hotel	4
Boogie Hostel	6
Boogie Hostel Deluxe	5
Cinnamon	9
DoubleTree by Hilton	7
Hart Hostel	2
Hotel Monopol	11
Mleczarnia	8
Stop Wrocław	3
The Granary – La Suite	10

■ DRINKING

Ale Browar	6
Barbarka	2
Eter	9
Manana Café	4
Mleczarnia	11
Niebo	7
Nietota	12
Pod Kalamburem	3
Spiż	5
Stu Mostów	1
Szajba	10
Szynkarnia	8

● EATING

BLT & Flatbreads	8
Bułka z masłem	12
Café Targowa	4
JaDka	5
Karczma Lwówska	7
Kawiarnia Literatka	6
Konspira	11
KRVN	10
Miś	3
Pod Fredrą	9
Polish Lody	13
Powoli	1
Znasz Ich	2

10

WROCŁAW DWARFS AND THE ORANGE ALTERNATIVE

One thing you can't help but notice while ambling around central Wrocław is the strange profusion of **dwarf figurines** scattered around major squares and junctions. These began appearing in 2005 and have grown to number over 350, in a municipally-supported project to brighten up the streets and amuse tourists – maps available from the tourist office help you find your way from dwarf to dwarf.

The adoption of the dwarf as a Wrocław symbol is a tribute to a 1980s group of anti-establishment activists called the **Orange Alternative** (Pomorańczowa alternatywa), who stenciled their logo of an orange dwarf on city walls throughout Poland. Led by student activist **Waldemar "Major" Fydrych**, the group organized street happenings which, while clearly satirizing the nature of authoritarianism, were organized in such a way that made it difficult for the police to identify and arrest the participants. For example, they appeared on the streets giving away sheets of toilet paper to passersby – a clear refrence to the communist regime's inability to produce and distribute basic household goods. On another occasion activists wore lettered T-shirts which spelled out either highly innocuous or extremely subversive slogans, depending on which way they lined up. The so-called **Dwarf Revolution**, held on June 1, 1988, brought an estimated 10,000 people onto the streets of Wrocław in joyous, surreal protest against the grey, incompetent communist regime of the day.

Fydrych is nowadays regarded as one of the key figures in twentieth-century subversion, his choice of street-theatre tactics having had a profound influence on protest movements elsewhere. He is not so happy about Wrocław's kitsch recycling of his dwarfs, however, and has taken the city to court at least once for using his hallowed protest symbol for present-day promotional gain.

---

south aisle was added and the whole thing decorated in an elaborate late-Gothic style. The **east facade** is the one that figures in all Wrocław's promotion material, featuring an astronomical clock from 1580 and an elaborate central gable decorated with intricate terracotta patterns and exquisite pinnacles. In contrast, the west facade (the main entrance) is relatively plain, save for the octagonal Gothic belfry with its tapering Renaissance lantern. The intricate carvings embellishing the **south facade** are worthy of more protracted scrutiny, lined up between the huge Renaissance windows crowned with their spire-like roofs. Along its length are filigree friezes of animals and foliage as well as effigies of saints and knights, mostly nineteenth-century pastiches, overshadowed by an old crone and a yokel.

Museum of Bourgeois Art

ul. Sukiennice 14/15 • Wed–Sat 10am–5pm, Sun 10am–6pm • 15zł; free on Sun • ☎ 71 347 1690, ⊕ muzeum.miejskie.wroclaw.pl

Relieved of its municipal duties by the adjoining nineteenth-century offices, the town hall now serves as the misleadingly translated **Museum of Bourgeois Art** (Muzeum Sztuki Mieszczańskiej; what they probably mean is something like "museum of urban applied arts"), a collection of paintings, furniture and handicrafts which provides an excellent excuse to visit the building's evocatively restored interior. The kernel of the town hall, dating back to the 1270s, is the twin-aisled **Burghers' Hall** (Hala Mieszczańska) on the ground floor. Not only the venue for important public meetings and receptions, the hall doubled as a covered market, functioning as such for 450 years. Upstairs is the resplendent three-aisled **Great Hall** (Sala Wielka), its vaulted ceiling studded with bosses depicting all kinds of real and imaginary creatures.

At the far end of the hall are two stone portals, the one on the right adorned with hairy wild men and giving access to the elegantly panelled fifteenth-century **Chamber of Council** (Izba Rady). Behind the left doorway lies the **Duke's Hall** (Sala Książęca), a pure example of fourteenth-century Gothic, with a vault resting on a single central pillar.

Pan Tadeusz Museum

Rynek 6 • Tues–Sun 10am–6pm • 20zł (1zł on Sun); audio guide free • ☎ 71 755 640, ⊕ muzeumpanatadeusza.ossolineum.pl

Polish national poet Adam Mickiewicz (1798–1855) never had any connection with Wrocław, but the city can at least claim ownership of the original manuscript of his greatest work – *Pan Tadeusz* (see page 475), his lyrical poem of life on the Polish-Lithuanian borderlands. The manuscript is now the star exhibit of the **Pan Tadeusz Museum** (Muzeum Pana Tadeusza), an ambitious multimedia affair occupying the Baroque house known as **Under the Golden Sun** (Pod Złotym Słońcem).

Employing a mixture of original objects, modern visuals and recreated period interiors, the main body of the museum presents a magnificent panorama of Polish society in the nineteenth century, a time when national independence seemed a distant dream but national culture was alive with inspired, patriotic creativity. An additional section entitled **Mission: Poland** tells the story of twentieth-century political struggle through the lives of former Auschwitz inmate and post-1989 foreign minister Władysław Bartoszewski (1922–2015), and World War II resistance courier and subsequent Radio Free Europe broadcaster Jan Nowak Jeziorański (1914–2005). All in all, it's an uplifting and visually ravishing display – and one that you don't need to know a great deal about *Pan Tadeusz* to enjoy.

10

Plac Solny

The southwest corner of the main square leads to a second, smaller square, **plac Solny**. Its traditional function as a market has been revived, with the salt from which the market takes its name now replaced by flowers. The square itself is a minor sensory delight, girdled by restored nineteenth-century town houses painted in a range of vivacious colours.

St Elizabeth's Church

Św. Elżbiety 1 • Tower open daily: May–Sept 10am–7pm; Oct–April 10am–4pm • 5zł

Just off the northwest corner of the main square are two curious Baroque houses known as **Hänsel and Gretel** (Jaś i Małgosia), linked by a gateway giving access to **St Elizabeth's Church** (Kościół św. Elżbiety). Since the mid-fifteenth century the church's huge 90m-high **tower**, under construction for 150 years, has been the city's most prominent landmark. Originally, a lead-sheeted spire added another 36m to the steeple's height, but this overambitious pinnacle was blown down by storms a year after completion and never rebuilt. Ill fortune has continued to dog the church, which having been destroyed by a hailstorm in 1529 was burnt out under suspicious circumstances in 1976. The lofty, bright interior is well worth a peek. Climbing the tower's 300-plus steps may be exhausting, but is well worth it for great views of the Old Town and beyond.

St Mary Magdalene's Church

ul. Szewska 10 • Mon–Fri 10am–7pm, Sat & Sun 10am–8pm (no visiting during Mass)

The twin-towered **St Mary Magdalene's Church** (Kościół św. Marii Magdaleny) is another illustration of the seemingly inexhaustible diversity of Wrocław's brick churches: this fourteenth-century example is unusual in having flying buttresses, giving it a French feel. It survived the war, only to be destroyed just three days after liberation, when the munition that the Soviet army had stored inside accidentally exploded. Rebuilt in the 1970s, the exterior has a bevy of funeral plaques and epitaphs from the fifteenth to eighteenth centuries, though the most striking adornment is the twelfth-century Romanesque sandstone **portal** on the south side. The Büsserinnen ("Penitents") bridge between the two church towers was only rebuilt in 2001 and can be visited for excellent views. In medieval times unfaithful wives were punished by carrying two buckets of water up to this bridge to clean it – adulterous men were chained and mocked in the main square.

White Stork Synagogue

ul. Włodkowica 9 • Mon–Thurs 10am–5pm, Fri 10am–4pm, Sun 11am–4pm • Free • ☎ 504 905 358, ⓦ wroclaw.jewish.org.pl

Wrocław's **Jewish quarter** was located around ulica Włodkowica, a ten-minute walk southwest of the Rynek. The glowingly restored Neoclassical **White Stork Synagogue** (Synagoga pod Białym Bocianem), tucked away on a tiny square off the southern side of ulica Włodkowica, has a small but informative exhibition about Wrocław's Jewish population on the first floor and an art exhibition area above, which is not always devoted to Jewish art. It's the only synagogue in Wrocław to have survived the Nazi destruction on Kristallnacht, and takes its name from an inn which once stood here. The building is again being used as a place of worship today.

Kolejkowo

pl. Orląt Lwowskich 20B • Daily 10am–6pm • 19zł • ☎ 880 008 004, ⓦ wroclaw.kolejkowo.pl

The biggest model railway layout in the country, **Kolejowko** ("Train Town"), is located in the former suburban train station of Wrocław Świebodzki, just west of the centre. The layout features recognizable bits of Wrocław and the highland resort of Karpacz (see page 393), as well as an impressive roster of O-scale locomotives. Over 2000 miniature figures bring life and humour to the scene.

City Historical Museum

ul. Kazimierza Wielkiego 15 • Tues–Sat 10am–5pm, Sun 10am–6pm • 10zł • ☎ 71 391 6940, ⓦ muzeum.miejskie.wroclaw.pl

Occupying the grand interiors of the former Prussian **Royal Palace** (Pałac Królewski), the **Historical Museum** (Muzeum Historyczne) contains a well-presented collection of artefacts illustrating the city's history, plus an art collection focusing on the works of local painters. The richly ornamented Baroque interiors provide an additional reason to visit.

St Dorothy's Church

pl. Wolności

The lofty Gothic **St Dorothy's Church** (Kościół św. Doroty), also known as the "Church of Reconciliation", was founded in 1351 by Charles IV, king of Bohemia and the future Holy Roman emperor, in thanks for the conclusion of his negotiations with Kazimierz the Great, which secured Bohemia's rule over Silesia. Unlike most of Wrocław's other brick churches, it stayed in Catholic hands following the Reformation, becoming a Franciscan monastery. Its bright interior is littered with gigantic Baroque altars, giving it a decidedly opulent appearance in comparison to many of the city's other churches.

The National Forum of Music and around

pl. Wolności 1 • ☎ 71 715 9700, ⓦ nfm.wroclaw.pl

Looking like a carefully stacked pile of timber, the layered brown bulk of the **National Forum of Music** (Narodowe Forum Muzyki, or NFM) brings a touch of contemporary style to the southern reaches of the city centre. Opened in 2015 to provide the Wrocław Philharmonic with a state-of-the-art new home, it also hosts a wide variety of choral and chamber-music concerts as well as some leading international festivals – notably the internationally-renowned Wratislavia Cantans (see page 385). The lobby, whose contrasting dark and light surfaces are supposed to evoke a piano keyboard, is well worth a quick peek – there's a café and well-stocked CD shop inside.

Recent re-landscaping of the adjoining **plac Wolności** revealed several bits of medieval Wrocław, which can be glimpsed through glass-covered gaps in the paving. From here you can follow the **Staromiejska promenade** for some wonderful leafy walks along the town moat (Fosa Miejska).

THE PETERSDORFF STORE

The former **Petersdorff store** – now an office building – at the junction of ulica Oławska and ulica Szewska, is a classic of twentieth-century design, built by German Expressionist architect **Erich Mendelsohn** in 1927. The concrete-and-glass building relies for its effect on the interplay between the bold horizontals of the main street fronts and the dramatically projecting cylinder on the corner. Mendelsohn's many other buildings include the Einstein Tower in Potsdam, Germany (1917–21), and – together with Serge Chermayeff – the De La Warr Pavilion (1935) in Bexhill-on-Sea on the south coast of the UK.

10

Galeria Awangarda

ul. Wita Stwosza 32 • Tues & Thurs–Sun 11am–6pm, Wed noon–8pm • 8zł; free on Wed • ☎ 71 790 2582, ⓦ bwa.wroc.pl

The **Galeria Awangarda** (Avant-garde Gallery), Wrocław's leading contemporary art gallery, is a good place to catch high-profile exhibitions of Polish and international art. The building itself is worth a look, too, incorporating the surviving Neoclassical remnants of a bombed-out nineteenth-century town house into a modern, glass-and-steel pavilion.

Bernardine monastery: the Museum of Architecture

ul. Bernardyńska 5 • Tues & Fri–Sun 11am–5pm, Wed 10am–4pm, Thurs noon–7pm • 10zł • ☎ 71 344 8279, ⓦ ma.wroc.pl

The gargantuan former **Bernardine monastery** is the last important example of Gothic brickwork in the city. The monastery was begun in the mid-fifteenth century and finished only a few years before the Reformation, whereupon it was dissolved. The **Museum of Architecture** (Muzeum Architektury) makes excellent use of the former monastery church, with a display of models and photos documenting the historic buildings of the city – many of which perished in the war. Keep an eye out for temporary exhibitions on global architectural themes.

The Racławice Panorama

ul. Purkyniego 11 • Mid-April to Sept daily 9am–5pm; Oct to mid-April Tues–Sun 9am–4pm • 30zł; also valid for the National Museum • ☎ 71 344 1511, ⓦ panoramaraclawicka.pl

Housed in a specially-built rotunda beside the Juliusz Słowacki Park, the **Racławice Panorama** (Panorama Racławicka), is one of the wonders of nineteenth-century patriotic art. At 120m long and 15m high, it's a truly enormous painting, commissioned in 1894 to celebrate the centenary of the Battle of Racławice, when a Russian army was defeated by Tadeusz Kościuszko's people's militia. The painting is stretched round the inner wall of the rotunda to form a perfect circle, with much attention being paid to a natural foreground of soil, stones and shrubs, which greatly adds to the uncanny appearance of depth. Visitors are admitted at thirty-minute intervals, and supplied with headphones employing English-language commentary and appropriate sound effects. Afterwards you can study the scale model of the battlefield downstairs at leisure.

Painters Jan Styka and Wojciech Kossak were the chief "authors" of the picture, although they were assisted by many of the leading artists of the day – Teodor Axentowicz and Włodzimierz Tetmajer among them. The painting was initially put on show in Lwów, which was then part of Austria – the only one of the Partitioning powers that would have tolerated such nationalist propaganda. It remained there until 1944, when it was substantially damaged by a bomb. Although allocated to Wrocław, it was then put into storage – officially because there were no specialists to restore it and no money to build the structure the painting would need, although the truth was that it was politically unacceptable to allow Poles to glory in their ancestors' slaughter of Russians. That all changed with the events of 1980, when the rise of Solidarity forced the Polish authorities to place more emphasis on Polish patriotic traditions. Within five years the painting had been immaculately restored and was on display in a snazzy new building.

The National Museum

pl. Powstańców Warszawy 5 • April–Sept Tues–Fri 10am–5pm, Sat & Sun 10.30am–6pm; Oct–March Tues–Fri 10am–4pm, Sat & Sun 10am–5pm • 15zł; free on Sat; also free with Racławice Panorama ticket • ☎ 71 372 5150, ⓦ mnwr.art.pl

Diagonally opposite the Racławice Panorama is the ponderous neo-Renaissance home of the **National Museum** (Muzeum Narodowe), which unites the collections of Breslau and Lwów. An important collection of medieval stone **sculpture**, housed on the ground floor, includes the delicately linear carving *The Dormition of the Virgin*, which formed the tympanum of the portal of St Mary Magdalene's Church (see page 371). The other major highlight is the poignant early fourteenth-century **tomb** of Henryk IV, the armour-clad effigy of the prince surrounded by a floor-level frieze of weeping mourners.

Upstairs lies an impressive display of medieval Silesian art, with a colossal set of late fourteenth-century saintly statues, several rooms of fifteenth-century altarpieces and a comprehensive collection of **Polish paintings** on the top floor. A leading exhibit here is an unfinished blockbuster by Matejko, *Vows of King Jan Kazimierz Waza*. Set in Lwów Cathedral, it illustrates the monarch's pledge to improve the lot of the peasants at the end of the war against his invading Swedish kinsmen.

Along the River Odra

One of the best ways to admire the city's architecture is from the banks of the **River Odra**. The recently landscaped area on the south side of the river along **bulwar Dunikowskiego** is the ideal place to start a stroll, beginning behind the red-brick Bastion Ceglarski, immediately west of the National Museum. Heading west from here takes you along an attractive park-side path, with excellent views of Ostrów Tumski's Gothic spires on the opposite bank. Stepped seating arranged on the riverside slope provides an excellent opportunity to sit and enjoy the scenery. At the western end of bulwar Dunikowskiego, overlooking the Piaskowski Bridge, is the **Market Hall** (Hala Targowa), a preformed concrete update of the brick church idiom built in 1908. Piled high most days with seasonal fruit and veg, flowers and deli products, it's one of the city's most colourful corners.

The university quarter

Dominating much of the Odra's southern bank, Wrocław's **university quarter** comprises a handsome cluster of Baroque and Neoclassical structures, many of which date back to the period of Austrian rule over the city. The university was founded as a Jesuit college by Austrian Emperor Leopold I in 1702.

The Collegium Maximum and the University Museum

pl. Uniwersytecki 1 • May–Sept Mon, Tues, Thurs & Fri 10am–5pm, Sat & Sun 10am–6pm; Oct–April daily except Wed 10am–4pm • 14zł • ☎ 71 375 2618, ⓦ muzeum.uni.wroc.pl

The university's main building, begun in 1728, is the so-called **Collegium Maximum**, with an impressive 171m-long facade. Its wide entrance portal bears a balcony adorned with statues symbolizing various academic disciplines and attributes; more can be seen high above on the graceful little tower. Inside, the **University Museum** (Muzeum Uniwersytetu Wrocławskiego) offers a small but well-arranged display of scientific instruments and old books. Included in the ticket is a chance to see the celebrated **Aula Leopoldina** or main assembly hall, one of the greatest secular interiors of the Baroque age, fusing the elements of architecture, painting, sculpture and ornament into one bravura whole. The huge illusionistic ceiling frescoes show the Apotheosis of Divine and Worldly Wisdom above the gallery and auditorium. Continue upstairs to reach the **Mathematicians' Tower** (Wieża Matematyczna), where there's an exhibition on the astronomical and meteorological research that was done here, and a terrace offering some of the best views over the Old Town.

Church of the Blessed Name of Jesus
pl. Uniwersytecki 1 • April–June, Sept & Oct Mon–Sat 11am–3.30pm, Sun 1.30–3.30pm; July & Aug Mon–Sat 10.30am–5.30pm, Sun 1.30–5.30pm; Nov & March Wed–Sat 11am–3.30pm, Sun 1.30–3.30pm; Dec–Feb closed except for Mass • Donation requested • ☎ 71 344 9423, Ⓦ uniwersytecki.archidiecezja.wroc.pl

The **Church of the Blessed Name of Jesus** (Kościół Najświętszego Imienia Jezus), immediately east of the Collegium Maximum, was built in the Jesuit style at the end of the seventeenth century, one of the rash of Counter-Reformation religious buildings in the Habsburg lands. Its most arresting feature is the huge allegorical ceiling fresco by the most celebrated Austrian decorative painter of the day, Johann Michael Rottmayr. A free audio guide provides a ten-minute documentary.

The Ossolineum
ul. Szewska 37 • Ⓦ ossolineum.pl

Just east of the Collegium Maximum stands one of Wrocław's most distinguished buildings, the **Ossolineum.** Founded by Józef Maksymilian Ossoliński in Lwów in 1817, this famous library was moved (at least in part) to Wrocław in 1947, where it took up residence in the Baroque former convent where it remains today. The collections can only be viewed during special exhibitions, but the building itself is a real treat – the best **views** are from the beautifully restored walled garden on the south side of the building or from the Wyspa Słodowa on the other side of the river.

Wyspa Piasek, Wyspa Słodowa and Nadodrze
From the city centre the Most Piaskowy bridge leads north across a branch of the River Odra to **Wyspa Piasek** (Sand Island), its cluster of historic buildings dominated by the fourteenth-century **Church of St Mary on the Sands** (Kościół NMP na Piasku). Accessible via footbridge to the northwest, the grassy lawns of **Wyspa Słodowa** (Malting-House Island) are used for impromptu picnics by the city's sizeable youth and student population, while indie rock and dub reggae are pumped out by the converted-barge café-bars moored nearby.

Another graceful foot- and cycle-bridge leads from Wyspa to the northern bank of the Odra and **Nadodrze**, a sprawling, up-and-coming residential suburb with a reputation for boho-meets-working-class authenticity. There are a few pockets of café culture here, and a handful of large apartment-block-covering murals; it's a rewarding place to stroll if you want to get away from the tourist-poster Poland of ryneks and cathedrals.

Ostrów Tumski
Two elegant little bridges, Most Młynski and Most Tumski (the latter decorated with padlocks, placed there for luck by newly-wed couples), connect Wyspa Piasek with **Ostrów Tumski**, or Cathedral Island. For those not already sated by medieval churches, there's a concentration of five more here. With its massive bulk, giant buttresses and pair of dissimilar towers, the imperious **Holy Cross Church** (Kościół św. Krzyża) is particularly interesting, as it's really two churches, one on top of the other; the lower one was originally dedicated to St Bartholomew.

Cathedral of St John the Baptist
pl. Katedralny 18 • Mon–Sat 10am–5pm, Sun 2–5pm

The slender twin-towered **Cathedral of St John the Baptist** (Katedra św. Jana Chrziciela) was Poland's first cathedral built in the Gothic style, completed in 1272. Grievously damaged in 1945, it has been restored to its thirteenth-century form. Three chapels behind the high altar make a visit to the gloomy **interior** worthwhile: on the southern side, **St Elizabeth's chapel** dates from the seventeenth century, its integrated architecture, frescoes and sculptures created by Italian followers of Bernini; next comes

10

the Gothic **Lady chapel**, with the masterly Renaissance funerary plaque of Bishop Jan Roth; and last in line is the **Corpus Christi chapel**, a perfectly proportioned and subtly decorated Baroque gem.

St Giles's Church and Archdiocesan Museum

pl. Katedralny 16 • Museum: Tues–Sat 9am–3pm • 10zł • ☎ 71 322 1755, ⓦ muzeum.archidiecezja.wroc.pl

Opposite the northern side of the Cathedral of St John, the tiny thirteenth-century **St Giles's Church** (Kościół św. Idziego) is the only one in the city to have escaped destruction by the Tatars, and it preserves some finely patterned brickwork. Next door, the **Archdiocesan Museum** (Muzeum Archidiecezjalne) is a treasure-trove of religious art, with late-medieval wooden sculptures from all over Silesia, and a wonderful array of altarpieces.

Botanical Gardens

ul. Sienkiewicza 6 • April–Oct daily 8am–6pm • 15zł • ☎ 71 322 5957, ⓦ ogrodbotaniczny.wroclaw.pl

For some respite from sightseeing, head to the **Botanical Gardens**, established at the beginning of the twentieth century. Set over several acres, the gardens include a small lake, cactus and palm houses, a plant shop and café, and offer great views of Ostrów Tumski's towering spires.

Plac Grunwaldzki and around

The eastern end of Ostrów Tumski is marked by the elongated avenue of **plac Grunwaldzki**, a busy main road famous for being used as an **airstrip** during the Siege of Breslau in 1945. The runway was exposed to enemy artillery, and almost 13,000 died in its construction and maintenance. Overlooking the oval tram intersection that marks plac Grunwaldzki's central point is a cluster of six residential tower blocks that go under the collective name of **Wrocław Manhattan** (Wrocławski Manhattan). Designed in the 1970s by leading Polish modernist Jadwiga Grabowska-Hawrylak, they are famous for their organic-looking facades made up of bowed, curving balconies.

Marking plac Grunwaldzki's southwestern end is the most famous of the city's bridges, **Most Grunwaldzki**, built in 1910 and opened by Kaiser Wilhelm II. An iconic construction with blue-painted steel arcs suspended from stone, fortress-like gates, it leads back towards the National Museum (see page 374).

Szczytnicki Park

ul. Wróblewskiego • Take trams #2 and #10 from ul. Szczytnicka, or #4 and #10 from ul. Kazimierza Wielkiego in the Old Town

Wrocław's most enticing stretch of greenery is the **Szczytnicki Park**, 1km east of plac Grunwaldzki across Most Zwierziniecki, a fine old bridge completed in 1897. The park's focal point is the huge modernist masterpiece known as the Centennial Hall, although there is plenty more to see in the vicinity. Food trucks and snack stalls are frequently positioned outside the Hall.

Centennial Hall and around

ul. Wystawowa 1 • **Centennial Hall** ⓦ halastulecia.pl • **Discovery Centre** April–Oct Mon–Thurs & Sun 9am–6pm, Fri & Sat 9am–7pm; Nov–March daily 9am–5pm • 12zł • ☎ 71 347 5047, ⓦ centrumpoznawcze.pl

Wrocław's one contribution to the UNESCO World Heritage List list is the **Centennial Hall** (Hala Stulecia), a vast rotunda built in 1911–13 to celebrate the centenary of the liberation of the city from Napoleon. Designed by the innovative Max Berg, it combines traditional Prussian solidity with a modernistic dash – the unsupported 130m-wide dome is an audacious piece of engineering even by present-day standards. The Hall is still in regular use as a venue for rock-pop concerts, conferences and trade exhibitions.

Visitors can take a peek at the **Discovery Centre** in the foyer, which documents the building's construction with animated videos and original photos. There are also plenty of pictures of the other things built in Wrocław in the 1920s and '30s, including the cool-as-a-white-cube suburban houses thrown up by the Bauhaus-inspired arts-and-architecture group the *Werkbund*.

On the western side of the Centennial Hall, the ribbed steel prong known as the **Wrocław Needle** (Wrocławska iglica) soars skywards. This 96m-high construction was erected to mark the Recovered Territories Exhibition of 1948, when it served as a symbol of the new "people's" Poland.

Pavilion of the Four Domes

ul. Wystawowa 1 • April–Sept Tues–Thurs 10am–5pm, Fri 10am–7pm, Sat 10am–8pm, Sun 10am–6pm; Nov–March Tues–Thurs 10am–4pm, Fri & Sun 10am–6pm, Sat 10am–8pm • 20zł • ☎ 71 712 7182, ⓦ pawilonczterechkopul.pl

10

Built at the same time as the Centennial Hall but in more eclectic style, the exhibition space known as the **Pavilion of the Four Domes** (Pawilon Czterech Kopuł) is very much the masterpiece of Max Berg's teacher Hans Poelzig, who went on to build acclaimed modernist buildings all over Germany. It's now used as an extension of the **Contemporary Art Museum** (see page 378), hosting a small but growing permanent collection focusing on the classics of contemporary Polish art, alongside themed exhibitions bringing in a lot of leading international names.

Wrocław Fountain

ul. Wystawowa 1 • April–Oct daily 10am–10pm; sound-and-light shows start on the hour and last 4–20min • Free • ⓦ wroclawskafontanna.pl

Splurting its stuff from the middle of an artificial lake behind the Centennial Hall, the huge **Wrocław Fountain** (Wrocławska Fontanna) was opened on June 4, 2009, to mark the thirtieth anniversary of the epochal 1989 elections. The **sound-and-light show** is at its most impressive at dusk or after dark, when the spurting waters are coordinated with rock-show lighting and projected visuals.

The Japanese Garden

April–Oct daily 9am–7pm • 4zł • ☎ 71 328 6611

Occupying a swathe of Szczytnicki Park just beyond the Wrocław Fountain, the **Japanese Garden** was initially laid out (by bona-fide Japanese gardener Mankichi Arai) as a temporary attraction in 1913, and returned to its former splendour by local enthusiasts at the end of the 1990s. Featuring a beautiful array of shrubs, grasses and rocks set beside a lily-filled pond, it's a blissfully restful place.

The Afrykarium and Wrocław Zoo

ul. Wróblewskiego 1–5 • March & Oct Mon–Thurs 9am–5pm, Fri–Sun 9am–6pm; April–Sept Mon–Thurs 9am–6pm, Fri–Sun 9am–7pm; Nov–Feb Mon–Thurs 9am–4pm, Fri–Sun 9am–5pm • 45zł • ☎ 71 340 7119, ⓦ zoo.wroclaw.pl

Manatee-watching in Poland may not immediately spring to the top of your holiday bucket list. Until, that is, you've heard about the **Afrykarium**, a state-of-the-art **aquarium** complex bang in the middle of **Wrocław Zoo** (and included on the same ticket). With different zones covering different parts of the African continent, the aquarium includes recreated rainforests, deserts, seacoasts and swamps. As well as observing manatees sashaying gracefully around their tanks, you can admire hippos basking beneath an artificial waterfall, and crocodiles eyeing passing children from behind thick glass. Dating from 1865, the zoo itself is the oldest in Poland, and contains over six hundred species, from lions to flamingos. The grounds are vast and it's wise to factor in a rest or two.

Hydropolis

Na Grobli 19–21 • Mon–Fri 9am–6pm, Sat & Sun 10am–8pm • 18zł • ☎ 71 340 9515, ⓦ hydropolis.pl • Tram #0L, #0P or #5 to pl. Wróblewskiego, then a 10min walk down ul. Wałońska and onto Na Grobli

In an underground nineteenth-century reservoir, **Hydropolis** is a hands-on science museum-cum-learning zone that looks at numerous aspects of water, particularly its

> ## THE TALE OF THE EIGHTY MILLION ZŁOTYS
>
> In 1980–81, the independent trade union Solidarity deposited **eighty million złotys** in a local Wrocław bank, but when activists got wind of the imminent imposition of martial law in December 1981, they rushed to withdraw the money before their assets were frozen by the state. The bank manager was supposed to report all large withdrawals to the authorities, but delayed his phone call long enough to allow the activists to get away – which they did employing the usual tricks of a bank heist, switching vehicles on route. They left the money for safekeeping with the Archbishop of Wrocław, who took the precaution of changing the money into dollars in order to avoid the fall in value that would have inevitably been brought about by high Polish inflation. The whole thing was made into an entertaining caper-movie by Waldemar Krsystek in 2012.

importance to all forms of life, the human impact on the environment, and the use of water in big cities like Wrocław. The nine different exhibition zones contain plenty of technology-aided visual drama – with the chance to descend to the bottom of the ocean in a virtual submarine, observe a video installation of sharks attacking smaller fish, and watch a ten-minute planetarium-style projection about the history of the Earth – as well as traditional exhibits such as a collection of model boats.

Jewish cemetery

ul. Ślężna 37/39 • Daily 8am–6pm • 7zł • Tram #9 or #16 (direction Park Południowy) from the train station

The **Jewish cemetery** (Cmentarz Żydowski), an atmospheric walled area 3km south of the city centre, is a poignant reminder of Wrocław's Judaic heritage. Many important figures have been laid to rest here, and it's useful to purchase the informative booklet (15zł) at the entrance so you can find them amongst the vines creeping over the gravestones and monuments.

Zajezdnia History Centre

ul. Grabiszyńska 184 • July & Aug Tues & Wed 10am–6pm, Thurs 11am–6pm, Fri–Sun 11am–7pm; Sept–June Tues & Wed 9am–5pm, Thurs 10am–5pm, Fri–Sun 10am–6pm • 10zł • ☎71 715 9682, ⊛ zajezdnia.org • Tram #4, #5, #11 to Centrum Zajezdnia from ul. Piłsudskiego

Opened in 2016, the **Zajezdnia History Centre** (Centrum Historii Zajezdnia) is one of the finest of Poland's new-generation history museums, providing numerous insights into social, cultural and family history alongside the hard narrative of political events. Zajezdnia means "depot" in Polish, a reference to the red-brick tram and bus garage in which the museum is housed; strikes in favour of the independent trade union Solidarity took place here in August 1980, making the building itself part of the story.

Visitors pass through an antechamber filled with pictures of Polish society in the interwar years before emerging into a display devoted to Breslau/Wrocław in 1945. The museum goes on to recount how the city was rebuilt and reinvented by a population that had by-and-large moved here from somewhere else. The development of society and culture is handled in colourful manner: helping to illustrate the 1960s and '70s is a chamber filled with a seductive array of period theatre posters, magazine covers and LP sleeves. The museum documents the unrest-ridden 1980s in some detail, focusing in particular on the story of the Eighty Million Złotys (see above).

Contemporary Art Museum Wrocław

pl. Strzegomski 2A • Mon 10am–6pm, Wed–Sun noon–8pm • 10zł • ☎71 356 4257, ⊛ muzeumwspolczesne.pl • Tram #3, #10, #20, #23, #31, #32, #33 to pl. Strzegomski

Two kilometres west of the city centre, a former anti-aircraft gun tower from World War II looms over the busy traffic ribbon of ulica Legnicka, providing a dramatic home to the **Contemporary Art Museum Wrocław** (Muzeum Współczesne Wrocław or MWW). Thematic exhibitions and group shows are mounted in the gritty, grey-concrete environment of the tower's rotunda-like interior. There are superb views from the terrace of the top-floor café.

ARRIVAL AND DEPARTURE

WROCŁAW

By air Wrocław airport (☎71 358 1381, ⓦ airport. wroclaw.pl) is 10km to the west of the centre in the suburb of Strachowice. Bus #106 from the airport (every 20–30min; 40min depending on traffic) drops passengers off on ul. Podwale, near the Old Town, before terminating at the train station.

By train The main train station, Wrocław Główny, faces the broad boulevard of ul. Piłsudskiego, a 20min walk south of the centre.

Destinations Bolesławiec (8 daily; 2hr); Bydgoszcz (5 daily; 4hr 20min); Dresden (2 daily; 3hr 50min); Gdańsk (3 daily; 4hr 20min); Jelenia Góra (15 daily; 2hr 20min); Katowice (5 daily; 2hr 20min); Kłodzko (7 daily; 1hr 45min); Kraków

(8 daily; 3hr 30min); Łódź (2 daily; 4hr 30min); Poznań (hourly; 2-3hr); Przemyśl (4 daily; 7hr 30min); Rzeszów (5 daily; 6hr); Świdnica (4 daily; 1hr 10min); Szczecin (6 daily; 5hr 10min); Szklarska Poręba (6 daily; 3hr 30min); Wałbrzych (hourly; 1hr 20min); Warsaw (5 daily of which one overnight; 4hr 45min–5hr 15min); Zielona Góra (7 daily; 2hr 40min).

By bus The main bus station, Dworzec PKS (☎71 361 6135, ⓦ polbus.pl), is in the Galeria Wroclavia shopping centre on ul. Sucha, at the back of the train station.

Destinations Jawor (hourly; 1hr 10min); Jelenia Góra (hourly; 2hr); Karpacz (1 daily; 3hr); Sobotka (every 30min; 1hr); Świdnica (every 30min; 1hr 15min).

GETTING AROUND

By tram and bus The tram and bus network provides comprehensive coverage for Wrocław. Tickets are bought in advance from newspaper kiosks and cost 3zł each; night services are 3.20zł.

By taxi A central taxi rank is on ul. Wita Stwosza;

otherwise try MPT (☎19191) or ZTP (☎19622).

By bike Bikes can be hired from Bike Tours, at the tourist information centre at Rynek 14 (April–Oct daily 9am–7pm; Nov–March ring in advance to reserve; 60zł/day; ☎534 100 780, ⓦ seewroclaw.pl).

INFORMATION

Tourist information The tourst office at Rynek 14 (daily: May–Sept 9am–9pm; Oct–April 9am–7pm; ☎71 344 3111, ⓦ visitwroclaw.eu) has plenty of maps and leaflets.

ACCOMMODATION

Wrocław has accommodation to suit every taste and pocket, with a new generation of chic **design hotels** joining an already generous roster of business-oriented places and mid-range tourist establishments. There's a relative lack of B&B-type accommodation, but Wrocław has been well and truly "discovered" by backpackers and the city's **hostels** offer good-value double rooms as well as dorm beds.

HOTELS AND B&BS

Akira pl. Strzelecki 28, Nadodrze ☎71 323 0888, ⓦ hotelakira.pl; tram #0L, #0P, #8 to pl. Staszica; map page 368. Friendly B&B north of the river with neat but ascetic rooms, a cute breakfast room and a small garden patio out the back. 180zł

Art Hotel ul. Kiełbaśnicza 20 ☎71 787 7400, ⓦ art hotel.pl; map page 368. Comfortable hotel in a superb location just off the main square, with modern interiors and (despite the name) not a lot of art. Doubles are spacious and modern. 400zł

Boogie Hostel Delux ul. Białoskórnicza 6 ☎71 342 1160, ⓦ boogiehostel.com; map page 368. Despite its name, this sister place to *Boogie Hostel* (see page 380) is really a budget hotel with attitude. The rooms (all en suite) are designed with hipness in mind, and come in brash colours with plenty of space and light. The vibrating massage seat in the reception is

a nice touch, as is the sauna in the basement. 140zł

★ **DoubleTree by Hilton** ul. Podwale 84 ☎71 777 0000, ⓦ doubletree3.hilton.com; map page 368. Bulging up against the city centre like an ocean liner arriving at port, the *DoubleTree* belies its international-chain status with a highly individual approach to architecture and design. Social areas and many of the rooms feature organic, curvy-walled interiors; design is on the modern minimalist side without abandoning any of the creature comforts you would expect from the name. Gym, spa centre and 18m pool. 600zł

Hotel Monopol ul. Heleny Modrzejewski 2 ☎71 772 3777, ⓦ monopolwroclaw.hotel.com.pl; map page 368. This nineteenth-century pile is one of the most palatial of Wrocław's grand historic hotels. Five-star luxury includes a spa and wellness centre with sauna and pool, an Italian delicatessen, wine boutique, business suites, a bar and a top-class restaurant. 500zł

10

10

Stop Wrocław ul. Sienkiewicza 31 ☎519 115 075, ⓦstopwroclaw.pl; map page 368. Just north of the centre across the river on Ostrów Tumski, this cute and welcoming guesthouse offers small but comfortable rooms, with access to a kitchen and free tea/coffee. Four-person apartments are also available. Doubles 139zł, apartments 260zł

★ **The Granary-La Suite Hotel** ul. Mennicza 24 ☎71 395 2600, ⓦgranaryhotel.com; map page 368. Outstanding boutique hotel situated in a sixteenth-century red-brick brewery, which lends the place lots of ambience. Custom-designed rooms are kitted out with all the extras, while luxury suites come with kitchenettes. 550zł

HOSTELS

Boogie Hostel ul. Ruska 35 ☎71 342 4472, ⓦboogie hostel.com; map page 368. Spacious and colourful hostel with clean, modern rooms, ultra-cool purple decor, and a tendency to attract a party crowd. Dorms 40zł, doubles 130zł

Cinnamon ul. Kazimierza Wielkiego 67 ☎71 344 5858, ⓦcinnamonhostel.com; map page 368. Pleasant, airy rooms with wooden floorboards and names like "Lavender", "Spice" and "Honey" (decorated accordingly), plus friendly, attentive staff, make this hostel a winner. Board games in the common room help to keep things sociable. Dorms 50zł, doubles 160zł

Hart Hostel ul. Rydygiera 25a, Nadodrze ☎533 755 822, ⓦfacebook.com/HART.Rydygiera25a; tram #0L, #0P, #8 from train station to Pomorska; map page 368. Located in a courtyard in the Nadodrze district, this hostel aims for cool design and a cultured atmosphere, with art exhibitions in the social areas. Dorms 45zł, doubles 110zł

Mleczarnia ul. Włodkowica 5 ☎71 787 7570, ⓦmleczarniahostel.com; map page 368. Comfortable, bohemian hangout, situated in an old building above a candlelit coffee bar (see below). The lovely dorms and doubles are furnished with antiques, and there's a spacious kitchen/sitting area and a covered courtyard with rocking chairs. Dorms 45zł, doubles 220zł

EATING

CAFÉS AND SNACK BARS

BLT & Flatbreads ul. Ruska 58/59 ☎71 796 3344, ⓦblt. wroclaw.pl; map page 368. Filling the gap in the sandwich market, *BLT* serves up excellent sandwiches, burgers and tortilla wraps, all with delicious fresh ingredients. Mon–Thurs & Sun 10am–10pm, Fri & Sat 10am–11pm.

Bułka z masłem ul. Włodkowica 8a ☎503 476 241, ⓦfacebook.com/bulkazmaslemwroclaw; map page 368. Charming, roomy café with a famously leafy garden terrace, serving everything from late breakfasts to gourmet burgers. It draws a crowd on weekdays due to the excellent two-course set lunch (28zł), and is also a fine place to drink in the evening. Mon–Sat 10am–midnight, Sun 11am–midnight.

★ **Café Targowa** ul. Piaskowa 17 ☎536 591 286, ⓦcafetargowa.pl; map page 368. A minimally decorated cubicle among the colourful (and blissfully aromatic) stalls of Wrocław's covered market, *Café Targowa* contrives to serve up some of the best coffee in the Polish southwest. They roast their own beans and offer the full range of espresso, filter, Chemex and aeropress options. Look out for a changing roster of home-made cakes and biscuits. Daily 8am–6.30pm.

Kawiarnia Literatka Rynek 56/57 ☎71 341 8013, ⓦkawiarnialiteratka.pl; map page 368. Bucking the trend on the Rynek for noisy, crowded bars, this café is an altogether more refined space, with an artsy, relaxed atmosphere created by shelves of old books, dark-wood decor and chandeliers. Two-course lunches are a steal at 21zł (Mon–Fri). Daily 10am–1am.

Miś ul. Kuźnicza 48; map page 368. Extremely popular and well-known milk bar that provides quick, filling grub

for the student crowd. Mains from 4zł. Mon–Fri 7am–6pm, Sat 8am–5pm.

Znasz Ich ul. Rydygier 25B, Nadodrze ☎794 967 872, ⓦfacebook.com/znaszich; tram #0L, #0P or #8 to Pomorska; map page 368. Tucked away in a Nadodrze courtyard, this café is best known for its toasted croissants with savoury fillings (cheese-and-pear croissant 13zł), although they also do a lot more in the soup and creative-salad line. Art exhibitions, freshly-squeezed fruit juices and a good wine list, too. Mon–Sat 10am–10pm, Sun 10am–8pm.

ICE-CREAM PARLOUR

★ **Polish Lody** pl. Kościuszki; map page 368. Join the queue at this fantastic ice-cream parlour, serving mainstream flavours as well as unique own-recipe originals – grapefruit with basil and tomato with raspberry have been known to grace the list of daily specials chalked up above the counter. Mon noon–9pm, Tues–Sun 10am–9pm.

RESTAURANTS

JaDka ul. Rzeźnicza 24/25 ☎071 343 6461, ⓦjadka. pl; map page 368. A meal at folksy-but-refined *JaDka* may not be cheap (though some classics like *pierogi* come in at 27–39zł), but you can be assured of world-class Polish cuisine and excellent service. Daily 1–10pm.

Karczma Lwówska Rynek 4 ☎713 439 887, ⓦlwowska. com.pl; map page 368. No-nonsense meat-and-potatoes mains, well-priced at around 25zł, served in an interior decked out with Ukrainian folk motifs and sepia photographs of old Lwów. Meats are grilled traditionally and are excellent. If you're a vegetarian, run. Daily 11am–midnight.

Konspira pl. Solny 11 ☎796 326 600, ⓦkonspira. org; map page 368. A theme restaurant that's actually serious about the theme, this memorabilia-stuffed place in a courtyard behind pl. Solny commemorates the 1980s generation of Solidarity activists and cultural subversives who turned Wrocław into a fortress of political disobedience. The whole thing is handled with humour: the photocopied menus look like the *samizdat* publications of the Martial Law period, while the food (superbly executed Polish standards) comes with funny names: *Danie wywrotowca* or "Wrecker's Dinner" is actually goulash with gnocchi-like dumplings (25zł). Mon–Wed & Sun noon–10pm, Thurs–Sat noon–11pm.

KRVN ("Karavan") ul. św. Antoniego 40/1a ☎575 791 757, ⓦkrvn.pl; map page 368. Distressed but arty-looking café-bar serving soups, salads, gourmet burgers (23–27zł) and a handful of mains, with at least one veggie choice. Two-course set lunches (Mon–Fri) clock in at 25zł,

while beer from the Litovel stable and local brewers like Stu Mostów (see page 381) may encourage you to linger. Mon–Thurs & Sun noon–midnight, Fri & Sat noon–2am.

Pod Fredra Rynek-Ratusz 1 ☎71 341 1335, ⓦpod fredra.pl; map page 368. One of the best places in town to sample traditional Polish food in ambient surrounds; duck, rabbit, goose and venison dishes (30–40zł, amongst many others, are lovingly prepared, while an impressive wine list accompanies the menu. Daily 11am–11pm.

Powoli ul. Rydygiera 25/27, Nadodrze ☎732 752 025, ⓦfacebook.com/sniadaniaiobiady; tram #0L, #0P or #8 to Pomorska; map page 368. The place to go for breakfasts and lunches in Nadodrze, with fried-egg breakfasts, soups, quiches and sandwiches, and a penchant for chilli-seasoned Mexican and Asian mains, with most dishes under 20zł. It's mostly vegetarian but there's usually a token dish for carnivores. The only problem is that it closes early. Daily 9am–6pm.

DRINKING AND NIGHTLIFE

Wrocław's drinking and nightlife scene is as vibrant as you would expect from a large university city. The Rynek is cluttered mainly with touristy bars and noisy clubs; exploring further afield, the area between the main square and the university is packed with bars, while the **Pasaż Niepolda** passageway between ul. Ruska and ul. św. Antoniego is a key pub-crawling zone. Many of Wrocław's bars and pubs feature DJs and dancing as the night wears on. Additionally, there's a handful of dedicated **music clubs** with a regular programme of disc-spinning events and/or gigs by local bands.

BARS AND PUBS

Ale Browar ul. Włodkowica 27 ☎533 944 823, ⓦface book.com/alebrowarwroclaw; map page 368. Corner pub with a bright, minimalist interior and a great choice of boutique beers – at 6–7zł for 0.25l you can sup your way through several brews. Mon–Thurs & Sun 2pm–midnight, Fri & Sat 2pm–2am.

Barbarka Wyspa Słodowa 6 ⓦfacebook.com/barbarka wroclaw; map page 368. Consisting of a riverside pontoon and a deckchair-scattered stretch of lawn, this popular "beach" bar attracts an outdoor café crowd in the daytime and bopping revellers at night. DJs are on hand to supply a range of niche rock-to-reggae sounds, and there's a good choice of beers from the Miłosław stable in the fridge. May–Sept Mon–Thurs & Sun 9am–midnight, Fri & Sat 9am–3am.

★ **Mleczarnia** ul. Włodkowica 5 ☎71 788 2448, ⓦmle.pl; map page 368. The most atmospheric bar in town is this dark, candlelit place, characterized by antique furniture, nineteenth-century knick-knacks and sepia family photographs, where a bohemian crowd sips coffee and cocktails. There's a lovely summer terrace overlooking the synagogue at the back. Daily 8am–4am.

Niebo ul. Ruska 51, Pasaż Niepolda ☎71 342 9867, ⓦfacebook.com/niebocafe; map page 368. This big pub-like venue with distressed furniture and a grungy vibe is the best of the many Pasaż Niepolda drinking options. It hosts occasional rock concerts, and attracts a healthy mix of

oblivion-seeking students crowding round the bar till very very late. Mon 5pm–4am, Tues–Sun 1pm–4am.

Nietota ul. Kazimierza Wielkiego 50 ☎733 233 992, ⓦfacebook.com/KlubNietota; map page 368. There's something going on almost every night of the week at this place, with a long bar, a stage for bands, DJs and occasional stand-up comedy. Mon–Thurs & Sun 5pm–2am, Fri & Sat 5pm–5am.

★ **Pod Kalamburem** ul. Kuźnicza 29a, ⓦkalambur. org; map page 368. Bohemian bar located between the Rynek and the university quarter, with beautiful Art Nouveau decor, some lethal cocktails and occasional concerts and exhibitions. A great place to kick off the evening, it's also a popular last-stop for early-hours revellers. Mon–Thurs & Sun noon–2am, Fri & Sat noon–4am.

Spiż Rynek-Ratusz 2 ☎71 344 7225, ⓦspiz.pl; map page 368. Superior cellar pub incorporating Poland's first boutique brewery, with several beers brewed on the premises. Bread-and-dripping (*chleb ze smalcem*) is the traditional side order. A wider range of Polish nosh is available in the rather more formal *Spiż* restaurant next door. Mon–Thurs & Sun 10am–midnight, Fri & Sat 10am–2am.

★ **Stu Mostów** ul. Jana Długosza 2 ☎501 822 305, ⓦ100mostow.pl; tram #6, #11 or #23 from the junction of Świdnicka and Piłsudskiego to the Kromera terminus; map page 368. Dedicated followers of Poland's craft beer revolution should head for *Stu Mostów*, a

10

brewery, restaurant and bar located in the former workers' cinema of a suburban factory 3km northeast of the centre. It's the ideal place to drink your way through an entire range of pilsners, rye beers and Schöps (a distinctive local ale of medieval vintage that has recently been recreated by *Stu Mostów*'s brewmasters). A substantial menu of snacks and mains ensures that you can make an evening of it. Daily noon–midnight.

★ **Szajba** ul. św. Antoniego 2/4 ☎ 660 404 270, ⓦ szajba.wroclaw.pl; map page 368. Hidden down one of the city's ubiquitous alleyways and decorated with bric-a-brac and old radios, this is a great find. There's a pleasant courtyard to sit in, or you can hang out inside amongst the hipsters – expect a colourful, young crowd. Mon–Thurs & Sun 5pm–2am, Fri & Sat 5pm–4am.

Szynkarnia ul. sw. Antoniego 15 ☎ 793 634 994, ⓦ szynkarnia.com.pl; map page 368. Part deli store, part multitap pub, this place has the current selection of

Polish and international craft beers chalked up beside the bar. Wraps and sandwiches with a variety of fillings cost 13–15zł. Daily 9am–midnight.

CLUBS

Eter ul. Kazimierza Wielkiego 19 ☎ 71 722 7100, ⓦ facebook.com/ClubEter; map page 368. Perhaps the biggest club in town, *Eter* ("Ether") also houses some of the biggest events, from visiting rock and pop acts to renowned international DJs. Two levels (one to relax, one to dance), five bars, one great night. Fri & Sat 8pm–4am.

Manana Café ul. św. Mikołaja 8–11 ☎ 71 3434 370, ⓦ mananacafe.pl; map page 368. The default choice for many late-night partying Wrocławians, *Manana* is a fun, let-your-hair-down kind of place which attracts an eclectic crowd of students, 30-somethings and tourists, and which plays a variety of cheese from the '70s, '80s and '90s. Mon–Thurs & Sun 5pm–4am, Fri & Sat 5pm–7am.

ENTERTAINMENT

Browar Mieszczański ul. Hubska 44 ☎ 71 367 7048, ⓦ browar.wroc.pl. Red-brick former brewery complex a 15min walk southeast of the train and bus stations, now a cultural hub hosting alternative theatre, gigs, club nights and daytime outdoor markets.

National Forum of Music (Narodowe Forum Muzyki) pl. Wolności 1 ☎ 71 715 9700, ⓦ nfm.wroclaw. pl. Home of the city's philharmonic orchestra and host to all

manner of jazz, choral and chamber concerts in a superb 1800-seater main hall or a variety of chamber spaces.

Opera Wrocławska ul. Świdnicka 35 ☎ 71 370 8880, ⓦ opera.wroclaw.pl. Top-notch warbling and superb stagecraft from the Lower Silesian Opera, one of Poland's best companies. Also the home of the city ballet.

Teatr Muzyczny Capitol ul. Piłsudskiego 72 ☎ 71 789 0451, ⓦ teatr-capitol.pl. Operetta, musicals and cabaret.

DIRECTORY

Hospital University Teaching Hospital (Uniwersytecki szpital kliniczny), ul. Borowska 213 (☎ 71 733 1110).

Left luggage There are lockers at the train and bus stations.

Pharmacy Pod Lwami, al. Jana Pawła II 7 (☎ 71 343 6724, ⓦ aptekapodlwami.com.pl), is open 24hr.

Police Grunwaldzka 6 (☎ 71 340 4358).

Post office There are post offices at Rynek 28 (24hr) and outside the train station at Piłsudskiego 12 (Mon–Fri 8am–8pm).

Świdnica and around

ŚWIDNICA, 50km southwest of Wrocław, and for centuries Silesia's second most important city, suffered little damage in World War II and preserves some of the grandeur of a former princely capital. For centuries an important centre of trade and commerce, Świdnica ranked as one of Europe's most renowned brewing centres, with its famous *Schwarze Schöps* forming the staple fare of Wrocław's best-known tavern and exported as far afield as Italy and Russia. Today's Świdnica is a forward-looking town with a tangible self-confidence, popular with visitors due to its attractive main square and splendid **Church of Peace**. There's another stunning Church of Peace at **Jawor**, an easy 35km side-trip from here.

The main square

The lively **main square** is predominantly Baroque, though the core of many of the houses is often much older. Two particularly notable facades are at no. 7, **Under** the Crown, and no. 8, **The Gilded Man**. In the central area of the square are two fine fountains and the handsome early eighteenth-century **town hall**, which preserves the tower and an elegant star-vaulted chamber from its Gothic predecessor.

Museum of Shopkeeping

Rynek 37 • Tues–Fri 10am–5pm, Sat & Sun 11am–5pm; Oct–April closes 4pm • 6zł • ☎ 74 852 1291, ⓦ muzeum-kupiectwa.pl

Round the back of the town hall, the **Museum of Shopkeeping** (Muzeum Dawnego Kupiectwa) sheds light on Świdnica's mercantile past, with re-creations of traditional shop interiors, their counters bearing the cumbersome but decorous weights and measures used by the town's traders.

Church of St Stanislaw

pl. Jana Pawła II 1

Off the southeastern corner of the main square, the main street, ulica Długa, curves gently downhill. The view ahead stretches past a number of Baroque mansions to the majestic **belfry** – at 103m the third highest in Poland – of the Gothic parish **Church of St Stanislaw** (Kościół św. Stanisława). The impressive facade features a sublime late Gothic relief of St Anne, the Virgin and Child.

After the Thirty Years' War the church was given to the Jesuits, who carried out a Baroque transformation of the **interior**. A massive high altar with statues of the order's favourite saints dominates the east end; the organ, with its carvings of the heavenly choir, provides a similar focus to the west.

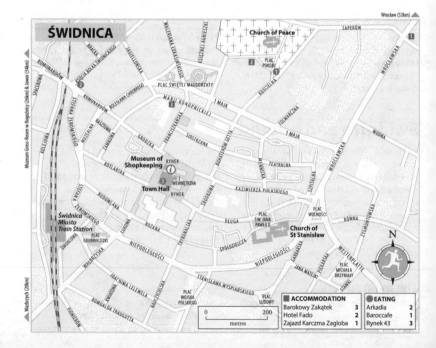

WROCŁAW FESTIVALS

Wrocław hosts several prestigious annual **festivals**, a profile enhanced by its stint as European Capital of Culture in 2017. The tourist office (see page 379) can provide details of all events.

Stage Songs Review (Przegląd Piosenki Aktorskiej) March–April ⓦ ppa.wroclaw.pl. Long-standing international music festival that showcases quality songwriters, cabaret and experimental theatre music, with after-show DJs.

Jazz on the Odra (Jazz nad Odrą) April ⓦ jazznad odra.pl. One of the great events of the European jazz calendar, featuring top international performers.

New Horizons (Nowe Horyzonty) July–Aug ⓦ nowehoryzonty.pl. International art-film festival with screenings in a variery of ambient, open-air locations.

Wratislavia Cantans Sept ⓦ wratislaviacantans. pl. Oratorios and cantatas, featuring specially commissoned works and choral groups from all over the world.

10

Church of Peace

pl. Pokoju • April–Oct Mon–Sat 9am–6pm, Sun 11.30am–6pm; Nov–March Sat 10am–3.30pm, Sun 11.30am–3.30pm • 10zł • ☎ 74 852 2814, ⓦ kosciolpokoju.pl

Set in a quiet walled close ten minutes' walk north of the main square, the **Church of Peace** (Kościół Pokoju) was built in the 1650s for the displaced Protestant congregation of the Church of St Stanislaw. Its name derives from the Peace of Westphalia of 1648, which brought to an end the morass of religious and dynastic conflicts known as the Thirty Years' War. The church was one of three that Silesia's Protestant minority were allowed to build following the cessation of hostilities – another of the three survives at Jawor (see page 386) – and the ruling Habsburg emperor demanded that it be built without stone or brick, without stone foundations or a church tower, and outside the town walls, but within range of the cannons. Thanks to the double two-tiered galleries, more than 3500 worshippers can be seated inside.

The church was sharply modified in the eighteenth century, as the Protestant community increased in influence after Silesia came under the rule of Prussia. A domed vestibule using the hitherto banned materials was added to the west end, and a baptistery to the east, while a picturesque group of **porches** serve as entrances to the private boxes of the most eminent citizens. At the same time, the church was beautified inside by the addition of a rich set of furnishings – pulpit, font, reredos and the large and small organs.

ARRIVAL AND DEPARTURE   ŚWIDNICA

By train Świdnica Miasto train station is a 5min walk west of the main square.
Destinations Jelenia Góra (8 daily; change at Jaworzyna Śląska; 2hr–2hr 45min); Rogoźnica (every 2hr; 40min); Wrocław (4 daily; 1hr 10min).
By bus The bus station is next to the train station.

Destinations Wałbrzych (hourly; 35min); Wrocław (minibuses every 10–30min; 1hr 15min).
Tourist information The tourist office is on the main square at ul. Wewnętrzna 2 (daily: May–Sept 10am–8pm; Oct–April 10am–6pm; ☎ 74 852 0290, ⓦ um.swidnica.pl).

ACCOMMODATION

Barokowy Zakątek pl. Pokoju 7 ☎ 0734 150 059, ⓦ kos ciolpokoju.pl/noclegi-barokowy-zakatek; map page 384. Right next to the Church of Peace in a half-timbered former schoolhouse, this six-room B&B offers a mix of old and new furnishings, with white walls establishing a meditative tone of seventeenth-century Protestant asceticism – it's all very tastefully done. 200zł

Hotel Fado ul. Marii Konopickiej 6 ☎ 074 666 6370, ⓦ hotelfado.eu; map page 384. One of the best places in town for a comfortable stay, thanks to crisply modern

en-suite rooms, a small but soothingly-lit swimming pool, decent breakfasts and an on-site sauna. 300zł

Zajazd Karczma Zagloba ul. Wrocławska 46 ☎ 74 851 2236, ⓦ zagloba.info; map page 384. Named after a Falstaffian seventeenth-century character from a Sienkiewicz novel, this is every inch the comfy traditional inn, complete with wooden beds, plumped-up pillows and exposed timber beams. The thematically-decorated restaurant downstairs serves up traditional Polish nosh. 200zł

10

EATING

Arkadia ul. Księcia Bolka Świdnickiego 4 ☎ 74 852 1225; map page 384. A couple of blocks northwest of the main square, this place does better-than-average food with a Hungarian slant; the goulash served in a traditional metal pot (45zł) will probably suffice for two. Daily lunch specials cost 15zł. Mon–Thurs & Sun 10am–10pm, Fri & Sat 10am–midnight.

Baroccafe pl. Pokoju 7 ☎ 534 065 609, ⓦ kosciolpokoju. pl/baroccafe; map page 384. Located in the former gatehouse of the Church of Peace, this is a cosy and atmospheric place with wooden furnishings and art on the walls. It's good for hot chocolate and cakes, while lunch

snacks include cold cheese-and-meat platters featuring local farm produce (20zł). There's also a lovely summer garden with a fountain. Daily 10am–11pm.

Rynek 43 Rynek 43 ☎ 74 856 8419, ⓦ rynek43.pl; map page 384. Situated on the ground floor of the town hall building, this minimalist white-cube restaurant (with a leafy courtyard in summer) serves up superbly prepared local food with a good mix of fowl, game and fish. There's a healthy handful of specialities that you don't often find elsewhere (carp soup 8zł; mushroom strudel 29zł), and the seasonal three-course set meals at 43zł are well worth a try. Desserts are exceptional. Daily noon–10pm.

The Church of Peace at Jawor

Park Pokoju 1, Jawor • April–Oct Mon–Sat 10am–5pm, Sun noon–5pm; Nov–March by appointment • 10zł • ☎ 516 493 990, ⓦ kosciolpokojujawor.pl • Trains run from Świdnica (every 2hr; 50min) via Rogoźnica (every 2hr; 10min) to Jawor station, from where it's a 5min walk to the church; alternatively, minibuses from Wrocław depart from the corner of ul. Joannitów & ul. Dawida, behind the bus station (hourly; 1hr 10min)

Some 35km northwest of Świdnica, the small town of **JAWOR** was formerly the capital of one of the independent Silesian duchies. Severely bashed up in World War II, the central square is now fairly modern and colourless, although it has retained its arcaded style. The town's one truly great monument is the barn-like, timber-framed **Church of Peace** (Kościół Pokoju) which, like its counterpart in Świdnica, was built following the Peace of Westphalia and according to the same strict conditions. Designed by the same engineer who worked on the Świdnica church and completed several years earlier, the church was cleverly laid out with four tiers of balconies in such a way that an enormous congregation could be packed into a relatively modest space.

Wałbrzych and around

An important transport hub on the Wrocław–Jelenia Góra rail line, the city of **WAŁBRZYCH** is a long, thin settlement that runs for some 8km along a wooded valley. The former coal capital of Lower Silesia, the city was blighted by mine closures in the late 1990s and became a by-word for post-industrial depression, but recent years have seen a complete turnaround in its fortunes: industrial-heritage tourism has taken off thanks to the **Stara Kopalnia** show mine and cultural centre; while the proximity of **Książ Castle** and the **Riese complex** of World War II-era tunnels has led to a boom in visitor numbers. Most importantly, the legend that a **Nazi Gold Train** (see page 387) lies secretly hidden beneath the hills has provided the city with bags of ready-made mystique.

Somewhere in the middle of Wałbrzych's 8km-long strip is a handsome **Old Town** consisting of two neat squares (plac Magistratski and the Rynek), although there's a lack of concrete sights here and most things of interest are a short bus ride to the north.

Stara Kopalnia

ul. Piotr Wysockiego 29 • Daily 10am–6pm; compulsory guided tours of the museum depart on the hour; English speakers are provided with an audio guide • Museum 20zł; art gallery free • ☎ 74 667 0970, ⓦ starakopalnia.pl

Opened in 2014, **Stara Kopalnia** ("The Old Mine") is a spectacular transformation of a former coal mine that now comprises mining museum, art gallery, concert hall and conference venue. Tours of the **mine museum** (frequently led by former mine workers)

THE WAŁBRZYCH GOLD TRAIN

Ever since the end of World War II, stories have circulated in the Wałbrzych region concerning a **gold-laden train**, hidden by retreating Nazis in the huge complex of tunnels that extends beneath the city and the neighbouring Owl Mountains. In the summer of 2015, two **treasure hunters** (the Polish Piotr Koper, and German Andreas Richter) claimed to have found evidence of the train's existence somewhere beneath the main Wałbrzych–Wrocław railway line, sparking a frenzy of media interest. The world's press descended on Wałbrzych looking for a story that subsequently turned out to be something of a red herring; after a year of talk, radar imaging and excavations, the researchers discovered precisely nothing. Wałbrzych, meanwhile, has extracted untold benefit from the surrounding aura of mystery, and tourism has risen enormously as a result.

Ultimately, there is such a huge network of unexplored tunnels in the Wałbrzych region that it remains perfectly reasonable to assume that there is something down there somewhere. The myth of the Gold Train, it seems, is set to run and run.

take in sections of the underground workings, along with the overground changing rooms, machine halls and social areas that made up a virtual mini-town servicing a workforce of several hundred. Also on display are the ceremonial uniforms worn by miners on special occasions – including Barbórka (St Barbara's Day) on December 4, when the patron of miners is honoured with solemn processions, followed by a lot of beer and singing. Included in the tour is a trip up the (modern) **lookout tower**, which provides great views of the surrounding hills. Contemporary exhibitions are held in Stara Kopalnia's **art gallery**, and frequent concerts take place in the yard.

ARRIVAL AND INFORMATION

WAŁBRZYCH

By train Wałbrzych has several train stations. Pending the construction of an integrated central bus and train station called "Wałbrzych Centrum" (at the time of writing still a building site), the most convenient station is Wałbrzych Fabryczny, 1km southwest of the Old Town along ul. Przemysłowa. Trains serving the southeast use Wałbrzych Główny, 4km south of the centre (connected by local buses #A and #6).

Destinations (from Wałbrzych Fabryczny) Jelenia Góra (hourly; 1hr); Wrocław (hourly; 1hr 20min).

Destinations (from Wałbrzych Główny) Głuszyca (6 daily; 20min); Kłodzko (Kłodzko Miasto: 3 daily; 1hr 35min; Kłodzko Główne: 6 daily; 1hr 15min); Kudowa Zdrój (4 daily; 2hr 40min).

By bus Buses and minibuses pick up and drop off on ul. Sikorskiego, 500m west of the Old Town.

Destinations Głuszyca (hourly; 30min); Kamienna Góra (hourly; 35min); Wrocław (1hr 30min; minibuses hourly; 1hr 15min).

From the Czech Republic Wałbrzych municipal transport bus #15 runs from Meziměstí train station on the Czech side of the border (accessible from Prague via Nachod) 4 times daily.

Tourist information The tourist office at Rynek 9 (daily 8am–4pm; ☏ 074 666 6068, ☏ cit.walbrzych.pl) is a great source of information on surrounding attractions.

ACCOMMODATION

Hotel Zamkowy Książ ul. Piastów Śląskich 1 ☏ 74 664 3890, ☏ hotelzamkowy.pl. Located in a trio of Książ Castle outbuildings (see page 388), this hotel offers old-school ruby-carpet and brown-cupboard en suites. Most are large, high-ceilinged affairs, and the hill-and-forest views are outstanding. **250zł**

★ **Stara Kopalnia** ul. Piotr Wysockiego 29 ☏ 74 667 0970, ☏ starakopalnia.pl. Neat, comfortable guest

rooms above the Stara Kopalnia reception building. It's a great place to stay, embracing post-industrial vistas of the centre's courtyard (lit up in changing colours at night), while still being within walking distance of the Old Town. Optional breakfast (25zł) in the *Café Sztygarówka* downstairs. **180zł**

EATING AND DRINKING

★ **Magiel Bar** pl. Magistracki 11 ☏ 7888 200 038, ☏ facebook.com/magielBAR. Cute café and lunch bar

that serves a well-rounded range of Polish staples and light Mediterranean dishes, including a legendary fish soup

10

(12zł). A great place for coffee too. Mon–Fri 10am–7pm, Sat noon–8pm.

Pasaż pl. Magistracki 8 ☎ 74 842 2946, ⓦ restauracja pasaz.pl. Welcoming basement restaurant with an Italian slant, serving serviceable pastas and pizzas in the 18–20zł range. The two-course weekday lunches (from 15zł) are not to be sniffed at. Daily 11am–10pm.

Zielona Sofa ul. Moniuszki 9 ☎ 663 166 040, ⓦ zielona sofa.pl. Perfect place for a daytime break with armchairs,

good coffee, hot chocolate and an exemplary apple pie (10zł). Daily 11am–10pm.

Złota Stacja ul. Rycerska 1 ☎ 74 847 0775, ⓦ zlota stacja.pl. Animated basement pub with craft beers and burgers. Named "Golden Station" in honour of the Gold Train (see page 387), it boasts a few quirky touches: the barkeepers are dressed like station staff, while the menu is listed above the bar in the form of a train departure board. Daily noon–midnight.

Książ Castle

12km west of Świdnica, just off the road to Wałbrzych • April, May, Sept & Oct Mon–Fri 9am–5pm, Sat & Sun 9am–6pm; June–Aug daily 9am–6pm; Nov–March Mon–Fri 10am–3pm, Sat & Sun 10am–4pm • Compulsory guided tour 39zł • ☎ 74 664 3872, ⓦ ksiaz.walbrzych. pl • Bus #8 from Wałbrzych (every 30min–1hr) goes right to the castle gates

One of the best-preserved castles in Silesia – and the largest hilltop fortress in the country – is to be found at **KSIĄŻ**, 8km north of Wałbrzych. The **castle** is well worth visiting for its setting alone, perched on a rocky promontory surrounded on three sides by the River Pełcznica, and tightly girdled by a belt of ornamental gardens. Despite a disparity of styles taking in practically everything from the thirteenth-century Romanesque of Duke Bolko I's original fortress to idealized twentieth-century extensions (Książ served as an HQ for both the German Wehrmacht and the Soviet Red Army), it's an impressive sight.

The tour takes in some of the beautifully restored palace interiors, including some of the oldest, Renaissance-period halls, as well as the **Maximilian Hall**, a glittering example of palatial Baroque. Things wind up with a visit to parts of the castle used by the German Wehrmacht in World War II, including sections of tunnel running under the castle. The castle's most famous inhabitant was **Princess Daisy von Pless**, an English-born aristocrat who died in Wałbrzych in 1943. As an outsider who became a local celebrity, Princess Daisy is one of the few personalities from Silesian history who continues to be cherished by both the Poles who came to live here after 1945 and the Germans who left at the same time. There's a local history foundation devoted to her legacy (ⓦ facebook.com/Fundacja.Daisy).

The Riese underground complex

Between November 1943 and the end of the World War II, the German Wehrmacht built a huge **underground complex** in the remote Góry Sowie ("Owl Mountains") near the town of Głuszyca, 15km southwest of Wałbrzych. Using prisoner labour supplied by the nearby Gross-Rosen concentration camp and its sub-camps, 213,000 cubic metres of bomb-proof tunnels and halls were carved out of the rocks under the code-name **Riese** ("giant"). The removal of all machines and documents by the retreating Germans and invading Soviets means that even today the ultimate purpose of the underground facilities is unclear, although it seems likely that it was intended as a bombardment-proof base for Hitler's high command and a secret manufacturing base for rockets and other experimental weapons. The project certainly had a top-priority status, requiring 28,000 prisoners to work on it; in 1944, it was allocated more concrete than all the civilian air-raid shelters constructed in Germany that year. Construction came to a halt in March 1945 when the area fell to the Red Army. The Soviet (and subsequently Polish) authorities ransacked the Riese complex for machinery but didn't map the entire tunnel system or keep proper records. It's believed that many more tunnels lie undiscovered – which is why stories of a Nazi Gold Train (see page 387) buried hereabouts still enjoy credence.

Of the sections of the Riese complex currently open to tourists, **Osówka** and **Walim** are the most impressive. The underground tunnels maintain a year-round temperature of 5–7°C, so bring warm clothing.

Osówka

ul. Świerkowa 29d, Sierpnica, 4km east of Głuszyca • Tours depart hourly, daily: March–Oct 10am–5pm; Nov–Feb 10am–4pm • 90min tour 18zł • ☎ 74 845 6220, Ⓦ osowka.pl

The **Osówka visitor centre** organizes various **guided tours** of the complex, most popular of which is the ninety-minute historical tour. There are several longer tours involving a bit more walking and step-climbing; see the website for details. Depending on the group size and guide, translations in English can be given; otherwise you need to book an English-language tour guide (an additional 120zł) in advance.

Walim Drifts: Rzeczka complex

ul. 3-ego Maja 26, Walim • May–Sept Mon–Fri 9am–6pm, Sat & Sun 9am–7pm; Oct–April Mon–Fri 9am–5pm, Sat & Sun 9am–6pm • 15zł • ☎ 74 845 7300, Ⓦ sztolnie.pl

On the other side of the mountain near **WALIM** is the smaller **Walim Drifts: Rzeczka complex** (Sztolnie Walimskie: Kompleks Rzeczka). The "drifts" are three parallel sloping shafts that lead into the hillside, towards large rock-hewn factory halls where slave-workers laboured – and frequently died. There's a model of a V2 rocket outside the entrance and a V1 inside, symbolizing one of the possible purposes of the Riese complex: a secret construction site for high-technology terror weapons.

ARRIVAL AND INFORMATION

By bus and train You can get to Głuszyca (for Osówka) from Wałbrzych by bus (10 daily; 35min) or train (from Wałbrzych Główny; 4 daily; 15min). There is no public transport to Walim.

RIESE UNDERGROUND COMPLEX

Tourist information The tourist office at ul. Grunwaldzka 20, Głuszyca (Mon–Fri 9am–4pm; April–Oct also Sat 9am–2pm; ☎ 74 845 6220), can help with accommodation and transport information to both complexes.

Jelenia Góra

Some 110km southwest of Wrocław, **JELENIA GÓRA** is the gateway to the Karkonosze (see page 392), one of Poland's most popular holiday and recreation areas. Its name means "Deer Mountain", but the rusticity this implies is scarcely reflected in the town itself, which has been a manufacturing centre for the past five centuries. Founded as a fortress in 1108 by King Bolesław the Wrymouth, Jelenia Góra came to prominence in the Middle Ages through glass and iron production, with high-quality textiles taking over as the cornerstone of its economy in the seventeenth century. Thankfully, Jelenia Góra's present-day factories have been confined to the peripheries, leaving the traffic-free historic centre remarkably well preserved.

Plac Ratuszowy and around

Jelenia Góra's **plac Ratuszowy** is one of Lower Silesia's most impressive market squares, its tall pastel-coloured mansions hovering above arcaded walkways. Occupying the familiar central position is the large mid-eighteenth-century **town hall**, its unpainted stonework providing an apposite foil to the colourful houses. To the east of plac Ratuszowy on plac Koscielny rises the slender belfry of the Gothic church of **Sts Elmo and Pancras** (Kosciól św. Erazma i Pankrackiego). Epitaphs to leading local families adorn the outer walls, while the inside is chock-full of Renaissance and Baroque furnishings.

Holy Cross Church

ul. 1 Maja • April–Oct Mon–Thurs 10am–6pm, Fri noon–4pm, Sat 10am–4pm • 4zł

Jelenia Góra's most imposing religious monument is the handsome, green-domed **Holy Cross Church** (Kościół św. Krzyża), built as a Protestant church – though it now serves a Catholic congregation – in the early eighteenth century on the model of St Catherine's in Stockholm. It is one of six "**Mercy Churches**" built for the Protestants of Silesia following the 1707 Peace of Altranstädt, when Charles XII of Sweden persuaded Emperor Joseph I of Austria to restore the religious rights of his Silesian subjects. The double-galleried **interior** is richly decorated with trompe l'oeil frescoes, and features an extravagant pulpit and an organ whose cluster of pipes appear to be held upright by carved figures. The grassy expanse surrounding the church was formerly the Protestant cemetery and is surrounded by **family chapels** which, following extensive restoration, constitute a wonderful outdoor gallery of late Baroque sculpture. Typically for the funerary art of the period, many of the memorials feature carved skulls, skeletons and decomposing bodies – this is how all earthly vanity ends up, seems to be the message.

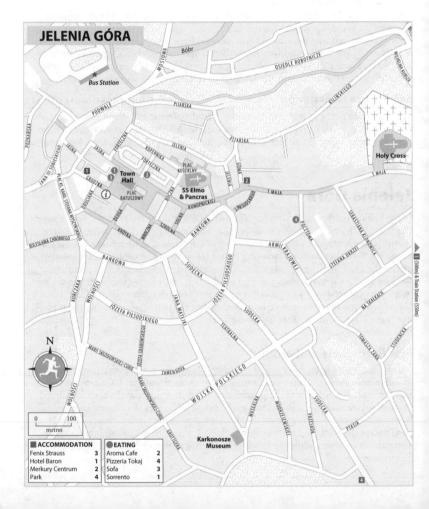

■ ACCOMMODATION		● EATING	
Fenix Strauss	3	Aroma Cafe	2
Hotel Baron	1	Pizzeria Tokaj	4
Merkury Centrum	2	Sofa	3
Park	4	Sorrento	1

Karkonosze Museum

ul. Jana Matejki 28 • Tues–Sun 9am–5pm • 10zł; free on Wed • ☎ 75 645 5071, ⓦ muzeumkarkonoskie.pl

South of the centre, just below the wooded Kościuszki Hill, the **Karkonosze Museum** (Muzeum Karkonoskie) is a small but superbly designed display, which starts with an entire pre-World War I cottage rebuilt in the museum lobby. The ethnographic section strikes the right balance between didacticism and sheer seductive colour – indeed, it's a shame that the embroidered Lower Silesian bonnets on show here are no longer in fashion. The first floor is given over to the history of **glass** from antiquity to the present day, with due emphasis on local examples and a particularly impressive twentieth-century section.

10

ARRIVAL AND INFORMATION

JELENIA GÓRA

By train Trains arrive at the station at the east end of ul. 1 Maja, about a 15min walk from the centre.
Destinations Świdnica (6 daily; change at Jaworzyna Śląska; 2hr 30min); Szklarska Poręba (7 daily; 50min); Wałbrzych (hourly; 1hr); Wrocław (15 daily; 2hr 20min).
By bus Jelenia Góra bus station is just northwest of the Rynek, behind a shopping mall on ul. Obrońców Pokoju.

Destinations Kamienna Góra (5 daily; 1hr); Karpacz (every 30min; 40min); Szklarska Poręba (hourly; 55min); Wrocław (hourly; 2hr).
Tourist information The tourist office at pl. Ratuszowy 6/7 (daily: June–Sept 8am–8pm; Oct–May 9am–5pm; ☎ 075 767 6925, ⓦ citik.jeleniagora.pl) offers a wealth of advice on tourism throughout the Karkonosze region.

ACCOMMODATION

Because there are plentiful buses to the nearby mountain resorts of Karpacz (see page 393) and Szklarska Poręba (see page 392), Jelenia Góra makes a canny alternative and excellent base for the Karkonosze, especially in summer and winter peak periods when those towns can be uncomfortably overcrowded.

Fenix Strauss ul. 1 Maja 88 ☎ 75 641 6600, ⓦ hotel strauss.com; map page 390. Reasonably large rooms in a well-maintained nineteenth-century building, conveniently placed for the train station (near enough for you to hear the bing-bang-bongs of the platform anouncements, although they won't keep you awake at night). 200zł
Hotel Baron ul. Grodzka 4-5 ☎ 75 752 3351, ⓦ hotel baron.pl; map page 390. Intimate and rather charming hotel just off the main square with a mix of en-suite rooms, some with muted decor, others rather loud. Decent buffet breakfast spread. 240zł

Merkury Centrum ul. 1 Maja 5 ☎ 75 718 5793, ⓦ merkurycentrum.eu; map page 390. An almost-boutique hotel offering neat, bright rooms, some displaying ancient exposed stonework, in an attractively restored historic house (if one excuses the pizza franchise occupying the ground floor). Good breakfast, and all-day access to tea and coffee. 230zł
Park ul. Sudecka 42 ☎ 75 752 4525, ⓦ camping. karkonosz.pl; map page 390. Clean en-suite rooms and year-round camping facilities at this site, located by a main road on the way out of town. Camping 43zł, doubles 125zł

EATING

★ **Aroma Cafe** pl. Ratuszowy 22 ☎ 508 147 841; map page 390. One of several excellent coffee shops in town, *Aroma* gets the nod because of its carefully selected single-origin coffees, great selection of world teas and revitalizing summertime smoothies (12zł). There's outdoor seating under the arcades. Mon–Fri 8am–8pm, Sat 10am–6pm, Sun noon–6pm.
Pizzeria Tokaj ul. Pocztowa 6 ☎ 75 752 4564, ⓦ tokaj bar.com.pl; map page 390. Great little pizzeria which doubles up as a locals' drinking den with a rock vibe, selling local brews. Daily 1pm–midnight.
Sofa pl. Ratuszowy 13/14 ☎ 75 742 3851, ⓦ sofa.jgora.

pl; map page 390. A big list of burgers (18–20zł) and a smattering of Mediterranean fare feature on the menu of this place, which has a terrace on the square and is an equally popular choice for an evening beer. Mon–Fri lunchtime specials are 15zł. Mon–Thurs & Sun 10am–11pm, Fri & Sat 10am–1am.
Sorrento pl. Ratuszowy 15–17 ☎ 75 765 0055, ⓦ sorrento.pl; map page 390. Italian restaurant with a superior Mediterranean menu featuring plenty of pasta and pizza but also a good selection of seafood – mussels in garlic sauce are recommended. Most mains are 30–40zł. Mon–Thurs & Sun 10am–10pm, Fri & Sat 10am–midnight.

10

The Karkonosze

The mountains of the **Karkonosze** are the highest and best-known part of the chain known as the Sudety, which stretches 300km northwest from the smaller Beskid range, forming a natural border between Silesia and Bohemia. Known for its raw climate, the predominantly granite Karkonosze range rises abruptly on the Polish side, and its lower slopes are heavily forested with fir, beech, birch and pine. At around 1100m, these trees give way to dwarf mountain pines and alpine plants, some of them endemic to the region. Primarily renowned as **hiking** country, these moody, mist-shrouded mountains strongly stirred the German Romantic imagination and were hauntingly depicted by the greatest artist of the movement, Caspar David Friedrich.

The upper reaches of the Karkonosze have been designated a **national park**, and trails are well-maintained. The two sprawling resorts of **Szklarska Poręba** and **Karpacz** make good bases from which to embark on hiking expeditions.

ESSENTIALS

Tickets Entry to the national park (ⓦ kpnmab.pl) costs 5zł per day; tickets are sold at booths at the major trailheads in both Szklarska and Karpacz.
Maps The 1:25,000 map of the park, available from kiosks and tourist information offices (see page 393), shows all the paths and viewpoints and is a must if you intend doing any serious walking.

Weather Like all mountain areas, the Karkonosze range has changeable weather; take warm clothing, even on a sunny summer's day, and plenty of water. Mist and clouds hang around on about three hundred days in the year; in such circumstances stick to the marked paths and don't expect to see much.

Szklarska Poręba

SZKLARSKA PORĘBA lies 18km southwest of Jelenia Góra, just to the west of a major international road crossing into the Czech Republic. On the way into town the main road passes through the Kamienna river gorge, and you can stop off to see the **Szklarka waterfall**, situated a short walk from the road in a beautiful canyon setting.

The River Kamienna slices Szklarska Poręba in two, with the main streets in the valley and the rest of the town rising high into the hills on each side. It's well worth following the stream all the way through the built-up part of the resort, as there's a picturesque stretch on the far side of the centre, with some striking **rock formations**, the Kruce Skalny, towering above the southern bank.

Szrenica

Chairlift: late April to mid-Oct & Dec–early April daily 8am–4pm • 31zł return • From the bus station, follow ul. 1 Maja, then turn right into ul. Turystyczna, continuing along all the way to the end

The quickest way from town up to the summits is on the Szrenica **chairlift**, which goes up in two stages and terminates a short walk from the summit of **Szrenica** (1,362m). From the top of the lift, you can walk back down following the red trail to the tourist office or the green and then blue trails to the eastern end of town. More ambitiously, follow the ridge east to the sister peak of Śnieżka and the resort of Karpacz beneath it (see page 393), a good day's walking.

Hauptmann House

ul. 11 Listopada 23 • Tues–Sun 9am–4pm • 6zł • ☏ 75 717 2611

Over on the northern side of town, the **Hauptmann House** (Dom Hauptmannów) has photographs and manuscripts of the German novelist and playwright Gerhard Hauptmann, one of the many artists and writers who spent their holidays in Szklarska at the close of the nineteenth century. It was here that Hauptmann wrote much of *The Weavers*, a drama of Silesian industrial life that helped bag the Nobel Prize for Literature in 1912.

| **ARRIVAL AND INFORMATION** | **SZKLARSKA PORĘBA** |

By train The main train station, Szklarska Poręba Gorna, is a cute half-timbered building on a hillside just north of the centre.
Destinations Jelenia Góra (7 daily; 55min); Liberec (Czech Republic; 3 daily; 1hr 50min); Wrocław (6 daily; 3hr 30min).
By bus The bus terminus is at the eastern entrance to the resort. There are regular buses to Jelenia Góra (hourly; 55min).
Tourist information The tourist office is at ul. Jedności Narodowej 1a (June–Aug & mid-Dec to mid-March Mon–Fri 8am–6pm, Sat & Sun 9am–5pm; rest of year Mon–Fri 8am–4pm, Sat 9am–5pm; ☎75 754 7740, ⓦszklarskaporeba.pl).

ACCOMMODATION AND EATING | **10**

As you'd expect, Szklarska Poręba has a great variety of accommodation. The Almar travel agency at ul. Jednosci Narodowej 6 (☎75 717 2123, ⓦbtalmar.pl) can fix up **pension** accommodation (160zł), including some worthwhile half-board deals. There's a cluster of inexpensive **snack huts** at the foot of the Szrenica chairlift; otherwise the central ul. Jedności Narodowej and ul. 1 Maja offer the main concentration of places to eat.

Camping Pod Mostem ul. Gimnazijalna 5 ☎75 717 306. The most convenient campsite in town, situated just west of the bus station. Its central location means you sacrifice peace and quiet, but the facilities are fine and it's good value. **45zł**
Hotel and Sound Bossa Nova ul. Kilińskiego 14 ☎75 761 5980, ⓦbossanova.pl. Lovely pre-World War I villa set in its own grounds, offering thoroughly modernized rooms with a subtly retro feel to the furnishings and fittings. **330zł**
Hotel Szrenicowy Dwór ul. Wzgórze Paderewskiego 12 ☎75 717 3461, ⓦhotelszrenicowydwor.pl. Certainly one of the best-looking hotels in Szklarska Poręba, this Gothic-turreted place is perched on a hill above the town. Rooms (featuring classic furniture and tasteful decor) and service are both top-notch, and there are large grounds with parking. The elegant restaurant serves Polish cuisine with a bit of classic French finesse (mains 40–60zł). Restaurant noon–10pm. **260zł**

Pensjonat Kanion ul. 1 Maja 18a ☎604 279 007, ⓦpensjonatkanion.pl. Modern building with smart, soothingly-decorated en-suite rooms and a ground-floor restaurant that opts for a middle way between Polish and Italian cuisine – with decent soups, pizzas (from 27zł) and baked *pierogi*. Restaurant noon–9pm. **300zł**
Pensjonat Trans ul. Turystyczna 21 ☎505 441 677, ⓦpensjonattrans.eu. Early twentieth-century building harbouring modern en-suite rooms in warm colours. It's ideally situated for walking routes and ski lifts, and the breakfast buffet is generous. **280zł**
Restauracja Kaprys ul. Jedności Narodowej 12 ☎793 117 179, ⓦkaprys-szklarska.pl. A pleasant place on the main street, with a relaxed vibe, a plant-filled interior and a large terrace at the back looking over the river. The menu runs from spicy tiger prawns (40zł) to some serious steaks (70–80zł). Mon–Thurs & Sun 10am–10pm, Fri & Sat noon–midnight.

Karpacz and around

KARPACZ, 15km south of Jelenia Góra, is an even more scattered community than Szklarska Poręba, occupying an enormous area for somewhere with only a few thousand permanent inhabitants. It's a fairly characterless place if the centre of town is all you see, but the sheer range of easily accessible hikes in the neighbouring mountains make this the most versatile of Silesia's highland resorts.

Karpacz is a long, thin settlement built along the main road, **ulica 3 Maja** (ulica Karkonoska in its upper reaches), which stretches and curves uphill for 5km. Most tourist facilities are located in **Karpacz Dolny** (Lower Karpacz), at the lower, eastern end of the resort, although **Karpacz Górny** (Upper Karpacz), up the valley to the west, has its fair share of hotels and pensions. In between lies the **Biały Jar** roundabout, which is the main starting point for most of the hiking trails (see page 394).

Wang Chapel

ul. na Śnieżkę 8 • Mid-April to Oct Mon–Sat 9am–6pm, Sun 11.30am–6pm; Nov to mid-April Mon–Sat 9am–5pm, Sun 11.30am–5pm • 8zł • ☎75 752 8290, ⓦwang.com.pl

Located in the upper reaches of Karpacz Górny is the most famous, not to say curious, building in the Karkonosze – the **Wang Chapel** (Świątynia Wang). Girdled at a discreet distance by souvenir stalls and snack bars, this twelfth-century wooden church with Romanesque touches boasts some wonderfully refined carving on its portals and capitals,

10

HIKES FROM KARPACZ

From Karpacz's Biały Jar roundabout, it's a twenty-minute walk to the lower station of the **Kopa chairlift** (daily: April–Nov 8.30am–5pm; Dec–March 8.30am–4pm; return 35zł), which leads up towards Kopa (1377m), just forty minutes from the Karkonosz's high point of Śnieżka (see below). A short detour west from the bottom lift station takes you to the upper of two **waterfalls** on the River Łomnica, which rises high in the mountains and flows all the way through Karpacz, defining much of the northern boundary of the town, as well as the course of ulica Konstytucji 3 Maja, which follows a largely parallel line. The second waterfall, below Biały Jar on a path waymarked in red, is less idyllic, having been altered to form a dam.

TO ŚNIEŻKA SUMMIT

The most popular goal for most walkers is the summit of Śnieżka, at 1602m the highest peak in the range and sometimes covered with snow for up to six months of the year. Lying almost due south of Karpacz, it can be reached by the **black trail** in about three hours from the Biały Jar roundabout, or in about forty minutes if you pick up the trail at the top of the Kopa chairlift. From the chairlift you pass through the Kocioł Łomniczki, where the abundant vegetation includes Carpathian birch, cloves, alpine roses and monk's hood. Access to the actual summit is by either the steep and stony "**Zigzag Way**" (the red trail) which ascends by the most direct method, or the easier "**Jubilee Way**" (the blue route), which goes round the northern and eastern sides of the summit.

At the top is a large modern weather station-cum-snack bar, where you can get cheap hot **meals**; refreshments are also available in the refuges on Kopa and *Pod Śnieżką*, and at the junction of the two trails. On a clear day, the **view** from Śnieżka stretches for 80km, embracing not only other parts of the Sudety chain in Poland and the Czech Republic, but also the Lausitz mountains in Germany.

GLACIAL LAKES AND ROCK FORMATIONS

Once at the summit, it's worth following the red trail immediately to the west above two glacial **lakes**, Mały Staw and Wielki Staw, just above the tree line. Assuming you don't want to continue on to Szklarska Poręba, you can then descend by the blue trail, which brings you out at Karpacz Górny. If you're feeling energetic you might like to go a bit further along the red trail and check out the Słonecznik and the Pielgrzymy **rock formations**, thereafter descending by the yellow and later blue trails back to Karpacz Górny. If the above routes seem too strenuous, a satisfyingly easy alternative is to take the blue trail from Karpacz Górny to the *Samotnia* refuge on the shore of Mały Staw, a round trip taking about three hours.

as well as an exterior of tiny wooden tiles. It stood for nearly six hundred years in Vang village in southern Norway, but by 1840 it had fallen into such a state of disrepair that the parishioners sought a buyer for it. Having failed to interest any Norwegians, they sold it to one of the most enthusiastic architectural conservationists of the day, King Friedrich Wilhelm IV of Prussia. He had the church dismantled and shipped to this isolated spot, where it was reassembled. The chapel is still used on Sunday mornings for Protestant worship; there are also organ recitals on alternate Sundays in summer.

Toy Museum

ul. Karkonoska 5 • Tues–Fri 9am–4.30pm, Sat & Sun 10am–5.30pm • 10zł • ☎ 75 761 8523, Ⓦ muzeumzabawek.pl

A couple of kilometres downhill from the Wang Chapel, above the Biały Jar roundabout, the **Toy Museum** (Muzeum Zabawek) is as much a tribute to local crafts as to the history of playthings, with a host of wood-carved animals, carriages and sleds.

Museum of Sport and Tourism

ul. Kopernika 2 • Tues–Sun 9am–5pm • 8zł • ☎ 75 761 9652, Ⓦ muzeumsportu.org

Down in Karpacz Dolny, just east of the main strip, the **Museum of Sport and Tourism** (Muzeum Sportu i Turystyki) has an enjoyable selection of archaic bobsleighs and crampons and, upstairs, a room full of lace, carved furniture and traditional dress.

ARRIVAL AND INFORMATION

By bus Most buses terminate at Biały Jar roundabout (picking up and dropping off at numerous stops along ul. 3 Maja on the way), although some continue all the way to Karpacz Górny.

Destinations Jelenia Góra (every 30min; 40min); Wrocław (1 daily; 3hr).

Tourist office The office at ul. Konstytucji 3 Maja 25 (daily 10am–6pm; ☎75 761 8605, ⓦkarpacz.pl) sells hiking maps and can help you find a bed in one of Karpacz's innumerable private rooms or pensions.

Karkonosze National Park Information Centre Housed in a lovely wooden house on high ground south of the centre, the park information centre at ul. Leśna 9 (Centrum Informacyjne Karkonoszkiego Parku Narodowego; Tues–Sun 9am–4pm; ☎75 700 0008, ⓦcikpn.kpnmab.pl) provides advice, sells maps and has a fascinating geology exhibition and a medicinal herb garden.

10

ACCOMMODATION

Hostel Krokus ul. Grzybowa 7 ☎515 970 980, ⓦkrokus.batur.pl. Attractive half-timbered villa with a garden, offering bright dorms, a couple of private rooms, plenty of social space and a big kitchen. Dorms __35zł__, doubles __90zł__

Hotel Gołebiewski ul. Karkonoska 14 ☎75 767 0741, ⓦgolebiewski.pl. Looking something like the *The Shining's* Overlook Hotel, this is as incongruous as anything you'll see in Karkonose. With 900 rooms it's the biggest hotel in Poland and the third biggest in Europe; five restaurants, three bars, a nightclub, gym, pool and children's play-area make it a family magnet, while its many business suites and meeting rooms will attract the suits. Bring a credit card. __500zł__

Pensjonat pod 5 ul.Kamienna 5 ☎882 753 300, ⓦrestauracjakarpacz.pl. On a hillside in the upper part of the resort towards the Wang Chapel, this timber-built meadow-side house offers simply but stylishly furnished doubles and triples, most with beautiful mountain views. The popular restaurant on the ground floor concentrates on familiar Polish flavours, but does it very well. __250zł__

Pensjonat Safir ul. Turystyczna 1a ☎516 983 675, ⓦsafir.karpacz.pl. Attractive three-storey house set against a wooded hillside a 10min walk west of the village centre. Rooms are bright with wooden floors, and the buffet breakfast is generous. __250zł__

★ **Rezydencja** ul. Parkowa 6 ☎75 761 8020, ⓦhotel rezydencja.pl. Handsome nineteenth-century villa in Karpacz Dolny, whose understated plushness makes it one of the most comfortable places to stay in town. Spa, bar and restaurant all help make it a top choice. __300zł__

EATING AND DRINKING

Bistro Aurora ul. Konstytucji 3 Maja 45 ☎75 761 6314, ⓦaurora.karpacz.pl. This communist-themed place feels a bit like dining in a museum (and might come across as rather tasteless to those who don't find Soviet totalitarianism particularly funny), with busts of Lenin and Stalin and various other Cold War-era memorabilia on show. Thankfully, the quality of the food is a few notches higher than what was on offer back then: Polish staples with some Russian specialities like *pielmieni* (stuffed little dumplings) and *blini* (small thick pancakes). Pretty much everything is priced under 30zł. Daily 11am–10pm.

U Ducha Gór ul. Olimpijska 6 ☎75 761 8563, ⓦkarpatka.com.pl. A rustic timber cottage with a folksy pine-log interior and grassy terrace, "In the Spirit of the Mountains" is a good place for Polish highland dishes such as *golonka* (roast pork knuckle), ribs and mountain trout. Mains 35–45zł. Daily 11am–10pm.

Wysące Tarasy ul. Konstitucji 3 Maja 23c ☎722 138 977. The "Hanging Gardens" offers excellent mountain views with deckchairs spread out on the terrace in summer. The menu focuses on Polish classics in decent-sized portions, with mains clocking in under 40zł. Daily noon–8pm.

The Kłodzko Region

Due south of Wrocław is a rural area of wooded hills, gentle valleys and curative springs known as the **Kłodzko Region** (Ziemia Kłodzka) after its largest town. It's surrounded on three sides by the Czech Republic, with the Sudety mountains forming a natural frontier. A sense of subtle grandeur prevails in the region's cluster of **spa resorts** (identified by the suffix *-zdrój*), which were fashionable throughout the nineteenth century among aristocrats and intellectuals from all over Europe. In the hills above the towns are some fine **hiking routes** passing through some dramatically bizarre rocky landscapes, especially in the **Table Mountains** above the health resort of Kudowa Zdrój. The southeast of the area is taken up by the **Śnieżnik Massif**, characterized by dark forest ridges and smooth, bare mountain tops.

Kłodzko

Spread out beneath the ramparts of a stolid Prussian fortress, the thousand-year-old town of **KŁODZKO** was for centuries a place of strategic importance. Situated on the main trade route between Bohemia and Poland, Kłodzko's ownership fluctuated between the adjacent nations until the eighteenth-century Prussian takeover. Today, its Old Town retains some of the charm of its medieval origins.

Plac Bolesława Chobrego and around

The Old Town's sloping main square, **plac Bolesława Chrobrego**, has a number of fine old houses from various periods, a grand nineteenth-century town hall and an ornate Baroque fountain which looks up to the fortress's walls. At its eastern side, Wita Stwosza leads south to the main survivor of the town's medieval fortifications, the Gothic **St John's bridge** (Most św. Jana). The oldest of its kind in Poland, it was adorned in the Baroque period by a collection of sacred statues which look pleadingly heavenward.

Kłodzko Regional Museum

ul. Łukasiewicza 4 • Tues–Sun: May–Sept 11am–5pm; Oct–April 10am–4pm • 8zł; free on Sat • ☎ 74 867 3570, ⓦ muzeum.klodzko.pl

The **Kłodzko Regional Museum** (Muzeum Ziemi Kłodzkiej) has a large collection of local glassware and an exhaustive assembly of more than four hundred **clocks** from the Świedbodzia and Srebrna Góra clock factories. The display features everything from ancient astronomical devices, working grandfather and irritating cuckoo clocks, to porcelain-backed kitchen clocks.

Underground passageway

ul. Zawiszy Czarnego • Daily: April–Oct 9am–6pm; Nov–March 9am–3pm • 12zł • ☎ 74 873 6477, ⓦ podziemia.klodzko.pl

Just east of the regional museum is the northern aperture of a 600m-long **underground passageway** (*podziemna trasa*), passing under the Old Town and emerging near Kłodzko Fortress. There are various instruments of torture to see along the way, including miniature French guillotines and even more barbaric Prussian methods of execution.

Kłodzko Fortress

ul. Grodzisko 1 • Daily: April–Oct 9am–6pm; Nov–March 9am–3pm; individual tourists will need to wait to join a guided tour of the fortress (roughly 1hr 30min) or tunnels (1hr); tours are in Polish unless English is reserved in advance • Fortress 12zł; tunnels 12zł; combined ticket 18zł; tunnels not recommended for children under 5 • ☎ 74 867 3468, ⓦ twierdza.klodzko.pl

Greatly extended by the Prussians in the eighteenth century from earlier defensive structures built on the rocky knoll, the squat **Kłodzko Fortress** (Twierdza Kłodzka) lost its reputation for impregnability when captured by the all-conquering army of Napoleon in 1807. Guides in seventeenth-century costume lead visitors around the upper part of the fortress, passing a number of audio-visual displays and allowing plenty of time to savour the panoramic views from the ramparts. Visitors can also descend into the stronghold's extensive **tunnels**, which were excavated by prisoners of war during the Prussian era.

ARRIVAL AND DEPARTURE

By train Kłodzko Miasto station is only a few minutes' walk east from the centre. Kłodzko Główne station, an inconvenient 2km to the north, handles additional trains to Wałbrzych (6 daily; 1hr 15min).

Destinations (from Kłodzko Miasto) Kudowa Zdrój (6 daily; 1hr 15min); Świdnica (3 daily; 2hr); Wałbrzych (3 daily; 1hr 40min); Wrocław (7 daily; 1hr 45min).

By bus Kłodzko's bus station is right next to Kłodzko Miasto train station.

Destinations Kudowa-Zdrój (hourly; 1hr 10min); Lądek-Zdrój (hourly; 50min); Międzygórze (5 daily; 1hr 20min); Wambierzyce (4 daily; 50min).

INFORMATION

Tourist information The tourist office is at the entrance to the tunnels below the fortress at ul. Czeska 24 (daily: April–Oct 9am–6pm; Nov–March 9am–3pm; ☎74 865 4689, ⓦ centrum.klodzko.pl).

PTTK You can buy local hiking maps at the PTTK office, ul. Wita Stwosza 1 (Mon–Fri 9am–3pm; ☎74 867 3740, ⓦ klodzko.pttk.pl).

ACCOMMODATION AND EATING

There's not a great choice of **accommodation** in town, so you're best advised to head for one of the spa resorts, such as Kudowa-Zdrój, if you're going to be staying in this part of Silesia for any length of time. For drinking, there's a handful of **beer gardens** on and around the main square in fine weather.

★ **Bar Dobrze** pl. Bolesława Chrobrego 32 ☎602 354 654, ⓦ facebook.com/BarDobrze. For good food at a reasonable price there are few places better than *Bar Dobrze*, an unpretentious daytime restaurant on the main square which puts together a daily menu, based on what's fresh, of local Silesian dishes with a contemporary-European twist; daily specials cost about 20zł. Daily 10.30am–5pm.

Casa D'Oro ul. Grottgera 7 ☎74 867 0216, ⓦ casadoro. com.pl. The best of Kłodzko's hotels, offering decent-sized en-suite rooms of a high standard in a nice old building between the station and the Old Town. The restaurant

downstairs serves hearty Polish fare (mains 30–40zł). Restaurant daily 11am–10pm. 180zł

Korona ul. Noworudzka 1 ☎74 867 3737, ⓦ hotel-korona.pl. Northwest of the town centre, this hotel may look dour on the outside but has cheerful little en-suite rooms inside. The pleasant wooden-beamed restaurant serves everything from pork ribs to lasagne, with mains in the 30–40zł region. Restaurant daily noon–10pm. 180zł

W Ratuszu pl. Bolesława Chrobrego 3 ☎74 865 8145, ⓦ wratuszu.pl. In the centre of the Rynek under the town hall, this is the place to go for a slap-up Polish meal. Mains hover around the 40zł mark. Daily noon–11pm.

Wambierzyce

Heading west from Kłodzko on the main road to Prague are a string of spa towns. The first of these, Polanica-Zdrój, is not in itself worth the detour, but a right turn at the west end of town leads 9km to the village of **WAMBIERZYCE**, a tiny rural settlement which is the site of huge religious institution.

The basilica

Daily 7am–7pm • ☎ 887 155 155, ⓦ wambierzyce.pl

Wambierzyce's Baroque **basilica**, perched above a broad flight of steps above the village square, has been the site of pilgrimages since 1218, when a blind man allegedly regained his sight by praying at a statue of the Virgin Mary enshrined in a lime tree. The impressive monumental facade of the basilica is all that remains of the third shrine built here at the end of the seventeenth century; the main body of the building collapsed soon after completion, at which point it was rebuilt with the interior you see today. The basilica is circumvented by a broad ambulatory with a variety of chapels and grottoes representing the Stations of the Cross and biblical scenes. Inside, the oval chancel has a cupola illustrating the fifteen Mysteries of the Rosary with a magnificent silver tabernacle from Venice bearing the miraculous image, accompanied by a profusion of votive offerings encased at its side.

Calvary

Moving Crib open daily: May–Sept 9am–6pm; Oct–April 10am–4pm • 8zł • ☎ 74 871 9197, ⓦ wambierzyce.pl

Found all around the village are nearly one hundred **shrines** depicting further scenes from the Passion, culminating at **Calvary**, the wooded hill facing the basilica, which is reached by a long series of steps also lined by shrines. At the foot of the hill is the wonderful **Moving Crib** (Ruchoma Szopka), a room with eight clockwork mechanical contraptions from the nineteenth century; hundreds of moving figures in miniature theatre sets present biblical scenes, some of them rather gruesome, as well as local themes such as coal mining.

By bus Kłodzko–Polanica–Radków buses pass through Wambierzyce four times a day (50min from Kłodzko).

Kudowa-Zdrój and around

Nestling at the foot of the Table Mountains some 40km west of Kłodzko, the border town of **KUDOWA-ZDRÓJ** is one of the most popular health resorts anywhere in Poland. Patronized by the internationally rich and famous in the nineteenth century, it's nowadays an appealing under-commercialized place which has preserved plentiful helpings of charm. A decent choice of accommodation and proximity to the mountains help to make Kudowa-Zdrój the best place to base yourself in the region.

Spa park

Grand old villas set in their own grounds give Kudowa its aristocratic air, yet it has no obvious centre other than the **spa park**. Here the huge domed **pump room** (*pijalnia*) houses the venerated marble fountain from which issue hot and cold springs. Nearby stalls cash in on visitors' health worries, selling the pipe-like *kóbki*, small flattened jugs with swan-necked spouts, from which the surprisingly refreshing water – slightly sweet and carbonated and allegedly good against obesity, fatigue and general weakness – is traditionally drunk.

Toy Museum

ul. Zdrojowa 46b • Daily: May–Sept 9am–6pm; Oct–April 10am–5pm • 12zł • ☎ 74 866 4970, ⓦ muzeum-zabawek.pl

Occupying a building on the south side of the spa park, the **Toy Museum** (Muzeum Zabawek) is a hands-off history of playthings through the ages. Absolutely fascinating for adults, but less rewarding for small kids, it harbours some wonderful examples of antique soft toys, train sets and costumed dolls.

Chapel of Skulls

1.5km north of Kudowa-Zdrój; follow ul. Moniuszki through the park and keep going • Tues–Sun: May–Sept 9.30am–5.15pm; Oct–April 10am–3.45pm • 5zł • ⓦ czermna.pl

Twenty minutes' walk north of town, the outlying hamlet of **CZERMNA** is host to the macabre **Chapel of Skulls** (Kaplica Czaszek). Its walls and ceiling are decorated with more than three thousand skulls and crossed bones from the dead of various wars and epidemics, amassed during the last decades of the eighteenth century by the chapel's priest, with the help of his devoted grave-digger. Their own remains are set in a glass case by the altar, and thousands more skulls are stashed in the crypt. Ossuaries are common in central Europe, often based on the belief that having one's bones stored in a suitably holy site will increase the chances of enjoying a favourable afterlife.

Museum of the Sudeten Foothills

5km north of Kudowa-Zdrój • May–Oct daily 10am–6pm • 7zł • No public transport

A walkable 3km north of Czermna, the village of **Pstrążna** plays host to an enjoyable open-air ethnographic collection, the **Museum of the Sudeten Foothills** (Muzeum Kultury Ludowej Pogórza Sudeckiego), with a wide-ranging collection of vernacular buildings from local villages. Among the more curious of these are the wooden, bell-topped watchtowers that used to be a feature of many a village, warning the local inhabitants of fire or avalanche danger.

By bus Buses drop you on ul. 1 Maja on the eastern side of the town centre.

Destinations Karłów (May–Sept 5 daily; 20min); Kłodzko (hourly; 1hr 10min); Náchod (Czech Republic; every 2hr;

25min); Wrocław (5 daily; 2hr 45min).

By train The train station, 2km south of the centre just off the main Kłodzko road, is unstaffed – buy tickets from the conductor.

Destinations Kłodzko (6 daily; 1hr 15min); Wałbrzych (4 daily; 2hr 40min); Wrocław (2 daily; 3hr 30min).

Tourist information The tourist office is in the centre of town at ul. Zdrojowa 44 (May–Sept Mon–Fri 9am–6pm, Sat 9am–5pm, Sun 10am–3pm; Oct–April Mon–Fri 9am–5pm, Sat 10am–1pm; ☏ 74 866 1387, ⦿ kudowa.pl).

ACCOMMODATION

Villa Pod gwiazdami ul. Słowackiego 4 ☏ 74 866 3603, ⦿ podgwiazdami.wkudowie.pl. Small boutique hotel just south of the centre, nicely done up in Art Deco style and equipped with a mini-spa. **190zł**

★ **Willa Lawenda** ul. Słoneczna 12 ☏ 784 075 125, ⦿ lawenda.com. Lovely brick-and-timber house with a lovely garden and cosy en suites with electric kettles. There

are some nice family rooms with wooden beams on the top floor. **180zł**

Willa Sanssouci ul. Buczka 3 ☏ 74 866 1350, ⦿ sanssouci-dauc.pl. Set back from the main street, this nineteenth-century villa contains thirty spacious en-suite rooms, including some handy triples and quads. There's a pretty back garden with gazebo and parking. **180zł**

EATING AND DRINKING

Ania ul. Zdrojowa 42 ☏ 74 866 12 28. This central place beside the tourist office serves up cheap Polish snacks, and some delicious desserts. Daily 9am–7pm.

★ **Café Sissi** Park Zdrojowy ☏ 728 404 880. Elegant café in the spa park with white-shirted waiting staff, all manner of hard-to-resist cakes and sweets, and a few cute tricks (such as teas and juices served in jam-jars). Open

10am–10pm.

W Starym Młynie ul. Fredry 10 ☏ 74 8663 601, ⦿ wstarymmlynia.com.pl. Set in attractive grounds, "In the Old Mill" features interesting variations on traditional Polish dishes, and is a great place to sample locally-caught trout and salmon. Mains cost around 30–40zł. Daily 1–10pm.

The Table Mountains

Rising above 900m and almost as flat as their name suggests, the **Table Mountains** (Góry Stołowe; ⦿ pngs.com.pl) boast some extraordinary rock formations, most of which can be accessed in a full day's walk from Kudowa. If you want to tackle Szczeliniec Wielki or the Stone Mushrooms without walking all the way from Kudowa, consider catching a shared taxi or a seasonal bus as far as Karłów, and starting from there.

The Erratic Rocks and Szczeliniec Wielki

The easiest way to access the area is to head northeastwards from the village of Pstrążna (see page 398), 5km north of Kudowa-Zdrój, picking up the well-signed **green trail**. This leads to the first of several fantastic rock formations in the range, the **Erratic Rocks** (Błędne Skały), where the trail twists and turns, squirming through narrow gaps between gigantic rocks. It then continues via Pasterka to the village of **Karłów**, from where a climb of nearly seven hundred steps leads to the **Szczeliniec Wielki**, the highest point in the range at 919m. Here the rocks have been weathered into a series of irregular shapes and are named after camels, elephants, and so on. There's a small entrance fee once you get to the top (daily 9am–6pm; 7zł), where a café offers refreshments, then you follow the trail that goes down through a deep chasm, on to a viewpoint and back by a different route.

The Stone Mushrooms

From the Erratic Rocks, the **red trail** leads directly to Karłów, continuing east 5km to the largest and most scattered group of rocks in the area, the **Stone Mushrooms** (Skalne Grzyby), rocks whose bases were worn away by uneven erosion producing the top-heavy appearance their name suggests.

Międzygórze and the Śnieżnik Massif

At the southeastern corner of the Kłodzko region is the enticing **Śnieżnik Massif** (Masyw Śnieżnika), which, unlike the overrun Karkonosze to the west, seems to be

10

THE ŚNIEŻNIK MASSIF AND THE BEAR'S CAVE

A signpost at Międzygórze's main junction indicates the many marked hiking routes in the area. One particularly good walk follows the **red trail**, which rises steeply through lovely wooded countryside for about two hours, leading to the *Na Śnieżniku* **refuge** (☎74 813 5130), an isolated PTTK hostel which offers dorm beds for 15zł per person and also serves inexpensive homely meals. From here it's then a much gentler ascent to the flat summit of **Śnieżnik** (1425m), the highest point in the Kłodzko region, set right on the Czech border.

From the summit it's worth descending north by the **yellow trail** towards the village of Kletno, which will bring you in about an hour to the **Bear's Cave** (Jaskinia Niedźwiedzia), which takes its name from the bear fossils found when the cave was discovered in 1966 during quarrying. Around 600m of the cave can be explored on a Polish-language **guided tour** (Feb–April & Sept–Nov Tues, Wed & Fri–Sun 10am–4.40pm; May–Aug Tues–Sun 9am–4.40pm; 40min; 25zł; advance booking advised; ☎74 814 1250, ⓦjaskinianiedzwiedzia. pl), on which you can see the usual wondrous stalactites and stalagmites. You can also get to the cave directly from Międzygórze in about two hours by following the red trail (see above) and then branching off northwards after a couple of kilometres when you see signs to the Bear's Cave and Kletno. The cave is also accessible by car via Kletno.

---

gratifyingly ignored by the crowds. The main jumping-off point is the charming hill resort of **MIĘDZYGÓRZE** ("among the hills"), 30km southeast of Kłodzko – well worth a couple of days' stay if rustic peace and hiking opportunities are what you need. The village is characterized by the **wooden villas** (*drzewnianki*) built to serve as rest homes at the beginning of the nineteenth century; ramshackle affairs with carved balustrades, neo-Gothic turrets and creaky interiors, they're still in use as tourist accommodation today.

Built around a central T-junction, Międzygórze is easy to find your way around. Five minutes' walk west of the junction, steps descend from the *Nad Wodospadem* hotel to a 27m-high **waterfall**, surrounded by deep forest. On the far side of the waterfall paths ascend towards the **Fantasy Garden** (Ogród Bajek) about twenty minutes away, a hilltop garden designed by local forester Izydor Kriesten before World War II. It's an attractive spot consisting of huts constructed from roots, branches and cones, each of which is inhabited by an assemblage of gnomes and model animals. Overlooking the village centre, the charming **St Joseph's Church** (św. Jozefa), a Baroque-style wooden building from 1742, has a lovely balconied interior which can be visited on Sundays after morning Mass.

ARRIVAL AND DEPARTURE   MIEDZYGÓRZE

By bus Międzygórze is served by five buses a day from Kłodzko (1hr 20min).

ACCOMMODATION AND EATING

Alpejski Dwór ul. Sanatoryjna 13 ☎505 280 324, ⓦalpejskidwor.pl. Much-restored Tyrolean-style chalet with cosy en-suite rooms and a popular rustic restaurant serving excellent local trout and game. Restaurant daily 1–9pm. __200zł__

Pizzeria Wilczy Dol ul. Sanatoryjna 9 ☎74 813 5286. A laid-back café with graffiti-style decor, simple snacks and

alternative music. Outdoor gigs are sometimes organized in summer. May–Sept daily noon–8pm.

Willa Trebla ul. Sanatoryjna 9 ☎516 916 805, ⓦwilla trebla.pl. This romantic nineteenth-century guesthouse, complete with spindly carved balustrades, is one of the most photogenic buildings in Międzygórze. The modern en-suite rooms come with beautiful woodland views. __500zł__

Lądek Zdroj and around

The waters of **LĄDEK-ZDRÓJ**, situated in a forested bowl 25km east of Kłodzko, have been exploited for their healing properties since at least the fifteenth century, and in later years attracted visitors as august as Goethe and Turgenev. Today the town, strung out along the Biała Lądecka river, retains a charm that other spa resorts in the area cannot match, though many buildings are still rather run-down. The renovated **main square** features a gaggle of pastel-coloured Baroque houses facing the octagonal tower of the town hall.

Wojciech Spa

Mon–Sat 6.30am–9pm, Sun 7.30am–9pm • Pump room free; Turkish bath 24zł for 30min • ☎ 74 811 5474, ⓦ uzdrowisko-ladek.pl.

Centrepiece of the **spa park** at the east end of town is the recently restored **Wojciech Spa** (Zdrój Wojciech), a handsomely domed Neobaroque building built directly above the hot-water springs. Visit the **pump room** to knock back a glass of the healing waters – good for strengthening bones, improving cholesterol levels and generally keeping you young and sprightly – or take a dip in the **Turkish Bath** (24zł), beautifully decorated with brightly-coloured ceramic tiles.

10

The Golden Mountains

Immediately to the east of the town, the **Golden Mountains** (Góry Złote) offer some good hiking routes. Check out the blue trail which leads southeast of the town, ascending within an hour to a ruined medieval castle near the summit of **Karpień** (776m), via a series of oddly weathered rocks of the type so often found throughout the region.

ARRIVAL AND INFORMATION

LĄDEK-ZDRÓJ

By bus The hourly bus from Kłodzko (50min) represents the only public transport in and out of town.

Tourist information The tourist office is in the centre at pl. Staromłyński 5 (Mon–Fri 8am–4pm, Sat 10am–2pm; ☎ 74 814 6245, ⓦ ladek.pl); it can point you in the direction of locals renting out rooms.

ACCOMMODATION AND EATING

Hotel Alhambra ul. Przechodnia 7 ☎ 74 631 7024, ⓦ alhambra.pl. A stately Neoclassical structure in the centre of Lądek Zdroj featuring serene rooms in neutral colours and a much-patronized ground-floor café and restaurant. Guest deals with nearby spa centres and swimming pools are available. The *Alchemia* restaurant has a small but well-chosen menu of quality local fare, usually with a decent vegetarian option among the mains (25–35zł). Restaurant Mon–Thurs & Sun 1–8pm, Fri & Sat 1–9pm. **300zł**

Rezydencja Grawert ul. Lipowa 4 ☎ 74 814 6079, ⓦ rezydencjagrawert.pl. Snug rooms in an elegant nineteenth-century villa, complete with retro furnishings and colourful reproduction wallpaper and textiles. The hotel's restaurant, *Londyn* (complete with Victorian-London thematic touches), concentrates on Polish favourites presented in style, with roast duck (55zł) and baked trout (35zł) among the stand-outs. Restaurant daily noon–9pm. **300zł**

Wielko-polska

ULICA TUMSKA, GNIEZNO

Wielkopolska

Halfway between Warsaw and Berlin, the gently undulating landscape of Wielkopolska may not offer much drama, but its human story is an altogether different matter, as its name – "Greater Poland" – implies. This area has been inhabited continuously since prehistoric times, and it was here that the Polish nation first took shape. The name of the province, and of Poland itself, derives from a Slav tribe called the Polonians, whose leaders – the Piast family – were to rule the country for five centuries.

11

Regional capital **Poznań** is one of Poland's great cities, the famously stately architecture of its main square serving as a fine backdrop to a wealth of up-to-date museums, a booming bistro scene and a don't-stop-till-you-drop attitude to nightlife. Just beyond the Poznań city limits are two of Poland's finest former aristocratic residences at **Kórnik** and **Rogalin**, the latter set in a famously leafy landscaped park. Both lie near the boundaries of the **Wielkopolska National Park**, a gently unulating area of lakes and forest which epitomizes the region's glaciated landscape.

The main city south of Poznań is **Zielona Góra**, a handsome historical centre that stands in the middle of Poland's one genuinely productive wine-making region. Zielona Góra serves as the gateway to **Wolsztyn**, a cute lakeside town that's also famous for being the site of one of the last few working steam locomotive depots in Europe; and Żagań, original location of the daring World War II prisoner-of-war breakout known as the "Great Escape". East of Poznań, **Gniezno** is home to a historic cathedral and remains an important archiespiscopal city, while relics of the early medieval period can be seen at mysterious **Lake Lednica**.

Poznań

Thanks to its position on the Berlin–Warsaw rail line, **POZNAŃ** is many visitors' first taste of Poland. In many ways it's the ideal introduction, as no other city is more closely identified with Polish nationhood. The inscription on the oldest surviving depiction of the town, *Posnania elegans Poloniae civitas* ("Poznań, a beautiful city in Poland"), has been adopted as a local catchphrase to highlight the city's unswerving loyalty to the national cause over the centuries. Nowadays, it's a place of great diversity, encompassing an animated centre focused on one of Europe's finest squares; a tranquil cathedral quarter; and a dynamic business district whose trade fairs are the most important in the country. Poznań may be a big city, but most of its primary attractions are grouped in a central core. A number of fine museums and a wealth of nightlife opportunities ensure that a few days are well spent here.

Poznań is also a good base from which to explore the region's other key attractions, with regular trains running to the Wielkopolska National Park, Gniezno and beyond.

MAIN SQUARE, POZNAŃ

Highlights

❶ Main square, Poznań One of Poland's classic public spaces, featuring fine buildings from all epochs and ringed by great places to eat and drink. See page 407

❷ Śródka neighbourhood, Poznań Home to the fantastic new Brama Poznania multimedia museum, the little suburb of Śródka boasts a handful of fabulous bistros and a celebrated street mural. See page 415

❸ Rogalin Palace One of Central Europe's great palaces, presiding over a lush park filled with ancient oaks. See page 419

❹ Wolsztyn Hop aboard a locomotive at one of Europe's few surviving steam-engine depots to still run regular passenger services to nearby towns. See page 423

❺ Stalag Luft III, Żagań A dignified museum commemorates the camp – and mass break-out – that inspired the Hollywood movie The Great Escape. See page 424

❻ Gniezno For centuries the seat of Poland's archbishops, this easy-going provincial town is still the site of a truly wonderful cathedral. See page 426

❼ Lake Lednica Visit one of the country's largest skansens or take a boat to Ostrów Lednicki to see the seat of the first Polish king. See page 429

HIGHLIGHTS ARE MARKED ON THE MAP ON PAGE 406

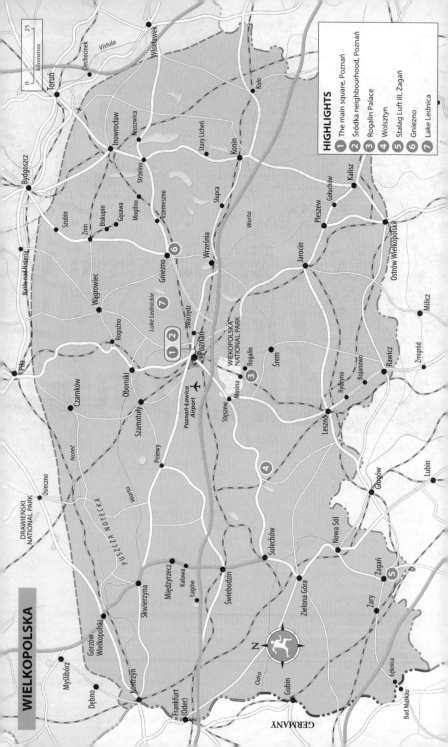

Brief history

In the ninth century the Polonians founded a castle on a strategically significant island in the River Warta, and in 968 Mieszko I made this one of the two main centres of his duchy, and the seat of its first bishop. The settlement that developed here was given the name **Ostrów Tumski** (Cathedral Island), which it still retains.

Although initially overshadowed by Gniezno, Poznań did not follow the latter's decline after the court moved to Kraków in the mid-thirteenth century. Instead, it became the undisputed capital of Wielkopolska and the main bastion of Poland's western border. Poznań's prosperity soared as it profited from the fifteenth-century decline of both the Teutonic Order and the Hanseatic League, and the city became a key junction of European trade routes as well as a leading centre of learning.

Regression set in with the ruinous Swedish Wars of the seventeenth century. Revival of sorts came during the Partitions period, when Poznań became the Prussian city of Posen, and shared in the wealth of the Industrial Revolution. It also consolidated its reputation as a rallying point for **Polish nationalism**, resisting Bismarck's Germanization policy and playing an active role in the independence movements. An uprising in December 1918 finally forced out the German occupiers, ensuring that Poznań would become part of the resurrected Polish state.

Poznań's rapid expansion during the interwar period has been followed by accelerated growth, with it doubling in population to its present level of 580,000, and spreading onto the east bank of the Warta. The city's association with the struggle against foreign hegemony – this time Russian – was again demonstrated by the **food riots** of 1956 (see page 413), which were crushed at a cost of 74 lives. Nowdays, as well as being a vibrant **university town**, Poznań is a brash, self-confident commercial centre which, with a relatively high standard of living, sems to epitomize Poland's post-communist progress.

The main square and around

For seven centuries the distinguished **main square** (Stary Rynek) has been the hub of life in Poznań. Badly damaged during World War II, it is now among the most attractive of Poland's rejuvenated old city centres, lined with a characterful mixture of facades, and at its best in the spring and summer months when pavement cafés crowd the cobblestones.

Archetypically Polish, the square's most important public buildings are sited in the middle, with the town hall in every way predominant. Running southwards from the town hall is a colourful line of buildings, once home of the market traders, many of whom sold their wares in the arcaded passageways on either side. The present structures date from the sixteenth century and are the oldest in the square. Outside the town hall stands a fine Rococo **fountain**, alongside a copy of the **pillory** in its traditional location.

The town hall

Originally a two-storey Gothic brick structure, the **town hall** (Ratusz) was radically rebuilt in the 1550s. The arcaded eastern facade presents the building at its most vivacious, its lime-green pilasters framing a frieze of Polish monarchs, who are accompanied here by **portraits** of statesmen and poets from ancient Greece and Rome – a propagandist attempt to present Poland's rulers as the guardians of classical wisdom. Every day at noon, the effigies of two goats emerge onto the platform of the **clock** above the facade and butt their heads twelve times. This commemorates the local legend in which the two animals locked horns on the steps of the town hall, and thereby drew attention to a **fire** which had just begun there, so saving the city from a potentially disastrous conflagration. Other sides of the building are inscribed with the words of Polish Renaissance sages, to which post-World War II restorers were forced to add extracts from the communist constitution.

Museum of the History of Poznań

Stary Rynek 1 • Tues–Thurs 11am–5pm, Fri noon–9pm, Sat & Sun 11am–6pm • 7zł; free on Sat

The interior of the town hall houses the **Museum of the History of Poznań** (Muzeum Historii Miasta Poznania), though the main reason for entering is to see the building itself. Surviving from the Gothic period, the vaulted **cellars** were transformed into a prison in the sixteenth century; they now contain the earliest objects in the display, notably the medieval pillory and items excavated on Ostrów Tumski. However, the

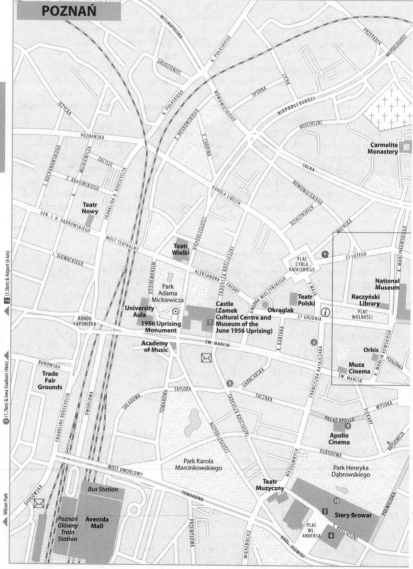

POZNAŃ

most impressive room is the Renaissance **great hall** (*wielka sień*) on the first floor, dating from 1555. Its coffered vault bears polychrome bas-reliefs which embody the exemplary civic duties and virtues through scenes from the lives of Samson, King David and Hercules. The southern section by the staircase depicts astrological and bestial figures, while the marble busts of Roman emperors around the walls are reminders of the weighty tradition of municipal leadership.

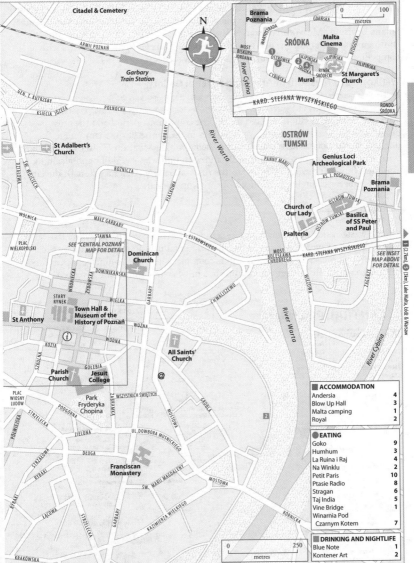

■ ACCOMMODATION	
Andersia	4
Blow Up Hall	3
Malta camping	1
Royal	2

● EATING	
Goko	9
Humhum	3
La Ruina i Raj	4
Na Winklu	2
Petit Paris	10
Ptasie Radio	8
Stragan	6
Taj India	5
Vine Bridge	1
Winarnia Pod Czarnym Kotem	7

■ DRINKING AND NIGHTLIFE	
Blue Note	1
Kontener Art	2

The Weigh House

Immediately behind the western side of the town hall is the **Weigh House** (Waga Miejska), once the most important public building in this great trading centre; what you see today is a reproduction of the original, the work of architect Giovanni Battista Quadro of Lugano.

The Guardhouse: Museum of the Greater Poland Uprising

Stary Rynek 3 • Tues–Sat 10am–5pm, Sun 10am–8pm • 4zł; free on Sat • ☎ 61 851 7289, ⓦ wmn.poznan.pl

Tucked behind the western side of the town hall is the sternly Neoclassical **Guardhouse** (Odwach), an eighteenth-century pavilion that now houses the **Museum of the Greater Poland Uprising** (Muzeum Powstania Wielkopolskiego 1918–19). The museum commemorates the postwar uprising against the region's German authorities with a compelling mixtue of photos, uniforms and sound effects.

Wielkopolska Museum of Arms and Arsenał Gallery

Wielkopolska Museum of Arms Stary Rynek 9 • Tues–Thurs 11am–5pm, Fri noon–9pm, Sat & Sun 11am–6pm • 7zł; free on Sat • ⓦ mnp.art.pl • **Arsenał Gallery** Stary Rynek 6 • Tues–Sat 11am–6pm, Sun 10am–3pm • 3zł • ☎ 61 852 9502, ⓦ arsenal.art.pl

Two low concrete pavilions erected during the communist period add the only discordant notes to the ensemble of buildings in the centre of the main square. In one, the **Wielkopolska Museum of Arms** (Wielkopolskie Muzeum Wojskowe) vividly documents the arms development in Poland with uniforms, weapons and gleaming armour. The other pavilion is home to the **Arsenał Gallery** (Galeria Arsenał), the city's prime venue for changing exhibitions of contemporary art.

Działyński Palace

Stary Rynek 78

On the western side of the main square stands the massive green-and-white **Działyński Palace**, its imposing facade topped by a monumental pelican which cranes its neck down towards the square. Cultural soirées took place here in the nineteenth century, helping to keep Polish-language culture alive in what was a Prussian-governed city.

CENTRAL POZNAŃ

0 — 200 metres

■ **ACCOMMODATION**
Brovaria	4
Garden Boutique	1
Hill Inn	2
Melody Hostel	5
Rzymski	3

● **EATING**
Brovaria	2
Cocorico	3
Drukarnia	4
Ratuszova	1

■ **DRINKING AND NIGHTLIFE**
Cuba Libre	7	La Rambla Nova	5
Czarna Owca	8	Lot Chmiela	1
Dragon	2	Meskalina	4
Kriek Belgian Pub	6	Pod Minogą	3

HENRYK SIENKIEWICZ (1846–1916)

Outside Poland, **Henryk Sienkiewicz**'s reputation has rested largely on *Quo Vadis?* an epic on the early Christians in the decadent days of the Roman Empire, which won him the 1905 **Nobel Prize for Literature** and quickly became a favourite subject with movie moguls. Yet the huge popular success of this tended to overshadow the remainder of his colossal oeuvre, which marks him out as Poland's answer to Charles Dickens.

Born in the Podlasie region to a minor aristocratic family, Sienkiewicz began his career as a **journalist** and **short-story writer**. His major contribution to Polish literature was the reinvention of the **historical epic**, which he used to explore major themes of national identity. His vast trilogy *With Fire and Sword*, *The Deluge* and *Fire in the Steppe* (all published between 1884 and 1888) is set against the heroic backdrop of Poland's seventeenth-century wars with the Cossacks, Swedes and Turks. Historical realism, however, was sacrificed in favour of Sienkiewicz's own Catholic, nationalist, chivalrous and anti-intellectual outlook. *Quo Vadis?*, which followed the trilogy, was always regarded as a fable about the Poland's oppression under the Partitions, despite its ancient-Roman setting. Sienkiewicz's final epic, *The Teutonic Knights* (1900), dramatized the 1410 Battle of Grunwald, when the Poles, Lithuanians and their East European allies smashed the power of the Teutonic Order.

Always an important part of the curriculum in Polish schools, Sienkiewicz's work has also provided the Polish **film** industry with a rich seam of blockbuster material. Director Jerzy Hoffman filmed hugely popular adaptations of *The Deluge* and *Fire in the Steppe* in the 1960s and 1970s, and returned with a lavish big-screen version of *With Fire and Sword* in 1999. The latter was at the time the most expensive Polish film ever made, although it was soon surpassed by Jerzy Kawalerowicz's opulent remake of *Quo Vadis?* in 2001. Mervin Le Roy's 1951 **Hollywood version** of *Quo Vadis?* remains the best-remembered Sienkiewiz adaptation outside Poland. Although nominated for eight Oscars, it didn't win any on the night, outmanoevred by *An American in Paris*, *A Streetcar Named Desire* and *African Queen*.

11

Henryk Sienkiewicz Literature Museum
Stary Rynek 84 • Tues–Fri 9am–5pm, Sat 9am–4pm • 5zł • ☎ 61 852 2496

Just north of the Działyński Palace, the house at no. 84 was once home to Giovanni Battista Quadro – a statue of the architect, sketchbook in hand, occupies a niche in the facade. The building now houses the **Henryk Sienkiewicz Literature Museum** (Muzeum Literackie im. Henryka Sienkiewicza), dedicated to Poland's most celebrated novelist (see above). Despite Sienkiewicz having only a rather tenuous connection with Poznań – he penned a few short stories here – this is the most important museum dedicated to his life and works. Inside lies a well-presented words-and-pictures account of the author's life, accompanied by first editions of his works.

Archeology Museum
ul. Wodna 27 • Tues–Thurs 10am–4pm, Fri & Sat 10am–5pm, Sun noon–4pm • 8zł; free on Sat • ☎ 61 852 8251, ⓦ muzarp.poznan.pl

East of the main square is the **Górka Palace** (Pałac Górków), which still preserves its intricate Renaissance portico and sober inner courtyard. The mansion now houses the **Archeology Museum** (Muzeum Archeologiczne), which traces the history of the region in entertaining fashion, with a sequence of dioramas illustrating the daily life of Wielkopolska inhabitants from the time of the nomadic hunters all the way to the early feudal society of the seventh century. Poznań University's **archeological expeditions** abroad – notably to Egypt and Sudan – are documented with an absorbing display of artefacts.

Parish Church of St Mary Magdalena
ul. Gołębia 1 • 10am–7pm daily

Leading off from the southeast corner of the main square, ulica Świętosławska ends in a cluster of gloriously salmon-coloured former Jesuit buildings, the finest examples

THE POZNAŃ CODE-BREAKERS

In front of the Zamek Cultural Centre stands a monument covered in numbers, commemorating the three Poznań University graduates who probably did more than anyone else to bring an end to World War II by cracking the **Enigma encryption codes** used by the Germans for communications. The trio (Marian Rejewski, Henryk Zygalski and Jerzy Różycki) first broke the Enigma cypher in 1934, intelligence that was passed on to the French and British in 1939. In the West, the wartime breaking of Enigma was often treated as the sole achievement of British boffins based at Bletchley Park – although the construction of a Polish Memorial in the grounds of Bletchley Park Museum has gone some way to restore the balance.

of Baroque architecture in the city. The end of the street is closed by the facade of the **Parish Church of St Mary Magdalene** (Kościół Farny św. Marii Magdaleny), completed just forty years before the expulsion of the Jesuits in 1773. Its magnificently sombre interior has a painting over the high altar illustrating a legendary episode from the life of **St Stanisław**. Then a bishop, Stanisław was accused by King Bolesław the Generous of not having paid for a village he had incorporated into his territories. In order to prove his innocence, the saint resurrected the deceased former owner of the land to testify on his behalf.

The Royal Castle: Museum of Applied Arts

Góra Przemysła 1 • Tues–Thurs 9am–3pm, Fri noon–9pm, Sat & Sun 11am–6pm • 12zł; free on Sat • ⓦ mnp.art.pl

Rising just to the west of the Rynek is an arresting red-brick structure that looks like a medieval fortress reimagined by twentieth-century architects –which is more or less exactly what the **Royal Castle** (Zamek Królewski) actually is: the castle was built by Poznań-born thirteenth-century Piast ruler Przemysł II, then subsequently ruined, rebuilt, ruined, then rebuilt again in the modern era. Inside, the **Museum of Applied Arts** (Muzeum Sztuk Użytkowych) houses an engrossing collection of costumes, ceramics and textiles. One room is devoted to modern design, with Ettore Sotsass kitchen utensils and Philippe Starck furniture rubbing shoulders with an alluring Polish Smaragd television set from 1962. Take the **lift** to the top of the tower for a superb panorama of central Poznań. There's a small display devoted to the history of the Piast dynasty on the ground floor.

The National Museum in Poznań

al. Marcinkowskiego 9 • Tues–Thurs 9am–3pm, Fri noon–9pm, Sat & Sun 11am–6pm • 12zł; free on Sat • ☎ 61 851 5898, ⓦ mnp.art.pl

The **National Museum in Poznań** (Muzeum Narodowe w Poznaniu) contains one of the best collections of Polish and international art outside Warsaw. From the entrance in the contemporary north wing on aleja K. Marcinkowskiego, steps ascend through an extensive display of Polish art, featuring examples of virtually every **art movement** to have impacted on the country. Nineteenth-century symbolist Jacek Malczewski features prominently, with his distinctive spade-bearded countenance peering from numerous large-format canvases, in each of which his self-portrait is joined by a host of mystical and metaphorical characters. The Art Nouveau-esque **Młoda Polska movement** (see page 270) is represented by monumental Mehoffer pastels and touching family portraits by Stanisław Wyspiański. Further up, look out for some explosive 1950s abstract art from Maria Jarema as well as cartloads of stuff by Jerzy Nowosielski, whose enigmatic daubs made him postwar Poland's most highly priced artist.

   International art is housed in the older, south wing of the museum, where an impressive Italian section includes panels from Gothic and Renaissance altarpieces, and an extensive display of Flemish art contains works by Massys and Joos van Cleve. The Monet painting *Beach at Pourville*, stolen in 2000 and recovered ten years later, hangs in pride of place.

Plac Wolności and around

West from the National Museum is the elongated space of **plac Wolności**. Here stands another seminal centre of the fight to preserve Polish culture, the **Raczyński Library** (Biblioteka Raczyńskich), founded in the early nineteenth century to promote Polish-language learning and literature, and still functioning as a library. Architecturally, it's one of the most distinguished buildings in the city, erected in the 1820s in cool Neoclassical style.

Heading into the business and shopping thoroughfares that branch out west from plac Wolności, you shortly come to the **Teatr Polski**, a charming wedding-cake of a building at ulica 27 Grudnia, erected in the 1870s by voluntary contributions. Overlooking the busy junction at the end of the street is the **Okrąglak** or "Big Log", an imposing ten-storey cylinder built in the mid-1950s to house the city's main department store; it's now occupied by a bank.

The Castle: Zamek Cultural Centre and Museum of the June 1956 Uprising

ul. św. Marcin 80/82 • **Zamek Cultural Centre** ☎ 61 646 5272, ⓦ ckzamek.pl • **1956 Museum of the June 1956 Uprising** Tues–Sat 10am–5pm, Sun 10am–4pm • 8zł; free on Tues • ☎ 61 852 9464, ⓦ wmn.poznan.pl

Looming over the western end of the bustling ulica św. Marcin, the **castle** (zamek) was built in 1910 to accommodate the German Kaiser whenever he happened to be in town. It now provides a home for both the **Zamek Cultural Centre** (Centrum Kultury Zamek), offering a varied menu of theatre, film screenings and concerts, and the **Museum of the June 1956 Uprising** (Muzeum Powstania Poznańskiego – Czerwiec 1956), which honours those who took part in the first insurrection against Poland's communist regime. Featuring various real-life objects from the event, including arms, stretchers, a Soviet tank and various propaganda posters, the museum is one of the few places in town you can get a flavour of communist times in Poznań.

Stary Browar

ul. Półwiejska 32 • Mon–Sat 9am–9pm, Sun 10am–8pm • ⓦ starybrowar5050.com

It's not often that a shopping mall qualifies as a tourist sight in its own right, but Poznań's **Stary Browar** (Old Brewery) – a stunning combination of nineteenth-century red brick and contemporary glass and metal – very much lives up to the billing. The building began life as the Hugger brewery in 1844, closing in 1980 when production moved to the outskirts of the city, and was transformed into its current temple-of-consumerism state in 2002–04 by developer Grażyna Kulczyk. Kulczyk's original idea was that the Stary Browar should fulfil both commercial and artistic functions – not only is the architecture stunning both inside and out, but there's a collection of sculptures and installations strewn around the premises, and landscaped gardens at the lower level. The building is also the site of one of Poland's most daring hotels, *Blow Up Hall* (see page 416).

THE 1956 UPRISING MONUMENT

West of the castle in the Park Adama Mickiewicza, two huge crucifixes bound together with heavy rope form a **monument** to the victims of the Poznań **food riots** of June 1956, in which up to eighty people were killed. The riots – and their brutal suppression by the security forces – sent shockwaves through Polish society, resulting in the return to power of the reform-minded communist Władysław Gomułka. The lesson that workers' protests could make and break regimes was not lost on future generations, helping to precipitate the rise of **Solidarity** in 1980. It was during Solidarity's extraordinary period of power and influence in communist Poland – before the declaration of martial law in December 1981 – that the monument was unveiled, in June 1981, marking the 25th anniversary of the riots.

The Citadel

The northern stretches of the city centre are overlooked by the **Citadel** (Cytadela), a vast earthwork fortress built by the Prussians in the nineteenth century and subsequently pressed into service by the interwar Polish state as the linchpin of their western defenses. The scene of bitter fighting in both 1939 and 1945, it is now an extensive, partly wooded park, the southern slopes of which are occupied by a **memorial garden** in honour of the six thousand Russians and Poles who lost their lives here. A stairway just off the northern end of aleja Niepodległości leads uphill through the graves towards a huge **memorial** to the Red Army. A couple of hundred metres east of the stairway lies a small British and Commonwealth **cemetery**; interred here are POWs from both World Wars, including those shot after the "Great Escape" (see page 424), as well as airmen shot down over Poland between 1939 and 1945.

Museum of Arms

Tues–Sat 9am–4pm, Sun 10am–4pm · 8zł; free on Tues · ☎ 61 820 4503, ⓦ wmn.poznan.pl

One of the Citadel's red-brick bastions harbours the **Museum of Arms** (Muzeum Uzbrojenia), with a small but absorbing collection of uniforms and firearms, and a large outdoor display of tanks, artillery pieces and armoured cars.

"The Undiagnosed" sculpture

The midpoint of the park is marked by **Nierozpoznani** ("The Undiagnosed"), arguably the best-known piece of modern outdoor sculpture in Poland. The work of artist Magdalena Abakanowicz (1930–2017), this cast-iron army of 112 larger-than-life headless figures is a powerful metaphor for life and its pressures in the constantly on-the-move mass society of today.

Ostrów Tumski

Trams #4, #8 and #17

Just east of the city centre between the River Warta and its minor branch, the Cybina, **Ostrów Tumski** (Cathedral Island) is thought to be the oldest part of Poznań, where the first royal palace and cathedral were constructed some time in the tenth century. Still the site of the cathedral, it's an area of quiet streets lined by handsome eighteenth-century houses, largely populated by priests and monks.

The Basilica of Sts Peter and Paul

Ostrów Tumski 17 · Daily 10am–5pm · Cathedral free; crypt 4zł · ☎ 61 852 9642

Ostrów Tumski is still very much in the shadow of the **Basilica of Sts Peter and Paul** (Basylika św. Piotra i Pawła), a largely Gothic structure framed by a fine pair of Baroque spires. Highlight of the interior is the ornate **Golden Chapel** behind the altar, where parts of the sarcophagi of the first two Polish kings, Mieszko I and Bolesław the Brave, currently rest. The **crypt**, entered from below the northern tower, has been extensively excavated, uncovering the thousand-year-old foundations of the pre-Romanesque and Romanesque cathedrals which stood on the site – two models depict their probable appearance.

Genius Loci Archeological Park

ul. Ks. I. Posadzego 3 · Tues–Thurs 10am–4pm, Fri & Sat 10am–6pm, Sun 10am–3pm · 6zł; free on Sun · ☎ 61 852 2167, ⓦ muzarp.poznan.pl

North of the cathedral is the **Genius Loci Archeological Park**, a contemporary piece of brick-and-glass architecture built on top of recent archeological excavations that uncovered parts of Poznań's tenth-century walls. Glass floors allow you to peer down at the diggings, while films and touch-screen visuals help to place relics in their historical context. Genius Loci is also the venue for some fascinating temporary exhibitions delving into aspects of urban history.

Środka and Lake Malta

Trams #4, #8 and #17 to Rondo Środka

East of Ostrów Tumski lies **Środka**, a compact residential neighbourhood that finds itself on the cusp of fashionability due to the emergence of several quirky restaurants and cafés. It's the oldest part of the city apart from Ostrów Tumski itself, a fact referenced by the award-winning **mural** that covers a bulding on the corner of Rynek Środkecki and ulica Filipiński: entitled A Środka Tale with a Trumpeter on the Roof and a Cat in the Foreground, the colourful scene contains a jumble of the medieval and Baroque buildings that once characterized Środka – until the last of them were knocked down to make way for the Rondo Środka roundabout. Unveiled in 2015, the mural was designed by architect Radosław Barek and executed by local cultural organization Puenta.

Brama Poznania

ul. Gdanska 62 • Tues–Fri 10am–6pm, Sat & Sun 10am–7pm • 21zł • ☎ 61 647 7634, ⓦ bramapoznania.pl

A short stroll north of Środka (also accessible via footbridge from Ostrów Tumski), a striking, pale-grey cube of a building houses the **Brama Poznania** museum. There are no exhibits as such: the museum is basically a state-of-the-art storytelling exercise that employs projections, models, touch-screen displays and sound to conjure up the key moments of Wielkopolska history. The top-floor observation deck offers great views back towards the spires of Ostrów Tumski.

Lake Malta

Zoo ul. Krancowej 81 • Daily 9am–7pm • 18zł Mon–Fri, 24zł Sat & Sun • ☎ 61 870 9502, ⓦ zoo.poznan.pl • **Narrow-gauge rail line** Mid-May to mid-Sept 10am–7pm: Mon–Fri every hour, Sat & Sun every 30min • 6zł • Trams #4, #8 and #17 to Rondo Środka

The eastern end of Środka is dominated by the Rondo Środka traffic roundabout, the starting point for paths leading down to the western end of **Lake Malta** (Jezioro Maltańskie), the city's most popular summertime playground. This 2km-long stretch of water was built to accommodate rowing regattas and is surrounded by pleasant footpaths. At the eastern end of the lake a couple of grassy strands are equipped with bathing piers, alongside children's play areas and an all-weather toboggan run. Just beyond the lake's eastern shore is the sizeable, open-plan **zoo**. The **Maltanka narrow-gauge rail line** runs from Rondo Środka to the zoo, passing alongside the northern shore of the lake on the way.

ARRIVAL AND DEPARTURE   POZNAŃ

By air Poznań airport (☎ 61 849 2343, ⓦ airport-poznan. com.pl) is 7km west of the city. Bus #59 (every 20–30min; 30min; 4.60zł) runs to Poznań Główny train station between 5am and 11pm; outside these hours night bus #242 goes to Rondo Kaponera, near the station.

By train Poznań Główny train station is a striking contemporary building joined on to the Avenida shopping mall, 1.5km southwest of the old town. Tram #5 heads from here to al. Marcinkowskiego, 300m short of the main square; while tram #8 delivers you to pl. Ratajskiego in the western part of the downtown area.

Destinations Berlin (3 daily; 2hr 45min–3hr); Bydgoszcz (10 daily; 1hr 40min–2hr 30min); Gdańsk (4 daily; 3hr 45min); Gniezno (every 30min–1hr; 30–50min); Kraków (6 daily; 5–6hr); Łódź (4 daily; 4hr); Mosina (8 daily; 25min); Szczecin (12 daily; 2hr 30min); Toruń (6 daily; 1hr 30min–2hr 15min); Warsaw (10 daily; 3hr 30min–4hr); Wrocław (hourly; 2–3hr); Zielona Góra (8 daily; 1hr 30min–2hr); Wolsztyn (every 2hr; 2hr).

By bus The bus station, Dworzec autobusowy (ⓦ pks. poznan.pl), is directly beneath the ticket hall of Poznań Główny train station.

Destinations Gniezno (hourly; 1hr 15min); Kórnik (hourly; 30min).

GETTING AROUND

By tram and bus The city is well served by a dense and efficient network of tram and bus routes, with services running from about 5.30am until 10.45pm – after which infrequent night buses run on selected routes. Tickets (bought from kiosks or ticket machines at stops and inside vehicles) cost 3zł for a trip of 10min or under, or 4.60zł for a trip of 40min. If you are sticking around it pays to invest in a PEKA card, a pre-paid card that charges the user according to how many stops you travel; it can be bought from kiosks.

Taxis Euro Taxi (☎ 61 811 1111, ⓦ euro-taxi.com.pl); Hallo Taxi (☎ 61 19623, ⓦ hallotaxipoznan.pl).

INFORMATION

Tourist information The main tourist office is in the Arkadia building at ul. Ratajczaka 44 (Mon–Fri 10am–7pm, Sat 10am–5pm; ☎ 61 851 9645, ⌨ cim.poznan.pl); there's another branch at Stary Rynek 59/60 (May–Sept Mon–Fri 10am–8pm, Sat & Sun 10am–6pm; Oct–April Mon–Fri 10am–6pm, Sat & Sun 10am–5pm; ☎ 61 852 6156). Both offices hand out free maps and will help reserve hotel and hostel accommodation.

ACCOMMODATION

Poznań has a good range of accommodation, with hotels in all categories and a reasonable range of hostels too. Note that hotel rates can rise by an additional fifty percent or more during **trade fairs**, and Poznań can be fully booked during the four biggest fairs (late Jan, early April, late May and mid-Sept).

HOTELS

Andersia pl. Andersa 3 ☎ 61 667 8000, ⌨ andersia hotel.pl; map page 408. Top-end tower-block hotel offering luxury and style in abundance, with an indoor pool, spa, gym and well-appointed rooms, some with window-seat views of Stary Browar. There's a slinky bar and rather fine restaurant downstairs. 860zł

★ **Blow Up Hall 5050** ul. Kościuszki 42 ☎ 61 657 9980, ⌨ blowuphall5050.com; map page 408. Located inside the Stary Browar building (see page 413), *Blow Up* pushes the envelope with its avant-garde design and creative approach to customer service. Guests are given smart phones to enter rooms, complete transactions or call for service. The 22 rooms are all different; one includes a jacuzzi at the end of the bed. 600zł

Brovaria Stary Rynek 73/74 ☎ 61 858 6868, ⌨ brovaria. pl; map page 410. Popular boutique hotel right above the boutique brewery and restaurant (see page 416), offering spacious, cream-coloured rooms with all the creature comforts. Some rooms have views of the square. 350zł

Garden Boutique ul. Wroniecka 24 ☎ 61 222 2999, ⌨ gardenhotel.pl; map page 410. Homely, cosy and bang in the centre, this place offers great mid-range value for those who want to avoid the chain hotels. Rooms are a little chintzy, but are all individual, and service is great. 400zł

★ **Royal** ul. św. Marcin 71 ☎ 061 858 2300, ⌨ hotel-royal.com.pl; map page 408. Characterful renovated place with bags of charm, tucked into a quiet courtyard just off the main downtown street. The en-suite rooms are on the small side but are cosily furnished in warm colours. 300zł

Rzymski al. K. Marcinkowskiego 22 ☎ 061 852 8121, ⌨ hotelrzymski.pl; map page 410. Spruced-up hotel with a good restaurant, just a couple of minutes' walk from the main square. Doubles with shower are uninspiring but adequate, and there are also some plushed-up business-class rooms. 380zł

HOSTELS

★ **Hill Inn** ul. Zamkowa 1/2 ☎ 61 853 0910, ⌨ hillinn. pl; map page 410. Located in a nineteenth-century villa, this is the hostel to come to if you want the combined luxury of peace and quiet and a great location. Staff are attentive and friendly, and there's a good choice of singles, doubles (some of which are en suite) and four-person doorms. The first-floor patio is a great place to sit and people-watch. Dorms 40zł, doubles 120zł

★ **Melody** Stary Rynek 67 (entrance ul. Kozia 16) ☎ 61 851 6060, ⌨ melody-hostel.com; map page 410. A great option just off the main square, this musically-themed hostel has lots of character. It's decked out with old vinyl records and guitars, and each room has a different colour scheme depending on the style of music it's named after; the largest, the four-bed "Classical", is decorated with staves and an effigy of Mozart. Friendly service and cleanliness throughout make this a top choice. Dorms 50zł, doubles 160zł

CAMPSITES

Malta ul. Krańcowa 98 ☎ 61 876 6203, ⌨ camping malta.poznan.pl; tram #6 or #8 to ul. Warszawska, 600m north of the site (get off after passing the Novotel on your right); map page 408. Situated at the northeastern end of the eponymous lake, this campsite offers tent pitches as well as en-suite bungalows that are just as comfy (and expensive) as most downtown hotel rooms. Camping 65zł, bungalows 230zł

EATING

CITY CENTRE

Brovaria Stary Rynek 73–74 ☎ 61 858 6868, ⌨ brovaria.pl; map page 410. Poznań's very own microbrewery (which brews three main varieties: a pilsner, a honey beer and a wheat beer) has a huge restaurant attached, decked out in cool post-industrial style and serving some of the best meat and fish dishes in the city: pan-fried salmon weighs in at 48zł, pork tenderloin 38zł. Mon–Sat noon–11pm, Sun noon–10pm.

Cocorico ul. Świętosławska 9 ☎ 61 852 9529, ⌨ cocorico.pl; map page 410. An exceptionally relaxing café-restaurant, with twin rooms (one slightly more formal and old-fashioned than the other), serving everything from *croque monsieur* to an excellent fillet of cod with lentils (45zł). There's a great garden out back. Daily 10am–11pm.

Drukarnia ul. Podgórna 6 ☎61 850 1420, ⓦwinoi chleb.com; map page 410. This relatively new restaurant gets the mix of post-industrial decor and comfy intimacy just right. The menu ranges from burgers (29zł) to steaks (60–70zł), although some delicate pasta and fish dishes ensure that this is more than just an upmarket meaty grill. Daily 7am–10pm.

Goko ul. Ratajczaka 18 ☎61 639 0639, ⓦgoko.com.pl; map page 408. Arguably the best and most varied sushi option in town, with an impressively large number of mixed sets to choose from, plus some intriguing exercises in fusion (for example, bacon and plum sushi; 22zł for six pieces). The soups, tempura dishes and ice-cream desserts are not to be sniffed at, too. Mon–Sat noon–11pm, Sun noon–10pm.

★ **Petit Paris** ul. Półwiejska 42 ☎61 667 1555; map page 408. It may be in a shopping mall (the Stary Browar) but don't let that put you off; this ooh-la-la bakery excels when it comes to fresh-baked bread, croissants, eclairs and light-lunch fare such as baguette sandwiches and quiche. Mon–Sat 8am–9pm, Sun 9am–9pm.

★ **Ptasie Radio** ul. Kościuszki 74/3 ☎61 853 6451, ⓦptasieradio.pl; map page 408. A favourite with the arty elite, this sophisticated, cosy café occupies an upstairs room with distressed walls and birdcages hanging from the ceiling. The menu covers everything from breakfast and bruschettas to burgers and a small selection of Polish-Mediterranean mains (including pork tenderloin with beetroot puree for 35zł). Mon–Fri 9am–11pm, Sat 10am–11pm, Sun 10am–10pm.

Ratuszova Stary Rynek 55 ☎61 851 0513, ⓦratuszova. pl; map page 410. Imaginative variations of traditional Polish meals served below artfully decorated cellar vaults. This is a great place to try classy numbers like wild boar with dumplings (35zł), seabass with lentils (70zł) or steak cooked sous-vide (99zł). Daily noon–11pm.

Stragan ul. Ratajczaka 31 ☎789 233 965, ⓦfacebook. com/StraganKawiarnia; map page 408. Home to one of the best espressos in the city, this café serves aeropress, Chemex and other brews in a setting that looks more like a chemistry lab than a café. Scrambled-egg breakfasts, bagels and cakes settle the tummy rumbles. Daily 8am–9pm.

WEST OF THE CENTRE

Winarnia Pod Czarnym Kotem ul. Wolsztynska 1 ☎506 041 700, ⓦfacebook.com/poznanpodczarnym kotem; map page 408. This welcoming suburban wine bar a 20min walk from the centre draws dedicated diners thanks to its mix of global fusion mains (20–30zł) and Mediterranean tapas. Live gigs, open-air film screenings and a great choice of wine provide extra reasons to venture out this far. Daily 1pm–11.30pm.

ŚRÓDKA AND LAKE MALTA

Hum Hum ul. Ostrówek 15, Śródka ☎793 798 491; map page 408. Informal Lebanese café-restaurant with a scattering of benches and cushions. They specialize in hummus (the traditional kind, plus a few own-recipe variations), but also rustle up soups, Mediterranean salads and Middle Eastern mains such as kefta meatballs and chicken in pomegranate sauce. The "Lebanese Platter", featuring a generous mixture of everything, is well worth the 47zł shell-out. Daily noon–10pm.

La Ruina i Raj ul. Śródka 3, Śródka ☎666 152 555; map page 408. Characterful café run by folks who have travelled a lot and designed a menu around what they discovered on the road – Vietnamese baguette sandwiches, Thai curries and Moroccan tajine come particularly recommended. Mains are in the 30–40zł bracket, and there's also excellent coffee if you just want a quick break. Daily 11am–9pm.

Na Winklu ul. Śródka 1, Śródka ☎796 145 004, ⓦfacebook.com/NaWinklu; map page 408. The place to go for *pierogi*, especially the baked, crispy variety. Expect traditional stuffings and also a few Mediterranean-influenced variations, including a particularly tempting tomato and basil. The baked *pierogi* are big so don't order too many (three pieces 15–18zł; six-piece mix 23zł). They also do soups and salads. Daily noon–9pm.

Taj India ul. Wiankowa 3, Lake Malta ☎61 876 6249, ⓦtajindia.pl; map page 408. Tucked away at the far end of Lake Malta, this Indian-run restaurant is well worth a trip. Fine views of the lake from the balcony complement a great southern-Indian based menu (mains 30–40zł). Butter chicken and lamb *mughalai* are recommended. Daily noon–11pm.

Vine Bridge ul. Ostrówek 6, Śródka ☎61 875 0934, ⓦvinebridge.pl; map page 408. Once famous for having just three tables, *Vine Bridge* has since expanded but remains an intimate and unique little place, offering a creative blend of fresh regional products and modern European technique. Simple things like burgers and *pierogi* are turned into something imaginative and exquisite; main dishes (35–45zł) depend on what the chef has found at the market. Mon–Sat 4–11pm, Sun noon–8pm.

DRINKING AND NIGHTLIFE

Blue Note ul. Kościuszki 76/78 ⓦbluenote.poznan.pl; map page 408. Renowned jazz club underneath the castle, hosting frequent gigs (rock as well as jazz) and club nights. Tickets (15–80zł) can also be bought at the tourist office. Mon–Wed & Sun 7pm–midnight, Thurs–Sat 7pm–3am.

Cuba Libre ul. Wroclawska 21 ☎61 855 2344; map page 410. A Latin dance club popular with the student crowd, offering the best late-night party in town (0.5lt beer costs 8zł). Mon–Wed 9pm–3am, Thurs–Sat 9pm–5am, Sun 9pm–1am.

Czarna Owca ul. Jaskółcza 13 ☎502 287 755, ⓦfacebook.com/czarnaowcaclub; map page 410.

POZNAŃ'S FESTIVALS

Pride of place in the Poznań festival calendar goes to the **St John's Fair** (Jarmark Świętojański), a traditional knees-up of medieval origins, with handicraft stalls and folk-music performers taking over the main square in the days leading up to St John's Day (June 24). **St Martin's Day** (Nov 11) is marked by the mass-consumption of *rogale świętomarcińskie* – locally produced croissant-like pastries which can be bought in bakeries and food shops. Diversions of a different kind are provided by the **Malta Festival** (ⓦmalta-festival.pl) in late June, a celebration of contemporary theatre that also includes art exhibitions and outdoor gigs.

11

Welcoming warren of subterranean rooms just around the corner from the main square, with mainstream music and a hedonistic crowd. Mon–Wed & Sun 6pm–1am, Thurs–Sat 6pm–3am.

★ **Dragon** ul. Zamkowa 3 ☏61 853 0819, ⓦface book.com/klub.dragon.poznan; map page 410. This rambling pub with countless nooks and crannies, mix-and-match furniture and a buzzing beer garden is the chosen late-night hang-out of the city's artists, musicians and dreamers. Regular live music in the basement, anything from free jazz to freak folk. Mon–Thurs & Sun 10am–3am, Fri & Sat 10am–5am.

Kriek Belgian Pub ul. Wodna 23 ☏508 267 570, ⓦfacebook.com/kriek.poznan; map page 410. Cute, enjoyable place with a choice of 170 Belgian beers, several on tap. With so many to sample, you might leave the pub a little light-headed. Daily 1pm–1am.

★ **Kontener Art** ul. Ewangelicka ⓦkontenerart. pl; map page 408. This summer-only spot is unique in Poznań: an outdoor venue that supports local art and music projects. Set on an otherwise-deserted stretch of the River Warta, there's an artificial beach, a makeshift stage for DJs and deckchairs or wooden pallets to sit on. Child-friendly during the day; live music and DJs at night.

Daily noon–2/3am.

La Rambla Nova ul. Woźna 5/6 ☏61 852 3721, ⓦlaramblanova.pl; map page 410. This bar-cum-café-cum-restaurant is a welcome addition to Poznań's nightlife scene. Stocking over forty fine wines from Spain (even Withnail wouldn't be able to drink this cellar dry), it serves smashing tapas too. Daily 1pm–midnight.

Lot Chmiela ul. Żydowska 4 ☏601 686 692; map page 410. A mellow and relaxing take on the craft-beer pub experience, with a cute loungey interior, an intimate garden terrace, a live-music programme that tends towards the acoustic, and a carefully curated selection of ales and spirits. Daily 4pm–2am.

Meskalina Stary Rynek 6 ⓦmeskalina.com; map page 410. Dive into the Arsenal art gallery on the main square to find this throbbing hipster pub popular with a student and post-university set. There's a menu of soups and bites, and frequent live gigs. Mon–Thurs & Sun 5pm–1am, Fri & Sat 5pm–4am.

Pod Minogą ul. Nowowiejskiego 8 ☏61 852 7922; map page 410. Perennial student favourite, featuring a club-like back room and upstairs section where DJs play alternative music. Mon–Fri noon–5am, Sat & Sun noon–5pm.

ENTERTAINMENT

There's always a great deal going on in Poznań when it comes to highbrow culture. **Tickets** to performances are reasonably priced and easy to come by, and are sold at the tourist offices (see page 416).

CONCERT AND DANCE VENUES

Filharmonia Poznańska Box office at ul. św. Marcin 81 ☏61 853 6935, ⓦfilharmoniapoznanska.pl. Regular performances by the Poznań Philharmonic (usually on Fri or Sat), interspersed with chamber concerts and solo recitals. Concerts take place at the University Aula (Aula Uniwerzytecka), ul. Wienawskiego 1.

Teatr Muzyczny ul. Niezłomnych 1e ☏511 433 616, ⓦteatr-muzyczny.poznan.pl. The city's main venue for musicals and operetta.

Teatr Wielki ul. Fredry 9 ☏61 659 0231, ⓦopera. poznan.pl. Home of the Poznań opera. There are usually several operas running concurrently throughout the

season, with performances several nights a week.

Zamek Cultural Centre ul. św. Marcin 80/82 ☏61 646 5260, ⓦckzamek.poznan.pl. Venue for concerts featuring all kinds of music, from classical recitals to pop.

FOOTBALL

Inea Stadium ul. Bułgarska 17 ☏61 886 3050, ⓦineastadion.pl; tram #13 from the centre. Local side Lech Poznań (ⓦlechpoznan.pl) play at the 43,000-capacity Inea Stadium, 4km west of the centre, a curvaceous contemporary beauty built for the Euro 2012 football championships. The season runs Aug–May.

CINEMA

Apollo ul. Ratajczaka 18 ⓦapollo.poznan.pl. Mainstream movies and comfy atmosphere in a traditional two-screen cinema.

Malta ul. Filipińska 5, Śródka ⓦkinomalta.pl. A student cinema across the river, a good 20min east of the main square, this has the widest range of art movies and cinema classics.

Muza ul. św. Marcin 30 ⓦkinomuza.pl. Mainstream films and special film series in a central location.

DIRECTORY

Hospital ul. Chełmońskiego 20 ☎61 866 0066.

Left luggage There are lockers at the train station (24hr) and the bus station (8am–10pm).

Pharmacies There's a 24hr pharmacy just northwest of the main square at ul. 23 Lutego 18.

Post office The main office is at ul. Kościuszki 77 (Mon–Fri 7am–8pm, Sat 8am–3pm). The train station branch, just outside the western entrance at Głogowska 17, is open 24hr.

Around Poznań

It's easy to escape the big-city feel of Poznań, with its outskirts soon giving way to peaceful agricultural villages set in a lake-strewn landscape. Within a 25km radius of the city is some of the finest scenery in Wielkopolska, along with two of Poland's most famous **stately homes**.

11

Kórnik Castle

ul. Zamkowa 5 • **Castle** Tues–Sun: May–Sept 10am–5pm; Oct–April 10am–4pm; closed mid-Dec to mid-Jan • 15zł • ☎61 817 0081, ⓦbkpan.poznan.pl • **Arboretum** Daily: April & July–Sept 10am–6pm; May–June 10am–7pm; Oct 10am–5pm; Nov–March 10am–4pm • 7zł • ☎61 307 2423, ⓦidpan.poznan.pl • Kombus #501 (hourly) runs from Poznań's suburban Rondo Rataje bus station, 1.5km east of the centre along ul. Królowej Jadwigi, to **Kórnik**'s main square, a well-signed 5min walk from the castle

The lakeside village of **KÓRNIK**, 22km southeast of Poznań on the main road to Katowice, is the site of one of the great castles of Wielkopolska. **Kórnik Castle** (Zamek Kórneckie) stands amid extensive parkland at the southern edge of the village. Originally built for the Górka family in the fourteenth century, the castle was rebuilt in neo-Gothic style in the nineteenth century for its then owner, Tytus Działyński, whose aim was as much to show off his collection of arms, books and *objets d'art* as to provide a luxurious home for himself. In contrast to the affected grandeur of the exterior, with its mock defensive towers and Moorish battlements, the interior is rather more intimate. On the ground floor, the **drawing room** with its superb gilded ceiling and huge carved wooden portal bears Działyński's coat of arms, and none other than Chopin once ran his fingers across the keyboard of the nearby grand piano. On the first floor the **Moorish Hall** attempts to mimic Granada's Alhambra.

Stretching away behind the castle is Działyński's **arboretum**, a landscaped collection of more than three thousand types of tree. The lakeside offers an even more pleasant stroll, particularly the western bank with its fine distant views.

Rogalin Palace

ul. Archiszewskiego 2 • May–June Tues–Fri 9.30am–4pm, Sat & Sun 10am–5pm; July & Aug Tues–Sun 10am–5pm; Sept–Nov & mid-Jan to April Tues–Sun 9.30am–4pm • Garden free; palace 15zł; picture gallery 15zł; coach house 5zł; palace, gallery and coach house free on Fri • ☎61 813 8800, ⓦrogalin.mnp.art.pl • It's not possible to get to Rogalin and back by bus so your own transport is needed

With your own transport, it's easy to combine a visit to Kórnik with a look round the **Rogalin Palace** (Pałac Rogalinskie), 10km to the west on the road to Mosina. Long-time seat of the eminent Raczyński family, it's one of Poland's finest mansions, a truly palatial residence forming the axis of a careful layout of buildings and gardens. Begun in 1768 and only finished 47 years later, the palace represents a remarkable tasteful fusion of the Baroque and Neoclassical styles. Two bowed palace wings feature some

11

WALKS IN THE WIELKOPOLSKA NATIONAL PARK

It's best to stick to the official **hiking paths** , which are colour-coded blue, red, black and yellow. Signage within the park is good and the trails cross each other at certain key points of the park, so there is no reason why you shouldn't start exploring one trail and then switch to another. Crossing the entire park from east to west takes about two hours, although you can spend a lot longer in the park by varying your itinerary.

Walking **from Mosina** gets you into the best of the terrain quickly. Heading out of town on the road to Stęszew, turn right at the *Morena Hotel*, then left at the top of the hill (waymarks – orange-red for cyclists and blue for walkers – point you in the right direction); the path descends to the small **Lake Kociołek,** which is beautifully shaded by trees.

BLUE TRAIL

If your plan is to cross the park west to Stęszew, your best bet is to follow the **blue trail** from Lake Kociołek. This leads north round the lake before continuing through the forest to the southern end of Lake Górecke. It then climbs through thick woods before passing through open countryside to Lake Łódźkie. The route then leads along the northern shore of Lake Witobelskie to Stęszew.

RED TRAIL

The **red trail** runs south along the shore of Lake Kociołek before travelling circuitously uphill, skirting the small Lake Skrzynke just before crossing the blue trail. It arrives at the bend in the sausage-shaped Lake Góreckie, from where there's a view across to an islet with a ruined castle – a former fortress of the Działyński family, and a meeting point for the Polish insurgents of 1863. The path then leads round the perimeter of the lake as far as Jeziory, where there's a car park plus a restaurant and café. Two separate paths proceed to Puszczykówko, while a third follows the long northerly route to Puszczykowo via Lake Jarosławieckie.

BLACK TRAIL

The **black trail** begins at the station of **Trzebaw-Rosnówko** (just north of Stęszew, on the Poznań–Wolsztyn rail line), then traverses the fields to the hamlet of Trzebaw, before continuing through the woods to Lake Łódźkie. It's wise to skip the last part of this trail, as it passes Lake Dymaczewskie to end at Stare Dymaczewo on the Mosina–Stęszew road, which has no convenient public transport connections.

fine furniture and house the **picture gallery**, a well-laid-out collection of nineteenth-century Polish and German works. Jacek Malczewski was a frequent guest at Rogalin and his works are well represented here, as are those of **Jan Matejko**, his epic *Virgin of Orleans* taking up an entire wall.

Fronting the palace courtyard is a long forecourt, to the sides of which are the stables and **coach house**, the latter now a repository of carriages once used by owners of the estate, along with the last horse-drawn cab to operate in Poznań. Passing outside the gates, a five-minute walk brings you to the unusual **chapel** which houses the mausoleum of the now defunct Raczyńskis.

At the back of the main palace, the English-style park is famous for its **oak trees**, three of which have been fenced off for protection and are known as the **Rogalin Oaks**. They are at least one thousand years old – and thus of a similar vintage to the Polish nation itself. Following World War II they became popularly known as Lech, Czech and Rus, after the three mythical brothers who founded the Polish, Czech and Russian nations.

EATING   ROGALIN PALACE

Dwa Pokoje z Kuchnią ul. Arciszewskiego 28 ☎508 167 215, ⓦdwapokojezkuchnia.pl. Pleasant restaurant beside the entrance to the Rogalin Palace grounds, with a small but well-executed menu, ranging from *pierogi* (22zł) to local-favourite duck breast with liver (44zł). April–June & Sept–Oct Fri–Sun 11am–10pm; July & Aug Tues–Sun 11am–10pm.

Wielkopolska National Park

The **Wielkopolska National Park** occupies an area of some 100 square kilometres to the south of Poznań, and is a popular day-trip destination from the city. A post-glacial landscape of gentle ridges and lakes, the park is largely taken up by pine and birch forest planted as replacements for the original hardwoods. The twin villages of **PUSZCZYKOWO** and **PUSZCZYKÓWKO**, on the west bank of the snaking River Warta 15km south of Poznań, serve as the starting points for trails heading into the northern section of the park. Puszczykówko is marginally the more appealing of the two, if only because it's the site of the Arkady Fiedler Museum. Another 2km south of Puszczykówko is **MOSINA**, the best starting point for exploring the eastern reaches of the park. **STĘSZEW** is the obvious trail head for those approaching the park from the west.

Arkady Fiedler Museum

ul. Słowackiego 1, just east of Puszczykówko train station • Tues–Sun: May–Oct 9am–6pm; Nov–April 10am–3pm • 10zł • ☎ 61 813 3794, ⓦ fiedler.pl

The **Arkady Fiedler Museum** (Muzeum Arkadego Fiedlera) is housed in the former house of Fiedler, one of the most popular travel writers in Polish history. The museum is full of the personal knick-knacks brought back from his sojourns in Africa, South America and the East, while the delightful **garden** has an impressive array of replica Aztec, Easter Island and other sculptures as well as a scale replica of Columbus's *Santa Maria* boat.

11

ARRIVAL AND GETTING AROUND

WIELKOPOLSKA NATIONAL PARK

BY TRAIN

Access to the park from Poznań is fairly easy, with a dozen daily trains passing through a sequence of settlements on the fringes of the park, from where you can pick up hiking trails into the park itself.

From the east Settlements on the eastern side of the park – Puszczykowo, Puszczykówko and Mosina – are served roughly hourly by the regional trains (marked

'R' on timetables) running on the Poznań–Leszno and Poznań–Wrocław routes. The journey from Poznań to Mosina takes 25min.

From the west The western border of the park is served by the Poznań–Wolsztyn rail line, which passes through the trailhead town of Stęszew (every 2hr; 30min). Some of the services are still pulled by steam engines from the Wolsztyn depot (see page 423).

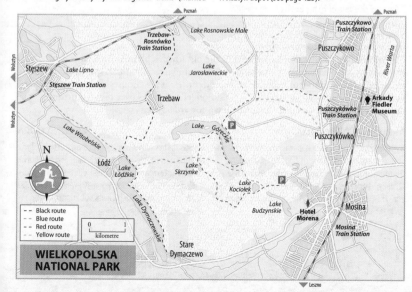

BY BIKE

Bike trails open to cyclists have orange-red waymarks.

Bike rental You can rent good bikes at Puszczykowo's train station (Mon–Fri by appointment, Sat & Sun 9am–7pm; 20zł/3hr or 40zł/day; ☎ 600 040 581, ⓦ rowerowo.com.pl) though make sure to book in advance.

South Wielkopolska

The flat farmland south of Poznań is punctuated by occasional lakes, villages and sleepy small towns. This is a great area for cycling, while for train enthusiasts there is the last working steam train line in Europe at **Wolsztyn**. A visit to **Zagan** and the prisoner-of-war camp made famous in **The Great Escape** is a must for war-movie buffs, while nearby **Zielona Góra** is one of Poland's most pleasant small cities.

Zielona Góra

A hundred kilometres southwest of Poznań, the medium-sized city of **ZIELONA GÓRA** makes a good base from which to explore nearby Wolsytzn and Żagań. The city presents an engaging patchwork of pre-World War I architectural styles, with quirky neo-Gothic turrets poking from the corners of some town houses, Art Nouveau decoration dripping from the facades of others. Few of the buildings around the eighteenth-century town hall on the main square are of any great vintage, but their pastel colour schemes give the city a cheerful air. Most imposing of the monuments is the **Church of Our Lady of Częstochowa** (Kościół Matki Boskiej Częstochowskiej), just north of the main square, an eighteenth-century half-timbered building. The beautiful interior has two levels of galleries and a pulpit standing on a carved palm tree.

Lubuskie Regional Museum

al. Niepodległości 15 • Wed–Fri 11am–5pm, Sat 10am–3pm, Sun 10am–4pm • 10zł; free on Sat • ☎ 68 327 2345, ⓦ mzl.zgora.pl

Northeast of the main square, the **Lubuskie Regional Museum** (Muzeum Ziemi Lubuskiej) contains an overview of the local **winemaking** industry – Zielona Góra being one of the few places in Poland where the tipple is produced. A separate section devoted to the history of torture covers the witch trials which took place in Zielona Góra in the sixteenth century.

The Wine Park

ul. Wrocławska 12 • Palmiarnia daily 10am–11pm • Free • ☎ 68 478 4550

The **Wine Park** (Park Winny) southeast of the old town is planted with vines and crowned by the **Palmiarnia** (palm house), containing over 200 plant species and an aquarium with various tropical fish and some turtles; it also houses a pleasant café and very decent restaurant (see page 423) which offers fine views over town. Surrounding the palm house, the vineyard stretches down towards the city.

ARRIVAL AND INFORMATION

ZIELONA GÓRA

By train Zielona Góra's train station is on the northeastern edge of the centre, a 15min walk from the main square.

Destinations Poznań (8 daily; 1hr 30min–2hr); Wolsztyn (2 daily; change at Zbaszyn; 2–3hr); Wrocław (7 daily; 2hr–2hr 40min); Żagań (1 daily direct; 4 daily changing at Żary; 1hr 30min–2hr 30min).

By bus The bus station is adjacent to the train station. There are regular services to Żagań (every 30min–1hr; 1hr 40min).

Tourist information The tourist office at Stary Rynek 1 (Mon–Fri 9am–5pm, Sat & Sun 10am–2pm; ☎ 68 323 2222, ⓦ cit.zielona-gora.pl) gives out information on the whole region.

ACCOMMODATION

★ **Betti** ul. Drzewna 1 ☎ 509 246 205, ⓦ apartamenty betti.pl. Renovated town house offering colourful en-suite rooms and fully equipped apartments. The friendly welcome and a cute breakfast room create a family atmosphere. Doubles 180zł, apartments 250zł

Ruben al. Konstytucji 3 Maja 1 ☎ 68 456 7070, ⓦ ruben hotel.pl. Just south of the centre, this modern glass-fronted building offers spacious and stylish en suites, with TV and minibar in each room, and a very respectable restaurant. Weekend reductions are available. 383zł

Śródmiejski ul. Żeromskiego 23 ☎ 68 415 2415, ⓦ srodmiejski.pl. In the pedestrian area just northeast of the main square, this hotel has friendly staff and neat en-suite rooms decorated in light, calming colours. 270zł

EATING AND DRINKING

Haust Plac Pocztowy 9 ☎ 68 325 6670, ⓦ haust.pl. A cheerful microbrewery serving its own rather excellent beers (ranging from "Snotgreen" Irish-style porter to pale ales and lagers) and a sizeable food menu featuring burgers and Polish mains. Tues–Thurs & Sun noon–11pm, Fri & Sat noon–2am.

Jazzgot al. Niepodległości 25 ☎ 600 217 021. Suave, contemporary space combining cool music (occasional jazz concerts) with a light and tasty Polish/international menu and a selection of microbrew beers. Three-course lunchtime specials (Mon–Fri) are particularly good value at 20zł. Daily 8.30am–midnight.

★ **Kawon** ul. Zamkowa 5 ☎ 68 324 4386, ⓦ kawon. zgora.pl. A great place, either to chill out in for an afternoon beer or to stumble home from after a marathon session, this roomy pub-restaurant combines a modern concert space with granny's-front-room nooks and crannies. There's a full food menu strong on pastas and steaks, and a regular schedule of gigs, cabaret and stand-up comedy. Daily 1pm–1am.

Palmiarnia ul. Wrocławska 12a ☎ 68 478 4550. With tables spread out both in the palm house and in the nineteenth-century building next door, this is Zielona Góra's best bet for refined dining. Traditional pork, fowl and fish dishes are beautifully prepared and presented (mains hover between 50zł and 80zł), and all washed down, of course, with local wines. There's also a café section serving some exceptional own-recipe cakes. Tues–Sun 10am–10pm.

Pizzeria Kawiarnia Gioconda ul. Mariacka 5 ☎ 68 324 6565. Just off the main square, this is the place to go for pizzas, pancakes and ice cream. The pizza toppings are for the most part traditional (a serviceable Quattro Formaggio clocks in at 27zł), although the fruit- and gunk-covered Pizza Nutella is a decidedly modern invention. Daily noon–10pm.

11

Wolsztyn

Those with a nostalgia for the days of steam should make tracks for the lakeside town of **WOLSZTYN**, midway between Poznań and Zielona Góra. It's the only remaining rail depot in Europe that still proudly uses **steam locomotives** to haul passenger services (see page 423).

Engine shed

ul. Fabryczna 1 • Daily 8am–3pm • 2zł; 10zł for camera • ☎ 68 419 1793, ⓦ parowozowniawolsztyn.pl

Wolsztyn's main attraction is the **engine shed** (*parowozownia*), 1km southeast of the train and bus stations, where there's a small museum and several working locomotives on display. Pride of the fleet is the green-liveried Piękna Helena (Beautiful Helena), built for the Polish state railways in 1937 and still going strong. An impressive row of old steam engines stretches along the tracks between here and the station.

WOLSZTYN STEAM TRAINS

At the time of writing, steam-hauled **passenger train services** were operating the Wolsztyn–Leszno route (Mon–Fri; 2 daily) and Wolsztyn–Poznań route (Sat only; 2 daily), although future changes are possible. In addition to the regular services, various special trips are made throughout the year, and a **parade** of steam locomotives (*parada parowozów*) is staged at Wolsztyn Station in late April or early May every year. Railway enthusiasts can follow train-driving **courses** organized by the UK-based Wolsztyn Experience (☎ 01842 860436, ⓦ thewolsztynexperience.org) – it's thanks to these activities that the steam trains keep running.

STALAG LUFT III AND THE GREAT ESCAPE

The area of pine forest and heath immediately southwest of Żagań was used by the Nazis as the site of several **POW camps** during World War II. The first, Stalag VIIIC, was established in 1939 to incarcerate captured Poles; other camps were added as the war progressed. Most famous of the Żagań camps was **Stalag Luft III**, built by the Luftwaffe in 1942 to house allied air officers, who were considered a high-risk category due to their dedication to the idea of escape. Concentrating officers together, however, turned the camp into a veritable academy of escapology, with numerous tunnelling operations underway at any given time.

One group used a wooden vaulting horse to hide their digging activities, making a successful getaway in October 1943 – an exploit subsequently immortalized in escapee Eric Williams' best-selling account *The Wooden Horse*, which also became a hit film. A far more ambitious operation, masterminded by Squadron Leader **Roger Bushell**, aimed to get hundreds of prisoners out of the camp via a trio of **tunnels** nicknamed "Tom", "Dick" and "Harry". The first two were discovered by the Germans, but on the night of March 24, 1944, a total of 76 prisoners made their way out of Harry and into the surrounding woods. Three escapees eventually made it to freedom; the rest were rounded up by the enraged German authorities, who had fifty of them shot as an example to the others. The whole extraordinary episode was first dubbed **the Great Escape** in the big-selling book of that name written by Australian ex-POW Paul Brickhill in 1950, although it's thanks to John Sturges' 1963 film of the same name that the escape occupies such a memorable niche in Western popular culture.

11

Lake Wolsztyn

On the northwestern side of the town centre lies **Lake Wolsztyn**, where there's a small sandy beach and secluded lakeside paths. The al fresco cafés by the beach offer the best places to grab a quick meal and a drink in summer.

Skansen of Western Wielkopolska Folk Architecture

ul. Bohaterów Bielnika 26 • Mid-April to mid-Oct Tues–Sat 9am–5pm, Sun noon–5pm; mid-Oct to mid-April Tues–Fri 10am–4pm • 5zł • ☏ 68 384 2619, ⊕ muzea-wolsztyn.com.pl

Following the shore of Lake Wolsztyn westwards through wooded parkland brings you after fifteen minutes to the **Skansen of Western Wielkopolska Folk Architecture** (Skansen Budownictwa Ludowego Zachodniej Wielkopolski), which has a small but impressive collection of sturdy traditional farm buildings, each topped by a thick thatch of reeds taken from the lake.

ARRIVAL AND DEPARTURE   WOLSZTYN

By train The train station is just south of the centre, near the engine shed. For details of steam train passenger services, see the "Wolsztyn steam trains" box (page 423).

Destinations Poznań (every 2hr; 2hr); Zielona Góra (2 daily; change at Zbaszyn; 2–3hr).

ACCOMMODATION AND EATING

Kaukaska Poniatowskiego 19 ☏ 68 347 1284, ⊕ kaukaska.pl. It's a bit ugly from the outside but this three-star hotel is right in the centre of town and has

pleasant en-suite rooms, as well as good inexpensive Polish food in its restaurant. **180zł**

Żagań

Some 50km southwest of Zielona Góra, the quiet town of **ŻAGAŃ** has two major attractions: a Baroque ducal **palace** set in an extraordinarily lush and inviting park; and a captivating museum commemorating the archipelago of German POW camps that once stretched southwest of town. One of these camps, **Stalag Luft III**, was the scene of the break-out that provided the inspiration for the film *The Great Escape* (see above).

ŁĘKNICA: THE BABINA MINE GEOTOURISTIC PATH

Straddling the River Neisse 55km west of Żagań, the Polish-German frontier town of **Łęknica/ Bad Muskau** is the starting point of the **Babina Mine Geotouristic Path** (Ścieżka geoturystyczna "Dawna Kopalnia Babina"; W geosciezkababina.pl), a 4.5km-long trail that leads through a rippling landscape of sandy-floored forest on the eastern (Polish) side of town.

Slightly more dramatic than your average nature walk, the trail takes you through terrain used until the 1970s to mine brown coal and clays, revealing abandoned **mine workings**, water-filled pits and spectacular turquoise or sunset-orange **lakes** discoloured by minerals and old industrial equipment. All in all it's one of Poland's most uncanny landscapes. You can get to Łęknica by bus from either Zielona Góra or Żagań, in both cases changing at Żary.

Wallenstein Palace

ul. Szprotawska 4 • **Palace** Admission by guided tour only (in Polish) Mon–Fri at noon; May–Sept additional tours on Sat & Sun at noon & 4pm • 7zł • **Park** Free access • ☎ 68 477 6464, W palacksiazecy.pl

The **Wallenstein Palace** (Pałac Wallensteina), just southeast of Żagań's frumpy main square, was begun in the Renaissance period by order of Albrecht von Waldstein (aka Wallenstein), the military genius who commanded Austrian forces during the Thirty Years' War and was awarded the Duchy of Żagań (then part of Austrian-ruled Silesia). Completed in Italianate Baroque style after Waldstein's death, it was badly damaged during World War II, although several rooms have been sumptuously restored and can be seen by occasional guided tour – although they're also frequently pressed into service for conferences and wedding receptions. The monumental winged facade, facing south across parkland towards the swan-patrolled waters of the Bóbr River, is an impressive sight.

Prisoners of War Camps Museum

St. Lotników Alianckich 6, beside the Żagań–Lubań road • March–Oct Tues–Fri 10am–4pm, Sat & Sun 10am–5pm; Nov–Feb Tues–Sat 10am–3pm • 5zł • ☎ 68 478 4994, W muzeum.eline2.serwery.pl • A taxi from Żagań bus station will cost about 15zł

Żagań's POW camps are remembered in the **Prisoners of War Camps Museum** (Muzeum Obozów Jenieckich), 3km southwest of the town centre. Inside, there's a **scale model** of Stalag Luft III (see page 424), a mock-up of the tunnelling techniques employed by the escapees, and a display devoted to the other camps established here – some 200,000 prisoners from all over the world were housed outside Żagań at one time or another, most of whom had to endure conditions far more squalid and brutal than those enjoyed by the relatively privileged air officers held at Stalag Luft III. Outside the museum building there's a newly built wooden **barracks** displaying the living conditions of the POWs and a reconstruction of a short stretch of tunnel Harry, complete with a wooden trolley.

You're free to explore the network of marked paths covering the site of the camps, although little remains save for a few scraps of brickwork poking up between the pine trees; all sites of interest now have English-language **information panels**. The most evocative spot is thirty minutes' walk northeast of the museum (and also signposted next to the industrial area on the main road), where a symbolical path indicates the exact length of tunnel Harry, with an engraved boulder – placed here on the sixtieth anniversary of the Great Escape – marking the spot where it emerged. From here it's possible to walk through the forest to the train station at the southern end of town in about twenty minutes.

ARRIVAL AND INFORMATION ŻAGAŃ

By train Żagań's train station is on the south side of the palace park, midway between the town centre and the POW camps.

Destinations Wrocław (2 daily; 2hr 10min); Zielona Góra (1 daily direct; 4 daily changing at Żary; 1hr 30min–2hr 30min).

11

By bus The bus station is on the west bank of the River Bóbr, a 5min walk from the main square. Buses run regularly to Zielona Góra (every 30min–1hr; 1hr 40min).

Tourist information The tourist office at the entrance to the palace park (Tues–Sun 9am–5pm; ☎ 068 477 1001) hands out a useful map of the town and lends bikes for free (100zł desposit).

EATING

Kepler Rynek 27/28 ☎ 502 299 133, ⓦ kepler.com.pl. The best place to eat in town, serving up traditional Polish fare (mains 20–35zł) in a nicely restored town house. Mon–Thurs noon–10pm, Fri–Sun noon–11pm.

Gniezno and around

Despite the competing claims of Poznań and Kruszwica, **GNIEZNO**, 50km east of Poznań, is generally credited as the first capital of Poland, a title based on the web of myth and chronicled fact that constitutes the story of the nation's earliest years. Nowadays Poland's ecclesiastical capital has a relaxing laid-back feel, with sufficient historical attractions to make it well worth a visit. It's a compact little place, with train and bus stations only ten minutes' walk from a quiet, cobbled **main square**. Just west of the city centre is **Lake Jelonek**, a peaceful spot with a wonderful view of the town. Gniezno is also an excellent base from which to visit the medieval archeological site at **Lake Lednica**, which is a short journey from town.

Brief history

Lech, the legendary founder of Poland, supposedly came across the nest (*gniazdo*) of a white eagle here; he founded a town on the spot, and made the bird the emblem of his people, a role it still maintains. Less fancifully, it's known for sure that Mieszko I had established a court here in the late tenth century, and that in the year 1000 it was the scene of a turning point in the country's history. In 997 **St Adalbert** (św. Wojciech), the first bishop of Prague, set out from Gniezno to evangelize the Prussians, a fierce

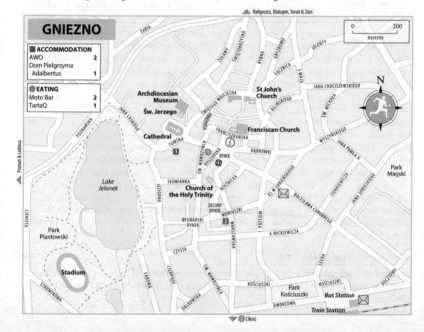

Baltic tribe who lived on Poland's eastern borders – and who quickly dispatched him to a martyr's death. In order to recover the body, Mieszko I's son, **Bolesław the Brave**, was forced to pay Adalbert's weight in gold, an astute investment as it turned out. At the pope's instigation, Emperor Otto III made a pilgrimage to Gniezno, bringing relics with him which would add to the site's holiness. Received in great splendour, he crowned Bolesław with his own crown, confirming Poland as a fully-fledged **kingdom**. Furthermore, Gniezno was made the seat of Poland's first archbishopric and Adalbert's brother Radim was the first to be appointed to the post.

Gniezno was soon replaced as **capital** by the more secure town of Kraków, and although it made a partial recovery in the Middle Ages, it never grew very big. Nevertheless, it has always been important as the official seat of the primate of Poland. It was while serving as Archbishop of Gniezno that **Cardinal Stefan Wyszyński** (1901–81) was arrested by the communist authorities in 1953, the culmination of a sustained campaign of intimidation and repression against the Catholic Church. Detained in a monastery at Komańcza in the remote Eastern Beskid Mountains, Wyszyński became a moral figurehead for generations of dissident Poles.

11

The Cathedral

Laskiego 9 • Mon–Sat 9–11.45am & 1–4pm • 5zł; bronze doors 5zł extra • ☎ 61 424 1389

Northwest from the main square along ulica Tumska lies Gniezno's **cathedral**, in front of which stands a statue of Bolesław the Brave. The basic brick structure was built in the fourteenth century in severe Gothic style, but was enlivened in the Baroque period by a ring of stone chapels and by the addition of steeples to its twin towers. The cathedral contains a sequence of richly decorated chapels, in which many of Poland's primates are buried. Behind the high altar lies the silver **shrine of St Adalbert** (św. Wojciech), the martyr seen here reclining on his sarcophagus surrounded by figures representing the different social classes. Other monuments to prominent local clerics include one to Primate Stefan Wyszyński (see above), in the north side of the ambulatory.

The cathedral's highlight is the magnificent pair of **bronze doors** located at the entrance to the southern aisle. Hung around 1175, these are among the finest surviving examples of Romanesque decorative art, and are unique in Poland. St Adalbert's life from the cradle to beyond the grave is illustrated in eighteen scenes, going up the right-hand door and then down the left, all set within a rich decorative border.

Archdiocesan Museum

ul. Kolegiaty 2 • May–Sept Mon–Sat 9am–5pm, Sun 9am–4pm; Oct–April Tues–Sat 9am–4pm • 6zł • ☎ 61 426 3778, ⓦ muzeumag.com

Just north of the cathedral, the **Archdiocesan Museum** (Muzeum Archidiecezjalne) houses a sumptuous collection of silverware, ecclesiastical sculpture and art. The star items are a copy of the cathedral doors and a tenth-century Byzantine chalice said to have belonged to St Adalbert (św. Wojciech).

ARRIVAL AND INFORMATION   GNIEZNO

By train The train station is about 500m south of the centre – walk straight down ul. Lecha to ul. Bolesława Chrobrego to reach the main square.

Destinations Bydgoszcz (10 daily; 1hr 10min); Poznań (every 30min–1hr; 30–50min); Toruń (6 daily; 1hr–1hr 20min); Trzemeszno (8 daily; 15–45min).

By bus The bus station is next to the train station.

Destinations Poznań (hourly; 1hr 15min); Trzemeszno (hourly; 35min).

Tourist information The tourist office at Rynek 14 (May–Sept Mon–Fri 8am–6pm, Sat 9am–3pm, Sun 10am–2pm; Oct–April Mon–Fri 8am–4pm; ☎ 61 428 4100, ⓦ informacjaturystycznagniezno.pl) has tons of information on Gniezno and eastern Wielkopolska.

THE PIAST ROUTE: TRZEMESZNO, STRZELNO AND KRUSZWICA

There are several jewels of medieval architecture waiting to be discovered east of Gniezno, many of which are associated with the early years of the **Piast dynasty** and are included on the so-called **Piast Route** (Szlak piastowski; @szlakpiastowski.pl), a touring itinerary promoted with great enthusiasm by local tourist boards.

The route is easiest to follow by car. Travelling by public transport, you can get to Trzemeszno by bus and train from Gniezno (see page 426); while Strzelno and Kruszwica are served by buses from Inowrocław, the main industrial city to the north.

TRZEMESZNO

Fifteen kilometres east of Gniezno, **Tremeszno** is a lightly industrialized town that was founded, according to tradition, by St Adalbert (św. Wojciech). The ancient church that St Adalbert is said to have established was succeeded by a Romanesque structure, parts of which are incorporated in the town's main sight, the Baroque **Assumption Basilica** (Basylika Wniebowzięcia NMP). The interior is a revelation of light and colour, with superb **paintings** in the dome and along the transept that for once take the attention away from the central altar, under which an effigy of Adalbert reposes. The ceiling frescoes vividly depict three crucial scenes from the saint's life and death: his vicious slaying by the Prussian pagans; the retrieval of his remains for their weight in gold, with Adalbert just a few body parts on a scale; and his eventual entombment in the basilica.

STRZELNO

The sleepy town of **Strzelno,** 28km east of Trzemeszno, is home to two outstanding Romanesque buildings. The **Monastery of the Holy Trinity** (Klasztor św. Trójcy) is a typically Polish accretion: brick Gothic gables and a monumental Baroque facade sprout from a late twelfth-century Romanesque shell. Two of the original nave pillars are adorned with figurative carvings, crafted with a delicacy found in few other European sculptures of the period.

Beside the monastery stands the slightly older little red sandstone **Chapel of St Procopius** (Kaplica św. Prokopa). In contrast to its neighbour, this has preserved the purity of its original form.

KRUSZWICA

Of all the sites associated with the Piast dynasty perhaps the oddest is in **Kruszwica**, a tranquil town straddling the pencil-slim **Lake Gopło**, 15km northeast of Strzelno. Dominating a shady tree-lined peninsula just east of the main square is a brick octagon known as the **Mice Tower** (Mysia Wieża), built during the reign of Kazimierz the Great but associated in the popular mind with the legendary King Popiel, a mean ruler who was devoured in this tower by rats. The sweeping views down the length of Lake Gopło make a trip to the top worthwhile.

Kruszwica's other key monument is the twelfth-century **Collegiate Church** (Kolegiata) on the far bank of the lake. A grim granite basilica with three apses, it has been stripped of most of its later accretions, except for the brick Gothic tower, and gives a good impression of what an early Christian church may have once looked like.

ACCOMMODATION

AWO ul. Warszawska 32 @61 426 1197, @hotel-awo. pl; map page 426. Mid-sized hotel located in a courtyard on a lively shopping street. Comfortable en-suite rooms with TV and warm colour schemes make this a welcoming pied-à-terre. 210zł

Dom Pielgrzyma Adalbertus ul. Tumska 7a @61 426 1360, @pietrak.pl; map page 426. Small but comfy modern en-suite rooms in a charming palace-like archdiocese building on Lech Hill, right opposite the cathedral. The on-site restaurant does a rather good line in pasta and pizza. 190zł

EATING

Moto Bar Jelonek 1 @61 424 7224, @facebook.com/ motobarjelonek; map page 426. Three kilometres out of town on the road to Konin, this cult eatery started out as a simple bar in a parked bus before morphing into the snug roadside diner that it is today. It's famous for serving an excellent *golonka* (roast pork knuckle) with cabbage, although you can also get burgers, sausages, pork chops and other flesh-chomping fare. Daily 9am–8pm.

TartaQ Tarciarnia Francuska ul. Tumska ☎ 790 800 966, ⓦ facebook.com/TartaQTumska; map page 426. Tasty quiches, savoury tarts, salads and some wonderful soups in a busy downtown spot. The terrace is good for coffee and cakes with views of the cathedral; *TartaQ*'s own-recipe lemonades are a hit in summer. Daily 11am–9pm.

Lake Lednica

One of the most worthwhile excursions you're likely to make in this corner of Poland is to the slender **Lake Lednica**, 18km west of Gniezno. Originally the site of a tenth-century courtly residence, the lakeshore is now home to both an absorbing **archeological site** and one of the largest *skansens* in the country.

Wielkopolska Ethnographic Park

Mid-April to mid-Oct Tues–Sun 10am–5pm (June–Aug till 6pm) • 12zł; combined ticket with Museum of First Piasts 18zł • ☎ 61 427 5040, ⓦ lednicamuzeum.pl • Take a Gniezno–Poznań bus (hourly) and alight at the turn-off for Dziekanowice and Lednica; from there it's a 10min walk north to the Wielkopolska Ethnographic Park

The **Wielkopolska Ethnographic Park** (Wielkopolski Park Etnograficzny) consists of about fifty traditional rural buildings including windmills, a Baroque cemetery chapel and several farmsteads. Some of the more eye-catching of the latter belonged to the Wielkopolska Dutch – **immigrants** from the Low Countries who were encouraged to settle here in the seventeenth and eighteenth centuries because of their superior knowledge of land irrigation techniques. They built solid, prosperous-looking farmhouses with red-tiled roofs, unlike their Polish neighbours, who preferred thatch.

Museum of the First Piasts and Ostrów Lednicki

Mid-April to mid-Oct Tues–Sun 10am–5pm (June–Aug till 6pm) • 10zł; combined ticket with Wielkopolska Ethnographic Park 18zł • ☎ 61 427 5010, ⓦ lednicamuzeum.pl

From the Wielkopolska Ethnographic Park, continue north through the village of Dziekanowice and turn left at the T-junction to reach the disparate tourist complex known as the **Museum of the First Piasts at Lednica** (Muzeum Pierwszych Piastów na Lednicy).

Just beyond the village you'll come across a small **exhibition hall** filled with replica tenth-century arms and armour. From here it's another ten-minute walk to an impressive wooden gateway that marks the entrance to another key part of the site, containing the **Under Medieval Skies** (Pod niebem średniowiecza) exhibition hall – presenting weapons and jewellery unearthed by archeologists – and the so-called **Small Skansen** (Mały skansen), featuring eighteenth-century granaries and a wooden windmill.

Take the **ferry** to **Ostrów Lednicki**, the largest of the three tiny islands in Lake Lednica, where it's believed that Mieszko I once held court. This unlikely site was once a royal seat equal to Poznań and Gniezno in importance – **Bolesław the Brave** was born here, and it may also have been where his coronation by Emperor Otto III took place, rather than in Gniezno (see page 426). Ostrów Lednicki began life in the ninth century as a fortified town and, in the following century, a modest **palace** was constructed, along with a church: the excavated remains only hint at its former grandeur, but the presence of stairways prove it was probably at least two storeys high. By the landing jetty a model of the former settlement gives an idea of how it may have looked, surrounded by the extant **earth ramparts**. The buildings were destroyed in 1038 by the Czech Prince Brzetysław and for centuries the island served as a cemetery, until it was lulled out of its sleep by tourism.

11

Pomerania

ODRA RIVER, SZCZECIN

Pomerania

Edged by gloriously long stretches of white-sand beach, Pomerania *(Pomorze)* attracts hundreds of thousands of Polish tourists every year. Due to the Pomeranian coast's northerly latitude the holiday season is rather short, but in July and August hordes of visitors arrive to soak up what sun there is, with fish-and-chip stalls and beer tents springing up to service basic gastronomic needs. Although relatively quiet, spring and early autumn can be rewarding times to visit, especially if beach strolling – rather than sunbathing – is your thing.

The fishing village of **Łeba**, gateway to the famed sand dunes of the **Słowiński National Park**, is the place to aim for in eastern Pomerania, although any number of other charming beachside settlements await exploration nearby. Over to the west, the island of **Wolin** offers yet more in the way of fine sands, as well as a much-visited bison reserve in the forested **Wolin National Park**. Pomerania's administrative and industrial capital, **Szczecin,** is never likely to make it into Polish tourism's top ten, but it nonetheless possesses an appealing urban vigour and a wealth of cultural diversions.

GETTING AROUND   **POMERANIA**

By public transport Szczecin is the region's main transport hub, with rail and bus services fanning out to serve the western half of the province. The beach resorts of central and eastern Pomerania are connected by bus to inland towns such as Koszalin, Słupsk and Lębork, all of which lie on the main Szczecin–Gdańsk rail line.

12

Szczecin

The largest city in northwestern Poland, with 405,000 inhabitants, **SZCZECIN** (pronounced "Shchechin") sprawls along the banks of the Odra in a tangle of bridges and cranes. A city with a long maritime and shipbuilding heritage, it's a gruff, workaday place that bares few of its charms to the passing visitor. However, it's also a fast-changing city boasting some landmark contemporary architecture and some attractive quayside walks. A full day should be enough to cover the main sights. The medieval **Old Town** (Stare Miasto) was heavily bombed in World War II, and **commercial** life has shifted northwestwards to the blandly grey thoroughfares of aleja Niepodległości and aleja Wyzwolenia. Further west lies an area of well-preserved nineteenth-century boulevards, lined with grand apartment blocks.

Brief history

The Slav stronghold established here in the eighth century was taken in 967 by the first Piast monarch, **Mieszko I**, and Szczecin became the residence of a local branch of Piast princes. German colonists were present from the earliest times, and came to dominate local life once the city joined the **Hanseatic League** in the mid-thirteenth century. The Swedes captured Szczecin in 1630 but sold it to the **Prussians** ninety years later. The city remained under Prussian rule until 1945, when it became an outpost on Poland's newly established western frontier. Long overshadowed by more glamorous Polish cities, Szczecin is beginning to step out into the limelight thanks to headline architectural projects such as the Szczecin Phiharmonic (2014) and the Upheavals Dialogue Centre (2016).

Empress Catherine the Great p.434   **Fauna in Słowiński National Park** p.451

THE BEACH AT MIĘDZYZDROJE

Highlights

❶ **Szczecin** Brash, bustling port city with varied nightlife and some genuine architectural gems hiding amid the industrial concrete. See page 432

❷ **Międzyzdroje** Charming, old-fashioned seaside resort town, conveniently located at the edge of the thickly forested Wolin National Park. See page 440

❸ **Świnoujście** A clutch of nineteenth-century Prussian era forts provide a gruff reminder of this town's former strategic importance, and a broad stretch of seashore makes it a tempting place to linger. See page 444

❹ **Mielno** A chic seaside settlement sandwiched between the Baltic and a saltwater lake, boasting a wonderful stretch of beach and excellent sailing. See page 446

❺ **Darłowo** Cute medieval town just a short hop away from the silky beaches and laid-back vibe of Darłówko. See page 446

❻ **Słowiński National Park** Poland's most alluring dunescapes, an area filled with reedy lakes and rich with birdlife, right next to the characterful fishing village and beach resort of Łeba. See page 450

HIGHLIGHTS ARE MARKED ON THE MAP ON PAGE 434

EMPRESS CATHERINE THE GREAT

Just west of Szczecin's Castle is ulica Farna, where the residence of the commandant formerly stood. This was the birthplace of Sophie von Anhalt-Zerbst (1729–96), a princess of a minor aristocratic line better known to history as **Empress Catherine the Great** of Russia. A character of extreme ruthlesness – she deposed her own husband and was probably behind his subsequent murder – she presided over an extraordinary period of Russian expansion, and played a leading role in the Partitions that wiped Poland off the map. That her native city is now Polish is truly ironic.

The modern centre

Central Szczecin is dominated by a grid of busy four-lane highways. The most obvious central landmark is the **Harbour Gate** (Brama Portowa), which stands in a traffic island on plac Zwycięstwa. Built by the Prussians in 1725, it comprises two deliciously ornate Baroque gables linked by a long hall. Downhill to the east looms **St James's Cathedral** (Katedra św. Jakuba), a massive Gothic church grievously damaged in 1945 and subsequently the victim of over-restoration. The oldest parts of the church date back to the fourteenth century and are the work of Hinrich Brunsberg, the finest of the specialist brickwork architects of the Baltic lands.

Trafo Centre for Contemporary Art

ul. Świętego Ducha 4 • Tues–Sun 11am–7pm • 10zł • ☎ 91 400 0049, ⊕ trafo.art

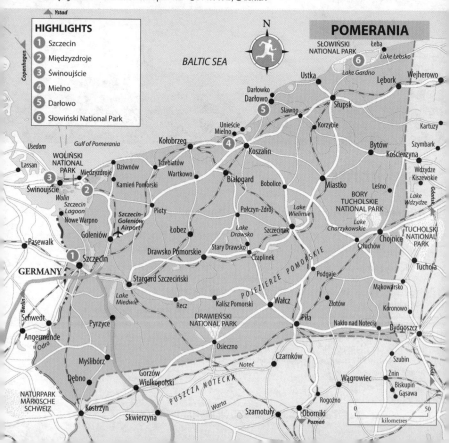

POMERANIA

HIGHLIGHTS
1. Szczecin
2. Międzyzdroje
3. Świnoujście
4. Mielno
5. Darłowo
6. Słowiński National Park

South of the cathedral in a tangle of streets leading down to the river, a pre-World War I power station provides the austere-but-chic venue for the **Trafo Centre for Contemporary Art** (Trafostacja Sztuki). It's arguably the best place on the Baltic coast to catch cutting-edge exhibitions involving international artists; there's also a well-stocked art-and-design bookshop.

Rynek Sienny and Nowy Rynek

Szczecin's old town square, broken into **Novy Rynek** and **Rynek Sienny** ("Haymarket"), is a rather odd affair, where concrete blocks and vacant lots rub shoulders with reconstructed burghers' houses gaudily decked out in bright blue and orange. By far the most personable of Szczecin's buildings is the gabled **old town hall** in the Rynek's centre, an artful reconstruction of the fourteenth-century original that was flattened in the war. The restorers opted to return it to something like its pre-war appearance, right down to the bulging lopsided walls.

Mariners' Avenue

A few steps east of Rynek Sienny, the Odra riverbank is the site of a recently re-paved foot- and cycle-path, dubbed **Mariners' Avenue** (aleja Żeglarzy), that runs past Szczecin's yacht moorings – quite a sight in summer, when a variety of swanky craft drop anchor here. A clutch of café-restaurant pavilions provide the riverbank with a year-round sense of social focus, and there are stirring views of cranes and warehouses on the other side.

Castle of the Pomeranian Dukes

ul. Korsarzy 34 • Tues–Sun 10am–6pm • Museum 6zł; bell tower 6zł • ☏ 91 489 1630, ⓦ zamek-szczecin.pl

From its hillside perch, the **Castle of the Pomeranian Dukes** (Zamek Książąt Pomorskich) enjoys commanding views of the river. An early medieval settlement rebuilt in stone in the mid-fourteenth century, the whole thing was given a Renaissance enlargement in the late sixteenth century, and again remodelled in the 1720s. Dukes aside, the building has been used as a brewery, barracks and anti-aircraft emplacement – the last being the reason it was flattened in an air raid in 1944. Reconstruction continued into the 1980s, and it has since been turned into a museum and cultural centre.

The **Castle Museum** (Muzeum Zamkowe) occupies a few vaults, displaying the sarcophagi of several dukes as well as photographs of the castle's restoration. It's worth climbing the two hundred or so steps up the **bell tower** (*wieża*) for the view over the city, with church spires and dockside cranes piercing the skyline.

Museum of Regional Traditions and the Contemporary Art Museum

Museum of Regional Traditions ul. Staromłyńska 1 • Tues–Thurs & Sat 10am–6pm, Fri & Sun 10am–4pm • 10zł • **Contemporary Art Museum** ul. Staromłyńska 27 • Same hours • 10zł • ⓦ muzeum.szczecin.pl

A branch of the National Museum, the **Museum of Regional Traditions** (Muzeum Tradycji Regionalnych) is housed in an elegant Baroque palace, formerly the Pomeranian parliament. The ground floor features an impressive display of medieval Pomeranian **sculpture**, highlights of which include delicately carved thirteenth-century columns from the Kołbacz monastery, and several fifteenth-century triptychs. Upstairs the emphasis is on Polish painters, along with the occasional token German work. On the other side of the street is another branch of the museum, the **Contemporary Art Museum** (Muzeum Sztuki Współczesnej), hosting changing exhibitions of modern art and photography.

Across the broad open space of plac Żołnierza Polskiego is the Baroque **Gate of Prussian Homage** (Brama Hołdu Pruskiego), whose design, with reliefs of military trophies, echoes that of the Harbour Gate (see page 434).

Upheavals Dialogue Centre

pl. Solidarności 1 • Tues–Thurs, Sat 10am–6pm, Fri & Sun 10am–4pm • 10zł • ☎ 91 817 1430, ⓦ przelomy.muzeum.szczecin.pl

Despite its cumbersome name, the **Upheavals Dialogue Centre** (Centrum Dialogu Przełomy) is actually a stunning museum of contemporary Polish history, which makes excellent use of sound, video and digital technology to deliver an informative and at times extremely moving narrative. It's initially rather difficult to ascertain where the museum actually is: built on a slope, it looks like a gently rising extension of the pedestrian square on which it is situated – indeed, you'd be forgiven for thinking that it's some kind of balustraded skateboard park. Once inside, the museum tells the history of twentieth-century Poland from Szczecin's point of view – a city of

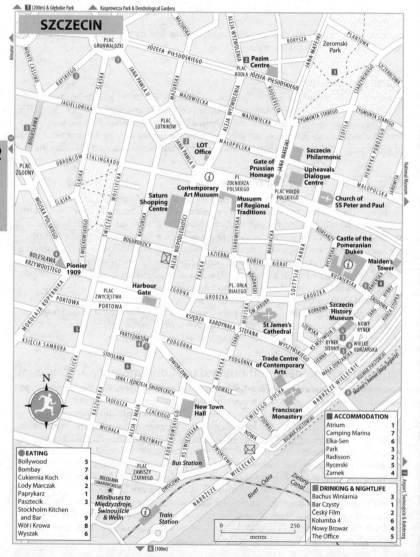

"upheavals" that went from German to Polish, Nazi to communist, industrial to post-industrial – and analyses the malevolent impact of ideology and political extremes and the will to resist that often results. Szczecin's place in recent Polish history – notably the regime-rocking shipyard strike of 1970 – gets full and gripping treatment.

Szczecin Philharmonic

ul. Małopolska 48 • ☎ 91 431 0720, ⓦ filharmonia.szczecin.pl

Like many great buildings, the **Szczecin Philharmonic** (Filharmonia w Szczecinie) is totally out of keeping with anything built in the city previously, and yet somehow succeeds in fitting in with its surroundings without losing the requisite amount of aesthetic shock. Barcelona-based architects Studio Barozzi Veiga took inspiration from local Gothic church gables, shipyard cranes and sailing ships to produce the corrugated-tent-from-space that rises above the intersection of Małopolska and Matejki. Step inside the über-chic, arctic-white lobby for a taste of contemporary Polish cool – or grab a concert ticket (see page 439) to enjoy the superb acoustics.

National Museum

Wały Chrobrego 3 • Tues–Thurs & Sat 10am–6pm, Fri & Sun 10am–4pm • 10zł • ⓦ muzeum.szczecin.pl

A grandiose Art Nouveau pile on Wały Chrobrego – a leafy promenade commanding an expansive panorama of the Odra River – the main building of the **National Museum** (Muzeum Narodowe) contains a wealth of material on seafaring Slavs and Celts. The museum's pride and joy is a large ethnographic collection devoted to non-European cultures, a colourful and varied display of objects from Pacific islands, South America and Africa. Much of it was brought back to Szczecin by enthusiastic members of Poland's merchant navy between the 1950s and 1980s, a programme of acquisition that nowadays stands as tribute to Szczecin's globe-spanning, mercantile past.

12

ARRIVAL AND GETTING AROUND

SZCZECIN

By plane Szczecin airport is located at Goleniów (☎ 91 481 7400, ⓦ airport.com.pl), 45km north of the city. Trains from the airport run to Szczecin Główny (3–4 daily; 40min), while minibuses (timed to coincide with arrivals and departures; 1hr 20min) run to and from Szczecin bus station.

By train Szczecin Główny train station is a two-storey building near the Odra river. Depart the upper level via ul. Owocowa to walk to the town centre (10min), or exit the lower level to catch a tram: #3 goes to the Harbour Gate (Brama Portowa), and #6 goes along the riverbank towards Wały Chrobrego. There are left-luggage lockers on the lower level.

Destinations Berlin (8 daily; change at Angermünde or Pasewalk; 2hr 30min); Gdańsk (4 daily; 5hr); Koszalin (8 daily; 2hr–2hr 30min); Kraków (3 daily; 8hr); Lębork (4 daily; 3hr 30min); Międzyzdroje (10 daily; 1hr 35min); Poznań (12 daily; 2hr 30min); Słupsk (4 daily; 3hr);

Świnoujście (10 daily; 1hr 50min); Warsaw (6 daily; 5hr 30min–6hr 50min); Wolin (10 daily; 1hr 20min).

By bus The bus terminal is a 5min walk downhill from the town centre at pl. Grodnicki.

Destinations Berlin Schönefeld and Tegel airports (8 daily; 3hr–4hr 30min); Kamień Pomorski (hourly; 1hr 20min); Kolobrzeg (3 daily; 3hr); Międzyzdroje (hourly; 1hr 30min); Świnoujście (hourly; 1hr 45min); Wolin (hourly; 1hr 10min).

By minibus Minibuses serve many of the same destinations as buses from stands on ul. Limanowskiego, just uphill from the train station.

Destinations Międzyzdroje (hourly; 1hr 20min); Świnoujście (hourly; 1hr 35min); Wolin (hourly; 1hr).

Public transport The tourist office (see page 437) can provide a free map of bus and tram city transport routes. Tickets can be bought at newspaper kiosks near stops, and cost 2zł for 15min travel or 3zł for 30min.

INFORMATION

Tourist information There are tourist offices in the castle courtyard at Korsarzy 34 (daily 10am–6pm; closed Sun mid-Oct to mid-April; ☎ 91 489 1630) and at pl. Żołnierza Polskiego 20 (Mon–Fri 9am–6pm; June–Sept also Sat 9am–3pm; ☎ 0891 434 0440, ⓦ szczecin.eu). Both have free town maps. There's also a branch at the train station (daily: May–Sept 8am–8pm; Oct–April 8am–6pm).

ACCOMMODATION

HOTELS

Atrium al. Wojska Polskiego 75 ☎ 91 422 1096, ⌨ hotel-atrium.pl; map page 436. Centrally-located, well-run hotel offering soothingly decorated rooms with desk space and electric kettle. Breakfast 35zł per person extra. **270zł**

Elka-Sen ul. 3 Maja 1A ☎ 91 433 5604, ⌨ elkasen.szczecin.pl; map page 436. Eccentric little place in the basement of a hotel-and-catering school, handy for both the city centre and the stations. The en-suite rooms are a bit dowdy and careworn, but eminently servicable as an inexpensive urban base. Breakfast 18zł per person extra. **135zł**

Park ul. Plantowa 1 ☎ 91 434 0050, ⌨ parkhotel.szczecin.pl; map page 436. The hotel of choice if you fancy a bit of old-school elegance, occupying an interwar villa in the middle of peaceful Żeromski Park. Pastel-coloured en suites include some nice attic-level rooms, and there's a small on-site spa centre. **495zł**

Radisson pl. Rodła 10 ☎ 91 359 5595, ⌨ radissonblu.com/szczecin; map page 436. Gleaming custom-built luxury hotel with its own casino, nightclub, fitness centre and swimming pool, plus all the other upmarket facilities you'd expect. **360zł**

Rycerski ul. Potulicka 2a ☎ 91 814 6601, ⌨ hotelewam.pl; map page 436. Smart, central place in a handsome nineteenth-century red-brick building, offering tastefully furnished en suites with TV. There's also a small sauna. Breakfast 35zł per person extra. **250zł**

Zamek ul. Panieńska 15 ☎ 91 852 2777, ⌨ hotelzamek.pl; map page 436. Boutique hotel just below the castle, offering fourteen richly decorated rooms. Modern bathrooms, a top-floor gym and good views of the river (from most of the rooms) complete the picture. **500zł**

CAMPSITE

Camping Marina ul. Przestrzenna 23 ☎ 91 460 1165, ⌨ campingmarina.pl; local train to Szczecin-Dąbie station, then bus #56, #33D or #79; map page 436. Year-round campsite by the waterside in Dąbie, 5km east of town. Camping **70zł**, chalets **160zł**

EATING

CAFÉS AND SNACKS

★ **Cukiernia Koch** al. Wojska Polskiego 4 ☎ 91 488 2828, ⌨ koch.com.pl; map page 436. Old-school patisserie with wooden fittings and browner-than-brown wallpaper – the ideal venue for relaxing over a cup of coffee or pigging out on the decadent range of pastries and cakes. Daily 9am–8pm.

★ **Lody Marczak** ul. Rajskiego 25 ☎ 509 746 785, ⌨ lodymarczak.pl; map page 436. Family-run ice-cream business producing excellent ice cream in seasonal fruity flavours – as well as the odd flavour-clash experiment – at 3.50zł per scoop. The inevitable queue outside is definitely worth joining. Daily noon–9pm.

RESTAURANTS

Bollywood ul. Panieńska 20 ☎ 91 433 3033, ⌨ bollywood.com.pl; map page 436. The food here is just as good as in sister-restaurant *Bombay* (see below) but the atmosphere is different, with a youthful, clubby atmosphere and screens showing sub-continental movies. *Thali* platters are well worth a shot at 45–50zł. Daily 1–11pm.

Bombay ul. Partyzantów 1 ☎ 91 812 1171, ⌨ india.pl; map page 436. Smoothly relaxing Indian restaurant with exemplary service and a long, authentic menu, including plenty for vegetarians – ask for extra spice if you like your food hot. Mains 40–50zł. Daily 1–11pm.

Paprykarz al. Jana Pawła II 42 ☎ 91 433 2233, ⌨ paprykarz.com.pl; map page 436. Seafood bistro in a bright space decked out with nautical memorabilia. The accent is on Mediterranean rather than Baltic fare, with tuna steaks (60zł) and grilled sea bass (50zł) among the stand-outs. Lobster, oysters and mussels also feature on the menu. Mon–Thurs noon–11pm, Fri & Sat noon–midnight, Sun noon–10pm.

Pasztecik al. Wojska Polskiego 46 ☎ 91 433 9606; map page 436. Hardly the ideal slimming aid but definitely worth trying at least once, the *pasztecik* is a unique Szczecin snack that looks like cholesterol on a stick – a deep-fried tube of pastry filled with minced meat or cheese. Order and pay at the till in this legendarily minimalist stand-up buffet. Mon–Fri 10am–9pm, Sat 10am–4pm.

Stockholm Kitchen and Bar ul. Piastowski 1 ☎ 789 303 879; map page 436. This riverside pavilion with floor-to-ceiling windows makes the perfect vantage point for observing goings-on along the quay. The modern-European menu has a Swedish slant – expect salmon grilled, smoked or in soup, and some to-die-for seasonal fruit desserts. Daily 2pm–1am.

Wół i Krowa ul. Wielka Odrzańska 20 ☎ 731 000 230, ⌨ wolikrowa.com; map page 436. Burgers and a bit more besides from this late-opening, enjoyably brash bar-restaurant just behind Rynek Sienny. Popular for late breakfasts, soups, salads and a wide range of burger options (23zł-ish), washed down with craft beers and cocktails. Daily 11am–2am.

Wyszak ul. Księcia Mściwoja II 8 ☎ 662 233 678, ⌨ browarwyszak.pl; map page 436. Upscale brew-pub and restaurant in the stunning brick-vaulted cellar of the old town hall – although there's also a summer terrace right on the Rynek Sienny. Mains (steaks, game and fish) are in the 50–70zł range. There is an excellent pils on offer and several seasonal brews on tap. Daily 1–11pm.

12

DRINKING AND NIGHTLIFE

BARS AND PUBS

Bachus Winiarnia ul. Sienna 6 ⓣ662 281 273, ⓦbit.ly/BachusWiniarnial; map page 436. Subdued lighting, domestic knick-knacks, old-school lampshades and a long list of wines makes this an eminently grand place to spend an evening of glass-cradling contentment. Eats range from salami-and-cheese platters to pastas and steaks – with most mains hovering around the 30–40zł mark. Daily noon–10pm.

Bar Czysty ul. Księcia Bogusława X 8 ⓣ512 808 912, ⓦbarczysty.com.pl; map page 436. Of the many bars on this increasingly popular drinking strip, *Czysty* is one of the more refined, with a long list of long drinks and shots, and a startlingly complete choice of whiskys and whiskeys. Mon & Sun 4pm–2am, Tues–Thurs 4pm–3am, Fri & Sat 4pm–4am.

Český Film al. Jana Pawła II 3–4 ⓣ608 359 007, ⓦceskyfilm.wordpress.com; map page 436. A bar themed around Czech cinema? It works very well, actually, with film posters on the walls, video projections of famous flicks, and beers from small-town Czech and Polish breweries. Sausage snacks and burgers play a supporting role. Daily 4pm–4am.

Nowy Browar ul. Partyzantów 2 ⓣ91 433 5484, ⓦnowybrowar.pl; map page 436. Modern beer hall with crisp minimalist decor, TVs with sport, a menu of pub food and large copper tanks brewing some distinctly quaffable lagers, wheat beers and one-off seasonal batches. Mon–Thurs 9am–midnight, Fri 9am–2am, Sat 11am–2am, Sun 11am–midnight.

The Office ul. Osiek 10 ⓣ798 630 760, ⓦthe-office.ontap.pl; map page 436. Relatively small and intimate place that's perfect for eager explorers of Poland's booming craft beer culture, with guest beers on tap and bottles from all over the place. They also serve Starka, Poland's legendary herbal vodka – but it's not cheap. Daily 4–11pm.

CLUB

Kolumba 4 – Szczecinski Loft Kultury ul. Kolumba 4 ⓦkolumba4.pl; map page 436. Warehouse club on several floors that spreads out into the courtyard on summer weekends, offering life gigs and DJ action. Fri, Sat & sometimes Sun.

ENTERTAINMENT

Filharmonia Szczecin ul. Małopolska 48 ⓣ91 431 0720, ⓦfilharmonia.szczecin.pl. A regular programme of classical music concerts performed in a fabulous new auditorium. The season runs Sept–May.

Opera na Zamku ul. Korsarzy 34 ⓣ91 434 8106, ⓦopera.szczecin.pl. Opera and ballet in a modern auditorium inside the castle.

Pionier 1909 al. Wojska Polskiego 2 ⓣ91 434 7702, ⓦkino-pionier.com.pl. Art-house cinema that was founded in 1909, and claims to be the oldest continuously operating cinema in the world.

Wolin island

A large, heavily indented island that separates the Szczecin Lagoon from the open sea, **WOLIN** offers a wonderfully varied landscape of sand dunes, lakes, forest, meadows and moors. The gap dividing it from the mainland is at times so narrow that Wolin is often described as a peninsula rather than an island; indeed, roads are built directly over the River Dziwna in two places: near its mouth at Dzwinów, some 12km from Kamień Pomorski; and at **Wolin Town** towards the island's southern extremity. These roads converge at the seaside town of **Międzyzdroje**, main access point to the hiking trails of the **Wolin National Park**. To the west is **Świnoujście**, an engaging mixture of bustling port and beach resort which straddles the channel dividing Wolin from the neighbouring island of Uznam.

Wolin Town

Squatting beside the Dzwina River on the island's southeastern tip, the town of **WOLIN** occupies the site of one of the oldest Slav settlements in the country. Pagan Slavs established themselves here in the eighth century, developing one of the most important early Baltic **ports** and carrying on a healthy trade with the Vikings (who called the place Jomsborg). Temples to Slav deities Światowid and Trzygłów existed here until the early twelfth century, when Bishop Otto of Bamberg arrived to persuade the locals that acceptance of Christianity would be good for business.

The Slav and Viking Centre

Recław 37 • Daily: April–June, Sept & Oct 10am–4pm; July & Aug 10am–6pm • 10zł • ⓦ jomsborg-vineta.com

A bridge just east of the village centre leads to the Wolińska Kępa island, where the **Slav and Viking Centre** (Centrum Słowian i Wikingów) is dedicated to the hybrid Slav-Viking culture that existed here a millennium ago. At the heart of the centre is a *skansen*-like recreation of a pre-Christian settlement featuring 27 houses (built from logs filled in with cow dung), each containing replica furnishings and kitchen utensils of the kind that would have been in use at the time. In summer, staff in period costume are frequently on hand to demonstrate iron-age crafts. A three-day **Festival of Slavs and Vikings** draws thousands of historical reenactment enthusiasts from all over Europe for a long weekend in August (see website for precise dates).

ARRIVAL AND DEPARTURE WOLIN TOWN

By train Ten trains a day head from Szczecin to Świnoujście, calling at Wolin (1hr 20min) along the way.

By minibus Szczecin–Wolin–Międzyzdroje–Świnoujście minibuses (hourly; 1hr to Wolin) operate from a stop on ul. Limanowskiego in Szczecin, dropping off on the northeastern side of Wolin Town, a 5min walk from the main street.

Międzyzdroje and around

Best base for exploring Wolin island is **MIĘDZYZDROJE**, which boasts a long sandy beach and the best hiking trails in the area. A favourite with the pre-war German middle class, it is now one of the west Baltic's busiest resorts. It may not look all that snazzy to the outsider, but Międzyzdroje was traditionally one of the places where Polish TV and film stars spent their holidays; there's a "Promenade of the Stars" (Promenadaa Gwiazd), complete with hand-prints of the famous, running behind the beach.

The centre of town, 1km inland from the sea, revolves around **plac Neptuna**, a modern, pedestrianized, café-filled square which brings to mind the mall-like plazas of Mediterranean holiday resorts. Main focal point of the beach is the nineteenth-century **pier**, the entrance to which is framed by an imposing pair of domed pavilions.

National Park Museum

ul. Niepodleglosci 3 • Tues–Sun: May–Sept 9am–5pm; Oct–April 9am–3pm • 6zł

Occupying a low hill immediately south of the town centre, the **National Park Museum** (Muzeum Przyrodnice Wolińskiego Parku Narodowego) houses a display of the island's flora and fauna which is worth visiting before heading into the park itself. The exhibits are mostly in Polish, but the taxidermied specimens of bison, birds and other endemic creatures are interesting nevertheless.

Baltic Miniature Park

ul. Nowomyśliwska 98 • Daily: Feb & March 10am–4pm; April & Oct 10am–5pm; May, June & Sept 10am–6pm; July & Aug 9am–7pm; Nov–Jan 10am–3pm • 19zł • ☎ 609 038 580, ⓦ baltyckiparkminiatur.pl • Bus #10 from Międzyzdroje, or free golf cart in season

Located at the western end of town some 3km from the centre, the open-air **Baltic Miniature Park** (Bałtycki Park Miniatur) displays model buildings from all over the Baltic region – from Rosenborg Castle in Denmark to St Petersburg's Cathedral of the Assumption, with loads of famous Polish landmarks inbetween. With model railways, seasonal flower displays and a lake for model boats, it will keep the family entertained for an hour or so.

The bison reserve

May–Sept Tues–Sun 10am–6pm; Oct–April Tues–Sat 8am–4pm • 6zł • Head east along ul. Kolejowa and turn left onto ul. Leśna when you see the signs; you'll pass through a park gate after about 5min after leaving the town outskirts, beyond which a trail leads through deep forest to the reserve itself

Wolin's densely wooded National Park starts right on the outskirts of Międzyzdroje, and the **bison reserve** (Zagroda pokazowa Żubrów) lies a twenty-minute walk through the park from the town centre. Bison died out here in the 1300s and the animals on show are descended from those brought from Białowieża in eastern Poland (see page 187). The aim of the reserve is to breed the shaggy beasts in captivity to save them from extinction. You'll also see deer, eagles and a clutch of wild boar who loll about in the mud, twitching their prodigious snouts.

ARRIVAL AND INFORMATION MIĘDZYZDROJE

By train The train station is at the southeastern fringe of town, a 5min walk uphill from the centre. Ten trains a day run to Szczecin (1hr 30min), Świnoujście (16min) and Wolin (16min).

By bus and minibus Both buses and minibuses pick up and drop off close to the centre, on al. Niepodległości. There are hourly minibuses to Szczecin (1hr 20min), Świnoujście (20mn) and Wolin (20min). In addition, the #10 bus runs

between Międzyzdroje train station and Świnoujście port (Mon–Fri 10 daily, Sat 8 daily, Sun 4 daily; 20min).

Tourist information The tourist office is in a pavilion next to the Dom Kultury at ul. Bohaterów Warszawy 20, and inside the Dom Kultury during the off-season (May–Sept Mon–Fri 9am–6pm, Sat & Sun 9am–5pm; Oct–April Mon–Sat 9am–7pm; ☎91 328 2778, ⍈mdkmiedzyzdroje.com). They have free maps of town and can help with accommodation.

ACCOMMODATION

Camping 24 ul. Polna 36 ☎91 328 0275, ⍈camping24.cba.pl; bus #10; map page 441. Large grassy site 2km west of the centre with pitches in the open meadow or under the trees. There's a restaurant and small shop on site; the beach is a 10min walk away. **64zł**

Marina Gryfa Pomorskiego 1 ☎91 328 0449, ⍈marina-miedzyzdroje.pl; map page 441. Smart new building

on the main road through town, providing smallish but extremely cosy en-suite rooms with TV. There's also a pleasingly old-fashioned restaurant serving seafood. **350zł**

Vienna House Amber Baltic Promenada Gwiazd 1 ☎91 322 8500, ⍈viennahouse.com; map page 441. This outwardly ugly piece of seafront concrete is bright, colourful and luxurious inside, with well-equipped,

12

balconied rooms and a host of on-site extras, such as spa facilities and indoor and outdoor pools. __800zł__
Willa 777 ul. Krasickiego 8 ☎ 91 328 1644, ⓦwilla777.

pl; map page 441. A smart pension with contemporary en suites that come with balconies and TVs, in a large, centrally located house. The attic rooms are particularly cosy. __340zł__

EATING

Heaven pl. Neptuna 8 ☎ 502 583 999, ⓦpubheaven.pl; map page 441. This place offers the Polish soup, *pierogi* and pork-chop repertoire but handles Mediterranean fare competently, too, with some good pizzas and (rarely in Poland) an eminently edible salad Nicoise. Mains are around 25–30zł. Daily noon–midnight.
Restauracja Willa 777 ul. Krasickiego 8 ☎91 328 1644, ⓦwilla777.pl; map page 441. Simple but smart canteen restaurant with a wide choice of *pierogi*, Polish-style cabbage-heavy salads, and pork-based mains, all at

low prices. Pile your plate high for less than 25zł. Daily 11am–8pm.
★ **Strzecha** ul. Promenada Gwiazd 38; map page 441. Located at the northeastern end of town where fishermen pull up their boats, *Strzecha* is one of the best of several huts serving excellent fried fish. It's a simple order-at-the-counter affair but has a pleasant covered terrace facing the sea. Food is priced by weight; a succulent fillet of halibut shouldn't set you back more than 30zł. Summer daily noon–10pm; out of season hours are limited.

DRINKING

★ **Roza Wiatrów** pl. Neptuna 7 ☎91 328 1544, ⓦfacebook.com/TawernaRozaWiatrow; map page 441. Dark, cosy pub-restaurant with nautical prints and model boats stashed around the place. Thanks to a good choice of bottled beers and several shelves of spirits, it's a great place to drink, plus it also has a serviceable food menu concentrating on the tried-and-

tested repertoire of pork, chicken and fish dishes. Daily noon–midnight.
Scena ul. Bohaterów Warszawy 20 ☎608 866 766, ⓦfacebook.com/disco.scena; map page 441. Large and comfortable basement pub, with karaoke nights and a regular programme of DJ-led events in season. Summer daily 8pm–3am; out of season open weekends only.

Wolin National Park

ⓦwolinpn.pl

An area of richly varied landscapes, **Wolin National Park** (Woliński Park Narodowy) is the habitat of more than two hundred different types of bird – the sea eagle is its emblem – and numerous animals such as red and fallow deer, wild boar, badgers, foxes and squirrels. It would take several days to cover all its many delights, but a reasonable cross-section can be seen without venturing too far from Międzyzdroje. A good aid to walking in this region is the 1:75,000 *Zalew Szczeciński* **map** of the red, blue and green trails, all clearly marked, which meander through the surrounding forest; it's readily available in Międzyzdroje, notably from the National Park Museum (see page 440).

The red trail

Some of the most impressive scenery in the park can be seen by following all or part of the 19km-long **red trail** along its eastward stretch from Międzyzdroje, which passes for a while directly along the beach. You soon come to some awesome-looking tree-crowned **dunes**, where the sand has been swept up into cliff-like formations up to 95m in height – the highest to be seen anywhere on the Baltic. Quite apart from its visual impact, much of this secluded stretch is ideal for a spot of swimming or sunbathing away from the crowds.

After a few kilometres, the markers point the way upwards into the forest, and you follow a path skirting tiny Lake Gardno before arriving at the village of **WISEŁKA**, squeezed between its eponymous lake and a popular stretch of beach. Here there's a **restaurant**, snack bars and several shops. The trail continues east through the woods and past more small lakes to its terminus at **KOŁCZEWO**, set at the head of its own lake, the only other place along the entire route with **refreshment facilities**. From either here or Wiselka you can pick up a bus (the Emilbus Kamień Pomorski-Świnoujście service runs through both places) back to Międzyzdroje.

The green trail

Also terminating at Kołczewo is the 17km-long **green trail**: if you're prepared to devote a very long day to it, you could combine this with the red trail in one circular trip. The green trail begins in Międzyzdroje and passes by the bison reserve (see page 440) before continuing its forest course, emerging at a group of glacial **lakes** around the village of Warnowo (also reachable by train) where there's another reserve, this time for mute swans. Five lakeshores are then skirted en route to Kołczewo.

The blue trail

The third route, the **blue trail**, 26km in total, follows a southerly course from Międzyzdroje's train station, again passing through wooded countryside before arriving at the northern shore of the Szczecin Lagoon. Following this to the east, you traverse the heights of the Mokrzyckie Góry, then descend to the town of Wolin (see page 439).

Świnoujście

Occupying both sides of the channel that divides Wolin from the island of Uznam, the bustling fishing port, naval base and beach resort of **ŚWINOUJŚCIE** is a popular entry point into Poland, thanks to the passenger ships that sail here from Sweden and Denmark. It's also 3km away from the land border with Germany, to whom the vast bulk of the island of Uznam belongs.

Świnoujście's gruff semi-industrialized appearance makes it slightly less attractive as a base than nearby Międzyzdroje, but it is worth at least a day-trip thanks to the trio of well-preserved Prussian-era fortifications guarding the mouth of the River Świna. The town centre is fairly nondescript, so it's best to head directly to the town's superb white-sand **beach** twenty minutes north on the far side of the spacious spa park.

Western Fort and Angel Fort

ul. Jachtowa • **Western Fort** Daily: April & Oct 10am–5pm; May & Sept 10am–6pm; June–Aug 10am–8pm • 10zł • ☎ 508 738 118 • **Angel Fort** Daily: May–Sept 9am–dusk; Oct–April 10am–3pm • 8zł • ☎ 601 767 171, ⓦ fortaniola.pl

At the eastern end of Świnoujście's seaside park, on the west bank of the River Świna, are two of the brick-built forts erected by the Prussians in the mid-nineteenth century. Set in the northeastern corner of the park, nearest the sea, **Western Fort** (Fort Zachodni) contains a small history museum and an open-air display of artillery pieces. A ten-minute walk south, **Angel Fort** (Fort Anioła), so named because of its alleged resemblance to Castel Sant'Angelo in Rome, is worth a look for its attractive, cylindrical exterior – although the exhibition on Vikings inside is rather throwaway.

Fort Gerhard and the lighthouse

ul. Bunkrowa • **Fort Gerhard** Daily: May–June 9.30am–5pm; July–Sept 9.30am–7pm; Oct–April 10am–4pm • 15zł; combined ticket with Underground City 26zł • ☎ 91 321 8626, ⓦ fort-gerharda.pl • **Lighthouse** Daily 10am–6pm • 6zł • ☎ 91 321 6063 • 30min walk or 5min ride on bus #1 from Świnoujście train/bus stations

Over on the eastern bank of the river, the ruddy **Fort Gerhard** (Fort Gerharda) was the pride and joy of the Prussian defence system, and today functions as an entertaining historical attraction. From May to September individual visitors are formed into "platoons" and marched around the courtyard and gun emplacements by staff in nineteenth-century Prussian uniforms (complete with *Pickelhaube* spiked helmets). Whatever time of year you come, you can also look around the **Museum of Coastal Defences** (Muzeum Obrony Wybrzeża; same times and ticket), a collection of militaria held in a wing of the fortress.

Next door to Fort Gerhard, the 68m-high **lighthouse** (*latarnia*) offers excellent views of the surrounding coast from the top of its steep 300-step staircase.

Underground City

4km east of Fort Gerhard, just north of the Świnoujście–Międzyzdroje road • Tours: May & June Mon–Fri at 3pm, Sat & Sun at 12.30pm & 3pm; July & Aug daily at 10.30am, 12.30pm, 1.30pm, 3pm & 4.30pm; Sept daily at 12.30pm & 3pm; Oct–April Sat & Sun at 12.30pm & 3pm • 15zł; combined ticket with Fort Gerhard 26zł • ☎ 789 072 244, ⓦ podziemne-miasto.pl • Bus #10 to Przytór, then a 500m walk

Set in woods east of Świnoujście, the **Underground City** (Podziemne Miasto) was originally a World War II German artillery bunker before being chosen by the Polish army as the site of a large subterranean HQ. It consists of over a kilometre of corridors and an extensive complex of storage rooms and sleeping quarters. The ninety-minute tour, led by appropriately uniformed staff, leads past radio rooms, power generators and Cold War-era charts illustrating plans for attacking Denmark.

ARRIVAL AND DEPARTURE ŚWINOUJŚCIE

All main points of arrival (except road and rail crossings with Germany) are on the eastern bank of the River Świna. A half-hourly car ferry (on which pedestrians travel free) runs over to the centre of town on the western bank.

By train The train station is **right by the ferry port**. Ten trains a day run to Międzyzdroje (1hr 15min), Wolin (30min) and Szczecin (1hr 50min).

By bus and minibus The bus station is also by the ferry port. There are hourly minibuses to Międzyzdroje (20min) and Szczecin (1hr 40min). The #10 bus runs to Międzyzdroje (Mon–Fri 10 daily, Sat 8 daily, Sun 4 daily; 20min).

By ferry Both Unity Line (☎ 91 880 2909, ⓦ unityline.

eu) and Polferries (☎ 91 322 6140, ⓦ polferries.pl) operate daily car ferries to Ystad in Sweden, while Polferries also runs ferries daily to Copenhagen.

By train from Germany The Usedomer Bäderbahn railway (UBB) connects Świnoujście with a string of towns on the German side of the border. The station is at the western end of town on ul. Konstytucji 3 Maja. There are no facilities at the station – buy tickets (in euro) from the conductor.

Destinations Ahlbeck (every 30min; 10min); Heringsdorf (every 30min; 20min); Peenemünde (hourly; change at Zinnowitz; 1hr); Stralsund (every 2hr; 2hr 30min).

INFORMATION

Tourist information The tourist office, ul. Słowiański 6/1 (Mon–Fri 9am–5pm, Sat 10am–2pm; ☎ 91 322 4999, ⓦ swinoujscie.pl), can help with accommodation, including private rooms.

ACCOMMODATION

Camping Relax ul. Słowackiego 1 ☎ 91 321 3912, ⓦ camping-relax.com.pl. Well-located campsite between the spa park and the beach, offering both tent sites and basic chalets. Open mid-June to mid-Sept. Camping 49zł, two-person bungalows 170zł

Cis ul. Piłsudskiego 26 ☎ 91 321 2114, ⓦ hotelcis.pl. A century-old villa close to the beachfront with bright en suites in pastel tones, a small garden and breakfast delivered to your room. 450zł

Pod Kasztanami ul. Paderewskiego 14/1 ☎ 91 321 3947, ⓦ pod-kasztanami.pl. This intimate little pension in the town centre provides elegant en-suite rooms in a nicely restored nineteenth-century villa, in a peaceful location next to a leafy park. 420zł

Villa Jedynak ul. Piłsudskiego 35 ☎ 91 880 7111, ⓦ villajedynak.pl. Pleasant pre-World War I villa with neat, mildly chintzy en suites – as usual, the cosiest ones are in the attic. 370zł

EATING

Café Wieża ul. Paderewskiego 7 ☎ 788 883 992. Occupying the surviving belfry of a former church, the "Tower" serves excellent tortes and meringues in a uniquely Gothic space, stuffed with comfortingly old furniture. Daily 10am–8pm.

El Papa – Café Hemingway Bohaterów Września 69 ☎ 510 400 551, ⓦ facebook.com/elpapacafe. Arty, homely café serving some of the best cakes in Pomerania; cheesecake with seasonal fruits is the specialit. A selection of artworks on the wall creates a gallery atmosphere. Daily 10am–8pm.

Kurna Chata ul. Piłsudskiego 20 ☎ 501 177 125, ⓦ bit. ly/KurnaChata. Almost (but not quite) a tourist trap, *Kurna Chata* serves traditional Polish fare in a chamber packed with colourful textiles and with a crowd of ornaments hanging from the ceiling. Decent *pierogi*, local fish and all kinds of pork are on the menu. Mains 25–35zł. Daily noon–10pm.

Neptun ul. Bema 1 ☎ 91 888 8001. Roomy restaurant-pub with something for everyone: Polish pork-chop staples, pastas and salads, and a long list of shots and cocktails. Mon–Thurs & Sun 11am–10pm, Fri & Sat 11am–midnight.

12

The central Pomeranian coast

East of Wolin island, the central Pomeranain coast boasts a string of relaxing and laid-back resorts. Give overdeveloped Kołobrzeg a miss – although it's Poland's most popular beach resort and health spa, it's also the one that foreign visitors are least likely to want to visit – and head instead to **Darłowo** or **Mielno**, both of which offer the kind of small-town charm and unspoiled surroundings that Kołobrzeg largely lacks. If you're Darlowo-bound, there's a good chance you'll pass through **Słupsk**, a pleasant inland town famous for the collection of paintings by Stanisław Ignacy Wikiewicz ("Witkacy") in the local museum.

Mielno and Unieście

The resort of **MIELNO**, some 12km northwest of the provincial capital Koszalin, is a straggling beachside settlement that bleeds into **UNIEŚCIE**, the next village to the east. Popular with sailors due to the large saltwater lake just inland from the beach, Mielno is one of the more laid-back resorts on the coast, although the construction of gated apartment complexes is increasingly giving the place a Warsaw-by-the-sea reputation.

From the western edge of the resort, ulica 1 Maja leads down to a seaside promenade overlooked by a smattering of *belle-époque* holiday villas – including some attractively rickety timber constructions. It's roughly a half-hour's walk from here to Unieście, which has a comparatively sleepy, village-like feel, with wooden fishing boats parked up on the dune-fringed beach. The beach gets more unspoilt (and more deserted) the further east you go – once you've cleared Unieście, it's 10km to the next settlement.

12

ARRIVAL AND INFORMATION

MIELNO

By minibus Minibuses run to and from Koszalin train station **every 15–20min and** pass through Mielno (15min) before terminating in Uniescie 5min later.

Tourist information The tourist office is on ul. Lechitów 23, by Mielno's bus stop (June–Aug Mon–Fri 8am–8pm, Sat & Sun 9am–5pm; Sept–May Mon–Fri 8am–4pm; ☎ 94 318 9955, ⓦ cit.mielno.pl); it has details of private rooms and pensions throughout the two villages.

ACCOMMODATION

★ **HT Houseboats** ul. 6 Marca 2 ☎ 669 855 769, ⓦ hthouseboats.com. This is the most imaginative accommodation option in Pomerania and one that's well worth travelling to Mielno in order to stay in: a series of box-shaped cottages (ranging in size from two-person to eight-person) mounted on pontoons floating on Mielno's lake. They're beautifully appointed inside, feature wonderful views, and breakfast is delivered to your boat. The only problem: they're frequently booked up well in advance. Two-person houseboat <u>450zł</u>

Lesny Resort ul. Chmielna 4 ☎ 502 565 874, ⓦ lesny resort.mielno.pl. A collection of cute, tastefully decorated wooden cabins sleeping two to four people, in a forested setting complete with BBQ pits and children's playgrounds. Open May–Sept. <u>170zł</u>

Willa Focus ul. 1 Pionerów 7 ☎ 606 283 199, ⓦ focus. mielno.pl. Close to the beach in the centre of Mielno, this guesthouse spread over two buildings offers neat simple rooms with electric kettles or use of a communal kitchen. <u>180zł</u>

EATING

La Palma Wojska Polskiego 1 ☎ 512 685 667. Café-restaurant in a part-timber pavilion with a palm tree in the middle, serving baked fish, pizza and pasta (35–35zł), and some excellent *szarlotka* (apple pie). Daily noon–11pm.

Meduza ul. Nadbrzezna 2 ☎ 94 348 0890, ⓦ meduza. mielno.pl. A refined if slightly pricey restaurant with a lovely seaside patio, serving duck with cranberry sauce and good pork dishes. Mains 35–50zł. Daily 10am–11pm.

Darłowo

Thirty kilometres northeast of Mielno, **DARŁOWO** is the one town along the coast that preserves its medieval Rynek and street plan more or less intact. The beaches just north of the town, around the coastal suburb of **Darłówko**, are as popular as any.

The Rynek

Darłowo's **Rynek** is the site of a gracefully reconstructed **town hall**, complete with a Renaissance doorway and an unusual fountain. On one side of the Rynek sits the Gothic **St Mary's Church** (Kościół NMP), an attractive brick building with a relatively restrained Baroque interior. Inside there's an eighteenth-century wooden pulpit decorated with scenes from the Last Judgement, while in among a clutch of royal tombs beneath the tower is that of the notorious **King Erik VII** (1397–1459). A local-born aristocrat who acceded to the thrones of Denmark, Sweden and Norway, Erik married Henry V of England's daughter Phillipina, whom he later tired of and banished to a nunnery. Deposed in 1439, he returned to Darłowo and spent the last years of his life here as the Duke of Słupsk, living off piracy in the Baltic Sea.

Regional Museum

ul. Zamkowa 4 • May, June & Sept daily 10am–4pm; July & Aug daily 10am–6pm; Oct–April Wed–Sun 10am–4pm • 13zł • ☎ 94 314 2351, 🖰 zamekdarlowo.pl

South of the Rynek lies the well-preserved fourteenth-century **castle** of the Pomeranian dukes, now home to the **regional museum** (Muzeum regionalne), which contains exhibits on local folklore as well as furnishings from the castle itself – notably the ornate seventeenth-century limewood pulpit that once graced the castle chapel.

St Gertrude's Chapel

ul. Ojca Damiana Tyneckiego 23

About 400m northeast of the Rynek sits the extraordinary white-walled **St Gertrude's Chapel** (Kaplica św. Gertrudy), a twelve-sided seventeenth-century structure squatting beneath a tapering, inverted ice-cream cone of a roof covered in slender wooden shingles. The galleried interior is decorated with pictures of shoes and boots donated by pious tradesmen – St Gertrude being, among other things, the patron saint of cobblers.

Darłówko

On the coast 3km west of Darłowo (and served by regular shuttle service from the bus station) lies **Darłówko**, a low-rise, leafy resort straddling the mouth of the Wieprza. Clogged by fishing boats, the river is spanned by a pedestrian **drawbridge**, whose control tower – a mushroom-shaped affair resembling something out of a 1960s sci-fi movie – is very much a local attraction. There are the usual expanses of sand backed by woods, making this a restful place if you're in need of a seaside breather.

ARRIVAL AND INFORMATION | DARŁOWO

By train Darłowo's train station is just west of town: walk down ul. Boguslawa X to reach the centre.
Desinations Koszalin (3 daily; change at Slawno; 55min); Słupsk (5 daily; change at Slawno; 50min–1hr 20mn).
By bus The bus station is next to the train station.
Desinations Koszalin (3 daily; 1hr 5min); Słupsk (8 daily; 1hr 25min).

By minibus Minibuses run to and from Koszalin train station (14 daily; 50min).
Tourist information The tourist office is just off the Rynek at ul. św. Gertrudy 8 (Mon–Fri 10am–7pm, Sat & Sun 10am–4pm; ☎ 519 303 032, 🖰 darlot.pl). It can help find private rooms and pensions in Darłowo and Darłówko.

ACCOMMODATION AND EATING

Apollo ul. Kapielowa 11, Darłówko ☎ 94 314 2453, 🖰 hotelapollo.pl. This historic beachside establishment is in a completely different league from anything else in town, with plush, modern en-suite rooms offering gorgeous sea views. The elegant restaurant has a terrace overlooking the sea, where you can dine on roast wild boar, pork ribs or duck. Restaurant daily 11am–9pm. **520zł**
Camping 243 ul. Conrada 20, between Darłowo and Darłówko ☎ 94 314 2872, 🖰 camping243.com. Campsite offering grassy tent pitches and comfortable bungalows, in a park-like spot a few kilometres from the sea. Camping **46zł**, two-person bungalows **95zł**
Tivoli ul. Wladyslawa IV 17, Darłówko ☎ 794 068 332. Uncomplicated but cosy seafront pizzeria offering a wide selection of thin crust pies in the 23–27zł range, plus soups, pastas and bruschetta sandwiches. Daily 10am–10pm.

12

Słupsk

Well worth a leisurely exploration before pressing on to the coastal resorts of Darłowo or Łeba, **SŁUPSK** is one of the region's more handsome inland towns, boasting broad tree-lined avenues, a smattering of surviving red-brick architecture and a couple of good art museums.

Museum of Central Pomerania

ul. Dominikańska 5–9 • Mon 11am–3pm, Tues–Sun 10am–6pm • 14zł • ☏ 59 842 4081, ⊚ muzeum.slupsk.pl

Słupsk's main claim to fame is Poland's biggest collection of paintings by Stanisław Ignacy Witkiewicz, better known as "**Witkacy**" (see page 328), the interwar artist and playwright famous for taking narcotics while painting. The collection is housed on the second floor of the **Museum of Central Pomerania** (Muzeum Pomorza Środkowego), sited in the former Renaissance castle, and covers all stages in Witkacy's career; the portraits crowding the walls (many of them full of fanciful symbolist details) add up to a stunning display. The museum ticket is also valid for the next-door castle mill, which holds an absorbing collection of folk costumes.

Baltic Gallery of Contemporary Art

ul. Nullo 8 • Tues–Sun 9am–5pm • Free • ☏ 59 841 2621

On the banks of the Słupia River, round the corner from the Museum of Central Pomerania, the surviving fortification known as the **Witches Tower** (Baszta Czarownic) is named after the eighteen innocent women tortured and executed here during a seventeenth-century witch hunt. Inside is the highly worthwhile **Baltic Gallery of Contemporary Art** (Bałtycka Galeria Sztuki Współczesnej), devoted to edgy, contemporary stuff.

ARRIVAL AND INFORMATION

SŁUPSK

By train Słupsk's train station is at the western end of al. Wojska Polskiego, 1km from the town centre. Destinations Darłowo (5 daily; change at Sławno; 50min–1hr 20mn); Gdańsk (6 daily; 2hr–2hr 20min); Lębork (12 daily; 30min–1hr); Szczecin (7 daily; 2hr 50min–3hr 45min).

By bus The bus station is next to the train station. Buses to Darłowo leave regularly (8 daily; 1hr).

Tourist information The tourist office is just off the eastern end of al. Wojska Polskiego at ul. Starzyńskiego 8 (mid-June to mid-Sept Mon–Fri 9am–6pm, Sat & Sun 10am–3pm; mid-Sept to mid-June Mon–Fri 9am–4pm, Sat 10am–3pm; ☏ 59 728 5041, ⊚ slupsk.pl).

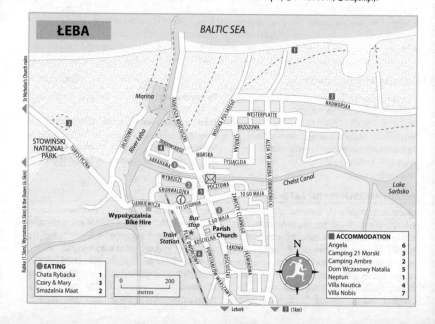

ŁEBA

BALTIC SEA

ACCOMMODATION

Angela	6
Camping 21 Morski	3
Camping Ambre	2
Dom Wczasowy Natalia	5
Neptun	1
Villa Nautica	4
Villa Nobis	7

EATING

Chata Rybacka	1
Czary & Mary	3
Smażalnia Maat	2

EATING AND DRINKING

Repeta ul. Starzyńskiego 11 ☎ 533 370 401, ⓦ repeta.eu. Swish café-restaurant serving everything from breakfasts to cocktails, with main courses ranging from steak and burgers to pasta. A T-bone will set you back 65zł, while most other dishes are in the 25–35zł range. Mon–Thurs 10.30am–9pm, Fri &

Sat 10.30am–10pm, Sun 10.30am–8pm.
Vega Bistro & Café ul. Nowobramska 2 ☎ 577 837 608. All kinds of meat-free goodies: hummus dips, tortillas and soups for the snackers; and tasty risottos and lasagnes (16–24zł) for those in need of a good lunch. Daily 10am–6.30pm.

Łeba and around

Of all the Pomeranian seaside resorts, **ŁEBA** is the most celebrated – an attractive old fishing settlement presiding over kilometre upon kilometre of irresistible dune-backed beaches. Small enough to preserve a village-like feel, it nevertheless receives enough summer visitors to generate an invigorating holiday bustle. The bigger of the local **dunes** (*wydmy*), just west of town in the **Słowiński National Park**, forms one of Poland's prime natural attractions, and draws hordes of sightseers as a result. There are plenty of unspoiled Baltic pine forests and silvery sands nearby if you want to escape the crowds.

Łeba village

The **village** is set a kilometre back from the sea; dunes and beach cover the original site of the settlement, which was forced to move inland in the late sixteenth century because of shifting sands. Łeba's main street, **ulica Kosciuszki**, is still lined with several of the one-storey, brick-built fishermen's houses once common to the region. A little further north, Kościuszki bridges a canalized branch of the River Łeba – where trawlers and pleasure boats moor – before veering eastwards and becoming **ulica Nadmorska**, which leads to the bigger hotels and campsites.

12

The beaches

In summer the area around ulica Nadmorska is busy with cheerful holidaymakers heading for unbroken sandy **beaches** widely regarded as among the cleanest on the Baltic coast. Another stretch of beach, to the west of town, can be reached by walking down ulica Turystyczna, which passes a swanky yachting marina and the turn-off to Rąbka (see page 450) before arriving at another clutch of beachside campsites. Just before the access to the beach, a path leads off into the forest towards the meagre ruins of **St Nicholas's Church** (Kościół św. Mikołaja), a lone reminder of the village's former location.

ARRIVAL AND DEPARTURE   ŁEBA

Main point of access for public transport is the provincial town of **Lębork** just to the south, which stands on the main east–west road and rail routes connecting Szczecin to Gdańsk. Buses and minibuses to Łeba leave from the forecourt of Lębork train station.

By train Łeba's train **station is** two blocks west of ul. Kościuszki.
Destinations Lębork (July & Aug 8 daily; Sept–June 1 daily; 50min); **Warsaw (1 daily; 7hr).**
By bus The bus stop is next to the train station. Buses to and from Lębork run hourly (40min).

INFORMATION

Tourist information There are two very helpful tourist offices; one in the centre of town at ul. Listopada 5A (July & Aug Mon–Fri 9am–7pm, Sat 10am–4pm, Sun 10am–3pm; Sept–June Mon–Fri 8am–4pm; ☎ 59 866 2565, ⓦ lotleba. pl); and the other 2km south of the centre at the main-road entrance to town at ul. Kościuszki 121 (July & Aug Mon–Fri 7.30am–5pm, Sat 9am–5pm, Sun 10am–2pm; Sept–June

Mon–Fri 7.30am–3.30pm; ☎ 504 247 615, ⓦ leba.eu). Both can help book one of the innumerable private rooms and pensions.
Bike hire From Wypożyczalnia on ul. Sienkiewicza (☎ 696 042 119) or from a stand at the entrance to the national park, for 15–20zł/day.

ACCOMMODATION

HOTELS AND B&BS

Angela pl. Dworcowy 2a ☎59 866 2647, ⓦangela. afr.pl; map page 448. A largish place right by the train station with cosy rooms that are slightly old-fashioned, but come equipped with balconies. There's also a neat garden restaurant out front. **200zł**

Dom Wczasowy Natalia ul. Kościuszki 38 ☎605 420 072, ⓦdomwczasowynatalia.com; map page 448. Simply furnished but neat studios and apartments grouped around a central patio. All have electric kettles and fridges, and there's a guest kitchen. **200zł**

Neptun ul. Sosnowa 1 ☎59 866 1432, ⓦneptunhotel.pl; map page 448. Upmarket hotel right on the beach among the pine trees, in a hundred-year-old villa with a mock castle turret. Many of the plush en-suite rooms have sea views, and there's a tennis court and swimming pool on site. **850zł**

Villa Nautica ul. Dzerdowskiego 13A ☎792 390 000, ⓦnauticaleba.pl; map page 448. Neat modern, family-oriented B&B offering en-suite rooms with small wooden balconies, TV and electric kettle. **330zł**

Villa Nobis ul. Kolorowa 4 ☎866 1876, ⓦvillanobis.pl; map page 448. Family house on a quiet street southeast of the centre, with neat en-suite rooms, many with small balconies. **200zł**

CAMPSITES

Camping 21 Morski ul. Turystyczna 3 ☎664 258 806, ⓦcamping21.pl; map page 448. Near the entrance to the national park but also handy for the beach, this is a big campsite with sports facilities, a shop and lots of pine trees. Camping **56zł**, four-person apartments **200zł**

Camping Ambre ul. Nadmorska 9 ☎59 866 2472, ⓦambre.leba.info; map page 448. A large, well-organized campsite stretched out beneath birch trees by the seaside, which also has four-person bungalows and a sauna on site. Camping **63zł**, four-person bungalows **360zł**

EATING

There's a surfeit of **fish-fry stalls** (*smażalnia ryb*) selling fresh cod or halibut with chips, particularly concentrated by the Chełst canal where local boats unload their catch. In addition, there's a clutch of tourist-oriented restaurants scattered throughout the town centre. **Opening hours** fluctuate widely according to how many visitors are in town, and many places close their doors altogether outside the tourist season (roughly May–Sept).

Chata Rybacka ul. Abrahama 8 ☎690 010 250, ⓦchata rybacka.pl; map page 448. Right on the port, this is a wonderful place to try local fish – not just fried in batter in the usual Polish-seaside manner, but also grilled and baked (cod baked with spinach and mozzarella is a particular favourite; 32zł). Good fish soups, too. Daily noon–10pm.

Czary & Mary ul. Kościuszki 41 ☎737 728 888, ⓦface book.com/CZARYMARYLEBA; map page 448. Bright, breezy café-restaurant serving up a succulent range of burgers (20–25zł), dependable pizzas (28–32zł) and a great choice of cocktails and craft beers. Daily noon–10pm.

Smażalnia Maat ul. Kosciuszki 30 ☎59 866 2977; map page 448. Order-at-the-counter fish-fry establishment, though it's not really a budget option. Succulent fillets of halibut or turbot are priced by weight; expect to pay 35–45zł for a decent portion with fries. Daily 10am–8pm.

Słowiński National Park

ⓦ slowinskipn.pl

West of Łeba stretches **Lake Łebsko** (Jezioro Łebsko), the largest of several lagoons separated from the sea by a belt of mobile **sand dunes** that form the centre of **Słowiński National Park** (Słowinski Park Narodowy) – one of the country's most memorable natural attractions, included in UNESCO's list of world Biosphere Reserves. The park gets its name from the **Slovincians**, a small ethnic group of Slav origin who, like the Kashubians, retained a distinctive identity despite centuries of German influence.

Abandoned to the elements by its original human inhabitants, the expanse of shifting, undulating sand provided an ideal training ground during World War II for units of the Afrika Korps, who drilled here in preparation for the rigours of Rommel's North African campaigns. In the latter stages of the war the spit west of Łeba was turned into a **rocket research station**; the missiles tested here were distant cousins of the fearsome V1 and V2 rockets that later bombarded London.

The eastern entrance to the park is at **Rąbka**, a small cluster of houses and snack bars on the shores of Lake Łebsko, 1.5km west of Łeba. To get there on foot from Łeba, head down ulica Turystyczna and take the signed left turn about 400m beyond the canal; from here, it's a 1.5km walk through the birch trees. The pathway to the dunes begins on Rąbka's western edge.

FAUNA IN SŁOWIŃSKI NATIONAL PARK

The shores of Lake Łebsko are covered with thick reeds that provide ideal cover for **birds**, and sanctuaries at several points protect the main breeding sites. **Birds** in the park are classified into three main groups: nesting, migratory and wintering. Nesters include such rare species as the white-tailed eagle, crane, eagle owl and black stork. This is also a popular area for the more common white stork. During the late autumn migration period large flocks of wild geese wing over the lakes, and in winter you'll find ducks and other fowl from the far north of Europe sheltering – velvet scoters, mergansers, auks and whooper swans included.

Mammals are numerous too. The shores of the lakes harbour deer and boar, while elks, raccoons and badgers live in the surrounding woods. Shy red squirrels are a common sight in among the trees surrounding Łeba.

ESSENTIALS   SŁOWIŃSKI NATIONAL PARK

Tickets and maps A kiosk in Rąbka, by the pathway to the dunes, sells tickets to the park (May–Sept dawn–dusk; 6zł), as well as local maps.
Bike hire and golf carts You can hire a bike at the park

entrance (15–20zł/day) – assuming you haven't already done so in Łeba (see page 449) – or jump aboard a golf cart (depart when full; 12–15zł depending on where you want to get off).

Wyrzutnia
Museum: April–Oct daily 8am–8pm • 14zł

Three kilometres west of Rąbka lies a small clearing known as **Wyrzutnia** ("Launchpad"), the site of the World War II base where the German military experimented with various forms of rocket between 1943 and 1945 – part of Hitler's strategy of producing terror **weapons** that would give Germany a psychological advantage over its adversaries. A **museum** inside one of the observation bunkers contains photographs of pre-war Łeba, alongside diagrams of the **rockets** developed here. The first of these was the stumpy *Rheintochter* (Rhine Daughter), although this was soon superseded by the larger *Rheinbote* (Rhine Messenger), a sleek 11m-long affair that resembles the ground-to-air missiles in use today. Despite more than eighty test launches, the *Rheinbote* never saw active service, the Germans instead opting for the V2 rockets developed by a separate team.

Ranged beside one of the launchpads are replicas of the two rockets, together with post-war Polish rockets that look very similar to the German missiles on which they were modelled.

The dunes
Beyond Wyrzutnia, the path forges westwards through deep forest for a further 2km before emerging at the base of the **Biała Góra** (White Mountain). At 40m, this is the first and highest of the **dunes**, which stretch westwards for about 5km. Even a brief hike will give you the flavour of the terrain. Dried by the sun and propelled by the wind, the dunes migrate over 10m per year on average, leaving behind the broken tree stumps you see along the path. Out in the middle of the dune area, there's a desert-like feeling of desolation with the rippling sands giving an eerie sense of fluidity.

Crossing the dunes northwards will bring you down onto the **seashore** within ten minutes: from here you can walk back to Łeba along the beach (8km) or return the way you came.

Kluki
Skansen: May–Aug Mon 11am–3pm, Tues–Sun 10am–6pm; Sept–April Mon 11am–3pm, Tues–Sun 9am–4pm • 14zł • ⑩ muzeumkluki. pl • Kluki is accessible by bus from Słupsk (5 daily; 1hr; last one back at 2.50pm)

Twenty kilometres southwest of Łeba, on the southern edge of Lake Łebsko and entirely surrounded by woods, the little Slovincian village of **KLUKI** has a charming **skansen**, the **Museum of Slovincian Timber-framed Architecture** (Muzeum Wsi Slowinskiej w Klukach); you'll see similar, if more dilapidated, buildings still in use in several villages in the region.

12

SAUSAGE STAND, KRAKÓW

Contexts

History

Few other European countries have had so chequered a history as Poland. At its mightiest, it has been at the heart of a huge commonwealth stretching deep into the Baltics, Russia and Ukraine; at its nadir, it has been a nation that existed only as an ideal, its neighbours having conspired to wipe it off the map. Yet, for all this, a distinctive Polish culture has survived and developed without interruption for more than a millennium.

The beginnings

The great plain that is present-day Poland has been inhabited since the **Stone Age**. However, it did not sustain anything more socially advanced than a tribal culture until a relatively late date. The exact period when this plain was first settled by **Slav tribes** is uncertain, but it may have been as late as the eighth century.

It was the **Polonians** (the "people of the open fields"), based on the banks of the River Warta between Poznań and Gniezno, who were responsible for forging a recognizable nation, which thereafter bore their name. From the ninth century, they were ruled by the **Piast** dynasty, whose early history is shrouded in legend but emerges into something more substantial in the second half of the tenth century. In 965, the Piast **Mieszko I** married the sister of the Duke of Bohemia and underwent public baptism, thus placing himself under the protection of the papacy. Mieszko's motives appear to have been political: Otto the Great, the Holy Roman Emperor, had extended Germany's border to the Odra and would have had little difficulty in justifying a push east against a pagan state. By 990, Mieszko had succeeded in uniting his home area of **Wielkopolska** (Great Poland), with that of the Vistulanian tribe, which took the name of **Małopolska** (Little Poland). **Silesia**, settled by yet another Slav tribe, became the third component of this embryonic Polish state.

Mieszko's policies were carried to their conclusion by his son **Bolesław the Brave**. In 1000, Emperor Otto III was dispatched by the pope to pay tribute to the relics of the Czech saint, Adalbert, which Bolesław had acquired. During his stay, the emperor crowned Bolesław with his own crown, thus renouncing German designs on Polish territory. Subsequently, Bolesław established control over Pomerania and Mazovia; he also began Poland's own easterly drive, pushing as far as Kiev. The name "Poland" came into general use, and its status as a fully-fledged kingdom was underlined by Bolesław's decision to undergo a second coronation in 1022.

Piast Poland

By the middle of the eleventh century, Małopolska had become the centre of the nation's affairs and Kraków had replaced Gniezno as capital. The power of the Catholic Church remained a major factor in the Polish state: when **Bishop Stanisław** of Kraków was murdered in 1079 on the orders of **Bolesław the Generous**, the clergy not only gained a national saint whose cult quickly spread, but also succeeded in dethroning the king.

996	1025	1049
Baptism of Mieszko I	Coronation of Bolesław the Brave	Archbishop (later Saint) Stanisław of Kraków murdered by Bolesław the Generous

In the early twelfth century, centralized monarchical power made a comeback under **Bolesław the Wrymouth**, who repulsed German designs on Silesia. However, he undid his life's work with a decision to divide his kingdom among his sons; for the rest of the century and beyond, Poland lacked central authority and was riven by feuds as successive members of the Piast dynasty jostled for control over key provinces. Pomerania fell to Denmark, while Silesia began a long process of fragmentation.

In 1225 Duke Konrad of Mazovia, under threat from the heathen Prussians and Lithuanians on his eastern border, invited the **Teutonic Knights**, a quasi-monastic German military order, to help him secure his frontiers. The knights duly based themselves in Chełmno, and by 1283 they had effectively eradicated the Prussians. Emerging as the principal military power in northern Europe, the knights built up a theocratic state defended by some of the most awesome castles ever built, ruthlessly turning on their former hosts in the process. They captured the great port of Gdańsk in 1308, renaming it Danzig and developing it into one of Europe's richest mercantile cities. At the same time, German peasants were encouraged to settle on the fertile agricultural land all along the Baltic. Poland was left cut off from the sea, with its trading routes severely weakened as a result.

The **Tatar invasions** of 1241–42, when the Poles were decisively defeated at the Battle of Legnica, spelt the beginning of the end for Silesia as part of Poland. It gradually split into eighteen tiny duchies under the control of Bohemia, then the most powerful part of the Holy Roman Empire.

It was only under the last Piast king, **Kazimierz the Great** (1333–70), that central political authority was firmly re-established. Kazimierz established Poland's first university at Kraków, introduced a new silver currency and secured his borders with a line of castles. He extended his territories east into Red Ruthenia and Podolia, which meant that, although the Catholic Church retained its prominent role, the country now had sizeable Eastern Orthodox minorities. Even more significant was Kazimierz's encouragement of **Jews**, who were protected from persecution by a law of 1346 – a major factor in Poland's subsequent position as home to the largest Jewish community in the world.

The Jagiellonians

On Kazimierz's death, the crown passed to his nephew Louis of Anjou, king of Hungary, but this royal union was short-lived, as the Poles chose Louis' younger daughter **Jadwiga** to succeed him in 1384, while her sister ascended the Hungarian throne. This event led to the most enduring alliance in Polish history – with **Lithuania**, whose grand duke, Jogaila (henceforth known to history by his Polish name, Władysław Jagiełło), married Jadwiga in 1386. Europe's last pagan nation, Lithuania had resisted the Teutonic Knights and developed into an expansionist state that now stretched from its Baltic homeland all the way to the Crimea.

After Jadwiga's death in 1399, Jagiełło reigned over the two nations for the next 45 years, founding the **Jagiellonian dynasty** – which was to remain in power until 1572. One of the first benefits of the Polish-Lithuanian link was a military strength capable of taking on the Teutonic Knights, and at the **Battle of Grunwald** in 1410, the order was defeated, beginning its long and slow decline. By the 1466 Treaty of Toruń, the Lower Vistula was awarded to the Polish crown, and Danzig became an independent city-state, run by a merchant class of predominantly German and Flemish origins, but

c.1175	1225	1241
Bronze doors of Gniezno cathedral cast by Romanesque masters	Konrad of Mazovia invites the Teutonic Knights to garrison his borders	Polish army defeated by Tatars at Battle of Legnica

swearing fealty to the Polish king. The knights were left only with the eastern territory thereafter known as Ducal Prussia or East Prussia.

Towards the end of the fifteenth century, Poland and Lithuania began to face new dangers from the east. First to threaten were the Crimean Tatars, whose menace prompted the creation of the first Polish standing army. A far more serious threat – one which endured for several hundred years – came from the **Muscovite tsars**, the self-styled protectors of the Orthodox faith who aimed to "liberate" the Ruthenian principalities to their west.

The Renaissance and Reformation

The spread of **Renaissance** ideas in Poland was most visibly manifested in the number of Italianate buildings constructed throughout the country. Science and learning also prospered under native Polish practitioners such as Nicolaus Copernicus. The period also saw a collective muscle-flexing exercise by the Polish nobility (*szlachta*). In 1493, the parliament, or **Sejm**, was established, gaining the sole right to enact legislation in 1505 and gradually making itself an important check on monarchical power.

The **Reformation** had a significant impact on Poland, not least because it precipitated the final collapse of the Teutonic Order in 1525, when grand master Albrecht von Hohenzollern accepted Lutheranism and converted his state into a secular duchy under the Polish crown. Lutheranism also took a strong hold in Danzig and the German-dominated cities of Royal Prussia. Poland became home to a number of refugee sects: along with the acceptance already extended to the Jewish and Orthodox faiths, this added up to a degree of **religious tolerance** unparalleled elsewhere in Europe.

The Republic of Nobles

The last of the Jagiellonians, **Sigismund August**, spent his final years trying to forge an alliance strong enough to withstand the ever-growing might of Moscow. The result of his negotiations was the 1569 **Union of Lublin**, whereby Poland and Lithuania were formally merged into the Commonwealth of the Two Nations. Lithuania, whose aristocracy was by now almost wholly Polish-speaking, retained much of its internal autonomy, but ceded large parts of what is now Ukraine to the Polish crown. In the same year the Sejm moved to **Warsaw**, a more central location for the capital of this new agglomeration; its capital status became official in 1596.

Sigismund August died without heir in 1572, leading to the creation of what became known as the **Republic of Nobles** – thenceforth kings were to be elected by an assembly of the entire nobility, from the great magnates down to the holders of small estates. The nobles also insisted on their Right of Resistance, a licence to overthrow a king who had fallen from favour. The Sejm had to be convened at two-yearly intervals, and all royal taxes were subject to ratification by the nobles.

The **Compact of Warsaw** of 1573 guaranteed the constitutional equality of all religions, although the ongoing Counter-Reformation ensured that few Protestant strongholds survived in Poland: a large section of the aristocracy was reconverted, while others who had recently switched from Orthodoxy to Calvinism were persuaded to change allegiance once more. The Orthodox Church was weakened by the creation of the Uniate Church in 1596, in which Orthodox believers on Poland's eastern borders recognized the authority of Rome.

1386	1410	1484
Marriage of Queen Jadwiga of Poland to Grand Duke Jogaila of Lithuania	Poland and Lithuania defeat Teutonic Knights at Battle of Grunwald	Death of pious Polish prince (and subsequently national saint) Kazimierz

The Republic of Nobles achieved some of its most spectacular successes early on, particularly under the second elected king, the Transylvanian prince Stefan Bathory who waged a brilliant campaign against the Russians between 1579 and 1582, neutralizing this particular threat to Poland's eastern borders for some time to come.

The Waza dynasty and its aftermath

The foreign policy of the next three monarchs, all members of the Swedish Waza dynasty, was less fortunate. **Sigismund August Waza**, the first of the trio, was a Catholic bigot who soon came into conflict with the almost exclusively Protestant population of his native land and was deposed from the Swedish throne in 1604. Though his ham-fistedness meant that Poland now had a new (and increasingly powerful) enemy, he continued as the Polish king for the next 28 years, having fought off a three-year-long internal rebellion.

In 1618, Ducal Prussia was inherited by **John Sigismund von Hohenzollern**, who set about weakening Poland's hold on the Baltic seaboard. A couple of decades later, the Hohenzollerns inherited much of Pomerania as well, with another section being acquired by Sweden. Poland managed to remain neutral in the calamitous series of religious and dynastic conflicts known as the **Thirty Years' War**, from which Sweden emerged as Europe's leading military power.

The reign of the third of the Wazas, **Jan Kazimierz**, saw Poland's fortunes plummet. In 1648, the year of his election, the Cossacks revolted in Ukraine, allying themselves with Moscow in 1654. This diversion inspired the Swedes to launch an invasion of Poland, soon overrunning the country in what came to be known as the **Swedish Deluge** ("Potop"). A heroic fightback was mounted, and the 1660 Treaty of Oliwa saw Poland recover most of its former territories. Three years earlier, however, the Hohenzollerns had wrested Ducal Prussia from the last vestiges of Polish control, merging it with their other territories to form the state of **Prussia**.

As well as the territorial losses suffered, these wars had seen Poland's population reduced to four million, less than half its previous total. A further crucial development of this period had been the first use in 1652 of the liberum veto, whereby a single vote in the Sejm was enough to stall any piece of legislation. Once established, the practice soon became widespread in the protection of petty interests, and Poland found itself on the slippery slope towards **ungovernability**.

Jan Sobieski

Before repeated use of the liberum veto led to the final collapse of political authority, Poland had what was arguably its greatest moment of glory in international power politics. A huge offensive by the Ottoman Turks was beaten back by the Poles, under the command of **Jan Sobieski**, at the **Battle of Chocim** (in southwestern Ukraine) in 1673 – as a reward for which Sobieski was elected king the following year. In 1683 Sobieski defeated the Ottomans outside Vienna, marking the end of Turkish designs on Central Europe.

However, Sobieski had concentrated on the **Turkish campaign** to the exclusion of all other issues. His relief of Vienna exhausted Poland's military capacity while enabling Austria to recover as an imperial power; it also aided the rise of the predatory state of Prussia, which he had intended to keep firmly in check. His neglect of domestic policy led to the liberum veto being used with impunity, while Poland and Lithuania grew apart as the nobility of the latter engaged in a civil war.

1518	1543	1569
Sigismund the Old marries Milanese Bona Sforza, who brings Italian style to Kraków	Nicholas Copernicus publishes *On the Revolutions of the Celestial Spheres*	Union of Lublin creates the Polish-Lithuanian Commonwealth of the Two Nations

The decline of Poland

Known as "Augustus the Strong", owing to his fathering of more than three hundred children, Sobieski's successor, **Augustus Wettin**, was in fact a weak ruler, unable to shake off his debts to the Russians who had secured his election. In 1701, Friedrich III of Prussia openly defied him by declaring Ducal Prussia's right to be regarded as a kingdom, having himself crowned in Königsberg. Augustus's lack of talent for power politics was even more evident in his dealings with Sweden, against whom he launched a war for control of Livonia. The victorious Swedes deposed Augustus in 1704, securing the election of their own favoured candidate, **Stanisław Leszczyński**, in his place.

Augustus was reinstated in 1710, courtesy of the Russians, who reduced Poland to the role of a client state in the process. The **Silent Sejm** of 1717, which guaranteed the existing constitution, marked the end of effective parliamentary life. When Leszczyński won the election to succeed Augustus the Strong in 1733, the Russians intervened immediately to have him replaced by the deceased king's son, who proved to be an even more inept custodian of Polish interests than his father.

When the younger Augustus Wettin died in 1763, the Russians again intervened to ensure the election of **Stanisław-August Poniatowski**, the former lover of their empress, Catherine the Great. However, Poniatowski proved an unwilling stooge, even espousing the cause of reform. Russian support of the Orthodox minority in Poland led to a growth of Catholic-inspired nationalism, and by obstructing the most moderately liberal measures, Russian policy led to an outbreak of revolts.

The Partitions

Russia's Polish policy was finally rendered impotent by the revolt of the **Confederacy of Bar** between 1768 and 1772. A heavy-handed crackdown on these reformers would certainly have led to war with Prussia, probably in alliance with Austria; doing nothing would have allowed the Poles to reassert their national independence. As a compromise, the Russians decided to support a Prussian plan for the **Partition of Poland**. By a treaty of 1772, Poland lost almost thirty percent of its territory. White Ruthenia's eastern sectors were ceded to Russia, while Austria received Red Ruthenia plus Małopolska south of the River Vistula – a province subsequently rechristened Galicia. The Prussians gained the smallest share of the carve-up in the form of most of Royal Prussia, but this was strategically and economically the most significant.

Stung by this, the Poles embarked on a radical programme of reform, including the partial emancipation of serfs and the encouragement of immigration from the three empires that had undertaken the Partition. In 1791, Poland was given the first codified **constitution** in Europe since classical antiquity and the second in the modern world, after the United States. It introduced the concept of a people's sovereignty, this time including the bourgeoisie, and adopted a separation of powers between executive, legislature and judiciary, with government by a cabinet responsible to the Sejm.

This was all too much for the Russians, who, buying off the Prussians with the promise of Danzig, invaded Poland, defeating them the following year. By the **Second Partition** of 1793, the constitution was annulled; the Russians annexed the remaining parts of White and Red Ruthenia, with the Prussians gaining Wielkopolska, and parts of Mazuria and Toruń in addition to the star prize of Danzig.

In 1794, Tadeusz Kościuszko launched a national insurrection, achieving a stunning

1578	1610–12	1647
Polish-Lithuanian forces destroy the Russian army at the Battle of Wenden	Polish-Lithuanian forces occupy Moscow	Astronomer Johannes Hevelius publishes *Selenografia*, a pioneering work about the moon

victory over the Russians at the **Battle of Racławice** with a militia largely composed of peasants armed with scythes. However, the rebellion was put down, Poniatowski forced to abdicate, and Poland wiped off the map by the **Third Partition** of 1795. This gave all lands east of the Bug and Niemen rivers to Russia, the remainder of Małopolska to Austria, and the rest of the country, including Warsaw, to Prussia. By an additional treaty of 1797, the partitioning powers agreed to abolish the very name of Poland.

Napoleon and the Congress of Vienna

Revolutionary France was the country that Polish patriots looked to in their struggle to regain independence, and Paris became the main headquarters for exiles and conspiratorial groups. Hopes eventually crystallized around **Napoleon Bonaparte**, who assumed power in 1799, but when three Polish legions were raised as part of the French army, Kościuszko declined to command them, regarding Napoleon as a megalomaniac who would use the Poles for his own ends.

Initially, these fears seemed unfounded: French victories over Prussia led to the creation of the **Duchy of Warsaw** in 1807 out of Polish territory annexed by the Prussians. This seemed the first step in the recreation of Poland and encouraged **Józef Poniatowski**, nephew of the last king and one of the most brilliant military commanders of the day, to throw in his lot with the French. Poniatowski played a key role in Napoleon's advance on Moscow in 1812, a campaign which ended in humiliating retreat. Cornered by the Prussians and Russians near Leipzig, Poniatowski refused to surrender, preferring to lead his troops to a suicidal defeat. This act of self-sacrifice was to serve as a symbol to Polish patriots for the rest of the century.

The **Congress of Vienna** of 1814–15, set up to organize post-Napoleonic Europe, awarded the main part of the Duchy of Warsaw (now renamed the **Congress Kingdom**) to the Russians. The Poznań area was detached to form the Grand Duchy of Posen, in reality no more than a dependency of Prussia. Austria was allowed to keep most of Galicia, which was governed from Lwów (renamed Lemberg). After much deliberation, it was decided to make Kraków a city-state and "symbolic capital" of the vanished nation.

The struggle against the Partitions

As the most liberal part of the Russian Empire, the Congress Kingdom enjoyed a period of relative prosperity under the governorship of **Adam Czartoryski**, preserving its own parliament, administration, educational system and army. However, this cosy arrangement was disrupted by the arch-autocrat **Nicholas I**, who became tsar in 1825 and quickly imposed his policies on Poland. An attempted **insurrection** in November 1830, centred on a botched assassination of the tsar's brother, provoked a Russian invasion. By the end of the following year, the Poles had been defeated; their constitution was suspended and a reign of repression began. These events led many to abandon all nationalist hopes; the first great wave of Polish **emigration**, principally to America, began.

An attempted insurrection against the Austrians in 1846 also backfired, leading to the end of Kraków's independence with its reincorporation into Galicia. The last major uprising, against the Russians in 1863–64, was hopelessly limited by Poland's lack of a regular army. Its failure led to the abolition of the Congress Kingdom and its formal incorporation into Russia as the province of "Vistulaland". However, it was immediately followed by the **emancipation of the serfs**, granted on more favourable

1648	1683	1791
Bogdan Hmelnitsky launches Cossack uprising in Ukraine	Jan Sobieski defeats Ottoman Turks outside Vienna	Great Sejm passes the Constitution of May 3

terms than in any other part of the tsarist empire – in order to cause maximum ill-feeling between the Polish nobility and peasantry.

Following the crushing of the 1863–64 rebellion, the **Russian sector** of Poland entered a period of quiet stability, with the abolition of internal tariffs opening up the vast Russian market to Polish goods. For the next half-century, Polish patriots, wherever they lived, were concerned less with trying to win independence than with keeping a distinctive culture alive. They had the greatest success in Galicia, because they were the second-largest ethnic group in the **Habsburg Empire**, and because the Habsburgs had a laxer attitude towards the diversity of their subjects. The province was given powers of self-government and, although economically backward and ruled by a reactionary upper class, flourished once more as a centre of learning and the arts.

Altogether different was the situation in **Prussia**, the most efficiently repressive of the three partitioning powers. Poles made up a large percentage of the workforce in some of its technologically most advanced areas, notably the rich minefields of Upper Silesia. The price to be paid for this relative prosperity was a severe clampdown on Polish culture, seen at its most extreme in the **Kulturkampf**, whose main aim was to crush the power of the Catholic Church, with a secondary intention of establishing the unchallenged supremacy of the German language in the new nation's education system. It misfired badly in Poland, giving the clergy the opportunity to whip up support for their own fervently nationalistic brand of Catholicism.

Meanwhile, an upturn in political life came with the establishment of representative assemblies in Berlin, Vienna and St Petersburg. This led to the formation of various new Polish **political parties** and movements, the most important of which were the Polish Socialist Party (PPS), active mainly in the cities of Russian Poland; the Nationalist League, whose power base was in the peripheral provinces; the Peasant Movement of Galicia; and the Christian Democrats, a dominant force among the Silesian Catholics.

The resurrection of Poland

World War I destroyed the Russian, German and Austrian empires and allowed Poland to rise from the dead. Some of the groundwork was done right at the start of the war, when founder-member of the PPS **Józef Piłsudski** formed a Polish Legion to fight alongside the Austrians, assuming that the defeat of the Russians would allow him to create the new Polish state on his own terms. In this, he favoured a return to the great tradition of ethnic and religious diversity of centuries past. Piłsudski's great rival was **Roman Dmowski**, leader of the Nationalist League, who had a vision of a purely Polish and staunchly Catholic future, in which the Jews would, as far as possible, be excluded. He opted to work for independence by exclusively political means, in the hope that victory over Germany would lead the Western allies to set up a Polish state under his leadership.

In the event, Piłsudski came out on top: the Germans, having held him in internment for well over a year, released him the day before the armistice of November 11, 1918, allowing him to take command of a Regency Council. He was sworn in as head of state three days later. Dmowski had to accept the consolation prize of head delegate to the Paris Peace Conference, though his associate, the concert pianist **Ignacy Jan Paderewski**, became the country's first prime minister.

1795	1825	1830
Third Partition of Poland wipes Poland off the map	First cotton mill built in Łódź	November Uprising against Tsarist rule

Poland redefined

The new Poland lacked a defined territory. Initially, it consisted of the German and Austrian zones of occupation, centred on Warsaw and Lublin, plus Western Galicia. Wielkopolska was added a month later, following a revolt against the German garrison in Poznań. The Paris Conference played only a minor role in all this, but did take the key decision to give the country access to the sea by means of the **Polish Corridor**, a strip of land cut through the old Royal Prussia, which meant that East Prussia was left cut off from the rest of Germany. **Danzig** was excluded from the corridor on the grounds that its population was overwhelmingly German; instead, it reverted to its former status as a city-state – an unsatisfactory compromise that was later to have tragic consequences.

The **Polish–Soviet War** of 1919–20 was the most significant of the conflicts that determined the country's borders. Realizing that the Bolsheviks would want to spread their revolution to Poland and then to the industrialized West, Piłsudski aimed to create a grouping of independent nation-states stretching from Finland to Georgia to halt this new expansionist Russian empire. Taking advantage of the civil war between the Soviet "Reds" and the counter-revolutionary "Whites", his army marched deep into Belarus and the Ukraine. He was subsequently beaten back to Warsaw, but skilfully regrouped his forces to pull off a crushing victory, regaining a sizeable chunk of the old Polish-Lithuanian Commonwealth's eastern territories.

The fate of Upper Silesia was decided by **plebiscite**, although a series of Polish uprisings in Upper Silesia helped to force the international community's hand. In the end the province was partitioned: Poland gained most of the Katowice conurbation, thus ensuring that the country gained a solid industrial base.

The interwar years

The fragility of the new state's political institutions became obvious when Piłsudski refused to stand in the 1922 presidential elections on the grounds that the office was insufficiently powerful. Worse, the victor, **Gabriel Narutowicz**, was hounded by the Nationalists for having won as a result of votes cast by "non-Poles", and assassinated soon afterwards. For the next few years, Poland was governed by a series of weak governments presiding over hyperinflation, feeble attempts at agrarian reform and a contemptuous army officer class.

In May 1926, Piłsudski staged a military coup, ushering in the so-called **Sanacja** regime, named after a slogan proposing a return to political "health". Piłsudski functioned as the state's commander-in-chief until his death in 1935, though he held no formal office after an initial two-year stint as prime minister. Parliamentary life continued, but opposition was emasculated by the creation of the so-called **Non-Party Bloc for Co-operation with the Government**, and disaffected groups were brought to heel by force if necessary.

Having a country led by **Stalin** on one frontier was bad enough, but when **Hitler** seized power in Germany in 1933, Poland became a sitting target for two ruthless dictators. Hitler had always been open about his ambition of wiping Poland off the map again, regarding the Slavs as a race who were fit for no higher role than to be slaves of the Aryans. He also wanted to unite all ethnic Germans under his rule: a foreign policy objective that was quickly put into effect by his annexation of Austria in March 1938 and of parts of Czechoslovakia – with British and French connivance – in September of the same year. As Hitler's attentions turned towards Poland, his foreign minister Joachim

1834	1849	1861
Adam Mickiewicz publishes epic national poem *Pan Tadeusz*	Frederic Chopin dies in Paris aged 39	January Uprising against Tsarist rule

POLAND 1938

POLAND 1945

1896	1901	1903
Henryk Sienkiewicz publishes epic novel *Quo Vadis*	Stanisław Wyspiański premieres his play *Wesele* ("The Wedding")	Marie Skłodowska Curie wins Nobel Prize in Physics

von Ribbentrop and his Soviet counterpart Vyacheslav Molotov concluded the notorious **Nazi–Soviet Pact** in August 1939, which allowed either side to pursue any aggressive designs without the interference of the other. It also included a secret clause which agreed on a mutual partition of Poland, thereby clearing the way for Hitler to start **World War II**.

World War II

On September 1, 1939, Hitler invaded Poland, beginning by annexing the free city of **Danzig**. The Poles fought with great courage, inflicting heavy casualties, but were numerically and technologically in a hopeless position. On September 17, the Soviets invaded the eastern part of the country, claiming the share-out agreed by the Nazi–Soviet Pact. France and Britain declared war on Germany on September 3, but had no strategic plan to come to Poland's aid; by the first week of October, the country had capitulated. A government-in-exile was established in London under **Władysław Sikorski**.

Millions of Polish civilians were to be imprisoned, enslaved or murdered by the occupiers over the next six years. Right at the start of the war, Nazi death squads known as the **Einsatzgruppen** were given the task of mopping up resistance – which basically meant shooting civilians (Polish and Jewish alike) out of hand. Meanwhile the Soviets **deported** thousands of Poles to Siberia, while killing outright the potentially troublesome elements – hence their murder of 22,000 Polish officers, known as the **Katyń massacre** (see page 73).

Nazi control of western Poland entailed further territorial dismemberment. Some parts of the country were simply swallowed up by the Reich, with northwestern districts forming part of the newly created Reichgau of Danzig-West Prussia, and west-central territories around Poznań being absorbed into the Warthegau. Everything else – Warsaw and Kraków included – was placed under a German-controlled administration known as the **General-gouvernement**, an ad hoc structure designed to exploit the economic and labour potential of Poland while the war lasted. Poles everywhere were subjected to dislocation and hardship. Those living in the Warthegau were forced to emigrate to the Generalgouvernement in an attempt to Germanize the province; while those in Danzig-West Prussia were allowed to stay where they were providing they adopted German names and passports.

The Final Solution

The Nazi invasion of the Soviet Union in June 1941 drove the Soviets out of eastern Poland and paved the way for the introduction of an even more vicious regime of occupation. Most importantly it made possible the so-called **Final Solution**, in which the Jews of Europe were systematically murdered at **extermination camps** (rather than being shot, starved, worked to death or forced to emigrate, as was the pre-existing plan). Most of the extermination camps were built in occupied Poland – largely because large numbers of Jews had already been deported to ghettoes in these areas. The Nazi determination to eliminate the Jews was matched by a belief that millions of Poles and other Slavs should also be shot or starved in order to provide German colonizers with living space. A vast infrastructure of camps and slave-labour factories was established to facilitate these megalomaniac goals. The huge facility at **Auschwitz (Oświęcim)** had many functions – including slave-labour camp, POW camp, Gestapo torture centre and extermination camp (predominantly for Jews but also for Gypsies and other undesirables) – which is why the site subsequently became such an important symbol for all levels of Nazi terror.

1906	1918	1924
Foundation of Cracovia Kraków, Poland's oldest football club	Re-establishment of an independent Poland	Stanislaw "Witkacy" Witkiewicz opens his Portrait Painting Company in Zakopane

Nazi defeat and Soviet victory

Hitler's attack on the USSR failed to deliver the expected lightning victory and turned instead into a long violent failure, with Nazi Germany's defeat the only possible outcome. **Stalin** began by cooperating with the Polish government in exile but gradually came to realize that he didn't need to; Poland's fate would be decided by the advancing Red Army, not by politicians sitting in London or the underground resistance movement in the country itself. At the **Tehran Conference** in November 1943 Britain and America basically agreed that Eastern Europe now fell within the Soviet sphere of influence, making it almost inevitable that postwar Poland would be forced into the Soviet camp. Stalin also insisted that the Soviet Union would retain the territories it had annexed in 1939. Allied support for this was obtained by reference to the current border's virtual coincidence with the so-called **Curzon Line**, which had been drawn up by a former British Foreign Secretary in 1920 in an unsuccessful attempt at mediation in the Polish–Soviet War.

During the **liberation of Poland** in 1944, any possibility of reasserting genuine Polish control depended on the outcome of the **uprising in Warsaw** against the Nazi occupiers (see page 70). On July 31, with the Soviets poised on the outskirts of the city, the Home Army was forced to act. The Red Army lay in wait during the ensuing bloodbath. When the insurgents were finally defeated at the beginning of October, Hitler ordered that the city be razed before leaving the ruins to the Red Army. In early 1945, as the Soviets pushed on through Poland, the Nazis set up last-ditch strongholds in Silesia. Wrocław (then known as Breslau) held out until May 6, two days before Germany's final surrender.

The aftermath

No country suffered so much from World War II as Poland. In all, around 25 percent of the population died, and the whole country lay devastated. Moreover, although the Allies had originally gone to war on its behalf, it found itself reduced in size and **shifted west** across the map of Europe by some 200 kilometres, with its western frontier fixed at the lines of the Odra and Nysa rivers. Stalin had in effect achieved his twin aims of moving his frontiers and his sphere of influence well to the west.

The losses in the east – including Lwów and Wilno, both great centres of Polish culture – were painful, and involved the transfer of millions of people across the country in the following two years. There were compensations, however: Pomerania and the industrially valuable Silesia were restored after a gap of some seven centuries; and the much-coveted city of Danzig, which had been detached since its seizure by the Teutonic Knights, was also returned – and, as Gdańsk, was later to play a major role in postwar Polish history.

Polish communism: the early years

The Polish communists took power gradually and methodically over the next two to three years, their progress guaranteed by the presence of the Red Army. Already in 1943 Stalin had formed the **ZPP** (Union of Polish Patriots) from Polish communist exiles and Russian placemen with polonized names in order to bring the country under political control. As the Red Army drove the Germans west, the ZPP established a **Committee for National Liberation** in Lublin, under the leadership of **Bolesław Bierut**. This was to form the core of the Polish government over the next few years.

Political opposition was fragmented and ineffectual. From the government-in-exile, only

1935	1939	1944
Death of Polish leader Józef Piłsudski. His body is buried in Kraków, his heart in home-city Vilnius	Poland is invaded by Nazi Germany and the Soviet Union	The Warsaw Uprising is put down by the Germans; the city is almost totally destroyed

a single prominent figure returned to Poland after 1945 – **Stanisław Mikołajczyk**, leader of the prewar Peasants' Party. A coalition government was formed in which the communist-controlled **Polish Workers' Party** held the Interior Ministry, thereby controlling the police. The communists falsified the results of a 1946 referendum on the future direction of the state, and did the same again in the 1947 general election. After the forcible merger of the socialists and communists in 1948 as the **PZPR** (Polish United Workers' Party), it only remained for the external pressures of the emerging **Cold War** to lock Poland completely into the Soviet sphere of influence and model of economic and political development.

The birth of the PRL

In 1952 a new Constitution enshrined the leading role of the PZPR in every aspect of Polish society, designating the country as the Polish People's Republic or Polska Rzeczpospolita Ludowa – nowadays remembered by its acronym, **PRL**. While the trappings of democracy were retained, the other parties – the Democratic Party (SD) and the reconstituted Peasants' Party (ZSL) – were under the effective political control of the PZPR. Only the **Catholic Church**, although harassed by the authorities, retained a degree of independence – although its leader, **Cardinal Wyszyński**, was arrested in 1953 for "anti-state" activities and imprisoned for three years.

Nationalization continued throughout this period, although the collectivization of agriculture proved impossible given the traditional independence of Polish farmers. Major iron and steel industries were established, and an entire **shipbuilding** industry developed along the Baltic coast – most notably in Gdańsk. There were, inevitably, costs: standards of living remained almost static, food was scarce, and unrestrained industrialization resulted in terrible pollution. Perhaps the most significant achievement of the period was the creation of an urban industrial working class. Paradoxically, these very people proved to be the backbone of almost every political struggle against the Party in the following decades.

1956 – the Polish October

In Poland, as in Hungary, 1956 saw the first major political crisis of the communist era. It was in February 1956 that **Khrushchev** made his famous "secret" speech to the Twentieth Congress of the Soviet Communist Party, denouncing Stalin and his crimes; the speech was a bombshell, unmasking the lie of the absolute correctness of Stalin's every act. In June, workers in Poznań took to the streets over working conditions and wages. The protests rapidly developed into a major confrontation, and up to eighty people were killed in the ensuing **Poznań riots**. Initial government insistence that "imperialist agents" had instigated the street battles gave way to an admission that some of the workers' grievances were justified and that the Party would try to remedy them.

The Poznań riots further divided an alarmed and weakened Party. In October, the Party plenum elected as leader the reform-minded **Władysław Gomułka**, a former victim of Stalinist purges who had spent the 1951–54 period in prison. Moscow had not been consulted about the appointment and an enraged Khrushchev flew to Warsaw in person to demand an explanation. Soviet troops were mobilized along Poland's borders, in response to which Polish security forces prepared to defend the capital. In the end, Gomułka assured Khrushchev that Poland would remain a loyal ally and maintain the essentials of communist rule. Khrushchev returned to Moscow, Soviet troops withdrew, and four days later Gomułka addressed a huge crowd in Warsaw as a national hero.

1949	1954
Spontaneous mass pilgrimages to witness a weeping icon of the Madonna in Lublin are hushed up by communist authorities	Bohemian beat writer Marek Hłasko publishes his first short stories in the Warsaw press

The **Soviet invasion of Hungary** to crush the national uprising there in early November 1956 provided a clear reminder to Poles of how close they had come to disaster.

The **Polish October**, as it came to be known, raised high hopes of a new order, which initially seemed justified. Censorship was relaxed, Cardinal Wyszyński was released and state harassment of the Church and control over the economy eased. A **cultural thaw** encouraged an explosion of creativity in art and theatre – much of it wildly experimental – and opened the doors to "decadent" Western preoccupations such as jazz and rock and roll. But the impetus for political reform quickly faded, and the 1960s saw a progressive return to centralized planning, a stagnant economy and sporadic attempts to reassert some measure of control over an increasingly disaffected populace. **Student protests** in March 1968 were met with a clampdown; the fact that some student leaders were of Polish-Jewish heritage provided government leaders with an excuse to mount a shamelessly anti-Semitic campaign against cosmopolitan elements and supposed "Zionists", who were accused of being disloyal to Poland and encouraged to emigrate.

1970–79: from Gomułka to Gierek

In December 1970, huge **food price rises** were announced, provoking **strikes** and demonstrations along the Baltic coast, centring on Gdańsk. When troops fired on demonstrators, killing many, the protests spread like wildfire, to the point of open insurrection (Gomułka's defence minister, **Wojciech Jaruzelski**, was to be put on trial for the killings some twenty years later). A traumatized Central Committee met five days before Christmas, hurriedly bundling Gomułka into retirement and replacing him as first secretary with **Edward Gierek**, a member of the Party's reformist faction in the 1960s. Price rises were frozen and wage increases promised, but despite a Christmas calm, strikes broke out throughout January 1971, with calls for free trade unions and a free press accompanying the more usual economic demands. Peace was only restored when Gierek and Jaruzelski went to the Gdańsk shipyards by taxi to argue their case and admit their errors to the strikers.

The Gierek period marked out an alternative route to social stability, borrowing heavily from Western banks throughout the early 1970s. Food became cheaper and more plentiful as internal subsidies were matched by purchases from the West and the Soviet Union. Standards of living rose and a wider range of **consumer goods** became available. However, the international economic recession and oil crises of the mid-1970s destroyed the Polish boom at a stroke. Debts became impossible to service, new loans harder to obtain, and it became apparent that earlier borrowing had been squandered in unsustainable rises in consumption or wasted in large-scale projects of limited economic value. By 1976 the wheel had turned full circle. The government announced food price rises of almost treble the magnitude of those proposed in the early 1970s.

This time the ensuing **strikes** were firmly repressed and many activists imprisoned. In response to the imprisonment of strikers, the **KOR** (Committee for the Defence of Workers) was formed. Comprising dissident intellectuals, it was to provide not only valuable publicity and support for the opposition through Western contacts, but also a degree of strategic sophistication that the spontaneous uprisings had so far lacked. Perhaps even more decisive was the election of Karol Wojtyła, archbishop of Kraków, as **Pope John Paul II** in 1978. A formidable opponent of the communist regime, he visited

1964	1967	1978
Sprinter Irena Szewińska wins first of her three career gold medals at the Tokyo Olympics	The Rolling Stones play in Warsaw	Mirosław Hermaszewski, flying in a Soviet Soyuz spacecraft, becomes the first Pole in space

Poland in 1979 and was met by the greatest public gatherings that Poland had ever seen. For the Polish people, his visit provided a public demonstration of their potential power.

1980–89: Solidarity

Gierek's announcement of one hundred percent price rises on foodstuffs in July 1980 led to more strikes, centring on the **Gdańsk shipyards**. Attempts by the authorities to have a crane operator, Anna Walentynowicz, dismissed for political agitation intensified the unrest. Led by a shipyard electrician, **Lech Wałęsa**, the strikers occupied the yards and were joined by a hastily convened group of opposition intellectuals and activists, including future prime minister **Tadeusz Mazowiecki**. Together they formulated a series of demands – the **Twenty-one Points** – that were to serve as the intellectual template for the opposition in both Poland and Eastern Europe in general.

Free trade unions, the right to strike and freedom of speech were the first three points on the list. However, the opposition was careful to reiterate that they "intended neither to threaten the foundations of the Socialist Republic in our country, nor its position in international relations". The Party caved in, signing the historic **Gdańsk Agreements** in August 1980, after which free trade unions, covering over 75 percent of Poland's 12.5 million workforce, were formed across the country, under the name Solidarność – **Solidarity**.

Gierek and his supporters were swept from office by the Party in September 1980, but the limits of Solidarity's power were signalled by an unscheduled Warsaw Pact meeting later in the year. Other Eastern European communist leaders perceptively argued that Solidarity's success would threaten not only their Polish counterparts' political futures, but their own as well. Accordingly, Soviet and Warsaw Pact units were mobilized along Poland's borders. The Poles closed ranks: the Party reaffirmed its Leninist purity, while Solidarity and the Church publicly emphasized their moderation. Throughout 1981 deadlock ensued while the economic crisis gathered pace. Solidarity, lacking any positive control over the economy, was only capable of bringing it to a halt, and repeatedly showed itself able to do so.

General Jaruzelski took control of the Party in July 1981 and, in the face of threats of a general strike, continued to negotiate with Solidarity leaders, but refused to relinquish any power. A wave of strikes in late October 1981 were met by the imposition of **martial law** on December 12: occupations and strikes were broken up by troops, Solidarity banned, civil liberties suspended and union leaders arrested. However, these measures solved nothing fundamental, and in the face of creative and determined resistance from the now underground Solidarity movement, still actively supported by large segments of the populace, martial law was lifted in the wake of Pope John Paul II's second visit to his home country in 1983.

The period 1984 to 1988 was marked by a final attempt by the Jaruzelski government to dig Poland out of its **economic crisis**. The country's debt had risen to an astronomical $39 billion, wages had slumped, and production was hampered by endemic labour unrest. After a devastating wave of strikes in 1988 Jaruzelski finally admitted defeat and called for a "courageous turnaround" by the Party, accepting the need for talks with Solidarity and the prospect of real **power sharing** – an option of political capitulation only made possible by the election of Mikhail Gorbachev as secretary general in the Kremlin.

1980	1984
Strikes in Gdańsk lead to the formation of free trade union Solidarity	Pro-Solidarity priest Jerzy Popiełuszko is murdered by rogue elements of the security forces

1989–2005: the new Poland

The **round-table talks** ran from February to April 1989, government representatives ultimately agreeing to the opposition's demands for the legalization of Solidarity, the establishment of an independent press and the promise of what were termed "semi-free" elections. All hundred seats of a reconstituted upper chamber, the Senate, were to be freely contested; while 65 percent of seats in the lower house, the Sejm, were to be reserved for the PZPR and its allied parties.

The communists suffered a humiliating defeat in the elections of 1989, with Solidarity winning almost every seat it contested. Thus, while the numerical balance of the lower chamber remained with the PZPR, the unthinkable became possible: a Solidarity-led government. The parties that had been allied to the PZPR broke with their communist overlords and voted to establish journalist **Tadeusz Mazowiecki** as prime minister in August 1989, installing the first non-communist government in Eastern Europe since World War II. Subsequently the PZPR disintegrated, voting to dissolve itself in January 1990.

President Wałęsa and the first free elections

After a period away from the political limelight, **Lech Wałęsa** re-emerged to win the presidential elections of 1990, promising a faster pace of reform and the removal of the privileges of the communist elite. In January 1991 he appointed business-oriented liberal **Jan Krzysztof Bielecki** as prime minister, although it was finance minister Leszek Balczerowicz who earned the headlines with an austerity programme that led to rising prices and rocketing unemployment. Balczerowicz's "shock therapy" won the confidence of Western financial institutions, resulting in an agreement with the International Monetary Fund (IMF) about the reduction of Poland's $33 billion debt.

Elections – the first fully free ones since World War II – were held in October 1991. A spectacular array of parties took part, of which 29 entered the new Sejm, with the highest scorer, the Democratic Union (UD), gaining a meagre 14 percent of the alarmingly low (43 percent) turnout. A succession of right-of-centre coalition governments followed, mixing liberal economic policies with the kind of social conservatism that went down well with the increasingly influential Catholic Church. The 1993 elections represented something of a turnaround, with victory for a coalition between the former-communist Democratic Left Alliance (SLD) and the Peasants' Party (PSL). The new government continued with market reforms, but at the same time pledged to do more to address its negative social effects.

The Kwaśniewski era

In 1995 an increasingly crotchety and quarrelsome Wałęsa lost the presidential elections to the SLD's **Aleksander Kwaśniewski**, a polished, consensus-building character whose accessible blokeishness appealed strongly to the average Pole.

The September 1997 **elections** handed victory to a new right-of-centre grouping, the Solidarity-led AWS, but with just 34 percent of the vote they had to forge a **coalition** with Leszek Balcerowicz's neo-liberal Freedom Union (UW). The main planks of the government's programme were little different from those of its predecessor, emphasizing continuing privatization and economic retrenchment. However, the government was hamstrung by the split between the Balcerowicz faction, which was committed to free market reforms and public spending cuts, and those closer to

1988	1989	1999
Wrocław-based art subversives Orange Alternative stage the "Revolution of the Dwarfs"	Poland forms its first non-communist government since 1945	Poland joins NATO

Solidarity, who favoured a less radical style. The economic growth of the mid-1990s was beginning to slow down by the end of the decade, unemployment was rising, and those in work were frustrated by having to put up with negligible pay rises from one year to the next. In these conditions, the SLD bounced back into popular affections; Kwaśniewski won a landslide in the presidential elections of 2000.

The volatile nature of party politics throughout this period had little impact on the main goals of Polish **foreign policy**: membership of **NATO** and the **European Union**. The weak international position of Russia allowed Poland unexpected freedom of manoeuvre, signing up to NATO's newly formed **Partnership for Peace** in 1994 and, together with the Czech Republic and Hungary, becoming a full member of the alliance in March 1999.

Decline of the SLD

Profiting from government mistakes rather than presenting a radically different programme of its own, the SLD won the **parliamentary elections** of September 2001, although with 200 of the Sejm's 460 seats it still needed the support of the PSL to form a government. Both the AWS and the Freedom Union were wiped out entirely and replaced by the Civic Platform (PO).

The new administration of **Leszek Miller** proved just as ineffectual as its predecessors' in fulfilling the huge public expectations invested in it. Despite clear evidence that the Polish economy was becoming more efficient and attracting increasing levels of foreign investment, unemployment remained high and average wages low. In foreign policy the SLD remained true to the pro-Western line and supported the American-led invasion of **Iraq** in spring 2003 by sending several thousand troops.

However, it was domestic policy that led to serious strains in the ruling coalition, and Miller resigned as prime minister in March 2004 – ironically, on the eve of what should have been his greatest triumph, Poland's entry into the **European Union** in May 2004. A referendum on EU membership held in June 2003 had produced a huge majority in favour, the result symbolizing for many Poland's extraordinary voyage from Soviet satellite to equal member of the wider European family.

The main beneficiary of the SLD's declining support was the right-of-centre **Civic Platform** (PO). However, the lack of ideological differences between Poland's main political groupings encouraged the emergence of new populist parties eager to exploit those discontents which the mainstream, pro-market and pro-European politicians seem unable to face head-on. Winning their first-ever seats in the parliamentary elections of 2001 were **Samoobrona** (Self-Defence), a peasants' rights party led by Andrzej Lepper, a maverick populist notorious for his controversial and often anti-democratic outbursts, and the **League of Polish Families** (LPR) headed by Roman Giertych, a much more openly anti-European, anti-liberal party combining a left-wing social programme with a right-wing mix of nationalism and reactionary moral values.

2005–14: PiS versus the PO

The rightward shift in the balance of political forces culminated in elections held in September 2005. The traditionalist-conservative **Law and Justice (PiS)** party, led by Jaroslaw Kaczynski, scored a narrow victory over the Civic Platform (PO), with

2001	2004	2007
Ski jumper Adam Malysz wins the first of his four World Cup gold medals.	Poland joins the EU	Tennis player Agnieszka Radwańska wins her first WTA tournament in Stockholm

the SLD suffering near electoral wipeout. Completing the political turnaround, one month later **Lech Kaczynski**, twin brother of the PiS leader, triumphed over the PO's Donald Tusk in the second round of presidential elections. The PiS formed a minority government with Samoobrona and the LPR, and focused on a staunchly **anti-communist programme** of national renewal aimed at sweeping away what the party saw as the moral and political corruption of the post-1989 era. PiS activists saw the post-1989 political establishment as a smokescreen for a powerful network of organized crime, politicians, business people and a security service suspected of being dominated by communist-era functionaries. The Kaczynskis' foreign policy strove to put national interests first, introducing a Eurosceptic note to relations with Brussels and vetoing EU efforts to sign a cooperation agreement with Russia.

Less than two years into its period of office things took a decided turn for the worse for the PiS when continued infighting with its smaller radical allies culminated in the collapse of the government coalition in July 2007. Early elections in October 2007 resulted in an emphatic victory for **Donald Tusk**'s PO. A Tusk-led coalition government between the PO and the Polish Peasant's Party (PSL) pursued pro-business, pro-EU policies that proved popular at a time when the Polish economy was expanding. The financial crisis was not felt as keenly in Poland as in other European countries, helping to maintain the optimistic mood.

Smoleńsk

On April 10, 2010, a Polish plane carrying President Lech Kaczyński and 95 other dignitaries and crew crashed in thick fog while approaching the Russian airport of Smoleńsk, killing everyone on board. They were on their way to take part in commemorations marking the 70th anniversary of the Katyń massacre (see page 73), an event that symbolized more than any other Poland's suffering at the hands of powerful neighbours. The Smoleńsk crash briefly brought the country together in shock and mourning, and also led to an outpouring of international goodwill – not least from Russia, the country that was only just coming to terms with its original culpability in the Katyń crime of 1940. However, Russia and Poland gradually fell out over what had caused the crash: for the Russians it was simply a matter of Polish pilot error; the Polish government investigation concluded that pilot error had been compounded by misleading information from the Russian air traffic controllers on the ground. The tragedy gradually became a major bone of contention in Polish society too, with those connected with the late president's PiS party dissatisfied with both the official investigation and the way the event was commemorated – with particularly bitter arguments breaking out about the placing of memorial crosses in central Warsaw.

For a time, the ruling PO remained master of the situation. The PO's **Bronisław Komorowski** was elected president in July 2010, while Tusk triumphed again in the parliamentary elections of 2011. Poland's transformation continued apace, with new sports stadiums and transport infrastructure developed in time for the **Euro 2012** football championships (co-hosted with Ukraine), and **EU funding** changing the face of urban Poland with everything from new museums to railway stations. However, the EU was also perceived as forcing changes on Polish society that conflicted with traditional conservative values – especially the increased emphasis on secularism, women's equality and gay rights. The EU also enabled international capital to gain

2010	2012
President Lech Kaczynski and 95 others killed in an aeroplane crash at Smoleńsk	Poland co-hosts Euro 2012 football tournament with Ukraine

control of large sections of the Polish economy, provoking an **anti-EU**, anti-liberal backlash that united traditional conservatives and a new breed of radical populists.

The political present

By 2014, the PO government was running out of steam; Tusk resigned as PM in September to become President of the EU Council, to be replaced by **Ewa Kopacz**. A coming change in the political climate was signalled in May 2015, when Komorowski narrowly lost the presidency to PiS candidate **Andrzej Duda**.

Aware of his own lack of charisma, PiS party chairman Jarosław Kaczyński allowed close ally **Beata Szydło** to lead the party into the October 2015 elections. Thanks to the increasing fragmentation of the political centre, the PiS won an absolute majority in the Sejm on the basis of 37.6 percent of the vote. The elections also saw another right-wing populist party, **Kukiz'15** (led by anti-establishment, anti-EU former rock singer Paweł Kukiz) enter the Sejm for the first time.

Under PiS, Polish politics immediately took a more right-wing turn. The new government lost no time in transforming national TV and radio into a mouthpiece for PiS policies and adopting a cultural policy that prioritized traditional **patriotic themes**. The investigation into the Smolensk disaster was reopened, along with suggestions that the previous administration had somehow covered up the causes of the crash – fueling unsubstantiated speculation that some kind of Polish-Russian conspiracy had downed the plane. Prime minister Szydło made repeated attacks on EU **immigration policy** and argued that, by refusing to take in refugees, Poland was defending the traditional culture of Europe. Uniting all of these threads is that the idea that liberal, left-wing and internationalist ideas have eroded Polish values and that a radical return to national conservatism represents the only salvation.

With the centre of Polish politics fragmenting into a handful of rival parties, opposition to PiS rule has come from citizens' groups and single-issue protests. A bill calling for a total ban on **abortion** was voted down by the Sejm in October 2016 after mass protests by women (known as the Black Protests due to the attire worn by the demonstrators) persuaded MPs to distance themselves from the legislation.

Before losing power in 2015 the PO government had appointed five new members of the constitutional court in order to present the incoming government with a fait accompli. PiS resolved not only to overturn these appointments but also to decrease the independence of the **judiciary**, placing it under the increased control of government ministers. This provoked a long-running crisis that saw huge protests inside the country and a series of high-level complaints from the EU. In July 2017 President Duda vetoed two of the PiS amendments that would have allowed the justice minister control over the supreme court, but allowed a third reform that gave the minister control over the lower courts.

In some senses Poland is a politically divided country, with major cities (many of which are ruled by independent mayors with a local power base) belonging to a liberal-cosmopolitan culture which is not entirely shared by large areas of the countryside. One thing on which almost all Poles agree is strong **support for NATO** and the enduring need for a functioning Euro-Atlantic alliance. For a country situated between an economically dominant Germany and a resurgent imperial Russia, few other foreign-policy options are on the table.

2015	**2017**
Ida, directed by Paweł Pawlikowski, picks up the Oscar for best foreign-language film	Footballer Robert Lewandowski becomes Poland's all-time top scorer with his 50th goal for the international side

Polish music

Poland is a musical superpower that doesn't always get the credit it deserves. And these traditions don't just boil down to Chopin, Szymanowski and the folklore proudly nurtured by heritage societies across the country. Poland is also one of the heartlands of European jazz, a major centre of contemporary classical music and a hotbed of rock and roll.

Indeed, there was a time when Poland was the Liverpool of Central-Eastern Europe, producing a stream of guitar-wielding mop-tops and warbling starlets whose music was exported all over the Soviet bloc. In the 1960s Poland developed a home-grown version of Western pop which went under the name of **Bigbeat** – with groups like Czerwone Gitary and Skaldowie providing the local answer to the Beatles and the Rolling Stones. However, the biggest name to emerge from the 1960s was **Czesław Niemen** (1939–2004), a national institution who began with earthy rhythm-and-blues and moved on through psychedelia, then prog-rock. Niemen introduced a new breadth of vision to Polish pop, although his voice – a cross between Otis Redding and a castrated wildebeest – is very much an acquired taste.

Poland's strong cabaret tradition also fed into the pop mainstream, with bards like **Marek Grechuta** (a stalwart of the *Pod Baranami* club in Kraków) producing wistful, well-constructed songs that bear comparison with the likes of Jacques Brel, Serge Gainsbourg and Leonard Cohen. By the early 1980s punk and reggae came to the fore, the popularity of both due in part to their rebel stance – anything gobbing at authority went down particularly well in post-martial-law Poland. Nowadays the Polish pop scene resembles that of any other European country, with hardcore, rap, reggae and death-metal subcultures coexisting with a mainstream diet of techno. **Jazz** has had a well-established pedigree in Poland ever since the 1950s, when bebop broke through in a country hungry for free expression. This explosion of interest in jazz brought forth a wealth of local talent, most notably **Krzysztof Komeda**, who wrote edgy, experimental scores for Roman Polański's early movies, including the satanic lullaby theme tune of *Rosemary's Baby* (1968). Other home-grown musicians who made it into the international big league include alto saxophonist Zbigniew Namysłowski, violinist Michał Urbaniak, trumpeter Tomasz Stańko and singer Urszula Dudziak – the latter responsible for ultra-catchy 1976 jazz-disco hit *Papaya*.

TEN ESSENTIAL ALBUMS

The list of albums below is a subjective attempt to cover as many aspects as possible of the Polish musical spectrum – although there are plenty of other fans of Polish music who would come up with lists radically different from this one.

Monika Brodka *Clashes* (2016). Echoes of trip hop, Americana and pop-noir characterize the fourth album by Brodka, a former winner of the local edition of Pop Idol whose frequent Bowie-esque image changes are discussed eagerly by the tabloids. Her most recent incarnation sings in English and paints melancholy alt-rock from a broad palette. This is as rich and accomplished as Polish pop gets.

Cool Kids of Death *Cool Kids of Death* (2002). One of the few Polish bands to successfully pick up the electro-punk gauntlet thrown down by Siekiera (see page 472) eighteen years before, Łódź-based Cool Kids of Death (CKOD) mixed razor-sharp guitars with throbbing synthesizers to create a squall of paranoid noise – articulating perfectly the

frustrations of a society that went through the economic shock therapy of the 1990s without quite achieving the world of opportunity they imagined. Despite the schoolboy nihilism suggested by the band's name (actually taken from a track by British popsters St Etienne), it's the typically Polish poetic melancholy lurking within the songs that makes this album a classic.

Henryk Górecki *Symphony No. 3* (1992). A stalwart of the Polish experimental scene until turning towards contemplative minimalism, Górecki premiered this piece to moderate acclaim in the mid-1970s – only to find it given a commercial release by Elektra records fifteen years later, when it became an international bestseller. It's a haunting orchestral work with soprano voice, inspired by the need to mourn the missing and the murdered of Poland's twentieth-century conflicts. One key passage was taken from words scrawled on the wall of a Gestapo prison by a torture victim (the prison in question is now a rest home in Zakopane).

Marek Grechuta and Anawa *Korowód* ("Parade"; 1971). A product of the Kraków intellectual cabaret scene, Marek Grechuta (1945–2006) was probably the greatest exponent of what Poles call "sung poetry" – a subtle and intelligent lyricist who put his words to well-crafted, top-drawer pop. Containing elements of chanson, jazz and prog rock – plus philosophical lyrics that students would ponder well into the night – Grechuta's second album *Korowód* would have been a global classic on a par with Dylan or Cohen had it not been sung in Polish.

Krzysztof Komeda *Astigmatic* (1966). Jazz pianist Komeda (1931–69)'s first and best album, *Astigmatic* was an important signpost for European jazz, marking the end of its dependence on American forms and its movement towards a broader-based communion between contemporary classical, bebop and free jazz. It's Komeda's compositional and ivory-tinkling skills that make this album, although his backing band (saxophonist Zbigniew Namysłowski and trumpeter Tomasz Stańko included) also let rip in spectacular fashion. Invited to Hollywood by Roman Polański, Komeda was on the verge of a great international career when he died of head injuries received when accidently pushed over by Polish beat writer Marek Hłasko.

Leszek Możdżer *Piano* (2004). Poland's reputation for keyboard-bashing runs from Chopin through film soundtracks to free-form jazz – a complex heritage that runs fluently through the fingers of Gdańsk-born pianist Możdżer. He was a key member of outstanding 1990s jazz outfit Miłość before emerging as one of the outstanding individual figures of Polish music in the 2000s. This is his best-known album, showcasing an organic, almost velvety playing style which never loses its idiosyncratic jazz-is-mad-really edge.

Czesław Niemen *Niemen Enigmatic* (1969). National treasure Niemen's finest moment, this is arguably one of the greatest prog-rock albums of all time – all the more remarkable for being recorded a year or two before the Western prog scene really got going. The album saw Poland's greatest hollering soul-man setting classic Polish poetry to an ambitious mix of rock, gospel and jazz, crowned by some great (but never show-off) musicianship: Niemen himself on Hammond organ, and Namysłowski and Michał Urbaniak on saxophones.

Republika *Nowe sytuacje* ("New Situations"; 1983). Poland experienced a rock boom at the beginning of the 1980s, and Republika, led by charismatic Grzegorz Ciechowski (1957–2001), was its most outstanding product. Somehow the gritty sound of post-punk and new wave provided the perfect accompaniment to the bleak years of martial law and its aftermath, and Republika's debut album – complete with angular guitars, rebelliously pouty attitude and great pop tunes – sold an incredible 300,000 copies. Such was their success that they were viewed as a pro-regime band by hardcore alternative types, who pelted them with tomatoes at the Jarocin festival of 1985. That Republika played on and won the crowd over earned their place in legend.

Siekiera *Nowa Aleksandria* ("New Alexandria"; 1986). Another band associated with the rock boom of the 1980s, Siekiera ("The Axe") started out as a classic three-chord punk band before developing into a strange hybrid of hurtling riff-driven rock and machine-noise electronica. Their only studio album is a dark, angst-ridden but also melodic and danceable affair – a monument to what it was like to be a youth in the Jaruzelski years. The most focused and fully realized product of the Polish new wave, it still sounds raw, fresh and slightly dangerous.

Warsaw Village Band *Wykorzenienie* ("Uprooting"; 2004). One of the key exponents of present-day Polish roots music, this ironically titled outfit ("Kapela ze wsi Warszawa" as they are known at home) combines reverence for traditional folk with a contemporary urban taste for large-scale noise. This 2004 release sees the traditional music of central Poland brought thrillingly up to date, with an authentic love of ancient tunes and instruments blending nicely with anarcho-punkish attitude and energy. The 2008 album *Infinity* goes several steps further, blending Slav folklore with jazz, blues and hip-hop.

Books

A vast amount of writing both from and about Poland is available in English, far too much to be listed here. What follows is a subjective list taking account of what's currently available in bookshops and online stores. Those indicated by the ★ symbol are particularly recommended.

HISTORY, POLITICS AND MEMOIRS

★ **Anne Applebaum** *Iron Curtain: the Crushing of Eastern Europe*. How did communists tighten their grip on the societies of Poland, East Germany and Hungary? The story is told here in a solidly-researched and revealing narrative full of telling detail. The same author's *Between East and West* is a well-informed, vividly written account of her travels through Eastern Europe's borderlands in 1991. Applebaum's broad-ranging cultural-historical frame of reference means the book suffers less than others from being too close to immediate events.

David Cesarini *Final Solution: The Fate of the Jews 1933–1949*. Nazism, the Holocaust and its aftermath chronicled in exhaustive detail, with an earnest and thoughtful analysis of how the Final Solution took place – was it planned years in advance by Hitler or did it emerge from the murderous logic of total war?

★ **Norman Davies** *God's Playground*. Epic history of Poland written by a renowned Poland specialist who is also an engrossing writer with an infectious enthusiasm for Polish history. The same author's *Rising '44: The Battle for Warsaw* is an impeccably researched and eminently readable account of the ill-starred Warsaw Uprising. The question of whether the insurgents were the victims of allied betrayal is treated in balanced, meticulous fashion.

Timothy Garton Ash *The Polish Revolution: Solidarity 1980–82*. Garton Ash was the most consistent and involved Western reporter on Poland during the Solidarity era, displaying an intuitive grasp of the Polish mentality, and this book is a vivid record of events from the birth of Solidarity. Garton Ash's *The Magic Lantern: The Revolution of 89* contains his gripping reportage on the climactic events of 1989, documented as an eyewitness in Warsaw, Budapest, Berlin and Prague.

Martin Gilbert *The Holocaust*. A standard work, providing a trustworthy overview on the slaughter of European Jewry – and the crucial role of the Nazi extermination camps, many of which were sited in occupied Poland. Gilbert's *Holocaust Journey* is an account of a study trip undertaken by Gilbert and his students in the 1990s, taking in the towns and cities where Polish Jews once lived, as well as the key memorial sites associated with Nazi crimes. A moving and ultimately uplifting read.

Peter Hayes *Why?: Explaining the Holocaust*. A professor of Holocaust Studies at Northwestern University, USA,

Hayes analyzes with surgical precision how the German Nazis arrived at the idea of a Final Solution, and what made such a huge exercise in mass murder possible. A valuable book with important lessons.

Primo Levi *If This Is a Man; The Truce; Moments of Reprieve; The Drowned and the Saved; The Periodic Table; If Not Now, When?* An Italian Jew, Levi survived Auschwitz because the Nazis made use of his training as a chemist in the death-camp factories. Most of his books, which became ever bleaker towards the end of his life, concentrate on his experiences during and soon after his incarceration in Auschwitz, analyzing the psychology of survivor and torturer with extraordinary clarity. *If Not Now, When?* is the story of a group of Jewish partisans in occupied Russia and Poland; giving plenty of insights into eastern European anti-Semitism, it's a good corrective to the mythology of Jews as passive victims.

Laurence Rees *The Holocaust: a New History*. A documentary film maker responsible among other things for BBC series The Nazis: a Warning From History and Auschwitz: The Nazis and the Final Solution, Rees focuses on individual lives, human stories and a wealth of interview material in this moving and frequently harrowing book. The same author's *Auschwitz* is a grave and unflinching look at the most notorious death-camp of all.

Alexandra Richie *Warsaw 1944: Hitler, Himmler and the Warsaw Uprising*. Exhaustive narrative of Warsaw's doomed but heroic anti-Nazi uprising, placing detailed and moving emphasis on individual stories and human costs.

Radek Sikorski *The Polish House: An Intimate History Of Poland* (o.p.). Highly personalized and passionately penned account of modern Polish history by former Solidarity activist, UK exile and journalist who became Poland's Foreign Minister in 2007.

Timothy Snyder *Bloodlands*. Outstanding work that weaves Soviet and Nazi crimes into a single narrative, making the point that Poland, the Baltic States, Belarus and Ukraine were the areas where both regimes committed most of their mass-murders. The Final Solution is set against the wider context of war, dislocation and killing, in which the citizens of Central-Eastern Europe were targeted by two competing forms of totalitarianism.

Władysław Szpilman *The Pianist*. Wartime memoirs of concert pianist and composer Szpilman (1911–2000), who miraculously survived the Warsaw Ghetto. Originally published as *Smierć Miasta* (*Death of a City*) in 1945, Szpilman's book was initially buried by a postwar Polish regime unwilling to recognize the full extent of Jewish suffering during World War II. Now available again in both Polish and English versions, *The Pianist* has already made it onto celluloid courtesy of Kraków Ghetto survivor Roman Polański.

POLISH LITERATURE

THE POLISH CANON

Jerzy Andrzejewski *Ashes and Diamonds*. Spring 1945: resistance fighters, communist ideologues and black marketeers battle it out in small-town Poland. A gripping account of the tensions and forces that shaped postwar Poland, and the basis for Andrzej Wajda's film of the same title.

★ **Tadeusz Borowski** *This Way for the Gas, Ladies and Gentlemen*. These short stories based on Borowski's Auschwitz experiences marked him out as the great literary hope of communist Poland, but he committed suicide soon after their publication, at the age of 29.

Witold Gombrowicz *Ferdydurke*; *Pornografia*; *The Possessed*. The first two experimentalist novels concentrate on humanity's infantile and juvenile obsessions, and on the tensions between urban life and the traditional ways of the countryside. *The Possessed* explores the same themes within the more easily digestible format of a Gothic thriller.

Bolesław Prus *Pharaoh*; *The Doll*. A late-nineteenth-century epic set in ancient Egypt, *Pharaoh* offers a trenchant examination of the nature of power in a society that was of more than passing relevance to Partition-era Poland. *The Doll* is probably the most famous of the "Polish Tolstoy's" lengthier works: widely regarded as one of the great nineteenth-century social novels, it is a brilliantly observed story of obsessive love against the backdrop of a crisis-ridden *fin de siècle* Warsaw.

Władysław Reymont *The Peasants* and *The Promised Land* (both o.p.). Reymont won the Nobel Prize for *The Peasants*, a tetralogy about village life (one for each season of the year), but its vast length has led to its neglect outside Poland. *The Promised Land*, which was filmed by Andrzej Wajda, offers a comparably unromanticized view of industrial life in Łódź.

★ **Bruno Schulz** *Street of Crocodiles*; *Sanatorium under the Sign of the Hourglass*. These kaleidoscopic, dream-like fictions, vividly evoking life in the small town of Drohobycz in the Polish Ukraine, constitute the entire literary output of their hugely influential author, who was murdered by the SS.

Henryk Sienkiewicz *Quo Vadis?*; *With Fire and Sword*; *The Deluge*; *Fire in the Steppe*. Sienkiewicz's reputation outside Poland largely rests on *Quo Vadis?* (which won him the Nobel Prize), treating the early Christians in Nero's Rome as an allegory of Poland's plight under the Partitions. Until recently, Sienkiewicz's other blockbusters existed only in inadequate and long out-of-print translations, but the Polish-American novelist W.S. Kuniczak has recently rendered the great trilogy about Poland's seventeenth-century wars with the Swedes, Prussians, Germans and Turks into English in a manner that at last does justice to the richly crafted prose of the originals.

Isaac Bashevis Singer *The Magician of Lublin*; *The Family Moskat*; *The Slave*; *Satan in Goray*. Singer, who emigrated from Poland to the US in the 1930s, wrote in Yiddish, so his reputation rests largely on the translations of his novels and short stories. Only a selection of his vast output is mentioned here. *The Magician of Lublin* and *The Family Moskat*, both novels set in the ghettos of early twentieth-century Poland, are masterly evocations of life in vanished Jewish communities. *The Slave* is a gentle yet tragic love story set in the seventeenth century, while *Satan in Goray* is a blazing evocation of religious hysteria in the same period.

CULT FICTION AND CONTEMPORARY CLASSICS

★ **Pawel Huelle** *Who Was David Weiser?*; *Moving House*; *Mercedes-Benz*. The first novel from the award-winning Gdańsk-based writer centres on an enigmatic young Jewish boy idolized by his youthful contemporaries. The author's themes and style show an obvious debt to fellow Danziger Günter Grass. Huelle's magic-realist propensities are further developed in *Moving House*, a marvellous collection of short stories, with the intersecting worlds of Polish and German/Prussian culture again providing the primary frame of reference. *Mercedes-Benz* is a hugely entertaining four-wheeled meditation on Polish history, the much-loved metal crate of the title having been requisitioned from the narrator's grandfather by the Soviets outside Lwów in 1939.

Marek Hłasko *Killing the Second Dog*; *All Backs Were Turned*; *The Graveyard*. Once considered Poland's "Angry Young Man", Hłasko articulated the general disaffection of those who grew up after World War II, his bleak themes mirrored in a spare, taut prose style.

★ **Bruno Jasieński** *I Burn Paris*. Interwar futurist Jasieński was expelled from France for writing this darkly fantastical, visionary novel about the collapse of bourgeois society in a maelstrom of chaos. *The Legs of Izolda Morgan* is an equally scintillating collection of Jasieński's short stories and essays.

★ **Tadeusz Konwicki** *A Minor Apocalypse*. A convinced Party member in the 1950s, Konwicki eventually made the break with Stalinism, and since then a series of highly respected novels, films and screenplays have established him as one of Poland's foremost writers. Describing a single day's events, *A Minor Apocalypse* is narrated by a character who constantly vacillates over his promise to set fire to himself in front of the Party headquarters.

Dorota Masłowska *Snow White and Russian Red.* Published in 2002 when Masłowska was just 21, this is a dark, funny, surreal and compelling portrait of Poland's blank generation, with a cast of going-nowhere-fast characters fuelled by alcohol, cheap drugs, hormones and bad language. Edgy vernacular writing at its best.

Jerzy Pilch *The Mighty Angel.* Leading Polish novelist Pilch delves deep into the life of an alcoholic who is constantly in and out of rehab, weaving a mordantly witty tale of all-too-human yearnings and failures. The ten short stories that form Pilch's *My First Suicide* provide further glimpses of the author's richly idiosyncratic imagination.

Olga Tokarczuk *House of Day, House of Night.* Award-winning novel from one of the most distinctive voices in contemporary Polish fiction, evoking the small-town world of Nowa Ruda (a real-life mining settlement in the Polish-Czech-German borderlands) through a dream-like mixture of narrative fragments, extracts from the life of a medieval saint, and recipes for forest mushrooms. Tokarczuk's *Flights* is a fragmentary, essayistic novel about travel, living at speed, and the compulsion to be constantly on the move.

GENRE FICTION: CRIME, SF AND FANTASY

Marek Krajewski *Death in Breslau.* Compellingly noir crime thriller set in 1930s Wrocław (then part of Germany and known as Breslau), bringing the interwar city to life with a thrilling mixture of grime, seediness and political extremism. *End of the World in Breslau* and *Phantoms in Breslau* continue the Breslau series; *The Minotaur's Head* moves the action to Lwów and sees Breslau detective Mock hand over to new chief protagonist Edward Popielski.

★ **Stanisław Lem** *Solaris; The Futurological Congress.* The only recent Polish writing to have achieved a worldwide mass-market readership, Lem's science fiction focuses on the human and social predicament in the light of technological change. An author of considerable range and invention, Lem's best-known work, *Solaris*, is a disturbing and meditative account of a spiritual quest, while *The Futurological Congress* is a sophisticated satire on the absurdity of our times.

Zygmunt Miloszewski *Entanglement; Grain of Truth; Rage.* Well-drawn characters, a jaundiced view of modern Polish institutions and a bleak sense of the everyday grotesque characterize this fine crime series. Contemporary Warsaw is the setting for *Entanglement*, the first in a series of investigations involving world-weary public prosecutor Teodor Szacki; the action moves to Sandomierz and Olsztyn in *Grain of Truth* and *Rage*.

Andrzej Sapkowski *The Last Wish.* The first in a series of fantasy novels about the Witcher ("Wiedźmin" in Polish), a monster-slayer with supernatural powers who roams a fictional continent populated by humans, elves, dwarves and werewolves. The hugely entertaining cycle has spawned a video game, graphic novel, TV series and film.

POLISH POETRY

Zbigniew Herbert *Selected Poems.* Arguably the greatest contemporary Polish poet, with a strong line in poignant observation; intensely political but never dogmatic. The widespread international mourning occasioned by Herbert's death in 1998 confirmed the man's special place in contemporary literary affections.

Adam Mickiewicz *Pan Tadeusz; Konrad Wallenrod; Grażyna. Pan Tadeusz* is Poland's national epic, set among the gentry of Lithuania at the time of the Napoleonic invasion – the most engaging and accessible translation is that by Leonard Kress, available as a download from ⓦ leonardkress.com. In contrast to the self-delusion about Polish independence shown by the characters in *Pan Tadeusz, Konrad Wallenrod* demonstrates how that end can be achieved by stealth and cunning; like *Grażyna*, its setting is Poland-Lithuania's struggle with the Teutonic Knights.

Czesław Miłosz *New and Collected Poems.* A writer of massive integrity, Miłosz in all his works wrestles with the issues of spiritual and political commitment; this collection encompasses all his poetic phases, from the Surrealist of the 1930s to the émigré sage of San Francisco.

Wisława Szymborska *View With a Grain of Sand; Poems New and Collected 1957–1997; Sounds, Feelings, Thoughts: Seventy Poems.* Nobel Prize-winning Szymborska remains one of the most distinctive modern (female) voices. *View With a Grain of Sand* is an excellent introduction to the Szymborska oeuvre; *Poems New and Collected 1957–1997* is a large, well-translated selection of her poems spanning the last four decades; *Sounds, Feelings, Thoughts: Seventy Poems* covers similar territory, albeit less comprehensively.

POLISH NON-FICTION

Kazimierz Brandys *Warsaw Diary 1977–81.* The diary of this major Polish journalist and novelist brilliantly captures the atmosphere of the time, and especially the effect of John Paul II's first papal visit in 1979. During martial law, possession of this book carried an automatic ten-year prison sentence.

Jacek Hugo-Bader *Kolyma Diaries: A Journey into Russia's Haunted Hinterland.* Seasoned reporter Hugo-Bader travels along the Kolyma highway in the Russian Far East, site of a notorious archipelago of labour camps during the Soviet period. The author weaves encounters with the hardy present-day inhabitants with a chilling evocation of Kolyma's unforgiving past.

★ **Ryszard Kapuściński** *Another Day of Life.* For many years Kapuściński was Poland's only full-time foreign correspondent, his elegant, essayistic reportage setting a standard for all other journalists of his generation. This, his first book, covers the Angolan wars of the mid-1970s, and is full of impressionistic description and insightful comment. Of his subsequent works, *Emperor* is a gripping behind-the-scenes take on Haile Selasse's doomed regime in the Ethiopia of the 1970s; *The Soccer War* recounts travels in South and Central America; while *Imperium* traces his travels in the former Soviet Union and contains revealing reflections on Poland's historically fraught relationship with near-neighbour Russia.

★ **Mariusz Szczygieł** *Gottland*. A cult work of non-fiction that has launched many imitations, *Gottland* presents an idiosyncratic and fragmentary history of twentieth-century Czechia, told with insightful humour by a leading Polish journalist who is not afraid of stylistic experiments.

CHILDREN'S BOOKS

Aleksandra Mizielińska & Daniel Mizieliński *Maps*. A contemporary classic in Poland and something of an international hit, this picture atlas follows a well-established format – maps of various countries and continents filled with drawings of what kind of people and animals live there. However, award-winning illustrators the Mizielińskis bring a disarming mixture of charm and eccentricity to the project – it's a kids' book that is also an art book well worth keeping.

Mikołaj Pasiński & Gosia Herba *Elephant on the Moon*. A young lady astronomer espies an animal on the moon and, despite the ridicule of her colleagues, sets off on a daring mission to investigate. Beautifully illustrated by Herba, this is one of a series of lovely books produced by Polish-English graphic publishers Centrala.

LITERATURE BY FOREIGN WRITERS

★ **Isaac Babel** *Red Cavalry*, from *Collected Stories*. A collection of interrelated short stories about the 1919–20 invasion of Poland, narrated by the bizarrely contradictory figure of a Jewish Cossack communist, who naturally finds himself torn by conflicting emotions.

★ **Günter Grass** *The Tin Drum*; *Dog Years*; *Cat and Mouse*. These three novels, also available in one volume as the *Danzig Trilogy*, are one of the high points of modern German literature. Set in Danzig/Gdańsk, where the author grew up, they hold up a mirror to the changing German character this century. The later *The Call of the Toad* provides a satirical commentary on post-communist Polish and German attitudes towards the same city's past.

★ **James Hopkin** *Winter Under Water*. Poetic, sophisticated and powerful piece of writing with an east-west love affair at its heart and the city of Kraków as its setting. Unusually for novels written about eastern Europe since 1990, modern Poland is not reduced to a collection of post-communist clichés.

Thomas Keneally *Schindler's List*. Originally entitled *Schindler's Ark* before becoming the subject of Spielberg's film, this powerful, 1982 Booker Prize-winning novel is based on the life of Oskar Schindler, a German industrialist who used his business operations to shelter thousands of Jews.

Joseph Roth *Hotel Savoy*. Austrian-Jewish writer Roth's nightmarish look at Europe in the wake of World War I is set in an unnamed industrial city that is clearly based on Łódź. The hotel of the title still stands (see page 102), although is no longer the nest of paranoia described by Roth.

Steve Sem-Sandberg *The Emperor of Lies*. Epic, forceful historical novel centred on the career of Chaim Rumkowski, the Jewish elder who became leader of the Łódź ghetto in World War II and ruled over his people as a self-aggrandizing dictator. Employing a vast array of (mostly real) characters, Sem-Sandberg creates a convincing picture of ghetto life and its daily moral challenges, especially the compromise between opportunism and evil that forms the book's main theme.

Art Spiegelman *Maus*. Spiegelman, editor of the cartoon magazine *Raw*, is the son of Auschwitz survivors. *Maus* is a brilliant comic-strip exploration of the ghetto and concentration camp experiences of his father, recounted in flashbacks. The story runs through to Art's father's imprisonment at Auschwitz.

Polish

Polish has a reputation for being one of the most difficult European languages to learn, although this turns out to be something of a misconception once one gets over the initial hurdle of weird-looking Polish letters and the question of how to pronounce them. It's certainly a beautiful language to listen to, and any attempts to speak it yourself will be much appreciated by the locals.

Polish grammar is a remorselessly logical affair once you begin to pick up the rules. There are three **genders** (masculine, feminine and neuter) and no word for "the". **Prepositions** (words like "to", "with", "in" and so on) take different cases, and the case changes the form of the noun. Thus, the name *Kraków* changes its shape in sentences such as *do Krakowa* ("to Kraków") and *w Krakowie* ("in Kraków"). You don't have to learn this sort of thing off by heart, but it can be useful to be able to recognize it.

Finally, a brief word on how to **address people**. The familiar form used among friends, relations and young people is *ty*, like French *tu* or German *du*. However, the polite form which you will usually require is *Pan* when addressing a man and *Pani* for a woman ("Sir" and "Madam"). Always use this form with people obviously older than yourself, and with officials.

Pronunciation

While Polish may look daunting at first, with its apparently unrelieved rows of consonants, the good news is that it's a phonetic language – that is, it's pronounced exactly as spelt. So, once you've learnt the rules and have a little experience you'll always know how to pronounce a word correctly.

Stress

Usually on the penultimate syllable, eg *Warszawa, przyjaciel, matka*.

Vowels

a: as "a" in "cat".

e: "e" in "neck".

i: "i" in "Mick", never as in "I".

o: "o" in "lot", never as in "no" or "move".

u: "oo" in "look".

y: unknown in Standard English; cross between "e" and Polish "i, eg the "y" in the Yorkshire pronunciation of "Billy".

There are three specifically Polish vowels:

ą: nasalized – like "ong" in "long" or French "on".

ę: nasalized – like French "un" (eg Lech Wałęsa).

ó: same sound as Polish "u".

Vowel combinations include:

ie: pronounced y-e, eg nie wiem (I don't know): ny-e vy-em (not nee-veem).

eu: each letter pronounced separately, eg "E-u-ropa" (Europe).

ia: rather like "yah", eg historia (history): histor-i-yah.

Consonants

Those which look the same as English but are different:

w: as "v" in "vine", eg "wino" pronounced "vino" (wine).

r: trilled (as in Scottish pronunciation of English "r").

h: like the "ch" in Scottish "loch".

Polish-specific consonants include:

ć and **ci**: "t" as in "future".

ł: "dark l" sounding rather like a "w".

ń and **ni**: soft "n", sounding like "n-ye", eg koń (horse): kon-ye.

ś and **si**: "ss" as in "mission".

ź and **zi**: like the "j" of French journal.

ż and **rz**: as in French "g" in gendarme. (Note that the dot over the "z" is sometimes replaced by a bar through the letter's diagonal.)

Consonantal pairs

cz: "ch" as in "church".

sz: "sh" as in "ship".

dz: "d" as in "day" rapidly followed by "z" as in "zoo", eg dzwon (bell): d-zvon. At the end of a word it's pronounced like "ts" as in "cats".

dź: "d-sh", eg dźungla (jungle): d-shun-gla.

dż: sharper than the above; at the end of a word is pronounced like "ć".

szcz: this fearsome-looking cluster is easy to pronounce – "sh-ch" as in "pushchair", eg szczur (rat): sh-choor.

USEFUL WORDS AND PHRASES

WORDS

Yes Tak

No/not Nie

Please/you're welcome Proszę

More emphatic than proszę Proszę bardzo

Thank you Dziekuję/dziekuję bardzo

Where Gdzie

When Kiedy

Why Dlaczego

How much Ile

Here, there Tu/tam

Now Teraz

Later Później

Open Otwarty

Closed/shut Zamknięty

Earlier Wcześniej

Enough Dosyć

Over there Tam

This one (masc/fem/neuter) Ten/ta/to

That one (masc/fem/neuter) Tamten/tamta/tamto

Large Wielki

Small Mały

More Więcej

Less Mniej

A little Mało

A lot Dużo

Cheap Tani

Expensive Drogi

Good Dobry

Bad Zły/niedobry

Hot Gorący

Cold Zimny

With Z

Without Bez

In W

For Dla

How are you? (informal) Jak się masz?

How are you? (formal) Jak się Pan/Pani ma?

Fine Dobrze

Come what may (usually used as a positive exhortation to follow your instincts and not worry about the consequences) Jakoś to będzie

Do you speak English? Czy Pan/Pani mówi po angielsku?

I understand Rozumiem

I don't understand Nie rozumiem

I don't know Nie wiem

Please speak a bit more slowly Proszę mówić trochę wolniej

I don't speak Polish very well Nie mówię dobrze po polsku

What's the Polish for that? Co to znaczy po polsku?

I'm here on holiday Jestem tu na urlopie

I'm British (male/female) Jestem Brytyjczykiem/ Brytyjką

Irish Irlandczykiem/Irlandką

American Amerikaniniem/Amerikanką

Canadian Kanadyjczykiem/Kanadyjką

Australian Australyjczykiem/Australyjką

I live in... Mieszkam w…

Today Dzisiaj

Tomorrow Jutro

Day after tomorrow Pojutrze

Yesterday Wczoraj

Moment!/ Wait a moment Chwileczkę

In the morning Rano

In the afternoon Po południu

In the evening Wieczorem

Where is…? Gdzie jest…?

How do I get to…? Jak dojechać do…?

What time is it? Która (jest) godzina?

How far is it to…? Jak daleko jest…?

PHRASES

Good day/hello Dzień dobry

Good evening Dobry wieczór

Good night Dobra noc

"Hi!" or "'Bye" (like Italian ciao) Cześć!

Goodbye Do widzenia

Excuse me (apology) Przepraszam

Excuse me (requesting information) Proszę Pana/Pani

ACCOMMODATION

Hotel Hotel

Lodgings Noclegi

Is there a hotel nearby? Czy jest gdzieś tutaj hotel?

Do you have a room? Czy Pan/Pani ma pokój?

Single room Pokój jednoosobowy

Double room Pokój dwuosobowy

For one night (doba: 24hr) Będziemy jedną dobę

Two nights Dwie noce

Three nights Trzy noce
A week Tydzień
Two weeks Dwa tygodnie
With a bath Pokój z łazienką
With a shower Z prysznicem
With a balcony Z balkonem
How much is it? Ile kosztuje?
That's too expensive To za drogo
Does that include breakfast? Czy to obejmuje śniadanie?
Do you have anything cheaper? Czy nie ma tańszego?
Can I see the room? Czy mogę zobaczyć pokój?
Good, I'll take it Dobrze, wezmę
I have a booking Mam rezerwację
Campsite Pole namiotowe/kemping
Tent Namiot
Cabin Schronisko
Youth hostel Schronisko młodziezowe
The menu, please Proszę o jadłospis
The bill, please Proszę o rachunek

TRAVELLING

Car Auto, samochód
Aircraft Samolot
Bicycle Rower
Bus Autobus
Ferry Prom
Train Pociąg
Train station Dworzec kolejowy
Bus station Dworzec autobusowy
Taxi Taksówka
Hitchhiking Autostop
On foot Piechotą
A ticket to…, please Proszę bilet do…
Return Bilet powrotny
Single W jedną stronę
I'd like a seat reservation Proszę z miejscówką
When does the Warsaw train leave? Kiedy odjeżdża pociąg do Warszawy?
Do I have to change? Czy muszę się przesiadać?
Which platform does the train leave from? Z jakiego peronu odjedzie pociąg?
How many kilometres is it? Ile jest kilometrów?
How long does the journey last? Ile czasu trwa podróż?
Which bus is it to…? Jakim autobusem do…?
Where is the road to…? Gdzie jest droga do…?
Next stop, please Następny przystanek, proszę

SIGNS

Entrance; exit/way out Wejście/wyjście
No entrance Wstęp wzbroniony
Toilet Toaleta
Men Dla panów; męski
Women Dla pań; damski

Occupied Zajęty
Free, vacant Wolny
Arrival; departure (train, bus) Przyjazd; odjazd
Arrival; departure (aircraft) Przylot; odlot
Closed for renovation/stocktaking Remont
Pull; push Ciągnąć; pchać
Out of order; closed (ticket counters etc) Nieczynny
Platform Peron
Cash desk Kasa
Stop Stop
Polish state frontier Granica międzynarodowa
Republic of Poland Rzeczpospolita Polska
Beware, caution Uwaga
Danger Uwaga; niebezpieczeństwo
Police Policja
Information Informacja
No smoking Nie palić; palenie wzbronione
Do not touch Nie dotykać

DRIVING

Car Samochód, auto
Left Na lewo
Right Na prawo
Straight ahead Prosto
Parking Parking
Detour Objazd
End (showing when a previous sign ceases to be valid) Koniec
No overtaking Zakaz wyprzedzania
Petrol/gas Benzyna
Petrol/gas station Stacja benzynowa
Oil Olej
Water Woda
To repair Naprawić
Accident Wypadek
Breakdown Awaria
Speed limit Ograniczenie prędkości

DAYS, MONTHS AND DATES

Monday Poniedziałek
Tuesday Wtorek
Wednesday Środa
Thursday Czwartek
Friday Piątek
Saturday Sobota
Sunday Niedziela
January Styczeń
February Luty
March Marzec
April Kwiecień
May Maj
June Czerwiec
July Lipiec
August Sierpień

September Wrzesień
October Październik
November Listopad
December Grudzień
Spring Wiosna
Summer Lato
Autumn Jesień
Winter Zima
Holidays Wakacje
Bank holiday Święto

NUMBERS
1 Jeden
2 Dwa
3 Trzy
4 Cztery
5 Pięć
6 Sześć
7 Siedem
8 Osiem
9 Dziewięć
10 Dziesięć
11 Jedenaście
12 Dwanaście
13 Trzynaście
14 Czternaście
15 Piętnaście
16 Szesnaście
17 Siedemnaście
18 Osiemnaście
19 Dziewiętnaście
20 Dwadzieścia
30 Trzydzieści
40 Czterdzieści
50 Pięćdziesiąt
60 Sześćdziesiąt
70 Siedemdziesiąt
80 Osiemdziesiąt
90 Dziewięćdziesiąt
100 Sto
200 Dwieście
300 Trzysta
400 Czterysta
500 Pięćset
600 Sześćset
700 Siedemset
800 Osiemset
900 Dziewięćset
1000 Tysiąc
1,000,000 Milion

FOOD AND DRINK

COMMON TERMS
Filiżanka Cup
Gotowany Boiled
Grill/z rusztu Grilled
Jadłospis Menu
Kolacja Dinner
Kwaśny Sour
Łyżka Spoon
Marynowany Pickled
Mielone Minced
Na zdrowie! Cheers!
Nadziewany Stuffed
Nóż Knife
Obiad Lunch
Śniadanie Breakfast
Święży Fresh
Słodki Sweet
Smacznego! Bon appetit!
Surowy Raw
Szklanka Glass
Sznycel Escalope/schnitzel
Talerz Plate
Wegetariański Vegetarian
Widelec Fork

BASIC FOODS
Bułka Bread rolls
Chleb Bread
Chrzan Horseradish
Cukier Sugar
Drób Poultry
Frytki Chips/French fries
Jajko Egg
Jarzyny/warzywa Vegetables
Kanapka Sandwich
Kołduny Lithuanian ravioli-like parcels stuffed with meat
Kotlet Cutlet
Makaron Macaroni
Masło Butter
Mięso Meat
Ocet Vinegar
Olej Oil
Owoce Fruit
Pieczeń Roast meat
Pieprz Pepper
Potrawy jarskie Vegetarian dishes
Ryby Fish
Ryż Rice
Śmietana Cream
Sól Salt
Surówka Salad
Zupa Soup

SOUPS

Barszcz czerwony (z pasztecikem) Beetroot soup (with pastry)
Barszcz ukraiński White borsch
Bulion/rosół Bouillon
Chłodnik Sour milk and vegetable cold soup
Fasólka po bretońsku Spicy bean soup with bacon bits
Kapuśniak Cabbage soup
Krupnik Barley soup
Żurek Soup made from fermented rye flour and potatoes
(zupa) Cebulowa Onion soup
(zupa) Fasolowa Bean soup
(zupa) Grochowa Pea soup
(zupa) Grzybowa Mushroom soup
(zupa) Jarzynowa Vegetable soup
(zupa) Ogórkowa Cucumber soup
(zupa) Owocowa Cold fruit soup
(zupa) Pomidorowa Tomato soup

MEAT, FISH AND POULTRY

Baranina Mutton
Bażant Pheasant
Befsztyk Steak
Bekon/boczek Bacon
Cielęcina Veal
Dziczyzna Game
Dzik Wild boar
Gęś Goose
Golonka Leg of pork
Indyk Turkey
Kaczka Duck
Karp Carp
Kiełbasa Sausage
Kotlet schabowy Pork cutlet
Kurczak Chicken
Łosoś Salmon
Makrela Mackerel
Pstrąg Trout
Śledź Herring
Salami Salami
Sardynka Sardine
Sarnina Elk
Szaszłyk Shish kebab
Wątróbka Liver with onion
Węgorz Eel
Wieprzowe Pork
Wołowe Beef

FRUIT AND VEGETABLES

Ananas Pineapple
Banan Banana
Ćwikła/buraczki Beetroot
Cebula Onion
Cytryna Lemon
Borówki Blackberries
Czarne porzeczki Blackcurrant
Czereśnie Cherries
Czosnek Garlic
Fasola Beans
Groch Peas
Gruszka Pears
Grzyby/pieczarki Mushrooms
Jabłko Apple
Kalafior Cauliflower
Kapusta Cabbage
Kapusta kiszona Sauerkraut
Kasza Buckwheat
Kompot Stewed fruit
Maliny Raspberries
Marchewka Carrots
Migdały Almonds
Morele Apricots
Ogórek Cucumber
Ogórki Gherkins
Orzechy włoskie Walnuts
Papryka Paprika
Pomarańcze Orange
Pomidor Tomato
Śliwka Plum
Szparagi Asparagus
Szpinak Spinach
Truskawki Strawberries
Winogrona Grapes
Ziemniaki Potatoes

CHEESE

Bryndza Sheep's cheese
Oscypek Smoked goats' cheese
Twaróg Cottage cheese
(ser) Myśliwski Smoked cheese
(ser) Tylżycki Mild yellow cheese

CAKES AND DESSERTS

Ciastko Cake
Ciasto drożdżowe Yeast cake with fruit
Czekolada Chocolate
Galaretka Jellied fruits
Lody Ice cream
Makowiec Poppyseed cake
Mazurek Shortcake
Pączki Doughnuts
Sernik Cheesecake
Tort Tart

DRINKS

Cocktail mleczny Milk shake
Gorąca czekolada Drinking chocolate

Herbata Tea
Kawa Coffee
Miód pitny Mead
Mleko Milk
Napój Bottled fruit drink
Piwo Beer
Sok Juice
Sok pomarańczowy Orange juice

Sok pomidorowy Tomato juice
Winiak Polish brandy
Wino Wine
Wino słodkie Sweet wine
Wino wytrawne Dry wine
Woda Water
Woda mineralna Mineral water
Wódka Vodka

Glossary

Aleja Avenue (abb. al.)
Biuro Zakwaterowania Accommodation office
Brama Gate
Cerkiew (pl. cerkwie) Orthodox church, or a church belonging to the Uniates (Greek Catholics), a tradition loyal to Rome but following Orthodox rites that date back to the 1595 Act of Union.
Cmentarz Cemetery
Dolina Valley
Dom House
Dom Kultury Cultural House, a community arts and social centre
Dom Wycieczkowy Cheap, basic type of hotel
Droga Road
Dwór Country house traditionally owned by member of the szlachta class
Dworzec Station
Główny Main as in Rynek Główny, main square
Góra (pl. góry) Mountain
Granica Border
Jezioro Lake
Kantor Exchange office
Kaplica Chapel
Kawiarnia Café
Katedra Cathedral
Klasztor Monastery
Kościół Church
Ksiądz Priest
Książę Prince, duke
Księgarnia Bookshop
Kraj Country
Las Wood, forest
Masyw Massif
Miasto Town (Stare Miasto – Old Town; Nowe Miasto – New Town)
Most Bridge
Naród Nation, people
Nysa River Neisse
Odra River Oder
Ogród Gardens
Pałac Palace

Piwnica Pub
Plac Square (abb. pl.)
Plaża Beach
Poczta Post office
Pokój (pl. pokóje) Room
Pole Field
Prom Ferry
Przedmieście Suburb
Przystanek Bus stop
Puszcza Ancient forest
Ratusz Town hall
Restauracja Restaurant
Ruch Chain of newspaper kiosks also selling public transport tickets
Rynek Marketplace, commonly the main square in a town
Rzeka River
Sejm Parliament
Shtetl Yiddish name for a rural town, usually with a significant Jewish population
Skała Rock, cliff
Skansen Open-air museum with reconstructed folk architecture and art
Stocznia Shipyards
Święty Saint (abb. św.)
Starowiercy (Old Believers) Traditionalist Russian Orthodox sect, small communities of which survive in east Poland.
Stary Old
Szlachta Term for the traditional gentry class, inheritors of status and land
Ulica Street (abb. ul.)
Województwo Administrative district
Wieś (pl. Wsie) Village
Wieża Tower
Winiarnia Wine cellar
Wodospad Waterfall
Wzgórze Hill
Zamek Castle
Zdrój Spa
Ziemia Region

Small print and index

A ROUGH GUIDE TO ROUGH GUIDES

Published in 1982, the first Rough Guide – to Greece – was a student scheme that became a publishing phenomenon. Mark Ellingham, a recent graduate in English from Bristol University, had been travelling in Greece the previous summer and couldn't find the right guidebook. With a small group of friends he wrote his own guide, combining a contemporary, journalistic style with a thoroughly practical approach to travellers' needs.

The immediate success of the book spawned a series that rapidly covered dozens of destinations. And, in addition to impecunious backpackers, Rough Guides soon acquired a much broader readership that relished the guides' wit and inquisitiveness as much as their enthusiastic, critical approach and value-for-money ethos. These days, Rough Guides include recommendations from budget to luxury and cover more than 120 destinations around the globe, from Amsterdam to Zanzibar, all regularly updated by our team of roaming writers.

Browse all our latest guides, read inspirational features and book your trip at **roughguides.com**.

Rough Guide credits

Editor: Claire Saunders
Cartography: Katie Bennett, Ed Wright
Managing Editors: Monica Woods, Rachel Lawrence

Picture Editor: Tom Smyth
Senior DTP Coordinator: Dan May
Head of DTP and Pre-Press: Rebeka Davies

Publishing information

This eighth edition published in 2018 by
Rough Guides Ltd

Distribution

UK, Ireland and Europe
Apa Publications (UK) Ltd; sales@roughguides.com
United States and Canada
Ingram Publisher Services; ips@ingramcontent.com
Australia and New Zealand
Woodslane; info@woodslane.com.au
Southeast Asia
Apa Publications (SN) Pte; sales@roughguides.com
Worldwide
Apa Publications (UK) Ltd; sales@roughguides.com
Special Sales, Content Licensing and CoPublishing
Rough Guides can be purchased in bulk quantities
at discounted prices. We can create special editions,
personalised jackets and corporate imprints tailored to
your needs. sales@roughguides.com.

roughguides.com
Printed in China by CTPS
All rights reserved
© Jonathan Bousfield, 2018
Maps © Apa Digital AG and Rough Guides Ltd
All rights reserved. No part of this publication may be
reproduced, stored in or introduced into a retrieval system,
or transmitted in any form, or by any means (electronic,
mechanical, photocopying, recording or otherwise) without
the prior written permission of the copyright owner.
A catalogue record for this book is available from the
British Library
The publishers and authors have done their best to
ensure the accuracy and currency of all the information in
The Rough Guide to Poland, however, they can accept
no responsibility for any loss, injury, or inconvenience
sustained by any traveller as a result of information or
advice contained in the guide.

Help us update

We've gone to a lot of effort to ensure that the eighth
edition of **The Rough Guide to Poland** is accurate and up-
to-date. However, things change – places get "discovered",
opening hours are notoriously fickle, restaurants and
rooms raise prices or lower standards. If you feel we've got
it wrong or left something out, we'd like to know, and if
you can remember the address, the price, the hours, the
phone number, so much the better.

Please send your comments with the subject line
"Rough Guide Poland Update" to mail@uk.roughguides.
com. We'll credit all contributions and send a copy of the
next edition (or any other Rough Guide if you prefer) for
the very best emails.

Reader's update

Thanks to all the readers who have taken the time to write in with comments and suggestions (and apologies if we've
inadvertently omitted or misspelt anyone's name):
Francis Beresford, Robert Broad, Daniel, James Harris, Roger Kennington, Igor Kucera, Joanna Lewandowska, Marcin
Piasek, Andrew Rowe, Karl von Schoultz, Jane Shepard, Marion Stone, Susan Swatek, Kate Thomas, Alan Thornhill, John
Wernet, Artur Wieznowski

ABOUT THE AUTHOR

Jonathan Bousfield has been making regular visits to Poland
for the best part of twenty years. As well as Poland he has
authored Rough Guides to Croatia and the Baltic States, and co-
authored guides to Austria and Bulgaria. In-between times he has
been a rock critic for a UK newspaper, edited a listings magazine
in Bulgaria, and is the co-author (with artist Igor Hofbauer) of
graphic novella *Crimson Quays*. He is currently the chief navigator
of Ⓦstraysatellite.com and his book on Adriatic history *Adria Blue*
is due to be published by Profil in 2019.

Acknowledgements

In a way I embarked on this edition of the book for my nephew Joseph whose maternal grandparents come to the United Kingdom from Poland in 1945. Helping me along the road were Jamie Howard, Robert Krygsman, Joanna Bernacka, Bianca Torossian, Iga Winczakiewicz, Marcel Andino Velez, Marta Jablkowska, Marlena Paszkiewicz and Katarzyna Winczewska in Warsaw; Daniel Muzyczuk, Tamara Skalska, Leszek Karczewski, Anita Treścińska and Michał Pernikowski in Łódź; Krystyna Hartenberger, Magdalena Mistat, Arkadiusz Bilecki, Adam Czubaszek and Tomasz Rakowski in Gdańsk; Kamil Piaskowski in Toruń, Malgorzata Stanek in Lublin; Stuart Wadsworth, Nick Hodge, Ania Dyga, Marta Bosak, Sabina Potaczek-Jasionowicz, Marek Swierad and Agata Odziewa in Kraków; Maciej Krupa, Michał Pietrzak, Szymon Rolnik and Magdalena Łukaszczyk in Zakopane; Alicja Knast, Danuta Piękoś-Owczarek, Łukasz Kałębasiak and Karol Piekarski in Katowice; Anita Nowak, Adriana Kondratowicz, Kejal Ashra and Matthias Herd in Wrocław; Anna Żabska and Matt Mykytyszyn in Wałbrzych; and Jonasz Piorunek in Poznań. Thanks to editors Monica Woods and Claire Saunders for breathing new life into a Frankenstein's Monster of a book; and to Rachel Lawrence for steering the project to completion. Finally, love to Jura, Niko and Gordana for enduring long absences and putting up with the author when he got home.

Photo credits

(Key: t-top; c-centre; b-bottom; l-left; r-right)

Index

Main references are in **bold** type

N

Map Symbols

The symbols below are used on maps throughout the book

International boundary	✉ Post office	🐘 Zoo	⚲ Church/cathedral
Chapter boundary	ⓘ Information office	Museum	Abbey
Motorway	Ⓟ Parking	Castle	Synagogue
Dual carriageway	@ Internet access	Palace	Building
Main road	Ⓜ Metro station	Point of interest	Church
Pedestrianised road	★ Bus stop	Forest	Market
Railway	Ferry dock	Cave	Stadium
Funicular	Boat landing	Mountain range	Park/forest
Path	Gate	Mountain peak	Beach
Wall	Monument	Airport	Christian cemetery
River	Garden/fountain	Border crossing	Jewish cemetery
Ferry route	Lighthouse	Mosque	

Listings key

■ Accommodation

● Eating

■ Drinking/nightlife

● Shopping